Public speaking for a global society

INTERACTIVE
APPLIED
COMPREHENSIVE
EMPOWERING
INTEGRATED

Groundbreaking and critically acclaimed from the first edition, **Public Speaking: Concepts and Skills for a Diverse Society** trains students to be effective speakers and listeners in the context of our multicultural society. Now, in this comprehensive Third Edition, author Clella Jaffe further explores the intertwined nature of diversity and public speaking—with expanded coverage of basic public speaking skills, rhetorical foundations, and technology.

With a keen sense of what students need to excel, Jaffe infuses each chapter with the concepts, skills, theories, applications, and critical thinking proficiencies essential for success in today's world.

"Overall, this is a thoughtful, well-written, comprehensive text.... This text does give more foundational material coming from classical rhetoric than many other texts, which is nice."

Cheri Campbell, Keene State College

"Good examples of cultural diversity... excellent discussion of cultural differences in communication styles."

Paula Rodriquez, Hinds Community College

PREVIEW

1

INTERACTIVE

The Internet and interactive technology have made the world a smaller place. Whether or not your classroom is as culturally diverse as others, we all have increasing contact with people from diverse backgrounds through online communication. In order to succeed in this new environment, students not only need to understand diversity, but also the technology that is making co-cultural interactions more frequent. This same technology reinforces public speaking instruction by connecting content and delivery. Students can simultaneously listen to and watch the speech exemplars they read. In this third edition, Clella Jaffe arms students with the knowledge and tools they need to take full advantage of the dynamic technological resources available to them, from Web sites to an interactive CD-ROM — and they're all seamlessly woven into the content of the text.

PREVIEW

New!

Jaffe Connection CD-ROM

This new edition of Jaffe's **Public Speaking: Concepts and Skills for a Diverse Society** expands student learning into a multimedia environment. Accompanying each student text is the ***Jaffe Connection CD-ROM***. This CD-ROM consists of five integrated components: *InfoTrac College Edition*, Internet Exercises, access to chapter-by-chapter resources at the Public Speaking Resource Center at Wadsworth's Communication Café, *Jaffe Speech Interactive* and a preview of *Thomson Learning Web Tutor*™. Each component of the CD-ROM is represented in the text with an icon. Integrated throughout the chapter and expanded upon at the end of chapters, these integrated icons direct students to numerous digital/electronic activities and reinforce and enrich concepts presented.

■ **The engaging and practical Internet and *InfoTrac College Edition* exercises** expand chapter content and guarantee currency of presentation. Through these exercises, students are encouraged to use the Internet and are introduced to *InfoTrac College Edition*, a tremendous topic selection and research resource. *InfoTrac College Edition* is a Wadsworth exclusive and is bundled FREE with the text (see page 6 for more information on *InfoTrac College Edition*).

> *"Very strong—especially for the chapters on culture and ethics. The consistent use of Web-based materials . . . is a very useful part of the text."*
>
> **Hal Fulmer, Georgia Southern University**

■ **Access to the Wadsworth Public Speaking Resource Center** provides students with dynamic chapter-by-chapter resources as well as the opportunity to participate in an expert-monitored, threaded discussion on a variety of contemporary public speaking topics. For each chapter in the text, students can access hotlinks, quizzes, glossary terms, speech preparation and evaluation checklists, *InfoTrac College Edition* questions, and interactive activities. The interactive activities, including several that focus on speech organization and outlining, are based on the in-text *Stop and Check* feature (see page 3 for more information).

■ ***Speech Interactive* for *Jaffe Connection CD-ROM* icons prompt students to view the sample student speeches** from the text that are included on the CD-ROM. This multimedia tool—a Wadsworth/Thomson Learning™ exclusive—maximizes student experience by enabling them to read, watch, listen to, critique, and analyze the models provided. After completing the speech evaluation checklists and speech improvement plans for each speech, students can compare their work to an expert's suggestions.

Jaffe Speech Interactive

■ **Thomson Learning Web Tutor**™
Highlighted by icons throughout the text, students are encouraged to take their learning online! A great tool for studying and course management, *Web Tutor* helps professors take the public speaking course beyond classroom boundaries to an anytime, anywhere environment. This Web-based learning companion maximizes the *Jaffe Connection CD-ROM* and is available on both *WebCT* and *Blackboard* bundled with the text. See page 8 for more information on *Web Tutor*.

This text's skills-based focus gives your students ample opportunity to test and apply their knowledge. From exercises they can do on their own to those that are well-suited to a group environment, students are constantly encouraged to take their understanding further.

STOP AND CHECK

Begin to Evaluate Your Classroom Audience

Use the following form to analyze your classroom audience.

Audience Motivations and Demographics

In general, your audience is:

_____ pedestrian	_____ passive	_____ selected
_____ concerted	_____ organized	_____ absent
_____ hostile to	_____ neutral about	_____ interested in your subject

What strategies will you use to relate your topic to their interests and keep their attention?

_____

_____

Ethnically, _____ listeners are similar _____ from two groups _____ diverse

Mainly, _____ Christian _____ Jewish _____ Muslim _____ Buddhist _____ Other

Probably holds their religious _____ beliefs _____ very strongly

_____ moderately _____ weakly

_____ % women _____ % men

Mostly _____ mature _____ baby boomers _____ Gen Xers

New!

Stop and Check

Students are encouraged to *Stop and Check* their progress at various points in each chapter. These critical thinking and skill-building exercises are the ideal way for students to test their knowledge of key concepts and skills. Many of the *Stop and Check* features are in the student workbook and available online at both the *Public Speaking Resource Center* and through Jaffe *Web Tutor*™.

Self-Assessment Exercises

A number of introspective self-assessment exercises help students assess their skills, helping them build on and improve their public speaking abilities. Chapter 2's *Assess Your Public Speaking Anxiety* is based on the "Personal Report of Public Speaking Anxiety" and helps students assess their own level of communication apprehension and make a plan for improvement. Chapter 4's *Listening Self-Assessment* helps students create a personal plan to become more effective listeners.

STOP AND CHECK

Assess Your Public Speaking Anxiety

Take this test to self-assess your anxiety regarding public speaking. In the blank beside the statement, write the number of the response that best reflects your feelings.

(0) Strongly disagree
(1) Disagree
(2) Agree
(3) Strongly agree

___ 1. I begin to get nervous the moment the speech is assigned.
___ 2. I feel panicky because I don't know how to create a speech.
___ 3. I usually feel nervous the day before I have to speak.
___ 4. The night before the speech I can't sleep well.
___ 5. I'm afraid people will think I'm dumb or boring or weird in some way.
___ 6. On the morning of the speech, I am really tense.
___ 7. I find it difficult to think positively about giving a speech.
___ 8. I think my physical reactions are greater than those that other people experience.
___ 9. During my speech I actually think I'll faint.
___ 10. I continue to worry even after the speech is over.

Add your scores.

Application and Critical Thinking Questions

1. Sometimes people do not see themselves as public speakers, because they define the word *public* too narrowly. They think of public speakers as politicians speaking at conventions but not as homemakers testifying before a local school board. Write your definition of "publics." Then, make a list of specific publics you have already addressed and those you may address someday.

2. Interview a person working in the field you hope to enter when you graduate. What opportunities exist for public speaking within that occupation? Ask if and how public speaking is related to the higher-paying, more prestigious jobs within the field.

3. What stereotypes do you hold about the word *rhetoric*? Throughout this term, listen for the word *rhetoric* as it is used on radio or television. Watch for it as you read newspapers or magazines. Each time you encounter the word *rhetoric*, decide whether it's being used negatively, positively, or in a neutral manner. Note if any of the sources speak of rhetoric as essential in a free society.

4. In a small group, make a list showing how public speaking is similar to everyday conversation and how it differs. Use the communication model to guide your thinking.

5. Work with a group to evaluate the role of public speaking in creating and maintaining your college or university.

   ■ What role did public speaking have as the founders launched your institution?

   ■ How does your school currently use public speaking to recruit newcomers?

   ■ What role does ceremonial speaking, such as convocations or commencement addresses, have in maintaining the vision and the values of your institution?

   ■ When issues threaten to divide your campus? How do groups and individuals use public speaking to negotiate differences?

Application and Critical Thinking Questions

This popular feature, replete with a number of new and revised questions, helps students understand and critically evaluate the chapter content and skills they've learned. These end-of-chapter questions are flexible in that they can be used for individual or group assignments, or as launchers for in-class discussion.

"Very good, useful, and thought-provoking springboards to further discussion."

Paula Rodriquez, Hinds Community College

COMPREHENSIVE

INTERACTIVE APPLIED EMPOWERING INTEGRATED

In content and approach, **Public Speaking: Concepts and Skills for a Diverse Society, Third Edition** *leads the way with its expanded coverage of key public speaking topics, new research, and diversity.*

New!
Timely Content
From the incorporation of the latest research findings to a host of new exercises and activities, this Third Edition is unparalleled in its coverage of the topics and ideas that are making headway in public speaking. Explore this new edition and find:

■ An integrated discussion of diversity in Chapter 1, *Introduction to Public Speaking and Culture.*

■ A new chapter, *Ethics and Diversity* (Chapter 3), that helps students explore their responsibilities as ethical speakers and listeners in a diverse society.

■ A chapter on *Telling Narratives* (Chapter 15) that explores the importance of storytelling to all cultures.

■ The most current research on topic areas such as critical thinking, public speaking anxiety, culture, learning styles, technology, listening, and narrative speaking.

■ Comparative coverage of communication apprehension and speech anxiety that highlights the differences between the two phenomena.

■ Numerous new examples throughout the text to help illustrate key content and skills.

■ Expanded and updated coverage of small groups in the appendix.

> ### DIVERSITY IN PRACTICE
> ### The Homosexuals and the Baptists
>
> In October 1999, Jerry Falwell, a Baptist pastor and founder of the Moral Majority, invited 200 gay men and lesbians to meet with 200 members of his Thomas Road Baptist Church. His wanted to bring church members face to face with homosexual people for a discussion of ways to tone down anti-gay rhetoric in light of the rise in hate crimes against gays and lesbians.
>
> The Reverend Mel White, Falwell's long-time friend and ghostwriter of Falwell's biography, had come out of the closet and now heads a ministry to gays. Over the years, White has repeatedly asked Falwell to avoid anti-gay rhetoric that might incite violence against homosexual people. Falwell himself realized the impact of hate after several shootings occurred in which gunmen expressed anti-Christian sentiments, and he set up the October gathering between the two divergent groups.
>
> Jerry Falwell predicted "For the first time in history, we will have talked with...
> ...Mel White mused "Ho...

 Check the Internet for cultural topics. For example, you can find excellent resources on race and ethnicity at http://www.georgetown.edu/crossroads/asw/ract.html. Georgetown University manages this web page, which provides links to sites for Native Americans and Americans of African, Asian, and Latino origin. A category designated "other" links you to additional information such as immigration, Italian American resources, and cultural institutes for specific groups.

A word of caution: If you choose an international or cultural topic, be sure to make connections to your listeners' here-and-now concerns. For example, suppose your subject is land mines. This may seem pretty far removed from your campus world, but think of ways your classmates could identify with the topic. Would they empathize with the plight of innocent villagers who lose feet or even legs when they step on a mine? Do any of your listeners have friends or relatives who are military personnel and thus at

New!
Expanded Technology Coverage
With updated and expanded coverage of technology and the Internet, this Third Edition helps students fully exploit the technological resources available to help them select a topic, research, write, and present their speeches.

Updated!
Global Perspective
As the book's subtitle reveals, the diversity of individuals in our society has a profound impact on how we communicate. More than ever before, it is essential that students understand how individuals of different backgrounds speak and listen. Updated and expanded diversity topics are woven throughout the narrative of the book and further explored in new *Diversity in Practice* boxes that bring to light public speaking traditions from a range of perspectives.

> ### DIVERSITY IN PRACTICE
> ### Public Speaking in Ancient Cultures
>
> Public speaking has its place in every society. For example, fragments of the oldest book in existence, *The Precepts of Kagemni and Ptah-hotep,* which date back to 2100 B.C., instructed young Egyptian men and women in the wisdom of the culture (Gray, 1946). Not surprisingly, these writings stressed the importance of public speaking and give guidelines for both speaking and listening:
>
> ■ Speak with exactness; however, there is a time for silence.
>
> ■ Keep in mind that listeners who lack "good fellowship" cannot be influenced by the speeches of others.
>
> ■ Do not be proud of your learning.
>
> ■ Keep silent in the face of a better debater; refute the false arguments of an equal, but let a weaker speaker's arguments confound themselves.
>
> ■ Do not pervert the truth.
>
> ■ Do not give or repeat extravagant speech that is heated by wrath.

EMPOWERING

Apprehension about public speaking isn't something endured only by students — it affects everyone from the first-time speechmaker to the experienced executive. By helping students build skills and knowledge, Jaffe empowers them with the confidence to express their ideas through speechmaking. This new-found assurance serves students well on campus and in their future careers.

principles of invention help you analyze your audience, select an appropriate topic and purpose, gather evidence, and develop reasonable and logical arguments. Obviously, the content of any speech is vital; that is why this text devotes nine chapters to the norms found in the canon of invention.

2. **Canon of disposition (arrangement).** The standards in this canon help you arrange your ideas so that they connect logically and flow coherently. You will learn how to organize major points, create introductions and conclusions, and connect ideas to one another and to the speech as a whole. Seven of the following chapters discuss the principles of disposition or arrangement.

Canon of Disposition or Arrangement
Guidelines for organizing a speech.

3. **Canon of style.** The guidelines and principles in the canon of style help you choose the language that is best suited to your audience and to the occasion. Chapter 13 elaborates on style or language norms.

Canon of Style
Principles for choosing effective language.

4. **Canon of memory.** Ancient orators lacked the "technology" (pens, note cards, highlighters) that you have available to cue memory. Thus, they developed extensive principles for memorizing their speeches. Today we no longer need to learn speeches by heart. Consequently, there is no chapter in this text dedicated to the canon of memory, although Chapter 14 provides some guidelines for rehearsal.

Canon of Memory
Guidelines to help you remember your ideas.

5. **Canon of delivery.** The rules or standards for actually presenting your speech to an audience are found in the canon of delivery. Chapter 14 describes delivery skills (eye contact, gestures, vocal variety) that you can use to present your ideas with poise and polish.

Canon of Delivery
Rules or standards for presenting your speech.

For additional material on the canons of rhetoric, check the Internet website sponsored by Brigham Young University: http://humanities.byu.edu/rhetoric/canons.htm. The remainder of this chapter details an aspect of each canon that you can use as you create and perform your first speech.

Consider Your Audience (Invention)

Developing Confidence
Chapter 2, *Giving Your First Speech: Developing Confidence*, features an abundance of guidelines and suggestions for overcoming public speaking anxiety. Building upon a foundation of 2500-year-old principles of rhetoric—the five canons of invention, disposition, style, memory, and delivery—Jaffe provides students with a start-to-finish guide for preparing their first speeches. Her approach transforms the fear of the unknown into the confidence to succeed.

STUDENT OUTLINE WITH COMMENTARY

Self-Introduction *by Jason Kelleghan*

Since the beginning of time people have had the burning desire to explore unknown territory, seek out new lands, and go where no one has gone before. Men such as Lewis and Clark and Neil Armstrong have inspired us all to expand our boundaries. These men have risked injury, humiliation, and even death. I have been one of those men, and this is my story.

The summer before my senior year in high school, the feeling of invincibility had already set in. I was working as a camp counselor at a park called "Castle Rock," named after a gargantuan stone deep inside the park. Every Friday my best friend Keith would drive down and visit. We would spend the time hiking the trails behind the park. Every time we passed Castle Rock, we admired its size and majesty and discussed how wonderful it would be to climb it—all the while knowing we were too scared to actually make an attempt. And, every time, Castle Rock would look us in the eye and mock our cowardice.

Finally, I couldn't take it anymore. We were going to climb the rock or die trying. Now this rock was huge, almost five stories in height—mostly vertical, with a slight slope about three-quarters of the way up. Keep in mind that Keith had no experience rock climbing, let alone did we have the proper equipment. We both knew that a mistake on this rock could mean death, but that wasn't going to stop us.

The morning of the climb I loaded my backpack with food, water, and an old rope I found in the garage. I don't know why I brought the rope, it just seemed like a good idea for rock climbing. We hiked a short way to the base and, without saying a word, solemnly made our way up the rock. I went first; Keith followed. Keith and I both

He gains his classmates' attention by alluding to well-known explorers and to the *Star Trek* motto.

Jason's assignment was to introduce himself by telling a personal experience narrative that taught him a lesson.

Jason piles up details when he describes the setting of his adventure. Notice how he personifies the mountain (gives it human characteristics). Also, look at the way he clarifies an ambiguous

---

Updated!
Safety in Numbers— Sample Speeches
Because public speaking creates anxiety in so many people, it can be comforting to see how others tackle the challenge. Through their exploration of 14 student speeches (a dozen of which are new or updated) as well as five sample outlines, students gain an understanding of how to apply what they've learned to their own speech-making process. Several of the sample speeches are included

on the *Speech Interactive* component of the *Jaffe Connection CD-ROM*. Now, students can not only read the model speech but can watch, listen, critique, and compare their critique to an expert's model. Additional outlines and speeches are available in the *Student Workbook* (see page 8).

PREVIEW

INTEGRATED

Exploit the full resources available on the Internet with these dynamic teaching and learning resources exclusive to *Wadsworth/Thomson Learning*™!

InfoTrac® College Edition

Ignite discussions or augment your lectures with the latest development in public speaking! Packaged FREE with Jaffe's text, *InfoTrac College Edition* gives you and your students 4 months of free access to an easy-to-use online database of reliable, full-length articles (not abstracts) from hundreds of top academic journals and popular sources. Among the journals available 24 hours a day, seven days a week are *Commentary, Communication Quarterly, Communication World, Communication Daily, Argumentation and Advocacy*, and *Vital Speeches*.

The possibilities for incorporating *InfoTrac College Edition* into your course are virtually limitless, from putting together reading assignments to using articles to launch your lectures, jump-start discussions, or open whole new worlds of information and research for students. If you want your students to have access to a custom, no-cost set of online *InfoTrac College Edition* readings that feature the latest research and findings in communications and public speaking, you can work with your Wadsworth representative to create an up-to-the-minute resource. And, Wadsworth makes incorporating *InfoTrac College Edition* so easy— references to this virtual library are built into Jaffe's text. Contact your Wadsworth/Thomson Learning representative for more information. Offer available to North American colleges and universities only. Specific journals subject to change.

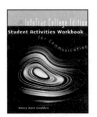

InfoTrac College Edition Student Activities Workbook for Communication 1.0
by Nancy Rost Goulden (Kansas State University)
ISBN: 0-534-52464-8
With a focus on public speaking, this workbook features extensive individual and group activities that utilize *InfoTrac College Edition*. Available bundled with the text, the workbook includes guidelines for faculty and students on maximizing this resource.

InfoTrac College Edition Student Activities Workbook for Communication 2.0
ISBN: 0-534-52993-3
With a focus on human communication topics (interpersonal, small group, public speaking), this workbook features extensive individual and group activities that utilize *InfoTrac College Edition*. Available bundled with the text, the workbook includes guidelines for faculty and students on maximizing this resource.

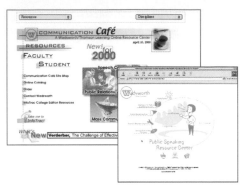

Communication Café
and the Public Speaking Resource Center
http://communication.wadsworth.com
When you adopt Jaffe's text, you and your students will have access to a rich array of teaching and learning resources that you won't find anywhere else. The *Communication Café* and the *Public Speaking Resource Center* feature everything from online quizzing to interesting links. It's the ideal way to make teaching and learning an interactive and exciting experience.

For instructors:
■ A faculty exchange area and dynamic faculty links

■ The ability to download supplements online

■ Custom publishing options

■ Product tours that let you explore new titles

For instructors and students:
■ Links to a rich array of relevant and interesting sites on the World Wide Web

■ Online activities that clarify communication course work and inspire further studies

ONLINE RESOURCES

INTEGRATED

Take your **classroom presentations** *further—and make preparation easier—with these outstanding tools.*

Instructor's Resource Manual
by Clella Jaffe
ISBN: 0-534-52995-X
Written by Clella Jaffe, this manual features course guidelines and sample syllabi. For each chapter there are transition notes to the new edition, chapter goals and an outline, suggestions for correlating supplements and online resources, supplementary research notes, suggested discussion questions and specific suggestions for integrating student workbook activities, *SpeakLink* PowerPoint slides, and videos including the exclusive *CNN Today* video series. The comprehensive Test Bank features questions built upon the concepts inherent to Bloom's *Taxonomy of Thinking.* Questions are labeled according to the *Taxonomy* and include rejoinders with page references.

ExamView® CD-ROM

CD-ROM for Windows® and Macintosh®
ISBN: 0-534-52997-6
This cross-platform CD-ROM provides a fully integrated collection of test-creation, delivery, and classroom management tools that feature all the test items found in the Instructor's Resource Manual.

SpeakLink: Lecture Presentation Tool for Public Speaking, v 1.0
by Linda Loomis Steck, Indiana University-South Bend
CD-ROM for Windows® and Macintosh® ISBN: 0-534-52996-8
This dynamic presentation tool contains a searchable database of PowerPoint slides that feature text art and CNN video clips plus the ability to import information from previously created lectures.

A Wadsworth/Thomson Learning exclusive!
CNN Today: Public Speaking Videos

Volume I ISBN: 0-534-52212-2; Volume II ISBN: 0-534-52213-0; Volume III ISBN: 0-534-52214-9
Launch your lectures with riveting footage from CNN, the world's leading 24-hour global news television network. *CNN Today: Public Speaking* videos allow you to integrate the newsgathering and programming power of CNN into the classroom to show students the relevance of course topics to their everyday lives. Organized by topics covered in a typical course, these videos are divided into short segments—perfect for introducing key concepts.

Wadsworth Communication Video Library
When you adopt this text, you can select from a variety of videos covering key communication topics such as public speaking, discussion, debate, and family and gender communication. Contact your Wadsworth/Thomson Learning representative for a more information and a complete listing of titles. Titles in the Video Library include:
- Foundations of Communication Series
- Student Speeches for Analysis
- Business and Professional Communication
- Gender Communication
- Great Speeches: The Video Series
- Great Speeches: Today's Women
- Great Speeches: The Presidents

Student Speeches for Critique and Analysis Video

Volume I ISBN: 0-534-56258-2;
Volume II ISBN: 0-534-56262-0
Volume I features a speech of introduction, two impromptu, four informative, and two persuasive speeches, this video is a great tool for helping students learn to analyze and provide effective feedback on imperfect speeches. Selected speeches feature non-native English speakers and the use of visual aids. A video outline including running time of each speech and video/chapter correlation guide is provided with each cassette. Volume II provides even more opportunities for critique and analysis!

The Teaching Assistant's Guide to the Basic Course
by Katherine G. Hendrix, University of Memphis (Ph.D., University of Washington)
ISBN: 0-534-56778-9
This guide is designed for the new communication teacher. Based on leading communication teacher training programs, the guide covers general teaching and course management topics as well as specific strategies for communication instruction. Topics include surviving the first week of class, considering the context of your teaching, lecturing and group discussion, grading oral performance, managing sensitive class discussions, and the value of self-assessment.

INSTRUCTOR'S RESOURCES

INTEGRATED

*These learning aids will help your **students** make the most of their study time away from the classroom.*

Jaffe Connection CD-ROM

Accompanying each student text is the *Jaffe Connection CD-ROM*. This CD-ROM consists of five integrated components: *InfoTrac® College Edition*, Internet Exercises, access to chapter-by-chapter resources at the Public Speaking Resource Center at Wadsworth's *Communication Café*, *Jaffe Speech Interactive* and a preview of *Thomson Learning Web Tutor™*. Each component of the CD-ROM is represented in the text with an icon. Integrated throughout the chapter and expanded upon at the end of the chapter, these integrated icons direct students to numerous activities and reinforce and enrich concepts presented.

Speech Interactive: Student Speeches for Critique and Analysis CD-ROM

CD-ROM for Windows® and Macintosh® ISBN: 0-534-52999-2

Exclusively developed for Wadsworth/Thomson Learning™, *Speech Interactive* helps students prepare for their own speech performance and effectively provide feedback to their peers by critiquing the impromptu, introductory, informative, and persuasive speeches of the students featured on the Wadsworth *Student Speeches for Critique and Analysis* video. Students can complete speech evaluation checklists and speech improvement plans compare to expert models. Jaffe *Speech Interactive* (described on page 2) is a text-specific version of this CD-ROM featuring select speeches from Wadsworth's student speech video and others from the Jaffe text.

Student Workbook

by Clella Jaffe
ISBN: 0-534-52998-4

This workbook complements and expands students' understanding and use of the book. Part I features a welcome letter to the student and an introductory overview about the benefits of taking a Public Speaking course. Part II features chapter-by-chapter activities, many of which are based on the text's *Stop and Check* activities and include *scenario-based* learning that facilitates both individual and group work. Chapter review self-tests with answer keys are also included. Part III features guidelines, checklists, and sample speeches representing a multitude of speech types. Speech preparation forms and checklists are formatted so they can be pulled out of the workbook and submitted.

Take your course beyond classroom boundaries!
Thomson Learning Web Tutor™
on WebCT and Blackboard

Web Tutor™ on WebCT ISBN: 0-534-53000-1
Web Tutor™ on Blackboard ISBN: 0-534-53044-3

WebTUTOR™

Designed to complement Jaffe's text, this content-rich, Web-based teaching and learning tool helps students succeed by taking the course beyond classroom boundaries to an anywhere, anytime environment. *Web Tutor* is rich with study and mastery tools, communication tools, and course content. You can use *Web Tutor* to provide virtual office hours, post your syllabi, set up threaded discussions, track student progress with the quizzing material, and more.

For your students, *Web Tutor* offers real-time access to a full array of study tools, including flashcards (with audio), practice quizzes, online tutorials, and Web links. Professors who have tried *Web Tutor* have been especially pleased with the way *Web Tutor* allows students—even those in very large classes—to participate in class discussions online. This student-to-student interaction has enormous potential to enhance each student's experience with the course content.

Guide to the Basic Course for ESL Students

by Esther Yook, Mary Washington College
ISBN: 0-534-56779-7

This student guide is designed to assist the non-native speaker. Features FAQs, helpful URLs, strategies for accent management, and overcoming speech apprehension.

Service Learning in Communication Studies: A Handbook

by Rick Isaacson, San Francisco State University, with Bruce Dorries, Radford University, and Kevin Brown, Montana State University
ISBN: 0-534-56631-6

The handbook provides guidelines for connecting service learning work with classroom concepts and advice for working effectively with agencies and organizations. The handbook also provides model forms and reports and a directory of online resources.

www.wadsworth.com

wadsworth.com is the World Wide Web site for Wadsworth and is your direct source to dozens of online resources.

At wadsworth.com you can find out about supplements, demonstration software, and student resources. You can also send e-mail to many of your authors and preview new publications and exciting new technologies.

wadsworth.com
Changing the way the world learns.®

From the Wadsworth Series in Speech Communication

Public Speaking

*Concepts and Skills for a
Diverse Society*

THIRD EDITION

CLELLA JAFFE
George Fox University

Wadsworth
Thomson Learning

Australia • Canada • Mexico
Singapore • Spain • United
Kingdom • United States

Executive Editor: Deirdre Cavanaugh
Publisher: Clark Baxter
Executive Marketing Manager: Stacey Purviance
Signing Representative: Tamy Stenquist
Editorial Assistant: Aimee Lilles
Project Editor: Cathy Linberg
Print Buyer: Mary Noel
Permissions Editor: Joohee Lee
Technology Project Manager: Jeanette Wiseman
Production Service: York Production Services

Text and Cover Designer: Lisa Mirski Devenish, Devenish Design
Photo Researcher: Laurel Anderson, Photosynthesis
Copy Editors: Judy Johnstone and Karen Slaght
Illustrators: Carole Lawson and 17th St. Studios
Cover, Title Page, Diversity in Practice Boxes, and CD-ROM
    Images: Details from "Culture of the Crossroads" ©1998 By
    Susan Kelk Cervantes. Sponsored by Precita Eyes.
Cover and Chapter-Opening Murals Photographer: Jonathan Fisher
Compositor: York Graphic Services
Printer: Transcontinental Printing

Printed in Canada
1 2 3 4 5 6 7 04 03 02 01 00

Library of Congress Cataloging-in-Publication Data
Jaffe, Clella Iles
    Public speaking: concepts and skills for a diverse society/ Clella
    Jaffe.—3rd ed.
        p. cm.
    Includes bibliographical references and index.
    ISBN 0-534-52992-5
    1. Public speaking. 2. Multiculturalism. I. Title.
PN4121 .J25 2000
808.5'1—dc21   00-032497

Wadsworth/Thomson Learning
10 Davis Drive
Belmont, CA 94002-3098
USA

For more information about our products, contact us:
Thomson Learning Academic Resource Center
1-800-423-0563
http://www.wadsworth.com

International Headquarters
Thomson Learning
International Division
290 Harbor Drive, 2nd Floor
Stamford, CT 06902-7477
USA

UK/Europe/Middle East/South Africa
Thomson Learning
Berkshire House
168-173 High Holborn
London WC1V 7AA
United Kingdom

Asia
Thomson Learning
60 Albert Street, #15-01
Albert Complex
Singapore 189969

Canada
Nelson Thomson Learning
1120 Birchmount Road
Toronto, Ontario M1K 5G4
Canada

Brief Contents

List of Speeches

Contents

Jaffe Speech
Interactive

Preface

The civilization of the dialogue is the only civilization worth having and the only civilization in which the whole world can unite. It is, therefore, the only civilization we can hope for, because the world must unite or be blown to bits.

Robert Hutchins, 1967

It is a pleasure to write a preface to the third edition to this text. I am grateful to all who used the first two editions and contributed helpful suggestions to improve the book. You'll find substantial revisions in this edition—changes that improve the text's overall readability and usefulness in a digital age. This edition continues to be a culturally informed book that never loses sight of its fundamental purpose: to train students to be effective public speakers and listeners. It applies 2,500-year-old principles of public speaking in a way that is sensitive to our rapidly changing pluralistic society. The recognition of diversity doesn't detract from building basic public speaking skills; rather, it broadens the repertoire of concepts, skills, theories, applications, and critical thinking proficiencies essential for listening and speaking in today's world.

Public Speaking and Diversity

I wrote this text because I believe that public speaking and diversity are intertwined. Through public speaking, we express, reinforce, transmit, influence, and blend diverse cultures. In fact, the very human characteristics speakers aim to influence—beliefs, values, attitudes, and actions — are precisely the basic elements of diversity. In the classroom, cultural backgrounds influence students' perceptions of the role of public speaking, their perceptions of themselves as speakers, their perceptions of their audiences, and their perceptions of other speakers. Culture also influences topic selection, research methods and resources, and reasoning styles.

More than ever before, students need to understand diversity, because the world now features unprecedented interaction between individuals of widely varying backgrounds and experiences. Also, people from one cultural background increasingly find themselves speaking to audiences from other cultural backgrounds. As media and transportation technologies become ever more sophisticated, the pace of cross-cultural interaction will only quicken. All of us need to tune in to the different ways in which people from diverse backgrounds speak and listen.

Technology has not only quickened the pace of cross-cultural interaction but also transformed the way teachers teach and students learn; thus, it is critical that the text support today's dynamic and interactive course experience.

In short, I believe that a book that teaches public speaking without strongly emphasizing diversity and fully integrating technology gives today's students an incomplete education. Consequently, this book continues to emphasize diversity while expanding coverage of basic public speaking skills and harnessing the power of technology resources. Throughout, I present public speaking and listening as a form of dialogue or public conversation in which speakers and listeners co-create mutual meanings.

Features of the New Edition

Three new chapters and the Jaffe Connection CD-ROM are at the core of this text's approach.

- **Chapter 1,** *Introduction to Public Speaking and Diversity,* now integrates a discussion of diversity (previously Chapter 3), reflecting an evolving definition of communication and culture that includes technology.

- **Chapter 3,** *Ethics and Diversity,* helps students explore their responsibilities as ethical speakers and listeners in a diverse society.

- **Chapter 15,** *Telling Narratives,* emphasizes the importance of narrative (storytelling) to all cultures, describing the function of and specific guidelines for creating narrative speeches.

- **JAFFE CONNECTION** This new edition of Jaffe, *Public Speaking: Concepts and Skills for a Diverse Society,* expands student learning into a multimedia environment. Accompanying each student text is the Jaffe Connection CD-ROM. This CD-ROM consists of five integrated components; access to chapter-by-chapter resources at the Public Speaking Resource Center at Wadsworth's Communication Café, access to InfoTrac College Edition, hyperlinked Internet Exercises, Jaffe Speech Interactive, and a preview of WebTutor. Each component of the CD-ROM is represented in the text with an icon. Integrated throughout the chapter and expanded upon at the end of the chapter, these integrated icons direct students to numerous activities and reinforce and enrich concepts presented.

Wadsworth Public Speaking Resource Center, hyperlinked from Jaffe Connection, provides students with dynamic chapter-by-chapter resources as well as the opportunity to participate in an expert monitored threaded discussion on a variety of contemporary public speaking topics. For each chapter in this edition, students can access hotlinks, quizzes, glossary terms, speech preparation and evaluation checklists, InfoTrac College Edition questions, and interactive activities. The interactive activities, including several that focus on speech organization and outlining, are based on the *Stop and Check* feature included in the text and described below
http://communication.wadsworth.com/publicspeaking/index.html.

InfoTrac College Edition

Students who purchase Jaffe Connection receive a free four-month subscription to this fully searchable, online library with extensive holdings in communication. **InfoTrac College Edition** exercises are included in the text and at the end of each chapter. These exercises expand chapter content and guarantee currency of presentation. InfoTrac provides access to complete articles from over 900 scholarly and popular periodicals, is updated daily, and dates back four years, including the journal *Vital Speeches,* a key resource of contemporary model speeches. Look for the InfoTrac College Edition logo in the text and in the Jaffe Connection section at the end of each chapter. See below for more about how to use InfoTrac College Edition in your course.

Internet Activities are located throughout the text and at the end of each chapter. These activities, marked by a web icon, introduce students to Public Speaking on the World Wide Web with practical and engaging activities that mirror the chapter content and include suggestions for small-group work. Hyperlinked from the text to Wadsworth's Public Speaking Resource Center via the Jaffe Connection CD-ROM, currency and functioning of Internet links is assured.

Jaffe Speech
Interactive **Jaffe Speech Interactive**

Jaffe Speech Interactive is the primary resident program on the Jaffe Connection CD-ROM. Speech Interactive helps students prepare for their own speech performance and effectively provide feedback to their peers by critiquing sample impromptu, introductory, informative, and persuasive speeches. Equipped with general guidelines for critiquing speeches, students have the opportunity to watch and listen to four different types of speeches from six different speakers. Students are then prompted to complete a Speech Evaluation Checklist and Speech Improvement Plan for each speech. Finally, students are presented with the opportunity to compare their critique and suggestions for improvement with that of an expert. Four of the speeches—an introduction, two informative, and a narrative speech—are included in the text.

WebTUTOR **Highlighted by icons throughout the text, students are encouraged to take their learning online!** Web Tutor is a web-based learning companion to the third edition and is previewed in Jaffe Connection. Professors who require Web Tutor provide students with a great tool for studying and course management. Features include presentation of chapter objectives and lessons; flashcards with audio; exercises that can be downloaded, completed, and returned to the instructor; discussion topics integrated within the chapter; online review questions and tutorials; links to real-world locations for timely information; real-time chat; calendar of syllabus information; e-mail connections (using existing e-mail accounts); and an announcement board. For a demonstration of this product please visit the website www.itped.com. This state-of-the-art class management and study tool is available bundled with the text.

In addition to three new chapters and Jaffe Connection, the following content enhancements and text features are included in the third edition:

■ **New Research.** This new edition integrates the most current research on areas such as critical thinking, public speaking anxiety, culture, learning styles, technology, listening, and narrative speaking. References are now provided in APA Style, for ease of use. You will also find a complete Bibliography at the end of the text, complete with online source references.

■ **Expanded Technology Coverage.** This new edition provides updated and expanded coverage of the impact of technology and the Internet on the speechmaking process.

    ■ Coverage includes using the Internet and electronically stored sources to research speech topics, critically evaluating Internet materials, and using technology to enhance visual aids.

    ■ In the text of each chapter, URLs have been added to help students further investigate chapter topics online. Consult the Jaffe Connection section at the end of each chapter and look for the accompanying icons in text.

■ **Communication Apprehension.** Chapter 2 now provides increased coverage of communication apprehension, including a new student self-assessment.

- **Quick Start Chapter.** Chapter 2, *Giving Your First Speech: Developing Confidence*, gets students off to a fast start with an overview of the speechmaking process and decreases their speech anxiety with a series of helpful tips and exercises.

- **Awareness of diverse learning styles and languages.** Where appropriate, I specifically address students whose first language is not English. Further, students will find specific guidelines for speaking through an interpreter, and Appendix C features a classroom speech given in Spanish and interpreted into English. In addition, the Student Resource Workbook contains an assignment for a speech using an interpreter. I've continued my focus on a variety of learning styles featuring both linear and nonlinear ways of learning.

Chapter-by-Chapter Features

- **Chapter Objectives.** Each chapter begins with a preview of the chapter's goals, then pauses every few pages to provide an opportunity to probe these key concepts through *Stop and Check* activities and *Diversity in Practice* boxes.

- **Margin Definitions.** Key terms are highlighted in bold throughout each chapter (when the term is first mentioned) and definitions are provided in the margins. These glossary terms are also provided on the Public Speaking Resource Center and in an audio and text format on Web Tutor.

- *Stop and Check.* These critical thinking and skill-building exercises help students check their progress throughout the chapter. Several of these activities are available in the Student Workbook and in an interactive format at the Public Speaking Resource Center and on Web Tutor.

- *Diversity in Practice.* These boxes enhance the book's emphasis on diversity by presenting brief summaries of public speaking traditions from a range of perspectives.

- *Key Terms.* The perfect complement to the in-chapter Margin Definitions, a list of key terms at the end of each chapter helps students check their acquisition of important vocabulary. Using the page number provided, students can easily reference the term with its definition in context.

- **Application and Critical Thinking Questions.** Due to their success with students, we've retained this popular feature. These end-of-chapter questions help students understand and critically evaluate the chapter content and skills they've learned. Instructors may use them in a variety of ways: as individual assignments, as group assignments, or as topics for in-class discussion.

- **Chapter Summary.** Each chapter concludes with a brief summary, highlighting the key topics covered in the chapter

- **Sample Speeches.** To provide you with exemplary models of the speech techniques taught in this text, this new edition has almost three times as many sample speeches and five times as many sample outlines as the previous edition. You will find 14 annotated sample student speeches or outlines and three speeches by professionals. Many of these are available on the Jaffe Connection CD-ROM, and additional student speeches will be made available online (http://communication.wadsworth.com). The five sample content outlines with commentary, plus expanded speaking outlines and outlines for alternative patterns, enhance the usefulness of this edition. You will find additional outlines and speeches in the Student Resource Workbook. (See below for more information about the Student Resource Workbook and Speech Interactive, a video and CD-ROM that has more sample speeches for critique and analysis.)

Resources for Students and Instructors

This edition has the most comprehensive array of supplements ever to assist in making this course as meaningful and effective as possible. The anchor of this program is the Jaffe Connection CD-ROM described earlier. This CD-ROM and many of the resources listed below are new to this edition. Please contact your local Wadsworth/Thomson Learning representative for an examination copy and demonstration, or call our Academic Resource Center at 1-800-423-0563. You may also visit us online at http://communication.wadsworth.com/.

Student Resources

- **Wadsworth Communication Café** http://communication.wadsworth.com. Pull up a chair, grab an espresso (or tea!), and log on to the Communication Café, *the* online resource for communication students and faculty. Our newly redesigned website features everything from online testing to tutorials to discussion forums. It's the ideal way to make teaching and learning an interactive and enlivening experience.

- *InfoTrac College Edition Student Workbook for Communication 1.0* (0-534-52464-8). Written by Nancy Rost Goulden of Kansas State University, this saleable workbook can also be bundled with the text. It focuses on public speaking and features extensive individual and group activities that utilize InfoTrac College Edition. The workbook also includes guidelines for students and faculty on maximizing this resource.

- *InfoTrac College Edition Student Workbook for Communication 2.0* (0-534-52993-3). This saleable workbook can also be bundled with the text. It focuses on human communication topics (small group, interpersonal, public speaking) and includes guidelines for faculty and students on maximizing this resource.

- *Student Workbook* by Clella Jaffe (0-534-52998-4). This workbook compliments and expands students' understanding and use of the book. Part I features a welcome letter to the student and an introductory overview about the benefits of taking a public speaking course. Part II features chapter-by-chapter activities, many of which are based on the text's *Stop and Check* activities and include scenario-based learning that facilitates both individual and group work. Chapter review self-tests with answer keys are also included. Part III features speech assignment options, examples, and checklists. Speech preparation forms and checklists are formatted so they can be pulled out of the workbook and submitted.

Instructor Resources

- **Instructor's Edition** (0-534-52994-1). This edition—produced for especially for the instructor—includes a visual preface that explains the book's key features and the ancillary package.

- **Instructor's Resource Manual** (0-534-52995-X). Written by Clella Jaffe, this manual features course guidelines and sample syllabi. For each chapter there is a chapter-at-a-glance grid that correlates supplements and online resources, transition notes to the new edition, chapter goals and outline, suggested discussion questions and specific suggestions for integrating student workbook activities, and videos including the exclusive CNN Today video series. The comprehensive Test Bank features questions built on the concepts inherent to Bloom's Taxonomy of Thinking. Question areas are labeled according to the taxonomy and include rejoinders with page references.

- **ExamView for Windows and Macintosh** (0-534-52997-6). This cross-platform CD-ROM provides a fully integrated collection of test creation, delivery, and classroom management tools that feature all the test items found in the Instructor's Resource Manual.

- **Web Tutor on WebCT** (0-534-53000-1). Harnessing the power of the Internet to deliver public speaking aids that support various learning styles, Web Tutor is a web-based learning companion to this text. Features include presentation of chapter objectives and lessons; flashcards with audio, still images, and video; exercises that can be downloaded, completed, and returned to the instructor; discussion topics integrated within the chapter; online review questions and tutorials; links to real-world locations for timely information; real-time chat; calendar of syllabus information; e-mail connections (using existing e-mail accounts); and an announcement board. For a demonstration of this product, please visit the website www.itped.com. This state-of-the-art class management and study tool is available bundled with the text, as a stand-alone, or via online subscription.

- **SpeakLink: Lecture Presentation Tool for Public Speaking** (0-534-52996-8). This cross-platform CD-ROM—developed by Linda Loomis Steck, Indiana University, South Bend—is a dynamic presentation tool. It contains a searchable database of PowerPoint slides that feature text art, CNN video clips, plus the ability to import information from previously created lectures.

- **Videos.** Also available to instructors adopting this book is a wealth of video resources. Video policy is based on adoption size; contact your Wadsworth/Thomson Learning representative for more information.

  - **Student Speeches for Critique and Analysis Video** (Vol. I: 0-534-56258-2; Vol II: 0-534-56262-0). Featuring a speech of introduction, two impromptu speeches, four informational, and two persuasive speeches, Volume I is a great tool for helping students analyze and provide effective feedback on imperfect speeches. Select speeches feature non-native English speakers and include the use of visual aids. Volume II offers additional opportunities for critique and analysis.

  - **CNN Today Public Speaking Videos.** Updated yearly, these high-interest, 45-minute videos can help you launch a lecture, spark a discussion, or demonstrate an application. The following series of public speaking videos are available to qualifying adopters. Ask your Wadsworth/Thomson Learning representative for more information. (CNN Today videos are also available for Human Communication, Interpersonal Communication, and Mass Communication.)

    - Volume 1 (0-534-52212-2)

    - Volume 2 (0-534-52213-0)

    - Volume 3 (0-534-52214-9)

  - **Wadsworth Communication Video Library.** This library has over 30 videos covering key communication topics, including "Oral Critiques of Student Speeches," "Public Speaking: Knowing Your Audience," "Effective Speeches," and "Great Speeches: The Video Series."

- **Service Learning in Communication Studies: A Handbook** (0-534-56631-6). Prepared by Rick Isaacson, Bruce Dorries, and Kevin Brown, this handbook describes ways to integrate service learning into the basic communication course and prepares students to work effectively with agencies and organizations.

- **The Teaching Assistant's Guide to the Basic Course** (0-534-56778-9). Katherine G. Hendrix, who is on the faculty at the University of Memphis, prepared this resource specifically for new instructors. Available to instructors who adopt this new edition, this useful guide is based on leading communication teacher training programs. It discusses some of the general issues that accompany a teaching role and offers specific strategies for managing the first week of classes, leading productive discussions, managing sensitive topics in the classroom, and grading students' written and oral work.

■ **A Guide to the Basic Course for ESL Students** (0-534-56779-7). This saleable item can be bundled with the text and is designed to assist the non-native speaker. It features Frequently Asked Questions (FAQs), helpful URLs, and strategies for accent management and overcoming speech apprehension.

How to Use InfoTrac College Edition

We have mentioned access to InfoTrac College Edition quite a bit. For the latest news and research articles online—updated daily and spanning four years—we strongly encourage you to make *InfoTrac College Edition (ICE)* a vital part of your public speaking course.

Once you request and receive your new edition bundled with InfoTrac College Edition, you will be able to access this valuable resource. Simply log on to www.infotrac college.com/wadsworth and enter your account ID number, which came with your text, and begin your search. If you did not receive a password, please contact your local Wadsworth representative or call our Academic Resource Center at 1-800-423-0563.

Ways to Search

You can use InfoTrac College Edition to search in three ways:

■ **Subject Guide.** Subject Guide pages display every indexed topic in which the word you typed in the search box appears, as well as the number of references indexed under each topic. This lets you see exactly what matches your search before you view the citations and enables you to choose a single aspect or topic.

■ **Key Words.** Entering one or more key words will give you the broadest range of citations. Literally any citation that includes your word or words in the title and/or abstract will appear. This is helpful if you have a very specific search word, but less helpful than the Subject Guide if your topic word is broad.

■ **PowerTrac.** PowerTrac lets you create complex search expressions that combine different search methods, such as author and topic, or find articles from a particular publication and issue date. You will find suggestions for PowerTrac searches in this new edition.

Search Tips

1. Be as specific as possible with search words, so you get citations that are useful to you.

2. If you don't get a lot of matches, try different words. For example, many articles use "public speaking" as a Subject Guide, but many other articles using "communication" as the subject might also be useful in speech preparation.

3. After you open an article, use the Link feature to get a list of related articles and topics.

4. When your search results are too broad, use the Limit Search button. This button will allow you to limit the search, for example, to within a specified range of dates, making your material more timely.

5. Please don't wait until the last minute to do your research on InfoTrac! As with any other library system, it takes time to get to know how the system works and the many ways it can help you do research.

Acknowledgments

Every book is in some way a co-created product in which an author relies on the insights and encouragement of others. Victoria O'Donnell (Montana State University), Sean Patrick O'Rourke (Vanderbilt University), and Anne Zach Ferguson (Oregon State University, Willamette University) initially encouraged me to undertake this project. In addition, many reviewers across the country provided insightful comments at various stages of the manuscript — some of which I incorporated into the text.

Reviewers for the Second Edition

Thomas E. Diamond, Montana State University; Kevin E. McClearey, Southern Illinois University at Edwardsville; Susan Messman, Pennsylvania State University; Karla D. Scott, Saint Louis University; Jessica Stowell, Tulsa Community College; and Lori Wisdom-Whitely, Western Washington University. I have also had support and suggestions from my valued colleagues and students at Oregon State University, St. John's University (Queens), and George Fox University.

Reviewers for the Third Edition

Clifton Adams, Central Missouri State University; Linda Anthon, Valencia Community College; Wm. Jay Baglia, University of South Florida; Carol M. Barnum, Southern Polytechnic State University; Lorin Basden Arnold, Rowan University; Julie Benson-Rosston, Red Rocks Community College; John S. Bourhis, Southwest Missouri State University; Sharman Brown, University of Rhode Island; Cheri Ellis Campbell, Keene State College; Faye L. Clark, Georgia Perimeter College; Risa E. Dickson, California State University, San Bernardino; Hal W. Fulmer, Georgia Southern University; Matthew Girton, Florida State University; Sherrie L. Guerroro, San Bernardino Valley College; Robert Gwynne, University of Tennessee, Knoxville; Fred E. Jandt, California State University, San Bernardino; Ben Martin, Santa Monica College; Cathy Sargent Mester, Penn State at Erie – The Behrend College; Laura L. Nelson, University of Wisconsin–La Crosse; Mark D. Nelson, University of Alabama; Jean E. Perry, Glendale Community College; Susan L. Richardson, Prince George Community College; Paula Rodriquez, Hinds CC; Scott Rodriquez, California State University, San Bernardino; Kristi A. Schaller, Georgia State University; Ann M. Scroggie, Santa Fe Community College; Karni Spain Tiernan, Bradley University; Susan Z. Swan, University of South Dakota; David E. Walker, Middle Tennessee State University; June D. Wells, Indian River Community College; Nancy J. Wendt, Oregon State University; L. Keith Williamson, Wichita State University; and Marianne Worthington, Cumberland College.

Finally, my daughter, Sara Jaffe Reamy, provided a student's perspective on manuscript drafts; my nephew, Mark Iles, contributed several pieces of art; and my husband, Jack, provided moral support throughout the hectic months of revision! The editors and designers at Wadsworth paid special attention to necessary details at each stage of manuscript revision. Beginning with Holly Allen who saw the project most of the way through the first edition, Randall Adams, Michael Gillespie, Vicki Friedberg, Sherry Symington, and Megan Gilbert who oversaw the second edition, and especially Kim Johnson and

Deirdre Cavanaugh in the third edition, these editors were patient and supportive throughout the revision process. Special thanks go to the designer, Lisa Devenish; and the copy editors, Judy Johnstone and Karen Slaght.

You can help make the next edition of this book even more useful. Please contact me through the Wadsworth Communication Web site at http://communication. wadsworth.com/ or send your comments, suggestions, and other thoughts to:

Dr. Clella Jaffe
c/o Deirdre Cavanaugh deirdre.cavanaugh@wadsworth.com
Executive Editor, Communication
Wadsworth Publishing Company
10 Davis Drive
Belmont, CA 94002

1

Introduction to
Public Speaking and Culture

This chapter will help you:

- Explain three ways you can be empowered by studying public speaking

- Define culture in the context of public speaking

- Give reasons for studying public speaking from a cultural perspective

- Identify three ways culture affects public speaking

- Know how public speaking influences culture

- Identify elements of the transactional model of communication

"Culture of the Crossroads"
©1998 By Susan Kelk Cervantes.
Sponsored Precita Eyes.

In her junior year of college, Amber becomes self-employed. She gives public speeches to sell her product and to recruit other salespeople. Tomas coaches a middle school soccer team—a job that requires him to explain basic skills and to inspire his players with pep talks. Aaron sits on the Supreme Court at his university where he critically hears and evaluates student reasoning about disputed issues. Indira selects and narrows her topics, conducts research, and organizes her ideas for papers and presentations in upper-division classes. All four of these students commonly use skills they developed through the study of public speaking.

You've listened to public presentations most of your life; you may have even given a number of speeches. Now you are enrolled in a course that will help you become more mindful of the skills involved in creating and evaluating public speeches. A major purpose of this course is to help you think your way through the process of creating effective speeches. You will evaluate your current skills, identify specific areas to improve, and then plan strategies to deal with your particular speaking and listening challenges. As you create, first one speech, then another, you will improve along the way, adding competencies and refining those you already have (Jensen & Harris, 1999).

Although this course will prepare you to give speeches, more often you will be an audience member who hears and evaluates public messages in a world that is increasingly diverse. Consequently, you need to evaluate critically the messages you hear each day. The skills needed for effectiveness in these two roles—as speaker and as listener—are the focus of this text.

Why Should You Study Public Speaking?

Stop for a moment and envision "public speakers." Do you see a man in a suit and tie standing at a podium? A woman in a spacesuit presenting her mission goals to members of the press? Do you picture a group of campers sitting around a fire listening to a scary story? What about a police officer explaining bicycle safety to a group of third-graders? A kayak instructor outlining the basics to a group of beginners? All of these are public speakers, people who prepare and deliver a presentation to a group that listens, generally without interrupting the flow of ideas. If you broaden the scope of public speaking to include introductions, toasts, and project briefings, you will probably have covered many of your own potential speechmaking opportunities. The study of **public speaking** principles can empower you in a number of ways, as this section discusses.

Our Culture Values Public Speaking Skills

Most employers of college graduates value the listening, speaking, and critical thinking skills that are developed in a public speaking course. For instance, researchers have documented the importance of public speaking classes for many occupations, including teaching (Johnson & Roellke, 1999) and accounting (Stowers & White, 1999). In fact, Kendall (1988) showed that more than half of a randomly selected sample of people gave at least one speech during the previous two years. Seventy percent of them gave four or more speeches, often on work-related topics. People with higher incomes and higher educational levels spoke more frequently. In a recent survey, 98 percent of personnel interviewers agreed that both verbal and nonverbal communication skills significantly impact hiring decisions; 91 percent agreed that higher-level positions require more effective communicators; and 92 percent agreed that increased skills will be necessary in the twenty-first century. In short, personnel managers said they were more likely to hire and to promote people who communicate well orally, who listen effectively, and who exude enthusiasm—all skills you can develop in this course (Peterson, 1997).

Public Speaking

One person prepares and delivers a speech to a group that listens, generally without interrupting the flow of ideas.

This kayak instructor is giving an informative speech. He is only one of thousands of people who regularly prepare talks as part of their occupational duties. (Joel Rogers/Off-Shoot Stock)

In addition to job success, the ability to present ideas clearly and persuasively gives people a voice in society. Rather than remaining silent, they freely join the ongoing cultural conversation that takes place in politics, religion, education, business, the arts, and all the other arenas of their lives. You can probably come up with numerous examples of people whose speaking out made a difference: A Canadian teenager, Craig Kielburger, formed "Free the Children," an organization with 5000 members in 20 countries whose purpose is to prevent child labor abuses in Third World countries (Greenhouse, 1999). Jaime Escalante argued for calculus classes in his inner-city high school; Christa Wilcox, a high school senior, told her church about lessons she learned on a trip to Costa Rica. These people all used their public speaking skills to influence local, national, and even international decisions.

Training in Public Speaking Builds Confidence

Many people dread the prospect of giving speeches. It is said that George Washington was more afraid of public speaking than he was of facing a cannon or a musket (Podell & Angovin, 1988). Harrison Ford and Bridget Fonda reportedly took up acting to overcome their fears. Although many people learn to speak well in public, they continue to experience *apprehension,* the dread or fear of having something bad happen to you. **Communication apprehension (CA)** is the fear of negative reactions you might experience because you speak out (Richmond & McCroskey, 1995). A specific type of CA is **public speaking anxiety (PSA)** (Behnke & Sawyer, 1999).

Communication Apprehension (CA)

The fear or dread of negative responses you might experience because you speak out.

Public Speaking Anxiety (PSA)

Fear or dread specifically related to speaking in public.

FIGURE 1.1 Communication competence combines three overlapping elements: motivation to communicate, knowledge about communication, and skills in speaking and listening.

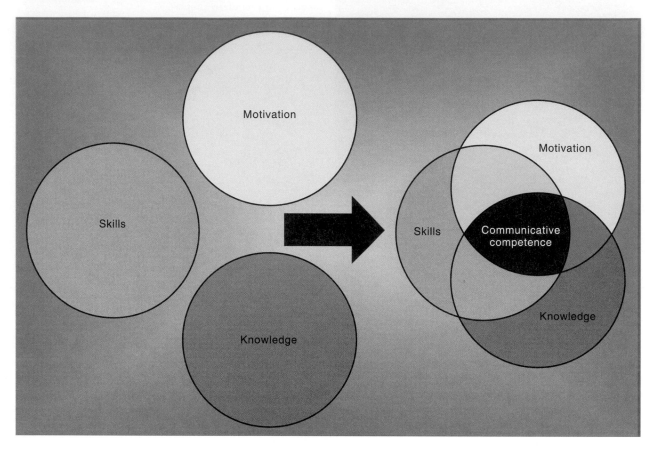

If you enter this class with some apprehension, don't worry—you're in good company. A recent poll, commissioned by the National Communication Association (Roper Starch, 1999), found that most people feel quite comfortable with their ability to communicate in face-to-face contexts, over the telephone, and in writing. However, only 24 percent (and only 13 percent of eighteen- to twenty-four-year-olds) have confidence in their public speaking abilities, while 40 percent express some level of PSA. Interestingly, 38 percent of educated people feel "very comfortable" about public presentations, in contrast to only 10 percent of high school dropouts in this category. Communication apprehension is linked to learning style preference (Dwyer, 1998), to inborn temperament traits (Beatty, et al., 1998), and to gender. Marjorie Jaasma (1997) found that, in general, women are more apprehensive than men. Chapter 2 presents information about recognizing and dealing with your own apprehension.

Remember that competence and confidence may be related, but they are not identical. Competence is the ability to succeed or to do something well; you can be *competent* without feeling *confident*. Brian Spitzberg (1994) identified three elements in **communication competence:** motivation, skills, and knowledge (see Figure 1.1). Motivation must come from within you, but studying this text, participating in classroom activities, fulfilling assignments, and actually giving speeches will help you develop the knowledge and skills you need to perform competently. Many people, especially those with high levels of PSA, feel more confident as well as more competent after they complete the course (MacIntyre & MacDonald, 1998).

Communication Competence
The ability to communicate appropriately and successfully.

Public
Speaking
Resource
Center

Public Speaking Important to a Liberal Arts Education

In ancient Greece, persuasive speaking or **rhetoric** was one of the most important subjects in the curriculum. This may seem surprising, given the general negative feeling people today have about the word. For instance, when asked to define *rhetoric,* Paula responded:

> Rhetoric is just talking. It's a negative word nowadays, but I don't think it always was. But presently it implies speaking just to fill up space, I think.
>
> *Paula*

She was probably thinking of terms such as "empty rhetoric" or "cut the rhetoric and get to the action." However, *rhetoric,* by definition, is the art of persuasive public speaking, and public speaking has been an important part of every culture and every generation. (The accompanying box on diversity addresses the historical importance of public speaking.) The ancient Greeks and Romans identified many elements of successful speechmaking; contemporary scholars continue to develop theories and models that describe both speaking and listening. Consequently, this text covers both ancient and modern principles of rhetoric.

   A major goal of a modern liberal arts education is the development of critical thinking skills. Critical thinkers can analyze information and sort through persuasive appeals. They can discriminate between faulty arguments and valid reasoning, follow ideas to their logical conclusion, and appreciate a diversity of opinions and presentation styles. Studying the principles of public speaking can help you increase your critical thinking competencies (Allen, et al., 1999).

   In short, a course in public speaking offers many advantages. You can increase your speaking and listening abilities within a culture that values them. Your confidence will increase as you face your fears and meet the challenge of preparing and giving speeches. Finally, the critical thinking skills you develop along the way will help you sort through the ideas and persuasive appeals that surround you daily.

Why Take a Cultural Perspective?

We are communicating in an age of globalization, with ever-increasing cultural contact. Consequently, you will be a more effective person if you understand how diversity impacts communication, even if your community or your school is not especially diverse. Speech professor Esther (Eunkyong) Lee Yook (1999) explains: "Diversity is no longer a buzzword to ponder, no longer an abstract concept for the future; diversity is now a fact of life". That is why this text presents both the forms of public speaking most common to the United States and the speaking traditions of other cultures, in this country and abroad.

   What exactly is culture? **Culture** is the integrated system of learned beliefs, values, attitudes, and behaviors that a group accepts and passes from older to newer members. Don Smith (1996), founder of Daystar University in Kenya, compares culture to an onion. Its outer layers represent visible elements such as clothing, art, food, and language; its deeper layers include ideology, folk beliefs, attitudes, values, and other em-

Rhetoric
The art of persuasive public speaking; a term often used negatively.

Culture
The integrated system of learned beliefs, values, behaviors, and norms that include visible (clothing, food) and underlying (core beliefs, worldview) characteristics of a society.

bedded perceptual filters that affect the way the culture's members view the world (Galvin & Cooper, 2000). In short, culture exists at a conscious as well as an unconscious level; it tends to be so pervasive that its members hardly see its effects (*Columbia Encyclopedia,* 1993; Wehrly, et al., 1999).

Members of a complex society like the United States share many common beliefs, practices, and values. For example, in educational, political, and economic arenas a variety of individuals sit side by side in classrooms, vote next to one another in polling booths, and get cash from the same ATM machines. However, within this commonality there are subgroups or **co-cultures,** comprised of people who are diverse in visible ways as well as in the embedded areas of belief or behavior. Think of all the co-cultural groups you can identify (for example, skinheads, the Amish, gays and lesbians, the Nation of Islam). Then log on to www.yahoo.com, click on the Society & Culture category, and follow the link to Cultures and Groups. When you have done this, you will better understand why this text takes a cultural perspective.

A cultural perspective will enable you to be a more competent communicator. Identifying audience expectations regarding the specific setting and determining what is most appropriate in it will make you a **rhetorically sensitive** person who "can adapt to diverse social situations and perform reasonably well in most of them" (Hart & Burks, 1972). Put simply, you will give each speech to an audience that has certain expectations regarding its length, appropriate delivery, and so on. You will be more effective if you understand and adapt to these cultural norms.

Co-culture

Subgroup of culture, characterized by mild or profound cultural differences, that co-exists within the larger culture.

Rhetorical Sensitivity

The ability to adapt to a variety of audiences and settings and perform appropriately in diverse social situations.

DIVERSITY IN PRACTICE

Public Speaking in Ancient Cultures

Public speaking has its place in every society. For example, fragments of the oldest book in existence, *The Precepts of Kagemni and Ptah-hotep,* which date back to 2100 B.C., instructed young Egyptian men and women in the wisdom of the culture (Gray, 1946). Not surprisingly, these writings stressed the importance of public speaking and gave guidelines for both speaking and listening:

- Speak with exactness; however, there is a time for silence.
- Keep in mind that listeners who lack "good fellowship" cannot be influenced by the speeches of others.
- Do not be proud of your learning.
- Keep silent in the face of a better debater; refute the false arguments of an equal, but let a weaker speaker's arguments confound themselves.
- Do not pervert the truth.
- Do not give or repeat extravagant speech that is heated by wrath.
- Avoid speaking of that which you know nothing.
- Bear in mind that a covetous person lacks persuasiveness in speech.

Other traces of well-developed public speaking traditions remain throughout the world. In ancient Mesopotamia (2700–2550 B.C.), for instance, evidence remains of a public speaking tradition involving an "Assembly of Elders" that judged cases and made policy decisions. Women probably participated in this assembly or had their own courts (Wills, 1970). Greeks, Romans, Persians, Hebrews—all these cultures developed principles for speaking in public.

FIGURE 1.2   Core cultural resources—beliefs, values, attitudes, and actions.

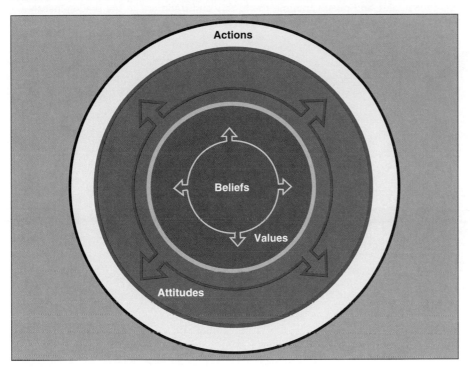

FIGURE 1.2   Core cultural resources—beliefs, values, attitudes, and actions.

Culture Affects Public Speaking

Some cultural influences on public speaking are easy to identify. For instance, a podium is common in the United States but not in Papua New Guinea. We commonly use overhead projectors in classrooms; we almost never use them at funerals. But our societies also influence our speaking in less visible ways. This section discusses core resources, technological aids, and expectations that vary from culture to culture and influence public speaking.

Cultures Provide Core Resources

According to communication professor W. Barnett Pearce (1989), our cultures supply us with a pool of **core cultural resources** or "logics of meaning and action" that define our obligations as well as our taboos. Cultural resources include a system of beliefs, attitudes, and values, as well as a set of predictable behaviors that provide a foundation for every area of life including public speaking. **Beliefs** are the ideas we mentally accept as true or reject as false. **Values** are our underlying evaluations of what's important, significant, moral, or right. **Attitudes** are our predispositions to evaluate—either negatively or positively—persons, objects, symbols, and the like. Finally, **behaviors** are the actions we consider appropriate or normal within our cultural groups. For instance, mainstream culture in the United States:

- *believes* we can change our society by speaking out and creating public policies (in contrast to cultures that consider it useless to fight fate);

- *values* individuality (in contrast to cultural groups that emphasize conformity);

- promotes positive *attitudes* about open forums (rather than to suppress dissenting opinions);

- holds standards for predictable speaking and listening *behaviors* that vary according to context.

Core Cultural Resources
Beliefs, values, attitudes, and behaviors that provide a logical basis for a culture to define what is necessary, right, doubtful, or forbidden.

Belief
Mental acceptance that something is true or false, valid or invalid.

Value
Ideal by which we judge what is important and moral.

Attitude
Predisposition to evaluate, either positively or negatively, persons, objects, symbols, and the like.

Behavior
Action considered appropriate or normal within a cultural group.

Storytellers in Niger recount the stories of that culture's heroes and villains. Their stories, proverbs, genealogies, and poems transmit the history and traditions of the predominantly oral culture. (Jeremy Hartley/Panos Pictures)

These core cultural resources, and others like them, combine to create public speaking expectations. For example, the value we place on freedom and uncoerced choice leads us to respect one another's ideas. Our beliefs that individuals are intelligent and reasonable leads us to choose persuasion rather than force as the dominant way to influence others. In contrast, cultures with different core beliefs and values may discourage their members from expressing their ideas freely and their leaders may use force to control the populace (Wallace, 1955).

Cultures Provide Technological Aids

Oral Cultures

Cultures with no writing and no way to record and send messages apart from face-to-face interactions.

The technology available to a culture greatly influences how its members create and exchange messages. For instance, if you lived in an **oral culture** with no writing and no technology to record and send your ideas to another person, you and your audiences would have to meet face to face, and you would memorize everything you know. In an oral culture, poems and chants, proverbs and sayings, stories and genealogies summarize the culture's values, beliefs, and history. Public performers in these cultures are like "walking libraries"; they must pass on their knowledge to someone in the next generation (Ong, 1982; Goody & Watts, 1991).

Literate Cultures

People record their ideas in words that can be sent across space and time; this leads to linear thinking and outlining of ideas.

The invention of writing brought about a communication revolution. Communicators in **literate cultures** can store their ideas in writing and send them to audiences separated by both distance and time. Literacy eliminates the need for face-to-face interactions; thus, you can read the ideas of someone from another country or from another century. In addition, you can use print resources as you gather speech material, and writing your own speaking notes frees you from the limitations of memory.

Literacy affected public speaking. Letters and words follow one another in a linear fashion, so speakers in print cultures tend to "outline" their ideas in a linear manner and to trace "lines" of thought. Consequently, scholars developed rules for organizing outlines and developing linear arguments. Because readers can pause and think, can analyze written claims and weigh evidence, they expect speakers as well as writers to provide support for any claims they make.

In a culture with a bookstore in every mall and a newsstand in every grocery store, we can easily see the importance of literacy. However, instead of picking up a newspaper today, you probably turned on a radio or television or went online to receive information. Twentieth-century inventions have created an **electronic culture** full of media that can bring voices, faces, images, and printed messages from around the globe into your home. You can also store and retrieve information on floppy disks, computer memory banks, and videotapes.

The electronic revolution is changing the ways we think. The rapid-fire words and quick-cut images typical of television may be replacing the structured lines of thought typical of literacy. Cultural norms for public speaking are changing as well. Professor Kathleen Hall Jamieson (1988) argues that speeches in a media-saturated society are more conversational, personalized, dramatic, and emotional.

Few cultures have only one type of media. For instance, an oral culture that is making the transition to literacy may contain a few scribes who have mastered reading. Theirs is an *oral-literate* culture. Many people in modern oral cultures cannot read but they have radios and, perhaps, television sets. Thus, they inhabit an *oral-electronic* culture. Most people in the United States can read, but they freely use electronic devices, which results in a *print-electronic* culture. Figure 1.3 illustrates this idea (McClearey, 1997).

Electronic Culture
A culture with technology that can store ideas in audiotapes, videotapes, CDs, and so on. Technology shrinks the globe and allows people to communicate instantly across great distances.

Cultures Provide Expectations About Speaking and Listening

Your cultural background influences your ideas about public speaking; your expectations, in turn, affect your comfort and often your competence when you speak in public. Cultures vary not only in the value they place on *expressiveness* and explicitness but also in the *who, how,* and *what* of public speaking.

Cultures Vary in Expressive and Nonexpressive Dimensions

Some cultural groups are comparatively *nonexpressive,* meaning that the members place a high value on privacy and encourage people to keep their emotions and ideas to themselves rather than expressing them publicly. Children in **nonexpressive cultures** learn negative attitudes toward verbalization (Marsella, 1993). Imagine how a person from a society described in the following quotation would feel if asked to speak in a typical U.S. classroom:

Nonexpressive Cultures
Members value privacy and encourage people to keep their emotions and ideas to themselves rather than to express them publicly.

> Speech is not equally valued in all societies, or even consistently throughout the United States. The qualities of cogency [the ability to be convincing], precision, and delivery which may be encouraged in speech communication classes in the United States may, in some other cultures, be regarded negatively (Condon, 1978, p. 386).

For example, many Native Americans are comfortable with a lack of conversation, even between friends (Weider & Pratt, 1990). Japanese people often associate silence with wisdom, and in some Asian cultures, silence expresses power. If you think about it, it is easy to understand how people who tell their secrets might be considered less powerful than those who keep their personal opinions and knowledge private. If your cultural group is comparatively nonexpressive, speaking in public may seem overwhelming (Jaasma, 1997; Kao, Nagita, & Peterson, 1997).

In contrast, **expressive cultures** encourage their members to give their opinions, speak their minds, and let their feelings show. To illustrate, many African cultures—the Anang tribe, for example—value fluency. In fact, the tribal name *Anang* means "the ability to speak wittily yet meaningfully upon any occasion" (Messenger, 1960). People

Expressive Cultures
Members are encouraged to give their opinions, speak their minds, and let their feelings show.

FIGURE 1.3 The three types of culture generally overlap. Can you name a culture, contemporary or historical, that is entirely oral? Can you name an oral-literate culture? How would you classify the culture of the United States? The culture in which your great-grandparents grew up?

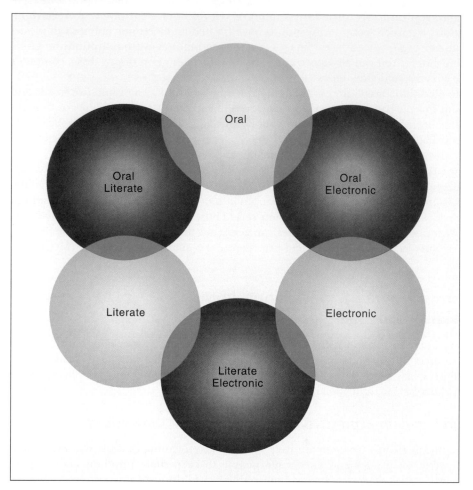

of African descent who share this value are some of our country's most skilled speakers. Congressional Representatives Maxine Waters and J. C. Watts, entertainers Bill Cosby and Oprah Winfrey, and religious leaders such as Martin Luthur King, Jr. and Jesse Jackson are among them.

Differences exist within cultures and among individuals, however. One recent cross-cultural study showed that southerners are statistically more expressive than northerners even within the same country (Pennebaker, et al., 1996). Furthermore, your culture may encourage emotional expression—both verbally and nonverbally—but you may have a reserved personality that prefers to maintain privacy. Interestingly, research shows that people can regulate their expressiveness to appear more or less outgoing, depending on the circumstances (DePaulo, et al., 1992). For example, African American speakers are encouraged to express their emotions and verbalize their ideas and opinions in order to create a dramatic image. However, at times, the same speakers withhold expression in order to "be cool" and not let others know what they are thinking or feeling (Kochman, 1990).

Although women and young people may have influence in private settings in a society such as Bahrain, they are expected to keep silent and let respected men speak in public. A Bahrainian woman who moved to the United States might have difficulty speaking in public. (Associated Press)

Cultures Influence Who Speaks

Some cultures limit the people who may make their ideas public—to adult men, for example, and sometimes just the oldest, wisest, or most knowledgeable among them (Weider & Pratt, 1990). Consequently, children, young people, nonexperts, and women may speak among themselves, but they are expected to keep silent in public arenas. If you're from such a culture, you may feel that nobody wants to hear what you have to say because you have not yet proved your wisdom or you really don't know much.

Cultures silence specific voices for a variety of reasons. For instance, the voices of the poor and oppressed, of gays and lesbians, of victims of incest and of other sufferers may be punished, ridiculed, or misunderstood if they are expressed (Jenefsky, 1996). Although the ideal of free speech that is embedded in our Bill of Rights is not always realized, it holds out the possibility for silenced individuals to find their voices. Public speaking classrooms can be safe places for previously "speechless" people to find their voices.

Cultures Guide the "How To" of Speaking

A culture's core assumptions and norms work together to produce a preferred **communication style** (Stewart & Bennett, 1991). Elements of the communication style typically used in public presentations in the United States include the following:

Communication Style
A culture's preferred ways of communicating, given its core assumptions and norms.

- *Problem orientation.* Because of core cultural assumptions that the world is rational and ordered and that individuals can act on problems and solve them, you will hear speeches—and probably give some yourself—that attempt to resolve issues or problems (gun control, financing a college education).

- *Directness.* In our action-oriented society, speeches tend to move in a logical way to an explicit conclusion without including a lot of side issues. This is why you often hear a "first . . . next . . . and finally" organizational pattern. Even when you tell a joke you are expected to "get to the point."

■ *Explicitness.* Speakers in public settings commonly use clear, concise, precise language rather than depending on nonverbal messages or indirect allusions. In fact, if you say "like" or "you know" a lot or give hints rather than direct instructions, you will probably be less effective in many speaking contexts.

■ *Personal involvement.* In line with cultural emphases on equality and individuality, speakers typically relate to their audiences by sharing personal experiences. This means that you should look for common ground with your listeners in order to establish a relationship with them. If you act like a know-it-all who is superior to everyone else, you will almost surely fail!

■ *Informality.* You will be more effective if you communicate conversationally. However, you should be more formal than you are when talking with friends.

Cultures Influence the What of Public Speaking

Cultures also differ in what is considered appropriate for public discussion. In some traditions, speakers give their opinions and show their personalized, emotional involvement with their topics rather than approaching the subject from an objective distance (Kochman, 1990; Sullivan, 1993; Weirbecka, 1991). In contrast, other cultures consider it inappropriate to discuss personal feelings and viewpoints in public. In college classrooms, students from many traditions bring their contrasting expectations of "how to" speak well. Clearly, if they judge each other by their own culture's standards, misunderstandings and negative evaluations may result.

In the United States, we separate speakers from their words, meaning that it's possible—even likely—that you will disagree with someone's ideas and still remain friends. This may result in a lively exchange of differing opinions after speeches on controversial topics. But Chinese and Japanese people traditionally do not argue in public. This reluctance to confront others in public may be traced to the Confucian idea of *hsin,* in which speakers and their words are inseparable. Thus, if you disagree with someone's words, you cast doubt on his or her honesty in general (Becker, 1988).

As you can see, factors from your background may determine how comfortable you feel in a public speaking classroom that teaches Euro-American cultural norms. What is considered competent in your classroom or in a corporate boardroom may be quite different from the expectations of your cultural tradition. If so, you may have to become **bicultural,** knowing the rules for competent speaking in the dominant culture while appreciating and participating competently in your own ethnic speech community. In the following example, a Nigerian woman living in the United States explains how she accomplishes this:

Bicultural
Knowing and applying different rules for competent behaviors in two cultures.

> At work, . . . I raise my voice as loud as necessary to be heard in meetings. At conferences where I present papers on "Women From the Third World," I make serious arguments about the need for international intervention in countries where women are deprived of all rights. . . . Yet as easily as I switch from speaking English to Ibo [her African language], . . . I never confuse my two selves.
>
> Hundreds of thousands of women from the third world and other traditional societies share my experience. We straddle two cultures, cultures that are often in opposition. Mainstream America, the culture we embrace in our professional lives, dictates that we be assertive and independent—like men. Our traditional culture, dictated by religion and years of socialization, demands that we be docile and content in our roles as mothers and wives—careers or not. (Ugwu-Oju, 1993)

In summary, our cultures provide us with a range of appropriate behaviors, both verbal and nonverbal, for our communicative acts. These are the standards we often use to judge speakers as competent or incompetent. But they are not the only way of sharing ideas publicly.

STOP AND CHECK

Recognize Your Cultural Speaking Traditions

What public speaking traditions do you bring from your cultural heritage? Evaluate the expressiveness of your heritage. In what ways does your culture encourage or discourage you from speaking because of your ethnicity, your age, or your gender? What topics are sensitive or taboo? How might your cultural traditions affect your participation and your comfort in this course?

To investigate this topic further, log on to InfoTrac College Edition and perform a subject search using the terms *culture* and *intercultural communication*.

You can also answer these questions online under Chapter 1: Activities for Jaffe Connection at the Public Speaking Resource Center at the Wadsworth Communication Café, http://communication.wadsworth.com/publicspeaking/study.html

Public Speaking Influences Culture

Although cultures have predictable elements, they are not static. We continue to shape and mold our way of life, often through public speaking. History demonstrates this: our views of slavery, women's roles, and homosexual partnerships have been modified as activists insisted on reforms in speech after speech. For instance, slavery, once legal and institutionalized, was abolished by a constitutional amendment. Laws now protect women, but activists are still seeking legal rights for partners in homosexual unions.

Public speakers attempt to influence society in a number of ways (Pearce, 1989):

■ Some hope to transmit cultural beliefs, values, attitudes, and behaviors to people who do not currently hold them. Think about it: If no one were to explain our core beliefs or inculcate our values, attitudes, and expected behaviors, children and newcomers to our society would not know how to behave appropriately. Consequently, teachers present information about the Bill of Rights, speakers prepare immigrants to take the citizenship test by explaining the way our government functions, and pastors hold catechism classes to teach their church's beliefs.

■ Other speakers reinforce or support cultural elements in our existing communities. That is, they encourage listeners to "keep on keeping on" with their current behaviors or beliefs. For instance, a politician urges people to keep voting, a pastor urges her congregation to continue feeding the hungry, and a teacher provides parents with tips for helping children with their homework.

■ When events threaten to tear apart our communities, speakers step up to restore matters to a healthy state. President Clinton addressed the nation after a series of school shootings made us question some of our basic beliefs and values, and in one city a large, diverse group of citizens gathered to hear speakers condemn the desecration of a Jewish cemetery there.

■ Societies can have dysfunctional elements, and speakers often attempt to change or transform cultural patterns when current ways no longer seem adequate or appropriate. For instance, animal rights activists argue *for* vegetarianism and *against* wearing fur; environmental activists argue for a change in attitude toward sports utility vehicles that pollute the environment more than smaller vehicles.

■ Even in a society that is stable and relatively functional, people perceive ways in which it could be improved. Public speakers appeal to us for attention to health care and literacy issues, for example.

In short, cultures are dynamic and changing. We speak in order to transmit cultural beliefs and behaviors, to strengthen or reaffirm what our audience already knows or does, to repair our cultures when they are in danger, and finally, to persuade audiences to change their ways of thinking or acting.

Visualizing the Communication Process: The Transactional Model of Communication

The word *communication* is so common that you may not think much about what actually happens when people communicate. The most common model for communication is called the **transactional model,** because it presents communication as a process in which speakers and audience members act together to create mutual meanings. This model, shown in Figure 1.4, is one way to think about what is going on when you interact with others. It includes the following components, which I will define by showing how they appear in my teaching:

Transactional Model of Communication

Represents communication as a process in which speakers and listeners work together to create mutual meanings.

- As a *sender–receiver* (or source), I originate or *encode* a message—meaning I select English words (a verbal code) to represent my ideas. As I work on my lesson plans, I keep my class in mind (receiving, in a sense, their messages from our last time together). For instance, I remember yawns from my 8 A.M. students and thankful looks from international students when I displayed key words on transparencies. I also check my e-mail before class to see if I've received questions or comments from students that might influence what I should define or emphasize as I speak.

- My *messages* are intentional, meaning that I try to inform my students as well as persuade them to value public speaking and to develop their skills. I choose language they understand, reasoning they accept, and illustrations related to their lives.

- I could use a variety of *channels* to send my message. My classroom setting calls for face-to-face, voice-to-ear interactions, but when I have 400 students in one room, I use a microphone. In addition, I use nonverbal channels such as gestures or tone of voice, which are part of the overall message. I could use closed-circuit television if my school has the equipment. Or, if I felt comfortable with the Internet as a channel, I could offer the course online.

- *Receivers–senders,* my students, hear my words and *decode* (interpret) them. Each person brings a personal background and heritage, plus individual beliefs, values, worries, and judgments to class. Each one filters my words through personal perceptions, thoughts, and feelings, and sometimes through the influence of other listeners. Some bring laptop computers, and others take paper-and-pencil notes as they listen.

- The students send messages of their own, called *feedback.* They ask questions and discuss how to apply ideas I've presented; they nod, frown, or smile. I then decode (translate) this feedback and adapt my response: too many yawns and I ask a question or introduce a visual aid; too many frowns and I define my terminology and provide an illustration. In this transactional process of mutual sending-receiving-responding, I learn from my students and they learn from me and from one another.

- *Noise,* or static, can interfere with message production or reception. For instance, if I have a sore throat, I may not produce enough sound to be heard. Or, in the middle of an important definition, a fire truck may go by the building (external noise). Internal noise, such as worries over being overdrawn at the bank or hunger pangs, can also disrupt the process.

- Our class takes place within a situational context that includes a five-sided classroom within a small, private university. I also speak and listen in other contexts—in faculty meetings, in discussions with my husband, in family councils, and in educational workshops. I communicate differently in each context. Students, too, choose different strategies in classroom interactions than they do in everyday conversations.

FIGURE 1.4   The transactional model of communication.

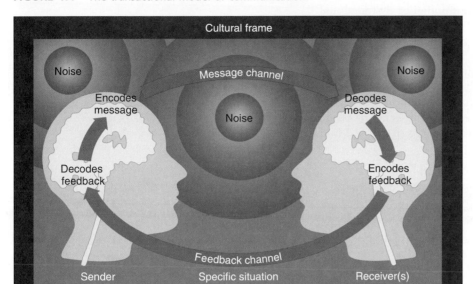

- Finally, our classroom communication exists in a larger cultural framework, in which expectations about higher education influence what is appropriate and what is not. Earlier, this chapter discussed some ways that these cultural expectations affect our beliefs, values, attitudes, and behaviors within our technologically advanced culture.

In summary, communication is a complex, dynamic process. The transactional model attempts to depict and clarify some of the many variables that affect the way humans cooperate with one another to create meanings.

Summary

This chapter introduced you to the benefits of studying public speaking from a perspective of cultural diversity. This is a course that will prepare you for participating actively in a culture that values speaking and listening skills. You will be able to increase your competence and, perhaps, your self-confidence. Finally, the study of rhetoric—a cornerstone of a liberal arts education—can equip you with critical thinking skills useful in everyday interactions.

By definition, culture includes both the visible and the underlying (embedded) aspects of a society, and culture influences public speaking in a number of ways. Your cultural and co-cultural traditions provide you with a set of core resources that include beliefs, values, attitudes, and behaviors that influence how you go about creating your own speeches and responding to the messages of others. In addition, this technologically advanced society provides you with a variety of resources that you can use to research your topic and present your speech. Finally, your cultural heritage provides you with expectations regarding the *who*, the *how*, and the *what* of public speaking. Of course, within each culture individual personalities and preferences also influence the ways we communicate.

Not only does culture affect public speaking but public speaking also affects culture. Speakers transmit core cultural beliefs, values, and attitudes to newcomers who must learn appropriate behaviors in specific contexts. Some speakers reinforce or support culture as it is; others repair or restore community when it is threatened.

Speakers can also influence the removal or transformation of cultural elements that are outmoded or dysfunctional.

The chapter closed with a model that depicts in visual form the transactional nature of communication. This model emphasizes that both the originator of the message and the receiver must cooperate to *transact* or negotiate meaning. That is, a public speaker originates the message, but remains aware of the audience and adapts to their feedback both in preparing and speaking. Listeners participate actively by decoding the information and encoding feedback. Their communication, which can be negatively affected by both internal and external noise, takes place within a specific situation and cultural frame.

JAFFE CONNECTION

Key Terms

public speaking (4)

communication apprehension (CA) (5)

public speaking anxiety (PSA) (5)

communication competence (6)

rhetoric (7)

culture (7)

co-culture (8)

rhetorical sensitivity (8)

core cultural resources (9)

belief (9)

value (9)

attitude (9)

behavior (9)

oral cultures (10)

literate cultures (10)

electronic culture (11)

nonexpressive culture (11)

expressive cultures (11)

communication style (13)

bicultural (14)

transactional model of communication (16)

Application and Critical Thinking Questions

1. Sometimes people do not see themselves as public speakers, because they define the word *public* too narrowly. They think of public speakers as politicians speaking at conventions but not as homemakers testifying before a local school board. Write your definition of "publics." Then, make a list of specific publics you have already addressed and those you may address someday.

2. Interview a person working in the field you hope to enter when you graduate. What opportunities exist for public speaking within that occupation? Ask if and how public speaking is related to the higher-paying, more prestigious jobs within the field.

3. What stereotypes do you hold about the word *rhetoric?* Throughout this term, listen for the word *rhetoric* as it is used on radio or television. Watch for it as you read newspapers or magazines. Each time you encounter the word *rhetoric,* decide whether it's being used negatively, positively, or in a neutral manner. Note if any of the sources speak of rhetoric as essential in a free society.

4. In a small group, make a list showing how public speaking is similar to everyday conversation and how it differs. Use the communication model to guide your thinking.

5. Work with a group to evaluate the role of public speaking in creating and maintaining your college or university.

   ■ What role did public speaking have as the founders launched your institution?

   ■ How does your school currently use public speaking to recruit newcomers?

   ■ What role does ceremonial speaking, such as convocations or commencement addresses, have in maintaining the vision and the values of your institution?

   ■ When issues threaten to divide your campus? How do groups and individuals use public speaking to negotiate differences?

   ■ How is your campus preparing for the next century? How does public speaking function to move your school from the present to the future?

Internet Activities

1. Using your InfoTrac College Edition, look up "public speaking." You will get many hits. Go to one of the subdivisions and find an article that discusses public speaking in a job setting. What does this article say about the importance of speaking and listening skills in that occupation?

2. Go to your InfoTrac College Edition and type in "cultural diversity." Link to multiculturalism, then read a specific article that interests you in one of the subdivisions under that topic. What did you learn about cultural diversity that you did not already know?

3. Test your Multicultural IQ. Go to Article A16877149 on the InfoTrac College Edition and take a test to assess your knowledge about cultural diversity.

4. See for yourself the results of the poll regarding public speaking anxiety that the National Communication Association commissioned. It's available on the Internet at http://www.natcom.org/research/Roper/how_americans_communicate.htm.

5. Visit Craig Keilberger's website at http://www.freethechildren.org and note the ways he uses public speaking to spread his message.

Hot Links at the Public Speaking Resource Center

Public Speaking Resource Center

The following links are maintained and can be accessed easily via Jaffe Connection at the Public Speaking Resource Center on the Wadsworth Communication Café web site at http://communication.wadsworth.com/publicspeaking/study.html

http://www.nsaspeaker.org
This site of the National Speakers Association gives you an idea of the kinds of work opportunities available for public speaking in businesses.

Speech Interactive

Jaffe Speech Interactive

It's a good time to preview the contents of Jaffe Speech Interactive on your Jaffe Connection CD-ROM.

Giving Your First Speech:

Developing Confidence

This chapter will help you:

- **Develop your speechmaking skills**

- **Explain the five canons of rhetoric: invention, disposition, style, memory, and delivery**

- **Develop strategies to deal with nervousness**

- **Understand physiological and psychological anxiety**

- **Learn skills for effective rehearsal**

- **Deliver your first speech**

Detail from "Family Life and The Spirit of Mankind" ©1977 by Susan Kelk Cervantes.

Chapter 1 pointed out the importance of public speaking in today's world. Until now, you may not have thought of yourself as a speechmaker. Nevertheless, you find yourself in a class where you will be a public speaker, for in the next few weeks you will make several presentations. If you are typical, you feel at least somewhat apprehensive about the prospect of giving a speech, and you may experience some of the same hesitancy that Caleb expresses here:

> Public speaking has always been hard for me, mainly because I'm shy and very self-conscious. I'm afraid of making a mistake and looking stupid in front of others. I also have the problem of not being able to bring across the message I want because I always stumble in speeches.
>
> *Caleb*

Public Speaking Anxiety (PSA) is common—in fact, one study reported that 20% of students in public speaking courses have severe PSA (Robinson, 1997). This study also showed that learning the how-to of public speaking helps demystify the speechmaking process, providing students with the skills they need to create good speeches. In addition, knowing a number of specific strategies for dealing with nervousness related to speech delivery increases students' overall competence. In this chapter, we will first look at the skills you need to create a speech, then we will turn to commonly suggested strategies for reducing anxiety.

Develop Speechmaking Skills: Overcome Public Speaking Anxiety (PSA)

Public
Speaking
Resource
Center

Students commonly experience anxiety as soon as an instructor gives a speech assignment (Benhke & Sawyer, 1999). What causes this anxiety? For many, it's fear of the unknown. In public speaking, this translates into the fear of not knowing what to say or how to say it (Bippus & Daly, 1999). To an extent, you can lessen your dread by learning the process of making a speech from start to finish. Through observation, study of speech principles, and actually speaking, you will learn how to create a public speech. As speechmaking becomes more familiar you will feel less panicky. (To assess your PSA, take the self-assessment on p. 33 or online under Chapter 2: Activities for Jaffe Connection at the Public Speaking Resource Center http://communication.wadsworth.com/publicspeaking/study.html.)

Think of it this way: When you are learning any new skill, you follow the guidelines fairly closely at first. Only after you have mastered the basics and feel more confident do you begin to take liberties. Remember when you first learned to drive a car? You concentrated on every move; later, the process of shifting, steering, and braking became automatic. Public speaking is similar. Early on, your instructor may ask you to follow the guidelines closely. After you are more experienced, you will feel freer to be creative in your preparation.

Use Principles from the Five Canons of Rhetoric

Canons of Rhetoric
Principles, standards, norms, or guidelines for creating and delivering a speech.

In the Greek and Roman academies, educators closely studied the "how to" of speechmaking. They divided the entire process into five major categories: (1) creating the speech, (2) organizing speech materials, (3) choosing effective language, (4) learning the major ideas, and (5) delivering the speech. In each category they identified a *canon* (a set of principles, standards, norms, or guidelines) that students need to master in order to become effective orators. They called these five categories, and the principles within them, the five **canons of rhetoric** (Cicero, 1981).

1. **Canon of invention.** In this canon are guidelines relating to the content of the speech. Just as an inventor designs a product that solves a particular problem, you must design a speech that meets a need for a specific audience and situation. The principles of invention help you analyze your audience, select an appropriate topic and purpose, gather evidence, and develop reasonable and logical arguments. Obviously, the content of any speech is vital; that is why this text devotes nine chapters to the norms found in the canon of invention.

   Canon of Invention
   Principles for designing a speech that meets a need a specific audience has.

2. **Canon of disposition (arrangement).** The standards in this canon help you arrange your ideas so that they connect logically and flow coherently. You will learn how to organize major points, create introductions and conclusions, and connect ideas to one another and to the speech as a whole. Seven of the following chapters discuss the principles of disposition or arrangement.

   Canon of Disposition or Arrangement
   Guidelines for organizing a speech.

3. **Canon of style.** The guidelines and principles in the canon of style help you choose the language that is best suited to your audience and to the occasion. Chapter 13 elaborates on style or language norms.

   Canon of Style
   Principles for choosing effective language.

4. **Canon of memory.** Ancient orators lacked the "technology" (pens, note cards, highlighters) that you have available to cue memory. Thus, they developed extensive principles for memorizing their speeches. Today we no longer need to learn speeches by heart. Consequently, there is no chapter in this text dedicated to the canon of memory, although Chapter 14 provides some guidelines for rehearsal.

   Canon of Memory
   Guidelines to help you remember your ideas.

5. **Canon of delivery.** The rules or standards for actually presenting your speech to an audience are found in the canon of delivery. Chapter 14 describes delivery skills (eye contact, gestures, vocal variety) that you can use to present your ideas with poise and polish.

   Canon of Delivery
   Rules or standards for presenting your speech.

For additional material on the canons of rhetoric, check the Internet website sponsored by Brigham Young University: http://humanities.byu.edu/rhetoric/canons.htm. The remainder of this chapter details an aspect of each canon that you can use as you create and perform your first speech.

Consider Your Audience (Invention)

Begin the process of invention by thinking of your classroom as *a mini-culture* (see Diversity in Practice on page 24). Look around and note factors that might influence your speaking choices. What can you tell about your classmates' backgrounds and interests? At first you will probably notice obvious categories like age or gender, but look for details such as wedding rings, books from other courses, or clothing choices. Strike up conversations before or after class as a way to become acquainted. In addition, consider the situation in which you will speak. Inspect the room itself. Is it well lighted and well ventilated? Will your speech compete with external noise? Consider the time of day your class is held. Will your classmates be sleepy, or hungry? Being mindful of details such as these will help you move to the next task—that of choosing your subject and purpose.

Choose Your Topic and Purpose (Invention)

Help! What will I talk about? Why am I doing this? These may be some of your biggest questions, and later chapters will provide you with detailed guidelines covering these concerns. Here, we examine how to choose a topic that you can discuss in a short period and how to identify a general purpose for your speech.

Consider your classmates' interests and their backgrounds as well as the situation in which you speak, and you'll be better able to create an effective speech. (Dick Blume/The Image Works)

Choose a Topic

Your first assignment will probably be an introduction—either of yourself or a class-mate. The task of introducing a classmate is fairly easy; you simply talk to the person, organize the information, then convey what you have learned to the class. If you are assigned a self-introduction, you may feel some anxiety. You must tell something about

DIVERSITY IN PRACTICE

Your Classroom Culture

We generally think of cultures as large national entities or as smaller co-cultural groups within them. However, various groups—even groups as small as your class—develop distinct ways of doing things; consequently, each becomes a *mini-culture* with its own set of beliefs, values, and norms or rituals (Staley & Staley, 2000). For example, one class may develop a warm, open climate in which students feel supported. Everyone believes that each student can succeed, values each person's feelings, and creates rituals—such as learning each other's names and greeting one another as the class gathers. In contrast, another class might develop a closed, hostile, or competitive culture wherein its members feel defensive and unsuccessful; these students reveal their values when they ignore one another and sleep or study during speeches. Instructors generally state their core beliefs, values, and behavioral norms during the first class session. They typically emphasize their belief that public speaking is important, their values regarding openness, honesty, and the acceptance of varying viewpoints, and their expectations about respectful listening and speaking behaviors. What you believe about your classmates, what you value, and how you act all contribute to the culture your classroom develops.

yourself within a fairly rigid time frame, and you have to decide what personal information you are willing to share. With either type of speech, consider these guidelines:

- *Be sure you understand the assignment.* It is embarrassing to prepare a speech and come to class only to find that everyone else has understood the assignment differently (and correctly!).

- *Choose to reveal something unusual.* Avoid boring your audience with something everyone has experienced. Here are some topics that have been successful: a student who had a stroke when he was seventeen talked about the day he fell, stricken, on the high-school track; another student discovered that the classmate she was to introduce had built a house with Habitat for Humanity; a third student missed the winning basket at the state basketball tournament and described the agony of his failure and the lessons he had learned; a fourth student described his job as a pyrotechnician, or a person who sets off fireworks displays.

- *Consider your listeners' sensibilities.* Your purpose is not to shock your audience by revealing things that are too personal or embarrassing.

- *Select a significant incident.* Perhaps you have learned something that you could teach others. Maysun described the changes in her life that resulted from working with Special Olympics athletes. Tim related the lesson he learned when he mixed skiing and drinking, with a near-disastrous outcome.

- *Try out your ideas on people you trust.* Discuss your audience and your assignment with them. If you have two or three ideas, ask your friends to give their opinions about each one.

If you have been thinking of your audience all along, you will have a good sense of what are and aren't appropriate subjects for your speech.

Identify a Purpose

When you have selected your topic, identify your reason for speaking by considering your audience once again. What response do you want from them? Answering this question will provide you with your general purpose. Your early speeches will probably focus on one of the following three goals:

- Do you want them to learn something? If so, your general purpose is *to inform.*

- Do you want them to respond by believing or doing something? Then, your general purpose is *to persuade.*

- Do you want them simply to laugh and enjoy themselves? Your purpose is *to entertain.*

As you might imagine, these purposes often overlap. In your introductory speech, your major goal will be to inform the class about either yourself or another classmate, but you will also want to be at least somewhat entertaining!

Gather Speech Materials (Invention)

Wouldn't it be convenient if you already knew all there was to know about your topic? For a speech of introduction, you will mainly rely on an interview or on your personal experiences, although you may also consult library resources. When your subject is yourself, obviously you have all the information you need. However, for other topics, you must begin gathering materials that provide supporting information for your speech. These materials will come from oral, print, and electronic sources (see Chapter 7).

In your speeches, highlight interesting and unusual events such as this disaster relief effort in which volunteers traveled to the Midwest to help shore up Mississippi River levees during a flood. (Alan Weiner/Liaison Intl.)

When interviewing, schedule your meeting for an uninterrupted time in a quiet place. After class, over e-mail, or by telephone, arrange the details regarding place and time you will meet—then be on time. Bring a list of questions and tape record your conversation (with permission only) or take notes as you talk. Be sure you understand your interviewee by asking questions such as "Did I hear you correctly when you said you worked side by side with former President Carter?" or "I'm not sure I know what Habitat for Humanity is. Could you clue me in?" Summarize at the end so you don't leave with misconceptions.

For additional information, consult print sources. For example, if you don't know anything about Habitat for Humanity, or you would like to know more about President Carter's role in that organization, go to books or magazines and fill in the gaps. You might even look up background information on a topic when you are introducing yourself! For instance, Maysun found additional facts about the Special Olympics program.

If you have an encyclopedia on CD-ROM, look there for information. Videos or television are other resources for speech materials. If you have access to the Internet, you can explore various websites to locate interesting or significant background information. A word of caution, however: Internet sources can provide both excellent and poor or even fraudulent data; Chapter 7 provides guidelines for thinking critically about information you find online.

Organize Your Materials (Disposition or Arrangement)

After you have gathered information, you must arrange the ideas so that they will make sense to your listeners. Of course, there are many ways to organize a speech, and cultures vary in their "patterns" or organizational styles. Before organizing your speech, consider the culture, and thus the expectations, of the people you will be addressing.

Most speeches in the Western speaking tradition have three major parts: the introduction, the body, and the conclusion. To be an effective speaker, you first orient your audience toward the subject in an introduction. This leads to the body of the speech, the part that generally takes up most of your speaking time, where you explain and develop your major ideas. After your major points, leave your listeners with a memorable conclusion. Taken as a whole, the outline looks like this:

I.   Introduction
II. Body
III. Conclusion

I. Introduce Your Topic

Your first speech may vary slightly from this pattern, but in general an introduction has these four major functions that date back to the first-century Roman educator Quintilian (trans. 1920–1922):

- Orient the audience by drawing their attention to your subject.
- Motivate them to listen by relating the topic to their concerns.
- Demonstrate that you are a credible speaker on the subject by linking yourself with the topic.
- Preview the major point of the speech by stating the central idea.

II. Develop the Body of Your Speech

In the body of your speech, present and develop your major ideas, using sufficient evidence for clarification and support. There are many ways to organize speeches: topical, problem–solution, cause–effect, and so on. Using these patterns results in a linear arrangement, as shown by this outline of a cause–effect speech:

A. Causes
   1. First cause
     a. Support
     b. Support
   2. Second cause
     a. Support
     b. Support

B. Effects
   1. First effect
     a. Support
     b. Support
   2. Second effect
     a. Support
     b. Support

Although linear patterns are common, your cultural background, your learning style, or your personality traits may lead you to visualize your speeches as moving in wavelike patterns or in spiraling forms. Chapter 9 illustrates both traditional and alternative organizational forms. (If your first assignment is to give a narrative speech, see Chapter 15.)

III. Conclude Memorably

To be most effective as a speaker, don't stop abruptly; instead, provide a sense of closure that ties your ideas together and leaves your audience with something to take away with them. Conclusions often have these elements:

1. A transition to the conclusion
2. A summary of the major ideas
3. A sense of psychological closure
4. A final memorable statement

Connect Your Ideas

Connectives
Words and phrases that you use to tie your ideas together.

Your major work is done, and it's time for weaving your ideas together so that your speech flows smoothly from point to point. The words and phrases that link your ideas with one another are called **connectives.** Simple connectives include words like *first, next,* and *finally.* More complex sentences, such as "After the initial shock of my accident, I began the painful rehabilitation process," summarize where you have been and where you are going in your speech. Put simply, connectives help your listeners keep their place in the speech by linking the various points to one another and to the speech as a whole.

Once you have your materials and the general framework or organizational pattern, you can begin to select precise wording and then learn your speech well enough to deliver it to an audience. The principles for these aspects of speechmaking are found in the final three canons of rhetoric: style, memory, and delivery.

Choose Suitable Language (Style)

Style
In rhetoric, style means language.

Many people think of your style as the way you walk, talk, and dress. So the guy who says "I really like your style" is probably referring to the way you present yourself. However, in rhetoric, **style** means language; the canon of style contains the principles for using language effectively in both speaking and writing. (That's why you may have seen style manuals in your writing classes.)

Put the finishing touches on your ideas by polishing the words you use, always with an ear tuned to your listeners. Here are a few general guidelines for effective use of language in public speaking:

- Choose appropriate vocabulary and grammar for both the occasion and the audience. This means adapting your vocabulary to audience characteristics such as occupation, age, or educational level.

- Omit language that may offend your listeners. Eliminate swear words, as well as language that demeans people on the basis of their sex, race, or age.

- Choose words that listeners understand. Either define technical terms or eliminate them and choose more familiar language.

- Use fewer slang expressions. The language used in public speeches is generally more formal than the language used in everyday conversation.

More information on the canon of style is found in Chapter 13.

Memorized Delivery
Learning the speech by heart, then reciting it.

Manuscript Delivery
Reading a speech.

Impromptu Delivery
Speaking with little advanced preparation.

Extemporaneous Delivery
Preparing a speech carefully in advance, but choosing the exact wording during the speech itself.

Learn Your Speech (Memory)

Because they lacked TelePrompTers and the like, Roman educators taught young orators elaborate techniques for learning their speeches by heart. In fact, memory is often called the lost canon because so few people in this culture rely on memory alone. In fact, **memorized delivery** is highly risky. Forgetting even a few simple words can lead to public embarrassment—something you definitely want to avoid! Also in your first speech stay away from **manuscript delivery,** in which you prepare your entire speech beforehand, down to the exact words, then read it to your audience. As you might imagine, reading your speech means you will lose important eye contact with listeners. Also avoid **impromptu delivery,** in which you stand up and speak with little preparation beforehand. Instead, make it your goal to use **extemporaneous delivery,** in which you have determined in advance the organizational outline and the major ideas. Before you speak, you have put key ideas on note cards. Rather than writing complete sentences, you wrote single words, phrases, and statistics to jog your memory as you deliver your speech. Then, during the speech itself, choose your words as you go. Chapter 14 elaborates on these four delivery methods, and Chapter 11 gives you additional ideas to help you remember your speech.

You will be more competent in creating your speech if you follow the guidelines found in the five canons of rhetoric. To summarize, begin by analyzing your audience, selecting a topic and purpose, and gathering materials (invention). Then organize or arrange your ideas into meaningful patterns (disposition), choose appropriate language (style), and learn your major points (memory). Now you are prepared for the rehearsal that will enable you to deliver your speech effectively.

STOP AND CHECK

Use the Canons to Assess Your Public Speaking Skills

Rank from 1 to 5 (easiest to hardest), the five canons of rhetoric in order of difficulty for you personally.
___ Invention: audience analysis, topic selection, purpose, research
___ Disposition: organization or arrangement and connection of ideas
___ Style: choice of appropriate language
___ Memory: remembering what you want to say
___ Delivery: actually presenting the ideas
Which is easiest? Why? Which is hardest? Why?
Identify specific strategies you can use to work on the areas that challenge you most. You'll find a speech development plan under Chapter 2: Forms and Checklists for Jaffe Connection at the Public Speaking Resource Center, http://communication.wadsworth.com/publicspeaking/study.html. You can use this form to record your strategies. For more information on this topic, log on to the Internet at www.alltheweb.com and search for the exact phrase *canons of rhetoric.*

Public Speaking Resource Center

Develop Strategies to Deal with Nervousness

Anxiety comes in two forms: physiological and psychological. **Physiological anxiety** is your bodily response to the feared event itself. **Psychological anxiety** manifests itself in worry, dread, and feelings of inadequacy that may start when your speech is assigned and peak about the time you open your mouth to speak. This section discusses a number of specific skills you can use in combination to overcome both kinds of nervousness (Sawyer & Behnke, 1999).

Understand Physiological Responses to Anxiety

Knowing how your body may react to stress can help. In any threatening situation, your body automatically prepares for survival by what is called the **fight-or-flight mechanism.** This means it energizes you either to fight against the threat or to run away from the dangerous situation. Unfortunately, your body doesn't distinguish between physically threatening situations, where you actually need the extra physical energy to make your escape, and psychologically threatening experiences, where your increased heart rate, butterflies, and adrenaline rush only add to your stress! This type of anxiety is typically highest just before and during the first few minutes of your speech (Sawyer & Behnke, 1999). As you progress, you will probably begin to feel more relaxed, becoming even

Physiological Anxiety
Bodily responses to a perceived threat (increased heart rate, adrenaline rush).

Psychological Anxiety
Mental stress about a perceived threat.

Fight-or-Flight Mechanism
Physiological mechanism your body automatically activates when threatened to enable you to fight or to flee.

more at ease during the conclusion (see Figure 2.1). If you are like most people, your stress will be minimal during the question-and-answer period immediately following the speech, although some physiological symptoms may linger.

To counteract physical tension, engage in some form of physical exercise before class—lift weights, walk, or run your tension away. Listen to soothing music. Don't skip breakfast or lunch, and limit sugar and caffeine if these substances make you feel wired. When you get to the classroom, focus on relaxing your major muscle groups and breathe slowly and deeply just before you speak.

These additional tactics may ease your anxiety:

- Plan a compelling introduction to help carry you through the anxiety peak at the beginning of the speech. When you arrive in the classroom, silently repeat the goal of the speech, the main ideas, and your introduction so you will start well.

- Use visual aids when appropriate, especially at the start of your speech. These ease tension because they give the audience something to look at besides you!

- Deliver your introduction from notes rather than reading it or reciting a memorized text. If you read a prepared text, you risk failing to engage your audience. A memorized introduction is hazardous because this is such a high-anxiety point in your speech.

Plan to Deal with Your Psychological Anxiety

Internal Monologue (I-M)
Self-talk.

Even though you know better, you may still hear a little internal voice say "I don't know what I'm doing. I'll forget halfway through. I probably won't get my ideas across. They'll see my knees shake." Self-talk is called **internal monologue (I-M)** (Howell, 1990), and negative self-talk adds to your discomfort, but it's not fatal. Recent research shows that two areas typically cause anxiety: your level of confidence (I'm not very well organized; I've never done this before; I'm embarrassed about my crooked teeth; I'll flunk) and your expectations regarding the audience's reactions (they'll make fun of me; they don't want to hear what I have to say; they won't pay attention; they'd rather be somewhere else) (MacIntyre & MacDonald, 1998; Bippus & Daly, 1999).

Control Your Internal Monologue

Cognitive Modification
Identifying negative thoughts and replacing them with positive ones.

You can learn to control I-M by a process called **cognitive modification** in which you identify negative thoughts and replace them with positive ones (Robinson, 1997). Think positively in three areas: about the message, about the audience, and about yourself:

- To think positively about the message, select a topic that interests you and is beneficial to your audience. Give yourself enough time for research and organization. Be sure of your pronunciation; check the dictionary to make sure you know how to say unfamiliar words.

- To promote positive thoughts about the audience, remember that other students are probably just as nervous when they speak, and they are not experts in your subject. Assume that they want you to succeed, and focus on the purpose of your speech. (If your first language is not English, think of how your audience would feel if they had to give a speech in your native language.)

- Maintain a positive self-image by focusing on the things you do well. Remind yourself that your worth as a person is unrelated to your skill as a novice public speaker and that competence develops with experience.

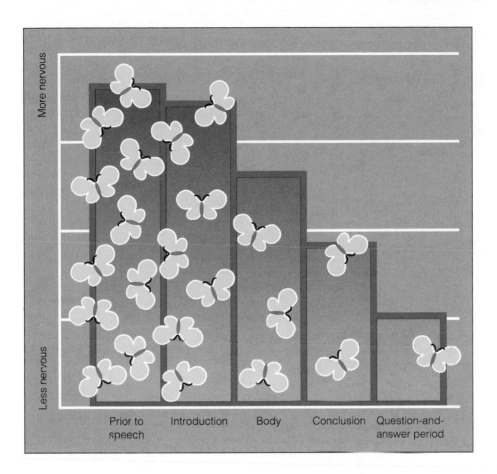

FIGURE 2.1 Knowing that anxiety is greater in certain periods can help you control your nervousness by planning strategies that enable you to get through these periods. [From Brownell & Katula (1984). Reprinted by permission of The Eastern Communication Association.]

Use Visualization

Another helpful strategy, one that many athletes use before performances, is called **visualization.** Visualization is a form of positive self-talk or mental strategizing in which you see yourself successfully performing a complex task. Professors Joel Ayers, Theodore Hopf, and their associates have guided many students to use visualization techniques to ease their PSA. They found that students who use these techniques during their preparation are less apprehensive and report fewer negative thoughts during their speeches (Ayers & Hopf, 1989; Ayers, Hopf, & Ayers, 1994).

Ayers and Hopf suggest that you:

1. Find a quiet place and picture all the details from the beginning to the end of your speech.

2. Seat yourself mentally in the audience and pretend you are watching yourself give the speech.

3. Imagine your speaking self as a competent, well-prepared performer who stands confidently, stresses important words, pauses effectively, and makes appropriate gestures.

4. Think about the audience responding positively with nods, smiles, and interest.

5. Continue to visualize yourself finishing your speech, gathering your notes, making final eye contact with the audience, and leaving the podium or other speaking space.

6. Finally, imagine yourself back in the audience, delighted to be through!

Two key elements accompany successful visualization: You must create vivid images, and you must control the images you generate (Ayers, Hopf, & Edwards, 1999).

Visualization

Rehearsing by using your imagination to envision your speech from start to finish.

Before you speak, find a quiet place and rehearse, so that you know the main ideas you intend to discuss, instead of trying to memorize your speech word-for-word. (Todd Eckelman)

Rehearse

After your speech is fully planned and outlined and you have taken steps to deal with your nerves, find a quiet place where you can deliver your speech out loud, using your note cards. Recruit friends, family, roommates—anyone who can act as an audience, provide feedback, troubleshoot problems, and give you practice speaking in front of a group. Plan to rehearse several times, each time selecting slightly different wording. Focus on looking away from your notes and communicating in a conversational manner. Remember, practice may not make perfect, but the more prepared you are, the better you will feel about your presentation.

Now that you have learned some strategies for dealing with PSA, take the assessment on page 33. If you took it at the beginning of the chapter, compare your two scores. Identify strategies you can use to deal with your specific fears.

Finish Up: Deliver Your Speech

Rehearsal is over, and the day comes when you actually perform your speech. Principles found in the canon of delivery provide guidelines on nonverbal behaviors, such as gestures and eye contact, that strengthen your performance. More details on delivery are covered in Chapter 14. Briefly, you will be more skillful if you remember the following:

STOP AND CHECK

Assess Your Public Speaking Anxiety

Take this test to self-assess your anxiety regarding public speaking. In the blank beside the statement, write the number of the response that best reflects your feelings. This test is available online under Chapter 2: Activities for Jaffe Connection at the Public Speaking Resource Center, http://communication.wadsworth.com/publicspeaking/study.html.

Public Speaking Resource Center

(0) Strongly disagree
(1) Disagree
(2) Agree
(3) Strongly agree

____ 1. I begin to get nervous the moment the speech is assigned.
____ 2. I feel panicky because I don't know how to create a speech.
____ 3. I usually feel nervous the day before I have to speak.
____ 4. The night before the speech I can't sleep well.
____ 5. I'm afraid people will think I'm dumb or boring or weird in some way.
____ 6. On the morning of the speech, I am really tense.
____ 7. I find it difficult to think positively about giving a speech.
____ 8. I think my physical reactions are greater than those that other people experience.
____ 9. During my speech I actually think I'll faint.
____ 10. I continue to worry even after the speech is over.

Add your scores.
_____Total score

0–5   You're virtually fearless.
6–15   Your level of anxiety is quite normal.
16–25   Your level of anxiety may give you problems.
26–30   Consider making an appointment with your professor. Go back and look at the areas that bother you most, then develop specific strategies from the chapter as a whole to help you with your unique stresses.

- Make eye contact with your listeners.
- Have pleasant facial expressions.
- Avoid a monotone voice.
- Smile at appropriate times.
- Be conversational.
- Stay within the time limits!

Focus throughout, not on giving something to your audience but on creating something with them. Believe it or not, research shows that most highly anxious students finish a speech class feeling more confident (MacIntyre & MacDonald, 1999). Here are a few students' experiences:

> Getting up in front of the class . . . built up my confidence.
>
> *Martina*

> I think it was really good that we did so many speeches because when we did it so many times, I was less nervous each time.
>
> *Jennifer*

> This class is almost like a hands-on class. You learn to give speeches by giving speeches.
>
> *Victoria*

Summary

It is not enough simply to get up in front of an audience and talk; good speaking requires thought and preparation. The Greeks and Romans identified a set of principles or standards—a canon—for each of five areas of speechmaking: invention, disposition, style, memory, and delivery. Use guidelines from the canon of invention to consider your audience's characteristics and interests and take into account their responses to the time of day and temperature in your classroom. After that, select a unique, significant, and appropriate topic. Decide whether your major purpose is to inform, persuade, or entertain, then gather materials that will provide the information you need to present your topic adequately. Consult oral, print, or electronic resources as you do your research.

Organize your ideas into a culturally meaningful pattern using norms from the canon of disposition to create an introduction, body, and conclusion. Choose appropriate wording (canon of style) and learn your major ideas (canon of memory) so that you can extemporaneously deliver your speech (canon of delivery).

Finally, deal with your nerves by rehearsing wisely. Know when to expect the highest levels of anxiety and plan accordingly. Then work to control your internal monologue by cognitive restructuring or substituting positive thoughts for negative ones. Visualize yourself performing your speech successfully from beginning to end. Use vivid images and control your imaginary scenario so that you succeed in giving your speech. Finally, plan specific activities to counteract the physical tension brought on by the fight-or-flight mechanism.

Doing these steps thoughtfully and thoroughly allows you to walk into your classroom with confidence on speech day. Thus, you will be able to deliver your speech more competently.

JAFFE CONNECTION

Access

for Audio Flashcards of Key Terms

Key Terms

canons of rhetoric (22)
canon of invention (23)
canon of disposition or arrangement (23)
canon of style (23)
canon of memory (23)
canon of delivery (23)
connectives (28)
style (28)
memorized delivery (28)

manuscript delivery (28)
impromptu delivery (28)
extemporaneous delivery (28)
psychological anxiety (29)
physiological anxiety (29)
fight-or-flight mechanism (29)
internal monologue (I-M) (30)
cognitive modification (30)
visualization (31)

Application and Critical Thinking Questions

1. Consider the role of preparation and rehearsal in increasing your speaking competence. What effect does last-minute preparation have on competence? What effect does it have on anxiety? Knowing this, how do you plan to prepare for your next speech?

2. At the top of a sheet of paper write the name of an occupation that interests you. Then, down the left side of the page, list the five canons of rhetoric, leaving several spaces between each one. Beside each canon, identify ways that the skills developed within the canon will be useful in the job you named. For example, how will identifying a purpose or doing research help a nurse or an engineer? How will organizing ideas help a teacher or computer programmer?

3. Work with a group to analyze your classroom audience, using the suggestions on page 23. In light of material from Chapter 1, and from your experiences, discuss some adaptations you might make in order to be successful with this group. For instance, how might the group influence your choice of topics? How might you adapt to diversity? How might the classroom itself, the time of day of the class, and other outside factors affect your speaking?

4. Within your classroom, you will generally use extemporaneous delivery; however, the other modes of delivery are sometimes more culturally appropriate. With a group, write down the four modes: memorized, manuscript, impromptu, and extemporaneous. Beside each, identify specific instances in which that mode would probably be the most effective. For instance: impromptu delivery—most wedding toasts; manuscript delivery—graduation speeches. After you have identified several specific examples, discuss with your group some guidelines that you think speakers should follow for each type of delivery.

5. Many famous people are anxious about speaking. In this excerpt from an article entitled "Speak for Yourself," published in *The New York Times Magazine*, Susan Faludi (1992), author of *Backlash: The Undeclared War Against Women* and *Stiffed: The Betrayal of the American Man*, shares her experiences with anxiety. As you read through it, see if you can identify the anxiety process and how she overcame her shyness to become a competent speaker. Then answer the questions that follow.

> "Oh, and then you'll be giving that speech at the Smithsonian Tuesday on the status of American women," my publisher's publicist reminded me as she rattled off the list of "appearances" for the week. "What?" I choked out. "I thought that was at least another month away." But the speech was distant only in my wishful consciousness, which pushed all such events into a mythical future when I would no longer lunge for smelling salts at the mention of public speaking.
>
> Like many female writers with strong convictions but weak stomachs for direct confrontation, I write so forcefully precisely because I speak so tentatively.
>
> "Isn't it wonderful that so many people want to hear what you have to say about women's rights?" the publicist prodded. I grimaced. "About as wonderful as walking down the street with no clothes on." Yes, I wanted people to hear what I had to say. But couldn't they just read what I wrote? Couldn't I just speak softly and carry a big book?

It has taken me a while to realize that my publicist is right. It's not the same—for my audience or for me. Public speech can be a horror for the shy person, but it can also be the ultimate act of liberation. For me, it became the moment where the public and the personal truly met.

While both sexes fear public speaking (pollsters tell us it's the public's greatest fear, rivaling even death), women—particularly women challenging the status quo—seem to be more afraid, and with good reason. We do have more at stake. Men risk a loss of face; women a loss of femininity. Men are chagrined if they blunder at the podium; women face humiliation either way. If we come across as commanding, our womanhood is called into question. If we reveal emotion, we are too hormonally driven to be taken seriously.

Public speech is a more powerful stimulus because it is more dangerous for the speaker. An almost physical act, it demands projecting one's voice, hurling it against the public ear. Writing, on the other hand, occurs at one remove. The writer asserts herself from behind the veil of the printed page.

The dreaded evening of the Smithsonian speech finally arrived. I stood knock-kneed and green-gilled before 300 people. Was it too late to plead a severe case of laryngitis? I am Woman, Hear Me Whisper.

I cleared my throat and, to my shock, a hush fell over the room. People were listening—with an intensity that strangely emboldened me. It was as if their attentive silence allowed me to make contact with my own muffled self. I began to speak. A stinging point induced a ripple of agreement. I told a joke and they laughed. My voice got surer, my delivery rising. A charge passed between me and the audience, uniting and igniting us both.

Afterward, it struck me that in some essential way I hadn't really proved myself a feminist until now. I knew public speaking was important to reform public life—but I hadn't realized the transformative effect it could have on the speaker herself. Women need to be heard not just to change the world, but to change themselves.

I can't say that this epiphany has made me any less anxious when approaching the lectern. But it has made me more determined to speak in spite of the jitters—and more hopeful that other women will do the same.

a. Pick out specific sentences that illustrate Faludi's progress through the anxiety process.
b. What specifically does she do to deal with her apprehension?
c. What can you learn from her experiences about conquering your own apprehension?

Internet Activities

1. Use your *InfoTrac College Edition* to look up public speaking anxiety. Note the number of hits you get. Sometimes researchers do not use terminology commonly used by the public. In a new search, look up the familiar term *stage fright*. How many hits do you get? Read an article under either term and summarize some tips for controlling your PSA.

2. Take advantage of the Internet as a source for research or for speech topics. For example, go to a search engine such as Yahoo! http://www.yahoo.com to research a topic such as Habitat for Humanity.

3. If you have a specific assignment, such as a birthdate speech, use a text engine such as alltheweb.com. http://alltheweb.com You can use "the exact term" search and type in the day, month, and year of your birth. You will likely get many hits.

4. Go to the Student Resources section of the Communication Café sponsored by Wadsworth at http://communication.wadsworth.com. Link to the Online Activities for Public Speaking, and do Activity 1: Managing Speech Apprehension.

Hot Links at the Public Speaking Resource Center

Public Speaking Resource Center

The following links are maintained and can be accessed easily via Jaffe Connection at the Public Speaking Resource Center on the Wadsworth Communication Café website at http://communication.wadsworth.com/publicspeaking/study.html.

http://www.clc.cc.il.us/home Follow links to cou052, then type SPEECHweb.html in the URL. You'll get a very detailed Speech Anxiety Workbook developed by counselor Dave Ross at College of Lake County.

http://www.tcnj.edu/~rhetoric Click on the link to "anxiety" on this site for information prepared by faculty in the rhetoric department at the College of New Jersey.

Log on to http://www.whitehouse.gov and explore the site. How might links found on this site help you apply principles of invention such as topic selection and research?

Speech Interactive

Jaffe Speech Interactive

Watch and listen to the following speech via Jaffe Speech Interactive on the Jaffe Connection CD-ROM. You will have an opportunity to critique Jason's speech and offer suggestions for improvement. Then, compare your Speech Evaluation Checklist and Speech Improvement Plan with the author's.

STUDENT SPEECH WITH COMMENTARY

Self-Introduction *by Jason Kelleghan*

Since the beginning of time people have had the burning desire to explore unknown territory, seek out new lands, and go where no one has gone before. Men such as Lewis and Clark and Neil Armstrong have inspired us all to expand our boundaries. These men have risked injury, humiliation, and even death. I have been one of those men, and this is my story.

The summer before my senior year in high school, the feeling of invincibility had already set in. I was working as a camp counselor at a park called "Castle Rock," named after a gargantuan stone deep inside the park. Every Friday my best friend Keith would drive down and visit. We would spend the time hiking the trails behind the park. Every time we passed Castle Rock, we admired its size and majesty and discussed how wonderful it would be to climb it—all the while knowing we were too scared to actually make an attempt. And, every time, Castle Rock would look us in the eye and mock our cowardice.

He gains his classmates' attention by alluding to well-known explorers and to the Star Trek motto.

Jason's assignment was to introduce himself by telling a personal experience narrative that taught him a lesson.

Jason piles up details when he describes the setting of his adventure. Notice how he personifies the mountain (gives it human characteristics). Also, look at the way he clarifies an ambiguous word such as huge.

Finally, I couldn't take it anymore. We were going to climb the rock or die trying. Now this rock was huge, almost five stories in height—mostly vertical, with a slight slope about three-quarters of the way up. Keep in mind that Keith and I had no experience rock climbing, let alone did we have the proper equipment. We both knew that a mistake on this rock could mean death, but that wasn't going to stop us.

The morning of the climb I loaded my backpack with food, water, and an old rope I found in the garage. I don't know why I brought the rope, it just seemed like a good idea for rock climbing. We hiked a short way to the base and, without saying a word, solemnly made our way up the rock. I went first; Keith followed. The climb was surprisingly easy. Keith and I both started wondering what we'd been so scared of. Then, about three-quarters of the way up, I was stuck. There were no handholds within a reasonable distance. Fortunately, there was a small ledge right above me. Unfortunately, the only possible way I could reach it was to let go of everything I was hanging on to, jump up, and grab the ledge. My shaking body and aching shoulders told me that I had no other choice. Mustering all the spring in my legs, I jumped, grabbed the ledge, and pulled myself to safety. After saying a quick prayer, I turned around to guide Keith through the maneuver.

The vivid descriptions help the audience share Jason's emotions.

Keith, however, is a little bit shorter than I am. When he jumped, he missed the ledge and began sliding down the rock. Just before he reached the falling-off point, Keith found a handhold and hung on to it with all his might. Good news! I had a rope! I threw off my backpack, untangled the rope, and threw it down to him. Bad news! It was too short. In the meantime, Keith was yelling "Hurry up, I am going to die!" I gathered the remaining slack in the rope and threw it again. This time it reached Keith, and I pulled him to safety.

After what felt like an hour of shaking we realized we had no way down; our only choice was to keep climbing. Again, I went first, but I couldn't find a path. However, Keith somehow found a way, and twenty minutes later we stood on top of the rock we had conquered. There we were rewarded with a magnificent view of the valley— and the knowledge that we had gone *where no man had gone before.*

Jason's use of humor helps the audience relax after the tense moments he's just brought them through.

Well, not quite. Looking behind a large rock, we spotted a trail that led to the summit on which we were standing. *Anyone* could climb that trail. To console ourselves we decided that taking a trail wasn't nearly as much fun or as rewarding as climbing the rock's face had been.

Nevertheless, we thankfully took the trail down to safety.

On the way back to the park Keith and I argued about who was the better rock climber. I naturally said I was because I had saved his life. Keith argued that he was the one who found the way up the rock. Without him we'd still be stuck on the ledge. But, I reminded him, without me he wouldn't have *been* on the ledge.

He doesn't hammer his point home, but he does provide his classmates with a metaphor that they can adapt to their own life challenges.

We decided to solve the argument with another climb—this time up a canyon wall. This wall was relatively short, and it was grooved, so there were plenty of handholds. The agreement was simple: first one up the rock was the better climber. We started up. After about ten feet I slipped and fell, spraining my ankle. I looked up and saw Keith still climbing. No way could I let him beat me, so I started again. About halfway I heard someone yelling. It was Keith, standing on the ground, telling me to come back down. Then I realized why. The canyon wall, although it appeared solid, was actually hardened dirt. The higher up the wall, the softer the dirt became. Nothing was solid; I was stuck. Now it was Keith's turn to get the rope and help lower me to safety. We silently went back to the park before either of us had another bright idea.

I have matured greatly since that day. I don't climb rocks without equipment, nor do I chance death just for the fun of it. But I learned two important principles. First, life presents two types of rocks. One is tall, and it appears scary and impossible to climb. However it is solid, and with perseverance we can make it to the top. The other is short and rough. It appears to be an easy climb, but we eventually realize it isn't solid and it crumbles all around us. We can choose which rock we'll climb. The second principle is this: No matter which rock you climb, the solid or the soft, make sure you always take along a friend.

3

Ethics and Diversity

This chapter will help you:

- Define ethics

- Describe three responses to diversity

- Identify characteristics of dialogical speaking and listening

- Distinguish between monologue and dialogue

- Explain three guidelines for speaking in a democracy

- Discuss ethical responsibilities of listeners

- Give examples of two kinds of unethical research

In November 1999, Hillary Rodham Clinton visited the Middle East, where she sat at the head table during a speech in which Suha Arafat, wife of the Palestinian leader, charged that Israel directed poisonous water and gas toward Palestinians. After the speech Mrs. Clinton kissed Mrs. Arafat on each cheek, as is customary. Rodham Clinton's critics immediately sprang into action. Why didn't she denounce Mrs. Arafat's assertions as baseless? Or, why didn't she walk out? Was her kiss an implied acceptance of the speech? Later, Mrs. Clinton issued a formal statement that "inflammatory" and "excessive" rhetoric did not help the peace process, but reporters continued their buzz (Schweid, 1999).

Mrs. Clinton faced an **ethical dilemma.** When confronted with information she believed to be unfounded, what should she have done? What obligation did she have to the truth? What was appropriate behavior for her as a visitor to the West Bank when a Palestinian speaker who was her host was addressing a Palestinian audience? Would her obligation have been different had the speech taken place in Washington?

Most of the situations you face are not so dramatic, but you make ethical communication choices every day. When you stand up for what you believe to be true, when you respectfully invite someone who has a different perspective to speak, when you check facts so that you don't pass on faulty information, when you resist the temptation to plagiarize a speech, you are making positive ethical choices.

Professor Vernon Jensen (1997) defines **ethics** as your

> moral responsibility to choose, intentionally and voluntarily, oughtness [what you should do] in values like rightness, goodness, truthfulness, justice, and virtue, which may, in a communicative transaction, significantly affect [yourself] and others (p. 4).

Put another way, when you communicate ethically, you make a conscious decision to speak and listen in ways that you, in light of your cultural ideals, consider right, fair, honest, and helpful—to others, as well as to yourself. This is not always easy, especially in a pluralistic culture.

In a society—indeed, a world—with so many sources of information and belief, you probably know both individuals and groups who believe and behave in ways almost opposite your own. These differences may seem irreconcilable, leading to tension between you and those with whom you otherwise have much in common (Pearce, 1989). Fortunately, the U.S. Constitution protects the free expression of a wide range of ideas, even those others find offensive or disgusting; however, you are not free to say just anything. You can't legally yell FIRE! in a crowded theater, for example; nor can you intentionally slander another person's reputation by spreading information you know to be false. Consequently, you must balance tensions between your rights and your responsibilities to others. Jensen suggests you concentrate on both, and he coins the term **rightsabilities** to emphasize this double focus.

This chapter discusses ethical communication in a pluralistic society, first examining common responses to diversity and then providing guidelines for ethical speaking, listening, and researching in a complex culture.

Diversity

Ideally, our culture allows expression of a wide variety of viewpoints; indeed, you've probably heard this famous expression: "I may not agree with what you say, but I will defend to the death your right to say it." Noble as this sounds, we as a society don't always live up to our highest values, occasionally suppressing some voices and shouting down others.

This raises questions. How do we determine right and wrong in public speaking? Should some things be left unsaid? Who decides? How? These ethically challenging questions are common in a multicultural world, and they have led us to develop principles for ethical speaking.

Ethical Dilemma

Ethical question or problem that arises when a communicator must balance important but competing beliefs and values.

Ethics

Making a conscious decision to communicate in ways that you, in light of your cultural ideals, consider right, fair, honest, and helpful to yourself and others.

"Rightsabilities"

Phrase coined by Professor Vernon Jensen to highlight the tension that exists between our right to free speech and our responsibility for our speeches.

Encountering Diversity

To illustrate the range of differences between individuals and national groups, Porter and Samovar (1994) created a maximum-minimum scale (see Figure 3.1). At the end marked "minimum" appear variations within the United States; for instance, environmentalists and developers share educational, monetary, and legal systems (they may even sit side by side in church and eat at the same restaurants) but they disagree about the balance between environmental and business interests. At the "maximum" end of the range are national groups with different languages, histories, religious traditions, forms of government, and core philosophies. Diversity, even at the minimum end of the scale, can be divisive and lead to hearings, open disputes, or marches. This section discusses three common responses to diversity: resistance, assimilation, and accommodation.

Resisting Diversity

Groups or individuals resistant to diversity try to minimize change and defend their own beliefs and traditions; in extreme situations, they attack people who differ from them (Berger, 1969). Attacks can range from active persecution and intolerance to milder challenges that ignore, discount, or ridicule divergent ideas. In the extreme, **resisting** leads to physical attacks, terrorist bombings, or even war. It is easy to see that hate crimes are unethical, but what about taunting or ignoring people who differ from you?

Sometimes resistant groups speak out against perceived injustices in the majority system. For instance, the 1960s were characterized by Black Power, anti-war, and feminist protests. Today, resistance is expressed as activists rally on behalf of the environment, animal rights, gay rights, abortion, and so on. Activists often justify their methods by reasoning that the ends they seek warrant the means they use. To read more about resistant groups, check the Internet at www.alltheweb.com. Search for the exact phrase "protest movement" and read an article about a local or global resistance movement.

Assimilating Diversity

In contrast to the practice of defending one's own ways and attacking others, people who are **assimilating** reject or surrender their background beliefs and practices to embrace those of another group (Berger, 1969). For example, a woman whose parents are both physicians rejects the medical establishment and embraces alternative healing practices. A Christian becomes a Buddhist. An immigrant learns English and never again speaks her first language. Individuals and co-cultural groups often assimilate in one area or another, but they rarely change entirely. Ethical implications arise when people passively allow themselves to be coerced or manipulated into changing without critically examining good reasons for the change.

To understand assimilation in greater depth, search your *InfoTrac College Edition* for the subject "cultural assimilation," and skim a couple of the articles you find there.

Accommodating Diversity

People who show a willingness to hear and evaluate diverse views are **accommodating** to diversity. This means they will openmindedly rethink their ideas, surrendering some, modifying others, and keeping still others relatively intact. Accommodation results in a **multivocal society** that actively encourages a variety of voices. In this sense, **voices** means ideas, opinions, and wishes of a person or group that are expressed openly and formally (Gates, 1992).

In their book *Transcultural Leadership*, Simons and colleagues (1993) describe individuals who acknowledge real differences between groups, but who learn enough about other cultures to communicate effectively while remaining rooted in the values and language of their own traditions. They actively look for shared cultural checkpoints with others and cooperate with different people and groups to adapt and create new forms

Resisting
Response to diversity in which you refuse to change, defend your own positions, or attack others.

Assimilating
Response to diversity in which you surrender some or most of your ways and adopt cultural patterns of another group.

Accommodating
Response to diversity in which you listen and evaluate the views of others; both sides adapt, modify, and bargain to reach mutual agreements.

Multivocal Society
Society that actively seeks expression of a variety of voices or viewpoints.

Voice
Ideas, opinions, and wishes of a person or group that are expressed openly and formally.

FIGURE 3.1   The minimum-maximum scale of sociocultural differences. (Samovar & Porter, 1994)

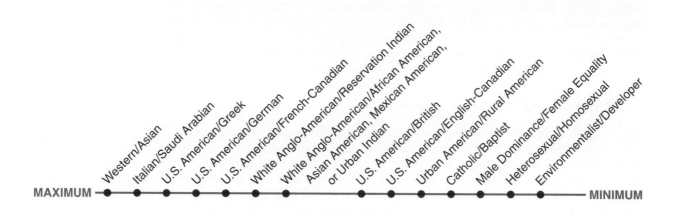

that transcend a single tradition or worldview. Gates (1992), who is chair of Harvard University's department of Afro-American studies, summarizes the ideals of such a society. In it, co-cultural groups recognize that they hold divided opinions, yet individuals and groups work together to forge a civic culture that accommodates both differences and commonalities. The meeting described in the box, Diversity in Practice: The Homosexuals and the Baptists, is an attempt between two groups to confront some of their differences in face-to-face conversations.

In summary, your decisions to resist new ideas or to embrace them with relatively few questions, to block voices from being heard or to create space for a multivocal society, have ethical implications for both speaking and listening in a pluralistic society.

We now turn to specific resources offered within our culture for people who want to be ethical communicators.

Speaking Ethically

Vir Bonum, Dicendi peritus
"The good person, skilled in speaking."

The emphasis on ethical speaking goes back thousands of years. The Latin motto *vir bonum, dicendi peritus* (the good person, skilled in speaking) inspired generations of orators. Roman educators, for example, urged their students to combine good character with knowledge about the world and skill in speaking. These instructors knew the power of words and the ethical implications of persuasive public speaking. Put simply, speakers can urge their listeners to behave abominably, or they can inspire them to better their world.

Your concern with ethics should begin as soon as you receive your speech assignment. What responsibilities do you have to your audience? To your topic? To yourself?

Differences in beliefs and values often lead people to protest, demonstrate, and, in some cases, openly attack people from the other side. (Left: Andrew Holbrooke/The Stock Market; right: L. Quinones/Black Star)

A number of speech scholars have set forth the cultural resources you can use when you are concerned about speaking ethically. This section presents two: dialogical principles, and democratic principles.

Use Dialogical Principles

Think back to how you first learned to communicate. Chances are, you spent a lot of time listening and then practicing words and phrases with parents and older relatives. According to the **dialogical theory** of communication, these first conversations or dialogues formed the foundational pattern for all your other communication, even public speaking (Schwandt & Soraya, 1992; McGuire & Slembek, 1987). Although public speaking is different from conversations in many ways, you and your listeners can at least take a dialogical, rather than a monological, attitude toward each other.

Dialogue involves authenticity, honesty, inclusiveness, and openness. The dialogical speaker tries to take listeners' perspectives and responses seriously. In contrast, **monologue** imposes an agenda, hides ulterior motives, and discounts the needs of the audience. Avoiding monologue and thinking dialogically is one way to incorporate ethics into your communication.

Avoid Monologue

Monological speakers treat listeners as objects to command or dazzle rather than as equals with whom they have a relationship, and a purely monological approach goes against our cultural values of equality and uncoerced choice. Johannesen (1996) explains that monological speakers are concerned

> with what others think of [them], with prestige and authority, with display of [their] own feelings, with display of power, and with molding others in [their] own image (p. 69).

Some speakers act as if listeners were clay that can be modeled or puppets that will respond if only they pull the right strings. You've probably listened to these monologues—or given some of your own. For instance, a manager does all the talking to his employees: "Now you listen to me," he snaps, attempting to dictate their every thought and behavior. The workers feel frustrated and angry because they have no say; their boss ignores their perspective. Similarly, a financial planner convinces a group of Chinese immigrants with limited English to risk their savings on investments that he knows are shaky. He is playing on his listeners' desire for financial security to satisfy his own desire for profit. In short, these monological speakers show varying degrees of "self-centeredness, deception, pretense, . . . domination, exploitation, and manipulation" (Johannesen, 1996, p. 68). In order to succeed, however, monological speakers need cooperative audiences who let themselves be swayed by their words or their impassioned

Dialogical Theory
Theory that conversation is the foundation for all communication; speakers and listeners work together actively to co-create meaning.

Dialogue
Speakers and listeners come together as equals who empathize with each other and examine their own assumptions with an open mind.

Monologue
The speaker manipulates the audience; listeners allow themselves to be swayed.

The Homosexuals and the Baptists

In October 1999, Jerry Falwell, a Baptist pastor and founder of the Moral Majority, invited 200 gay men and lesbians to meet with 200 members of his Thomas Road Baptist Church. He wanted to bring church members face to face with homosexual people for a discussion of ways to tone down anti-gay rhetoric in light of the rise in hate crimes against gays and lesbians (Cloud, 1999).

The Reverend Mel White, Falwell's long-time friend and ghostwriter of Falwell's biography, had come out of the closet and now heads a ministry to gays. Over the years, White has repeatedly asked Falwell to avoid anti-gay rhetoric that might incite violence against homosexual people. Falwell himself realized the impact of hate after several shootings occurred in which gunmen expressed anti-Christian sentiments, and he set up the October gathering between the two divergent groups.

Jerry Falwell predicted "For the first time in history, we will have talked without fighting" and Mel White mused "How do two people who see each other as a threat talk to each other in nonhate language" (Rossellini, 1999)? The answer is unclear, but the question highlights the difficulties inherent in communicating ethically when people disagree on fundamental issues.

To investigate the topic of inflammatory rhetoric directed toward a group, go to the Internet at www.alltheweb.com. Search for the exact phrase "gay bashing" or "Japan bashing" or "evangelical bashing," and read an article written from the perspective of a person whose co-cultural group is being bashed.

delivery. The historical example of Hitler shows the devastating results that can occur when a speaker treats his audience as automatons that can be organized and energized for evil purposes. It is noteworthy that Hitler was actually opposed by many Germans who were willing to die rather than follow his rhetoric.

Choose Dialogue

In *The Magic of Dialogue,* Yankelovich (1999) describes several instances in which dialogue helped change history for the better. For example, Mikhail Gorbachev, former head of the Soviet Union, said that the turning point in the Cold War was a conversation in which he and President Reagan respectfully discussed their values and aspirations for their respective countries. Dialogue also helps people at local and regional levels. A project called San Diego Dialogue, sponsored by the University of California at San Diego (UCSD), regularly brings together businesspeople and community leaders from Mexico and San Diego to deal with once-intractable border and regional problems.

Dialogue involves not so much a set of rules as a mindset about communication that corresponds closely to cultural values on freedom of choice, honesty, and openness (Jensen, 1997). Dialogue requires three conditions: equality, empathy, and examination. *Equality* means that you and your listeners respect one another; *empathy* means you all try to understand the others' perspectives; *examination* means that you are all willing to scrutinize your own and the others' assumptions with an open mind (Yankelovich, 1999). Invitational rhetoric, described in Chapter 17, is a dialogical method of speaking that Foss and Griffin (1995) say is typical of women's speech.

This drill sergeant is engaging in monological rather than dialogical communication with these recruits. (John C./ Liaison International)

In a dialogue, you expect the other speaker to respond: to pay attention, to consider your ideas, and to contribute ideas of her or his own. Similarly, in dialogical public speaking you hope your listeners will be mentally involved and responsive, reflecting the communication model in Chapter 1. Geissner uses the term *respons-ibility* to describe this speaker-listener involvement (McGuire & Slembek, 1987). Put simply, dialogical listeners work with you, and everyone gains as a result.

In contrast to monologue, dialogical speakers relate to their listeners. For instance, a dialogical manager has a definite point of view and clear ideas of what he wants for his workers. He shares his perspectives, opinions, and insights, but he also asks for their opinions, and he listens; they then negotiate a mutually acceptable solution. A dialogical financial planner similarly tries to see her audience's concerns and goals, then guides them toward investments that meet their needs as well as hers.

If you are committed to dialogue, you don't have to give up your personal biases or strong beliefs; in fact, you may *never* agree with your listeners, and you may try to persuade others to share your viewpoints. But you won't manipulate or trick them; you'll be honest and seek the common ground that benefits everyone. The Baptists and the gays of the Diversity in Practice box on page 46 may still have disagreed after their meeting, but they attempted to be honest about and respectful in their differences.

Stewart and Thomas (1995) summarize the traits of a dialogical attitude as applied to public speaking:

- Both you and your listeners value and build mutuality; that is, you all realize that you have much to learn from one another.

- You are actively involved with one another. You, of course, prepare and deliver the speech. But they actively listen, evaluate, and form their own conclusions.

- You are all genuine, authentic, openminded, and willing to change.

- You believe in synergy (the whole is greater than the sum of its parts). What you generate together is greater than what you or your listeners could produce alone.

In short, a commitment to dialogical principles involves authenticity, honesty, and openness. You take seriously your audience's perspectives and responses. Most people evaluate a dialogical attitude as more ethical than a monological approach.

Respons-ibility
Speakers and listeners respond to one another and come to mutual understandings.

STOP AND CHECK

Ethical Topic Selection in Diverse Settings

Several categories of subjects, if not taboo, at least require sensitivity when they are discussed in settings whose population is diverse. Such topics as sex, religion, and money (how much you have or don't have) are among them. Consider how you would apply dialogical principles in these examples.

Example 1

Taiwanese students Sharon Cheng and Mia Lee are embarrassed throughout Gerard's classroom speech about condoms. In their culture, to talk about sex publicly, much less to demonstrate how to use a condom, is highly inappropriate.

■ Would Gerard modify his speech if he thought of it as a conversation with each listener? If so, how?

■ What does it mean to respect diversity? When, if ever, is it appropriate to make people feel embarrassed?

■ Does this topic meet a need, or do most college students already know birth-control methods? If not, is the classroom the place to learn, or are other sources of information preferable?

■ How should Gerard consider his listeners who are not sexually active?

■ How should Sharon and Mia respond to Gerard's speech?

Example 2

Jamal, a Muslim, wants to talk about his religion, but he knows that religion — especially a faith his classmates don't share — is a sensitive topic.

■ How would Jamal approach his speech if he took a conversational or dialogical approach?

■ What arguments can be made that Jamal, honestly believing in his faith, should choose this topic for his classroom speech? What arguments can be made against this choice?

■ How should he best share with a diverse audience the beliefs most important to him?

■ Do the same arguments apply to Christians? Buddhists? Scientologists? Others?

Practice Democratic Principles

Dialogical principles focus on your relationship with your audience; democratic guidelines focus more on the ethical issues you face when you create the speech itself. Events in the twentieth century often highlighted the tension between free speech and responsible expression within a democracy. The McCarthyism of the 1950s, anti-war and black power protests of the 1960s, disputes over music lyrics, the Ku Klux Klan march in New York City in 1999, all brought the freedom vs. responsibility issue to the fore, and speech scholars labored to create principles for ethical speaking in a republic. The NCA Credo for Ethical Communication presents the principles endorsed by the National Communication Association in 1999. (This organization represents hundreds of speech professors.) Following this credo are common guidelines for ethical speaking (Wallace, 1955; Johannesen, 1996; Credo, 1999).

DIVERSITY IN PRACTICE

NCA Credo for Ethical Communication

Questions of right and wrong arise whenever people communicate. Ethical communication is fundamental to responsible thinking, decision making, and the development of relationships and communities within and across contexts, cultures, channels, and media. Moreover, ethical communication enhances human worth and dignity by fostering truthfulness, fairness, responsibility, personal integrity, and respect for self and others. We believe that unethical communication threatens the quality of all communication and consequently the well-being of individuals and the society in which we live. Therefore we, the members of the National Communication Association, endorse and are committed to practicing the following principles of ethical communication:

- We advocate truthfulness, accuracy, honesty, and reason as essential to the integrity of communication.

- We endorse freedom of expression, diversity of perspective, and tolerance of dissent to achieve the informed and responsible decision making fundamental to a civil society.

- We strive to understand and respect other communicators before evaluating and responding to their messages.

- We promote access to communication resources and opportunities as necessary to fulfill human potential and contribute to the well-being of families, communities, and society.

- We promote communication climates of caring and mutual understanding that respect the unique needs and characteristics of individual communicators.

- We condemn communication that degrades individuals and humanity through distortion, intimidation, coercion, and violence, and through the expression of intolerance and hatred.

- We are committed to the courageous expression of personal convictions in pursuit of fairness and justice.

- We advocate sharing information, opinions, and feelings when facing significant choices while also respecting privacy and confidentiality.

- We accept responsibility for the short- and long-term consequences for our own communication and expect the same of others.

Endorsed by the National Communication Association, November 1999. Reprinted by permission of the National Communication Association. For further information on the Credo, log onto the Internet and go to www.natcom.org and do a search for "credo."

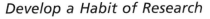

Develop a Habit of Research

Since you are the primary source of information for your audience, you owe it to your listeners to know what you're talking about. Consequently, you need to do your homework before you speak. For example, when you discuss a complicated issue such as educational vouchers, don't settle for just a surface understanding; instead, do research in a number of sources and seek out diverse perspectives. Find out positions that various Republicans and Democrats take. How do typical big-city mayors respond? How

The way people treat each other on television talk shows like *The Jerry Springer Show* is exaggerated, but the shouting and the physical attacks highlight the need for civility toward those who have different beliefs and behaviors. (Charlie Bennett, Associated Press/AP)

would vouchers affect inner-city education? Suburban schools? Rural education? Private schools? What ethnic or social-class issues are involved? Give your audience the breadth of information they need to make reasoned and wise choices.

Be Honest and Fair

Honest speaking means you present your information as truthfully as you know how. Don't exaggerate your material and make a problem seem greater than it actually is. Don't distort or twist information. For instance, statistics can be particularly misleading, so find out as much as you can about the numbers you present. Let's say you find statistics showing that wine, used in moderation, can be healthy, but the statistics come from studies funded by the wine industry. Does this mean they are inaccurate? Not necessarily, but probe further and see if impartial sources produce similar statistics.

Be fair and balanced. Give your subject an evenhanded treatment, rather than presenting only the arguments that support your position. You can hear examples of unbalanced presentations whenever you listen to talk radio. There, biased hosts and their carefully screened callers "discuss" issues and problems. In political ads, you'll also find slanted presentations full of emotional appeals aimed at scaring people. The movie *JFK* is still another example of a one-sided presentation. Director Oliver Stone's critics charged that Stone stacked the evidence supporting his assassination theory and omitted evidence that refuted it.

Practice Civility

Civility

Self-control or moderation, in contrast to pride or arrogance; civil speakers persuade, consult, and compromise rather than coerce and manipulate.

Talk-show host Jerry Springer's guests yell verbal insults and attack one another; talking heads on around-the-clock news programs interrupt and shout each other down; politicians use negative ads against their opponents. More and more often, cultural commentators lament the lack of civility in public discourse; one even used the term *drive-by debating* to describe the way citizens often discuss public issues (Hackney, quoted in Bartanen & Frank, 1999, p. 38).

Civility is a social virtue that involves self-control or moderation and contrasts with pride, insolence, and arrogance. Civil speakers and listeners are more than simply polite. They choose persuasion, consultation, advising, bargaining, compromising, and coalition building. Civility is related to two concepts presented earlier: accommodation and dialogical public speaking, both of which require people to understand, to appreciate opposing perspectives, and to accept the outcome when their own position does not prevail. Cultures across space and time, from the ancient Greeks to modern Asian cultures, have promoted civility as an ethical principle that is important in a diverse society (Barrett, 1991; Bartanen & Frank, 1999).

This is by no means a complete list of democratic principles. However, these guidelines will get you thinking about the importance of ethical speaking in a pluralistic culture. Since diversity is pervasive, you must decide how best you can respect (and live comfortably) with people who are different (Jensen, 1997).

To learn more about ethical speaking in a democracy, log on to the Internet and go to www.alltheweb.com; search there for the exact phrase "civility and diversity."

STOP AND CHECK

Would You Use Questionable Statistics?

Kilolo is researching the topic of breast cancer. She finds several sources that say women have a 1 in 9 chance of developing the disease. However, as she does more extensive research, Kilolo discovers a *New York Times* article that calls this figure "faulty," stating that, if a woman lives to be 110 then, yes, the cumulative probability that she will develop this type of cancer is 1 in 9. However, even eighty-year-old women are not at that high level of risk. And the chances are closer to 1 in 1,000 for women under fifty. A spokesperson for the American Cancer Society admits that the 1 in 9 figure is more metaphor than fact, but she argues that it is used for good ends—it makes women aware and concerned enough to seek early detection. Some physicians, in contrast, point to an "epidemic of fear" created by the inflated numbers (Blakeslee, 1992).

Questions

- Should Kilolo use the 1 in 9 figure because she's seen it in five or six sources? Why, or why not?

- What do you think of the American Cancer Society's decision to continue using the figure when they know it is inaccurate? Is this ethical?

Access

WebTUTOR

for an online discussion of the questions posed here

Listening Ethically

The dialogical attitude applies to listening as well as speaking. Certainly you cannot listen to everyone; you simply don't have the time. But listening to people empowers them. Although you may not agree with speakers' ideas, allowing them to speak recognizes them as significant persons whose ideas and thoughts are important enough to hear. Remember how good you feel when someone who disagrees with you still takes time to ask what you believe and how you came to your conclusions? Or, how listeners ask you questions after you speak on a controversial topic? Maybe the questions were tough, but they were not meant as personal attacks.

In contrast, there are many ways to silence speakers. Have you ever tried to talk to someone, only to have him say "I don't want to hear it" and walk away? You probably felt frustrated. The same thing can happen in the classroom or other public speaking settings. Someone leaves in the middle of a speech; or, two or more members of the audience, seated near the back, whisper and laugh throughout. These people are doing two things: (1) indicating disrespect for the speaker and the ideas being presented, and (2) being disrespectful of fellow listeners who wish to hear the speech. In addition, a **heckler** shouts down the speaker in an attempt to keep others from hearing the speech.

Heckle
Taunt, insult, ridicule, or shout down another person.

Heckling or shouting down speakers is only one way to silence them. Refusing to hear someone out and interfering with other people's ability to listen are additional ways to suppress unwelcome voices. (Wide World Photos)

Choosing not to listen when you could do so implies that the speaker's ideas are not significant or worth your time.

What do you do when you hear something you know to be false? Do you confront the speaker in front of others? Do you plan a speech to counter the ideas and present more accurate information? Do you ask questions that enable other listeners to detect the misinformation? These are all possible responses. Thinking about your ethical responsibilities as a listener, ask yourself these questions:

■ In a society in which issues are decided by informed people, do I expose myself to a number of arguments, or do I listen only to the side with which I already agree? In short, do I listen with an open mind?

■ Do I fulfill my ethical responsibilities to other listeners by not distracting them?

■ Do I fulfill my responsibilities to speakers by letting them know they are being heard?

■ Do I encourage speakers to meet ethical standards? This may mean that I ask for further information about their sources or that I point out relevant information the speakers omit (Holzman, 1970; Jensen, 1997).

Access

for an online discussion about heckling.

STOP AND CHECK

Heckling (Transcript, 1992)

During the 1992 campaign for the presidency, Bill Clinton faced hostile questioners on a number of occasions. Here is the transcript of an exchange he had with Bob Rafsky, who was dying of AIDS.

RAFSKY: This is the center of the AIDS epidemic—what are you going to do? Are you going to start a war on AIDS? Are you going to just go on and ignore it? Are you going to declare war on AIDS? Are you going to put someone in charge? Are you going to do more than you did as the governor of Arkansas? We're dying in this state. What are you going to do about AIDS?

CLINTON: Can we talk now?

RAFSKY: Go ahead and talk.

CLINTON: Most places where I go, nobody wants to talk. They want us to listen to them. I'm listening. You can talk. I know how it hurts. I've got friends who've died of AIDS.

RAFSKY: Bill, we're not dying of AIDS as much as we are from eleven years of government neglect.

CLINTON: And that's why I'm running for president, to do something about it. I'll tell you what I'll do. First of all, I would not just talk about it in campaign speeches, it would become a part of my obsession as President. There are two AIDS Commission reports gathering dust somewhere in the White House, presented by commissions appointed by a Republican president. There are some good recommendations in there. I would implement the recommendations of the AIDS Commission. I would broaden the HIV definition to include women and IV drug users, for more research-and-development and treatment purposes.

RAFSKY: [interrupting, unintelligible] . . . you know it's true.

CLINTON: Would you just calm down?

RAFSKY: You're dying of [unintelligible]. . . .

CLINTON: Let me tell you something. If I were dying of ambition, I wouldn't have stood up here and put up with all the crap I've put up with for the last six months. I'm fighting to change this country. And let me tell you something else. You do not have the right to treat any human being, including me, with no respect because of what you're worried about. I did not cause it, I'm trying to do something about it. I have treated you and all the people who've interrupted my rally with . . . more respect than you've treated me, and it's time you started thinking about that. . . . If you want something to be done, you ask me a question and you listen. If you don't agree with me, go support somebody [else] for president but quit talking to me like that. This is not a matter of personal attack, it's a matter of human wrong . . . Do not stand up here at my rally, where other people paid to come, and insult me without . . . Listen, that's fine, I'll give you your money back if you want it, out of my own pocket. . . .

Questions

- What do you think were Rafsky's motivations for attending the speech?

- What ethical responsibilities does Rafsky have toward Mr. Clinton? Toward the other listeners? Toward his cause? Which should assume the most importance in this setting? Explain your choice.

- Is there ever a place for heckling? If so, when or where might it be appropriate? If not, why not?

- In what ways, if any, could Rafsky have phrased his questions in order to participate and help the audience to share in the creation of understanding between himself and candidate Clinton?

 To hear an audio clip or see a video clip of a heckler in action, log onto the Internet and go to http://ntpaul.sprog.auc.dk/paul/research/heckle/heckle1.htm.

Researching Ethically

Thomas's speech started dramatically:

How would you react if I told you that inside this box there was a snake? Would you frantically jump up on top of your desk? Would you panic and let out a shrill scream? Would you run hysterically from the room? If you answered yes to one or more of these questions, chances are you have a phobia of snakes.

Students listened intently, but the professor frowned. This opening scenario sounded too familiar, and a quick check of department speech files turned up an identical outline submitted in a previous term. Obviously Tom's speech was plagiarized, which is a specific ethical breach. During the same term, Junko made up a statistic, which is an act of fabrication. In order to avoid these ethical mistakes, it is important that you understand just what plagiarism and fabrication are.

Avoid Plagiarism

Plagiarism

Presenting the words or ideas of others as if they were your own.

Plagiarism means that you present the ideas and words of others as if they were your own, without giving credit to the originators. Students plagiarize materials in two major ways. First, like Tom, they present as if it were their own work a speech written by someone else. In the handbook of your college or university you will probably find rules against this type of cheating, complete with penalties for students whose unethical behavior is discovered.

Second, speakers sometimes quote the words and ideas of others without giving credit to the source, either in the speech itself or in the outline. Often they do this out of ignorance, as in the following case. Jeremy spoke on cryonics, the process of deep-freezing a live creature then thawing it to return it to life. He vividly described a dog that was frozen and revived using this process. Throughout his speech his instructor kept thinking "I've heard this before," and she suspected that the student was using a "frat file" speech. After class, she checked the department files and pulled out an outline on cryonics submitted by a student in a previous term. When she examined the outlines side-by-side, she found that, although the two speeches were markedly different, both contained the identical passage on the frozen dog. She concluded that, while the second student was clearly not giving a frat file speech, he had used one source the previous speaker also used, and while both speakers lifted the word-for-word description, neither gave credit to the original source. Intentional or not, plagiarism is stealing.

In order to avoid this type of plagiarism, properly credit your sources as you speak. When you use a direct quotation, introduce it as such. Here are some examples of acceptable source information from student speeches:

> Faith Smith, President of the Native American Educational Services College in Chicago, argues that using Native American symbols in sports is derogatory, stereotypical, and often blatantly racist.

> According to an article in the *Wall Street Journal*, women in state and local governments held only 31% of the top administrative jobs.

In addition, when you write your outline, list your references at the end using a standard format like MLA or APA available on the Internet.

Avoid Fabrication

Fabrication

Making up information or repeating a rumor without sufficiently checking its accuracy.

Besides using the words and ideas of others, some speakers **fabricate,** or make up, information or guess at numbers and then present them as factual. They cite references they haven't consulted. In addition, they pass along rumors or unsubstantiated information. For instance, rumor mills report the alleged facelifts of famous entertainers, allegations the stars contend are fabrications. It would be easy to research the topic of plastic surgery, discover one of these rumors, and then use it as an example; however, doing this perpetuates a falsehood. The best way to avoid fabrication is to use a number of sources and to be alert for conflicting information. Thoroughly check any discrepancies before you present information as factual.

To further investigate the consequences of cheating, whether legal or personal, log on to your *InfoTrac College Edition* and search for "cheating."

Summary

People in pluralistic cultures have belief, value, attitudinal, and behavioral differences that range from superficial to fundamental. You can respond to diversity in a number of ways. If you choose to defy or resist, you will bolster your positions and (perhaps) attack or ignore diversity. If you choose to assimilate, you will surrender some aspect of your own cultural tradition and adopt a new way. Finally, when you accommodate diversity, you accept differences and work with others to create a society in which all can live together.

Our culture provides both dialogical and democratic resources that you can use to speak and listen ethically. Choose a dialogical rather than monological relationship with your listeners. That is, rather than impose your thoughts and ideas on others, respect your listeners as equals, have empathy with their perspectives, and examine both your own and your listeners' assumptions in an honest, open manner. Democratic principles remind you to develop a habit of research, to present your materials honestly and fairly, and to respond to diversity with civility.

Listening also calls for ethically responsible actions. Allowing people to speak empowers them, giving them a voice and allowing others to hear their ideas. However, when speakers present incorrect or misleading information, you are faced with ethical decisions in which you need to balance your rights and responsibilities against the rights and responsibilities of the speaker and other listeners. Vernon Jensen coined the term *rightsabilities* to highlight the tension you feel.

As you present your materials, be sure to cite your references and check a variety of sources in order to avoid the ethical problems of plagiarism or fabrication. Plagiarism occurs when you present the ideas or words of another person as your own without giving credit to the original source. Fabrication occurs when you make up material or present something as factual when it is not.

JAFFE CONNECTION

Key Terms

ethical dilemma (42)
ethics (42)
"rightsabilities" (42)
resisting (43)
assimilating (43)
accommodating (43)
multivocal society (43)
vir bonum, dicendi peritus (44)
voices (43)

dialogical theory (45)
dialogue (45)
monologue (45)
*respons-*ibility (47)
civility (50)
heckle (51)
plagiarism (54)
fabrication (54)

Access

for Audio Flashcards of Key Terms

Application and Critical Thinking Questions

1. Draw a minimum-maximum scale that represents the community (or the surrounding region) in which your college or university exists. Identify differences at the minimum end of the range. Work your way up the scale and identify increasingly greater areas of diversity that may be seen as conflicts. When and how do public speakers address this diversity?

2. Examine your own responses to diversity. In what areas do you resist diverse ways of believing and behaving? When, if ever, do you march or openly protest differences? What perspectives, if any, do you ignore or put down? In what areas, if any, have you changed your beliefs or behaviors and assimilated diverse perspectives into your personal life?

3. Use your own values and beliefs as well as the guidelines described in this chapter to write an ethical code that states the principles by which you want to live.

4. Evaluate yourself as a responsible listener. How do you avoid silencing speakers? Use the questions on page 52 to guide your self-evaluation.

5. With a small group of your classmates, discuss the following: What diversity issues on your campus provide opportunities for people with different beliefs, values, or behaviors to encounter one another? Which of the three ways of dealing with differences—resistance, assimilation, or accommodation—do they most commonly use? Assess the ethics of their responses.

6. With a small group in your classroom, discuss ways that people who hold diverse perspectives on a controversial topic might engage in dialogue. (For example, pro-choice advocates meeting pro-life activists; environmentalists having dialogue with developers; animal rights activists meeting with research scientists; the leaders of Iraq meeting with the leaders of the United States.)

7. With a small group of your classmates, discuss speakers who demonstrate opposite characteristics of one of the elements depicted in the Latin phrase *vir bonum, dicendi peritus:*

   ■ *A person, lacking in character, who is a skilled speaker.* Make a list of people who were skilled in speaking but were not "good" persons. (Hitler tops most people's list.) What problems did these skilled orators bring about in the world?

   ■ *A person of excellent character who is unskilled in speaking.* Identify situations, real or hypothetical, in which people who are good want to do something that will better their world, but lack the skills needed to present their ideas to others who could join their efforts.

Internet Activities

1. Use your *InfoTrac College Edition* and search for the subject "civility." Note how many hits you get. Skim the first couple of screens and see if you can find other terms that you could use to refine your search. Read one of the articles. How does the author apply principles of civility to a particularly frustrating communication situation?

2. Use your *InfoTrac College Edition* and look up heckling, then read one of the articles.

3. Use your *InfoTrac College Edition* and search for key terms "truth and false-hood." Read an article and identify the ethical dilemma described in it.

4. Using www.alltheweb.com, search for the exact phrase "fabricated story." Follow one of the links and come to your next class prepared to inform your fellow students about the impact the fabrication had on the people involved.

5. Karl Wallace (1955) wrote his ethical principles during the 1950s, when U.S. Senator Joseph McCarthy was searching out suspected communists in positions of influence. Use www.alltheweb.com and search for the exact phrases "Red Scare," "Joseph McCarthy," or the "McCarthy Era" (ignore links to Jenny McCarthy) and write a brief paper or create a report explaining why you think Wallace and other speech professors were so concerned about ethical speaking and freedom during this era.

Hot Links at the Public Speaking Resource Center

Public
Speaking
Resource
Center

The following links are maintained and can be accessed easily via Jaffe Connection at the Public Speaking Resource Center on the Wadsworth Communication Café web site at http://communication.wadsworth.com/publicspeaking/study.html

http://www.civnet.org
This site, sponsored by an organization called Civitas, provides international and national resources for civic education and civil society. Follow links to its journal for additional information about ethical communication.

http://newshour.com/newshour/gergen/august98/carter_8.5.html
David Gergen of *U.S. News & World Report* interviews Stephen Carter, Professor of Law at Yale University and author of *Civility, Morals, and the Etiquette of Democracy*. Carter, an African American, talks about his childhood move into an all white neighborhood and the lessons he learned about civility as a result of his experience as a member of a minority group.

Web Tutor

If you are using Web Tutor as part of your assigned coursework, you will find prompts for threaded discussion on the following topics: Ethical Topic Selection in Diverse Settings (Stop and Check, page 48), Would You Use Questionable Statistics? (Stop and Check, page 50), and Heckling (Stop and Check, page 53).

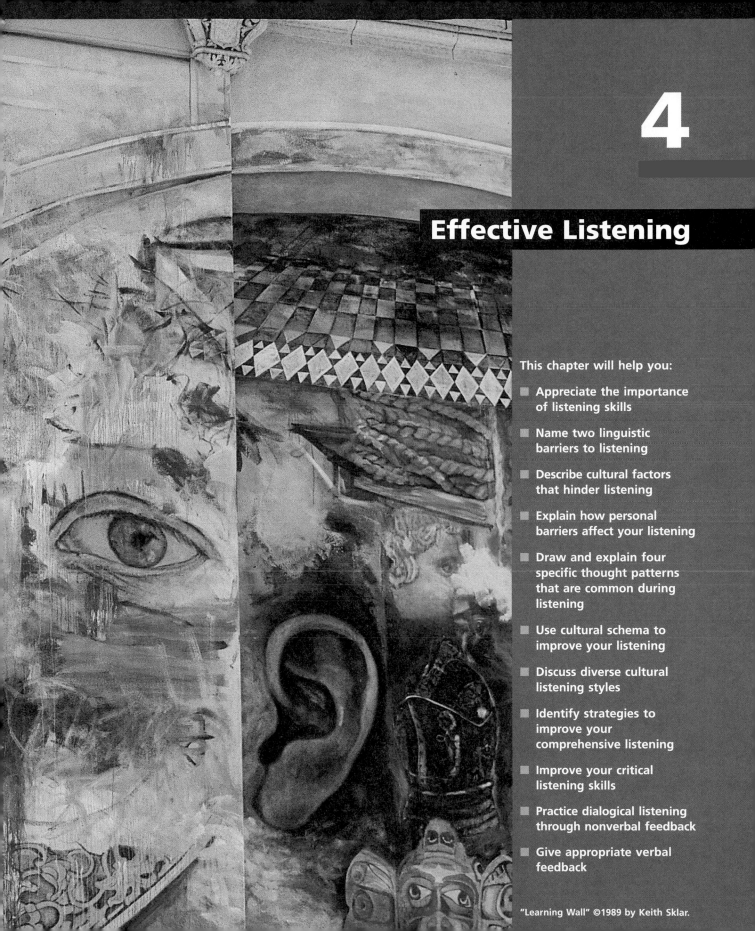

4

Effective Listening

This chapter will help you:

- Appreciate the importance of listening skills

- Name two linguistic barriers to listening

- Describe cultural factors that hinder listening

- Explain how personal barriers affect your listening

- Draw and explain four specific thought patterns that are common during listening

- Use cultural schema to improve your listening

- Discuss diverse cultural listening styles

- Identify strategies to improve your comprehensive listening

- Improve your critical listening skills

- Practice dialogical listening through nonverbal feedback

- Give appropriate verbal feedback

"Learning Wall" ©1989 by Keith Sklar.

Think about all your communication activities during a typical week. Then rank the following activities—reading, writing, listening, and speaking—in order according to the amount of waking time you normally spend doing each one:

_____ reading   _____ writing   _____ listening   _____ speaking

If you ranked listening first, you're like the average person, who spends more than 50% of time listening and less than 18% each reading, writing, and speaking. An ancient proverb, attributed to Zeno of Citium, endorses this bias toward listening: "We have been given two ears and but a single mouth in order that we may hear more and talk less."

If we listen so much, we should be pretty good at it, right? Unfortunately, we often fail to give this vital skill as much attention as we give other communication skills. Compare the number of reading, writing, and speaking courses to the number of _listening_ courses offered by your college or university. You are probably required to take at least one writing course, and literature course offerings are numerous. In addition, many schools provide informative speaking, persuasive speaking, and argumentation courses, but no listening-to-comprehend or critical-listening course. Instead, listening is incorporated into the speaking courses. Reading and writing are similar.

Because listening is so vital, this chapter begins by stressing its importance. Then it helps you identify areas of listening you may need to improve and, finally, it provides strategies to enable you to be a more effective listener.

Listening Skills Are Valuable

As the introduction pointed out, listening is the communication skill we use most and study least. However, good listening can be one of your most valuable assets. In fact, if you go to the website www.alltheweb.com and search for the exact phrase "listening skills," you will get almost 35,000 hits! Obviously, many people in this culture believe strongly in the importance of listening. However, they're typically overconfident about their abilities, thinking that they remember 75 to 80 percent of what they hear, when, in fact, average listeners recall only about 25 percent (Roach & Wyatt, 1995).

Listening skills are valuable in a number of ways:

■ We listen most. Recently, researchers found that listening is the skill most often used on the job, and that employers mention understanding and following instructions (skills linked to comprehensive listening) as the next most common (Maes, et al., 1997). Think of all the time you spend in college listening in order to comprehend information and follow directions; your skill determines whether you will succeed in your courses. Because listening takes up so much of your time, you are more productive if you do it well.

■ Listening and being listened to empowers people and aids personal relationships. An article available on _InfoTrac College Edition_ begins in this way: "Most people would agree that having someone listen to you makes you feel better—mentally and physically. In fact, according to Ralph G. Nichols, who is regarded as the father of listening, 'The most basic of all human needs is to understand and to be understood. . . . The best way to understand people is to listen to them.' Thus, being listened to is one of our most basic needs" (Bentley, 1998).

■ Good listening skills are good job skills. The better customer service representatives, salespeople, barbers, journalists, managers, doctors, and teachers are generally the better listeners. Even politicians understand the need to listen; during the 1999/2000 campaign season it was trendy for politicians to go on "listening tours."

These are only a few of the reasons listening is important; you can probably think of additional ways that good listening habits make life easier. Pause for a moment at the out-

Ears

Eyes

Heart

Listening

FIGURE 4.1 The Chinese character that translates as *listening* emphasizes its holistic nature by combining the symbols for ears, eyes, and heart.

set of this chapter and ask yourself how your listening helps or hinders your comprehension of coursework. What personal relationships benefit or suffer as a result of your listening behaviors? How is listening vital in a job you currently hold or plan to have someday? Keep these questions in mind as you study the remainder of the chapter.

Barriers to Listening

The Chinese character for listening (Figure 4.1) combines the symbols for ears, eyes, and heart, thus reinforcing the idea that good listeners are wholly involved in the listening process. Most of us don't start our days thinking "I'm going to be a terrible listener today." We intend to listen well; however, we face barriers arising from linguistic, cultural, and personal factors. Understanding these barriers and devising strategies to deal with them will help you more effectively take in the information you hear.

Linguistic Barriers

Diversity shows up in language variations within the United States. Walk down the streets of New York City, and you'll hear Spanish, French, Russian, accented English, Black English (ebonics)—more than 150 languages are spoken in that city alone. Compare the slang that teenagers invent and the phrases their grandparents use, the terminology that skateboarders use and the legalese that only lawyers understand. You can see the potential for linguistic misunderstandings.

Language Differences

A shared language is vital if you are to understand a speaker. (Chapter 13 develops in more detail the ways that language differences can affect comprehension.) Briefly, if you don't know a speaker's language, you'll need an interpreter or you won't be able to decode his message. Even then, because languages and the ideas they embody are so different, you probably won't understand everything the speaker is saying.

Accents or dialects can also hinder your ability to distinguish the words of the speech. Regional accents, ethnic dialects, accents influenced by a first language—all these require you to pay special attention in order to discriminate between words. Nonstandard syllable stress and pronunciation differences can create problems. For instance, in one class an international student gave a speech on *beerd* watching. His instructor was puzzled as to who watched beards, until he realized the speaker's pronunciation of the vowel sound in *bird* was confusing. A French speaker pronounced the word *atmosphere* as "at-MOS-feer." An African pronounced *alarm* as "AL-arm." These speakers' classmates had to concentrate carefully to understand each word.

Vocabulary Differences

Misunderstandings can also occur if you don't share the speaker's vocabulary. This may happen for a variety of reasons. For example, the speaker may use a highly technical jargon common to a particular field of study. A scholar at a convention read the following sentence:

> Urging a dialogue between neurology and culturalology, Turner suggests that the rhythmic activity of ritual, aided by sonic, visual, photic, and other kinds of "driving" may lead to specific neuronal activity that leads to social cohesion and feelings beyond verbalization (1992).

The scholars listening to her paper may have understood her, but you'd be lost, right?

Additionally, some people have large vocabularies due to their study of Latin or Greek, two languages that provide the roots for almost 80 percent of English words. Or they have learned new words through wide reading of literature or through a self-help book such as *Thirty Days to a More Powerful Vocabulary*. When you don't share a speaker's vocabulary, you will obviously have difficulty understanding the speech. For instance, in her speech to the 1992 Democratic National Convention, Barbara Jordan, former representative from Texas, said:

> We must frankly acknowledge our complicity in the creation of the unconscionable budget deficits, acknowledge our complicity and recognize, painful though it may be, that in order to seriously address the budget deficits, we must address the question of entitlements, also. . . . [T]he baby boomers and their progeny are entitled to a secure future (1992).

Because she was speaking to a relatively well-educated audience, most attendees could figure out what she was talking about, but some listeners, both those in the convention hall and those watching on television, would have a hard time defining such words as *complicity, unconscionable,* and *progeny*.

Cultural Barriers

Cultural Allusions
References to historical, literary, and religious sources that are familiar in a specific culture.

You may also misunderstand if you don't know a speaker's **cultural allusions,** or references to specific historical, literary, and religious sources. You can probably think of things that are familiar in your culture or co-culture that might confuse someone from a different group. Here are a few examples:

- A person who grew up in the Big Band era doesn't know who Ricky Martin or Jewel are.
- A Christian doesn't understand a Muslim speaker's reference to Ramadan.
- A student taking philosophy understands Kant's Categorical Imperative, but many of his classmates don't.

Nelson Mandela speaks English with British and South African syllable stress and pronunciation patterns; you may have to listen closely to understand his message. (Jacques Chenet/Woodfin Camp & Associates)

In our pluralistic society and multicultural world, each group draws from different historical events, cultural heroes, literary or oral traditions, and religious resources. In a pluralistic setting, you may be unfamiliar with these culture-specific references. It is up to the speakers to be sensitive to differences and explain allusions or choose areas of common knowledge.

Personal Barriers

Personal distractions can obstruct your listening. For example, William identified some of his listening problems:

> Sometimes I become aggressive; sometimes I get defensive when I feel attacked. I have attention deficit disorder; at times I am easily distracted by others around me. I let my feelings for people get in the way.
>
> *William*

His response is fairly typical. A number of personal factors can hinder your listening. *Physical factors* (hearing loss, sleep deprivation, hunger pangs, the flu) can affect your ability or your desire to focus on a speech.

Psychological factors can also keep you from listening closely: You just had an argument with a friend; you have a huge test coming up in your next class; you got a notice that you were overdrawn at the bank; you are concerned about a relative who is going in for medical tests. The mental worry that accompanies psychological stressors can take your energies away from listening.

Stereotype

Place someone in a category, then assume the person fits the characteristics of the category.

Prejudiced

Having pre-formed biases or judgments, whether negative or positive.

Stereotypes and prejudices can also hinder listening. You **stereotype** when you put people into a category, then assume that they will fit the characteristics of the category. If you are **prejudiced,** or biased, you listen to the speaker with pre-formed judgments, which may be either negative or positive. To illustrate, a student once remarked "He wore white socks! I can't take a guy seriously if he wears white socks with a suit!" Another student who supported abortion rights listened approvingly to a speaker from Planned Parenthood and blocked out one representing Right to Life.

Paying attention is another major factor in listening effectiveness. Here Gail discusses some of her thought patterns as she struggles to focus on the speech:

> I'm easily distracted. . . . It's easy for me to either focus on one particular thing that has been said, and then sort of drift off, exploring it further in my own mind, or—and this applies more specifically to someone whose speaking style or subject does not impress me—float off on unrelated topics ("I wonder where she gets her hair cut?"). Also, depending on the subject, I can get easily bored.
>
> *Gail*

Speech-thought Differential

The difference between the rate you think (about 500 words per minute) and the rate you speak (about 150 words per minute).

Leftover Thinking Space

Another term for the difference between your thinking rate and your speaking rate.

Often, listening is hard work. For one reason, you can think far more rapidly (about 500 words per minute) than the fastest speaker can talk (about 300 words per minute). Most speakers average about 150 words per minute, leaving you with 350 words per minute of a **speech-thought differential,** also called **"leftover thinking space"** (Lundsteen, 1993). Four specific thought patterns, illustrated in Figure 4.2, are common during listening:

- *Taking small departures from the communication line.* These small departures can hinder your comprehension, but they can also help you follow the message if, during them, you produce your own examples, relate the material to your personal experiences, answer the speaker's rhetorical questions, and otherwise interact with his ideas.

- *Going off on a tangent.* When this happens, you depart from the speaker's line of thinking and seize on one of her ideas, taking it in your own direction. You stop listening; one idea leads to another, and before you know it, you're in a daydream, several subjects removed from the topic at hand.

- *Engaging in a private argument.* Here, you begin to challenge and argue internally before you've heard the speaker out. Your thinking runs a parallel course to the speaker's ideas. You close your mind, stop trying to understand the speaker's reasoning, and carry on a running argument as you listen. In contrast, effective critical listeners identify arguments that don't make sense, but they withhold their final judgment of the overall argument until they have heard the entire speech.

- *Taking large departures from the communication line.* In this pattern your attention wanders off into unrelated areas; you bring it back and focus on the speech for a while; then, off it goes again, and you find yourself thinking about a totally unrelated topic. This cycle repeats indefinitely (Lundeen, 1993).

Public Speaking Resource Center

As you can see, listening can be difficult when linguistic, cultural, and personal factors get in the way. The remainder of the chapter discusses strategies you can use to become a better listener. Before moving on, do the Listening Skills Self-Assessment on page 70 and online under Chapter 4: Activities for Jaffe Connection at the Public Speaking Resource Center, http://communication.wadsworth.com/publicspeaking/study.html.

Strategies to Improve Listening

Being mindful of your thought patterns during the listening process will help you develop strategies for understanding and retaining material more effectively. Using resources from within your culture, along with nonverbal and note-taking skills, will help you become a better listener.

FIGURE 4.2 These four thought patterns are typical during listening. The first can be productive, but the rest characterize poor listening. (Wolvin, Andrew D., & Carolyn Gwynn Coakley, 1993, *Perspectives on Listening*, Ablex Pub. Co., Norwood NJ, p. 115.)

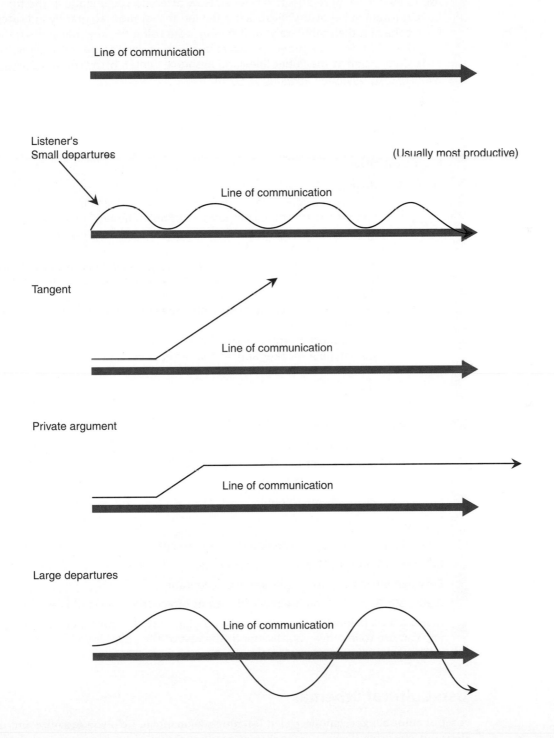

STOP AND CHECK

Listening Skills Self-Assessment

Evaluate your listening by taking this test. Then create a personal plan you can use to become a more effective listener. How often do you engage in the following listening behaviors? First, write the letter that most accurately indicates your behavior; then tabulate your listening score using the key that follows the questions. This Self Assessment is available online under Chapter 4: Activities for Jaffe Connection at the Public Speaking Resource Center, http://communication.wadsworth.com/publicspeaking/study/html.

A = almost always
B = usually
C = sometimes
D = rarely
E = almost never

How often do you

_____ 1. Get lost in a speech because your vocabulary is small.
_____ 2. Turn off a speaker who proposes a position different from one you hold.
_____ 3. Feel anger, defensiveness, fear, or other emotions when you disagree with the speaker.
_____ 4. Get distracted by external factors, such as noises outside the room.
_____ 5. Get distracted by internal preoccupations, such as personal worries or stresses.
_____ 6. Carry on a running argument with a speaker instead of hearing her out.
_____ 7. Go off on a tangent.
_____ 8. Have a short attention span and lose your place in a long speech.
_____ 9. Stereotype a speaker and let that affect how you listen.
_____ 10. Give up trying to understand a speaker's accent and tune the speaker out.

Key

For every A give yourself 2 points.

For every B give yourself 4 points.

For every C give yourself 6 points.

For every D give yourself 8 points.

For every E give yourself 10 points.

Total score _____

More than 90   Your listening skills are exceptional.

Between 76 and 90 You are above average.

Between 60 and 75 Your skills are about average.

Below 60   You are probably not as effective as you could be.

If you scored below 80, develop a listening plan that identifies specific strategies you can use to improve your listening. The rest of this chapter will provide you with some of these key strategies.

Schemas

Mental plans or models that guide your perception, interpretation, storage, and recollection of a speech.

Use Cultural Schemas

A set of cultural expectations, called listening schemas, can help you organize and understand messages (Figure 4.3). **Schemas** are the mental plans, blueprints, or models that you use, first to perceive information, then to interpret, store, and recall a speech

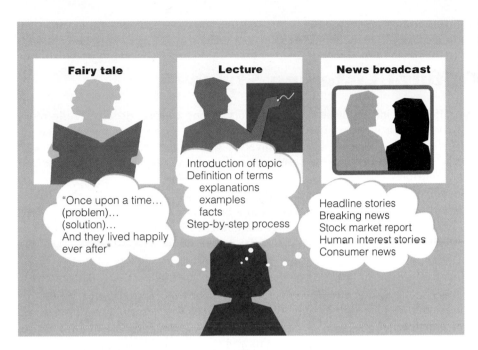

FIGURE 4.3 Our minds contain a number of schemas or models that help us listen and respond to specific types of speeches.

(Edwards & McDonald, 1993). Think of how you listen to a story. If you're typical, you have a mental model of what a good story is. You then use this model to interpret a specific story—whether to take it seriously, how to draw lessons from it, what parts are worth remembering, and so on.

You formulate schemas through listening to many and varying speeches. For instance, after you've heard several lectures, you have a pretty good mental picture of what to expect when a professor begins speaking because lectures follow a somewhat predictable pattern. Similarly, you learn what to expect from a demonstration speech, an entertaining story, a news report, a funeral eulogy, or an announcement because you've heard a number of speeches in each category.

The box on Cultural Listening Styles found on page 72 identifies some listening expectations that are common in other cultural and co-cultural groups.

Know Your Listening Purpose

Just as you have speaking goals, you also have goals for listening. You turn on the radio to be entertained; but, when a commercial comes on, you evaluate the claims critically, deciding whether the product interests you. You listen to a lecture to gain understanding of a topic, then have lunch with friends and listen to them vent about a test. For each type of listening, you shift your strategies in order to meet your listening goals more effectively. Here, we focus on listening to comprehend and listening to evaluate messages.

Improve Your Comprehension

Think of all the times you listen for information: A professor lectures; a lab instructor explains a process; your boss gives directions for your next assignment; a friend tells how to get to the financial aid office; a radio reporter tells you where an accident blocks traffic. Listening to learn, or **comprehensive listening,** is a vital skill in many areas of life.

Comprehensive Listening
Listening to learn, understand, get information.

DIVERSITY IN PRACTICE

Cultural Listening Styles

The differences in worldviews and behaviors among cultural groups is reflected in the ways their listeners approach public speeches. Researchers over the last three decades have been examining diversity in listening styles. Knowing some cultural variations will make you more mindful of listening differences. Here are a few examples:

■ A Javanese listening schema: On the island of Java, listeners repeat phrases they like to a neighbor. This results in a buzz of voices throughout the speech, signaling the speaker that the audience is receiving it well (Tannen, 1989).

■ An Asian listening tradition: In an Asian culture that emphasizes unity, listeners may expect speakers to develop oneness with them rather than present divisive ideas. Both speakers and audiences share the responsibility for making communication successful (Sitkaram & Cogdill,1976).

■ Another Asian tradition: An audience may listen in silence, feeling that noise breaks the concentration required to attend to a speech. Applause can signal suspicion, similar to booing by an audience in the United States; some listeners do not even applaud at the end of the speech in order to help the speaker remain modest (Sitkaram & Cogdill,1976).

■ An African-American schema: Within some contexts, the entire audience responds to the speaker's words. This schema, which reflects traditional African patterns, is termed "call and response." The speaker's statements (calls) are punctuated by the listeners' reactions to them (response), with the result that the audience is, in a real sense, talking back to the speaker. Because no sharp line distinguishes speakers and listeners, both cooperate to create the message (Smith, [Asanti], 1970; Daniel & Smitherman, 1990).

■ U.S. student preferences: In a recent cross-cultural study of student listening preferences, American students reported liking messages that are short and to the point. They tend to prefer speakers with whom they can identify (women more so than men).

■ German student preferences: German students prefer precise, error-free messages; disorganized presentations frustrate and annoy them. They are much less concerned about identifying personally with the speaker.

■ Israeli student preferences: Israeli students prefer complex and challenging information that they can think over and evaluate before they form judgments and opinions. The length of the message is relatively unimportant (Kiewitz, et al., 1997).

You can read the entire study of cross-cultural student listening preferences on your *InfoTrac College Edition*; go to PowerTrac and search for the author Kiewitz.

Several strategies can help you better comprehend material. Jot down the vocabulary words; to understand unfamiliar words and concepts, consult a dictionary. To develop skills for identifying major ideas and important supporting materials, study Chapter 8 (supporting information) and Chapters 9 through 11 (organization) in this text. Following are specific tips for overcoming those departures from listening presented earlier in Figure 4.2.

■ *Prepare in advance.* Prepare for class lectures by reading the related chapter in the text or by looking up related information. Study the list of major textual concepts usually found at the chapter opening; skim the chapter and notice headings and boldfaced terminology; read the summary. Look at the pictures and diagrams before you go to class. Or, go on the Internet and look for information.

■ *Attention directing.* To overcome departures and tangents from the speech, both large and small, focus on specific areas of the message and take notes on them. For example, listen for and write down the main ideas, or focus on practical "things I can use," or listen for what the speaker is *not* saying (what is being omitted).

■ *Enhance the meaning.* Use small departures productively by asking yourself questions that link the material to your personal experiences and ideas. For example: Who do I know who is like that? Isn't that what happened to my grandmother? How on earth does that work? What is the next step going to be? Does this match what I learned in another class? Elaborate on the ideas mentally by creating mental images or referring to what you already know or have experienced.

■ *Look for organizational patterns.* Use organizational skills from the canon of disposition to help you remember material. For instance, identify the main points and watch for signals such as "first," "next," or "finally" that will help you understand a series of steps. Be aware of words such as "therefore" or "in contrast" that connect one idea to another (Lundeen, 1993).

Use strategies that complement your personal learning style. For instance, if you learn best by hearing, get permission to tape the lecture or speech and replay it when you have time to go over the ideas again. If you learn best by creating linear outlines, then take a laptop computer or notebook with you and outline the main points and the most important supporting information. If you are more graphically oriented, make a mind map and draw connections between ideas. Draw useful illustra-tions in the margins of your notes. I personally include the lecturer's examples in my notes, because I learn and remember abstract ideas best when I tie them to real-life situations.

Don't ignore the manner in which the speaker presents her ideas. A confident, intense involvement with the subject may add a dimension that says "This is important, pay attention," or "I care about this topic and so should you." In contrast, a tentative, apologetic, or apathetic manner may lead you to conclude "This is not very important material," or "If this speaker isn't sure of this material, how can I be?"

In summary, comprehensive listening requires skill in understanding words and ideas, in identifying major ideas and supporting materials, in connecting new material with old, and in recalling information. This type of listening corresponds with the general speech purpose to inform. We now turn to critical listening skills that you'll employ when you hear a persuasive speaker.

Improve Your Critical Listening Skills

Persuasive speakers surround you and urge you to buy, to sign petitions, to donate, to vote, to accept a religious belief, or to use a particular product. You need to develop critical listening skills in order to sort out competing claims for your allegiance, your beliefs, your money, and your time. A critical approach means that you ponder and weigh the merits of various appeals rather than accepting them without reflection. **Critical listening** skills build on comprehensive listening skills, but add questions such as these:

■ What is this speaker's goal?

■ Does this message make sense?

■ Where does this information come from?

■ What are the benefits of adopting the speaker's ideas?

Critical Listening
Listening that requires you to reflect and weigh the merits of persuasive messages before you accept them.

Effective note-taking is one way you can improve your comprehensive listening skills. (J. Nordell/The Image Works)

- What problems, if any, go along with this position?
- Am I being swayed by my emotions?
- Should I trust this speaker?

In short, critical listening is one way to live out the cultural saying "Don't believe everything you hear." The skills it requires will guide you through all the persuasive appeals of the day. Chapters 8 and 17 provide tests you can use to evaluate evidence and reasoning.

In a diverse culture, as noted earlier, you are sometimes tempted to seek out speakers who affirm your ideas. Their support bolsters your beliefs and actions, especially if the dominant society challenges them. The following examples may clarify this listening purpose:

Public Speaking Resource Center

- People who give money to support needy children attend a banquet where they hear narratives describing how their gift literally saved lives. These stories convince them to continue their donations.

- Members of synagogues, churches, mosques, and temples gather weekly to reaffirm their beliefs about God.

- Every year on the anniversary of the Supreme Court decision *Roe v. Wade,* supporters on both sides of the abortion issue attend rallies to hear speakers who reaffirm their position.

- Members of Neo-Nazi groups organize gatherings in which speakers passionately argue for the merits of white supremacy.

If you find one of these settings comfortable, you may find yourself reacting enthusiastically by clapping, nodding, or verbally encouraging the speaker. Because you are involved with the topic, you may accept questionable arguments or emotional appeals that support your cause. However, you need to test these messages as you would any other persuasive speech. Think how different history would be had Hitler's listeners evaluated his messages critically (Ridge, 1993; Wolvin & Coakley, 1993).

STOP AND CHECK

Develop Strategies to Listen More Effectively

Return to the Listening Skills Self-Assessment you completed on page 70 and note each question you answered with an "A" or a "B." Then use materials from the section you just read (Strategies to Improve Listening) to develop strategies that will help you overcome the listening barrier implied in each question. You'll find a Listening Skills Development Plan under Chapter 4: Forms and Checklists for Jaffe Connection on the Public Speaking Resource Center. You can use this form to record your strategies. To investigate this topic further, log on to *InfoTrac College Edition* and perform a key word search for "listening tips."

Practice Dialogical Listening

Remember the diagram of communication from Chapter 1? As you listen to a public speech, you provide feedback, often nonverbal but sometimes verbal. This section will examine both nonverbal and verbal interactions. As you read, remember that cultural expectations influence appropriate feedback behaviors (refer to Cultural Listening Styles, on page 68).

Give Appropriate Nonverbal Feedback

Your posture, your movements, even the distance you sit from the speaker can all help you send feedback more effectively.

Posture

Your posture communicates involvement and helps you focus your attention. Face the speaker squarely. Even if you are sitting in the corner of the room, you can turn toward the speaker more directly. Lean forward slightly. When you are thoroughly engrossed in a speech, this posture—being "on the edge of your seat"—is natural. Let your body assume a relaxed, open position.

Distance

Think about the difference in your attentiveness if you sit in the far corner of the back row where people walk by an open door, or if you sit front-and-center where you have few outside distractions. Which seat contributes more to your learning? One study, illustrated in Figure 4.4, found that instructors interact more regularly with students who are sitting in the first two or three rows, toward the center (Hybels & Weaver, 1992). It makes sense that the more you interact with the speaker, the more you will understand and remember.

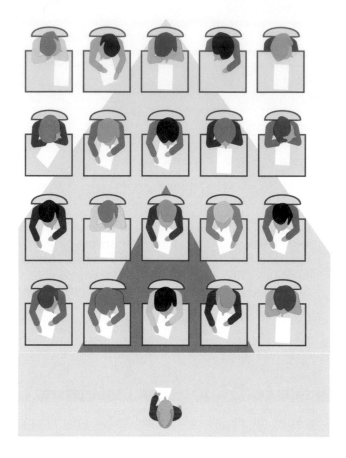

FIGURE 4.4 In the formal seating arrangement depicted in this classroom diagram, the "action zone" is shaded red. Students who sit in this zone interact more with the instructor. Those in the area shaded yellow interact less frequently, and those in the unshaded area have the fewest number of interactions.

Movements

Avoid disruptive behaviors such as fidgeting, shuffling papers, or drumming your fingers on the desk. Instead, support the speaker by making eye contact, which also helps focus your attention. Smiling at an amusing anecdote, nodding in support of a major point, or applauding when appropriate also increase your involvement and help the speaker.

A speaker who looks out at attentive listeners may actually become more interesting. One campus legend relates how a boring professor began the semester by standing only at the lectern and reading from his notes. His students decided to *act as if* he were a fascinating lecturer. Whenever he moved away from his notes, ever so slightly, they all leaned forward a bit, made eye contact, and used supportive motions. According to the story, the professor was eventually walking back and forth across the front of the room, lecturing animatedly!

Give Appropriate Verbal Feedback

What's her source of information? Where can I write for further facts? Hmmm . . . that happened to my sister! How is he defining that particular word? Questions and comments such as these arise as you engage the material of the speech. When you know that a question-and-answer period will follow a speech, jot down your questions and comments. Of course, there are many different types of questions, each of which influence the kind of response you will get. Make sure you choose the kind that suits your purposes. Here are a few common question types (Goodman & Esterly, 1990).

Loaded Questions

You can put a speaker on the defensive by the implicit assumptions it contains. These are **loaded questions.** Let's say a reporter asks the president "When are you going to start keeping your promises about Medicare reform?" The question is loaded because it implies (1) that the president made the promise, and (2) that he or she is failing to keep it. In addition, this question *when* is not really asking for a time. That is, the expected answer is not "Well, I thought I'd start that on the morning of June 16, just before lunch."

Loaded Questions
Questions containing implications intended to put the speaker on the defensive.

Closed Questions

Closed questions ask for brief, specific answers. Use them when you seek precise information or want to verify your understanding. The question "Did you read Alex Haley's entire book?" asks for a yes or no response. "When did the Mexican government ratify the treaty?" asks for a specific date. "What website do you use most?" asks for a specific Internet address. "Who wrote the *Chronicles of Narnia?*" requires a specific name.

Closed Questions
Requests for brief, specific answers.

Open Questions

Open questions invite more lengthy responses from a speaker. For instance, "How do you think the dean will respond to your proposal?" allows the speaker to select from a number of possible responses. Other examples include "What suggestions do you have for time management?" or "How will your spending habits change now that you've destroyed your credit cards?"

Open Questions
Requests for more lengthy responses.

Clarification Questions

When you are confused, you can ask for more information. Here are some examples of **clarification questions:** "Could you explain the difference between the Old Believers and the Molokan Russians?" "What did you mean when you said that without gays in the military we might not have been born?"

Clarification Questions
Requests to clear up confusing ideas.

Requests for Elaboration

If you want a speaker to further expand on her ideas, you can **request for elaboration:** "You told us that some of the Founding Fathers grew hemp. Could you elaborate on that?" "Can you tell us more about the Asian Americans' press coverage of the boycott of Korean storeowners?" "Could you give more details on theories about the causes of school shootings?"

Requests for Elaboration
Questions asking for more information.

Comments

Instead of asking questions, you can **comment** by providing information from your own experience or research. For instance, after a speech on bulimia, one person provided statistics she had heard on a television show. Another briefly shared a story about her bulimic sister's treatment. If you know some data in the speech is incorrect (for example, let's say the speaker gives outdated statistics) you can provide updated information. Your questions and comments are part of the co-creation of meaning that involves both a speaker and a participating audience. (Not all cultures participate equally in this co-creation of meaning process, as Diversity in Practice: Saving Face, on page 74, explains.)

Comment
Information from personal experience or research.

In summary, listening is not easy. Speakers can be boring, subjects are often complex and difficult, your emotions may get involved, and your daily stresses can influence how well you listen. Being aware of your thought processes during listening and actively working to focus your attention on the speech will help you become a better

By contributing comments and asking questions, dialogical listeners partner with a speaker to co-create meaning. (Anita Cirulis, George Fox University)

listener. Then, consider yourself a co-creator of meaning who actively interacts with the speaker, both nonverbally and verbally, to create mutual meanings.

DIVERSITY IN PRACTICE

Saving Face

Question-and-answer periods are not common in all cultural groups. For instance, in the context of traditional Chinese or Japanese public speaking, you are supposed to understand the speaker. Asking a question is an admission that you're not intelligent enough to unravel the shades of meaning provided. In addition, your questions reflect on the speaker's ability to communicate effectively; that is, if you're confused and have questions, the speaker failed to communicate. Finally, in order to preserve the speaker's "face," it's considered inappropriate to question a speaker's information—and thus, his or her character—in front of others (Becker, 1991; Sueda, 1995).

Summary

Listening is the communication activity that we do most and study least. Listening is important in your personal and occupational life. However, as a listener, you face a number of cultural as well as personal barriers that often impede effective listening.

Linguistic barriers can make it difficult to make sense of a message. Further, misunderstanding vocabulary or not knowing cultural allusions means that you will not fully understand the speech. In addition, personal and psychological factors, such as physical tiredness, stresses and worries, stereotypes and prejudices, and wandering attention patterns, can hinder your listening.

Fortunately, you can devise strategies to listen more effectively. Use cultural schemas or mental blueprints to guide the perception, interpretation, storage, and recollection of what you hear. Know your listening purpose and identify strategies to help you comprehend information or critically evaluate persuasive messages.

Finally, practice dialogical listening by contributing appropriate nonverbal and verbal feedback during the speech. Nonverbal actions communicate that you are interested in the speech; they also help you pay attention. Useful nonverbal elements include a posture that communicates involvement, a distance that helps focus your attention, and movements that support rather than disrupt the speech. When you have an opportunity to interact verbally with a speaker, you can ask questions or provide comments that elaborate on the topic. However, be aware that after-speech questions and comments are inappropriate in some cultures.

Key Terms

cultural allusions (62)
stereotype (64)
prejudiced (64)
speech-thought differential (64)
leftover thinking space (64)
schemas (66)
comprehensive listening (67)

critical listening (69)
loaded questions (73)
closed questions (73)
open questions (73)
clarification questions (73)
request for elaboration (73)
comment (73)

Access

**for Audio Flashcards
of Key Terms**

Application and Critical Thinking Questions

1. Think about the Chinese symbol that stands for listening (see Figure 4.1). In what way do you use your ears, eyes, and heart when you listen to your classmates? Your professors? A speaker whose ideas support your own opinions? A speaker with whom you totally disagree?

2. Practice the nonverbal skills of active listening in one of your courses. That is, use posture, space, and movement to help focus your attention on the lecture. Afterward, evaluate whether your nonverbal behaviors helped you pay attention and recall the class material.

3. Using the diagrams in Figure 4.2 as models, draw a diagram that depicts your listening pattern during the last lecture you heard. Next, draw a diagram that depicts your listening pattern during the last conversation you had with your best friend. Draw a third diagram that shows your thinking pattern during your last major conversation with a family member. Compare the three. What conclusions can you draw about your listening patterns in various contexts?

4. In the next group of classroom speeches, select one speech that you will follow by verbally interacting with the speaker. During the speech, jot down several questions you plan to ask.

5. Listen to a speaker who takes a position that differs dramatically from your views; you may find such a speaker on radio or television. (Examples: a person whose lifestyle differs from yours; one who disagrees about a political figure; someone whose views on a social issue such as capital punishment diverge from yours; a person with different religious beliefs.) As you listen, jot down your thoughts and your feelings, then evaluate your listening effectiveness.

Internet Activities

Reread the material in the box on Cultural Listening Styles, page 68, then log on to the Internet and read the study of cross-cultural student listening preferences available on your *InfoTrac College Edition* (Article A21283282). Discuss with a small group of classmates your understanding of the concept of "listening styles" and of cultural influences on them. After trying to identify your listening style, discuss your conclusions with them.

■ Log on to your *InfoTrac College Edition* and search for the subject "listening." Read an article in an online periodical that gives tips for better listening. Summarize its contents and come to class prepared to share guidelines for better listening.

■ Go to www.alltheweb.com and search for the exact phrase "listening skills." You will get tens of thousands of hits. Browse a few sites that contain .edu in the URL (see Chapter 7 for an explanation of URL) and summarize several reasons that developing good listening skills will help you personally.

Hot Links at the Public Speaking Resource Center

Public Speaking Resource Center

The following links are maintained and can be accessed easily via Jaffe Connection at the Public Speaking Resource Center on the Wadsworth Communication Café web site at http://communication.wadsworth.com./publicspeaking/study.

http://www.csbsju.edu/academicadvising/help/eff-list.html This page describes the "Five R's of Note Taking." It's sponsored by the Department of Academic Advising services at the College of St. Benedict/St. John's University.

http://online.sjsu.edu/COMM041/listen.html Dr. Stephanie Coopman of San Jose State University has excellent material about critical thinking on her site.

http://www.elmhurst.edu/library/effective-listening-skills.htm Elmhurst College Learning Center sponsors this site, which provides listening tests and definitions, as well as suggestions for and barriers to effective listening. Links to other sites online make it especially valuable.

Jaffe Speech Interactive

Jaffe Speech
Interactive

Review the Critiquing Guidelines on Speech Interactive on your Jaffe Connection
CD-ROM.

Do you see a correlation between the concepts presented in this chapter and the
Guidelines provided on the CD-ROM?

LIBERATE
EGYPT
SUDAN
CHAD
ETHIOPIA
CENTRAL AFRICAN REPUBLIC
CAMEROON
GABON
CONGO
ZAIRE
ZAMBIA
ZIMBABWE
MOZAMBIQUE
ANGOLA
BOTSWANA
NAMIBIA
SOUTH AFRICA
UNION
"The line of fire
is a place of honor."
~Lean Alejandro

5

Audience Analysis

This chapter will help you:

- **Describe various audience motivations**

- **Tell how demographic audience analysis helps you adapt your speech to the audience**

- **Explain how the situation affects your audience**

- **Develop a questionnaire to assess your listeners' psychological profile**

- **Analyze your audience's perception of your credibility**

"Educate to Liberate" ©1988 by
Miranda Bergman, Jane Norling, Maria
Ramos, Vicky Hamlin, and Arch
Williams

Every election provides another example. Candidates attempt, and fail, to identify with a specific audience's concerns. In 1992, H. Ross Perot blundered in a speech to the National Association for the Advancement of Colored People (NAACP); in 1996, Bob Dole similarly failed with an African American group. In 1999, Elizabeth Dole misread an audience that was much younger than she. The errors of these speakers resulted in national coverage, not of the candidate's ideas but of their blunders—with broad hints that the politicians were out of touch.

Perot and the Doles learned, the hard way, the importance of sensitivity to the audience at every step of the speechmaking process from initial topic selection through the final question-and-answer period. This process is often called **audience analysis** because it consists of analyzing a specific group of listeners and discovering resources that will most effectively communicate with them. When you take a dialogical perspective, you think of yourself as a **listening speaker** (Holzman, 1970), who hears audience interests and concerns before, during, and after your speech. Your relationship with your audience is complex, and this chapter examines both your perception of your audience and their perception of you.

Analyze Who Is Listening

A good speech is one you prepare for a specific group at a specific time; even politicians or university recruiters, who present the same material repeatedly, adapt their material to each group and each setting. This section explores ways you can think about a specific audience and a specific speaking situation.

Consider Audience Motivations

Why do audiences gather? What attracts them? What holds them? Why don't they all just walk out? Answering these questions provides clues about your audience's motivations and helps you prepare your speech more effectively. Audiences gather for a number of reasons. Many years ago, H. L. Hollingworth (1935) identified the following six types of audiences:

1. **Pedestrian audiences** randomly and temporarily gather because something grabs their attention—perhaps a salesman's flashy demonstration of a food processor, the impassioned voice of an activist in an outdoor forum, or the humorous stories of a sidewalk entertainer. Your challenge as a speaker? To attract listeners and keep their interest long enough to present your message.

2. **Passive audiences** listen to speeches in order to accomplish other goals. Most speech classes consist of passive listeners who attend class, not to hear your speeches but to receive academic credit. Some even take the course reluctantly. You will be most effective if you select an interesting topic and help your audience understand its relevance to their lives.

3. **Selected audiences** voluntarily and intentionally come to hear about a topic (such as getting a job after graduation) or to hear a particular speaker (a congressional candidate, for instance). When they are a **homogeneous audience,** they share an attitude—whether positive or negative. Speaking to an audience with a positive attitude can be fun, but you must develop your ideas clearly so that listeners understand and accept them. Facing a negative or **hostile audience** presents an entirely different set of challenges, which are discussed in Chapter 17.

4. **Concerted audiences** voluntarily listen because they more-or-less agree that the subject is important, but they don't know what they can do about it. They need you to

---

Audience Analysis

Identifying audience characteristics to communicate more effectively.

Listening Speaker

Dialogical speaker who hears audience interests and concerns before, during, and after a speech.

Pedestrian Audiences

Audiences that are random, temporary, and accidental, in that they did not intend to hear a speech.

Passive Audiences

Groups who listen in order to accomplish other goals.

Selected Audiences

Groups that choose to listen to a selected subject or speaker.

Homogeneous Audiences

Listeners who are similar in attitude.

Hostile Audiences

Listeners negative toward the topic or the speaker.

Concerted Audiences

Listeners who are positive toward a topic, but don't act; they need motivation and a plan.

Because they must create an audience out of people who are not intending to listen to a speech, speakers sometimes use unusual means to attract attention to their topic. (Jack Jaffe)

motivate them and to provide information about specific things they can do. Here's an example. After California voters struck down affirmative action programs, students gathered to protest. Organizers then stepped in to coordinate letter-writing campaigns, stage marches, and so on. A classroom audience may have some concerted characteristics. For instance, at one university, administrators decided to change the name of the team mascot against the wishes of most of the students in my speech class. In response, one student spoke up and organized a protest rally and a petition drive.

5. **Organized audiences** already know about the topic and are motivated and committed to act, but they need specific, "how to" instructions. The students in the example above knew about the mascot change and were committed to participating in a petition drive. So the leaders didn't rehash the problem and the need for action; instead, they focused on the where, when, and how of getting signatures on the petitions.

Organized Audiences
Motivated listeners who need specific instructions.

6. **Absent audiences** are separated from you by distance and, in some cases, time; they listen through radio, telephone conferencing, television, videotapes, or videoconferences—live, or days (even years!) later. Advances in technology make this type of audience more and more common. When you speak to absent audiences, focus on being interesting and relevant, and use conversational delivery as if you were speaking to one listener at a time.

Absent Audiences
Intentional listeners separated in distance and time who are reached through the media.

As you might imagine, an audience is not always homogeneous. For instance, a mostly passive audience such as your classroom may have several students who select both the topic and the instructor; a mostly organized audience may include passive listeners who are just tagging along with friends. Regardless, you'll be more effective if you consider the fundamental motivation of your audiences and plan speeches that are sensitive to their interests and needs.

Analyze Audience Demographics

One of the most common ways to consider your audience is through **demographic audience analysis,** in which you analyze listeners according to the groups or populations

Demographic Audience Analysis
Identifying audiences by populations they represent, such as age or ethnicity.

they represent. In some situations, demographic factors help you tailor your remarks specifically. However, if you are not careful, you may classify your listeners into categories and then stereotype them. Remember that each person belongs to many groups, and membership in a specific group is **salient** (it matters, or is significant) more in some situations than in others (Collier, 1994). Rothenberg (1998) summarizes the complexity of demographic analysis:

> When we engage in [demographic analysis], we should never lose sight of the fact that (1) any particular woman or man has an ethnic background, class location, age, sexual orientation, religious orientation, gender, and so forth, and (2) all these characteristics are inseparable from the person and from each other. . . . It is also true that . . . we may have to make generalizations about the experience of different groups of people, even as we affirm that each individual is unique (p. 2).

Figure 5.1 illustrates the complicated nature of demographic analysis. Because no one is simply a "woman" or a "Latina" or a "senior citizen," analyze your listeners' identification with various groups *in light of your specific speaking situation*. The following categories are common in demographic analysis: ethnicity, race, religion, gender, marital status, age, group affiliation, occupation and socioeconomic status, and region.

Ethnicity

Ethnicity refers to a group's common heritage and cultural traditions usually having national and religious origins (O'Neil, 1999; Collier, 1994). For example, the Russian Old Believers who live in the Willamette Valley of Oregon are a distinct ethnic group, distinguished from their European-American and Mexican-American neighbors by language, clothing, cultural heroes, and religious traditions (Jaffe, 1995). The United States is comprised of people from many historical and geographical backgrounds. Its urban areas are especially diverse. For example, members of more than 150 ethnic groups (speaking 114 languages) residing in Queens, New York. Ethnicity is a complex concept, in part because many people have ancestors from more than one ethnic group.

Ethnic identity assumes more or less salience depending on the context. Listeners in a fairly homogeneous audience—such as an all-Irish group whose members are debating a St. Patrick's Day parade—are probably thinking of themselves as Irish. However, an Irish student in a diverse speech class probably considers her educational and occupational goals to be more important than her ethnicity.

Race

Ethnicity is often linked to **race,** but the two are not the same. Racial categories are generally based on physical characteristics such as skin color or facial features; however, races are not clearly distinct, and characteristics that supposedly identify a particular race are also found in other populations. For example, dark-brown skin color is found among unrelated populations in Africa, India, Australia, New Guinea, and the Southwest Pacific (O'Neil, 1999). In addition, millions of Americans come from mixed racial backgrounds that blur the lines between groups (Marmor, 1996; Wehrly, et al., 1999). President Clinton addressed racial issues in his State of the Union Address (2000) by citing scientists such as Alan Templeton, an evolutionary and population biologist at Washington University who wrote *Racial Differences* (1999). According to these scientists, there is no such thing as race; genetically we are "99.9 percent the same." Instead, race is a "social category," and unfortunately such categories are often associated with stereotypes. If you assume that a person or group will have specific abilities, skills, or behaviors associated with these stereotypes, you are being **racist.**

Salient
Important or significant.

Ethnicity
Heritage and cultural traditions usually stemming from national and religious origins.

Race
Categories, often associated with stereotypes, based on physical characteristics.

Racist
Assuming someone has certain traits or behaviors because of race.

FIGURE 5.1 SILHOUETTES   These silhouettes represent a single audience member who is influenced by many demographic factors that are interwoven with individual traits and personality characteristics. In one situation, the listener's age is the more salient factor; in another, her region and group affiliation matter more.

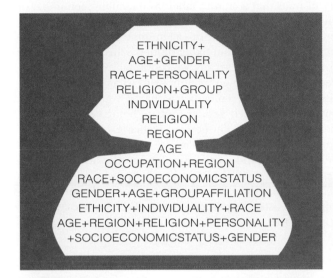

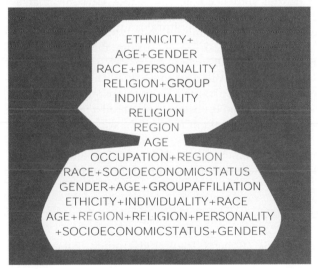

Religion

It is an old saying that it is better to avoid both religion and politics in social conversation. This is a reflection of the deep feelings many people have on these topics. Of course it is permissible to speak publicly on religion, but it is necessary *in every speech* to be sensitive to the possible range and intensity of religious beliefs within your audience. I've heard students, totally oblivious to their Jewish classmates, talk about "when we all go home to celebrate Christmas." Some listeners identify themselves as members of a particular faith yet see their religion as peripheral to their identity. For others, religion is a central factor that influences many other areas of their lives. Religious traditions are often linked to ethnicity, and disparagement or dismissal of a group's sacred texts, heroes, or rituals often evokes intense emotional reactions.

Gender

Don't confuse sexual differences, which are biological, with gender differences, which are cultural. **Gender** is a cluster of traits that a culture labels as masculine, feminine, or androgynous (containing both masculine and feminine characteristics). To illustrate, women often cook, and some cultural groups consider this a feminine task; however, nothing in a man's biological makeup prevents him from fixing dinner. Thus, cooking can be an androgynous activity. In our rapidly changing society, we continually examine and negotiate gender-associated characteristics, changing our notions of what are "proper" behaviors for men and for women. The point to remember is that, if you assume people will think or act in a certain way because of their gender, you are being **sexist.**

Gender identity is salient only at agreed-upon gender-exclusive events: a Million Man March or a Promise Keepers rally; a "Women in Science" conference or a mother-daughter banquet. For these events, gender identity is one reason the audience gathers. At other times, you may speak to all-male or all-female groups who are drawn to your subject by their political affiliation, educational level, or another factor. For example, engineers at a workshop on disaster preparedness may all be females, but it is their interest in safety that motivates them to attend, not their gender.

Marital Status/Sexual Expression

Another demographic category of your audience is marital status. Certainly, married people may differ from singles in some perspectives. In addition, rapidly changing cultural mores regarding sexuality dictate that you consider your listeners' sexual orientation (and their sexual activity in some instances). Do not assume that all your listeners are heterosexual—or that they are all sexually active. (In fact, in a 1990 Associated Press survey of sexual behavior, 3 percent of Americans identified themselves as lifelong virgins.) One student speaker made unwarranted assumptions in this area on a campus with an active Greek system. He advised his listeners to attend a fraternity party, scope out interesting women, persuade one of them to drink heavily, then invite her to an upstairs bedroom to "look at the goldfish." Many listeners laughed, but others were offended by his assumptions about women, fraternities, drinking, and heterosexuality. Married students in the class were amused at his immaturity but bored with his speech.

Age

In his classic work on rhetoric, Aristotle (Roberts, trans. 1984) noted that age influences an audience's motivations and concerns. Globally, cultures distinguish between generational groups, and ours is no exception. Modern market researchers in the United States identify age cohorts who were brought up differently, who experienced different events, and who pursue different social missions (Morton, 1998). Here are some common labels for, and descriptions of, these generations:

- ▪ *Mature Americans* born before 1924 have adapted to enormous cultural changes. As young people, these seniors lived through the Great Depression and World War II, listened to the radio but not television, drove Model Ts instead of SUVs. Those born between 1925 and 1945 tend to be adventurous and determined to remain youthful. Their teachers read the Bible, prayed in school, and fretted about students who chewed gum!

- ▪ *Baby boomers,* 77 million of them, were born between the end of World War II and the early 1960s. Older boomers lived through the assassinations of President Kennedy and Martin Luther King, Jr. Boomers tend to be individualistic, driven, and "me"-centered. Some avoided the draft, experimented with drugs, and organized protests. Boomers grew up with television, but they took along typewriters, not computers, when they went off to college.

■ *Generation Xers,* the first latchkey generation, are a racially and culturally diverse group whose 44.5 million members were born between 1963 and 1978 (or 1980). They came of age in a media-dominated society with access to network television and cable, CD-ROMs, VCRs, and videogames (Israel, 1993; O'Donovan, 1997). Socially, they grew up in the face of high divorce rates, legalized abortion, a huge national deficit, and a series of political scandals. Some researchers describe them as fun-loving and routine-hating, reactive and angry. Younger Gen Xers have used personal computers since they were six years old, so their outlook on life and their view of technology is vastly different from that of seniors (Halstead, 1999).

■ *The millennium generation,* born after 1978 (or 1980, according to some sources), inherited many social and environmental problems; consequently, they tend to be more civic-minded (and less angry) than Gen Xers. The millenium generation was born into the "twitch speed" era of MTV and personal computers, in which technology makes everything seem to move faster (Prensky, 1998). One student speaker referred to 18- to 24-year-olds as the "I-generation," or Internet generation.

Although people in each group have individual differences, members of a generational cohort tend to be moved by appeals and allusions that another generation might not understand. On an occasion referred to earlier, when Elizabeth Dole was running for president she addressed a group of young, female students at Harvard Law School, her alma mater. In her speech she described her 1950s struggle to convince her mother that she should go to Harvard Law and have a career. Her listeners couldn't relate to her story. Most of them grew up in achievement-oriented families within a society that now encourages women to plan for a professional life.

Group Affiliation

People often join with others who share their interests, experiences, or hobbies. Veterans of Foreign Wars, Wheelchair Athletes, Alcoholics Anonymous, the debate team, and members of fraternities or sororities are examples. Often these groups invite guest speakers to meetings. Because group identity is highly salient in these situations, as a speaker you need to draw on common experiences and shared beliefs and values. For instance, if you're at the Young Republicans, find heroes within that party that you can praise, even if your political instincts lie with another party.

Occupation/Socioeconomic Status

Differences in educational level, in income, in occupational choices, in social class status can all be salient in particular situations. Knowing your classmates' job experiences and their academic majors can help you adapt more specifically to unique elements within your classroom. In addition, consider the educational range within your class; seniors and sophomores may differ in their perspectives. In the world of work, computer engineers or physicians may differ in gender, ethnicity, religion, and sexual orientation, but similar interests and experiences give them commonalities that you can draw upon when you speak. Furthermore, comfortably middle-class individuals may have little in common with those who struggle to make ends meet when the topic is stock market investing; however, a topic such as cheating is relevant across economic lines.

Regions

You know that Japanese or Nigerian audiences require different speaking strategies, but what if you move from one geographic region to another in North America? While people on this continent share many commonalties, North Americans in various regions tend to have somewhat different characteristics due to climate, history, language, economic base, politics, and other regional features. This can, therefore, in-

Renee Firestone described her experiences in the Auschwitz concentration camp to a group of teenaged skinheads. She and her listeners differed in ethnicity, gender, age, and group affiliation. (Courtesy of the Simon Wiesenthal Center)

fluence audience interests and perspectives (Andersen, et al., 1987). Rosemarie found this to be true:

> I really found a lot of cultural differences among regions as I moved from Florida, to Wyoming, then to Oregon!

Rosemarie

You can see this principle in practice if you follow a presidential candidate around the country. He discusses hurricane damage with Florida residents, but not with Oregonians. His emphasis in Silicon Valley differs from that in the ranchlands of the West. He recognizes that an inhabitant of New York City may have more in common with a San Franciscan than she does with a person from upstate New York. The rural New Yorker may be more similar to an Iowan than to her Manhattan cousin—a point made clear to Hillary Rodham Clinton when she went on her "listening tour" of New York state in the summer of 1999.

In summary, demographic audience analysis is a way of considering your listeners in terms of categories, based on such elements as ethnicity, gender, age, group affiliation, and regional identity. But, instead of stereotyping your listeners, try to use the more inclusive model of Figures 5.1–5.3. Know that demographic categories can guide you as you select materials and organize your speech, but in each individual these elements function together rather than separately.

Assess the Situation

You have considered your listeners' motivations, and you have thought about demographic categories. Now think about the specific situation in which your speech takes place. Many aspects of the situation can affect your audience. Time and the environment are two basic considerations.

Consider the Time

Two aspects of time affect public speaking. First, consider what time of day your class is held and the effect that may have on your audience. Think of those 8:00 A.M. listeners

STOP AND CHECK

Begin to Evaluate Your Classroom Audience

Use the following form to analyze your classroom audience. You can access this form electronically under Chapter 5: Forms and Checklists for Jaffe Connection on the Public Speaking Resource Center, http://communication.wadsworth.com/publicspeaking/study.html.

Audience Motivations and Demographics

In general, your audience is:

_____ pedestrian   _____ passive   _____ selected

_____ concerted   _____ organized   _____ absent

_____ hostile to   _____ neutral about   _____ interested in your subject

What strategies will you use to relate your topic to their interests and keep their attention?

_____

_____

Ethnically, _____ listeners are similar _____ from two groups _____ diverse

Mainly, _____ Christian _____ Jewish _____ Muslim _____ Buddhist _____ Other

Probably hold their religious beliefs _____ strongly   _____ very moderately

_____ weakly

_____ % women _____ % men

Mostly   _____ mature   _____ baby boomers   _____ Gen Xers

_____ millenium generation

_____ % single   _____ % married

Members of _____ interest groups

Interested in _____ majors

Job experiences _____

Mostly from _____ small towns_____ rural_____ suburban _____ urban areas

Which, if any, of these demographic issues will probably be salient in your classroom speaking situation? _____

_____

What strategies will you use to relate your topic to their interests and keep their attention? _____

_____

To further investigate the topic of demographic audience analysis, log onto *Info-Trac College Edition* and perform a subject search using the term "demographics."

who stumble into the room brushing sleep from their eyes. Does anyone come to class after working a night shift? What about classes just before lunch, when people are hungry? Or those just after lunch, when some students are sleepy? What differences might you identify between these time periods and an evening class? Asking yourself these questions about the time you are scheduled to speak helps you adapt your talk appropriately. For instance, you might be more animated when listeners are sleepy, or you might shorten your speech when it's very late.

Also, consider the *cultural* time system. In the dominant U.S. culture, time is seen as a line that is cut into segments, each lasting a specific duration, with distinct activities assigned to each (Jaffe, 1995; Hamid, 1997). Take this class, for example. You chose this particular class partly because it fills a time slot you had available. The clock tells you when class starts and when it is over. In this setting, the date and length of your speech are important. (You may be graded down if you don't appear on the assigned date, or give a speech of the assigned length.) Your listeners expect you to work within this time pattern.

In contrast, listeners from a culture or co-culture with a more relaxed sense of time often focus less on starting precisely on time and fitting their remarks into a rigid time frame, as the following example illustrates. An American professor went to Brazil to teach psychology in a 10:00 A.M.-to-noon class (Burgoon, et al., 1989). Of course, he carried with him the expectations of this society, and he began speaking close to 10. However, students arrived as late as 11 without signs of concern or apology. At 12:15, everyone was still in the classroom, asking questions. Finally, at 12:30, the professor ended the class and left. The students, however, seemed willing to stay even longer.

Consider the Environment

Once I taught in a small college theater that was painted black. Floors, ceiling, chairs . . . everything was black. We met there twice before I called the schedule desk and asked for a different room assignment! The black theater is only one of many instances where the room itself can work against you. Windowless spaces, those too small or too large, rooms located by a noisy stairwell—all are examples of places that may affect your audience, whether or not they recognize it.

Other environmental considerations include the room's temperature (too hot, too cold), the weather outside (sunny and beautiful, stormy and icy), noise (an air conditioner, heater), and other items that might affect your listeners' comfort or draw their attention. You'll be a better speaker if you consider these aspects of your situation and adapt accordingly.

In summary, you form perceptions of your listeners by analyzing the demographic categories and groups to which they belong and the specific situation in which the speech takes place. Some of the generalizations you make may be fairly accurate; however, many speakers are less effective than they could be because they make unwarranted assumptions. Audiences criticized Mrs. Dole for her age-related blunder. They found fault with Mr. Perot and Mr. Dole for treating them as a racial group rather than as individuals who happened to be of African origin—although both speakers surmised correctly that racial identity was highly salient at the NAACP convention. Your sensitivity in audience analysis will help you avoid embarrassing blunders.

Analyze the Audience's Psychological Profile

Psychological Profile
Assessment of an audience's beliefs, values, and attitudes.

Natalie really wanted to speak about a vegetarian diet, but she didn't want to repeat information everyone knew, so she decided to take a **psychological profile** of her classmates by creating a questionnaire before she prepared her speech. She asked herself what her listeners already knew, how they felt, what they considered important, and how they actually ate. In other words, she assessed their psychological approach to her topic. To determine your audience members' psychological profile, think about their beliefs, values, and attitudes regarding your subject.

Beliefs

Belief
Mental acceptance that something is true or false, correct or incorrect, valid or invalid.

A **belief** is a mental acceptance that something is true or false, correct or incorrect, valid or invalid (Rokeach, 1972). Our beliefs may be based on study or investigation or on conviction without much factual information or knowledge. And we may be wrong; misconceptions are common! When Natalie evaluated her listeners' beliefs, she used open questions like the following that allowed for a variety of responses:

> **STOP AND CHECK**
>
> *Continue Your Audience Analysis*
>
> **Assess Time and Environment**
>
> What time of day is the class held? _____
>
> How might this affect your audience? _____
>
> _____
>
> What date will you speak? _____
>
> What are the consequences if you aren't prepared to speak on that date? _____
>
> _____
>
> _____
>
> How long is the speech supposed to be? _____
>
> What are the consequences for being under or over time? _____
>
> _____
>
> What environmental considerations might affect your listeners? _____
>
> _____
>
> What strategies can you implement to overcome any obstacles inherent in the situation in which you must speak?
>
> _____
>
> _____
>
> You can access this questionnaire electronically under Chapter 5: Forms and Checklists for Jaffe Connection at the Public Speaking Resource Center, http://communication.wadsworth.com/publicspeaking/study/html.

■ What do you think are the benefits and drawbacks of a vegetarian diet?

■ If you don't eat meat, why not?

■ If you eat meat, what might convince you to stop?

■ What are some categories that vegetarians fall into?

She added some closed questions such as these:
Is a vegetarian diet healthy?

_____yes

_____no

_____I'm not sure

Natalie discovered that a few audience members avoided eating meat, but they didn't really understand the concept of combining proteins. Most of the audience couldn't identify three kinds of vegetarians, and half of her classmates thought that a vegetarian diet was too difficult to follow during college. However, three persons were confirmed vegans who ate no animal products at all and who regularly downloaded information about vegetarianism from the Internet. In short, three people had a fairly deep understanding of Natalie's topic, but most had little information, and many misconceptions, about a vegetarian diet.

Attitudes

Our tendencies to like or dislike, to have positive or negative feelings, are called **attitudes.** Attitudes have an emotional component that involves feelings and values, a mental component that involves beliefs, and a behavioral component that influences

Attitudes
Preferences, likes and dislikes; involve beliefs, feelings, and behaviors.

actions. For instance, Americans tend to *feel* positively toward work because they *believe* it's linked to success, which they *value*, so they *act* by setting personal goals and striving to accomplish them.

Scaled Questions

Questions asking for responses along a continuum; used to assess attitudes.

Researchers use **scaled questions** to measure attitudes along a range or continuum from highly positive to highly negative. Attitudes can also be neutral, meaning that listeners probably haven't thought enough about the subject to form an opinion. Here are typical scaled questions that Natalie might use to assess audience attitudes:

I admire vegetarians.

I———————I———————I———————I———————I———————I———————I
strongly   agree   mildly   neutral   mildly   disagree   strongly
agree   agree   disagree   disagree

All things considered, I would like to try a vegetarian diet.

I———————I———————I———————I———————I———————I———————I
strongly   agree   mildly   neutral   mildly   disagree   strongly
agree   agree   disagree   disagree

Vegetarian diets are actually healthier than diets containing meat.

I———————I———————I———————I———————I———————I———————I
strongly   agree   mildly   neutral   mildly   disagree   strongly
agree   agree   disagree   disagree

Notice that the first statement identifies feelings, the second looks at a predisposition to act, and the third assesses beliefs. All three—feelings, behaviors, and beliefs—work together to create attitudes. It is easier to speak when the audience shares your attitude toward your topic, whether it's negative or positive. However, your task becomes more complex when audience attitudes are increasingly diverse. Natalie, a vegetarian, knew that she'd have three sympathetic audience members, but most listeners were mildly or moderately negative toward vegetarianism. Two were downright hostile; one of them lived on a beef cattle ranch and the other's grandfather was a butcher. Knowing the range of attitudes within one audience, she could better plan ways to create an effective speech.

Values

Values

Ideals by which we judge what is important and, consequently, how we should behave.

Values are the standards we use to judge what is good or bad, right or wrong, moral or immoral, beautiful or ugly, kind or cruel, appropriate or inappropriate. U.S. cultural values include choice, individualism, fair play, progress, freedom, equality, and the like. Almost every topic you choose touches on your values because you at least consider the subject important enough to discuss. However, you directly address value questions when you use evaluative words such as right or wrong, beautiful or ugly, moral or immoral, important or insignificant. As with attitudes, it's helpful to think of value judgments as existing across a range. The **Ethical Quality Scale (EQS)** gives you a way to visualize gradations of opinion regarding ethical questions (Jensen, 1985). Although this scale deals with ethical or moral judgments, you could easily adapt it for judgments related to beauty, fairness, and other value issues.

Ethical Quality Scale (EQS)

Graphic to visualize gradations of opinion regarding issues of value.

Killing animals to use as food is:

I———————I———————I———————I———————I———————I———————I
highly   ethical   somewhat   morally   somewhat   unethical   highly
ethical   ethical   neutral   unethical   unethical

Natalie found that some classmates judged vegetarianism as highly ethical, whereas others felt it was morally neutral. Even the beef eaters didn't care what Natalie ate as long as she didn't try to push her diet on them. Because values are the assumptions we hold of what is good, value questions often generate strong emotional responses that are difficult to change. Natalie is passionate about vegetarianism, but the rancher's daughter may become equally passionate if Natalie implies that raising beef cattle is wrong.

Construct a Questionnaire

Figure 5.4 provides an example of a questionnaire that combines closed questions, open questions, and scaled questions on the topic of road rage. Using your topic, construct a questionnaire that you can use to analyze your classmates' psychological profile.

To investigate this topic further, log on to *InfoTrac College Edition* and perform a PowerTrac search for the subjects "opinion poll" and "questionnaires."

Although we have discussed beliefs, actions, attitudes, and values as separate entities, the truth is that they're intertwined. Keep in mind the interrelated aspect of these psychological factors because they affect your audience's interest in your topic. Take a listener who doesn't know much about writing a resumé but has a positive attitude because a good resumé will help him be more successful, which has value for him. Contrast him to a woman who knows she needs to wear seatbelts, who values safety, and who buckles up automatically. Her interest in a speech about seatbelts is probably minimal.

Consider Your Audience's Perception of You

Be aware that while you are forming impressions of your listeners, they are busily forming perceptions of your **credibility**—impressions regarding your character, your intentions, and your abilities that comprise your overall credibility. They begin their evaluation you before your speech, they modify their views while you speak, and they carry away a lasting impression after you're through (McCroskey, 1993).

> **Credibility**
> Listeners' impressions of your character, intentions, and abilities that make you more or less believable.

Be Aware of Prior Credibility

Let's say a former president comes to your campus to speak on foreign policy. You go to the speech assuming that he'll know about the subject. Or, one of your classmates is on the fencing team, so when she arrives on her speech day with fencing equipment in hand, you expect her to have an insider's perspective on the topic. This type of credibility, the reputation or expertise of speakers that makes them believable even before they say a word, is called **prior** or **extrinsic credibility.** Practically speaking, you probably won't have prior credibility within your classroom, for most students lack the credentials or reputation that make their classmates see them as experts. Therefore, you'll need to establish some link between the topic and yourself in your introduction; see the box, Diversity in Practice: Prior Credibility in Other Cultures, on page 94. Chapter 18 provides more detailed information about how to do this.

> **Prior or Extrinsic Credibility**
> Credibility speakers bring to the speech because of their experience and reputation.

Demonstrate Credibility in Your Speech

Regardless of your reputation, you will need to demonstrate credibility in your speech. Not surprisingly, this is called **demonstrated** or **intrinsic credibility.** Think of the student on the fencing team. If she couldn't name pieces of equipment or describe a fencing match, you would decide she was no expert. What will your audience look for as they decide whether you are credible? They will want evidence that you are knowledgeable about the subject. Consequently, it is important to do your research carefully and, throughout your speech, cite the sources you used. Define unfamiliar terminology, give examples, tell your personal experiences with the subject, and otherwise show your thorough understanding of the subject. Finally, be prepared to answer questions after you speak.

> **Demonstrated Credibility**
> Obvious knowledge the speaker shows during the speech.

FIGURE 5.2   This combination questionnaire contains open, closed, and scaled questions.

A Combination Questionnaire

Name (optional) _____

Age _____   Sex _____   Major _____

Have you experienced road rage?   _____ yes   _____ no   _____ not sure

Have you been the object of road rage?   _____ yes   _____ no   _____ not sure

Place an X on the point of the scale that best indicates your response to the sentence.
Use the following codes:

SA	=	strongly agree
A	=	agree
MA	=	mildly agree
N	=	no opinion
MD	=	mildly disagree
D	=	disagree
SD	=	strongly disagree

Sometimes I get so angry at other drivers, that I feel
I could do something that might endanger their safety.

```
|-----------|-----------|-----------|-----------|-----------|-----------|
SA          A           MA          N           MD          D          SD
```

Angry drivers in other cars pose threats to my safety.

```
|-----------|-----------|-----------|-----------|-----------|-----------|
SA          A           MA          N           MD          D          SD
```

Road rage is a serious national problem.

```
|-----------|-----------|-----------|-----------|-----------|-----------|
SA          A           MA          N           MD          D          SD
```

How would you define road rage?

What effect do you think it has on its victims?

What is the best way to deal with this phenomenon?

What kinds of road rage, if any, are worse than others?

Your listeners will also expect you to be calm and poised in a stressful situation. Think of it this way: If you're agitated during a classroom presentation, your audience may wonder why you can't control yourself. In contrast, if you are poised, they will perceive you more favorably.

Take Terminal Credibility into Account

Relief! Your speech is over and you're through! But wait! Your listeners continue to evaluate you. The overall impression you leave, your **terminal credibility,** is a balance between the reputation you brought to your speech and the expertise you demonstrated as you spoke.

> **Terminal Credibility**
> Final impression listeners have of a speaker.

Terminal credibility is not permanently fixed. If your listeners eventually discover that some of your information was incorrect, they will lose confidence in you. For example, suppose one of your classmates praises the pharmaceutical product Ritalin that is used to treat attention deficit disorder (ADD). In a previous speech, she mentioned that her little brother had ADD, so she had some prior credibility for this speech. In the speech itself, she provides facts and figures that describe the prescription drug: what it is, what it does, what doctors say about it. You're impressed. A month later, a physician suggests that your cousin take Ritalin, and you do further research on the drug. You learn that your classmate's speech was clearly one-sided; she presented only the positive side of the medication. Your final impression of her credibility plummets.

DIVERSITY IN PRACTICE

Prior Credibility in Other Cultures

Cultures vary in their evaluations of prior credibility. In Chinese and Japanese cultures, for instance, demographic categories such as age, gender, social rank, and maturity contribute to the audience's view of the speaker's trustworthiness. Similarly, age and gender loom large in some Native American cultures. When the occasion calls for "saying a few words," younger males and women in these cultures will seek out older males to speak for them. Weider and Pratt (1990) relate the story of a young woman who spoke for herself and her husband on a public occasion. Her elders scolded her for not knowing how to act!

Your age as a speaker will probably affect your audience, either positively or negatively. Because U.S. culture celebrates youth and actively looks for fresh ideas, young people often receive as much or more attention than older speakers. In contrast, listeners in a culture that respects the wisdom and experience that come only with age may pay less attention when you are young and more attention when you are older. Consider this potential difference whenever you adapt to a culturally diverse audience.

Summary

You and your audiences are involved in an interactive process in which you each form impressions of the other. As a speaker, you assess your listeners' motivations as well as demographic characteristics such as age, ethnicity, race, religion, gender, marital status, group affiliation, occupation and socioeconomic status, and region; however, you also realize that these characteristics are only salient at specific times and in specific circumstances.

Situational characteristics also have an impact on your audience. The time of day, the length of your speech, and the noise level or temperature in the room can all affect their interest and attention. Do what you can to minimize environmental distractions.

Finally, analyze your audience's psychological profile as it relates to your topic. What do they already know or believe? How do they feel about your subject? What attitudes and underlying values influence their interest? Developing a questionnaire with various types of questions will help you identify their responses to specific aspects of your subject.

Your listeners are actively evaluating you. Before your speech they assess your reputation. During your speech, they form impressions of your credibility and your overall trustworthiness based on cultural criteria such as sound evidence, source citation, overall knowledge, and composure. After you've finished, your listeners may continue to assess your credibility, either positively or negatively.

This is one of the most important chapters in this text. As Perot and the Doles found, to their chagrin, sensitivity to a specific audience is not an option. It is essential to good speechmaking.

JAFFE ◉ CONNECTION

Access

for Audio Flashcards of Key Terms

Key Terms

audience analysis (80)
listening speaker (80)
pedestrian audiences (80)
passive audiences (80)
selected audiences (80)
homogeneous audiences (80)
concerted audiences (80)
organized audiences (81)
absent audiences (81)
demographic audience analysis (81)
salient (82)
ethnicity (82)
race (82)

racist (82)
gender (84)
sexist (84)
psychological profile (88)
beliefs (88)
attitudes (89)
scaled questions (90)
values (90)
Ethical Quality Scale (EQS) (90)
credibility (91)
prior or extrinsic credibility (91)
demonstrated credibility (91)
terminal credibility (93)

Application and Critical Thinking Questions

1. Identify times when you have been a member of each type of audience: pedestrian, passive, voluntary, concerted, organized, and absent.

2. What occupation(s) most interest you? Think of opportunities you might have to address each type of audience listed in Exercise 1 within your chosen occupational field. Which type of audience is most common in that occupation? Which is least common?

3. Try to see yourself as would a member of your classroom audience. At this point in the term, what credibility do you bring to each speech? How can you demonstrate credibility in your next speech? How do you think your audience sees you after you are finished?

4. Using one of these topics, talk with a small group of your classmates about the different ways you would develop a speech for each of the following audiences:

Topic: Your school's administrators are discussing a policy that will abolish all competitive sports on campus.

Audiences:

■ Your classmates

■ A group of prospective students

■ Alumni who are consistent donors to the school

■ Basketball team members

Topic: The United States should double its foreign aid budget

Audiences:

■ Senior citizens

■ A high school government class

■ The local chapter of the League of Women Voters

Internet Activities

■ Log on to your *InfoTrac College Edition* and do a subject search for "audience analysis." Skim one of the articles and compare the ideas you find in the article with the material in this chapter.

■ Use your *InfoTrac College Edition* to search for "polling data." Link to one of the articles and read the information pollsters discovered about the targeted polling group. Who was polled? On what topic? What audience interests and attitudes did pollsters find that you would need to consider if you were planning a speech on the topic?

■ Go to a search engine such as www.yahoo.com and find information about your state and another that differs in a number of significant ways such as diversity of population, rural-urban population ratio, or age. Examples: California and South Dakota; Florida and Idaho. Skim the information you find when you browse through links on both sites. How might you adapt the topics of educational reform or health care reform for a general audience in each state?

Hot Links at the Public Speaking Resource Center

The following links are maintained and can be accessed easily via Jaffe Connection at the Public Speaking Resource Center on the Wadsworth Communication Café web site at http://communication.wadsworth.com/publicspeaking/study.html

Public
Speaking
Resource
Center

http://maine.maine.edu/~zubrick/AUDANAL.html Joe Zubrick, University of Maine at Presque Isle, defines audience analysis and provides an audience analysis worksheet.

For more information on the race-ethnicity distinction, visit the website located at http://daphne.palomar.edu/ethnicity/default.html

6

Selecting Your Topic

and Purpose

This chapter will help you:

- Choose your speech topic

- Narrow your topic to fit the situation

- Identify both a general purpose and a specific purpose for your speech

- Write a central idea that states the main concept of your speech

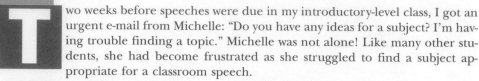

Two weeks before speeches were due in my introductory-level class, I got an urgent e-mail from Michelle: "Do you have any ideas for a subject? I'm having trouble finding a topic." Michelle was not alone! Like many other students, she had become frustrated as she struggled to find a subject appropriate for a classroom speech.

Is there a surefire method you can use to decide upon a topic that fits you, your audience, and the occasion? Probably not, but here are some techniques that worked well for a number of students:

> The way I usually come up with topics is by looking around and noting what things I see that I think are interesting. I evaluate whether or not they would make good speech topics. Also, I will take things that puzzle me or torque me off.
>
> *Amy*

> First, I try to clearly define the assignment. For example, what is an informative speech? What does that mean? Then I brainstorm topics I have enthusiasm about. After that, I narrow the topics down to ones that would best fit the speech type—informative or persuasive, etc.
>
> *Susanna*

> When I choose a topic, I analyze the parameters first: time limit, any given topic area, audience . . . then I think of something I'm interested in. If nothing comes to mind, I file the assignment in my thoughts—and often something during the day sparks an interest.
>
> *Joy*

> I spend a lot of time on the Internet, so I naturally go online and browse for topics. A site such as www.yahoo.com provides links to newspapers and magazines that include international and national topics, business and entertainment news. I always find several topics that interest me.
>
> *Terrence*

Regardless of method, eventually you will come up with a number of topics. The key—as Amy, Susanna, Joy, and Terrence point out—is to find something you are comfortable with, something that is significant enough to discuss publicly. This chapter will give you guidelines for choosing your topic, narrowing it to a manageable size, and then selecting your purpose and focus.

Choose Your Topic

Choosing a topic is generally up to you because most instructors don't assign specific subjects. You can avoid being overwhelmed at the openendedness of your assignment by examining five areas: the significance or need to discuss possible topics, your personal interests and experiences, other courses you're taking, current events, and international and cultural subjects.

Assess Your Audience's Need to Know

Topics are all around you. What did you eat for lunch? Who is your favorite recording artist or group? What is the traffic like in your town? Everyday topics such as these often result in interesting speeches (Christensen, 1998). However, look for a topic that's significant—one that you feel needs to be discussed in order to bring about some change, increase your audience's understanding, or highlight important cultural values and beliefs (Bitzer, 1999; Vatz, 1999). Evaluate possible topics from your audience's perspective. What do they already know about the subject? What more do they need to know? Does the topic affect their finances? Their future? Their health? Will your subject appeal to their curiosity?

One key to keeping audience interest is to provide novelty, presenting something unfamiliar or presenting a familiar topic in a different way (McKeon, 1998). For example, one student showed her audience how to make a peanut butter and jelly sandwich. (Take two slices of bread; put peanut butter on one slice and jam on the other; put them together). Her classmates felt this speech wasted their time; they'd known this recipe since kindergarten. Is this topic completely out of line? Not necessarily. Other students have researched the nutrients in peanuts, talked about their fat content, discussed vegetarian recipes that use peanuts, and explained the history of peanut butter. Many facts about peanuts would have been new to her audience and potentially valuable to listeners who were on a tight food budget.

In short, choosing a topic that meets your audience's need to know and presenting your subject in a novel way are two fundamental principles in speechmaking. Consequently, when audience members already know a lot about your subject, you'll be more successful if you dig for supplementary information or select another topic that will not waste their time.

Consider Your Personal Interests

Generally, good public speakers are curious about the world. They want to know what is going on, and they are concerned about how these happenings affect the lives of ordinary people. Use your natural curiosity to generate possible topics (Murray, 1998). What do you know and care about? What would you like to explore further? What is your major? What are your occupational goals? What pets do you own? What have you read about or seen on television that you found interesting? What irritates you? What changes would you like to see in society? Here are ways some students used personal interests to create speeches:

- Paula once spent a summer in Israel; she speaks about Israeli–Arab conflicts.

- Fadi works with the homeless; he believes they are not receiving enough attention, so he advocates increased funding for low-cost housing.

- Peggy saw a television show about the Bermuda Triangle; she wants to know more about it.

- Joshua built a telescope in high school; he explains the major constellations from a Native American perspective.

- Shawnelle is a pre-med major; she chooses Tay–Sachs disease as her subject.

In addition, consider your unique life experiences when searching for a topic. You are who you are because of what you know and what you've experienced (Christensen, 1998). Draw from knowledge arising from your family background, jobs, hobbies, or recreational interests. For instance, one student who fought forest fires one summer spoke about containment of fires. Another discussed neighborhood street fairs. Some students have drawn from their personal experiences with dyslexia. Others have discussed artists and writers from their ethnic group.

Speaking on topics that fascinate or concern you has obvious advantages. When you are truly interested in your subject, you are more enthusiastic about it. This enthusiasm often helps you concentrate on your topic rather than your insecurity as a speaker. In addition, if you appear to be bored by your topic, why should your audience be interested?

Look around you for topics about natural or manmade features. For example, novel information about the Space Needle in Seattle, Washington, could be worked into an interesting speech. (Jack Jaffe)

Look for Topics from Other Courses

Another good source for speech topics can come out of your major (or other) coursework. For example, if you're taking psychology, look at the table of contents in your psychology textbook and find potential topics such as Freud's theories of personality, defense mechanisms, memory, perception, or behaviorism. Giving a speech on an interesting topic from another class has the added advantage of helping you learn material for that course.

Don't hesitate to use research you have done for other courses if the subject is an appropriate speech topic. To illustrate, as part of a nursing course Jack wrote a paper on Cherokee beliefs and practices. He used some of the same material in his classroom speech on Native American medicine. Remember, however, if you adapt a paper, you must still tailor your information to your specific classroom audience.

Investigate Current Events

Newspapers, newsmagazines, and television shows are another excellent source of topics appropriate for beginning speakers. Skim headlines, jotting down current issues that interest you. Or surf Internet news sites, looking for something you find fascinating. Also, don't overlook television program guides as a source of subjects. This list came from just one day's television schedule:

Elton John	monks	problems on space station Mir
Pearl Harbor	eels	Women's World Cup soccer

Many students choose international subjects. Someone studying Asian cultures might speak about festivals like this spring festival that Indian students are celebrating by covering themselves with dye. (Steve Rubin/Image Works)

making hot dogs	amnesia	modern pirates
poisonous snakes	deafness	fortunetelling scams
floors as art	frontier doctors	the Panama Canal
Alaskan cruises	beach hockey	dog shows

Topics from current events usually address a need in society. The fact that they are important enough to discuss in the print or electronic media means that they are significant to many people. And, because these topics are publicly covered, you should be able to find information easily.

Consider International and Cultural Topics

You may find it easier to think of personal (how to write a resumé) or national (tax reform) topics because these are close to our lives and are regularly covered in news broadcasts. However, don't overlook international subjects, especially if you have traveled abroad or if you were born outside the United States. Explore your own cultural heritage and experiences for topics. For instance, someone of Swedish ancestry could examine the welfare system in Sweden, comparing and contrasting it to that in the United States. Someone who works at McDonald's might look at varying management styles in French or Russian businesses. A student with a Japanese heritage might speak about a famous Japanese film director. You can also go to newspapers, magazines, and television broadcasts that regularly report on topics such as trade, global investments, or international crime that will be increasingly important in the new century.

Check the Internet for cultural topics. For example, you can find excellent resources on race and ethnicity at http://www.georgetown.edu/crossroads/asw/. Georgetown University manages this web page, which provides links to sites for Native Americans and Americans of African, Asian, and Latino origin. A category designated "other" links you to additional information such as immigration, Italian-American resources, and cultural institutes for specific groups.

DIVERSITY IN PRACTICE

Does Requiring One Speech on "Communication and Culture" Increase Students' Empathy?

Lori Carrell (1997) reported the results of research done in a medium-sized Midwestern university. The goal of the study was to determine if student *empathy*, or the ability to take diverse perspectives, increased when diversity issues became part of the course. Underlying the research was the assumption that competent communicators are those who can view issues from multiple perspectives. Four groups participated in the study: A control group had no special treatment; another group took an entire course in intercultural communication; another discussed concepts related to diversity at several points during the term; finally, another group had a one-shot assignment to give a public speech on a "communication and diversity" topic.

The results indicated that students who studied intercultural communication for a whole term significantly increased in empathy. Those who discussed diversity issues often throughout the semester also increased in empathy. However, students who gave only one diversity speech had no significant gains in empathy.

What does this mean to you? How might an increase in empathy make you a more competent communicator? What connections can you see between the ability to take a variety of perspectives and the diversity concepts presented in this text and in your classroom? How might your topic choices make you more sensitive to issues of diversity?

A word of caution: If you choose an international or cultural topic, be sure to make connections to your listeners' here-and-now concerns. For example, suppose your subject is land mines. This may seem pretty far removed from your campus world, but think of ways your classmates could identify with the topic. Would they empathize with the plight of innocent villagers who lose feet or even legs when they step on a mine? Do any of your listeners have friends or relatives who are military personnel and thus at risk of injury from these weapons? What about your tax dollars that go to specialists who detonate the mines? Could you tie the topic into fundamental values, such as the desire for a world at peace or for freedom and justice for all? Your challenge is to find these connections and help your audience see the relevance of your topic to their lives.

Narrow Your Topic

Once you've selected a broad topic, your task is to narrow it sufficiently so that you can discuss it in a short classroom speech. As an example, let's consider the general topic of music. Obviously, you can't discuss all of music in seven minutes; however, you can focus on a single performer, a specific process, or a problem within the music industry. Consider using a mind map as a way of letting your ideas flow. Figure 6.1 illustrates how to start with a broad subject and narrow it to a series of much more realistic topics for a classroom speech. Use your creativity to approach the topic from a personal, national, or even international level.

FIGURE 6.1 A mind map of music topics.

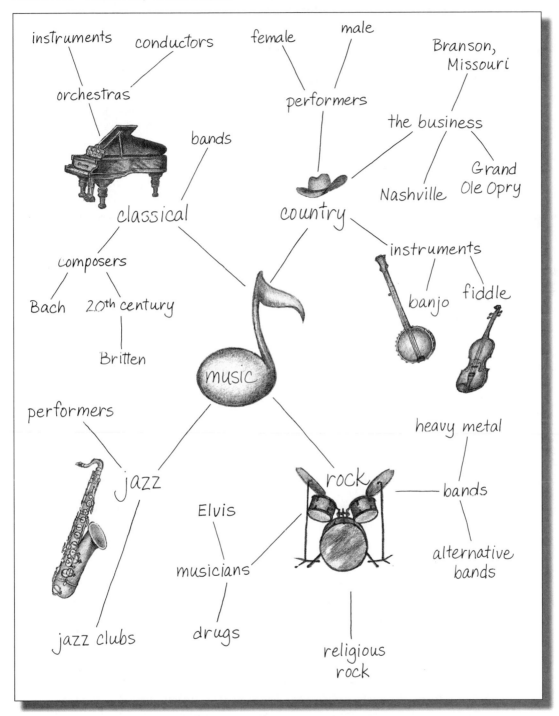

Careful work early in the term will produce several topics for you to use throughout the term. Let's say Figure 6.1 is Karen's mind map. She first gives an informative speech on buying a CD player. Later, she discusses the connection between drug use and the early deaths of famous musicians. In a third speech, she argues that *Time* magazine was right to name Courtney Love as one of the twenty-five most influential citizens in the United States. Karen's final presentation, a narrative speech, is based on an opera she attended at Lincoln Center in New York City.

> ### STOP AND CHECK
> ## Identify Several Usable Topics
>
> Make a list of 10 to 15 subjects that interest you, then narrow your list to two or three major topic areas. Make a mind map for each topic on your narrowed list.
>
> If you select these general areas early, you can be alert throughout the term for information to use in your speeches. Let's say you are looking for material on eating disorders; you can scan weekly TV schedules for shows that feature the topic. You can also set up interviews with professionals as well as people who have experienced eating disorders. Because you have the topic clearly in mind, you have plenty of time to gather up-to-date materials to create a good speech.
>
> If you begin early enough, you can create a file for each speech, photocopying or clipping articles from newspapers or magazines, taking notes on lectures, or videotaping related television programs. At speech time, you will have many resources available for a good presentation, including a number of audio-visual aids that a last-minute scramble might not produce!

Choose Your Purpose and Focus

You won't speak in public by accident; instead, you'll have specific goals or purposes in mind that lead you to speak (Scofield, 1999). Before you face your audience, you should have a clear idea of what you want to accomplish with your listeners. To accomplish this goal, you will need to first identify your general purpose and begin to formulate a specific purpose for your speech. You will continue to refine your specific purpose as you work on your speech. In addition, writing a summarizing statement will help both you and your listeners understand the central idea of the speech.

Identify Your General Purpose

Almost 2,000 years ago, St. Augustine, who was a rhetoric teacher long before he was a saint, identified three purposes for speaking publicly: to teach, to please, and to move (trans. Robertson, 1958). In the eighteenth century, George Campbell identified four purposes: to enlighten the understanding, to please the imagination, to move the passions, and to influence the will (ed. Bitzer, 1963). In this century, Alan Monroe said we attempt to inform, entertain, stimulate through emotion, or convince through reasoning (1962). Today, most speech instructors identify three **general purposes:**

General Purposes

A speaker's general purpose could be to inform, to persuade, or to entertain.

- To inform, in which your intention is to explain, teach, describe, or provide a basis for your audience to have a greater understanding of your topic. For example, you might inform your audience about Australian musicians, digital playback machines, or the Grand Ole Opry.

- To persuade, in which you intend to convince or motivate your audience in some way. You might gather evidence to convince your listeners that labels on rock music limit free expression or to persuade them to attend an upcoming piano recital.

■ To entertain, in which you help your audience release tension through laughter by taking a humorous look at your subject. You might tell a series of short, humorous narratives about the early days of rock and roll. Or you might relate your own funny experiences at concerts or with music lessons.

These purposes often overlap. Take the case of a university recruiter. She attempts to persuade her listeners to attend the school she represents, both by informing them about the university and by entertaining them with humorous accounts of campus life. In addition, she knows that a variety of listeners calls for a blend of purposes: She entertains the alumni (and encourages donations), informs the parents or spouses about financial aid, and persuades prospective students to fill out application forms.

Classroom instructors usually assign the general purpose for your classroom speeches. For instance, you may be assigned to give an informative speech. If so, focus your research on discovering and presenting factual material that will increase your audience's knowledge or understanding of your topic. When your general purpose is to persuade, you'll select convincing and motivating materials that will influence your listeners to believe and act in the ways you desire. (Chapter 17 looks further at ways you can narrow your persuasive speech purposes.) If you're asked to be entertaining, choose a ridiculous event or situation, and use strategies such as exaggeration and word plays to highlight humorous aspects of the topic. Although you may not be asked to give an entertaining speech in the classroom, maintaining interest rather than boring your audience will help you accomplish any other speech purpose. Figure 6.2 shows how to come up with a variety of speech purposes for a broad topic such as music.

STOP AND CHECK

Narrow Your Purpose

Make a diagram similar to the one in Figure 6.2, using one of the subject-area mind maps you made for the Stop and Check exercise on page 104.

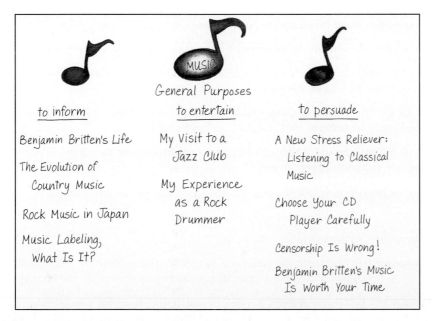

FIGURE 6.2 How to generate a number of musical topics for different purposes.

Identify Your Specific Purpose

Specific Purpose

The cognitive, affective, or behavioral responses a speaker desires.

Cognitive Effects

Influences on beliefs, understandings, and other mental processes.

Affective Effects

Influences on listeners' feelings.

Behavioral Effects

Influences on audience actions.

Patrick Barbo chooses to speak on tinnitus, a hearing problem he is having that was caused by listening to loud music over a period of time. Next, he must decide exactly what he wants to accomplish with his listeners, so he begins to focus on a **specific purpose,** the response he wants from his audience. He can focus on one of three areas: thinking, feeling, or doing.

- If his intention is to guide the thinking of his audience, he aims for **cognitive effects** that will inform their understanding or convince them to believe his claims.

- If he hopes to influence audience feelings, he'll target **affective** or emotional **effects.**

- Finally, **behavioral effects** are the actions he wants audience members to perform as a result of his speech.

In short, Patrick must clarify what he wants his listeners to know, feel, or do, and write his goals into a specific-purpose statement. He keeps the desired response in mind by using the words "my audience" within his statement, and he uses an infinitive phrase. Here are some specific-purpose statements he might formulate, depending on his general speech purpose:

- To inform my audience about three characteristics of tinnitus. (Cognitive effect: The audience will know more about the condition as a result of this speech.)

- To persuade my audience to believe that their choice of music volume now may lead to tinnitus later in life. (Cognitive effect: The audience will be convinced of the link between volume and ear damage.)

- To persuade my audience to care about tinnitus, permanent ear damage that is linked to loud music. (Affective effect: The audience will desire to protect their ears.)

- To persuade my audience to reduce the volume of their music in order to prevent tinnitus, a form of permanent ear damage. (Behavioral effect: The audience will be motivated to act as a result of this speech.)

Although many instructors ask their students to begin the specific purpose with the phrase "to inform my audience," some professors prefer that their students write the specific purpose as a statement of the outcome they want to produce in their listeners—one that specifies the desired audience response:

- As a result of my speech, my audience will *know* three characteristics of tinnitus.

- As a result of my speech, my audience will *believe* that a link exists between loud music and ear damage known as tinnitus.

- As a result of my speech, my audience will *care* more about their hearing and the ear damage known as tinnitus that is linked to loud music.

- As a result of my speech, my audience will *choose* to protect their ears from tinnitus by reducing the volume of their music.

At this stage of preparation, Patrick has this much of his speech formulated:

Topic: Tinnitus

General purpose: To persuade

Specific purpose: To persuade my audience to reduce the volume of their music in order to prevent tinnitus, a form of permanent ear damage

Patrick already has information from personal experience, from his physician's explanation, and from a pamphlet he got in the doctor's office. By formulating his gen-

Within a broad topic like rock music you can find many suitable subtopics for classroom speeches. Tinnitus, the career of a specific musician, and record labeling are three. (B. Daemmrich/Stock Boston)

eral and specific purpose early, he will be able to focus additional research more effectively. He would search out facts, descriptions, and explanations for most speech purposes, but especially if his goal is to inform; if he wants to prove links between music volume and tinnitus, Patrick will need scholarly studies and opinions from experts. In addition, examples and comparisons will help him motivate his listeners to care or to act.

After you've selected both your general and specific purposes, you are ready to begin formulating one statement that captures the major idea of your speech. This is known as the central idea.

Write Your Central Idea

The **central idea** is your summary statement of the main ideas of your speech. It's as if someone were to say "Tell me in one sentence what you're going to speak about. No details, just the bottom line. A complete sentence, not a question." The single-sentence digest or abstract you come up with is your central idea; it is also called the core idea, subject sentence, residual message or, for English essays, the thesis statement. This sentence states what you want your audience to remember after your speech is over. The following guidelines will help you formulate your central idea more effectively:

> Write a single declarative sentence
>> that makes a statement about the subject matter and
>>> summarizes the content of the speech
>>>> in a reasonably, simple manner
>>>>> that is precise enough to guide you and your audience (Engnell, 1999).

Notice, for example, the contrast between these correctly and incorrectly written central ideas:

Correct: Tinnitus has three major causes: obstruction of the ear canal, injury to the eardrum, and exposure to loud noise, either suddenly or over a period of time.

Central Idea

A single-sentence summary of the main idea of the speech.

Incorrect: Why should you turn down the volume on your CD player? (This is a question, not a declarative sentence.)

Incorrect: Tinnitus is a permanent ringing of the ears often caused by loud music. To prevent it, turn down the volume on your CD player. (The rule is one sentence, not two!)

Incorrect: Why you should avoid tinnitus. (This is a fragment rather than a complete sentence.)

Begin to formulate your central idea as soon as you've selected your topic and decided upon your general and specific purposes. Then allow yourself plenty of time to explore and develop your thesis—the approach, the slant, the point of view you'll develop, the general direction you'll take (Griffin, 1998). The process of invention takes time and energy; new ideas will emerge and others will seem less important, so don't be afraid to revise your direction as you do additional research, preparation, and organization. As this student explains:

> I tend to have running dialogues in my head, sometimes even out loud. While I talk to myself, I work out particulars. I answer questions I've posed to myself ("Well, really Gail, if you argue that, where will you go? It's too huge!" or "Now does that really make sense?"). My answers often lead me to modify my central idea as I continue my preparation.
>
> *Gail*

Here are some additional examples from student speeches that show the relationship between topic, general purpose, specific purpose, and central idea.

Topic: Dolphin communication
General purpose: To inform
Specific purpose: To inform my audience about studies in the area of dolphin-dolphin and human-dolphin communication.
Central idea: Dolphins are intelligent creatures who communicate with other dolphins and with human researchers.

Topic: Culture shock
General purpose: To inform
Specific purpose: To inform my audience of the five stages of the psychological phenomenon known as culture shock.
Central idea: Culture shock is a very real psychological process that typically progresses through five stages: honeymoon, disintegration, reintegration, autonomy, and interdependence.

Topic: Medical misinformation on the Internet
General purpose: To persuade
Specific purpose: To persuade my audience that medical misinformation on the Internet is a problem that can be solved if we take three corrective steps.
Central idea: Medical misinformation is rampant on the Internet, but a code of conduct for websites, government regulations, and personal action can protect consumers.

Topic: Sleep deprivation
General purpose: To persuade
Specific purpose: To persuade my audience that sleep deprivation is a national problem that can be solved through personal and societal effort.

Central idea: Sleep deprivation, which has several causes, affects millions of Americans every day; society can help, but most of the solutions are personal.

In the speech itself, usually in your introduction, state or paraphrase your central idea. This prepares your audience for what you are going to talk about and guides them as they listen. See how these students incorporated their central idea into the introduction of their speeches in order to inform their audiences directly of their purpose for speaking:

> According to experts, 30 to 50 percent of us will eventually suffer from tinnitus, a hearing condition resulting in permanent buzzing and whistling sounds. However, with attention to your ears today, you can prevent at least some of this ear damage tomorrow.

> We must first wake up to some of the alarming effects of sleep debts, then we can open our eyes to better understand their causes, and finally cozy up to some solutions at both the personal and the societal levels.

> Today, I will explain the concept of dolphin intelligence, dolphin-to-dolphin communication, and dolphin communication with humans.

In summary, topic and purpose selection is obviously one of the most important aspects of speechmaking; however, this process that can be frustrating. But you can focus your preparation more effectively if you select a subject that interests you, narrow it to a manageable subtopic, formulate general and specific speech purposes, then summarize your main concepts in a central idea or thesis statement that you want your audience to remember after your speech.

STOP AND CHECK

Putting It All Together

Choose three topics from this list (or select three topics that you can talk about without doing much research). Write out the general purpose, a specific-purpose statement, and the central idea for an impromptu speech you could create about each topic.

- Online shopping
- Stress relievers for college students
- Simple breakfasts
- Free things to do in our community
- Going to the movies
- Exercising regularly
- Study tips

You can complete this activity online under Chapter 6: Activities for Jaffe Connection at the Public Speaking Resource Center, http://communication.wadsworth.com/publicspeaking/study/html.

Public Speaking Resource Center

Summary

As you begin the process of choosing a speech topic, look for one dealing with something your audience needs to know. Then, examine your personal experiences, other coursework, current events, and international stories for topics that will contribute to your listeners' knowledge. Be sure to find a topic that interests you! By doing careful work early in the term, you can produce a list, or a series of files, on topics that would work for both you and your listeners.

After selecting your topic, focus on your intention or major purpose for the speech. Then, write the specific purpose that names the response you want from your listeners. The central idea comes next. This single sentence summarizes the major content of your speech in a way that guides both you and your listeners. Begin to formulate your central idea early in the speech, but be willing to revise it as you proceed in your research.

JAFFE CONNECTION

Access

**for Audio Flashcards
of Key Terms**

Key Terms

general purpose (104)
specific purpose (106)
cognitive effects (106)

affective effects (106)
behavioral effects (106)
central idea (107)

Application and Critical Thinking Questions

1. Design a mind map on the general topic of education after high school.

2. Some professors refer to the central idea by other names, including the core idea, the subject sentence, the thesis statement, or the residual message. If you were teaching this class, which terminology would you use to best clarify the concept? Why?

3. Work with a small group of your classmates to create a mind map based on a very general international topic such as Japan, world trade, ethnic wars, or the United Nations. Use a blank transparency or a large piece of paper to record your ideas; then, display your mind map for the entire class.

4. Discuss in a small group ways you could add the element of novelty to the following common topics: seatbelts, tea, President Clinton, television, weddings.

Internet Activities

1. Your *InfoTrac College Edition* is a great tool for narrowing your speech topic. Enter a general topic in the search bar.

2. Use your *InfoTrac College Edition* to look up information about St. Augustine's theories regarding speechmaking.

3. Do a PowerTrac search on your *InfoTrac College Edition*. Search for the key words "thesis statement" and read one of the articles aimed at teachers of college writing. Discuss with your classmates how the principles for selecting a thesis statement for a written paper are similar to selecting a central idea for a speech. Are they different? If so, how?

4. After you have selected a general topic area, search the Internet for subtopic categories by using a search engine such as Yahoo http://www.yahoo.com or

Dogpile http://www.dogpile.com. Type in a few key words ("greyhound AND adoption" for example), then follow promising links to other sites that might provide you with narrowed topics.

Hot Links at the Public Speaking Resource Center

The following links are maintained and can be accessed easily via Jaffe Connection at the Public Speaking Resource Center on the Wadsworth Communication Café web site at http://communication.wadsworth.com/publicspeaking/study.html

http://www.ilt.columbia.edu/k12/livetext/docs/semantic.html LiveText, Columbia University, The Institute for Learning Technologies at Teacher's College
This online resource presents an illustration of semantic mapping. You can choose to do an exercise if you wish to utilize semantic mapping for idea generation.
The following three sites define, explain, discuss, and assist you in developing your thesis statement:

http://www.wisc.edu/writing/Handbook/ThesisStatements.html University of Wisconsin, Madison Writing Center

http://www.grinnell.edu/individuals/dobbs/DrSyntax/index.html "Dr. Syntax," Grinnell College

http://www.hamilton.edu/academic/resource/wc/Intro_Thesis.html Hamilton College, Nesbitt-Johnston Writing Center

Jaffe Speech Interactive

Jaffe Speech Interactive

Watch and listen to one of the informative or persuasive speeches included in Jaffe Speech Interactive. Can you identify each speaker's thesis statement?

7

Researching Your Speech in an Electronic Culture

This chapter will help you:

- Plan your research
- Distinguish between primary and secondary sources
- Gather oral, print, and electronically stored resources effectively
- Include ethnic and international sources in your research
- Use the Internet critically
- Record your information in a way that is suited to your learning style

"Time After Time" ©1995 by Betsie Miller-Kusz

Chances are, you are not an expert on the subjects you will choose for your classroom speeches. For example, Rachel has spoken about the jury system; Rosa discussed ways to resolve conflicts in interpersonal relationships; Beth spoke about baldness. All these speakers had some experience with their topics, but none are recognized authorities. The challenge that faced them as they prepared their speeches is the one that faces you, once you have selected your topic: You must gather information to use as support for your ideas.

Gathering effective supporting materials is part of the canon that the Romans called *invention*. It combines several skills that contribute to your developing competence in speechmaking. As you select materials for use in your speech, you must:

- Know how to find the data you need to support your ideas
- Formulate a research plan
- Critically evaluate sources and choose the best materials available
- Record your findings in a systematic way

This chapter presents information on the research process, with the goal of helping you accomplish these four major tasks effectively.

Gather Materials for Your Speech

To gain a variety of perspectives about your subject, instructors usually recommend that you consult from three to seven sources, including both primary and secondary materials. You should be able to find oral, print, and electronic data easily; however, selecting the *best* information requires you to use your critical thinking skills throughout the research process. This section will discuss effective ways to plan, conduct, and evaluate your research.

Plan Your Research

Reference Librarian
Library specialist whose job is to help you find research information.

In a personal interview, Laurie Lieggi (1999), **reference librarian** at George Fox University, noted that students often wait until the last minute, thinking they can pop into the library once, spend a couple of hours in attack mode, get speech materials that are easy to find, and leave—choosing to be satisfied with whatever they can find immediately. Many go to the Internet first, and, because it's convenient, want to use it exclusively. Lieggi likened this type of research to eating at fast food restaurants. Fast food alone fails to provide the nutrients, variety, and quality of meals you carefully prepare at home.

You will use your research time more wisely if you sit down and plan a search strategy, even before you head to the library. The following tips will help you:

- *Budget enough time.* Good research is time consuming, and if you think you'll be able to get wonderful, usable information in one short library visit, you will be disappointed. Consequently, on your calendar, set aside more than one block of time for research.

- *Get to know your library.* Because each library is different, visit or tour the one you will use the most, and consult how-to pamphlets and brochures prepared by your campus librarians to explain specific features available in your library.

- *Include a librarian in your research plan.* Librarians are paid to help you, and if you run into problems at any stage of research, be sure to consult them. Laurie said, "I'm a reference librarian because I want to be available to students. That's what I enjoy. Every question is a puzzle, and I get to help a student solve a puzzle." Besides, who knows your campus library better than the people who work there daily? In larger academic libraries, subject librarians often have a library degree plus an advanced degree in another discipline.

Consult a reference librarian if you need help during any stage of your research.

■ *Let your topic guide your research.* This chapter suggests a number of research sources, but you won't use them all in a single speech. Instead, analyze your subject and identify the best sources for that topic. For instance, if you're speaking about a current event, include a nightly network or cable news program in your plan. For a topic like eating disorders, consider an interview with the campus nurse or a person who actually has an eating disorder. For a topic like whitewater rafting, helpful resources might include personal experiences, books, articles in sports magazines, and Internet websites.

■ *Identify key terms to use when you search computerized catalogs, databases, or the Internet.* Think creatively, consult a librarian, or go to the *Library of Congress Subject Headings.* Patrick searched for "hearing disorders" and "tinnitus" and found more than enough material for his speech. In contrast, Marcus searched for "disabled" and "housing" with little success until his librarian suggested he use the word "handicapped." Then he found all the information he needed (which is an indication that the headings are not always current in usage). Subject terms can be very specific. For example, to find material on the Civil War, type in "United States—History—1861–1865—battles," or you'll end up with sources about civil wars in ancient Greece, nineteenth-century Bolivia, and today's Congo. Some of the better online databases have browse, thesaurus, or index features that can help you identify specific key terms.

■ *Identify experts in the field (if known).* You'll save some research time if you know the names of people considered experts on your topic. Search for these names in the library's resources under "authors," or try to work an interview with a campus expert into your plan.

■ *Make critical evaluation a part of your plan from the outset.* Our culture provides so many oral, print, and electronic resources that you might feel you're drowning in data—some highly credible, some very questionable. Find out as much as you can about every source you use, whether book, article, website, or personal interview, and then compare sources. Some will be OK, some pretty good, and some excellent. Choose the best.

■ *Keep a running list of all your sources as you search.* This way, you can easily assemble your final bibliography and return to a source if necessary. If you are using the Internet, create a directory for your bookmarks if your computer has that feature.

■ *Plan to use a variety of sources.* Remember the fast food analogy? You wouldn't eat only Big Macs, so don't expect to use solely the Internet or newspapers or encyclopedias or any other credible source. Strive to find diverse perspectives so you can approach the topic from a number of viewpoints.

This is not an exhaustive planning list, but using these tips will help you focus your search more effectively. The rest of the chapter will guide you in carrying out your overall plan.

Public
Speaking
Resource
Center

STOP AND CHECK

Begin Your Research Plan

Before you even go into the library, use Figure 7.1, filling in sections A to G, to begin creating your research plan. Then read the rest of this chapter to identify and evaluate the best type of material for your specific topic. Additional Stop and Check activities in this chapter will help you refine your research strategies. The research plan featured in Figure 7.1 is also available online under Chapter 7: Forms and Checklists for Jaffe Connection on the Public Speaking Resource Center.

Distinguish Between Primary and Secondary Sources

Primary Sources

Created by people actually involved in the event.

Original Documents

Letters, news footage, minutes of a meeting, and other evidence recorded by a primary source.

Creative Works

Poems, dances, paintings, writings, and other aesthetic creations.

Relics or Artifacts

Culturally significant creations such as buildings, jewelry, or tools.

Secondary Sources

Produced by nonparticipants who summarize and interpret events or people.

Primary sources are created by individuals and groups who are directly involved in events at the time they take place. You'll find primary sources in several categories. **Original documents,** such as letters, interviews, news footage, and minutes of meetings, were written or created by insiders who were personally involved in events. **Creative works** include books, paintings, poems, and dance performances. **Relics or artifacts** are cultural objects such as jewelry, tools, buildings, clothing, and other created items.

Secondary sources are a step away from the actual persons or events under study, produced by nonparticipants who summarize and interpret the original reports. Although they may have been created when the events occurred, they can also appear months, decades, even centuries later. Examples include history books, critical reviews of artistic performances, and scholarly articles. Another example of a secondary source would be a quotation found in a book written by another author. Because scholars build on the knowledge of the past, they often refer to earlier experts as they create new material in their field. It is always preferable to go to the original source from which the quotation came.

As you do research, distinguish between primary and secondary sources. Although both are useful, you can appreciate the difference between a participant's account and an outsider's summary or interpretation of the same event. You can use three basic means to gather both primary and secondary materials:

■ Collect information in face-to-face interactions with both primary and secondary sources

■ Discover speech materials in print

■ Find data through media channels

Draw from Your Personal Experiences

You have probably chosen your topic because it relates in some way to your personal interests and experiences. Don't overlook your own experiences; instead, examine your personal connection with the topic for usable information. Drawing from personal experiences may make you more believable. Demonstration, or how-to, speeches are one example of topics in which personal know-how can translate into speech materials, but students have worked their personal experiences into speeches on immigration, Ritalin, bee keeping, cartooning, arranged marriages, and so on.

FIGURE 7.1   A research plan.

My Research Plan

A.   General topic: _____

B.   Narrowed topic: _____

C.   General purpose: _____

D.   Specific purpose: _____

E.   Tentative central idea: _____

F.   Budgeted time: (day) _____ (time) from _____ to _____ (place) _____

(day) _____ (time) from _____ to _____ (place) _____

(day) _____ (time) from _____ to _____ (place) _____

(day) _____ (time) from _____ to _____ (place) _____

G.   My questions for a librarian:

H.   Most promising resources:

_____interview with expert   _____ interview with layperson   _____ personal experiences

_____lecture or lecture notes   _____ televised interview   _____ videotaped or audiotaped interview

_____encyclopedias/books   _____ almanacs   _____ magazine/journal articles

_____newspapers   _____ Internet websites   _____ informational brochures

I.   Key experts: _____ _____ _____

_____ _____ _____

J.   Possible interviewee(s) _____   _____

K.   Date of interview _____ Time: from _____ to _____ Place _____

L.   Interview questions:

M.   Key search terms: _____ _____ _____

_____ _____ _____

N.   I plan to include diverse sources/options by:

O.   I plan to evaluate sources by:

P.   I plan to record my information by:

Consider Oral Sources

Oral Sources
Direct face-to-face informants.

When you get information in direct, face-to-face interactions, you are consulting **oral sources,** whether in a one-on-one interview or a one-to-many lecture. To record this information, use written notes, audio tapes, or videotapes.

Interview a Knowledgeable Person

Expert
Person whose knowledge is based on research, experience, or occupation.

Laypeople or Peers
Ordinary people whose knowledge comes from normal, everyday experience.

A well-planned interview with either an expert or a layperson can help you clarify confusing ideas by asking questions of someone with firsthand knowledge of your subject. A person who knows a subject through study, experience, or occupation is an **expert.** For example, to update this chapter, I interviewed a reference librarian; my students have talked with chiropractors, police officers, construction workers, and other people whose work experience makes them an expert. You can also interview **laypeople** or **peers**—ordinary people who have gained insights and formulated opinions through ordinary living rather than research. I could have interviewed some students who have learned to use library research tools effectively. Their insights, though not scholarly, often contain practical wisdom.

Most potential interviewees have full schedules, and you're really asking for a portion of their time. Because they're doing you a favor, consider these factors when you arrange your interviews:

- *Give your interviewee an idea of your speech topic and the kind of information you need.* This type of preparation is especially important if you are interviewing someone whose first language is different from your own. In order to think through and prepare their answers, these people may want you to submit written questions before you actually meet.

- *Be conscious of the time.* When you set up an appointment, specify the amount of time the interview should require, then respect those limits! Although different cultural groups have different norms regarding punctuality, arrive on time. If anyone is late, let it be your interviewee. If you absolutely can't keep your appointment, give the person as much notice as possible.

- *Prepare in advance.* Write out your questions so you will remember everything you want to ask. (Written questions also keep the interview focused.)

- *Take careful notes.* Then, make sure you've understood correctly by reading your notes back to the interviewee, who can then make corrections or additions. Ask questions such as "Is this what you mean?" or "Did I understand you correctly when you said . . . ?"

- *Aim to understand your topic from your interviewee's perspective.* If you interview someone whose ideas and actions clash with yours, practice civility.

- *If you want to tape the interview, ask for permission* in advance, and place the recorder in full view.

 When you cannot meet in person, consider a telephone interview, following the same guidelines regarding questions, advance preparation, and punctuality. Technology stretches our concepts of interviewing. E-mail, for instance, allows you to contact a source directly in a question-and-answer format similar to an interview. In fact, thousands of experts permit websites like http://www.expertcentral.com to list their e-mail addresses because they want to share their knowledge in hundreds of areas (Rodrigues & Rodrigues, 2000). In addition, you can regularly see or hear interviews on cable stations, on news programs, and over radio. Some shows even allow you to call or fax your questions to the expert.

This woman is interviewing a primary source for her speech on painting. (Karen Preuss)

Attend Lectures and Oral Performances

Don't overlook lectures or oral performances like poetry readings as sources of information. The key is to take careful notes or use a tape recorder—with advanced permission, of course. Some well-known lecturers are syndicated and their contracts prevent you from recording them; fortunately, they often sell tapes of their most popular lectures. Again, through electronic means such as television or videotapes, you can "attend" lectures or performances; camera close-ups may even give you the feeling of having a front-row seat.

STOP AND CHECK

Revisit Your Research Plan

You are now ready to fill in sections H to L of the research plan found in Figure 7.1 and online under Chapter 7: Forms and Checklists for Jaffe Connection on the Public Speaking Resource Center.

Public Speaking Resource Center

1. First, identify personal experiences that you can use to support your ideas. Think about places you might visit; for example, browse through a museum, tour a hospital, observe on a playground.

2. Consider using experts or laypeople who can provide helpful information, then plan an interview.

3. Think back on the classes you've taken, and identify lecture notes that might provide information.

4. Consider using video or audio taped interviews. Your public library, campus library, or media center probably has taped interviews or lectures on common topics such as eating disorders. For current topics, a news program will almost undoubtedly feature an interview. Check all-news cable channels (MSNBC, CNN, Fox News, and CNBC). In addition, the nightly *NewsHour with Jim Lehrer* on PBS, and the weekly *Face the Nation* (CBS) and *Meet the Press* (NBC) are generally considered credible.

To investigate this topic further, log on to *InfoTrac College Edition* and perform a keyword search using the term "interviewing" or "interview."

Use the Library

You'll find printed materials, pictures, maps, videotapes, and audio recordings in your library. Library materials have academic credibility because of the number of screenings they undergo before they are acquired. Book publishers employ editors and reviewers to validate each manuscript. Magazine and newspaper editors screen articles and hire fact checkers to correct errors. However, library materials still require critical evaluation. We expect opinions on editorial pages and in syndicated columns, but must stay alert to unsupported statements wherever they may be made. Also, specific publications have a bias, which is sometimes stated forthrightly; the *New Republic* proclaims its liberal bias, while the *National Review* proudly declares itself to be conservative. Other publications and books have an unstated bias that the reader must discern. Newspapers and book publishers tend to emphasize certain subjects or perspectives more than others. This is one reason your instructor asks you to consult several sources.

About 85 percent of college libraries have converted to online computerized programs to help you locate information quickly and easily (American Library Association, 1999). If you have not done so already, spend some time becoming familiar with your own library's cataloguing system. The research principles that follow are similar for libraries with card catalogs and those with computerized systems.

Books

Each library book is catalogued in three ways, by subject, author, and title. Traditional libraries that have only card catalogs reference each book on three separate cards. Thus, Doris Paul's book *The Navajo Code Talkers* is found under the author *Paul, Doris,* under the title *Navajo Code Talkers,* and under the subject *Native Americans, Navajo.* Online catalogs provide a menu of options including a subject, title, author, and keywords.

Look carefully at the copyright date that appears in the front of the book and in the catalog information. For some topics, up-to-date materials are essential. For example, a recent book on health care will provide current information about autism, whereas a book from the 1940s will be outdated. However, subjects such as *honesty* draw from philosophical, religious, and cultural traditions that go back thousands of years. For these subjects, a book written in 1910 may be as credible as one written in the 1990s.

The Reference Section

What was the murder rate in New York City in 1995? When was Jacqueline Kennedy Onassis born? Which horses have won the Triple Crown? To help you find specific information quickly, your library contains hundreds of reference works including encyclopedias, dictionaries, and sources for statistics.

General Encyclopedias
Collect and summarize information on a wide array of topics.

Encyclopedias **General encyclopedias,** such as *The Encyclopedia Americana* and *Collier's Encyclopedia,* collect and summarize information on thousands of topics. They provide a helpful overview of your topic early in your research. The *Encyclopedia Britannica* is especially useful for articles on international topics. An encyclopedia's index can often guide you to several related topics, and the bibliography at the end of each article suggests other sources of information. Many encyclopedias are available online, some for a fee; however, many libraries pay the fees so that you can find the information without charge.

Library books, magazines, and newspapers have a measure of academic respectability because of the selection process they undergo before they appear on the shelves. (Charles Gupton/Stock Boston)

In addition to general encyclopedias, the reference section includes **specialized encyclopedias** that provide information on specific subject areas. If you want to know about a particular bird, look in the *Encyclopedia of Birds*. Psychological depression? There is a whole encyclopedia on that topic alone. How about the *Encyclopedia of Computer Software*, or one on architecture? These are all available. Use your judgment in evaluating the publication date. The encyclopedia about computer software is rapidly outdated, whereas the one about birds remains useful for many years.

Computers with CD-ROM capacity can run encyclopedias such as Microsoft *Encarta* that contain thousands of articles and hundreds of sound clips, speeches, movie segments, and animations (Screen 7.1). Add to that 7,000 digitized photos, maps, and other illustrations, many of which are *interactive* (you can click on them with your mouse and get close-ups of specific sections) (Machrone, 1993). In addition, *Compton's Multimedia Encyclopedia* lets you view several articles simultaneously while taking notes on an accompanying word processor; encyclopedias such as these come already loaded into many personal computers.

Dictionaries are another type of reference materials. The most familiar type of **dictionary** provides definitions, historical sources, synonyms, and antonyms for words. However, you can find specialized dictionaries in the reference section, including ones devoted only to pianists, to psychotherapy, or to American slang. A number of dictionaries are also on the Internet. For instance, you can get to Webster's Dictionary's website by typing in http://www.m-w.com/dictionary. If your computer's software program has a built-in dictionary, simply type in a word and the definition and pronunciation will appear on your monitor.

Finally, your reference section includes many sources for statistics. Consult the *Statistical Abstracts of the United States* (a government document) for U.S. statistics on a variety of topics including population, health, education, crime, government finance, employment, elections, the environment, and defense. This book shows historical trends as well as current statistics. In addition, almanacs like *The World Almanac* provide statistical information. For information on national or global populations, you can access the U.S. Census Bureau's site at http://www.census.gov. This user-friendly, reliable site records each new birth automatically; consequently, population figures change regularly (Hawkes, 1999).

Specialized Encyclopedias
Summarize information in specific subject areas.

Dictionary
Provides definitions and other information about words or terms.

SCREEN 7.1 Take advantage of the information available in electronically stored resources such as this encyclopedia. It contains articles, charts, and pictures as well as sound clips, speeches, movie segments, and animations. (*Encyclopaedia Britannica Online* © Encyclopaedia Britannica, Inc.)

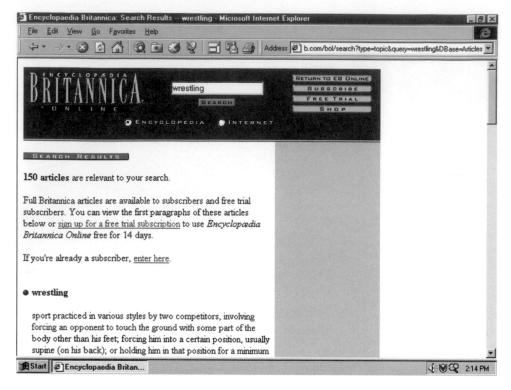

Periodicals

Periodicals

Magazines or journals issued at regular intervals.

Periodicals are issued once during a period of time—for example, weekly, monthly, quarterly, or annually. They range from popular or general-interest magazines, like *Time, Sports Illustrated,* and *MacLean's* (Canada), to more specialized periodicals such as *Hiker's World* or *Vital Speeches of the Day.* Popular magazines are easy to understand and have contemporary examples, up-to-date statistics, illustrations, and quotations from both experts and laypeople.

Trade or Professional Journals

Pertain to specific occupations or areas of academic research.

In addition, libraries also house **trade** and **professional journals,** such as the *Quarterly Journal of Speech,* which contain topics of interest to specific occupations and the research findings of scholars writing in academic areas. Some of these articles may be too technical for classroom speeches; others, however, provide excellent materials.

You'll find current issues on file and older issues archived, often on microfiche or microfilm. These two storage devices require that you use specialized machines, usually having a print capability so that you can copy articles you need. Currently, most major magazines and many scholarly journals are on the Internet, and you can easily download and print a hard copy of articles that you need. *InfoTrac College Edition* contains hundreds of magazines and journals.

Congressional Digest: The Pro and Con Monthly

Look at this periodical if you are researching a currently controversial topic because this independent storehouse of information represents multiple viewpoints. Each issue examines a single topic (affirmative action, farm policy, environmental protection) being discussed in Congress. For instance, a recent issue covers bankruptcy reform and examines both the interests of debtors and creditors. You will find a timeline of bankruptcy legislation and recent congressional actions. A glossary of terms, an overview of the issue, the current bankruptcy code, and directions to helpful Internet sites precede a presentation of pro and con arguments made by members of Congress.

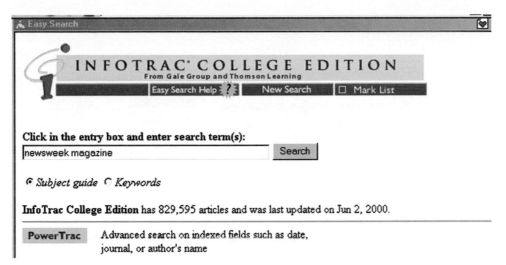

SCREEN 7.2 *InfoTrac College Edition* has hundreds of articles, updated continually. Use the password that accompanied a new copy of this text to access this database. (*InfoTrac College Edition* © Gale Group)

An annual index presents titles (for example, Drunk Driving: Setting National Standards) and subjects (healthcare, statehood proposals, foreign relations) from 1921 to the present. More helpful are the detailed tables of contents for topics covered from 1981 to the present. So, when you need to understand both sides of an issue, save valuable time and check this source early.

Indexes

An easy way to locate articles from both scholarly journals and popular magazines is to use indexes. Look in reference books or in computerized databases that index journals; the *ERIC* index for the field of education is one example. The *Readers' Guide to Periodical Literature* is invaluable for locating articles in popular magazines; its editors list each article in alphabetical order by subject, author, and title. Also indexed are broad topics with a number of subheadings, as this sample entry found under *Music* demonstrates:

> *Music and Sports*
> Swing time: music motivates and improves athletic performance. C. Krucoff. il
> The Saturday Evening Post v268 p151 Jl/Ag '96.

Each entry gives the title, author's name, magazine, volume, and page number. The 151 indicates that the story begins on page 151 but it may continue on later pages.

To use a computerized index, type in key words. You should get a number of hits; many will have an *abstract* (brief summary) that helps you decide which are worth looking up. For example, while researching his speech on the Promise Keepers (men who join together publicly to pledge that they will be faithful husbands and fathers), Diego typed in both "Promise Keepers" and "Men's Movement." He skimmed abstracts from over twenty articles, selected those that seemed suitable, printed the list of references, then went directly to the magazines and journals to read the articles.

Newspapers

Newspapers generally cover current events in greater depth than radio or television news broadcasts. You'll find reports on current issues and events, along with opinion pieces by editors, syndicated columnists, and readers who submit letters to the editor. Many newspapers also print humorous articles, obituaries, human interest pieces, and critical evaluations of movies, plays, books, art exhibits, and musical performances.

Daily, weekly, and monthly newspapers range in size from metropolitan papers with international circulation to small student papers. Some are specifically targeted

SCREEN 7.3 Don't settle for just one cultural perspective in your research; consult sources in the world of news that are available online. (© The Jerusalem Post)

toward various cultural and ethnic groups. (Diversity in Practice on page 125 discusses international periodicals.) A few are dubbed "the elite media" because they are known for excellent, detailed coverage of stories, and papers with smaller circulation often use their stories. Two major newspapers in this category are *The New York Times* and the *Washington Post*. Most school libraries carry at least one of these elite papers, and both are available over the Internet. If you don't regularly read such a paper, you might want to compare one day's edition with the same day's local newspaper.

The New York Times is an excellent source of primary documents because it reprints a number of them in part or in whole. Consequently, if you want to read the text of the president's inaugural address, you can find it in its entirety in the *Times*. You will also find excerpts of testimony given at Senate hearings, presidential remarks made at press conferences, and majority and dissenting opinions on significant Supreme Court decisions.

Newspaper Indexes

Major papers provide tools to help you locate specific articles. For instance, *The New York Times Index* provides the date, page, and column location of almost every news article that has appeared in its pages since 1851. The index lists articles alphabetically under one of four types of headings: subject, geographic name, organization, and personal name. Since 1962, the foreword of the annual *Index* has summarized each year's important events.

The index itself can be a source of information for brief answers to questions such as "Is the teenage birthrate rising or falling?" (It is falling—14.5 births per 1000 American girls, the lowest since 1909, according to the entry under "pregnancies" in the 1999 index.)

Use Mass Media Resources

Turn on your radio, catch the news on television, or watch a program like *60 Minutes* for speech materials. In fact, if your topic is current and is certain to be discussed on the day's news, plan to take notes, tape the portion of the program in which the topic is dis-

DIVERSITY IN PRACTICE

International and Ethnic Presses

Many libraries carry newspapers from around the world. Consulting one or more of these papers allows you to gain different perspectives, to hear other voices, than those you will find in local or national sources. Other sources have Internet web pages. For example, Osama bin Laden, who many leaders in this country consider an international terrorist, has an easily accessible homepage that allows you access to his perspective on conflict in the Middle East. Check out the *World Press Review,* a monthly magazine that prints excerpts of translated materials from international papers; its editors identify the bias of the source, whether conservative, liberal, or moderate.

Also search out materials representing diverse perspectives within the United States. Organized labor, African Americans, gays and lesbians, Catholics, and Muslims, to name a few, all publish periodicals that reflect their interests and perspectives. If your library doesn't subscribe to periodicals you need, look for them online. An Internet search engine like www.yahoo.com provides links to more than 8,000 newspapers and magazines, including alternative, regional, and international periodicals. Or log onto *InfoTrac College Edition* and do a Power-Trac Search for the list of journal names this resource provides; you'll find a wide variety of diverse perspectives there.

cussed, or purchase a videotape or transcript of the broadcast. That way, you can play back the tape or read the transcript carefully to check the accuracy of your information.

As you watch or listen, distinguish between primary and secondary sources, between factual news reporting and editorial opinion. For example, *The NewsHour with Jim Lehrer,* on public broadcasting stations, usually begins with factual information about a subject. Then Lehrer assembles experts who discuss the subject for as long as fifteen minutes. This part of the broadcast consists of opinions and interpretations as well as eyewitness accounts. Some guests, such as a representative of the Jordanian government, are primary sources. Others, like a U.S. professor of Middle Eastern studies, are secondary sources.

In addition, check your library's holdings of films, videotapes, and audio tapes, or contact one of the many organizations that circulate recordings and tapes of lectures, another good source for research information. For example, medical organizations provide tapes on such topics as ethical treatment of patients with highly contagious diseases. Action groups of all kinds offer audio and videotaped information about the issues that concern them. Other resources are as close as your local video store.

How to Use the Internet for Research

In the United States we are saturated with information, opinions, and persuasive appeals, and the **Internet** has multiplied the amount of available information by geometric proportions. In fact, there is so much information online that you could literally spend the rest of your life in front of your computer, skimming a screenful of data every ten seconds, and you wouldn't run out of material. Rather than become overwhelmed by all the available data or accepting it at face value, you should understand how to do research online. This section will focus on benefits and cautions relating to Internet research. The next section will show you how to evaluate the materials you find.

Internet
A system that links computers around the world; likened to a web or superhighway.

What Is the Internet?

Within the last decade, millions of people have gained access to this vast communication system that links computers globally. Originally designed for military and scientific purposes, today's Internet is somewhat like a spiderweb (the "World Wide Web"), a road system (the "Information Superhighway"), or a huge mall with numerous entrances, information centers, levels, concourses, and specialized areas (Harnack & Kleppinger, 1998). Wonderful as this tool is, finding credible information on the Internet is different from finding reliable resources in a physical library. Enormous advantages—and several disadvantages—result from the fact that the Internet is:

1. *Democratic.* Anyone who can gain access to the Internet has an equal chance of being heard. Personal or private e-mail, as well as public books, newspapers, and academic journals, are online. The information on some sites has not been checked for accuracy. Furthermore, no one organizes Internet documents or makes sure you will find a genuine match between your key words and the documents you find.

2. *Global.* You can access documents from your town or from around the world that are helpful—but potentially overwhelming.

3. *Up-to-the-minute.* Facts, such as weather information and breaking news, are as close as your computer terminal. In fact, the Internet is especially good for current topics related to popular culture, computer science, or government documents.

4. *Interactive.* You can send e-mail messages and join chat groups. If you like, you can play chess at any time of day or night with someone on the other side of the globe.

5. *Free.* Although you may have to pay for access to the Internet, most of the materials there are free. Furthermore, many, even most, public libraries as well as campus libraries and computer centers have terminals that anyone can use without cost (Hacker, 1998).

You've probably surfed the net before, but you may not have used it for serious academic research. Think of it as a cyberspace library where you can find printed materials, pictures, maps, videotapes, audio recordings, and public bulletin boards. However, enter this library cautiously. The net has highly screened, reputable material alongside and sometimes linked to unregulated sites. For instance, a university-sponsored and maintained site, such as the *Medieval Sourcebook* of Fordham University, may be just a few clicks of your mouse away from a medieval reenactment website created and maintained by a person who relies more on fantasy than fact. Another illustration: You can access the *Denver Post* online and find a serious, well-researched report about a political candidate. On the same site, you can link to a forum in which anyone can state an opinion about the same candidate, factually based or not, in complete anonymity.

You may find interesting, even accurate information on the medieval reenactment site or in the forum, but you'll be more credible to your audience if you present data that your listeners recognize as coming from quality institutions and organizations. For more information about the Internet, see the following websites:

- Walt Howe, When did the Internet start? A brief capsule history. http://www.delphi.com/navnet/faq/history.html.

- Internet Update at http://www.itworks.be/I_Update/current.html.

Researching Online

Browser
A software program that helps you find and display Internet information.

Taking the onramp to this electronic superhighway puts you into a system that links millions of electronic sites. However, your computer must follow a set of rules to access that information. First, you'll need a **browser**—a software program such as Netscape Navigator or Microsoft Internet Explorer that helps you find information and display it on your computer screen. Most Internet materials are stored on web pages written in a computer code or language called **hypertext markup language (HTML),** with highlighted links. Click on a link, and your computer connects you to the related site.

Each site has an address called a **URL (uniform resource locator).** When you know the address of a specific site, type it accurately into the address box on your browser; even one small mistake in capitalization or punctuation will result in a dead end. The URL has a number of elements, as these examples show:

http://www.nytimes.com
http://www.stemnet.nf.ca

http:	tells your computer the protocol or kind of link to make
//	shows that the link will be to another computer
www.	names the server where the file is located, in this case, the World Wide Web
nytimes/stemnet	names the owner of the website
.com	shows that the owner is a commercial site (*.org* is a nonprofit organization; *.edu* means an educational institution owns the site; *.gov* indicates a government site)
.nf.ca	signals a foreign site; *.nf* stands for Newfoundland; *.ca* means Canada (other foreign sites include *.fr* for France, *.jp* for Japan, and *.uk* for the United Kingdom)

Use a Subject Directory

Once you're on the Internet, you'll need search tools, which fall into two general categories: subject directories and text indexes. A **subject directory** is similar to your telephone book's *Yellow Pages* where your fingers do the walking to a general category such as physicians; there you look for more specific designations such as dermatologists. Finally, you home in on specific information such as the doctor closest to your home. When you want to find information about a broad topic, use a subject directory. A student interested in speaking about greyhound adoption, for example, can access a subject directory and type "adopt greyhound" in the search box. She'll get several hits— web pages of satisfied owners, links to adoption agencies, even a list of available dogs in her area.

Yahoo! (http://www.yahoo.com) is a popular subject directory. Its home page provides links to major categories such as education, entertainment, society and culture, reference, and health. Select a general category, then choose from successive menus until you come to websites that look promising. Or skip this route and simply type key words into the search box on the screen, then press SEARCH. Yahoo then provides a list of hits with links to other search tools. Check also the Argus Clearinghouse (http://www.clearinghouse.net), which monitors many subject guides or "webliographies." In addition, the Internet Public Library (http://www.ipl.org) and the Library of Congress home page (http://lcweb.loc.gov) provide excellent links to search tools with information on all Internet sources.

Finding the correct search term can be challenging, but you can turn to the librarians at http://www.ipl.org for assistance. They'll use their organizing skills to help you find interesting, useful information. Internet Public Library reference librarians at http://www.ipl.org/ref will even answer specific questions by e-mail.

Use a Text Index

For other types of searches, a **text index** is a better choice, especially if your topic is obscure or very limited, because text indexes allow you to search for exact phrases. Type in a key word, a series of words, or an entire line from a specific work. Here you'll need to use your skills for identifying and finding key terms. If your term is too broad, you may end up with over 100,000 hits. Not very helpful!

Hypertext Markup Language (html)

A computer code, or browser language, used to store material on the Internet.

Uniform Resource Locator (URL)

A set of letters, numbers, and symbols that function like an address for a specific web site.

Subject Directory

Searches the Internet by subject categories.

Text Index

Search engine that looks up specific phrases and obscure topics.

SCREEN 7.4   A subject directory. (© Yahoo! Inc.)

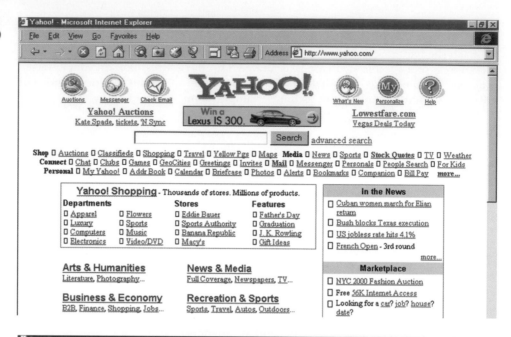

SCREEN 7.5   A text directory. (© Go2Net, Inc.)

   A powerful text index, *all the web.com,* was introduced in the fall of 1999; its URL is http://www.alltheweb.com. In a matter of seconds, this index will search more than 200 million of the 800 million sites on the Internet; developers eventually hope to search the entire web. Other text indices include AltaVista at http://altavista.com, Lycos at http://www.lycos.com, Metacrawler at http://www.metacrawler.com, and Dogpile at http://www.dogpile.com. Let's say your topic is bankruptcy reform; go to Dogpile and type in "bankruptcy reform" then press FETCH. You will probably get many hits, some of which overlap. Each hit comes with a short annotation so that you can make quick judgments about the source and usefulness of the site.

How to Evaluate Internet Resources

Powerful search tools will probably overwhelm you with information. How on earth can you sort through 4378 hits? You will probably be tempted to take the easiest material to access and get on with your life; however, this strategy may not be best, so exercise critical judgment about the sources and content they contain (Internet Source Validation Project, 1999).

Source

Even before you click onto a document, begin evaluating its source by looking at its URL. A document with a .gov or .edu sponsor is sponsored and maintained by an institution with a reputation to uphold; .com sites are commercial, and .org web pages are sponsored by organizations with varying reputations. When you enter the web page, look for the name and e-mail address of the person who created or maintains the site; this gives an additional basis for assessing source credibility. Try to determine the author's occupation, educational background, and expertise. Can you contact him or her? Would knowledgeable people consider the source to be accurate, expert, and reliable?

Content

First, look for a site rating. Teams of outsiders often evaluate sites to see if they provide complete, current, and thorough coverage of a topic. These evaluators also look at the way materials are organized to see whether or not the site is user friendly. A rating, although helpful, does not guarantee that the document contains accurate or high quality materials, so do your own site rating based on the following tips:

1. *Determine the intent or purpose of the site.* Is the page designed to provide information, to entertain, or to sway opinion? What audience does it appear to address?

2. *Look for a bias.* Does the material emphasize one perspective over another, or is it relatively objective? Is it free of gender or ethnic stereotyping? Does the creator or sponsor have a personal or commercial goal? Does the source have an established position on the topic?

3. *Check timeliness.* Is the information (especially statistical data) up-to-date? Is the site maintained regularly?

4. *Assess accuracy.* How is the material similar to what you've found in other sources? Would reputable sources accept the ideas as plausible and accurate? Look for links. Do these sites appear to be reputable as well? Does the document list its sources? Its methodology?

5. *Finally, consider organization.* If you have your choice between two sites that appear to be equal in accuracy and quality of information, choose the one that is easier to use (Hawkes, 1999).

For example, a search using www.dogpile.com for the topic "bankruptcy reform" turned up these promising documents:

■ *Nat'l Bankruptcy Review Commission Independent commission established pursuant to the Bankruptcy Reform Act. Access fact sheets, news and reports, with an archive and links.*

A government commission produces this site, which helps you establish its credibility. The site also provides links to other sources. Besides, you'll end up with other key terms to try if you need them.

■ *Idaho Credit Union League Home Page Idaho Credit Union League. April 20, 1999 Representatives Simpson Chenoweth cosponsor HR 833, the Bankruptcy Reform Act of 1999 Please join us in thanking Helen Chenoweth and Mike Simpson for their work on this bill. www.idahocul.org—Idaho Credit Union League*

Updated site; that's a plus. Gives an e-mail address; also good. Credit Union League will almost surely have a bias toward the lender.

> **STOP AND CHECK**
>
> ## Critical Thinking and the Internet
>
> Although the Internet is wonderful, use its information with care. Mixed in with verifiable facts and research data, texts of nineteenth-century British novels, and pictures of Roman architecture, you'll find commercials and rumors and opinions that you cannot verify because many Internet contributors are anonymous and not accountable.
>
> 1. Use the guidelines provided in the text to assess the reliability of the following sites. That is, evaluate the source and the content (the purpose, bias, timeliness, accuracy, and organization) of information you find on an organizational site for hang gliding, available at www.ushga.org, and on a specific commercial site such as www.hanggliding.com.
>
> 2. Then go to www.whitehouse.gov and read the biographical information you find there about the President of the United States. Assess the content. What is the purpose, the bias, the timeliness, and the accuracy of the biographical information you find there? Use a subject directory like www.yahoo.com and search for the president by name. Follow at least one link there and, using the same tests for site content, compare the biographical information you find there with the information the White House presents.
>
> 3. Of the sites you reviewed in 1 and 2, which materials are more apt to be verifiable? Which features more expert contributions? Which materials were probably not screened or edited? What are the strengths and limitations of each type of material? That is, when would you be likely to use each source effectively?
>
> Sometimes you will find hoax sites that look legitimate, but are really prank web pages that mimic and poke fun at the real thing. Internet activity 5 at the end of the chapter provides further information on one such a site.
>
> You can access these links and answer these questions online under Chapter 7: Activities for Jaffe Connection at the Public Speaking Resource Center.

■ *Juicy Lucy's Files for Protection from Creditors (PR Newswire) Juicy Lucy's drive-thru hamburger chain, a wholly owned subsidiary of Franchise Management International, Inc., announced today that it has decided to seek protection from its creditors by filing a Chapter 11 bankruptcy petition in Federal Court in Tampa, Florida.—[today's date] 8:00 AM EDT*

Juicy Lucy? What a name! Will surely gain audience attention. This article probably gives the consumer's perspective—at least to a degree. Juicy Lucy's is a real-life, up-to-date example. Newswire source seems credible.

■ *U.S. banks said to cut support for debt counselors (Reuters) By Andrew Clark WASHINGTON, [yesterday's date] (Reuters)—At the same time they are pushing Congress to pass tough new bankruptcy laws, U.S. . . .*

The title and opening phrase suggest an interesting occupation: debt counselors. Reuters is a top international news source; looks like it's worth reading.

Record Your Information

Obviously you won't remember everything you discover during your search, so you need a strategy for recording your findings. Then, when you sit down to organize your speech, you will have the necessary information at your fingertips and you can easily classify your ideas into themes and patterns. There are three common methods of recording research information: photocopied materials, mind maps, and note cards. Choose the one that matches your individual learning style. Then use a standard bibliographic format to list your sources at the end of your outline.

SCREEN 7.6 This site is sponsored by a commercial enterprise. (Raven Sky Sports)

SCREEN 7.7 An official organization sponsors this site. (United States Hang Gliding Association)

Photocopy or Print Your Materials

One advantage of photocopying your materials is that you have the entire resource in front of you. Use copy machines available in most libraries to copy articles from books, newspapers, and periodicals for one-time use. Or, download and print material from the Internet. Be sure you write the source (in standard bibliographic form) directly onto your photocopies or downloaded materials. Then, using highlighters, identify major ideas and salient information.

To see how this works, consider the speech topic "Hawaiian sovereignty." The prospective speaker photocopies pages from books and newspapers; she also clips articles from her own subscription newspapers and magazines. She makes sure to copy the entire reference at the top of each page. Then, using one color for major points and a second color for examples and quotations, she highlights the material relevant to her subject. When she finally organizes and outlines her ideas, she simply spreads out her photocopied and highlighted articles and weaves the materials together into a coherent speech.

Whenever you copy materials, you are using the intellectual property of another person who has a right to profit from its use. Fortunately, the **Fair Use provision** in the federal Copyright Act allows you to print and use materials for non-profit educational purposes; therefore, photocopying materials for one-time speech research is within your legal rights as a student (Kirshenberg, 1998).

Fair Use Provision
The provision in the federal Copyright Act that allows free use of materials for educational and research purposes.

FIGURE 7.2 A mind map.

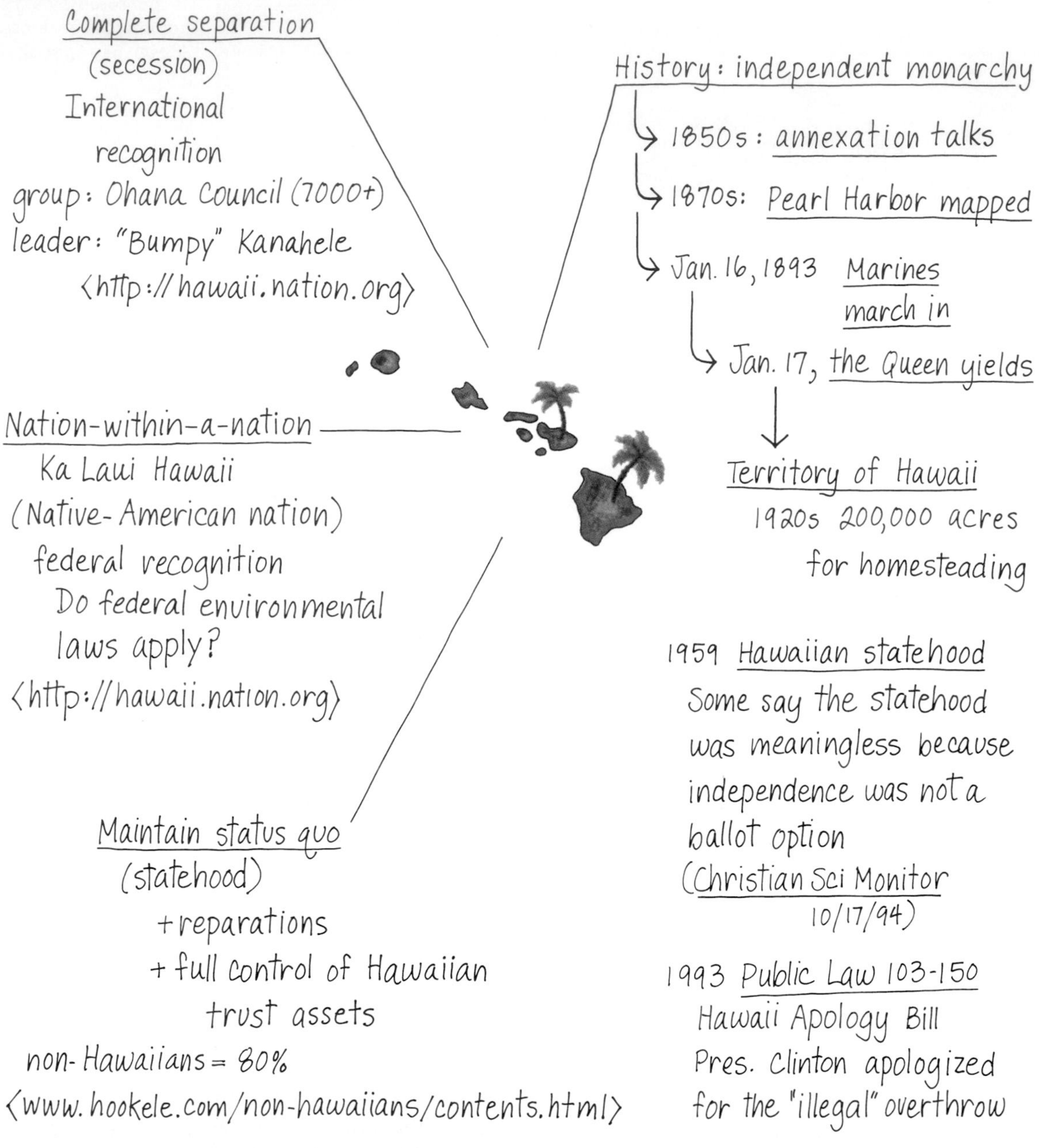

Complete separation
   (secession)
   International
      recognition
group: Ohana Council (7000+)
leader: "Bumpy" Kanahele
   <http://hawaii.nation.org>

History: independent monarchy
↳ 1850s: annexation talks
↳ 1870s: Pearl Harbor mapped
↳ Jan. 16, 1893   Marines
                     march in
↳ Jan. 17, the Queen yields
   ↓
Territory of Hawaii
   1920s 200,000 acres
      for homesteading

Nation-within-a-nation
   Ka Laui Hawaii
   (Native-American nation)
   federal recognition
      Do federal environmental
      laws apply?
   <http://hawaii.nation.org>

1959 Hawaiian statehood
   Some say the statehood
   was meaningless because
   independence was not a
   ballot option
   (Christian Sci Monitor
            10/17/94)

Maintain status quo
   (statehood)
      +reparations
      + full control of Hawaiian
            trust assets
non-Hawaiians = 80%
<www.hookele.com/non-hawaiians/contents.html>

1993 Public Law 103-150
   Hawaii Apology Bill
   Pres. Clinton apologized
   for the "illegal" overthrow

Create a Mind Map

If your learning style is more holistic, consider making a mind map. Chapter 6 showed how to use a mind map to generate speech topics, but you can use a similar process to record and sort topical information. One advantage of this method is that you can classify and subdivide your materials as you gather them.

Here's how a topical mind map works. First, identify the subject of your speech in the center of the page, using a diagram or drawing. Then, draw a line to attach each subtopic to this center. Show further subdivisions by drawing radiating lines under your subtopics. If you have a lot of material, you may have to make a separate page for each major point. See Figure 7.2 for a mind map about Hawaiian sovereignty. Be sure to list your sources. If

FIGURE 7.3 Source cards contain bibliographic information. Annotated cards also include a brief summary of the material found in the source.

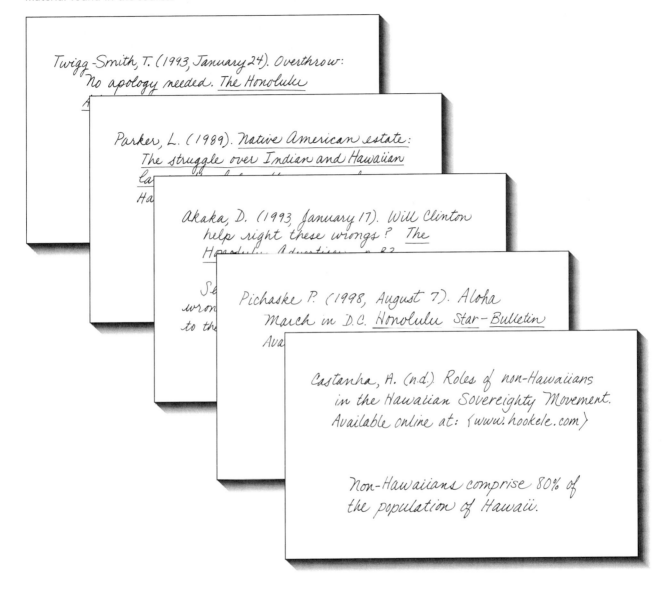

there's room, write your references directly onto your mind map; however, if your space is limited, make source cards or list your references on a separate piece of paper.

Write Note Cards

A more structured approach is to use 3 x 5 or 4 x 6 cards. This method has many advantages: The cards are small enough to handle easily, you can cite your sources directly on each card, and you can easily classify your information. Sort your material into major categories by using two basic kinds of note cards: source cards and information cards.

Source Cards

Begin by making a separate card for each source, using a standard bibliographic format. **Source cards** include the author, date, title, place of publication (for books), or news-

Source Cards

Cards used to record bibliographic information.

FIGURE 7.4 Use a different information card for each source, and classify each card according to the major idea the information supports. Include an abbreviated source citation on each card.

Arguments Against Hawaiian Sovereignty
Twigg-Smith, T, Overthrow: No apology
needed. B-1.

Thurston Twigg-Smith is president of a
Honolulu new
missionary a
time of the ov
throw of the

Arguments for Hawaiian Sovereignty
Akaka, D. Will Clinton help... B3

Daniel Akaka, U.S. Senator from Hawaii,
wrote a letter t
of the Hawaiian
terrible happeni
asks the Clinton
to correct a cen

Arguments For Hawaiian Sovereignty
Wood, D.B. ⟨http://hawaii.nation.org/nation/csm⟩

1. Even Pres. Clinton apologized, saying the
   overthrow was illegal in the 1st place.
2. Treaties were neither approved nor
   terminated by Congress.
3. The 1959 statehood vote is meaningless
   b/c independence was not a ballot option.

Annotate

To summarize a book or article's contents on a source card.

paper or magazine title, followed by the page number or URL where you found the information. You can **annotate** your bibliography, meaning that you write a brief description of the information you found in the book or article. Make source cards for materials gathered from interviews and films as well. Figure 7.2 shows examples of source cards for a speech about stages of culture shock. (See the entire outline in Chapter 11.)

Information Cards

Information Card

Card for recording and categorizing important data.

Next, copy down important data, creating a separate **information card** for each different idea, statistic, quotation, example, and so on. On the top of each card, write a heading that classifies the information into a category that may later become a main point. Also, label the card with an abbreviated source citation so that when you use the material in the speech, you can cite its source. Figure 7.3 shows examples of information cards.

The advantage of this method is that you can separate your cards into piles, then move them around, placing your major point at the top and arranging your supporting information below. You can easily change the order of both your points and your relevant supporting materials before writing the outline.

In summary, an important part of the research process is recording information so that it is readily available when you put your speech together. If you approach the research task holistically, you may download or photocopy your materials and use highlighters to identify important information. Or, you may make mind maps, using images as well as words to record the results of your research. If you like a structured, linear method, note cards may be your best choice. The important thing is that you find a way to remember your ideas.

Use a Standard Format to Cite Your Sources

To avoid plagiarism, give credit to the sources you use by creating a bibliography at the end of your outline. List all your sources in alphabetic order using a standard bibliographic format found in the style or publication manual your instructor recommends. The reference section of your library has many popular style manuals, including ones from the American Psychological Association (APA) and the Modern Language Association (MLA). To find specific sites online, go to www.alltheweb.com and search for the exact term "APA Style Manual," or "MLA Style Manual." You will get hundreds of hits that will link you to further information about bibliographic citations, much of which is furnished by professors and librarians. Good examples of APA source citations are http://puffin.creighton.edu/psy/TLB/writadv.html.

In summary, an important part of the research process is recording information so that it is readily available when you put your speech together. If you approach the research task holistically, you may download or photocopy your materials and use highlights to identify important information. Or, you may make mind maps, using images as well as words to record the results of your research. If you like a structured, linear method, note cards may be your best choice. The important thing is that you find a way to remember your ideas. Then use a standard bibliographic format to list your sources alphabetically.

> **STOP AND CHECK**
>
> ### Complete Your Research Plan
>
> Return a final time to your research plan, found on page 117 or online under Chapter 7: Forms and Checklists under Jaffe Connection at the Public Speaking Resource Center. Complete sections O and P. Make any other alterations that seem justified in light of having read this entire chapter.

Public Speaking Resource Center

Summary

Part of your competence in speechmaking is your ability to gather information. You'll be more effective if you set aside plenty of time to explore your topic using a research plan that is appropriate for the subject. Look for both primary and secondary sources of material: primary sources are original documents and other first-hand information; secondary sources interpret, explain, and evaluate the subject.

You can find both primary and secondary materials in face-to-face interactions, and in print sources such as books, periodicals, and newspapers, published in traditional library forms as well as online. Consider also the wide variety of visual and audio taped materials available to you. Throughout your research, search out diverse perspectives including international, ethnic, and alternative viewpoints.

Through the Internet, you can access literally millions of documents from local, national, and global sources—some highly credible, others useless. Use a subject directory to look up general topics. If you can't find information on specific or unusual topics or if you're looking for specific phrases, go to a text index. Sift through the materials you find by evaluating each source as well as the purpose, bias, timeliness, accuracy, and organization of each site's content. Constantly record your findings, using a method that meets your learning style preferences, whether photocopying, making a mind map, or using source and information cards. On the bibliography that accompanies your outline, cite your sources using a standard form that you can find in a style or publication manual.

JAFFE CONNECTION

Key Terms

reference librarian (114)
primary sources (116)
original documents (116)
creative works (116)
relics or artifacts (116)
secondary sources (116)
oral sources (118)
expert (118)
laypeople or peers (118)
general encyclopedias (120)
specialized encyclopedias (121)
dictionary (121)

periodicals (121)
trade or professional journal (121)
Internet (125)
browser (126)
hypertext markup language (html) (127)
uniform resource locator (URL) (127)
subject directory (127)
text index (127)
Fair Use provision (131)
source cards (133)
annotate (134)
information card (134)

Application and Critical Thinking Questions

If you have not already done so, visit your campus library. Locate and browse the reference books, the newspapers and periodicals, and the indexes and guides to them.

1. Make a file containing handouts prepared by the librarians in the library you'll use most often, and consult these during your research. (Examples: HOW TO: Locate U.S. Government Documents; HOW TO: Cite References According to the APA Manual; Periodicals Collection: A Service Guide.)

2. Make a list of library resources that provide an alternative perspective on subjects. That is, discover what subscriptions your library has to international, ethnic, and alternative newspapers and magazines. Read an article in at least one of the resources.

3. Think about the different ways to record information. Which method—photocopies, mind maps, or note cards—would you most likely use? Which would you least likely use? When might you combine methods? Discuss your research style with a classmate.

4. Cooperate with your entire class to research a current event or an issue such as gun control. Go to the library and find and photocopy a print article. Or, download information from an Internet site. Or, interview an expert or layperson. Make sure that some students consult mainstream sources and that others seek out diverse perspectives. Bring your information to the next class meeting and discuss and evaluate the various sources and data by determining the purpose, the source bias, the timeliness, the accuracy, and the organization of the material.

Internet Activities

■ Use your *InfoTrac College Edition* to look up the subject of fair use laws. Read an article that describes authors' rights, as well as your rights to use intellectual property in your speeches.

- Using *InfoTrac College Edition*, type in key words relating to your speech topic. Select a number of articles and skim those that appear interesting.

- If possible, set aside an hour to explore newspapers and magazines on the Internet. A subject index like www.yahoo.com or a site like www.drudgereport.com provides links to many news sites. Surf around, clicking on links that you find interesting. Then, discuss with your classmates the value as well as the drawbacks of doing research over the Internet.

- To learn more about ways to integrate library and Internet research, use a search engine such as Yahoo or Lycos and type in "library research tutorial" or "research tutorial."

- The Internet features many hoax sites; for example, making a small change such as typing *.net* instead of *.gov* in the White House URL leads you to a prank site set up to look very much like the official White House web page. Go to http://www.whitehouse.net and see for yourself.

Hot Links at the Public Speaking Resource Center

The following links are maintained and can be accessed easily via Jaffe Connection at the Public Speaking Resource Center on the Wadsworth Communication Café web site at http://communication.wadsworth.com/publicspeaking/study.html

Public Speaking Resource Center

http://www.orst.edu/dept/library/tutorial/library.htm Oregon State University sponsors this Library Research Process Home Page that provides you with valuable tips for planning your research. Many libraries sponsor similar sites especially aimed at writers of research papers; however, the principles apply to speech research.

http://bob.ucsc.edu/library/media/research.html Here is another tutorial site that's sponsored by a university, this time the University of California at Santa Cruz. It's titled, Using the Web for Research: Tutorial.

http://www.library.ucla.edu/libraries/college/instruct/web/critical.htm This site provides a librarian's advice on evaluating Internet sources. The librarians at U.C.L.A. sponsor it.

STUDENT SPEECH WITH COMMENTARY

Medical Misinformation on the Internet *by Quianna Clay*

Did you know that flaxseed oil and cottage cheese can now cure lung cancer? Or, that avoiding dairy products will dissolve cataracts? Well, neither did registered dietician Ira Milner, until he spent 60 hours online and found a plethora of such incorrect medical information. What Milner describes as mere pond scum is noted on the Internet as an excellent dietary suppressant. His findings were reported in the April 27, 1997 *Star Tribune*. According to the October 19 *Wall Street Journal*, the information source that is quickly becoming the most powerful, overwhelming, and fraught with danger is the Internet. While we might laugh at the idea of using pond scum as a dietary suppressant, incidences of people encountering incorrect medical information online are usually far less amusing. In fact they can be deadly. Medical information is one of the most sought after topics online. In fact, according to the National Health Council, a Washington-based coalition of health organizations, at least 46 percent of Internet users are looking for medical information. The previously cited *Star Tribune* also notes

I first heard Quianna's speech at a tournament. It summarizes this chapter very well.

Quianna gains attention with amusing examples of misinformation. She then spells out the problem and the need for consumers to be critical thinkers. Throughout she demonstrates credibility by citing respectable sources.

Here Quianna spells out the problem and the need for consumers to be critical thinkers.

Here she previews the three main ideas she'll develop in the speech.

By focusing on a single type of information, one that may actually result in life or death, Quianna spotlights the importance of Internet research savvy.

This section of her speech echoes the contrast between print and Internet sources highlighted in this chapter.

Quianna emphasizes that anyone with the basic skills and equipment can create a web page.

that users have an estimated 10,000 sites from which to choose. Unfortunately, much of this information is in error.

Today we will explore the dangers associated with medical misinformation on the Internet. First, as consumers we would be wise to know where incorrect medical information has been found. Second, we'll see why there is so much misinformation on the Internet. And, finally, we will all learn what we must do to avoid being misled when using medical information gained from the Internet or other online services.

The World Wide Web and the Internet are increasingly more accessible and are attracting many more users. In the 1998 *Consumer Health Information Source Book,* the Times Mirror Center for the People and Press reported that the number of web users has jumped from 5 million in 1994 to 12 million in 1995 and has grown by at least 2 million each year since then. Many of these users, at least 37 percent, as mentioned earlier, are seeking all sorts of medical information, including information on physical symptoms and diagnosis, treatments for specific disorders, medications and products, and surgical techniques and procedures. On September 29 and 30 of 1997, the Federal Trade Commission ran an event called the North American Health Claims Surf Day. It took just a few hours for participants from the FDA, CDC, Health Canada, and other organizations to find over 400 websites offering faulty information. The June 1998 *Journal of Pediatrics* addressed the accuracy of medical web pages, reporting that 80 percent of the pages examined for one study offered medical advice that did not agree with recommendations given by the American Academy of Pediatrics, the largest affiliation of pediatricians in the United States.

Not only are current Internet users seeking medical information, but many new users also seek Internet sites as the first places they turn. Internet users often assume university-based web pages to be high-quality, credible sources of information. But this is not always the case. The August 1997 *Journal of the American Medical Association* offers an illustrative example: one university web page suggested that children with diarrhea fast and drink sports beverages, advice that directly contradicts the recommendation of the American Academy of Pediatrics. The AAP cautions against drinking sports beverages, juice, or chicken broth because they are low in electrolytes, which the body loses as a result of diarrhea.

Having examined the problem of misinformation on the Internet, let's look at what causes the problem. There are many causes for the incorrect information that is available online. The main cause is lack of peer review on the Internet. In print, a publication's credibility is judged by standards that include the credibility of the author, the publication's editorial content vs. its advertising commitments and educational values vs. product promotion, and the number of scientific facts it presents. Such standards, unfortunately, are not applied to medical information on the Internet. Dr. H. Juhling McClung, of the Ohio State University Medical Center, argued "If our objective on the scientific side of the web is to have good science, then we are going to have to have peer review."

Not only is information not reviewed, but researchers often are not involved directly in the creation of web pages. Often clerical staff, who may not be familiar with the subject matter, create the pages. These inexperienced staffers may be one significant source of errors. In addition, anyone with a computer, modem, and twenty dollars can create his or her own web page. According to the April 1997 *Journal of the American Medical Association,* the resulting web pages may contain large amounts of incomplete, inaccurate, and misleading information. Web pages posted anonymously may contain faulty information for many reasons. The person posting the page may have a personal agenda, may be interested in making quick money off consumers, and may have no formal medical training.

Finally, Internet users themselves often contribute to the problem. The July 1995 *Annals of Internal Medicine* notes that many people trust search engines to lead them to quality sites on the Internet. As computer-savvy people know, searches do not distinguish among quality sites and those containing misinformation. They merely count the number of times the requested key words appear in the content of a given site, then direct the person to the sites with the most matches. While some of us may understand the nature of search engines, at least 2 million novice Internet users come online each year—many of them unaware of the pitfalls awaiting them.

Fortunately, the situation of medical misinformation on the Internet is not hopeless. Several steps can improve the quality of medical information on the Internet. In addition, we as consumers can determine if the information we are using is correct and reliable.

First, some standards should be in place to help ensure the safety of those who seek medical information on the web. The 1998 *Consumer Health Information Sourcebook* notes that the Geneva-based Health on the Net Foundation has already formulated a code of conduct for medical websites offered by the 1997 editors of the *Journal of American Medicine*. The code suggests that the creators should:

1. Identify a credible person or group who stands behind the information provided.

2. Name the authors and contributors as well as their affiliations and credentials.

3. Cite all references and copyright information used to create the site.

Additionally, governmental agencies need to take a more active role in regulating medical information on the Internet. They should follow the lead of the FDA, which is currently exploring new standards for pharmaceutical advertising on the Net. As Melissa Mancavage, public health advisor for the FDA notes, "Current regulations on prescription drugs differ between print and broadcast medium. The Internet presents additional challenges."

Along with formal standards for the industry, we consumers must determine if a site is credible. These suggestions, issued by the Department of Health and Human Services in 1996, were published in the June issue of the FDA *Consumer*. First, determine who maintains the site. Government sources sponsor some of the better sites, including those maintained by the National Institutes of Health or the Centers for Disease Control. Private practitioners or organizations may have financial or political agendas that influence their material and their links.

Next, look for a listing of names and credentials of people who contributed to the site; see if they can be contacted to answer questions or provide further information. Also, look for links to other sites. A good site will not consider itself the only source of information; however, be cautious about links. A reputable site has no control over who links to it. Consequently, an unscrupulous group could link to a more trustworthy source such as the Food and Drug Administration in an attempt to appear more credible.

In addition, you can log on to the "Internet Health Watch" site, which evaluates other health websites. Reuters Health Information Service sponsors this site, which is maintained by Dr. John Renner, founder of the Consumer Health Information Research Institute in Independence, Missouri. Dr. Renner evaluates three sites each week on their technical content, credibility, usefulness, and linkage characteristics.

Most important, have any information you find corroborated by a licensed physician. Remember, the Internet should complement, not replace, the physician-patient relationship.

With so many possible solutions to this problem, we need not fall victim to the incorrect medical information we encounter online. The Internet certainly has the potential to host innumerable sources of high-quality information. It is also full of opportunities to inform and teach consumers. However, because no regulations are currently in place to control the accuracy of medical information online, we should use anything we find on the Internet with caution.

Now, knowing where cases of inaccurate medical information have been found, knowing the causes of such misinformation, and being armed with tools that can correct the situation allows us to exercise such caution. So, next time you are on the Internet and you begin to consider pond scum or cottage cheese as a cure for what ails you, keep these words in mind: *Caveat emptor*—let the buyer beware.

Search engines are neutral, which requires each researcher to sift through numerous hits with care. The chapter used sample hits on the topic of bankruptcy reform to make this point.

Quianna points out that many people are concerned about erroneous materials available online and are creating standards and guidelines for website creators.

Quianna summarizes the guidelines for assessing Internet information found on page 129.

Choosing Supporting

Materials

This chapter will help you:

- **Distinguish between fact and opinion and know how to test factual data**

- **Use examples effectively**

- **Quote authoritative sources**

- **Select numerical data carefully**

- **Distinguish between literal and figurative analogies**

Detail from "Carnaval" ©1995 by
Joshua Sarantitis, Emmanuel Montoya,
and Precita Eyes Mural Arts Center

Think about how you make decisions. How did you decide to attend your particular college or university? Did you read a promotional brochure? Did you talk to a friend or a high school teacher? Did you go by the reputation of the school? Most people select a school only after they ask questions like "Why should I go there?" "What does it cost?" "What's so great about that place?" They want evidence—facts, figures, examples, recommendations—to support their decision. So it is with other decisions we make. When we make a decision, we want support for our actions and our ideas. When we hear a speech, we expect the same from the speaker.

Each culture has its own rules for determining what is acceptable as evidence. In the United States, we generally look for facts, examples, quotations, statistics, and analogies to support our ideas. In addition, rather than accepting all information at face value, we follow cultural standards for weighing evidence, accepting some as valid and rejecting other data as inadequate, irrelevant, or inaccurate. This chapter looks at the typical kinds of evidence used in public speaking. Following the presentation of each type of evidence you will find a Stop and Check section to help you think critically about the quality of the data or evidence, both when selecting materials for your own speeches and when listening to the speeches of others.

Provide Facts

Probably most of the information you discover about your subject will be factual, and in Euro-American culture people typically demand facts before accepting an idea or proposal. **Facts** are defined as data that can be verified by observation, and **established facts** are those consistently validated by many observers as true; they include definitions and descriptions that are generally accepted within a society. You judge factual information as true or false. Facts derive from a variety of sources, as these examples reveal:

Facts
Data verifiable by observation.

Established Facts
Data verified consistently by many observers.

- The origin of the word *coffee* is disputed. Some say it derives from the Arabic word *qahwah;* others say it comes from Kaffa, the province in southwest Ethiopia that is considered coffee's birthplace. [source: dictionary]

- The racehorse Secretariat won the Triple Crown of racing in 1973. [source: racetrack records]

- Cigarette smoking is statistically correlated with heart disease. [source: empirical research studies conducted by scientists]

Use Definitions

Define
Give the meaning of a word.

You can **define,** or give the meaning of a term, in a number of ways. Looking in a dictionary provides the meaning generally accepted in common usage. For her classroom speech on coffee, Annette paraphrased the definition she found in the *Oxford Dictionary,* one of the most respectable sources available:

Coffee is a drink made by infusion or decoction from the seeds of a shrub, roasted and ground; extensively used as a beverage and acting as a moderate stimulant.

Because her source is so well known, most people (if they could figure out what decoction meant!) would agree that, yes, this is what coffee is. However, the dictionary definition is fairly technical, so Annette supplemented it with one of her own:

This seems cold for what I consider an institution, so I've come up with my own definition. True coffee connoisseurs would agree that coffee really means: gathering with friends, memories of warming hands at a football game, late nights—cramming, Christmas break when I wake up to the smell of Dad making coffee.

Here, you can see that Annette interjects her personal **opinions** into her definition. Stating personal opinion, either yours or that of other people, adds a subjective interpretation that is open to question. For instance, not all "true coffee connoisseurs" associate the beverage with friends, family, studies, or Christmas break.

Opinions

Subjective interpretations of facts; can be questioned.

Provide Vivid Descriptions

Most people are familiar with the look and smell of a steaming cup of coffee, but we are less knowledgeable about coffee bushes. Knowing this, Annette used vivid words to **describe** factual information about coffee bushes:

Describe

Create an image or impression through vivid words.

> Coffee grows on evergreen bushes that are 26 to 33 inches high. When in bloom, they're covered with white flowers that have a jasmine-like smell. These blossoms turn into red berries that are eventually harvested and roasted.

By describing the coffee plants (color, size, smell), Annette provides her listeners with facts that help them form mental pictures of the bushes.

The danger in using factual material is that it is easy to pass on unverified or inaccurate material. For instance, Camilla quoted from the speech, "Brother Earth, Sister Sky," which she attributed to Chief Seattle speaking over one hundred years ago. Had she searched further, she would have discovered that the speech was actually constructed in 1972 by a screenwriter named Ted Parry for a film about ecology. (*Info-Trac College Edition* includes a number of articles that provide accurate information about the authorship of the speech.) With the current explosion of available information, especially through the Internet and other electronic sources, distinguishing facts from opinions is now more important than ever.

STOP AND CHECK

Think Critically About Facts

Sometimes Arab Americans say that they are stereotyped and misunderstood, and that a lot of incomplete or incorrect information circulates regarding them. For example, one Arab speech scholar pointed out that numerous books, even some textbooks, say that Arabs like to stand close enough to smell each other's breath—an idea she found laughable! If I wanted to test that factoid (which I had read in several books), I would apply the following three tests.

1. *Check for accuracy or validity.* Is it true that Arab people stand fairly close? Is the reason so that they can get a whiff of one another? How many observers or sources say so? (One advantage of reading widely and from a variety of sources is that conflicting information can alert you to misinformation.) What do Arabs themselves say?

2. *Are the facts up to date?* Do they reflect contemporary reality? Even if some groups of Arabs at one time stood very close, is this the practice today? Using the latest research can help avoid errors here.

3. *Consider the source.* Who says Arabs stand close? An Arab scholar? Arabs themselves? A tourist who visited one Arab city a single time? (Chapter 7 discussed additional ways to test source credibility.)

In short, test facts by asking three questions: Is this true? Is this true now? Who says so?

Chief Seattle did not make a speech that is often attributed to him. Checking a variety of sources can help you avoid passing on incorrect information. (E. Lochrie/The Museum of the Rockies)

Use Examples

Have you ever listened to a speech that seemed abstract and irrelevant until the speaker used an example showing how the topic affected someone like you? Chances are, your interest increased because of the illustration. In many cultures, including this one, we choose short or long, real or hypothetical **examples,** or specific instances, to support our ideas because of their numerous benefits. David explains:

Examples
Specific instances used to support ideas.

> The speeches that are interesting usually start with an example—often from that person's life. It shows the communicator is human. The story adds credibility . . . and leads the audience into the speech, almost like a conversation; this lets the speaker earn the audience's trust.
>
> *David*

In addition, examples attract attention. Narrative theorists argue that we listen for examples and stories that make abstract concepts and ideas more concrete and relevant (MacIntyre, 1981). Moreover, illustrations help listeners identify emotionally with your subject. When the example rings true to their personal experience, listeners respond with internal dialogue something like this: "Yes, I've known someone like that" or "I've seen that happen—this seems real." Finally, using examples can enhance your personal credibility. Your listeners want to know that you are involved in real-world experiences. Examples let your audience see that you understand the practical implications of your theories and ideas.

You'll find two major types of examples: real and hypothetical. Both types can be further differentiated by length. Some are very brief; others are longer and more detailed.

Use Real Examples

Real examples, those that actually happened, provide your listeners with concrete, real-life illustrations of your concepts. For instance, John's topic is culture shock. He defines the term, then begins his discussion of the first stage, the honeymoon stage. His audience listens politely, but their attention really perks up and they more clearly understand the emotions associated with this stage when he tells about Sara's experiences during her first few weeks as a nanny in Belgium.

As you gather materials, look for experiences of people, as well as events or happenings in institutions, countries, and so on to illustrate your ideas. Because real examples actually occurred, you can provide specific names, dates, and places. For instance:

- To illustrate a speech about the downside of winning the lottery, tell about William, whose brother hired a hit man to kill him; Daisy, whose friend sued for half her winnings because he had prayed that she'd win and she did; Debbie, whose sisters no longer speak to her because she refused to pay their bills.

- For a speech arguing that ethnic wars are not new, use examples from ancient Africa, medieval Europe, and contemporary Ireland.

- Support a freedom-of-speech topic by using examples of specific Supreme Court rulings that protect this fundamental right.

You can also use examples from your own experience, which bolsters your credibility. John used personal examples from his semester in Kenya to illustrate his progress through the stages of culture shock. As a result, his listeners found him to be more credible; he not only had book learning, he knew firsthand what culture shock was like.

Consider Hypothetical Examples for Sensitive Topics

Sometimes you may use a **hypothetical example,** which means that the specific incident did not really occur, but something like it did or could happen. This type of example contains elements of several different stories woven together to create a typical person whose experiences relate to the topic. For instance, in a speech about teen suicide, instead of revealing details about a specific person you actually knew, you might combine elements from the lives and deaths of various teenagers to create a typical victim. If you choose a hypothetical example, tell the audience you're doing so by saying something like "Let's say a thirteen-year-old girl named Susan lived in a large city . . . we'll make that Los Angeles."

Indeed, because of our cultural value on privacy, hypothetical examples may be more appropriate than real examples when you're dealing with sensitive issues such as mental illness or sexual behaviors. For this reason, speakers whose work involves confidentiality—physicians, ministers, counselors, or teachers, to name a few—often use hypothetical examples. Family counselors who present workshops on parenting, for instance, tell hypothetical stories of good and bad parenting skills without revealing incidents from the lives of specific clients, whose real predicaments are confidential.

You can also create an imaginary scene that invites your listeners to personalize your topic. These scenes are especially effective at attracting attention and getting audience members to become emotionally involved. The following scene could function as the opening illustration for a speech on problems that lottery winners face:

> Imagine that you just won the lottery. You can't sleep; you're so excited! You call everyone you know, and for a few days you bask in the joy of being an instant millionaire. Notice I said a few days. A week after you win, relatives you've never seen start asking for loans. A few days later, a friend sues for half the money, arguing that she encouraged you to buy the ticket, and without her urging, you'd still be poor. . . . The demands and the expectations pile up—so much so that you may almost wish you'd never bought that ticket!

Real Examples
Actual happenings.

Hypothetical Example
Not a real incident or person, but true to life.

Speakers whose work involves confidentiality often describe hypothetical characters whose predicaments typify their clients' problems. (Charles Gupton/The Stock Market)

Although hypothetical examples can work well in informative speeches, you will be more effective if you select a real example when your purpose is persuasive. Imaginary scenarios are generally the least persuasive. Think of it this way: your listeners will more likely be persuaded by something that *did* happen than by something that *might* happen.

Combine Brief Examples

Examples don't have to be long. In fact, you may prefer to use a series of short illustrations to support your major points. One brief example is easily missed or disregarded, so string together two or three—especially in the introduction, where you are gaining listener attention. By layering example upon example, you provide audience members with a number of mental images they can use to visualize your subject. Here are illustrations of three types of people who watch professional wrestling; a speaker could use one after another to show the variety that exists among wrestling spectators:

■ Members of the pro-wrestling club at American University in Washington, DC gather around a television set every Monday night to watch *Raw Is War*, a two-hour show featuring the likes of Stone Cold Steve Austin and the Undertaker, two superstars of the World Wrestling Federation (WWF) (Kleiner, 1999).

■ Ten-year-old Jim Sabo, a wrestling fan since he was two, sits by his mother in the New Haven Coliseum cheering as Vince McMahon, head of the WWF, gets "bashed" with a metal chair, leaving him sprawled, spread-eagled in the ring (Rosellini, 1999).

■ Paul Cantor, a professor of English at the University of Virginia, also follows professional wrestling. He is working on an essay that analyzes the cultural meanings of the characters and the narratives they act out weekly (Cantor, 1999).

Create Emotional Connections with Extended Examples

Extended Examples

Longer incidents whose many details make them more compelling.

Extended examples include many details, each of which gives your listeners another opportunity to identify emotionally with the subject of the story. Use them to clarify, to explain in depth, and to motivate your listeners. Look at how each detail in this illustration makes the story more poignant. The subject is the need for cheap AIDS medicines in Africa:

> Thirty-five-year-old Veronica Mngoma was diagnosed with AIDS more than a year ago, but her doctors in South Africa didn't even tell her that drugs could prolong her life. Why? She earns only $33 a week working in a furniture company, so she simply can't afford the $750 per month treatments that would make her condition a chronic disease rather than a death sentence. This mother of three is now pencil-thin and weak. She opens her sore-filled mouth to whisper, "I worry about my children." Like millions of other AIDS sufferers worldwide, Mngoma needs access to cheaper medicines (Mabry, 1999).

Listeners can identify with one or more of the details: Ms. Mngoma's three children, her money worries, her helplessness and hopelessness. These help them connect with her plight and care about her situation. Because extended examples provide more distinct elements that engage listeners, they are generally more compelling. (Chapter 15 provides detailed information about organizing and evaluating narratives or well-developed stories that can function as the entire speech.)

STOP AND CHECK

Think Critically About Examples

Let's say you're reading for a speech about social anxiety and you come across the example of Grace Dailey, who experienced panic attacks so severe that she often had to leave college lectures. To help her get her degree, her professors agreed to leave the classroom door open during lectures, and they let her take tests alone (Schrof & Schultz, 1999). To evaluate the usefulness of an example such as this, ask yourself the following questions:

1. *Is this example representative or typical?* That is, do Grace's responses represent typical responses in the population of students with social anxiety? Or does her case seem extreme? This test relates to the probability of occurrence. Although the example may be possible, how *probable* is it?

2. *Do you have a sufficient number of examples?* Are enough cases presented to support the major idea adequately? How many people like Grace are attending colleges? Your listeners should be able to see that the issue you discuss is extensive, affecting a lot of people.

3. *Is the example true?* Did Grace actually leave lectures? How did such a shy woman convince her professors to work with her? Or, if it is hypothetical, does it ring true to what we know about the world and the way it operates?

Quote Culturally Acceptable Authorities

Remember this childhood challenge?

You make a statement.

Your friend responds "Who says?"

"My teacher says!"

"Well, who's he? What does he know?"

Mentally reactivate this question-and-answer scenario as you gather speech materials. Whatever your subject, think of your audience as responding, "Who says?". Then identify the type of authority you think your audience would believe, given your topic and purpose. Would you look for opinions of scholars? Wise women? Practitioners? Literary or scriptural texts? Quoting the words of authoritative sources will bolster your ideas, if and only if your audience views the source as credible on the topic.

Every culture identifies sources it considers insightful enough to comment on particular topics; these can include seers, teachers, elders, academic experts, religious leaders, and written texts—authoritative sources vary among cultures and co-cultural groups. Quoting well-recognized and culturally appropriate sources can be valuable, especially if you are not known as an expert on your topic. By doing so, you demonstrate that knowledgeable, experienced people agree with your conclusions. Stating someone's exact words is a **direct quotation.** However, when the material is extensive, you're often better off summarizing the quotation in a **paraphrase.**

As Chapter 7 pointed out, two kinds of authorities can provide valuable material: experts and laypeople (peers). To show that your sources are credible, state in your speech just who they are, why you believe their testimony, and why your audience should believe them.

Direct Quotation

Presenting the exact words of the source.

Paraphrase

Summarizing the source's ideas in your own words.

Expert

Person considered an authority because of study or work-related experiences.

Quote Culturally Accepted Experts

This culture emphasizes both education and experience, so look for opinions of **experts**—people considered credible because they know about a topic from study or from work-related experiences. Expert testimony comes from scholars, elected officials, practitioners such as doctors or stockbrokers, journalists, and others like them. Here is expert testimony that fits well into a speech about professional wrestling (Rosellini, 1999):

■ Mythologist Joseph Campbell argues that every new generation of humans recreates the ancient myths; professional wrestlers act out these myths.

■ Characters such as the Undertaker, Mankind, or the rebellious son Shane are, according to Jungian psychologist Polly Young-Eisendrath, instantly recognizable "because everybody has had the same emotional experience" (p. 57).

■ "[Televised wrestling] shows are extremely inappropriate models for children," says Howard Spivak who chairs the American Academy of Pediatrics' task force on violence (p. 55).

■ Even WWF's superstar, Stone Cold Steve Austin, himself a father of two young daughters, says "I get a little turned off with some of the sexual overtones" (p. 56).

Because most people in the audience have probably never heard of Young-Eisendrath or Spivak, it's up to the speaker to provide information that will help listeners decide whether the experts are credible. Notice that these examples both paraphrase and directly quote the experts.

Sometimes well-known people hold opinions that differ from what we might expect. That is, we commonly expect people to agree with the conventional wisdom of others who are similar to them in some way. Consider these examples:

■ William F. Buckley, Jr., a well-known conservative writer and journalist, supports legalization of drugs, a position not generally associated with conservatives.

■ Nat Hentoff, a writer and editor associated for many years with the liberal New York newspaper *The Village Voice*, takes a pro-life position, one that surprises many readers of the *Voice*.

Using unexpected testimony such as this can be powerful evidence in persuasive speeches. Why? Because your listeners reason that persons who go against their peers have thought through their opinions carefully.

Quote Credible Peers or Laypeople

This culture puts emphasis on individual expression and on equality among people. Therefore, the opinions of "regular people" who are knowledgeable, not because of

Whatever your topic, you need to identify sources your audience will see as authoritative. Who is best qualified to talk about the impact of professional wrestling on society? The wrestlers? The fans? Researchers who study the sport? Others? (Bruce Ayres/Tony Stone Images)

their study or employment, but because of their firsthand experiences with a subject, also carry weight. These **peer** or **lay sources** may not know scientific facts and related theories, but they can tell you how it feels to be involved as a participant. How do laypeople view professional wrestling? Several nonexperts gave their opinions:

> **Peer or Lay Sources**
> People considered credible because of firsthand experiences with a topic.

- Ten-year-old Jim Sabo, who has watched wrestling since he was two, likes best "how they all get hurt" (Rosellini, 1999, p. 56)

- Jim's mother, Laurie, isn't so concerned about the violence. She believes her son knows it is all an act, but she confesses "I'm not happy with the nudity and swearing" (Rosellini, 1999, p. 56)

- American University student Nicholas Kowalski refers to a wrestling move as "art," and admits "Yeah, wrestling is fixed, but at least there are still superheroes" (Kleiner, 1999, pp. 56–57)

Put simply, the ten-year-old who loves the violence, the mother who worries about the nudity and swearing, and the student who views the sport as artistic and heroic all add participants' perspectives that a speaker can use to good advantage in developing a speech.

Quote Sayings, Proverbs, and Words of Wisdom

Every culture provides a store of sayings, proverbs, phrases, and words of wisdom that encapsulates ideas, beliefs, and values considered to be important. (The Diversity in Practice box on the next page gives additional details about the importance of proverbs

Proverbs in a West African Culture

An article, entitled "Your Mother Is Still Your Mother" (Tembo, 1999), is available on your *InfoTrac College Edition.* In it, the author describes the importance of proverb usage among the Igbo people of Nigeria, West Africa, where proverbs both contain and transmit cultural wisdom. Chinua Achebe, a famous African author, calls them the Igbo's "horse of conversation." Adults who have reputations as wise conversationalists invariably use proverbs effectively, and every full and functioning adult in the village community learned to use proverbs properly during childhood. Each competent user understands each proverb's meanings and discerns the situations wherein a specific proverb fits.

Use the information given and the skills you've developed through your usage of *InfoTrac College Edition* to find and read this entire article.

in a specific culture.) Cultural words of wisdom come from literature and oral traditions, from well-known and anonymous sources, from philosophical and political treatises. For example:

- Neither a lender nor a borrower be. (literature)
- It takes a village to raise a child. (African proverb)
- Do unto others as you would have them do unto you. (religious text)
- Ask not what your country can do for you; ask what you can do for your country. (political speech)
- The greatest good for the greatest number [of people]. (philosopher)

Sayings do not always originate from well-known sources. You can also quote authoritative figures in your own life, as long as your audience respects the source. This speech excerpt illustrates how this works:

> My parents—and especially my father—taught me to draw an invisible line. He said to me, "Farah, you decide how you want other people to treat you, and if somebody crosses that line and it's unacceptable to you, just walk away from it. Don't let people treat you the way that they feel you should be treated. Have people treat you the way *you* feel you should be treated."
>
> That was good advice then. It is good advice now (Walters, 1992).

Walters expects her audience to accept her father as a credible source of wisdom, because this culture respects (although we sometimes reject!) the advice of friends and families.

Religious writings also provide rich sources of materials when the audience accepts the text as valid. The evangelist Billy Graham, for example, commonly uses the phrase "The Bible says . . . " when he intends to invoke the ultimate authority. If his audience includes people of religious affiliation other than Christian, it is conceivable that they discount Graham's source to at least some degree.

 To find sayings, proverbs, and wise words you can use in your speeches, log on to the Internet and go to a search engine like www.yahoo.com. Yahoo! links to a "References" category that includes many sources for quotations. Follow the links that interest you.

Think Critically About Quoting Authorities

Look back at the quotations of experts and laypeople relating to wrestling. Ask yourself these questions about each source cited.

1. *What is the person's expertise?* Joseph Campbell's? Polly Young-Eisendrath's? Howard Spivak's? Stone Cold Steve Austin's? Is it relevant to the subject under discussion?

2. *Is the person recognized as an expert by others?* How could you determine his or her reputation?

3. *Is the peer or layperson stating an opinion commonly held by others like him or her?* In other words, is it a typical or representative view? Do Jim and Laurie Sabo typify families who watch wrestling? Does the college student seem to represent views you'd expect?

4. Because you don't have the entire article, you cannot assess the context for the person's words. However, whenever possible, *ask if the words are taken out of context.* That is, do they fairly represent the speaker's intended meaning? Words can be distorted so that the quoted person appears to hold a position not actually held.

To investigate this topic further, log on to *InfoTrac College Edition* and search for the exact words "taken out of context." Read one of the articles and identify the effect this has on the person quoted incorrectly.

Employ Statistics Carefully

In our society, people tend to like numbers. We begin measuring and counting in kindergarten. We publish the results of opinion polls and statistical research. Many consider numbers and measurements to be credible and trustworthy—hard facts. Because of this, effective use of numerical support may increase your credibility, causing you to appear more competent and knowledgeable. Commonly, numerical information enables us to understand the extent of an issue or problem or to predict the probability of some future happening.

In short, numerical data can be useful; however, it has unique drawbacks. In general, statistics don't involve listeners' feelings; thus, numbers are short on emotional appeal, and too many in a speech may bore your audience. Furthermore, numerical information can be misleading, and if you present obviously biased information your listeners may distrust you. Consequently, you should take extra care to use enumeration and statistics accurately but sparingly.

Provide a Count

Enumeration means counting. Providing a count helps your audience understand the extent of a problem or issue: how many people are injured in accidents annually, are diagnosed with a disease, have adopted a child over two years old, and so on. Two major tips will help you use enumeration more effectively.

Enumeration
A count.

1. *Round your numbers up or down.* There are two good reasons for doing this. First, listeners find it hard to remember exact numbers. For instance, instead of saying "251,342 people were diagnosed with this disease in 1999," it is better to say "more than a quarter of a million people," or "more than 250,000 people." In addition, numbers related to current topics are likely to change rapidly. For example, one

AIDS awareness ad announced that 129,001 lives had been lost as a result of the disease. However, that number was out of date even before it appeared in print, for the day's obituaries listed several additional people who died of AIDS-related diseases the previous day.

2. *Make numbers come alive by comparing them to something already in your listeners' experience.* Take pro wrestling, for example. The sport attracts 35 million cable viewers each week, but just how many people is that? A quick Internet search for statistics shows that it is approximately the population of Canada and Norway combined. Giving your audience something concrete, such as the population of two familiar countries, allows them to understand better the concept of 35 million.

Here's how Sonja Ralston explained the number of people killed in accidents caused by sleep-deprived drivers:

Micro-sleep is the instantaneous dozing off that lasts less than a minute, but at 60 miles per hour, five seconds is long enough. Micro-sleep is the attributed cause of . . . 25 to 50 [deaths] every day in this country. . . . That's like a 747 crashing every other week, with no survivors.

By showing her listeners what 25 to 50 people means in a way they could visualize, Sonja kept their attention and helped them feel the emotional impact of so many deaths. It is hard to imagine 25 to 50 deaths for 365 days per year. However, because the U.S. media cover a single plane crash for days afterward, it is easier for Americans to understand the shocking effect of a 747 crash every other week. (The entire text of Sonja's speech appears at the end of Chapter 18.)

Choose Statistics with a Critical Eye

The statistics most commonly used in speeches include means, medians, modes, percentages, and ratios. (See Figure 8.1, p. 154).

Mean

Mean
Average of a group of numbers.

The **mean** is the *average* of a group of numbers. To calculate the mean, you sum all the specific measurements then divide by the total number of units measured. For example, you might compare at your school the mean SAT scores of students who are going into education with those of students going into medicine. Be aware that the existence of extreme figures at either end of the range will skew the mean, making it less useful. Just average the annual incomes of nine people who work for minimum wage and one billionaire to understand the limitations of the mean.

Median

Median
Middle number in a set of numbers arranged in a ranked order.

The **median** is the middle number in a set of numbers that have been arranged into a ranked order; with half the numbers lying above it and half below it. In the example of the billionaire and the wage-earners, the median is a way to give a more realistic picture to your listeners.

Mode

Mode
Most frequently occurring number.

The **mode** is the number that appears most commonly. For example, a classroom of first graders on the opening day of school may include a few seven-year-olds, and one five-year-old whose birthday is imminent, but the modal age of the students is six. A few nurses in one hospital earn $25 an hour; and a few earn only $14, but the modal rate for nurses' pay is $18 per hour.

Presenting numerical information in a creative way helps your audience understand numbers better. William Dakin, a tax counsel for Mobil Corporation, could have simply said that the company's tax return was thousands of pages long; however, he made his point more dramatically by showing the pages stacked on end. (David Scull/*New York Times*)

Percentages

Use **percentages** to show the relationship of a part to the whole, which is represented by the number 100. Public speakers commonly use percentages, as in the following example (which is illustrated in Figure 8.2, p. 155):

> During the forty years from 1880 to 1920, at least 12 million immigrants fleeing poverty and persecution in European countries flocked to the United States. Since 1965, when the immigration laws were changed, at least that many more have entered the United States—both legally and illegally. Of legal immigrants, 79% go to one of seven states, as the map shows.

Often you'll find the percentage stated as a **rate of increase or decrease,** which compares growth or decline during a period of time to a baseline figure from an earlier period. Treat these rates with caution, for unless you know the baseline number the rate of increase or decrease is relatively meaningless. Case in point: If a company employs two people in the year 1998 and adds an additional employee in 1999, the rate of increase is 50 percent. However, if a company employs 100 people in 1998 and adds an additional employee in 1999, the number of new employees is the same, but the rate of increase in the larger organization is only 1 percent. The reverse is also true. The two-person company that loses one employee decreases by half, or 50 percent; the large company hardly notices a loss of one. As you can see, when baseline numbers are initially very low, the rate of increase is potentially astounding!

Public speakers often use such rates when they present information, as the following this example demonstrates:

Percentages

Figures that show the relationship of the part to the whole, which is represented by the number 100.

Rate of Increase or Decrease

A percentage that uses an earlier baseline figure to compare growth or decline.

FIGURE 8.1 This pictograph shows lottery winnings of 25 participants. The mean or average was $5,700; the median or the midpoint was $3,000. However, most people won $2,000—the mode or most common amount. When a few extreme instances lead to unrealistic conclusions, the median or the mode is often more useful than the mean.

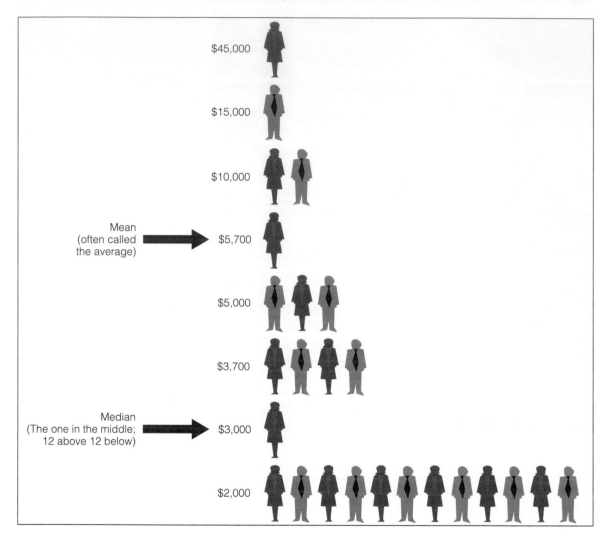

An AIDS activist spoke at a small town in a rural county of a Western state. He announced that AIDS increased by 34 percent in rural areas, while its rate of increase was only 5 percent in cities. However, he failed to show how that rate applied to the county in which he spoke. The total number of cases in the *entire county* was 8. A 34 percent increase meant that there had been 6 cases the previous year. However, a 5 percent increase in a city with 10,000 cases would mean that 500 additional people were afflicted with the disease.

Ratios

Ratio

A numerical relationship shown by numbers such as 1 in 10.

Often we present relationships between numbers as a **ratio,** rather than as a percentage; consequently, you may find 10 percent and 1 in 10 used interchangeably. Twenty-five percent, similarly, is stated as 1 out of 4. Ratios are most helpful when the percentage is very small; for example, .000001 percent equals 1 case in 100,000. As a result, you'll be more effective if you say, "18 out of 100,000 teens died of gunshot injuries in 1989, up from the 12 per 100,000 recorded in 1979," than if you give the figures as percentages.

FIGURE 8.2 Seventy-nine percent of legal immigrants to the United States go to one of seven states.

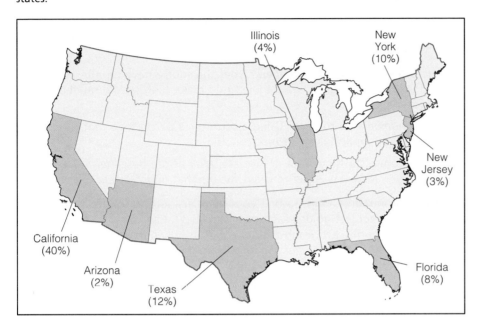

FIGURE 8.3 A table effectively depicts complex numerical data in a way that listeners can easily grasp.

Comparative Salaries of Child Care Workers

	Average for all men	Average for all women
College graduates	$51,804	$33,615
Some college	$33,161	$22,445
High school diploma	$27,865	$19,309
Highest paid child care worker	$15,488	

Use Visual Aids to Clarify Numerical Data

Because numerical data are sometimes difficult to understand, present them in visual form whenever you can. William Dakin, shown in the photograph on page 164, used stacks of paper to illustrate his point. The pictograph of Figure 8.1 and the map of Figure 8.2 are both visual aids. Figure 8.3 shows the value of a table to show complex numbers. Imagine trying to understand a speaker who simply says:

> Child care workers are underpaid. Men who graduate from college average more than $51,804 annually; women graduates average $33,615. Men who have some college earn an average of $33,161 compared to women in the same category who average $22,445. Even men with a high school diploma average $27,665 and women who have graduated from high school earn on the average $19,309. Compare all these salaries to the average of $15,488 that the highest paid child care workers earn.

Is your head spinning? Do you remember any of this data? Now, imagine that the speaker either gives you a handout or projects a transparency with Figure 8.3 on it. How are your responses different? In what ways does the visual enable you to grasp the material better?

You can see that different types of data call for different types of visual aids. Because visual aids are vital in American culture, this text devotes the entirety of Chapter 12 to the topic of creating and displaying visual materials.

Find Compelling Comparisons

Comparison or Analogy
Stating of similarities between two things.

We often learn new information or understand new ideas better if we can compare and contrast the new to something familiar. A **comparison or analogy** points out similarities between things: "The hail felt like a rain of golf balls" or "Her family is a circus and she's the clown." Put simply, we understand the unfamiliar better by finding points of comparison to something that's already in our experience. Comparisons can be literal or figurative.

Use Literal Analogies

Literal Analogies
Comparisons between two actual things that are alike in important ways.

When you compare things that are similar in important ways, you are using **literal analogies.** Political and military leaders who in 1999 debated U.S. military intervention in Serbia commonly used literal analogies in their rhetoric, as this example shows:

> Those who argued that the military should intervene, compared the dictator Slobodan Milosevic to Hitler and the "ethnic cleansing" of the Kosovo Muslims to the genocide of Jews, gypsies, and gays during the Holocaust.
>
> Opponents countered that Milosevic did not invade neighboring countries, nor did he have a plan to conquer Europe, so he was not comparable to Hitler. Also, the Holocaust killed millions, from Germany as well as from other countries, but Kosovo existed on a much smaller scale and essentially involved two ethnic groups that had longstanding historical conflicts.
>
> Opponents offered a competing analogy. Because Kosovo was part of Serbia, the war was really a civil war—more like Vietnam than the Third Reich. Involvement there would lead to another unwinnable quagmire that, like Vietnam, would require an American military presence for decades.

The *drama* of life, the *theater* of the mind, the statement "all the world's a stage"—these are all figurative analogies comparing life to dramatic productions. Can you identify other common examples? (Anita Cirulis)

Here's another example. In a classroom speech on the pros and cons of fetal-cell transplantation, Chris Patti showed how proponents on both sides of the controversial issue literally compare the dead fetus to other dead bodies:

> Supporters of transplantation believe that the fetus is essentially a cadaver. They reason that adult cadavers are used in research with the consent of their families. So why shouldn't fetal cadavers be used to develop more effective methods of treating debilitating diseases? John Robertson, a law professor at the University of Texas, says that the dead fetus is essentially an organ donor and that its usable organs should be used to treat horrible diseases.
>
> . . . Critics of fetal tissue research and transplantation believe that the fetus is essentially a victim. They ask, "Should we do harm so that good may come?" Their answer is no. Arthur Caplan, Director of the Center for Biomedical Ethics at the University of Minnesota, argues against using a victim to save the lives of others. "Society will not tolerate killing one life for another," he asserts.

Sometimes you will find that pointing out *differences*, or showing **contrasts** between a new concept and a more familiar one, is effective. For example, when Bett explained the Japanese educational system, she described its differences from schooling in the United States as well as its similarities. Andres explained lacrosse by contrasting it with the more familiar games of baseball and football.

Contrasts
Stating differences between two things.

Create Vivid Figurative Analogies

When you highlight similarities between otherwise *dissimilar* things, you're using **figurative analogies.** These analogies require your listeners to apply their imaginations and integrate

Figurative Analogies
Stated similarities between two otherwise dissimilar things; requires an imaginative connection.

likenesses between two otherwise different things or ideas. The rhetoric surrounding the Serbian conflict, for example, produced numerous figurative analogies alongside the literal ones. Milosevic was a *schoolyard bully* or a *thug; hawks* supported the war, but *doves* opposed it. The Serb forces had a *blueprint* for terror; the entire war was a *nightmare,* causing a *flood* of refugees. Each analogy framed the issue in a slightly different way.

In short, figurative analogies connect familiar images with those less known. Many Americans did not know much about Slobodan Milosevic or the situation in the Balkans, but they understood bullies and nightmares, blueprints and floods. Figurative analogies are effective only if the comparison makes sense to the audience.

STOP AND CHECK

Think Critically About Analogies

Evaluate your use of comparisons and contrasts by asking yourself these questions.

- To test literal analogies, make sure the two items are alike in essential details. For instance, you could mislead your audience by comparing the work of a police officer in Houston, Texas, to another in Sioux Falls, South Dakota. While they're alike in many ways, they are not fundamentally the same. Comparing the Houston officer to one in Los Angeles or Miami is more appropriate because all three operate in urban settings with diverse populations. Sioux Falls officers, on the other hand, have more in common with police officers in smaller cities in Michigan and Nebraska.

- To test figurative analogies, be sure the comparison is clear and makes sense. Can your listeners make the necessary connection of ideas?

- To learn more about both literal and figurative analogies, log on to your *InfoTrac College Edition* and do a subject search for analogies.

Summary

It is vital to support your ideas with evidence that listeners can understand so that they see reasons for your major ideas. Select facts, including definitions and descriptions, that you can verify in a number of sources. In addition, select facts that are up to date. Further, during your research, distinguish factual material from opinions and take care not to pass on distorted or incorrect materials.

Most listeners respond to examples, and using specific incidents as supporting material functions to make abstract concepts more concrete and relevant. In addition, illustrations help listeners identify emotionally with your topic by means of real or hypothetical, brief or extended, examples. To be effective, examples should be representative, sufficient in number, and plausible.

The use of quotations can enhance your credibility if you are not considered an expert on a topic. Directly quote or paraphrase the opinions of experts and lay or peer sources. In addition, quote cultural proverbs, written texts, and even words of wisdom from relatively unknown sources that your audience will accept as credible.

In a society that tends to be impressed by quantification, the judicious use of enumeration and statistics may increase your audience's acceptance of your ideas. However, be sure that your numerical support is understandable, up to date, and used in ways that do not create misleading impressions. Visual aids are often helpful in clarifying complex numerical data.

Finally, comparisons or analogies are an additional means of support. Literal analogies compare or contrast two actual things; figurative analogies compare two things that are generally considered different, but share one specific likeness. Both types add vividness to your speeches.

As you interweave facts, examples, numbers, testimony, and analogies, you give your listeners more reasons to accept the conclusions you present.

JAFFE CONNECTION

Key Terms

facts (142)
established facts (142)
define (142)
opinions (143)
describe (143)
examples (144)
real examples (145)
hypothetical examples (145)
extended examples (146)
direct quotation (148)
paraphrase (148)
expert (148)
peer or lay sources (149)

enumeration (151)
mean (152)
median (152)
mode (152)
percentages (153)
rate of increase (153)
rate of decrease (153)
ratio (154)
comparison or analogy (156)
literal analogies (156)
contrasts (157)
figurative analogies (157)

Access

**for Audio Flashcards
of Key Terms**

Application and Critical Thinking Questions

1. Bring to class a current edition of a newsmagazine or newspaper. With your classmates, choose an issue from the week's news. Collect and display information by dividing the chalk board into sections, one for each kind of evidence: facts, examples, quotations, numerical data, and analogies. Contribute information from your magazine or paper, cooperating with your classmates to fill the board. Evaluate the evidence using the tests presented in this chapter.

2. With a small group of your classmates, evaluate the effectiveness of the following pieces of evidence taken from student speeches. What kind (or kinds) of evidence does each excerpt represent? Is the evidence specific or vague? Does the speaker cite the source of the evidence adequately? Does it meet the tests for the type of evidence it represents?

A recent study showed that at least 3 out of 4 black children who were placed in white homes are as happy and have been successfully incorporated into their families and communities.

According to *The Natural History of Whales and Dolphins*, dolphins communicate through a system of whistles, clicks, rattles, and squeaks. These clicking sounds are not only used for navigation in the deep waters but they may also be used to convey messages. Pulsed squeaks can indicate distress, while buzzing clicks may indicate aggression.

As far as deaths [from killer bees] are concerned, Mexican officials report that only sixteen people have died in the last three years as a result of their stings. That number is similar to the number who die of shark bite. As one Texan put it, "The killer bee will be no more a threat to us than the rattlesnake."

According to New Jersey Congressman Frank Guarini, "American families play amusement ride roulette every time they go on an outing to an amusement park."

As reported by the *World Press Review Magazine*, the Japanese use of disposable chopsticks has resulted in the destruction of half of the hardwood forests in the Philippines and one-third of the forests in Indonesia. This trend will likely continue as long as the Japanese use 12 billion pairs of throwaway chopsticks a year, which is enough wood to build 12,000 average-sized family homes.

In 1988, fetal brain cells were implanted deep into the brain of a 52-year-old Parkinson's victim. Traditional treatments all failed this person. Now, he reports that his voice is much stronger, his mind is sharper and not confused, and he can walk without cane or crutches.

Internet Activities

■ Log on to your *InfoTrac College Edition* and do a simple search for the subject "African proverbs." Read one of the articles and summarize the importance of proverbs within a culture.

■ Do a PowerTrac search for the journal *Vital Speeches* on your *InfoTrac College Edition*. Read one of the speeches and identify the kinds of supporting materials the speaker uses. Evaluate the effectiveness of the strategies in gaining and keeping your attention. Where does your attention perk up? Where do you find yourself losing interest? How do you think the actual audience responded to the speech?

■ Do a PowerTrac search for a speech by Claire L. Gaudiani about the use of cultural wisdom as a way of supporting ideas. Read the speech and evaluate the impact of her suggestions.

Hot Links at the Public Speaking Resource Center

Public
Speaking
Resource
Center

The following links are maintained and can be accessed easily via Jaffe Connection at the Public Speaking Resource Center on the Wadsworth Communication Café web site at http://communication.wadsworth.com/publicspeaking/study.html

http://www.sru.edu/depts/artsci/ges/disco-4htm This site, supported by Slippery Rock University, is titled "Support Materials for Culture." Look on it for definitions, examples, facts, and the like related to cultural topics.

http://www.geocities.com/CapitonHill/senate/6970/ An excellent source for quotations, this continually updated site links to classic subjects such as "justice" and "friendship" as well as 21st century topics like "appreciating r & r."

http://www.bartleby.com/99/ Here you'll find *Bartlett's Familiar Quotations,* 9th edition.

http://www.ii.com/internet/faqs/ For FAQs (Frequently Asked Questions) and PIPs (Periodic Informational Postings), use links provided here to national and international information organized by category.

STUDENT SPEECH WITH COMMENTARY

What Is Real? Professional Wrestling and Children

by Terry Fredrickson

On May 27, 1999, while playing in their backyard, a seven-year-old Texas boy killed his three-year-old brother. The crime was so serious that police believed an adult had done it, according to Bill Wash of the Dallas Police department. When questioned, however, the seven-year-old stated, "I pushed him down." When asked why, he said, "I saw my heroes, Stone Cold Austin and the Undertaker [both pro wrestlers] do it on TV." The police asked him to demonstrate what he did, so the boy backed up ten feet, stuck out his arm at shoulder's length, and hit a life-sized doll at the neck, causing it to fall back and hit its head. The boy then jumped on the doll. The seven-year-old will not face criminal charges, but he was pretty shaken up because he had no intention of hurting his brother, said Bill Wash. This example shows how at least one child acted out the violence he saw on a televised wrestling program.

Today, I will argue that professional wrestling such as we see in the World Wrestling Federation (the WWF) and World Championship Wrestling (the WCW) is contributing to problems in today's society. We will first examine both social and physical problems that are worsened by professional wrestling, then we will look at possible solutions you and I can enact.

Whether we like it or not, pro wrestling is all around us. Wrestling is a collection of rock music, pyrotechnics, soap operas, and athleticism staged before a frenzied crowd. It has become the Number One show on cable TV, even outranking *Monday Night Football.* Its fifteen hours of weekly programming attract a whopping 35 million viewers. That's equivalent to the population of Canada and Norway combined. Wrestling has spawned two magazines, numerous videos and websites, T-shirts, action figures, and even a cologne. Wrestling is currently beamed to 120 countries and translated into 11 languages.

Pro wrestling is mostly programmed in the early evenings, allowing children to watch it before recommended bedtimes. Although WWF is rated PG 14, meaning that youth under the age of 14 should not view it, the WWF admits that a million viewers are 11 years old or younger. One example is ten-

Terry prepared this speech when he was on his college speech team. He begins with an extended example full of details that make it highly dramatic. He acknowledges that most young fans won't kill somebody, but physical harms can happen when naïve children emulate professional wrestlers.

Terry gains attention with a detailed horror story. Throughout he will demonstrate credibility by citing sources his audience respects. His vivid story involves listeners emotionally from the outset.

Here he states his claim and previews his points.

Combining vivid descriptions with numerical data, Terry builds a picture of the sport. He compares the number of viewers to a population his audience can grasp.

The facts in this section are followed by quotations from a fan and a physician—a layperson and an expert.

Enumeration is especially effective here. And the inclusion of an unexpected viewpoint—that of a wrestling superstar who says something negative about the sport—adds impact to the argument.

The details in these examples add emotional connecting points that make at least some audience members respond more negatively to the sport.

This factual description helps listeners understand how a particular wrestling move could be so harmful.

Most of Terry's solution section is factual. However, returning to the example of Jim Sabo and quoting his mother adds an element of psychological closure to the argument. Listeners briefly met Jim early in the speech, and they may have developed some questions about him. Adding to his story now may give them some answers.

year-old Jim Sabo, who has been a wrestling fan since he was two; he likes best "how they all get hurt." Fans like Jim alarm Dr. Howard Spivak, who chairs the American Academy of Pediatrics' task force on violence. "[Televised wrestling] shows are extremely inappropriate models for children," he says. Despite these concerns, no matter where we go or where we hide wrestling will be there influencing our youth.

Pro wrestling arguably contributes to social incivility. As *U.S. News* stated in an article, "Lords of The Ring," dated May 17, 1999, "Pro wrestling is filled with lewdness, simulated sex, prostitutes, and profanities." A recent study of 50 episodes done by researchers at Indiana University found 1,658 instances of grabbing or pointing to one's crotch, 157 instances of an obscene finger gesture, 128 episodes of simulated sexual activity, and 21 references to urination. Even WWF's superstar, Stone Cold Steve Austin, himself a father of two young daughters, admits, "I get a little turned off with some of the sexual overtones." In addition, professional wrestlers stereotype racial groups and gays, belittle and objectify women, and "bash" or yell crude remarks about opponents.

Pro wrestling harms some vulnerable youth physically. For example, a growing group of kids have formed what they call the Back Yard Wrestling Federation. They make rigs filled with nails and thumb tacks, then they portray their favorite wrestlers by hitting, jumping, body slamming, and even smashing light bulbs on one another's heads. In a Michigan newspaper, reporter Anthony Blunt tells a sickening story of backyard wrestling that turned deadly. On December 18, 1998, on the front lawn of his home in Port Austin, Michigan, Mark Moore an eighteen-year-old student, was fatally injured after being on the receiving end of a attempted Pile Driver by his friend Justin Tomis, age nineteen.

The Pile Driver works like this: Justin puts Mark's head between his legs; he then grabs Mark's legs, sits down and, using an up-and-down motion, pretends to drive Mark's head into the ground. While the move, known to wrestling fans across the world, is not done to cause injury to either man, it should never be attempted by those who have not been trained by a true professional. A dangerous move, in the hands of a novice, can be deadly. Moore's head slammed into the ground, injuring his spine and collapsing a lung; four hours later, he passed away. Justin did not come out of this unharmed; he suffered serious back injuries that will require him to wear a metal back brace for a long time. Once again, we see how some impressionable youth are mimicking what they see on television.

Some negative social effects can be minimized; in fact, you and I can act. Very simply, when we see pro wrestling on TV we should turn it off, because its income derives from viewership. We also need to let our cable representatives know that we support stricter ratings and later showings. Simply scheduling the broadcasts after most children's bedtimes would eliminate some very young viewers.

Most importantly, adults should sit down with children who watch pro wrestling and explain that it is not real life and wrestlers do not behave in ways we should behave. Jim Sabo's mother, Laurie, isn't so concerned about the violence. She believes her son knows it's all an act, but she confesses "I'm not happy with the nudity and swearing." By making sure that Jim knows wrestling violence is staged, and by explaining culturally appropriate ways to communicate, Laurie Sabo can at least help her son see the exaggerations that are typical in professional wrestling.

With all the violence and incivility in our society today, maybe it is time that we step back and realize that enough is enough. Pro wrestling is not just a multi-million-dollar TV show, it is also a source of influence that glamorizes violence and incivility. I hope after hearing my speech you realize that we can stand against negative messages being beamed to our youth. We can make it our solemn responsibility to do a Pile Driver on the harmful effects that professional wrestling has on impressionable young people.

Using the Pile Driver as a figurative analogy is a nice way to close this speech.

9

Organizing Your Speech

This chapter will help you:

- Organize your main points

- Identify and use a number of linear patterns, including topical, chronological, spatial, causal, problem-solution, and pro-con

- Identify and use more holistic, alternative patterns when they are appropriate, including the wave, the spiral, and the star

"Desaparecides Pero no Olvidados"
©1999 by Carlos Madriz, Josh Short, and Mabel Negrette

You have now chosen and carefully focused your topic. Even so, your research produced so much information that you feel overwhelmed. How do you sort through the facts and statistics, the quotations and analogies, to make an understandable speech—one that hangs together with a number of main points that have some sort of logical connection? Good speakers find ways to organize their thoughts and present their ideas in patterns that their listeners can follow and remember. Otherwise, they frustrate their listeners, as Heidi and Gail point out:

> If an audience is confused or overwhelmed with disarrayed information, not only is the speech difficult to understand but the whole underlying credibility of the rhetoric is diminished.
>
> *Heidi*

> Organization is *everything*. . . . I consider it being kind to your audience as well as yourself.
>
> *Gail*

Guidelines for organization fall into what the Romans called the *canon of disposition*. This chapter begins with general tips for identifying and organizing main points, moves on to explain some linear organizational patterns, and concludes with holistic, alternative methods of arranging the body of your speech.

Organize Your Main Points

Although the body is the middle part of your speech, it is the part that you plan first. As you collected information, you probably identified a number of subcategories such as causes or proposed solutions, or a chronological time line in which events occurred. Identifying these patterns can help you determine major points and focus supporting materials under each one. At the outset, consider the following general tips for organizing main points.

Limit the Number of Points You Use

Cognitive psychologists tell us we learn better when we portion blocks of information into 3–7 major units (which explains why your telephone number is divided into 3- and 4-digit segments). Consequently, your listeners will be better able to remember your speech if you develop a limited number of main ideas: most instructors recommend 3–5 points.

At this point in your preparation, return to the central idea you developed in Chapter 5. If you clearly identified the direction of your speech, you can now begin to flesh it out. For instance, Maria DiMaggio wanted to convince her classmates that the lottery winners are often unhappy, and people who want to be wealthy are better off spending their money elsewhere. So she initially set out this central idea:

> The lottery is a form of gambling that often leads to unhappiness.

During the research process, Maria's material seemed to cluster into three major points: (1) the lottery itself—its history, profitability, (2) the problems winners encounter, and (3) alternatives to buying lottery tickets. So she revised her central idea to read:

> The lottery, a form of gambling, raises money for good causes; however, winning often creates enormous problems for the winners, and they would be better off spending their money elsewhere.

Her major points are now easy to identify:

I. Lotteries are a form of gambling that raise money for good causes.

II. Lottery winners often have enormous problems as a result of winning.

III. Most people would be happier if they found an alternative to playing the lottery.

Support Each Point with Evidence

Chapter 8 described numerous ways to support the major ideas of a speech, among them facts, examples, quotations, numerical information, and analogies. At this stage, Maria sat down with her photocopied articles about lottery winners and arranged specific pieces of data under each main point. Here's an example of her first major point:

I. Lotteries are a form of gambling that raise money for good causes.

    A. *Webster's Dictionary* identifies the lottery as a popular form of gambling.

        1. Winners pay to participate, generally by purchasing tickets at a uniform price.

        2. Winners are determined by chance.

    B. Lotteries generate revenues for good causes.

        1. The earliest lottery, organized in London in 1680, raised money for a municipal water supply.

        2. A French lottery helped pay for the Statue of Liberty.

        3. Lotteries helped support the Jamestown Colony and the American Revolution.

        4. They provided funds for Harvard, Princeton, and Dartmouth.

        5. Current lotteries in New Hampshire and Oregon, among other states, provide educational funding.

Order Your Points Effectively

For some topics, the ordering of points flows logically. Obviously, starting with an explanation of lotteries in general, moving to the problems that winners encounter, and suggesting alternatives is more logically satisfying to Maria's audience than if she were to suggest alternatives, discuss the problems, then explain what lotteries are. For other speeches, the natural flow is less obvious. A topic such as saving money at the supermarket might have the following organization:

I. Saving in the produce department

II. Saving on meat

III. Saving money on bakery items

IV. Saving on the cereal aisle

No logical reason dictates that produce must come first and cereal last. In fact, the speaker might start with cereal (the breakfast food) then move to bakery, meat, and produce. Or he might move from the least expensive to the most costly, depending on the audience. If he were describing a market where everyone shopped, he could follow the progression a typical shopper makes on a typical trip. With these principles in mind, you can now choose from a number of organizational patterns that will best work for your speech.

Traditional Patterns

From listening to speakers throughout the years, you have developed some schema for organizational patterns. Some patterns work especially well for presenting facts and information; others are better for persuasive messages (see Chapter 17). This section presents six traditional patterns that can help you organize a wide variety of topics: topical, chronological, spatial, causal, problem-solution, and pro-con.

Topical Organization

The most widely used organizational pattern classifies major points into topics or subdivisions, each of which is part of the whole. Although every point contributes to an overall understanding of the subject, the points themselves do not have to occur in any particular order. For instance, Mary Lee used the following **topical arrangement** for her classroom speech on paralegal careers:

> A person can take three different routes in order to work in a paralegal career.
>
> I. Many colleges and universities offer the associate degree program.
>
> II. Another option is a four-year program.
>
> III. Nondegree certificate programs provide a third way to enter this career.

Mary could easily have presented her ideas in a different order. Indeed, another speaker might begin with the nondegree certificate route and end with the four-year program.

Topical Arrangement

A pattern that divides a subject into subtopics, each of which is part of the whole.

Chronological Organization

A second way to organize materials is to relate your points to one another in a **chronological pattern** in which the sequencing—what comes first and what follows—must occur in a given order. Because this pattern develops an idea as it transpires over a period of time, chronological organization is useful in biographical speeches, those that recount historical events, and those that explain processes, stages, or cycles.

It stands to reason that a biographical speech is often developed chronologically because an individual's life unfolds across a period of years. Here is a sketch of the main points of a speech about a person's life, organized chronologically:

> Mahatma Gandhi was a hero in the nonviolence movement.
>
> I. His early life in South Africa
>
> II. His public career teaching nonviolence
>
> III. His subsequent assassination

Chronological organizational patterns also function effectively when you describe historical events:

> The Civil War cost more lives than any other war.
>
> I. Events preceding the war
>
> II. The war years
>
> III. Reconstruction of the South

Process speeches generally feature a chronological pattern. In such a speech, a sequence of steps or stages follow one another in fairly predictable patterns. You might speak about natural as well as social processes. This skeleton outline shows the chronological organization of a natural process.

> The death of a star
>
> I. The star's early years
>
> II. One thousand years before its death

Chronological Organization

A pattern that presents points by time or sequence.

Process Speech

A speech that describes a sequence of steps or stages that follow one another in a fairly predictable pattern.

This speaker is creating a PowerPoint visual that lists the main points for a topical speech about five types of touch. (Anne Dowie)

III. The final year

IV. The star's collapse

V. One year later

Many social, psychological, or personal processes also occur in patterned sequences or cycles. Here is the way one student organized her speech on grief:

Five stages are typical in the grief process.

I. First is a period of denial.

II. Anger follows.

III. This is replaced by bargaining.

IV. Depression follows.

V. Finally, there is acceptance.

The key to chronological speeches is that events *must* occur in a sequence and follow a clear "first, next, finally" pattern. In a disease, for instance, symptoms follow rather than precede infection with a virus. Occasionally, however, speakers vary the pattern by beginning with the final point before showing the events that led up to it. For instance, the speaker could first describe Gandhi's assassination, then flashback and provide details from his early life and his career that led up to his murder.

Spatial Organization

You can also organize the points of your speech spatially by place or location. The **spatial pattern** is less common than some of the others, but it is good for speeches about places or about objects that are made up of several parts. For example, a guide showing a group how to use the campus library probably will provide a map and describe what is located on each floor. Beginning with the ground floor, she works her way up to higher floors. If you were to describe the effects of alcohol on the human body, you might move from the brain downward to the heart and other organs. The order in

Spatial Pattern
Presents points by place or location.

A spatial pattern is useful for organizing speeches about places such as Italy. Start at the top and move to the heel, then conclude at the toe of the Italian "boot." (Source: NRSC Science Library/Photo Researchers Inc.)

which you present your points doesn't matter with some topics, as this speech outline (which is divided geographically) demonstrates:

Major global earthquake areas

I. Eastern European fault lines

II. The Pacific "Ring of Fire"

III. The Rift Valley in Africa

Objects that you describe from top to bottom, bottom to top, or side to side lend themselves well to spatial organization. For example, because dams are constructed in layers, Bryant explained the process of dam building by beginning with the bottom layer and moving to the top of the dam. Similarly, exercise instructors often begin with head and neck exercises and work down the body spatially.

Causal Organization

Cause-Effect Pattern

Presents reasons (causes) and implications (effects) of a topic.

Because they have learned Euro-American thought patterns, people in the U.S. culture tend to look for causes that underlie events. For this reason, you might choose a **cause-effect pattern** to discuss problems by examining the reasons underlying the problem (the causes) and the implications it has for individuals or for society at large (the

effects). There are two basic causal organizational patterns: cause-to-effect and effect-to-cause. Here is a cause-to-effect outline for a speech on amusement park tragedies:

Amusement park tragedies injure thousands of people annually.

I. Causes

    A. Equipment failure

    B. Operator failure

    C. Rider behavior

II. Effects

    A. Personal risks

    B. Needless tragedies

Conversely, you can first look at the effects a problem has on an individual or group, then explore the causes of the problem. This is an effects-to-cause organization pattern.

The lack of available organs for donation affects many people in our society, and there are many reasons for this shortage.

I. Effects

    A. Scarcity of organs

    B. Length of waiting lists

    C. Deaths due to scarcity

II. Causes of organ scarcity

    A. Potential donor's fears

    B. The family's fears

    C. Health care provider's fears

Problem-Solution Organization

In line with their core beliefs that life presents a series of problems to be solved, people in the United States often approach global and national issues, as well as personal problems, as challenges to understand and solved through knowledge and effort. (Some cultures, in contrast, believe it is futile to fight fate.) Thus, a **problem-solution** organizational **pattern** is common among speakers in the United States. Not surprisingly, if you choose this pattern, you first look at the problem—sometimes examining its causes and effects—then propose solutions. Here is an example of an outline for an informative speech on elder abuse:

Problem-Solution Pattern
Describes a problem and a possible solution(s) to it.

Elder abuse is a social problem in the United States.

I. Elder abuse is an increasing problem.

    A. Causes of the problem

    B. Effects of the problem

II. Several solutions have been proposed.

    A. Day care for adults

    B. Support groups

    C. Senior advocates

Some speakers choose to present problem-solution approaches to personal as well as national or global topics. This outline shows the major points in a speech about a personal issue:

Hair loss affects millions of people.

  I. Women as well as men experience hair loss.

    A. Causes of the problem

    B. Effects of the problem

  II. There are several solutions on the market.

    A. Medications

    B. Hairpieces

    C. Bonding techniques

    D. Transplants

When the purpose of your speech is informative, introduce your listeners to a variety of solutions. In persuasive speeches, however, it is most effective to propose several solutions, then focus on the one solution you believe should be implemented. Chapter 17 returns to the problem-solution pattern and explains additional organizational plans commonly used for persuasive speeches.

Pro-Con Organization

Pro-Con Arrangement
Presents arguments in favor of and arguments against an issue.

In this culture, speakers and audiences commonly explore arguments both for and against controversial issues. If you give a speech that summarizes both sides of an issue, you may find **pro-con arrangement** to be useful. Classify all the arguments in favor of the issue under the pro label, then list the arguments against it under the con label. Here is an example of a pro-con organization:

The Hawaiian sovereignty movement has both proponents and opponents.

  I. Arguments in favor of an independent nation of Hawaii

    A. The 1989 annexation was illegal because the Senate never approved it.

    B. Promises made in the 1920s to return lands to Native Hawaiians have not yet been kept.

    C. The 1959 statehood vote is meaningless because independence was not a ballot option.

    D. In 1993, President Clinton apologized for the illegal overthrow of 1898.

  II. Arguments against an independent nation of Hawaii

    A. Most residents of Hawaii are not Hawaiian natives.

    B. Changing the current legal, economic, political, and military systems would be difficult.

    C. Other less drastic, solutions would solve the problems.

This organizational pattern works best in informative speeches, when your purpose is to enlighten people on the nature of an issue. By presenting both sides, your listeners can weigh the evidence and evaluate the arguments for themselves. When your purpose is persuasive (you are advocating acceptance of one set of arguments rather than another), you generally will choose a different pattern. Chapter 17 further examines persuasive techniques.

The major points of a speech on sovereignty for the Hawaiian Islands can be organized in a number of ways, including pro-con, topical, chronological, and spatial. (Ronen Zilberman/ Associated Press)

Choosing the Best Traditional Pattern

Because you can develop the same topic in a number of ways, choose the organizational pattern that best works, given your purposes and your supporting materials. For instance, in addition to the pro-con outline about Hawaiian sovereignty, just presented, other patterns would effectively organize an informative speech on the subject:

Topical: Supporters of sovereignty fall into three general categories.

   I. Independence, with international recognition as a sovereign nation

  II. Nation-within-a-nation status, similar to Native American tribes in the United States

 III. Status quo, but with reparations and full control of Hawaiian trust assets granted to Native Hawaiians

Chronological: The Hawaiian Sovereignty movement gained supporters during the 1990s.

   I. In the early 1990s, a few people supported Hawaiian sovereignty.

  II. In November 1993, President Clinton apologized for the U.S. treatment of Hawaii.

 III. In 1994, the Ohana Council members, led by "Bumpy" Kanahele, declared Hawaiian independence.

 IV. In August 1998, Native Hawaiians and supporters held an Aloha March in Washington, DC.

  V. In 1999, a sovereignty convention was held.

Spatial: Four Hawaiian regions are so different that each one would experience sovereignty uniquely.

   I. Ceded lands include 1.5 million acres of crown lands.

  II. Two hundred thousand acres were promised to homesteaders in the 1920s.

 III. Some islands have been purchased and developed by individuals such as Bill Gates.

 IV. Some islands have been developed for tourism and other industries.

STOP AND CHECK

Selecting Traditional Patterns

Identify the organizational pattern for the following main points on topics related to dogs. You can complete this activity online under Chapter 4: Activities for Jaffe Connection at the Public Speaking Resource Center, http//communication.wadsworth.com/publicspeaking.html

I. Drawings of greyhounds appear on Egyptian tomb art.

II. In the Middle Ages greyhounds became the dogs associated with nobility.

III. In the twentieth century, greyhound racing generates millions of dollars for racetracks.

Organizational pattern: _____

I. Hounds

II. Working dogs

III. Toy or miniature dogs

IV. Terriers

Organizational pattern: _____

I. Injured greyhounds or those too slow to race were killed by the thousands.

II. Greyhound adoption programs were developed to save these dogs.

Organizational pattern: _____

I. A number of dog breeds were developed in China.

II. Several dog breeds developed in Africa.

III. Mexico is the source for two breeds.

Organizational pattern: _____

Alternative Patterns

In addition to the traditional patterns usually taught in public speaking classes, researchers are looking at other organizational patterns commonly used by women and ethnic speakers. For example, Cheryl Jorgensen-Earp (1993) is exploring a number of alternative patterns that women have used historically. She argues that many speakers are uncomfortable with the standard organizational patterns due to cultural backgrounds or personal inclinations. As alternatives, she proposes several less direct and more **organic patterns** that provide a clear structure for a speech but have a less linear form. Jorgensen-Earp uses diagrams or pictures to describe these patterns, comparing them to a wave, a spiral, and a star (Zediker, 1993).

The Wave Pattern

This pattern, illustrated in Figure 9.1, consists of repetitions and variations of themes and ideas. Major points come at the crests of the waves. You follow each crest with a variety of examples leading up to another crest, then repeat the theme or make another major point. Use one of two types of conclusions: Either wind down and lead the audience gradually from your topic, or make a transition, then rebuild, so that your final statement is a dramatic peak. African Americans, as well as women, often use the **wave pattern** in speeches.

Perhaps the most famous wave-pattern speech is Martin Luther King, Jr.'s "I Have a Dream." King used this memorable line as the crest of a wave that he followed with

Organic Pattern

Alternative pattern that provides a clear speech structure in a less linear form.

Wave Pattern

A repetitive pattern that presents variations of themes and ideas with major points presented at the crest.

FIGURE 9.1   The wave pattern.

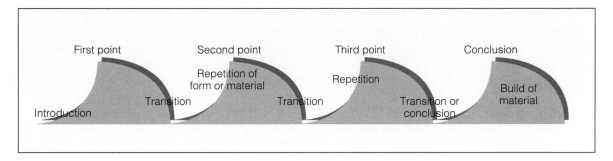

examples of what he saw in his dream; then he repeated the line. He concluded with a dramatic peak that emerged from the final wave in the speech—repetition and variation on the phrase "Let freedom ring." An excerpt from Sojourner Truth's "Ain't I a Woman?" speech illustrates this pattern:

> That man over there says that women need to be helped into carriages, and lifted over ditches, and to have the best place everywhere. Nobody ever helps me into carriages, or over mud-puddles, or gives me any best place!
>
> And ain't I a woman?
>
> Look at me! Look at my arm! I have ploughed and planted, and gathered into barns, and no man could head me!
>
> And ain't I a woman?
>
> I could work as much and eat as much as a man—when I could get it—and bear the lash as well!
>
> And ain't I a woman?
>
> I have borne thirteen children, and seen them most all sold off to slavery, and when I cried out with my mother's grief, none but Jesus heard me!
>
> And ain't I a woman?

One African-American student used the following outline to introduce a classmate. Who is this man?

    A. Example of his accomplishments

    B. Example of personal characteristics

Who is this man?

    A. Additional information about his accomplishments

    B. Another example of personal characteristics

Who is this man? . . . He's . . . [our classmate]!

In short, between the major points of your speech, use a barrage of specific and general examples that illustrate and support your main ideas. Employ repetition and variation throughout. Although the examples in this section repeat a phrase, this is not a requirement. You can use the repetitive style by stating main points that differ from one another. (For an example of this type of repetition, go to the appendix and read the excerpt from Elizabeth Cady Stanton's "The Solitude of Self.")

The Spiral Pattern

Shanna was asked to talk to high school students about selecting a college. She decided to create a hypothetical student, Todd, and have him appear in three scenarios, each

Spiral Pattern
Repetitive pattern with a series of points that increase in drama or intensity.

one costing more money and taking him further from home. She visualized a **spiral pattern,** illustrated in Figure 9.2, as she framed her speech. First, she described his choices and experiences at a local community college. Next, she sent Todd out of town but kept him at a public institution within the state. Finally, she placed Todd at a private university across the continent from his hometown. Because each major scenario was more difficult or more dramatic than the preceding one, her speech depicted Todd moving from smaller to larger adjustments. Figure 9.3 illustrates how she might write out her points in spiral form.

The spiral pattern is often useful for speeches on controversial topics that build in dramatic intensity. Euthanasia is one example. A series of narratives might revolve around a hypothetical character named Jake who suffers from painful terminal cancer. In the first scenario, Jake dies peacefully in hospice care where he is heavily sedated at the end. In the second, he is given less medication with the result that he suffers a great deal. In the final scenario, his physician and members of his family assist him in committing suicide. Each scene builds in tension, with the most controversial scenario reserved for the final spiral.

Star Pattern
Presents relatively equally weighted speech points within a thematic circle that binds them together; order of points may vary.

DIVERSITY IN PRACTICE

Speaking in Madagascar

In many areas of the world, speakers choose patterns markedly different from those presented in this text. For instance, elders in the Merina tribe of Madagascar use a four-part organizational pattern when they speak (Bloch, 1975):

1. First is a period of excuses in which the speaker expresses his humility and reluctance to speak. He uses standard phrases such as "I am a child, a younger brother, . . . " He sometimes relates well-known stories and proverbs.

2. He follows this by thanking the authorities for letting him speak at all. He uses a formula that thanks God, the president of the republic, government ministers, the village headman, major elders, and finally the people in the audience.

3. In the third section, he uses proverbs, illustrations, and short poems as he makes his proposal.

4. He closes by thanking and blessing his listeners.

The Star Pattern

Each point in a **star pattern** speech, illustrated in Figure 9.4, is more or less equally weighted within a theme that ties the whole together. You might use this variation on the topical pattern if you were to present the same basic speech to a number of audiences. By visualizing your major points as a star, you have the flexibility of choosing where to start and what to emphasize, depending on what's relevant for a specific audience. To illustrate, you might begin with a point your audience understands or agrees with, then progressively move to points that challenge their understanding and agreement. For inattentive audiences, begin with your most dramatic point. For hostile audiences, begin with your most conciliatory point. This pattern has the advantage of allowing you to make audience adaptations quickly and still have your speech work effectively.

There are two ways to develop the points of the speech. First, state the point, support or develop it, then provide a transition to the next point; or develop each point fully and then state it. Base your decisions on the type of audience and the nature of your various points.

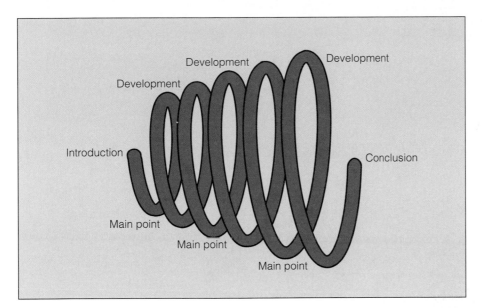

FIGURE 9.2 The spiral pattern.

FIGURE 9.3 The spiral pattern helps Shanna organize her points to show Todd's progress through increasingly dramatic situations.

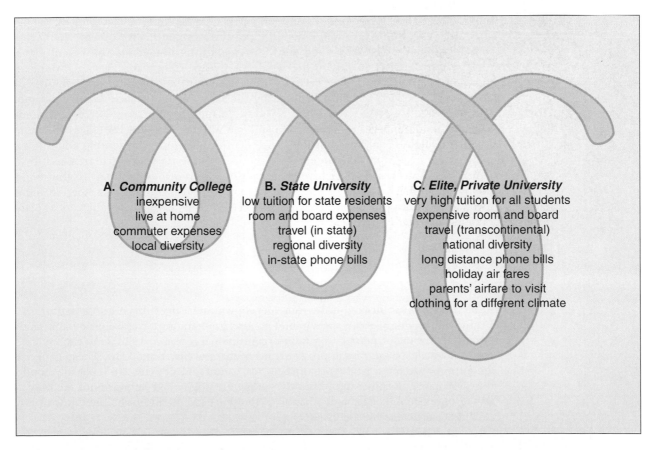

A. *Community College*
inexpensive
live at home
commuter expenses
local diversity

B. *State University*
low tuition for state residents
room and board expenses
travel (in state)
regional diversity
in-state phone bills

C. *Elite, Private University*
very high tuition for all students
expensive room and board
travel (transcontinental)
national diversity
long distance phone bills
holiday air fares
parents' airfare to visit
clothing for a different climate

FIGURE 9.4   The star pattern.

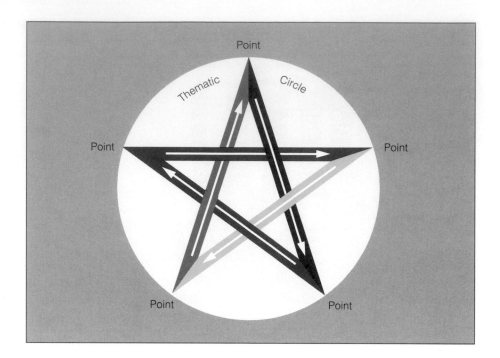

The final element in the pattern is a thematic circle that binds all your points together. By the close of the speech, your listeners should feel that the circle is completed and the theme is fulfilled. For instance, Jan presents seminars on investment management using the general theme of financial security, with points on retirement plans, medical insurance, growth investments, and global funds. With some audiences, she begins with retirement plans and ends with global investments; with others, she begins with growth and global funds and ends with medical insurance and retirement plans.

The star pattern is common during election years. Candidates share the underlying theme "Vote for me!" Furthermore, they stake out their position on a number of different issues. However, instead of giving the same "stump speech" to every group, they order the issues and target specific points to specific audiences. For soccer moms a candidate might begin with education and end with crime issues; for elders, the same candidate might begin by discussing social security and end by presenting educational policies. Figure 9.5 provides an example. Think of these repetition patterns as a form that is common in songs. Each verse provides a different development of the song's theme, while the lyrics are repeated exactly unchanged in the chorus. Keep in mind throughout your preparation that these patterns require as much organizational planning as the other more linear formats.

Summary

After you gather information for your speech, you must organize it into a pattern. Begin with the body of the speech, and choose from among several linear patterns to organize your major points. Common organizational frameworks include the topical, chronological, spatial, causal, pro-con, and problem-solution patterns. These patterns are appropriate for several types of speeches; causal and pro-con are especially good for informative purposes. However, the six patterns discussed here are not the only way to organize materials, and Chapter 17 presents several additional methods typically used in persuasive speeches.

FIGURE 9.5 This candidate visualizes her speeches as points of a star that is enclosed in the overall theme "Vote for me." When she addresses soccer moms, she begins with her education point. She chooses the balanced budget point when she talks to the Rotary Club.

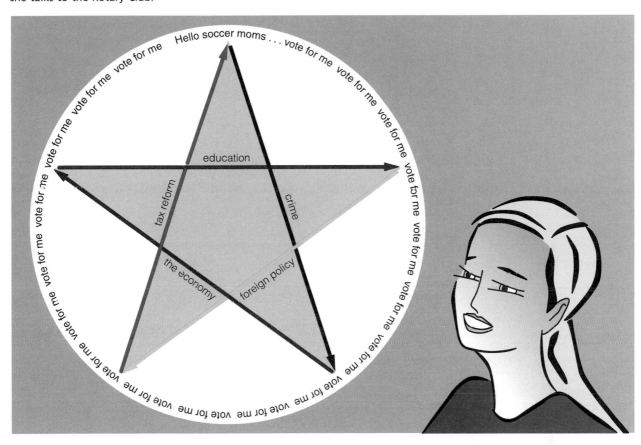

Furthermore, nonlinear patterns are typical in diverse settings, as the example from Madagascar and the alternative patterns show. Women and ethnic speakers, for example, commonly select holistic or organic patterns such as the repetitive wave or the spiral. Speakers who want flexible points within a major theme pattern may represent their ideas in the form of a star. Regardless of the pattern, traditional or alternative, you must carefully identify your main points and then develop them with supporting materials.

JAFFE CONNECTION

Key Terms

topical arrangement (168)
chronological pattern (168)
process speech (168)
spatial pattern (169)
cause-effect pattern (170)
problem-solution pattern (171)

pro-con arrangement (172)
organic pattern (174)
wave pattern (174)
spiral pattern (176)
star pattern (176)

Access

**for Audio Flashcards
of Key Terms**

Application and Critical Thinking Questions

1. Outline a speech given by one of your classmates. Is the organizational pattern easy to discern? What suggestions, if any, could you give the speaker about organizing the body of the speech?

2. Read or listen to a recording of a speech by an African-American speaker such as Vernon Jordan, Malcolm X, or Martin Luther King, Jr. (The speeches of Malcolm X can be found in his autobiography.) What basic organizational pattern does the speaker use? Can you find examples of the wave pattern within the speech?

3. To understand the wave pattern, read the excerpt and analysis of Elizabeth Cady Stanton's speech "The Solitude of Self" in the Appendix. Discuss your insights with a small group of your classmates.

4. With a small group of your classmates, take a topic such as abortion, divorce, alcohol on campus, or immigration and organize major points in as many of the following patterns as you can: topical, chronological, spatial, cause-effect, pro-con, problem-solution, spiral pattern.

5. Take the theme of creativity or the theme of perseverance. Then work with two or three classmates and discuss how you might create a speech organized around the wave, the spiral, or the star pattern. *Hint:* think of three famous people who persevered . . . each one in a more dramatic way. Or use examples from your school's sports teams, your personal lives, lives of entertainers, and so on.

Internet Activities

■ Use your *InfoTrac College Edition* to do a PowerTrac search for the journal *Vital Speeches*. Read several speeches and identify each speaker's main points and his or her organizational pattern.

■ Use the exact phrase option on http://www.alltheweb.com to search for "I have a dream." How many hits do you get? Read the script of Martin Luther King Jr.'s speech, making a list of all the wave "crests" you identify in it. Discuss your findings with your classmates.

■ "I have a dream" has inspired foundations and organizations as well as individuals. Using the hits you just found in the preceding activity, follow a link to a foundation or organization that is dedicated to living out the dream of racial reconciliation in the United States.

■ Isabella Baumfree, better known as Sojourner Truth, was similar to Martin Luther King, Jr. in that she, too, created a phrase that has become a familiar cultural allusion. Look up the exact phrase "Sojourner Truth" on www.alltheweb.com. Read about her life. Then look up "Ain't I a woman?" and note how many hits you get. (The sheer number shows the power of public speaking to influence a culture.) Follow a link that interests you.

Hot Links at the Public Speaking Resource Center

Public Speaking Resource Center

The following links are maintained and can be accessed easily via Jaffe Connection at the Public Speaking Resource Center on the Wadsworth Communication Café web site at http://communication.wadsworth.com/publicspeaking/study.html

http://web.utk.edu/~gwynne/organizing.html This great website reinforces the importance of organization. It was developed by Robert Gwynne, of the department of speech communication at the University of Tennessee, Knoxville. It defines and briefly discusses different types of organization. Professor Gwynne provides a number of questions you can ask yourself as you choose the most appropriate organizational pattern.

http://www.ukans.edu/cwis/units/coms2/vpa/vpa6.htm For a brief review of the six traditional speech organization patterns, visit this site.

STUDENT OUTLINE

You Have My Deepest Sympathy: You Just Won the Lottery *by Maria DiMaggio*

General Purpose:	To persuade
Specific Purpose:	To persuade my audience that winning the lottery is not as great as it's perceived to be and that they should invest their money in alternative ways.
Central Idea:	The lottery, a form of gambling, raises money for good causes; however, winning often creates enormous problems for the winners, and they would be better off spending their money elsewhere.

Introduction

I. You have my deepest sympathy; you just won the lottery.

II. Most of us would be shocked if someone said we'd won $20 million, then offered us condolences; however, hundreds of lotto winners have discovered the downside of winning big.

III. I used to think I'd be the happiest person in Brooklyn if I could just win a million dollars, but my research about lottery winners convinced me to spend my money elsewhere—and I hope you'll follow my example.

IV. Today, I'll explain what the lottery is, then describe various problems that winners face, and point out alternatives if you really want to spend money foolishly.

Body

I. Lotteries are a form of gambling that raise money for good causes.

   A. *Webster's Dictionary* identifies the lottery as a popular form of gambling.

   B. Winners pay to participate, generally by purchasing tickets at a uniform price.

   C. Winners are determined by chance.

II. Lotteries generate revenues for good causes.

   A. The earliest lottery, organized in London in 1680, raised money for a municipal water supply.

   B. A French lottery helped pay for the Statue of Liberty.

   C. Lotteries helped support the Jamestown Colony and the American Revolutionary War.

  D. They provided funds for Harvard, Princeton, and Dartmouth.

  E. Current lotteries in New Hampshire and Oregon, among other states, provide educational funding.

III. Unexpected problems arise for lotto winners.

  A. Their dreams of instant riches are not fulfilled.

   1. Money is given out over 20 to 25 years.

   2. A lotto "millionaire" gets about $50,000 annually—before taxes, delinquent taxes, past-due child support, and student loans are taken out.

   3. Winners who run short on cash cannot draw from their winnings.

   4. They cannot use their winnings as collateral to get a loan.

   5. They cannot liquidate their future winnings.

  B. Many suffer personal loss and rejection.

   1. William Post won $16.2 million but watched his brother go to jail, convicted of hiring a hit man to kill William.

   2. Debbie won $6.85 million but lost her sisters, who stopped speaking to her when she declined to pay their debts.

   3. Bernice took a day off work to claim her $1 million; her job was given to someone else.

   4. Daisy won $2.8 million but went through a painful lawsuit.

    (a) Her son's friend sued for half the winnings because she asked the friend to pray that she'd win.

    (b) He prayed, she won, so he thought he was entitled to some of her money.

    (c) The court ruled against him, saying he couldn't prove his prayers caused her to win.

  C. Lotto winnings don't necessarily bring happiness.

   1. A study of people with the best of luck and those with the worst of luck supported this conclusion.

   2. Accident victims weren't as unhappy as expected; however, lottery winners were more unhappy and took less pleasure in life than expected.

  D. Heaven help the heirs if a lotto-winning relative dies and leaves them a fortune.

   1. They must immediately pay estate taxes on the unpaid total, with monthly penalties added after nine months.

   2. Taxes on a $20 million lotto inheritance are more than $5 million.

IV. If you have extra money, you could spend it in far more profitable ways.

  A. Invest in the stock market.

  B. Donate your extra money to a charitable organization and claim a tax deduction.

  C. Indulge yourself: buy cable, eat lobster once in a while, buy season tickets to a sporting or a cultural event, get an exotic pet.

   D. If you like to think your lotto money supports education, you can donate to my college fund!

Conclusion

    I. I hope I've convinced you that playing the lotto is not all it's advertised to be.

   II. I've explained what the lottery is, the problems it can cause, and some alternative ways to get rid of money.

  III. So the next time you see a new lotto multimillionaire, consider sending your sympathies rather than your congratulations.

10

Beginning and Ending
Your Speech

This chapter will help you:

■ Develop an introduction for
your speech that gains
attention, motivates the
audience to listen,
establishes your credibility,
and previews the speech

■ Develop a conclusion that
signals the end,
summarizes, provides
psychological closure, and
ends with impact

■ Link the parts of the
speech to one another
through skillful use of
connectives such as
signposts and transitions,
internal previews and
internal summaries

"The Chant of the Earth, The Voice of
the Land" ©1991 by Betsie Miller-Kusz

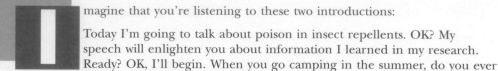

Imagine that you're listening to these two introductions:

> Today I'm going to talk about poison in insect repellents. OK? My speech will enlighten you about information I learned in my research. Ready? OK, I'll begin. When you go camping in the summer, do you ever slather your body with an insect repellent? . . .

> It's dangerous, it smells bad, and the National Capital Poison Center or the NCPC reports that last year 5,000 people were poisoned from it. And people living in the Midwest have developed a ritual before going out-of-doors. Before leaving the safety of the inside world, they must slather their body with it. It's a chemical called DEET found in popular insect repellents (Reynolds, 1995–1996).

Stop for a moment and think of the impression each speaker has created at the outset. How do you feel about being "enlightened"? Which introduction gains your attention? Arouses your curiosity? Which speaker seems more prepared? Which is more credible?

This chapter will help you lead your listeners skillfully into your subject and, at the end, conclude in a way that summarizes your thoughts and leaves a memorable impression. You will also learn how to connect your ideas to one another and to the speech as a whole.

Plan Your Introduction

After you have planned the body of your speech, then work on your introduction. As Chapter 2 pointed out, the Roman educator Quintilian (1920, 1922) identified four purposes for an introduction:

1. To draw the listeners' attention to the topic
2. To motivate them to listen
3. To establish yourself as knowledgeable about the topic
4. To preview the major ideas of the speech

In addition, remember to include the essential definitions or background information that listeners need in order to understand your subject. By including these elements in your introduction, you'll answer four basic listener questions up front: What's this all about? Why should I listen? Why should I listen to you? What will you be covering? Figure 10.1 depicts the function of the introduction as a way to answer these listener questions. We will look at each question in this section.

Gain Attention

Gaining attention is the first step in the listening process, so you must immediately answer your listeners' question, What's this speech about? Introduce your topic in a creative way. Some speakers—students as well as professionals—simply announce their subject like this: "Today, my speech is about polar bears." Although this does introduce the topic, it's not very creative; good speakers often choose more effective techniques. Here are a few strategies for introductions that will be discussed in this section.

- Ask a question.
- Provide a vivid description.
- Begin with a quotation.
- Use an audio or visual aid.
- Tell a joke or funny story.

FIGURE 10.1 The introduction functions to answer these four questions that your listeners have.

- Refer to a current event.
- Begin with an example.
- Start with startling numbers.

Ask a Question

Choose either a rhetorical or a participatory question. **Rhetorical questions** are the kind listeners answer in their mind; **participatory questions,** in contrast, call for an overt response, such as a show of hands or a verbal answer. A professional speaker used this rhetorical question with an interesting twist to open his speech, "Overworked Americans or Overwhelmed Americans? You Cannot Handle Everything" (Davidson, 1993).

Here is a multiple-choice question. Which word best describes the typical working American today:

A. Overworked

B. Underworked

C. Energetic

D. Lazy

Rhetorical Questions
The kind of questions that listeners answer in their minds.

Participatory Questions:
Questions that listeners answer overtly.

> Although much has been written of late as to whether A, B, C, or D is correct, the most appropriate answer may well be, "None of the above." . . . The best answer may well be that the majority of Americans are overwhelmed.

The audience responds internally to this rhetorical question by thinking of their own work-related experiences. Moreover, because they've encountered multiple-choice questions in their schooling, listeners may find the famous "None of the above" option amusing.

In contrast, sometimes you want a visible response from your listeners. If so, you must make it clear that you want them to respond physically. For instance, ask for a show of hands or call on a member of the audience to answer a question you pose, as Mary Beth demonstrates:

> Where do you think the following situations take place? Every person who leaves the house must carry a rifle. Every house has at least one gun easily accessible. No one leaves home after dark unless it is an emergency.
> [Pause—ask one or two people to venture an answer.]
> No, it's not Harlem or Bedford-Stuyvesant, but a quaint Arctic town in Canada called Churchill, Manitoba. And what these people fear is the polar bear.

For a question to capture the audience's attention, however, it must be sufficiently intriguing. Here are three examples of ineffective questions that came from actual speeches: The first is too broad; the second too specific; the third too unusual to relate to most people.

> How many of you have ever purchased an album, cassette, or compact disk?
> Have you ever had your finger almost sliced off and left hanging by a small piece of skin?
> Have you ever visited a harem?

Both types of questions, rhetorical and participatory, help establish dialogue between speakers and listeners because they invite audience response, whether mental or physical.

Provide a Vivid Description

Draw your audience's attention to your subject by describing a scene in such vivid language that your listeners are compelled to visualize it mentally. The scene can be either real or imaginary. Here is Danae's opening for her classroom speech on arachnophobia.

> Imagine yourself just hanging out one morning, minding your own business, when a large, monstrous body, fifty times your size, casually approaches you then, suddenly, lets out a blood curdling scream, hurls a giant bowl your way, and takes off running. Sound familiar? It would if you were the little spider that had the misfortune of getting just a little too close to Little Miss Muffet of nursery rhyme fame. I venture to say that we all have had to deal with spiders at some time in our lives. They seem to be everywhere, especially at this time of year. What causes this Muffet-type reaction? It just may be arachnophobia—the irrational fear of spiders.

Begin with a Quotation

You can often gain listener attention with a quotation or a familiar cultural proverb. These quotations or adages can be about a subject or, in the case of a biographical speech, by the subject. Choose a saying that encapsulates your overall theme and cite its source. For example, this professor began his commencement address with the following quotation (Foster, 1999):

> "He who exercises government by means of his virtue may be compared to the north polar star, which keeps its place and all the stars turn towards it." These words, from *The Analects of Confucius*, should have the status of received truth for those who serve in government—especially in a representative democracy such as ours, where ideally the best of us govern the rest of us.

Bob's speech on computerized drums, which you'll find at the end of Chapter 13, opens with a line from a cartoon character.

> According to a record producer in the cartoon strip Doonesbury, "Drummers are extinct."

Quotations can also come from song lyrics or poems. Or they may originate in family sayings or in memorable words spoken by someone such as a high school soccer coach. For instance, for a speech on perseverance, one such opening might be "My grandmother used to say, 'It's a great life if you don't weaken.'"

Use an Audio or Visual Aid

You can use posters, charts, tape recordings, and other visual and audio materials successfully in drawing attention to your topic. If you like humor, consider using an overhead projector or in-focus machine to display a relevant cartoon that you've transferred to a transparency or scanned onto a computer disk. For instance, you could begin a speech on buying a car by displaying a large poster of an automobile. Mary played seven seconds of a tape recording of sounds made by humpback whales and then began her speech.

> What do you think makes this gentle sound? Do you think of a fifty-foot-long, four-ton giant? Well, the source of this sound is just that: a humpback whale.

Draw listeners' attention to your topic at the outset of your speech. One effective attention-gaining strategy is to use a visual aid. (Bonnie Kamin/courtesy The Lindsay Museum)

Tell a Joke or Funny Story

Professional speakers often begin by telling a joke that creates an informal, humorous atmosphere at the outset of the speech. You may tell jokes and funny stories successfully; however, you may also embarrass yourself by beginning with a joke that flops. Make sure your joke relates to the topic of your speech. Otherwise, although you are gaining attention, you are not drawing it to your subject. The following riddle could be used to begin a speech on learning a second language:

> You know the word for a person who knows three languages? It's trilingual.
> What's the word for a person who knows two languages? Right, it's bilingual.
> What do you call a person who knows only one language?
> The correct answer is, "an American!"

Although most of the students in the rest of the world gain a measure of proficiency in English as well as in their own languages, most students who graduate from high schools in the United States know only English.

Refer to a Current Event

To identify with your listeners and establish common ground, you can refer to well-known current happenings—airplane crashes, campus controversies, well-publicized trials, elections, and the like. For example, this professional speaker began his commencement address during the middle of the investigation of President Clinton (Eckenhoff, 1998); he referred to the scandal humorously:

> . . . I wish to speak to you today on something few believe still exists, particularly in Washington, DC—character and the need to build it. The character I'm referring to is the ABLE character. . . . Now, I well realize that inviting someone from Washington, DC, to talk about character may flabbergast some of you, as the interior space of the Washington beltway is rarely associated with people building abled characters. But I hope that, in spite of my Washington mailing address, you will seriously consider my comments on character and I hope they may provide some utility in your lives.

 This speech or another that begins with a reference to a current event is available through your *InfoTrac College Edition.* Do a PowerTrac search for the journal *Vital Speeches.*

Begin with an Example

As Chapter 8 pointed out, examples provide your listeners with the opportunity to become emotionally involved with your topic. Everyone likes a good story, and when we hear of real people involved in real situations, we generally become more attentive. One speaker (Farmer, 1999) used this extended example in his introduction to a speech about the Internet.

> You may have heard the stunning story of the Russian sailor who had to practice telemedicine—on himself. This sailor was participating in a race in South Africa. He was alone in his boat when he became injured, with a major infection on his elbow. In true Internet style, he communicated his symptoms through satellite e-mail to an emergency room doctor in Boston. The Boston doctor became very alarmed, concerned that the sailor was in imminent danger. So he guided the sailor—via satellite e-mail—through surgery that the sailor performed on himself. He drained his abscess, stopped his bleeding, managed to survive all of this and then, for good measure, he won the race.

Start with Startling Numbers

Numbers and statistics can be dry; however, they can also capture and hold your listeners' attention if they are shocking enough or if they are put into an understandable context, as this example illustrates:

> Look at your watch. Before the hour is over, approximately 3,000 puppies and kittens will have been born—a supply that greatly exceeds the demand! The result is that nearly eight million unwanted animals must be euthanized annually.

Although this is not an exhaustive list of successful openings for speeches, it provides you with examples of openings commonly used by public speakers in a variety of settings. The purpose of an introduction is not simply to gain attention; it must draw attention *to your topic*. One student ignored this rule and slapped the podium loudly; when listeners jumped to attention, he said, "Now that I have your attention, I am going to talk about animal overpopulation." His introduction failed because, even though it attracted attention, it was not relevant to his subject.

Give Your Audience a Reason to Listen

Once you have your listeners' attention, it is important to answer their question, Why should I listen to this speech? You may think your topic is important and interesting, but your listeners may see it as boring or irrelevant. Jill faced this challenge when she came from Hawaii to study at Oregon State University; there she gave a speech on Hawaiian sovereignty. Most OSU students had never heard of the controversy about returning Hawaii to Hawaiian rule, and the issue was remote from their everyday lives. Jill met this challenge by relating to her Oregon audience as follows:

> Although you may not be aware of the issue of Hawaiian sovereignty, you may someday vote on whether or not to allow Hawaiians to again be a sovereign nation instead of a state.

You can frame your topic within a larger issue; for instance, caller ID is a privacy issue, and elder abuse is part of a nationwide problem of violence against the helpless. A speech on polar bears does not directly relate to listeners in most classrooms; however, treatment of polar bears is connected to larger issues such as animal rights and animal overpopulation. Here's one way to relate this topic to an urban audience.

> At this point, you may be curious about polar bears, but you may not think much about them. After all, the only polar bears in New York are in the zoo. However, the problem with polar bears in Canada is similar to problems here on Long Island with a deer population that is getting out of control. What do we do with animals that live close to humans?

One of the important characteristics of humans is their ability to learn new things. And at times, you give speeches to increase your audience's knowledge or to satisfy their curiosity. For instance, few people in the classroom will ever encounter a shark; however, many students have misconceptions about sharks due to their notoriety in the media. Joe appealed to his classmates' need to have more accurate information about sharks.

> I'm guessing that most people in this room share this basic opinion of sharks—that they are voracious man-eaters. This way of thinking is really incorrect, and is basically supported by overexaggerated films you may have seen and sensationalistic stories you may have read.

Organizational Culture
The way of life of a specific organization that includes its history, traditions, heroes, folklore, vocabulary, rituals, and ways of doing things.

DIVERSITY IN PRACTICE

Considering Organizational Culture

Chapter 1 pointed out that culture includes both the visible, stated aspects of a group's way of life as well as the more embedded beliefs and assumptions that guide group members. The concept of **organizational culture** extends this definition to recognize that organizations and institutions also have histories, traditions, hierarchies, rituals, folklore, and so on that make them function as small cultures within the larger society. Insiders know the group's way of life; newcomers must learn it. For example, Microsoft differs from IBM; St. John's University (Catholic sponsored) is unlike George Fox University (Quaker sponsored) in many ways.

Whenever you speak within an organization, learn as much as you can about its culture before you create your speech—even expectations for introductions can differ in specific settings. Today, for example, was graduation day at my university, and a business leader from the community gave the commencement address. She did not start with a statistic, a visual aid, or any other attention strategy mentioned in this chapter; instead, she first referred to the occasion, congratulated the graduates, and expressed respect for the university—acknowledging both the organization and the cultural event (graduation) before introducing the topic of her speech. It would have seemed abrupt and strange to the graduates and their families on this special occasion if she had launched into her speech immediately.

To see how speakers adapt their introductions to specific organizations, go to your library and look at several issues of the journal *Vital Speeches of the Day* or log on to your *InfoTrac College Edition* and do a PowerTrac search for the journal *Vital Speeches.* Read the brief summary given for each speech and select three or four talks given by a guest speaker at a ritual event. Read the introductions to see if and how the speaker recognizes elements of the organization's culture in opening remarks.

Many issues that don't seem to directly impact your listeners may actually affect their pocketbooks, whether or not they know it. National issues that rely on tax dollars for support are in this category—issues such as public radio and television, weapon development, and Medicare. Chapter 18 provides more details about some of the needs, wants, emotions, and values that motivate people to listen to speeches.

Establish Your Credibility

After you have the audience's attention and have given them a reason to listen to your topic, give them a reason to listen to you by linking yourself to your topic. Typically, you do this by briefly sharing your subject-related experiences, interests, and research findings. Mention your major, courses you have taken, television shows that first interested you, and so on. Joe linked himself to sharks through his personal experiences.

I first became interested in sharks when I was about twelve years old, and I was fishing at my uncle's house in the Florida Keys. There, for the first time, I encountered a shark in the wild. At first I experienced the normal anxiety people

Audiences recognize Mark Klaas's credibility when he speaks about crimes against children; his daughter Polly was kidnapped and brutally murdered. However, your listeners won't know your qualifications, so you'll have to explain your link to the topic. (Olivier Laud/Liaison Intl.)

feel when they see a shark almost the size of the boat, but as I observed it further, my fascination grew. Since then, I have been snorkeling many years, and I have seen sharks from underwater as well.

In a speech on the glass ceiling, the invisible barrier that prevents women and minorities from rising to the top in organizations, Victoria, an American of Chinese descent, linked herself to the topic in this way:

> I became interested in this topic when I read an article about Charlotte Beers, a woman who broke through the barrier to become the first woman to hold a top position in a multibillion-dollar advertising agency. I realized that this is the barrier I have personally encountered in a variety of managerial positions I have held at various firms.

Establishing your credibility is optional if another person introduces you and connects you with the topic or if your expertise is well established. However, even professionals who speak on topics outside their area would do well to link themselves with the topic. Let's say an engineer is speaking at a school board meeting about adoption of a districtwide sex education program. Her experiences as a parent are more salient in this context than her engineering expertise.

Preview Your Ideas

You may have heard the old saying, "Tell them what you're going to say; say it; then tell them what you said." The **preview** serves the first of these functions. It is the short statement you make as the transition between the introduction and the body of your speech in which you state some form of your central idea. Heidi explains the importance of a preview for listeners.

> It obviously helps to have an idea of where the speaker is headed. The preview provides a brief synopsis of what key points will be expanded upon. The speech then should continue in the order first declared.
>
> *Heidi*

Preview

The transition from the introduction to the body of the speech in which you state the central idea in some form.

DIVERSITY IN PRACTICE

A Navajo (Diné) Speech Introduction

Not all cultural groups begin their speeches by first gaining attention, next relating to audience interests, then establishing their credibility. Speakers at Diné Community College (formerly Navajo Community College) first answer the listeners' question, "Who are you and what's your clan affiliation?" Students thus begin their classroom speeches by telling their names (who they are) and identifying their clan affiliation (knowing this helps listeners understand the roots of their life). Until this personal, identifying information is shared, neither the speakers nor their listeners can feel at home (Braithwaite, 1997).

Here are three student previews that alert each audience to the speaker's organizational pattern. Previews like these aid listeners who are taking notes or outlining the talk.

Today I will show you that the reputation given the shark is based on stereotypes and misinformation and that we harm sharks more than they harm us.

Today, we'll explore specific ways that sleep deprivation affects our personal, relational, and occupational lives.

Let's now explore the wonderful world of Golden Seal Root by looking at what it is and how it is both used and misused.

In short, a good introduction draws attention to your topic, relates the subject to your listeners, links you to the subject, and previews your major ideas.

STOP AND CHECK

Create an Interesting Introduction

Select one or two of the following central ideas. Then work with a classmate to create an introduction that answers the four questions your listeners ask regarding any subject. You can also write these introductions online and email them to your classmates. Look for this activity under Chapter 10: Activities for Jaffe Connection at the Public Speaking Resource Center, http://communication.wadsworth.com/publicspeaking.html

Public Speaking Resource Center

- Arachnophobia, the irrational fear of spiders, has three major causes and two basic treatments.

- The five stages typical of the grief process are denial, anger, bargaining, depression, and acceptance.

- Elder abuse is an increasing problem in our society, but several solutions have been proposed.

- Many women, as well as men, experience hair loss, and they look to medications, hairpieces, bonding techniques, and transplants to solve the problem.

- You can save money at the supermarket on produce, meat, cereal, and bakery items.

■ Thousands of students default on federal student loans every year, leaving taxpayers with their school tabs.

The listener's questions are:

1. What's this about? Identify several strategies to gain attention to the topics you choose. Which do you think are more effective?

2. Why should I listen? How could you relate the topics to audience interests or experiences?

3. Why should I listen to you? How might a speaker establish credibility on each subject?

4. What will you be covering? How would you preview the main ideas of each topic you choose?

To learn more about different ways to begin a speech, log onto the Internet and go to http://www.gallaudet.edu/~engwweb/writing/introconslu.html. There you'll find one topic (deaf education) with several different opening options. Review the Introductions of the speakers featured on Jaffe Speech Interactive. Do the introductions fulfill the criteria described above?

Jaffe Speech
Interactive

Conclude with Impact

Your conclusion gives your audience a final impression of both you and your topic. This is the time to provide closure through a summary and a satisfying or challenging closing statement without adding new information. Appearing disorganized at the end can negate the positive impressions your audience held during the speech. Like the introduction, the conclusion has several important functions: to signal the end, to summarize the main points, to provide psychological closure often by a reference to the introduction, and to end with an impact.

Signal the Ending

Just as your preview provides a transition to the speech body, your signal makes the audience aware that you're concluding. Both beginning speakers and professionals use common phrases such as "In conclusion" or "Finally." However, Jen's transition is more creative.

> We now know that when we feel the need to escape from our world and enter into the zones of biting insects, dousing ourselves with DEET is not providing us with the protection it promises.

Don't overlook nonverbal actions as a way to signal to your conclusion. For instance, pause and shift your posture or take a step away from the podium. You may also slow down a bit and speak more softly. Combining both verbal and nonverbal transitions generally works well.

Review Your Main Ideas

Briefly summarizing or recapping your main points fulfills the "Tell them what you said" axiom, as the following reviews or summaries illustrate:

> We've explored ways that sleep deprivation affects us in three areas: in our personal lives, in our relationships, and in our workplaces.

I hope you have a better understanding of what Golden Seal Root is and how it can be used both effectively and ineffectively.

In contrast, Joe combined his transition statement with his summary:

Now that we have looked at the shark as it really is [transition phrase] maybe you now realize that its reputation is really inaccurate and that humans present a greater threat to the shark than sharks present to humans [restatement of the central idea].

Provide Psychological Closure

Looping back to something from your introduction—which one writing professor calls an "echo"—provides your audience with a sense of psychological closure. Here's the professor's explanation:

The echo is the inside joke of writing [or, in our case, speaking]. By repeating or suggesting a previous detail—a description, word, question, quote, topic or whatever—you make a point with that which is already familiar to your [audience]. It's a way of putting your arm around the [audience member] and sharing a bit of information that only the two of you can appreciate.

 Read this short article for yourself by logging on to the Internet and searching www.alltheweb.com for the exact phrase "Echo in introductions and conclusions." Look in your introduction for something that you could finalize here at the end. For instance, if you began with an example, complete it in the conclusion. Or, refer back to startling statistics or to quotations you presented in the opening. Here are some examples:

The inhabitants of Churchill, Manitoba, aren't wrong to fear the polar bears who wander into their towns, but carrying rifles may not be the best way to protect themselves against this already endangered species.

Five thousand needless deaths can be eliminated each year if people understand the dangers of DEET and protect themselves against its harmful effects.

Look at your watch again. In the seven minutes that I've spoken, more than 350 unwanted animals have entered the world only to face short lives and often painful deaths.

End Memorably

Finally, plan to leave a positive and memorable impression. During the few minutes you speak, audience members are focusing their attention on your subject. When you finish, however, each listener will return to his or her thoughts, moving away from the mental images you co-created throughout the speech. So end with impact by choosing some of the same types of material you used to gain attention in the beginning:

- End with humor.
- Ask a thought-provoking question.
- Use a quotation.
- Issue a challenge.
- Tie the subject to a larger cultural theme or value.

In summary, a good conclusion provides a transition to your conclusion, summarizes your major points, gains psychological closure, and finishes with a thought-provoking closing statement.

Using appropriate humor in your conclusion is one way to leave a favorable impression. (Paula Lerner/Woodfin Camp & Associates).

Public Speaking Resource Center

STOP AND CHECK

Evaluating Introductions and Conclusions

Here you'll find an introduction and conclusion for two different speeches. Read through each set, then answer the questions that follow it. You can complete this activity online under Chapter 10: Activities for Jaffe Connection at the Public Speaking Resource Center, http://communication.wadsworth.com/publicspeaking.html

Introduction: Six of the ten leading causes of death among Americans are diet related: heart disease, cancer, stroke, and diabetes mellitus, as stated by the *Vegetarian Times* magazine. Everyone here would like to live a healthy life, right? Today, I will explain the advantages of being a vegetarian to your health and to the environment.

Conclusion: Because I have this information, I have reduced my consumption of meat lately, and I ask you to do the same thing. Being a vegetarian is not that bad; you're improving your health and, at the same time, saving the environment. Don't forget, once you're old and suffering from a heart ailment or cancer, it will be too late. Take precautions now.

■ Does this introduction make you want to hear this speech? Why or why not?

■ How does he gain attention?

■ How does he relate to the audience? Is this effective?

■ Do you think he is a credible speaker on the topic?

■ Could you write a brief outline of his major points from his preview?

■ Is his conclusion as effective as his introduction? Why or why not?

Introduction: What is the easiest way to raise $125,000 for research for Multiple Sclerosis? That's right. Swim 1,550 miles down the Mississippi River like Nick Irons did. Nick, a 25-year-old, swam the murky waters of the Mississippi to raise money to research a disease his father has. Many people would think this was a crazy thing to do, because they don't know about the disease. Only one in ten George Fox students surveyed had the slightest idea of what MS was. My dad has had MS for eight years, and I really didn't know a lot about the disease until I researched it and found out a lot more than I expected. Since most people are unclear about MS, I will first define the disease, describe some of its effects, and tell you what is known about the cause, the cure, and the medications that are currently used.

Conclusion: In conclusion, little is known about the causes and cures of MS. It is a disease that attacks the central nervous system, impairing many senses. Next time you question why a person swam over 1,000 miles down a dirty river, make sure you know why and have a clear understanding of the cause. A lot is being done to find a cure for this debilitating disease. It will be found.

- What would you say is the most effective part of her introduction?

- What's the most effective element of her conclusion?

- Which is better: her introduction or her conclusion? Why? What improvements, if any, would you suggest she make?

To investigate this topic further, log onto the Internet and go to the site http://www.dc.peachnet.edu/~drobinso/students/concl.html. There you'll find a number of introductions and conclusions taken from student essays. Each one is followed by evaluative comments from other students in the class. Although this exercise was created for a writing class, you'll find insightful critiques that will help you evaluate your speech introductions and conclusions.

Jaffe Speech
Interactive

Review the conclusions of the Persuasive, Informative, and Narrrative Speeches featured on Jaffe Speech Interactive. Do the speakers signal the ending of the speech, review their main ideas, provide psychological closure, and end memorably?

Connect Your Ideas

After you plan the speech body and formulate the introduction and conclusion, you'll add the final touches to polish your speech. These are **connectives**—the words, phrases, and sentences that lead from one idea to another and tie the various parts of the speech together smoothly. They function as tendons or ligaments that hold your speech together and help your listeners keep their place as you talk. The most common types of connectives are signposts, transitions, internal previews, and internal summaries.

Signposts and Transitions

Signposts are similar to signs along a highway—those markers that help drivers know how far they've come and how far they must go. In much the same way, speech signposts help your listeners orient themselves to their place in your speech. Words such as *first, next,* and *finally* introduce new points and let your listeners sense the flow of your ideas. Other phrases that help your speech flow include *most importantly, in fact,* and *for example.* Here are some examples:

First, sleep deprivation affects your life in general.

The final step occurs when the case is submitted to the judge for a decision.

Connectives

Words, phrases, and sentences you use to lead from one idea to another and tie the various parts of the speech together smoothly.

Signposts

Simple connectives such as first, next, and finally that help listeners keep their place in your speeches.

On the other hand, the computer does have a lot of things going for it.

In addition, brain wave patterns can be measured and analyzed.

Transitions summarize where you have been and where you are going in the speech. You can use them both between points and within a single point. Here are some simple transitions *between* major points:

> We have seen the major arguments for dental implants [where you've been]; now let's turn to the arguments that opponents make against this type of dental work [where you're going].

> The problem, as you can see, is a complex one because both the people and the polar bears need protection [a summary of the last point]; however, two solutions have been proposed [a preview of the next main idea].

Transitions can also lead from subpoint to subpoint *within* a major point. For example, Tamara's major point, "There are several causes of amusement park tragedies," has three subpoints: equipment failure, operator failure, and rider behavior. After she describes the first two causes, she transitions to the final one by saying:

> While both equipment and operator failure cause accidents [first and second subpoint], a number of tragedies are additionally caused by rider behavior [third subpoint].

Here's another example. Jenny's speech about Golden Seal Root (GSR) has as one of its major points: People use GSR both internally and externally. She first describes the internal uses, then transitions to the second use by saying,

> Not only do people use Golden Seal Root internally [first use], they also apply the herb externally [lead-in to second use].

Internal Previews and Internal Summaries

Internal previews occur within the body of your speech, and briefly summarize the subpoints that you will develop under a major point. For instance, Tamara could say:

> Experts agree that there are three main causes of amusement park tragedies: equipment failure, operator failure, and rider behavior.

This internal preview helps her audience see the framework she'll use as she develops her major idea related to causes of accidents.

If you summarize subpoints after you've made them but before you move to another major point, you're using an **internal summary.** Thus, Tamara could have summarized her section on causes before moving on to the effects of amusement park accidents in this way:

> In short, we have seen that equipment failure, operator failure, and rider behavior combine to create thousands of tragedies annually.

After she finished discussing the uses of Golden Seal Root, Jenny could have summarized her entire point by saying:

> In summary, people use GRS both internally and externally.

Connectives, then, are words, phrases, and complete sentences you'll use to connect your ideas to one another and to your speech as a whole. They serve to introduce your points, to preview and summarize material within a point, and to help your listeners keep their place in your speech.

Transitions
Summaries of where you've been and where you're going in your speech.

Internal Previews
Brief summaries within the speech that foretell the subpoints you'll develop under a major point.

Internal Summary
Restatements of the ideas within a subpoint in the body of your speech.

Summary

After you've organized the body of your speech, plan an introduction that will take your listeners from their various internal mental worlds and move them into the world of your speech. Do this by gaining their attention, relating your topic to their concerns, establishing your credibility on the subject, and previewing your main points. Finally, plan a conclusion that provides a transition from the body, summarizes your major points, gives a sense of closure by referring back to the introduction, and leaves your listeners with a challenge or memorable saying. Throughout your speech, use connectives to weave your points and subpoints into a coherent whole.

JAFFE CONNECTION

Key Terms

Access

for Audio Flashcards of Key Terms

rhetorical questions (187)
participatory questions (187)
organizational culture (192)
preview (193)
connectives (198)

signposts (198)
transitions (199)
internal previews (199)
internal summary (199)

Application and Critical Thinking Questions

1. Before your next speech, trade outlines with others in your class. Use the guidelines in this chapter to evaluate your classmates' introductions, conclusions, and connectives—advising them on what you like and what you think they could improve. When you get your outline and suggestions back, make adjustments that would improve these sections of your speech.

2. Outline a speech given by one of your classmates. Evaluate the effectiveness of the introduction and conclusion. What suggestions, if any, would you give the speaker to improve the beginning or the ending?

3. Go back to Chapter 6 and review the section on credibility—what your audience thinks of you. How and why does a good introduction and conclusion affect audience perception of you? How and why does a poor start or finish influence their perception?

Internet Activities

1. Log onto your *InfoTrac College Edition* and do a PowerTrac Search for the journal *Vital Speeches*. Find three different speeches with interesting titles. Read each one and evaluate the effectiveness of the introduction by using criteria developed in this chapter.

2. Read the conclusions of the same speeches you studied in the previous exercise. Evaluate the conclusion using the criteria in the text. Does the speaker provide a

transition? Review the major points? Provide psychological closure? End memorably? What changes, if any, would you make that would improve the conclusion?

3. To see an example of an effective introduction, log on to your *InfoTrac College Edition* and use your PowerTrac skills to search for a speech by John Ramsay that's titled, "At home with books: Reading is fundamental." It's in *Vital Speeches* for March 15, 1999, vol. 65, no. 11.4.

4. Log onto the Internet and use the search engine www.alltheweb.com to search for the exact phrase "introductions and conclusions." You should find many sites that were created by both writing and speech instructors. Go to one of the sites for writers and compare and contrast the guidelines for writers with those for speakers that you find in this text. What are the similarities? The differences? How do you account for these differences?

5. Using the same search engine, search for "connectives." You may get over a thousand hits; some describe writing; others relate to computer programming. Look at a couple of the sites related to speaking or writing for ideas of ways to connect your ideas effectively.

Hot Links at the Public Speaking Resource Center

The following links are maintained and can be accessed easily via Jaffe Connection at the Public Speaking Resource Center on the Wadsworth Communication Café website at http://communication.wadsworth.com/publicspeaking/study.html.

http://saturn.atc.fhda.edu/instructor/cgreene/logical.html This interesting site provides examples of ways that connectives help link your ideas logically.

http://webpage.pace.edu/bmorris/will/clarity.htm This web page reviews material in Chapters 9 and 10. Follow the links to Introductions and Conclusions for examples and cautions regarding various beginning and ending strategies.

Public Speaking Resource Center

STUDENT OUTLINE WITH COMMENTARY

Peter Ilich Tchaikovsky *by Jennifer Gingerich*

General Purpose: To inform
Specific Purpose: To inform my audience about some of Peter Tchaikovsky's background and musical accomplishments.
Central Idea: Tchaikovsky was a great Russian composer who was, and is still, given much credit as a musician.

Introduction

I. Some of you may recognize this music [*The Nutcracker Suite*].

   A. If you do, go ahead and raise your hands as soon as you recognize it. [Play the recording.]

   B. [See how many recognize the music, and give an appropriate response.]

   C. You may have recognized the music as *The Nutcracker,* but do you know the composer—Peter Ilich Tchaikovsky, who was born in 1840?

In her introduction, Jennifer relates to her audience after she establishes her credibility. What do you think of the effectiveness of this? How well does her overall introduction fulfill the functions of a successful opening?

II. I first became interested in Tchaikovsky when I was a little girl.

    A. I heard the Portland Symphony perform the *1812 Overture* with live cannons.

    B. I grew up listening to works by Tchaikovsky, such as *The Nutcracker Suite* and his *1812 Overture.*

    C. I even played some of his music on my violin in orchestra class.

    D. The more I heard Tchaikovsky's music, the more I liked it, and he soon became my favorite composer.

III. Tchaikovsky even has distant connections to Goshen College!

    A. All of us have heard his music.

    B. Even more importantly, Tchaikovsky visited the United States a little over 107 years ago and performed in a place where some Goshen students will soon perform.

IV. Today I will share some things I've learned about Tchaikovsky including his background, his lasting works, and his concert that opened Carnegie Hall.

Body

I. First of all, Tchaikovsky was destined to be a musician.

    A. Peter had many musical talents as a young boy.

        1. He made up tunes and plunked them out on the piano.

        2. His mother taught him to play waltzes.

        3. Not only did he play tunes, he also tapped out rhythms.

    B. Although he showed talent, his destiny was not obvious to everyone, because at age 10 his father sent him to law school.

        1. Law was a stable and profitable career.

        2. In contrast, musicians led hard lives during that time.

    C. Tchaikovsky left law school at age 19 because his passion for music was too strong.

        1. In her 1942 biography, *Stormy Victory,* Claire Purdy quotes Tchaikovsky as saying, "My musical talent—you cannot deny it—is my only one."

        2. Because music was both his talent and passion, Tchaikovsky decided to focus solely on developing his musical gifts.

II. Composing full time was a wise career choice, for Peter Ilich Tchaikovsky began to write outstanding compositions that gained him lasting national and international adoration.

    A. Tchaikovsky was well loved in Russia for his talent.

    B. *The Nutcracker* is performed every Christmas to this day.

    C. In their 1940 book, *Living Biographies of Great Composers,* authors Henry and Dana Lee Thomas state that Tchaikovsky's music " . . . translates him into an entirely different world . . . in which he can . . . become an . . . instrument in the hands of a higher power."

III. Lastly, Tchaikovsky's talents were such that he was invited to conduct his works at the opening of Carnegie Hall.

Underline all the connectives you can find in the body of this outline. (Remember that an outline is not the same as a speech text. It's only the framework or skeleton that she'll elaborate on.) Jennifer builds connectives in her outlines so that her points hold together and her speech flows from point to point.

A. The *New York Times* article, "Music Notes," written on February 22, 1891, announced that Tchaikovsky was to open Carnegie Hall; the author added, "This Russian is one of the strongest composers of our time, and his appearance here will be a musical event of much importance."

B. According to the 1979 book *The Music Makers*, edited by Victor Stevenson, Tchaikovsky toured America, creating a musical sensation.

With all the information storage technology available today, Jennifer can actually locate and read newspaper articles that are more than 100 years old.

Conclusion

I. In conclusion, Tchaikovsky was a great composer who was destined to be a musician and who wrote great works that gained him a lasting recognition.

II. Tchaikovsky came to this country to open the great music hall that our own Goshen College Chamber Choir will be performing in on March 28.

III. I hope that I have helped you today to see the influence this wonderful composer has had on my life and the lives of many around the world.

Identify the ways this conclusion signals the end and reviews the main points. How effectively does she create psychological closure? What other ending choices could she have made? For example, what if she turned on *The Nutcracker Suite* as soon as she said "In conclusion," then played it softly throughout the rest of the speech?

References

Purdy, C. L. (1942). *Stormy victory: The story of Tchaikovsky*. New York: Julian Messner, Inc.

Stegmeister, E. (1973). *The new music lovers handbook*. New York: Harvey House, Inc.

Stevenson, V. (Ed.) (1979). *The music makers*. New York: Harry N. Abrams.

Thomas, H., & Thomas, D. L. (1940). *Living biographies of great composers*. Garden City, NY: Halcyon House.

Musical notes. (1891, February 22). *The New York Times*, 13.

11

Putting It All Together:

Outlining Your Speech

This chapter will help you:

- Outline the contents of your speech in a linear form

- Prepare note cards or a speaking outline

- Record your ideas in a more organic pattern

"Family Life and The Spirit of Mankind"
©1977 by Susan Kelk Cervantes.

When asked to create a formal outline, some students say, "Why should I write an outline? I'm preparing a speech, not writing an essay."

An outline is a requirement most instructors ask of their students. You've already done most of the work for creating an outline. That is, you've researched your topic (Chapter 7), selected supporting materials (Chapter 8) and identified ways to organize the body, introduction, and conclusion of your speech (Chapters 9 and 10). You've already seen the value of clearly identified points, each one supported by carefully chosen data. In fact, you may have already made a **rough draft outline** of your main points and supporting materials. This chapter will help you tie together all your efforts from preceding chapters and finish up a formal outline that will function as the framework or skeleton for your thoughts.

Outlines differ from **scripts,** which include every word you say. And both differ from the **speaking notes** you take with you to the podium. Compare and contrast the scripts of student speeches you find at the end of Chapters 2, 7, and 8 with the outlines at the end of Chapters 9 and 10 and the speaker's notes presented later in this chapter.

People who speak frequently know that there's no single way to outline a speech correctly; the more speeches you give, the more you'll find a way that works best for you, considering your individual learning style. This chapter presents tips for making conventional outlines, followed by a description of how to prepare speaking notes. It concludes with ideas for more holistic methods of pulling together a speech that take into account diversity in individual thinking styles.

How to Prepare a Content Outline

Most instructors ask students to turn in a **content outline,** a record of the speech's major ideas or materials and their relationship to one another. Although each instructor may require specific details, several general guidelines can help you prepare content outlines.

Begin with a Heading

Give your speech a title, then include the general purpose, the specific purpose, the finalized central idea, and the organizational pattern that you've developed using principles found in Chapters 5 through 9. The heading is a nutshell look at what you plan to accomplish. Here is the heading that John used for his speech describing the stages of culture shock.

Topic:	The Five Stages of Culture Shock
General Purpose:	To inform
Specific Purpose:	To inform my audience about the five stages of the psychological phenomenon known as culture shock and to demonstrate these stages with real-life examples
Central Idea:	Culture shock is a very real psychological process that typically progresses through five stages: honeymoon, disintegration, reintegration, autonomy, and interdependence
Organizational Pattern:	Chronological

Use a Standard Format

Before the advent of computers and word-processing programs, students had to use the tab feature on their typewriters to line up the points and subpoints on their outlines. Fortunately, most computer software programs now have a number of formatting features or style tools that automatically put in some of the formatting features discussed

---

Rough Draft Outline

A preliminary outline that's not yet formatted formally.

Scripts

The actual text of the speech; includes every word you say.

Speaking Notes

The key words and phrases you take with you to the platform when you speak.

Content Outline

A formal record of your major ideas and their relationship to one another in your speech.

in this section. Learning to use them will save you time and effort as you create your formal outlines.

Alternate Numbers and Letters

Show the relationship of the parts of your speech to one another by alternating numbers and letters in a consistent pattern. For example, identify your major points using one of the patterns described in Chapter 9. Then designate each major point with a Roman numeral. Under each main point, identify first-level supporting points and give each one a capital letter head (A., B., C., . . .). Second-level supporting points get Arabic numerals (1., 2., 3., . . .), and third-level points are designated with lowercase letters (a., b., c., . . .) The following system is typical:

I. Major point

   A. First-level supporting point

      1. Second-level supporting point

      2. Second-level supporting point

         a. Third-level supporting point

         b. Third-level supporting point

   B. First-level supporting point

II. Major point

   A. First-level supporting point

   B. First-level supporting point

Coordinate Points

Use the principle of **coordination;** this means that your major points have basically the same value or weight, as do your first-level and your second-level points. In the following outline, the problem and the solution are major points. First-level points—causes and effects—are coordinated approximately equally. Each first-level point is further supported by coordinated second-level points.

  I. Problem

    A. Causes

       1. First Cause

       2. Second Cause

    B. Effects

       1. First Effect

       2. Second Effect

       3. Third Effect

 II. Solution

    A. The plan

    B. Cost

    C. Benefits

Coordination
Points are arranged into various levels; the points on a specific level have basically the same value or weight.

Indent

Indentation is yet another way to help you see the interrelationship of your materials. For example, the A. and B. headings line up visually as do the second- and third-level supporting points. Consequently, the formatting itself helps you "see" your main ideas and the points under them.

Indentation
Formatting by spacing inward various levels of points.

Compare your finished outline to a completed puzzle. Here, the pieces are being fitted together to make a pleasing whole. Similarly, your outline shows how the pieces or elements of your speech fit together in a meaningful way. (Anne Dowie)

Write Your Points in Sentence Form

Complete sentences allow you to see the content included in each point. For example, John's introduction to his speech on culture shock *could* use only phrases, like this:

I. *Craik* in Ireland

II. Travelers abroad

III. My Kenyan experiences

IV. Five stages

It's obvious that someone reading his outline would not know what each point actually covers. His phrases might function adequately as a speaking outline; however, both John and his professor will have a better idea of his speech content if he uses the following full-sentence outline for the major points in his introduction.

I. You're in Ireland when a man offers you some *craik* (pronounced "crack"); should you be surprised or offended?

II. When you enter another culture, you can expect to go through culture shock before you feel comfortable.

III. I experienced this process when I spent the summer in Kenya.

IV. People typically experience five stages of adjustment when they enter a new culture: honeymoon, disintegration, reintegration, autonomy, and interdependence.

Parallel Points

Making the points similar in type.

Another key is to construct **parallel points.** That is, don't write out some points as declarative sentences and others as questions. Avoid mixing phrases and complete sentences, and don't put two sentences in a single point—all of which this student did when she originally outlined her major points:

I. What is Multiple Sclerosis (MS)? *a complete sentence in question form*

II. The Big Mystery! *a sentence fragment or phrase*

III. Who? *a single word in question form*

IV. Effects . . . Symptoms of MS. *an incomplete sentence*

V. There are three prominent medications being used right now to treat MS. These are talked about in the magazine, *Inside MS.* *two declarative sentences*

Here's how her rewritten points should look:

I. Multiple Sclerosis (MS) is a disease of the central nervous system.

II. The causes remain a mystery.

III. Its victims tend to share age, gender, and regional characteristics.

IV. The condition affects eyesight and bodily coordination.

V. Most physicians prescribe one of three major medications.

Use the Principle of Subordination

The word **subordination** comes from two Latin root words: *sub,* or under, and *ordinare,* or place in order. Simply stated, this means that all the first-level points support and are placed under the major points; all the second-level points support the first-level points and are put under them, and so on. Return to the previous example and think critically about the speaker's points. Are all her first-level points equal? Or do some seem more logically to follow others? What would happen if she were to use a problem-solution pattern for first-level points, then subordinate the other material to the second level of support? Her outline would now look like this:

Subordination
Placement of supporting points under major points.

I. [*problem*] Multiple Sclerosis (MS) is a disease of the central nervous system.

    A. [*causes of the problem*] Its causes remain a mystery.

    B. [*sufferers from the problem*] Its victims tend to share age, gender, and regional characteristics.

    C. [*effects of the problem*] It affects eyesight and bodily coordination.

II. [*solution*] Most physicians prescribe one of three major medications.

Coordinating her major points into a problem-solution pattern is a much more effective way to organize this speech. And subordinating three points—the causes, the sufferers, and the effects of MS—under the problem section of this speech is a more logical flow of ideas.

In summary, a good content outline begins with a heading and uses a standard format that includes coordinated points arranged by alternating letters and numbers and by indenting material in a way that shows the relationship of ideas to one another. It's written in complete sentences that are parallel in construction, and contains supporting materials that are arranged underneath the major ideas. The following student outline with commentary pulls all of these elements together, providing you with a good model outline and an explanation of how John organized and outlined his speech.

STUDENT OUTLINE WITH COMMENTARY

The Five Stages of Culture Shock *by John Streicher*

John was required to turn in this preparation outline for his informative speech. His professor asks for a list of references at the end of each speech, as well as an outline of both the introduction and conclusion. (Some instructors ask their students to write out the beginning and ending and outline only the body of the speech.) Here is John's complete content outline:

By writing out his heading, John made sure the focus of his speech is clear and that his outline accomplishes his stated purposes.

Topic:	The Five Stages of Culture Shock
General Purpose:	To inform
Specific Purpose:	To inform my audience of the stages of the psychological phenomenon known as culture shock and to demonstrate these stages with real-life examples.
Central Idea:	Culture shock is a very real psychological process that typically progresses through five stages: honeymoon, disintegration, reintegration, autonomy, and interdependence.
Organizational Pattern:	Chronological

Introduction

Specifically identify the introduction, the body, and the conclusion. The four major goals of this introduction are: gaining attention, relating to the audience, establishing credibility, and previewing the major points. Each goal is assigned a separate Roman numeral.

I. You're in Ireland when a man offers you some *craik* (pronounced "crack"); you're surprised and offended, but should you be?

II. Whenever you enter another culture, you can expect to go through culture shock.

A. According to Paul Peterson in *The Five Stages of Culture Shock,* culture shock is "an internalized construct or perspective developed in reaction or response to a new or unfamiliar situation."

B. Culture shock typically involves several stages of adjustment before you feel comfortable.

III. I experienced this process when I spent the summer in Kenya.

A. Customs were so different that I often felt I was missing what was going on.

B. However, working my way through several stages taught me valuable coping strategies.

C. My experiences have led me to be more aware of challenges facing newcomers to our culture!

Point iv., the preview, functions as the transition between the introduction and the body of the speech. It signals the audience to listen for chronologically organized information about the stages of culture shock.

IV. Today, I will identify and describe five stages people typically experience when they enter a new culture: the honeymoon, disintegration, reintegration, autonomy, and interdependence stages.

Body

John's outline specifically labels the body of his speech. His major ideas show the principle of coordination, because each identifies one of the stages of the overall process. In this first major point, John sets up a pattern he'll use, with modifications, to develop each major point. He defines the stage, explains typical feelings and experiences in it, provides examples, and ends with helpful tips for navigating the stage.

I. The first stage of culture shock, the Honeymoon stage, represents your initial contact with the culture.

A. Your previous cultural identity isolates you from belonging in that culture.

1. You'll be surrounded by strange sights, sounds, and smells.

2. You will not understand what others expect of you.

B. However, you'll typically feel excited and adventuresome—even confident—feelings that tourists experience.

1. People in the host culture may be kind and helpful.

2. You may be oblivious to errors you're making.

a. For example, students in a Venezuelan airport demonstrate unintentional errors.

b. In addition, a woman on a bus in the Bahamas shows a naïve attitude.

Subpoints B. and C. are first-level points that are made up of both second-level and third-level supporting materials.

C. You can take steps during this stage to help you through the later stages.

1. Begin a journal that you'll use throughout your entire stay to record both your positive and negative experiences.

2. Act like a tourist and find things you enjoy doing.

a. Look for cultural offerings in the area.

b. Find areas of natural beauty that can function as a retreat both now and later.

3. Plan a vacation for six months down the road.
4. Build a support system.
   a. Make contacts with people in the area.
   b. Maintain contacts with family and friends back home through letters, e-mail, telephone calls, and the like.

II. In about two to eight weeks, you enter the second stage—Disintegration–wherein the novelty has worn off, and unexpected things begin to happen.

A. You're no longer a spectator; you must now solve practical problems in the host culture.

1. Typically, you'll experience confusion (Help! What do I do now?), failure (I'm inadequate), and self-blame (It's all my fault).

2. A Texan visiting South African townships for the first time is an example.

B. You can take steps to help yourself through this stage.

1. Take care of yourself physically.
2. Continue to learn the language and the nonverbal communication system.

   a. When she was a nanny in Belgium, Sara worked on her language skills in her host family, but she also took a course in French at a nearby university.

   b. Look for cues to nonverbal expectations.

   c. Record your learnings in your journal.

III. Two to three months later, expect the third stage, Reintegration, in which you typically shed your self-blame and interact within the culture.

A. You may reject the feeling of being overwhelmed and begin to stand up for yourself.

B. However, you may feel intense anger and rejection toward the host culture.

1. For example, a student in Brazil took advantage of the language barrier and harassed a cabdriver.

2. An anthropologist in Africa strongly opposed an injustice she perceived in the legal system there.

3. Some people in this stage get together with others like them and exchange stereotypes about their hosts.

4. One form of rejection is to go home.

   a. Five to 30% of people on overseas assignments return early.

   b. Companies lose $250–$400,000 per returnee.

C. Plan ways to get through this stage as positively as you can.

1. Go on that vacation you planned during the Honeymoon stage.

2. Avoid or minimize meetings with your own group wherein you talk negatively about your hosts.

3. Take out your frustrations in your journal, not on the people in your host culture.

(Transition: You've faced the adjustments of the Honeymoon, Disintegration, and Reintegration stages; from here, you either regress toward maladjustment, or you move toward the greater understanding you'll find in the Autonomy and Interdependence stages.)

John develops this second point similarly, in that he first defines and explains the stage, then he ends with survival tips.

Here you can distinguish between his first-, second-, and third-level supporting points because they're subordinated by means of indentation and alternating numbers and letters.

Notice that all his points are phrased as declarative sentences and that he includes only one sentence per point.

Frustration climaxes in this, the third point, so here is a good place for John to write out a transition statement rather than use a signpost. He separates his transition from the lettering and numbering system.

IV. After three to six months, you'll find balance at the Autonomy stage in which you finally begin to see both the good and the bad in the culture.

A. You can relax more and understand, rather than criticize, the host culture.

B. You'll begin to feel like an "Old Hand" who can negotiate effectively in the setting that's foreign to you.

C. Some tips will help you through this stage.

1. Be careful: It's easy to overestimate your abilities and commit a blunder as two students in India discovered when they were invited into a local's home.

2. Now is the time to do some serious shopping, because you're less likely to be "taken."

V. Finally, after about nine months, you come to the last stage of culture shock—Interdependence.

John uses a signpost to lead into his last point.

A. Consider yourself bicultural or multicultural.

1. Your feelings aren't controlled or dominated by differences between your host culture and your home culture.

2. You can demonstrate trust and sensitivity.

3. This stage is best demonstrated by an American in Kenya.

B. You begin to assume responsibilities and privileges in your new culture.

Conclusion

By setting apart the conclusion, he makes sure that he's crafted a memorable ending that summarizes the speech and is both purposeful and brief.

I. I hope this information helps you understand the process of integrating into a new culture.

II. We've looked at five stages people typically experience upon entering a new culture: Honeymoon, Disintegration, Reintegration, Autonomy, and Interdependence.

III. You'll not only understand yourself in a foreign situation, you'll better understand people who immigrate to your neighborhood or your school.

IV. And through it all, have some *craik*—the Irish slang word for a good time!

Bibliography

This bibliography is formatted in the American Psychological Association (APA) style. Ask your instructor which format he or she prefers, but always include a list of the references you consulted during your speech preparation.

Coping with culture shock. (1999, March 23, last updated). Carnegie Mellon Office of International Education. Available at http://www.oie.studentaffairs.cmu.edu/students/guidebook.98/cultshock.htm.

Culture shock. (1999, December 2, last modified). Comox Valley International College—School of English Language. Available online at: http://www.cvic.bc.ca/c_shock.htm.

Culture shock: Survival manual. (1999). Technical University of Budapest International Education Center. Available online at: http://www.khmk.bme.hu/surv/studo1.ssi.

Drake, W. (1997). Managing culture shock: 25 slides with notes. Available online at http://www.culturebank.com/sepiv/realshock/.

Furnham, A., & Bochner, S. (1986). *Culture shock*. New York: Mcthuen.

Jordan, P. (1992). *Re-entry*. Seattle: Youth with a Mission.

Loss, M. (1983). *Culture shock*. Winona Lake, IN: Light and Life Press.

Pederson, P. (1995). *The five stages of culture shock*. Westport, CT: Greenwood.

Storti, C. (1990). *The art of crossing cultures*. Yarmouth, ME: Intercultural Press.

STOP AND CHECK

Evaluate Your Content Outline

This checklist is available online under Chapter 11: Forms and Checklists for Jaffe Connection at the Public Speaking Resource Center. Prepare your content outline, then evaluate it, using this checklist.

- ◾ _____ My heading provides important summary information about my speech.
- ◾ _____ The introduction, body, and conclusion are clearly identified.
- ◾ _____ My organizational pattern is clearly identifiable.
- ◾ _____ The points are coordinated.
- ◾ _____ I have subordinated supporting materials under them.
- ◾ _____ My indentation is accurate.
- ◾ _____ I've used complete sentences throughout.
- ◾ _____ Numbers and letters alternate.

I.
  A.
    1.
      a.
        (1)
          (a)

- ◾ _____ My references are in standard bibliographic form.
- ◾ _____ I have fulfilled any other requirement that my professor asks for.

To investigate this topic further, log onto the Internet and search for the exact term, "principles of outlining," on www.alltheweb.com. You should get hits for both writing and speaking outlines. Read the material on at least one speech-related site.

You can also hone your outlining skills by completing the outline analysis activity under Chapter 11: Activities for Jaffe Connection at the Public Speaking Resource Center.

Public Speaking Resource Center

How to Create Your Speaking Outline

Although content outlines help you organize your ideas and visualize your points in relationship to one another, they differ from your **speaking outline**—the outline you take with you to the podium. Content outlines are written in full sentences, but speaking outlines use full sentences in two places only: transition statements and direct quotations. Instead, they are **key word outlines,** using just enough important phrases or words to jog your memory as you speak. This section describes two major formats for key word outlines: note cards and speaking outlines.

Use Note Cards

Write your key words out on note cards—either 3" x 5" or 4" x 6" cards are most common. Using note cards in delivery offers several advantages. For one thing, they are smaller, less noticeable, and easier to handle than a standard sheet of paper. They are sturdy enough not to waver if your hand trembles. And if you deliver your speech without a podium, you can hold your cards in one hand and still use the other to gesture. Here are some tips for creating note cards:

Speaking Outline

The outline you take with you to the platform.

Key Word Outline

Uses the important words and phrases that will jog the speaker's memory.

FIGURE 11.1 Your note cards are highly individualized. That is, you make a personalized set of key term cards that will jog *your* memory.

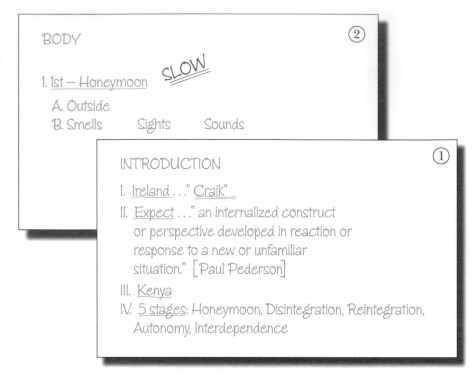

- Use purchased cards, or make your own.

- Write legibly; print or type key words in capital letters; double or triple space your lines.

- Number your cards so that you can put them in place quickly if they get out of order.

- Write on only one side of each card because turning note cards over can be distracting.

- Delete nonessential words—use only key words and short phrases.

- Use no more than five or six lines per card, and space your lines so that you can find your place instantly. For longer speeches, don't crowd additional information onto your cards; instead, use more cards.

- Highlight important ideas and circle or underline words you want to emphasize during delivery.

- Put words such as *pause* or *slow down* on your cards to serve as delivery reminders.

- Practice in front of a mirror using your note cards. Revise them if they are not as helpful as you would like.

- When you actually give your speech, use your cards unobtrusively. Never wave them around. However, when you read a direct quotation or give complicated statistics, hold up a card and look at it frequently to show your audience that you are being as accurate as possible (Preparing the delivery outline, 1999).

Figure 11.1 shows note cards for John's speech on culture shock.

Avoid this speaker's mistake, and keep your speaking notes largely invisible. Don't wave them around or tap the cards on the podium. Move from card to card or page to page unobtrusively; however, let your audience see you refer to your notes when you're giving direct quotations or complicated statistics. (Mark C. Burnett/Stock Boston)

Create a Speaking Outline

Another strategy is to create a speaking outline by typing out key terms on a standard-size sheet of paper. Many of the tips for creating note cards apply to key term outlines, but there are some minor differences as the following tips point out:

- Use plenty of space to distinguish between the various sections of your speech.

- Use highlighter pens to distinguish the sections easily. For example, underline signposts and transition statements in orange, and use a different colored highlighter for the introduction, the body, and the conclusion.

- Use different font sizes and formatting features to break up visual monotony and direct your eyes to specific places as you go along. For example, in Figure 11.2 the preview alternates lowercase and capitalized words.

- If you have several sheets of notes, spread them across the lectern in such a way that you can still see the edges of the lower pages. Then when you move from one page to another, slip the top sheet off in an unobtrusive motion and tuck it at the bottom of the pile.

- If a lectern is unavailable, place your pages in a dark-colored notebook or folder that you hold with one hand while gesturing with the other. (Angle your notebook so that the audience doesn't see your pages.)

Figure 11.2 shows the first page of a speaking outline for the culture shock speech.

FIGURE 11.2 Speaking outlines contain key words to remind you of your ideas and advice words to remind you of your delivery.

Introduction

    I. Ireland—**craik** ("crack")—offensive?   **RELAX !!**

    II. <u>expect</u> C.S.

        A. Paul Peterson *The Five Stages of Culture Shock*

        "an internalized construct or perspective
          developed in reaction or response
          to a new or unfamiliar situation."

        B. A progression.

    III. my **Kenyan** experiences.   **DON'T RUSH !!!**

        A. felt missing out.

        B. learned coping strategies.

        C. apply to newcomers here

    IV. <u>FIVE</u> stages:

        • honeymoon,

        • **DISINTEGRATION**

        • reintegration,

        • **AUTONOMY**

        • interdependence.

Body

    I. **First = Honeymoon**

        A. Don't belong

          1. <u>s</u>ights, <u>s</u>ounds, <u>s</u>mells.

        B. excited   adventuresome confident   <u>**like a tourist.**</u>

          1. helpful **hosts**

          2. **oblivious** to errors   **S - L - O - W !!**

            a. <u>**students**</u>   **Venezuelan**   **airport.**

            b. <u>**woman**</u>   **bus**   **Bahamas**

STOP AND CHECK

Evaluate Your Speaking Outline

Use your content outline to create a speaking outline or note cards, then use the following checklist to evaluate it. This checklist is available online under Chapter 11: Forms and Checklists for Jaffe Connection at the Public Speaking Resource Center.

■ _____ All the cards have key words or short phrases only — except for direct quotations.

■ _____ I can't find any other words I could still eliminate and have the notes remain useful.

■ _____ My introduction, body, and conclusion are clear.

■ _____ Transitions are written out; signposts are clearly marked.

■ ＿＿ I have used color effectively.

■ ＿＿ I have highlighted (underlined, etc.) the words I want to emphasize.

■ ＿＿ I numbered my cards or pages so that their order is clear.

■ ＿＿ Helpful delivery hints are scattered here and there.

■ ＿＿ After practicing with these notes, I have made changes as needed.

DIVERSITY IN PRACTICE

Individual Cognitive Style

Any discussion of diversity is incomplete without a mention of individuality, and in a chapter on outlining, it's important to note that each person's **cognitive style** (sometimes called thinking style or learning style) is unique. Consequently, every classroom contains "a diverse population of learners" (Thinking and learning skills, 1999). Your cognitive style is comprised of the modes you typically use to think, perceive, remember, and solve problems. Our cultures influence our styles to an extent, but your particular way of processing information is unique to you (Irvine & York, 1995).

In 1981, the cognitive scientist Roger Sperry won the Nobel Peace Prize for his research in brain hemispheric dominance. His studies revealed that the right brain processes information more globally, intuitively, and artistically; in contrast, left-brain processes are more linear, analytic, logical, and computational. Most people use both hemispheres of their brains, but one side or another tends to be dominant (Giller, n.d.; Riding & Cheema,1991). This text is obviously not intended to describe the finer points of cognitive science research. However, the diversity of cognitive styles and the fact that they reflect both a personal and a cultural orientation does fit the emphasis of this text.

What does this mean in a chapter on outlining? Well, the traditional form of outlining presented here and in most other public speaking texts involves a more left-brain way to frame a speech—a way that may or may not match your preferred cognitive style. Consequently, although you are required to produce a linear outline, your personal style may be more holistic—and when you organize speeches in contexts outside the classroom, you may want to know alternative, more organic ways of showing your points. The last section of this chapter describes some alternative ways of showing your speech ideas.

To learn more about this topic, log on to the Internet and do an *InfoTrac College Edition* PowerTrac search, or go to a subject directory (such as www.yahoo.com) or a text index (such as www.dogpile.com) and search for "thinking styles," "right-brain/left-brain," "learning styles," or other related terms. If you're interested in identifying your personal style, look for an online learning styles test on the site http://www.namss.org.uk/lstyles.htm.

Cognitive Style

Comprised of the modes you typically use to think, perceive, remember, and solve problems; it's influenced by your culture but unique to you.

FIGURE 11.3 This figure depicts the contents of the culture shock speech as visualized in a spiral form.

Introduction

I. If you're offered craik (crack) in Ireland, should you be offended?

II. Entering a new culture → culture shock.

III. I experienced this during my Kenyan summer.

IV. This speech describes the process:
Honeymoon, Disintegration, Reintegration, Autonomy, Interdependence.

Conclusion

I. Hopefully, you understand the process.

II. Typically, the stages are:
honeymoon, disintegration, reintegration, autonomy, interdependence.

III. You'll understand yourself and immigrants.

IV. Have some craik (Irish slang for a good time.)

So: protect yourself.
· Don't be overconfident
· Do serious shopping.
(won't be taken)

So: protect yourself
· Go on a vacation
· Avoid negative talk
· Use journal to vent

So: protect yourself
· Guard your heart
· Learn to communicate
  - verbally
  - nonverbally
  - in your journal

So: protect yourself
· Start a journal
· Act like a tourist
· Build a support system
· Plan a vacation

You feel like a tourist,
you don't really belong.

The culture
is interesting.

People
are nice.

You're a newcomer.
· excited
· adventuresome

Unexpected things
feel overwhelming.

You reject host culture.
· Stereotype hosts

You face problems.
· Help!
· I can't!
· It's my fault!

Go home.
· 5–30% go home
· Companies lose
$250–$400K
per return

The novelty wears off.
· confused
· anxious
· helpless

Find others like
yourself and gripe.

You stand up for yourself
"No" to victimhood

You reject your
discomfort and anger.

May, in confidence,
blunder.
· Students in India.

You find balance.
· relaxed
· less critical

Assume responsibilities
and privileges of
host culture.

You demonstrate
trust & sensitivity.
· An American
in Kenya.

You have bicultural
or multicultural
competencies
· not controlled
by differences

I. Honeymoon Stage (lasts 2–8 weeks)	II. Disintegration Stage (lasts 2–3 months)	III. Reintegration Stage (lasts 2–3 months)	IV. Autonomy Stage (lasts appx. 3 months)	V. Interdependence Stage (at about 9 months)

In short, speaking from brief notes, rather than reading from an outline or trying to memorize your speeches, allows you to remember your major ideas and supporting materials. Moreover, you can maintain eye contact with the audience, secure in the knowledge that if you lose your train of thought you can easily glance at these notes to regain your place.

How to Work with an Alternative Pattern

Diversity in Practice: Individual Cognitive Style on page 217 discusses thinking styles and their influence on outlining. If your cognitive style leans toward more global or imagistic thinking, you may choose one of the alternative patterns, such as the wave, spiral, or star described in Chapter 9. Consequently, your depiction of your speech's content will be less conventional, but you can still design an appropriate representation of your ideas and their relationship to one another by using the tips provided here (Jorgensen-Earp, n.d.):

- First, decide on the pattern you will use to organize your materials; you may find it useful to sketch the diagram.
- Then write out your main points.
- With your pattern in mind, indicate what you will use for developmental material, subordinating this material under the point it supports.
- Indicate how you plan to begin and end your speech; then write out key transition statements.
- Use standard indentation and numbering only if it's helpful.

Figure 11.3 provides an example of John's culture shock speech that's now formatted into a spiral pattern.

Summary

As part of the speechmaking process, it's important to understand and show the ways that your points and subpoints relate to one another. For this reason, you'll probably be asked to outline your ideas in a linear form, using alternating letters and numbers and careful indentation. Coordinate your main points and subordinate supporting materials under them. Write your content outline in complete sentences, and include a list of references at the end.

However, content outlines do not go with you to the podium. Instead, take a speaking outline that consists only of key words; this will enable you to remember your main points but prevent you from reading your speech verbatim.

A linear outline is not the only way to record your ideas; in fact, one way to recognize diversity is to admit that people with various learning styles may actually benefit from using an alternative way of recording the speech content. Experiment to find what works best for you. If you choose to use an alternative pattern, you may find it helpful to record your ideas as a simple diagram, then arrange your major ideas and supporting materials on it.

JAFFE CONNECTION

Key Terms

rough draft outline (206)
scripts (206)
speaking notes (206)
content outline (206)
coordination (207)
indentation (207)

parallel points (208)
subordination (209)
speaking outline (213)
key word outline (213)
cognitive style (217)

Application and Critical Thinking Questions

1. Select a sample student speech found elsewhere in this text and outline it. (Use a speech from the end of Chapter 7 or 8, or from Chapter 12 or 13.) Then have a classmate check your outline for both content and formatting.

2. Outline an in-class speech given by one of your classmates. After the speech, give the outline to the speaker and ask him or her to check its contents for completeness and faithfulness to the speech.

3. Using the same outline, ask another student to evaluate your formatting—use of indentation, alternating numbers and letters, complete sentences, and the like.

4. Before you give your next speech, work from your content outline and prepare a speaking outline. Let one of your classmates evaluate both outlines and make revisions that would improve either one or both.

Internet Activities

Public
Speaking
Resource
Center

1. Use your *InfoTrac College Edition* and do a PowerTrac search for the journal *Vital Speeches*. Create speaking note cards for one of the speeches you find on it.

2. Many speech instructors have created websites that provide information about content outlines and speaking outlines. Browse the Internet for such sites, and read the information you find on at least two of the better sites you find. For example, use www.yahoo.com and do an advanced search for "outlining a speech."

3. Using the sites you found above, look for a sample student outline. Read and critique it.

Hot Links at the Public Speaking Resource Center

The following links are maintained and can be accessed easily via Jaffe Connection at the Public Speaking Resource Center on the Wadsworth Communication Café web site at http://communication.wadsworth.com/publicspeaking/study.html

- http://owl.english.purdue.edu/Files/63.html Purdue University Online Writing lab developed this site to assist students in developing an effective outline for public presentations.

- http://owl.english.purdue.edu/Files/64.html This second site from Purdue University provides a sample outline for students who wish to view an actual outline.

12

Visual Aids:

From Chalkboard to Computer

This chapter will help you:

- Explain the value of visual aids in your public speeches

- Determine the advantages and disadvantages of using various presentation technologies, including overhead projectors, boards, handouts, poster board and flip charts, and slides

- Choose helpful visual aids for each speech, including objects, persons, models, lists, tables, charts, graphs, photographs, drawings, maps, videos, and audio equipment

- Explain the principles of computer-generated visuals

- Give guidelines for using visual aids

- Create your personal visual presentation plan

"Immigrant Pride Day Community Mural" ©1998 Precita Eyes Mural Arts Center

When asked to describe the best visual aids they had seen, several students responded.

The Key Club convention speaker first wore ramshackle clothing. Throughout his talk, he removed various items and replaced them with new ones. Shocking! But it made his point that we should shed bad habits. — Bethany

A classmate videotaped how to work through a computer program. It showed us what icons to click on and what kind of programs and neat features his computer had to offer. — Caleb

During a sermon on unity, a pastor gave everyone a handout about his white-water rafting trip; he then discussed how everyone was doing something different, but it took the efforts of all to make a successful trip. — Rachelle

They then described a number of worst examples.

I had a friend of mine hold up a book with my visual inside. He had to hold it for over fifteen minutes! — Jon

A teacher tried to describe a map. It was hard to visualize when you didn't know what he was talking about. — David

Some students used a sloppy graph on construction paper that was unreadable, due to size. — Rachelle

In this era of advanced technology, you'll almost certainly use visual aids when you make public presentations. The examples just given show that your visual aids can be memorable—either positively or negatively. Therefore, you'll be a more competent speaker if you know how to create and display visual support. The purpose of the chapter is to prepare you to use aids that will enhance your message and create positive impressions about you.

Visual Aids Transcend Culture

Despite a proliferation of media in this century, the use of visual aids is not new. In oral cultures, speakers used objects as well as words to clarify their ideas and to help their listeners better understand abstract concepts. For instance, in the sixth century B.C., the Jewish prophet Jeremiah used a ruined linen belt as an object lesson to symbolize the decay that would come to the kingdom of Judah as a result of disobeying God (Jer. 13). In addition to clarifying ideas, people learn and remember better when they use more than one sense to take in information, and in an image-saturated culture, they expect visual support. Think of your own listening experiences. Don't you learn more and remember more from speakers who use posters, charts, models, maps, objects, and graphs than from those who don't even use the chalkboard?

No, visuals are not new, but the number and kinds available are different from those used even ten years ago. And the future promises even greater technological diversity. For example, **multimedia presentations** involving text, audio, still images, and video are now commonplace. Visual support also enhances communication in pluralistic settings. Reynolds (1996) emphasizes their value as a tool in international marketing. And visuals can help presenters who must speak in a second language, as Diversity in Practice on the next page explains.

Multimedia Presentations
Combinations of text, music, still images, animation, and video

Choosing the Right Type of Presentation Technology

You can probably list a number of ways to display visuals—in fact some huge corporations exist for the sole purpose of providing machines and materials for creating and dis-

DIVERSITY IN PRACTICE

If Your First Language Is Not English

Nonnative speakers of English worry that their English will not be understood or that they will make mistakes when they address their American classmates. Visuals offer nonnative speakers the following advantages:

■ By putting key words on your visual, even if you have accented English, your listeners can see as well as hear your words. This enables them to understand you more clearly.

■ When you provide something for your audience to see, their focus—at least part of the time—will be on your visual rather than on you. This may help you overcome some anxiety.

■ Using visuals helps you remember your speech. Words on a list or pictures in a flow chart, for instance, remind you of your main points.

 playing visual aids. To prove this, log on to the Internet and go to www.alltheweb.com and search for the exact phrase "visual aids." (You should get somewhere around 40,000 hits!) The 3M Company, for example, makes transparencies, plastic envelopes to store them, frames to hold them, machines to project them, and so on. This section covers a number of common ways to display visual aids—each with advantages as well as disadvantages.

Overhead Projectors

Overhead projectors are everywhere—they're in classrooms, businesses, and other organizations throughout the United States and across the globe. They allow you to enlarge and display an image on a wall or a screen so that everyone can see it, even in a large auditorium. Using an overhead projector has many other advantages. Transparencies are simple and inexpensive to make; the film is available in most campus bookstores, print shops, or office supply stores—and it comes in colors. You can easily store and transport transparencies. You can also overlap them by simply placing one on top of another.

Draw freehand directly onto the transparency or trace a cartoon, map, or other drawing from any printed copy. For a more professional look, use a copier to transfer a printed image to the plastic transparency. Or insert a transparency into your printer and print onto it directly from your computer. I personally like to write directly onto a blank transparency, using it in place of a chalkboard, and eliminating the need to turn my back to the audience.

Skillful use of an overhead projector adds to your audience's perception of your competence. However, poor skills can have the opposite effect. For best results, here are a number of things to remember:

■ Before you begin speaking, turn the machine on and adjust the focus of your transparency. Then turn off the machine until you're ready to use your visual.

■ If you are using a list of words on a transparency, consider cutting the transparency into strips and displaying each strip as you discuss the point it makes (Becker & Keller-McNulty, 1996).

Using an overhead projector effectively is an important skill; this equipment is widely available and transparencies are easy to make. (The Image Works)

■ If you want to draw your listeners' attention to some part of your visual, point to your transparency instead of the screen. To avoid showing that you're trembling, use a pointed object, placing it where you want your listeners to focus; then move your hand away from the projector.

Chalk and White Boards

Chalkboards or white boards are part of the standard equipment in most educational settings. Boards have several advantages. They're almost always available in the classroom. They're great for explaining unfolding processes—working out a math problem, for example. They also encourage a level of informality that is appropriate in some public speaking settings. Finally, they are useful in settings that include speaker-audience interactions, such as brainstorming sessions (anonymous, 1994).

Unfortunately, the following three major drawbacks make boards less suitable for classroom speeches:

■ You can't prepare your visual beforehand. Having an unprepared visual creates additional anxiety for speakers who like to have everything, down to the visuals, ready and rehearsed in advance.

■ When you write on the board, your back is turned to your audience, and you're talking to the board. This is probably the major drawback of boards in general.

■ Most people don't write well on boards. Their visuals, consequently, look unprofessional.

Boards continue to evolve. Some have a copier machine button at their base. Push it, and the attached machine transfers what you wrote on the board onto an 8½-by-11-inch piece of paper suitable for making into handouts. Furthermore, technicians can set up electronically linked magnetic boards in several sites for use during a teleconference session. With this technology, for example, what you draw or write in Seattle appears simultaneously on boards in Hong Kong, Sao Paulo, and Cairo (Martel, 1984).

Handouts

You can provide each listener with a brochure, pamphlet, photocopy, or other hand-out. For example, with a health-related topic, get professionally made brochures from your campus health services or a local doctor's office or make your own information sheet. Although handouts are less common in classroom speeches, they're widely used in businesses and other institutions. Companies provide sales representatives with brochures and other handouts for potential customers. Committee members often receive an entire book of supplementary reports and visuals. Your primary challenge is to let the handout supplement your message, not replace it. To use handouts more effectively, do the following:

- Distribute them, face-down, before you begin speaking; then, at the point you discuss the material on them, ask your listeners to turn them over.

- Mark the points you want to emphasize with a letter or number so that you can easily direct your audience to specific places on your handout. Let's say you distribute a map of an entire state, but you want to talk about three areas. Mark the first with an A, the second with a B, and the third with a C. Then, as you discuss each point, draw your listeners' attention to it.

- Put identical material onto a transparency and project it as you speak—highlight on the transparency information you want them to find on their handout.

For a summary of characteristics found on effective handouts, log on to the Internet and go to the following .com site, sponsored by Kinko's Copy Service, http://www.am-city.com/buffalo/stories/1997/10/13/smallb3.html.

Poster Boards and Flip Charts

For convenience and economy, use large sheets of poster board to display your visuals. It's readily available in a variety of weights and colors at campus bookstores or art supply stores. You'll also need an easel of some sort to support your posters. If you watch Congress on C-SPAN, you've seen major public figures use poster board to display charts and graphs. Speakers who deliver the same speech over and over—financial planners, for example—regularly use professionally prepared posters. Posters are effective with relatively small audiences, but at greater distances, they're difficult to see. These tips will enable you to make more professional-looking posters.

- Use rulers or yardsticks to ensure straight lines and avoid a "loving-hands-at-home" look.

- Use more than one color to attract and hold audience interest.

- If you plan to use the poster more than once, stick-on letters will make it look more professional.

- Protect your poster from becoming bent or soiled by covering it with plastic when you transport it. If you use the same posters repeatedly, carry them in a portfolio.

Flip charts are tablets, lined or unlined, commonly used in businesses and organizations, but less frequently seen in classrooms. The paper in them can vary from tablet thickness to stiffer weights. They can be fairly large or relatively small for presentations to a few listeners only.

Flip charts can function similarly to a chalkboard, especially in brainstorming-type situations where you engage in a great deal of interaction with your audience. For example, ask listeners at the beginning of your presentation to contribute ideas that you will later incorporate into your talk. Tear off the series of lists you and your listeners create, and pin or tape them to the wall. If you use a flip chart in this way, you must

Flip Charts

Tablets you can prepare in advance or create on-the-spot; turn to a new page or tear off and display pages as you finish them.

Flip charts can be useful, especially if you repeat the same speech to various, fairly small audiences. You can even use small tabletop flip charts for presentations to individuals or small groups of people when other means of display are unavailable. (Jose Pelqez/Stock Market)

overcome the same disadvantages you faced with a chalkboard. When you turn to write on the chart, your back is turned toward the audience. In addition, they may not be neat or professional looking.

Flip charts are also good for "building" a diagram in front of the audience. Prepare the entire visual lightly in pencil. Then, during your presentation, simply trace over the lines for a professional-looking drawing that appears to be done on the spot. You can be sure that all the words are spelled correctly beforehand, and you can use the chart as a giant prompt card.

If you make the same presentation repeatedly for different, relatively small audiences, prepare a series of lists, charts, or drawings in advance on heavier weight tablets. Then use the flip chart much as you would use a series of posters, exposing each new visual as you discuss it. The separate visuals will stay in order. In addition, because the cover is very stiff, the tablet can stand alone on any table. This makes it a useful way to display your visuals when no other equipment, such as an overhead projector, is available (anonymous, 1994).

Slides

Slides, like overhead transparencies, can be projected onto a screen where fairly large audiences can see them. You can make slides from photographs; in addition, with a number of computer programs, you can make slides directly from your personal computer. One drawback: slides are less visible in well-lit rooms, and you may find yourself speaking in the dark when you use them.

Common slide projectors have a carousel-type tray in which you place your slides in order. Each time you want to project a different slide, press a button on your hand-held control. To enhance your professionalism, put a black slide between sections of content so that you can pause to talk with your audience while avoiding a blast of white light or leaving a picture or diagram up so long that it's distracting or boring (anonymous, 1994).

DIVERSITY IN PRACTICE

Traveling and Talking

Many students currently sitting in classrooms just like yours will someday create visual aids to use in another country. You may be among them. A lot of engineers, marketers, physicians, and computer specialists who today fly across oceans to speak never thought, when they took their beginning speech courses, that they'd eventually speak internationally.

In an issue of *Electronic Design Magazine,* columnist Bob Pease (1998) recounts a trip he took to South America and Asia where he presented a version of a lecture he'd given numerous times in the United States. He had supplemented his stateside talk with more than 400 transparencies (weighing over five pounds) of technical drawings and explanations. Before he left, he toyed with the idea of creating special transparencies with subtitles translated into Portuguese and Spanish. Good idea? Well, adding 400 transparencies per language would create bulk and add ten pounds of weight to his briefcase. Besides, he'd need a lot of help to create the subtitles. In the end, Pease ran out of time, so he used his English-language visuals.

Jeff Radel (1996), from the University of Kansas Medical School, reaffirms that the United States is not the center of the universe; thus, the size of slides available here is not globally uniform. As a result, slots in slide projectors and carousels differ in size, and the number of slots varies to accommodate thicker or thinner slides. He suggests that a speaker bearing slides make sure that standard U.S.-sized equipment will be available.

Pease and Seymour (1996) also address equipment problems. Before boarding an international flight, speakers should check the voltage used in the country's outlets and make sure their power-line cords can fit into foreign adapters. True, a wide prong that won't fit can be ground off with sandpaper or emery boards, but it's easier to check adapters and purchase appropriate equipment before departure. In short, presenters who depend on visual aids should carry a variety of backup equipment when they go on the road.

These articles, or others like them that deal with speaking internationally, are available on your *InfoTrac College Edition.*

Computer-Projected Visuals

A number of computer projection systems hook up directly to a computer and project what's on the monitor onto a screen. This technology allows you to prepare all your visuals using a presentation program such as Microsoft's PowerPoint. After you create your program of slides, put the entire series on a disk. Then on the day of your presentation, simply slip your disk into the computer and press any key to bring up the images you've created. To change a slide, click the mouse. Fit in a plain slide wherever you plan to discuss material that you don't plan to support visually. (The student speech at the end of the chapter illustrates this technique.)

This technology may or may not be readily available in your classroom, but workplaces of the future will certainly have highly developed machines to display computer-generated visual support. Keeping current with state-of-the-art display equipment is a real plus in the workplace.

Public
Speaking
Resource
Center

Choosing the Right Type of Visual Aids

A variety of visual aids can all function to make your ideas more understandable, although one type is often better than another. The key is to choose the *best* visual, not the one that's easiest to make. This section will discuss several types of visuals including:

- Three-dimensional objects, models, and people
- Lists, charts, and graphs
- Photographs, drawings, and maps
- Audio- and videotaped resources

Objects

Imagine a basketball coach trying to convey the finer points of dribbling without using a basketball. Or think of an origami instructor explaining how to fold a crane without giving the audience origami paper so they could do as well as hear about the project. These scenes are hard to visualize because we need to see as well as hear a verbal description of some subjects. For this reason, actual three-dimensional objects are useful, especially in speeches that demonstrate a process.

Your topic determines whether or not an object would be a realistic visual aid. For example, what object could you use for a speech about the Bermuda Triangle? Black holes? Welfare reform? It's nearly impossible to think of something appropriate. However, with a little creative thinking, you can sometimes come up with ideas for communicating your point through touch, smell, or taste. Here are some examples:

- Sky used beekeeping equipment for a speech on honey production.
- Shelly gave each listener a tuft of unprocessed wool and a piece of yarn to touch as she discussed yarn making.
- Melissa provided small samples of freshly ground coffee to smell for her talk on coffee roasting procedures.
- Juan had his classmates chew sticks of gum during his talk about the origins and evolution of gum.

However, objects are not always appropriate. For instance, it's illegal to bring in firearms, and it's unwise to use live animals that may be difficult to manage, as Denis found out. His nervous wolf dog detracted from his speech because wary listeners focused on the size of the animal's teeth, not Denis's words! Some objects are impractical. Marko couldn't think of a way to bring his motorcycle into the classroom. (Fortunately, his class was willing to walk to a nearby parking lot where he spoke from the seat of his bike.) In short, objects must be legal, accessible, and practical.

FIGURE 12.1 An audiovisual aid plan.

My Audiovisual Aid Plan

A. Topic _____

B. Organizational Pattern: _____

C. Available equipment—check all that apply:

_____ overhead projector _____ transparencies _____ boards _____ handouts

_____ posterboard _____ easel _____ flip chart _____ slides _____ slide projector

_____ computer software package to create visuals _____ projector for computer-generated visuals

Given this room and this audience, which would be best? _____

Where do I get materials (such as posterboard or transparencies)? _____

Do I have to reserve equipment? If so, how do I go about this? _____

_____

D. Most promising types of visuals (check those that apply, and write specifics in the blank):

_____ object (what, how used?) _____

_____ model (what, how used?) _____

_____ person (who, how used?) _____

_____ list (specifically?) _____

_____ table (of what?) _____

_____ chart type _____ that shows _____

_____ graph(s) type _____ depicting _____

_____ photograph(s) of _____

_____ drawings of _____

_____ maps of _____

_____ audio support of _____

_____ videotape of _____

Before you bring an object into the classroom, consider your audience's possible negative reactions. For instance, this student *could* bring in her snake, but *should* she? (Jerome Hart)

Objects can be invaluable or they can be detractions unless you follow a few guidelines for their use:

■ Be sure the object is large enough for everyone to see, or provide each listener with an individual object.

■ Don't pass your objects around. If you do, some members of the audience will focus their attention on the visual rather than on your speech, and by the time everyone actually gets the object you may have completed the speech.

Models

Model

A facsimile of an object that you can't easily bring to the speech.

When you can't bring actual objects into the classroom, use a **model** or realistic facsimile instead. Scaled-down models depict larger objects, like buildings, dinosaurs, or cars. In contrast, enlarged models show larger versions of very small objects such as atoms, ants, or eyeballs. Teachers often use models such as skeletons, brains, or hearts when they cannot bring the real objects into their classrooms. Sometimes you can make your own model, or you can borrow one from a professional to display during your speech.

One student's topic was his summer job as a pyrotechnician, or fireworks display technician. Because federal regulations prevented him from bringing explosives into the classroom, he made a model of the spherical explosive device, complete with a fuse. He also brought the actual cylinder into which he dropped lit explosives. Finally, he wore the actual jumpsuit and displayed the safety helmet that he wore.

People

Use friends, volunteers from the audience, even yourself to demonstrate a concept. For example, to point out the problems inherent in judging people by their looks, Nancy introduced her friend to the class. Then, during the course of the speech, she used makeup, hair gel, and black clothing to transform her friend from a "preppy" into a "Goth" in just a few moments. Also consider ways to use the audience as a whole—you might ask fellow students to stand and participate in an exercise of some sort. Don't overlook yourself as a visual aid. Consuelo, a first aid instructor, used her wrists and neck to show the location of major arteries.

In short, an object, a model, or a person is almost indispensable in certain types of speeches—especially demonstration speeches. However, when it's unrealistic to use them, turn to the many other types of visuals available to you.

Lists

Lists are **text-based visuals,** meaning that they rely on written words more than on visual images. Lists might incorporate clip art in a minor way, but their value depends on the words and numerical information they display. That is, without clip art, the message would still come through; without the words or numbers, it would not.

Text-based Visuals

Carry meaning in the written words rather than visual images.

Lists are popular for speeches organized chronologically because you can easily make a list out of anything that's done in stages or that occurs in steps. For example, a list of the stages of grief, as shown in Figure 12.2a, would help listeners better organize and remember the stages in the correct order. Lists can also summarize in words or phrases the key points of more detailed material used in topically arranged speeches. You'll use lists more effectively if you remember the following:

■ Don't put too much information on your visual. For instance, if your list is too detailed, your listeners may simply read it, discover the same information as in your speech, then stop listening.

■ Follow the six-by-six rule: Use no more than six lines, no more than six words per line (Davidson & Kline, 1999).

■ Use words and phrases rather than long sentences or whole paragraphs.

■ Avoid the impulse to write out your main points, then read them to your audience (Becker & Keller-McNulty, 1996).

Charts

The two basic types of charts are flowcharts and organizational charts. **Flowcharts** show the order in which processes occur. You can often recognize them by the use of arrows indicating directional movement. Flowcharts can include drawings (pictorial flowcharts), or they may simply be a series of labeled shapes and arrows. Figure 12.2b illustrates a portion of a flowchart.

Flowcharts

Show the order or directional flow in which processes occur.

Organizational charts show hierarchies and relationships. A family tree, for example, is an organizational chart showing the relationships among family members. The chart in Figure 12.2c shows the relationship among various individuals involved in television production.

Organizational Charts

Show hierarchies and relationships.

Graphs

Have you ever felt bombarded with statistic after statistic? Speeches full of dry numbers are often boring, difficult to follow, and impossible to remember unless you use graphs

FIGURE 12.2 Common visuals include (a) a list, (b) a flowchart, and (c) an organization chart.

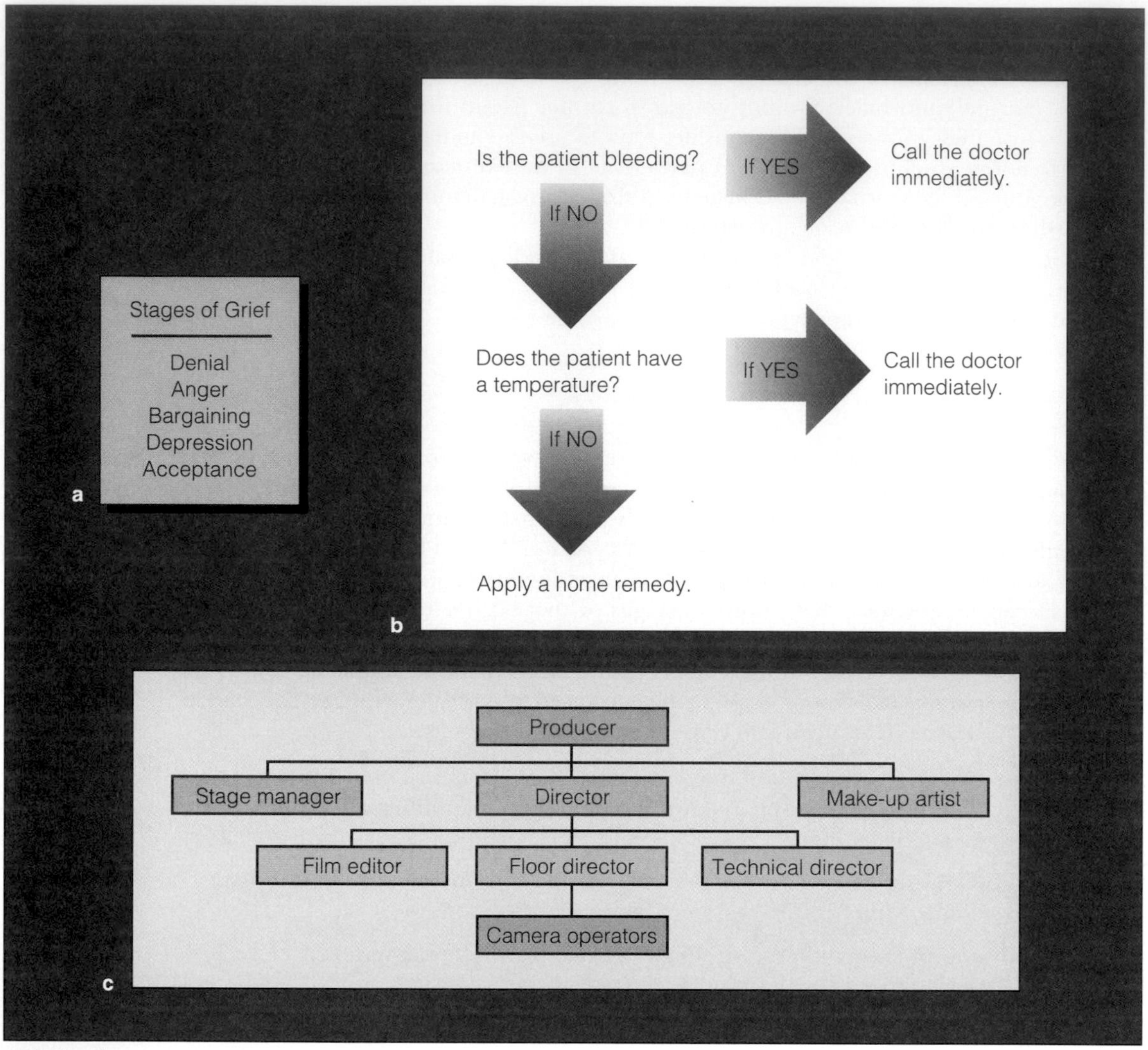

Image-based Visuals

Carry meaning in visual images; written words are only secondary.

Line Graphs

Show in a linear form one or more variables that fluctuate over a period of time.

Bar Graphs

Compare data from several groups by using bands of various lengths.

Pie Graphs

Circles divided into portions that represent parts of the whole or divisions of a population.

to represent the statistical data in diagram form. Graphs are a type of **image-based visuals** that communicate via a figure or other image. Depicting your material in one of four types of graphs allows your listeners to see how your numbers relate to one another.

1. **Line graphs** depict information in linear form; they are best for showing a variable that fluctuates over a period of time, such as the changes in college enrollment over two decades. Moreover, they are good for showing the relationship of two or more such variables—comparing the number of male and female students during the same period. (Figure 12.3a shows fluctuation in funding of three projects over a six-year period.)

2. **Bar graphs** are useful for comparing data from several groups. For instance, numerical information comparing the salaries of men and women with differing educational levels is displayed on the bar graph in Figure 12.3b.

3. **Pie graphs** are circular graphs that are especially good for showing divisions of a population or parts of the whole. The pie graph in Figure 12.3c depicts the way typ-

FIGURE 12.3   Major types of graphs: (a) a line graph, (b) a bar graph, (c) a pie graph, and (d) a pictograph.

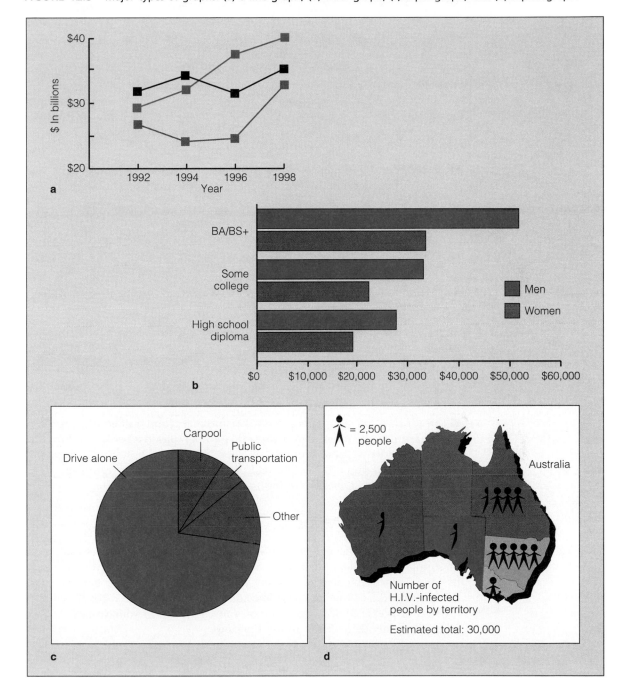

ical Americans get to work; you could use it in a speech about carpooling or public transportation.

4. **Picture graphs or pictographs,** the least common of the four types, are especially effective for data that relate to objects or people. Each picture represents a certain number of individual cases, as Figure 12.3d demonstrates.

Picture Graphs or Pictographs

Present data in pictures, each representing a certain number of individual cases.

Photographs

Although photographs provide an actual view of objects, persons, or scenes, the saying "A picture is worth a thousand words" is not necessarily true in your classroom speeches. Photographs are of little use unless they are large enough to be seen. Because of this, any photo you show to the class as a whole should be poster size. This ensures that each audience member can see the details of the picture.

However, because enlargements are sometimes difficult to acquire and because prints themselves are generally too small to be seen in even the smallest classrooms, you must figure out how best to show photographs you've deemed to be essential. Here are three effective ways students displayed photographs:

- Tricia found four pictures of Harry Truman at various stages of his life. She cut and taped them onto one piece of paper; then she made a photocopied handout for each classmate.

- Alene transferred a black-and-white photograph of a newborn baby to a transparency; then she used an overhead projector to project it onto a plain wall in the classroom. Throughout her speech on fetal development, the image of the baby framed her presentation.

- Bunnasakh brought six carefully selected slides to introduce her classmates to her country, Thailand.

Despite some successes, it's easy to use photographs ineffectively, and you should avoid two common mistakes:

- Don't pass photographs around. As with objects, the person closest to the speaker sees all the pictures and hears their explanation, but the person at the back of the room sees the photographs after the speech is over.

- Don't show pictures from a book. For instance, John walked back and forth across the front of the room, showing several photographs in a book that didn't fully open. Some students had to squint to see the pictures, and holding the book put John in an awkward posture. Also, he had to spend time flipping from page to page. This was obviously an ineffective way to present his pictures.

Drawings and Maps

Drawings can be invaluable, either alone or added to lists or other visuals as decorative or supplementary support. If you can't even draw stick figures, you can at least trace or photocopy a commercial drawing onto a transparency or a handout. Or let your computer come to your rescue. Most computer graphics packages have extensive clip art files of prepared drawings that you can easily add to your visuals. This partial list gives you some ideas of how to use drawings.

- Substitute drawings for illegal firearms, nervous wolf dogs, inaccessible motorcycles, buildings that are too large, or insects that are too small to bring into your classroom.

- Insert a cartoon when it perfectly illustrates your point and adds humor to your talk.

Diagram
A drawing or design that serves to explain, rather than realistically depict, an object or a process.

- Add a **diagram**—a line drawing or graphic design that serves to explain, rather than realistically depict, an object or a process—to illustrate the acid rain cycle or the circulatory system.

Maps are drawings that visually represent spaces. We map the heavens as well as the earth; we map weather; and we even talk about mind maps—maps of information. Choose from the following kinds of maps:

FIGURE 12.4 A floor plan of a building is a type of map. This Native American kiva is an example. (Mark Iles)

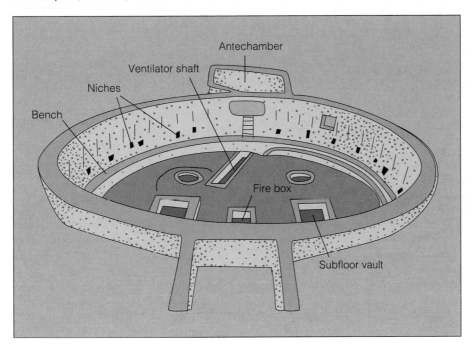

- **Political maps** show the borders between nations and states, but such maps are easily outdated in a rapidly changing world. For instance, any world map dated before 1990 is obsolete; since then, a number of countries, including the Soviet Union and Yugoslavia, have been dismantled, and new political boundaries have been drawn.

- **Geographic maps**—those showing mountains, deserts, lowlands, and other natural features—do not go out of date.

- Blueprints and floor plans of buildings, maps of routes between two points, city maps, campus maps—the list goes on. Figure 12.4 depicts a map of a Native American kiva.

If you want to draw your listeners' attention to specific features on the map, mark the spot with a letter or number. Then, during your speech, ask listeners to focus on that specific feature.

In short, we use a variety of visuals to illuminate ideas, clarify concepts, help audiences organize and remember material, and present abstract concepts more concretely. Three-dimensional objects, and text-based or image-based visuals can be indispensable in a visually oriented society. However, in some cases, recordings of sounds or images are even more effective support.

Political Maps

Show man-made borders for states and nations; rapidly outdated in fast-changing world.

Geographic Maps

Show mountains, deserts, and other natural features—not outdated.

Audio and Video Resources

Think of the difference between hearing a speech on jazz and actually hearing some jazz recordings. Or think of the greater understanding you get when you can see and hear a film clip showing the sights and sounds of a rodeo compared to a poster showing a list of its major events. Although audio and visual support take extra preparation and planning, they can be very helpful for conveying certain types of information.

Audio Resources

Audio support is particularly important if your topic is related to music. Portable electronic keyboards, guitars, ethnic musical instruments, and so on can add to your speech—as can tapes or CDs. All these allow your audience to hear the sounds you are explaining, ranging from reggae music to the music of a particular composer (as demonstrated in the speech about Tchaikovsky, outlined at the end of Chapter 10).

Although it's less commonly done, you can effectively use sounds other than music. In her speech on whales, for instance, Mary Beth played a tape of a whale song and asked her listeners to identify the source of the sound. Use your creativity to think of other ways to incorporate short sound clips—sounds from nature, traffic noises, conversations—to enhance your presentation.

Video Resources

College recruiters visit high school campuses, bringing along videos of their institutions, complete with background music and interviews with administration, faculty, and students. In many cases, the images themselves provide most of the message. The recruiter simply introduces the video, then fields questions afterward.

In the classroom, your goal with videotapes is not to replace your words but to supplement your ideas using some of the massive amounts of visual resources available to you—including television shows, feature films, advertisements, and home movies. By carefully selecting short clips to illustrate your points, you can clarify your ideas dramatically and memorably, as these examples demonstrate.

- Lisa made the *Guinness Book of Records* for being part of the largest tap dancing group ever assembled at one time for a performance. As she explained ways to get listed in the famous record book, Lisa used a fifteen-second video clip that her mother had recorded.

- Mary Beth's whale speech ended with a ten-second clip taken from a television program, showing a number of whales playfully leaping in and out of the water.

- Andrew discussed the difference between men's and women's gestures. To illustrate, he brought a fifteen-second commercial showing a male and female interacting. As he introduced his topic, he played the tape. Then, as he discussed each point, he again played the tape—this time with the sound turned off—pausing the tape at various places to illustrate the point he was making.

All these students were successful because they preplanned carefully. They selected short clips that illustrated, rather than substituted for, their words; they cued up their tapes in advance; and they planned carefully exactly when they'd start and stop the tape.

Enabling listeners to see or hear about your topic is important in many public speaking settings today. Indeed, it's almost necessary in some presentations, such as demonstrations. Skillful construction and use of visuals will distinguish good speakers from adequate ones, and as you learn to work with visuals, your competence will increase.

STOP AND CHECK

Continue Your Visual Presentation Plan

Return to the plan in Figure 12.1. Review your speech outline or think of the material in your speech and decide which ideas need to be supplemented by which types of visual or audio aids. Then fill in section D. On a separate sheet of paper, make a preliminary sketch of the material you plan to use on each visual.

For additional advice on choosing the best type of visual or sketching out your material, visit the online tutorial series sponsored by the University of Kansas Medical School, located at: http://www.kumc.edu/SAH/OTEd/jradel/effective.html

Use Computer Technology to Create Visuals

So much technology is available to create and display visuals that you may be tempted to overuse visual support and forget that oral delivery is still the key to a good presentation. Put simply, 400 visuals, fabulous though they may be, taken by themselves won't replace one well-prepared and polished speaker who explains her ideas clearly. In fact, a recent article in the *New York Times* (Zuckerman, 1999) suggested that overused bulleted points, bar graphs, flowcharts, and the like have taken the life out of public speaking and made some talks seem like old-fashioned grade school filmstrips. Perhaps he was overreacting, but his point was good: a flashy "presentation" cannot substitute for good ideas. Keep in mind that the technological tools and design principles described in this section are helpful only insofar as they help listeners understand your ideas.

Take Advantage of Technological Tools

Computers enable you to produce high-quality, professional visuals quickly and easily. Software packages currently on the market far surpass those used even a decade ago. The simplest way to create visuals on your computer is to use a word-processing program and type in the information that you will eventually transfer to a handout or a transparency. Although word processors are simple to use, the documents you create don't have to be boring. By adjusting fonts, letter sizes, line spacing, and formatting, you can create visually appealing lists, tables, and charts. You can add bullets, borders, and clip art to make your visuals even more attractive.

Let a **graphics program** do the hard work of converting your statistical data into graphs. Among the better-known graphics programs are Harvard Graphics, StatView, Delta Graph, Freelance Graphics, or Adobe Illustrator. You don't have to be a genius or a computer whiz to use these packages successfully, as their user's manuals are quite friendly.

Graphics Programs
Computer programs that convert statistical data into graphs.

Presentation programs are software packages written to help you create a series of lists, tables, graphs, and so on, then transfer them to slides, transparencies, or a computer disk for use with a special display machine. If you don't personally have a presentation program, visit your school's computer lab and search for Microsoft Power-Point, Adobe Persuasion, or a similar program.

Presentation Programs
Computer software to create a package of lists, tables, graphs, and clip art.

Experiment with backgrounds, fonts, and colors. By typing in a few easy directions, the computer will create line, bar, and pie graphs. It's also easy to create organizational charts. And you can either illustrate your visuals with clip art from more than 200 drawings and diagrams or use a **scanner,** a machine that lets you copy and store in electronic form photographs or other images from books, magazines, or other print sources. You can then add these images to your package of slides. Presentation programs also allow you to import or download images from the Internet, to add video clips or animation, or to use music and create a multimedia presentation. The speech at the end of the chapter shows how one student used a series of PowerPoint-created slides to support her ideas.

Scanner
A machine for converting a photograph or image from print to electronic data so that you can store it on a disk.

Design Your Visuals for Impact

If you work with a presentation program, you'll have access to so many design features that you may be tempted to use too many and create a series of slides that impress, but fail to enlighten your audience. For example, with PowerPoint you can create transitions between slides as well as build on individual slides. This means you could program every slide to **transition** onto the screen differently—one wipes from the left, another appears from the top down, another dissolves, a fourth appears in a checkerboard pattern. You could similarly program individual slides to **build,** which means that lines of text come onto a slide only when you press the mouse or touch a computer key. You can easily end up with slides and lines of text that fly in from the left, the right, the top, the corner, flashing on and off, one letter appearing at a time with clicking sound effects, and so on—creating a mishmash of movement that doesn't communicate your *ideas* at all.

You're better off to experiment with a presentation program for fun but, in the end, to follow rules for simple, well-designed visuals. This section describes a number of design principles that will help you make pleasing, but effective, visuals.

Choose a Readable Font

Whether you make your visuals by hand or rely on a computer, make readability your primary concern. One way to do this is to choose a **font**—a complete set of letters and numbers of a given design—that helps, rather than hinders, your audience's ability to read it. Here are some tips for readability that you can see illustrated in Figure 12.5.

Transition
The way each slide in a series appears on the screen.

Build
Lines of text appear on individual slides only when you touch a computer key or press the mouse.

Font
A complete set of letters and numbers of a given design.

FIGURE 12.5 Both serif and sans serif fonts are useful on classroom visuals. Avoid fancy display fonts that don't pass the readability test.

Serif fonts such as these are easier to read; using boldface makes them even more visible.

Palatino	**Palatino (bold)**
Times New Roman	**Times New Roman (bold)**
Bookman	**Bookman (bold)**

Sans serif fonts are useful for titles and headings.

Helvetica	**Helvetica (bold)**
Optima	**Optima (bold)**
Avant Garde	**Avant Garde (bold)**

Tempting as they may be, you're wise to avoid fancy display fonts that are difficult to read.

Zapf Chancery	*Zapf Chancery (bold)*
COPPERPLATE	COPPERPLATE (BOLD)
Template Gothic	Template Gothic (bold)

- Choose title or sentence case, and avoid all capital letters.

  - USING ALL CAPITAL LETTERS IS MORE DIFFICULT TO READ—BESIDES YOU'RE NOT SHOUTING AT YOUR LISTENERS, SO WHY CAPITALIZE?

  - Using Title Case (Capitalizing the First Letter of Important Words) is Easier to Read.

  - Using sentence case (capitalizing only what you'd capitalize in a sentence) is also readable.

- Use a **serif font** (with cross lines at the top and bottom of letters) rather than a **sans serif font** (with no cross lines) when you use a computer to create your visuals.

  - A serif font is easier to read because serifs lead your eyes from one letter to another (Readability, n. d., 2000).

  - Sans serif fonts are less readable; use them for titles.

- Avoid cutesy but hard-to-read display fonts, even if your computer program offers a plethora of choices, some very artistic and interesting. If you are handwriting your visual, write legibly in plain lowercase letters.

  - A font such as Template Gothic, besides being less readable, can draw attention to itself.

  - A font such as Oxford can be difficult to read.

  - *Cursive fonts such as Kauffman are generally less readable.*

- Remain consistent from visual to visual. That is, if you use Helvetica for your title on the first visual, use it on every visual. Do likewise for the subtitle and text fonts. Figure 12.6a shows a unified composition; Figure 12.6b illustrates an unfortunate mix of fonts.

For more information about fonts in general, log on to the Internet and go to www.alltheweb.com. Do a search for all the words "readability of serif fonts" or "font size."

Serif Font

A font with cross lines at the top and bottom of letters.

Sans Serif Font

A simple font with no cross lines on each letter.

Helvetica Is the Title Font

- Point #1 — Bookman
- Point #2 — Bookman
- Point #3 — Bookman

a

Template Gothic Is the Title Font

➤ **Point 1** — **Hobo**
➤ **Point 2** — **Gadget**
➤ Point 3 — Comic

b

FIGURE 12.6 Use the same fonts for each slide in your series.

Use Size and Space Wisely

Points
The unit of measurement for font size.

One key to well-designed visuals is font size, which is measured in **points (pt.)**. A good general rule is to use a 30–36 point font size for titles on computer visuals and overhead transparencies. Use 24 point for the next level of information and 18 point for the third level. Figure 12.7a shows a variety of font sizes. Figure 12.7b shows the three sizes recommended for a visual, simply typed onto a background.

FIGURE 12.7 This figure shows (a) a variety of font sizes, (b) the three sizes recommended for computer-created visuals, and (c) the information formatted in a balanced manner across the entire area.

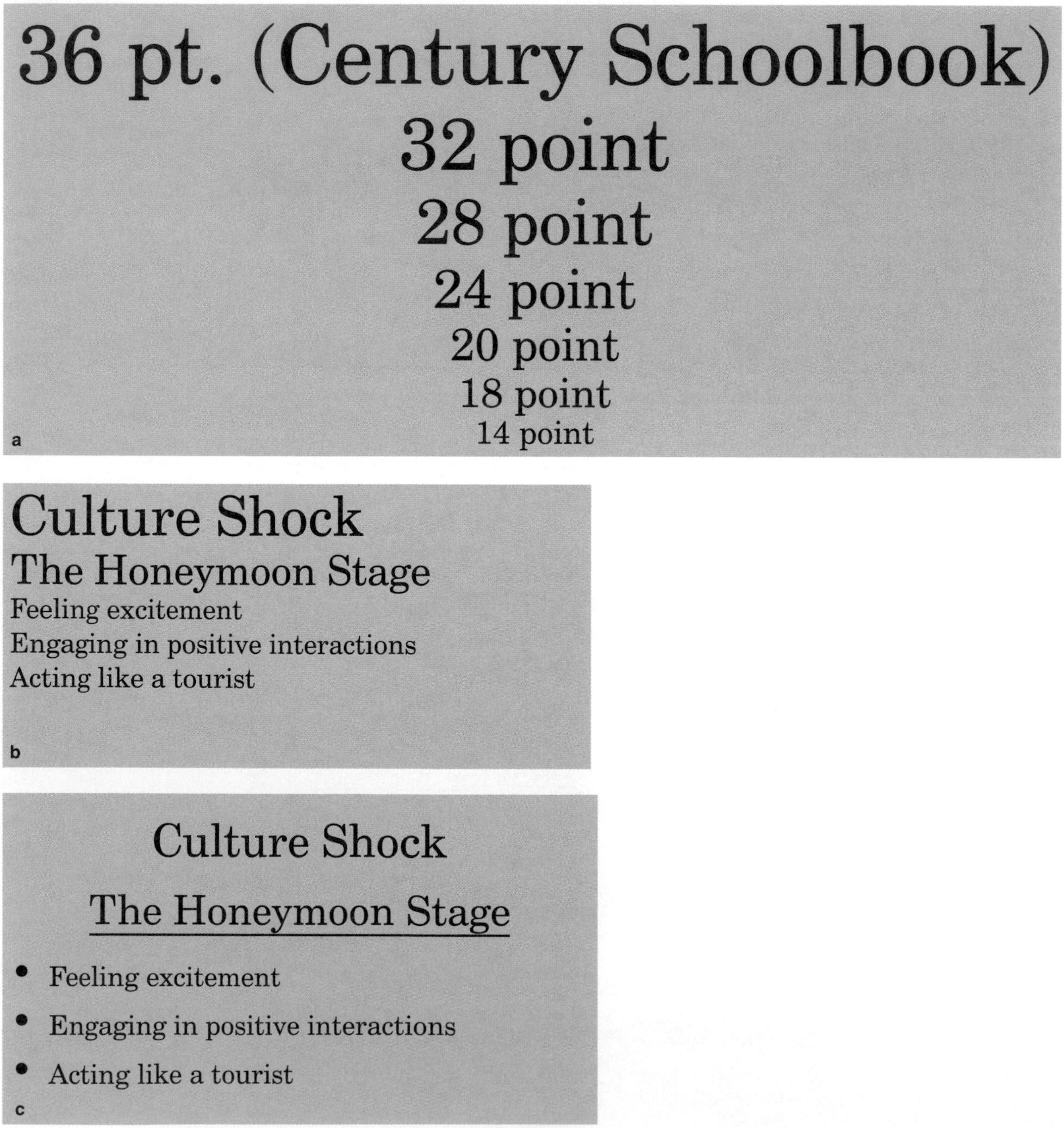

36 pt. (Century Schoolbook)
32 point
28 point
24 point
20 point
18 point
14 point

a

Culture Shock
The Honeymoon Stage
Feeling excitement
Engaging in positive interactions
Acting like a tourist

b

Culture Shock

The Honeymoon Stage

- Feeling excitement
- Engaging in positive interactions
- Acting like a tourist

c

Figure 12.7c then shows how centering the title, underlining the subtitle, and bulleting the points helps your audience to see the relationship of your ideas to one another better. This visual also shows the improvement in overall balance gained by spreading the information across more of the visual, rather than bunching the text in one corner.

Don't try to cram too much information on each visual; instead, limit yourself to one idea per visual, and leave plenty of white space so that your listeners' eyes can find their place easily. The *maximum* amount of material recommended is six lines, no more than 40 or 45 characters per line. While you're still planning out your visuals, write in your material, then go back and edit out every unnecessary word or figure. In other words: simplify, simplify, simplify.

Color and Emphasis

Use color to add interest and emphasis. According to the 3M Company, color has the following four advantages:

1. It attracts attention and holds audience interest.

2. It increases learning, retention, and recall of informative messages.

3. It adds persuasiveness to messages.

4. It motivates audiences to participate.

Select colors for your text words and images that contrast with the background color. For white or ivory-colored posters and clear transparencies, choose high-contrasting black or dark blue, not yellows or oranges. Red is a good emphasis color. For computer-generated slides, experiment until you find a color combination you like. Try yellow lettering, followed by white then lime green, on a dark blue background. Afterwards, try red or green on the same dark blue. In order to avoid a cluttered look, limit yourself to three colors for your entire series of slides.

Color is one way to emphasize ideas. For example, use brightly colored bullets to draw attention to a list. Or vary the color of a word or phrase you want to stand out. You can also underline or use italics or boldface fonts to highlight and accent something specific.

In summary, focus on principles of good design—on readability, on sizing and spacing your words and figures, and on choosing color combinations that will make your words readable and provide emphasis where you want it. These principles will keep you mindful of the fact that your aids are just that: aids—they aren't your message and they aren't a display of personal artistic or computer skills.

STOP AND CHECK

Complete Your Visual Presentation Plan

Return to your audiovisual plan. Make any revisions you'd like; next, sketch out each visual—paying attention to the size and spacing of your words and images. Select appropriate colors and decide which words or phrases you want to emphasize. Then go to work on your text- or image-based visuals. If you plan to use audio or video support, make arrangements now for the equipment you'll need. And have fun!

General Guidelines for Using Visual Aids

Although each type of visual aid has specific techniques for successful use, you can build your skills in preparing and presenting visual aids by applying these general guidelines.

■ Whatever type of visual you choose, be sure it can be seen in the room where you will speak.

■ Don't create a visual for its own sake. For example, a presenter who says, "Today, I'll talk about 'character,'" and the word "CHARACTER" appears on a slide is not clarifying a complex point or strengthening a bond with the audience. She's created what professional presenter Joan Detz (1998) calls a "dreaded" word slide that doesn't really add to a message.

■ Display visuals only when you discuss them; then cover them.

■ Talk to your audience, not to your visual.

■ Rehearse using your visuals. If you don't have access to a projector or easel during your practices, use a table as a "projector." Or visualize yourself using your posters or transparencies—where you'll stand in relation to them, how you'll point out specific features on them, what you'll do with them when they're not in use.

■ Don't violate your audience's norms or expectations to the point where you shock, offend, revolt, or anger listeners. One student killed, skinned, and cleaned a live fish in front of a horrified class. Another showed pornographic photographs to illustrate her speech about pornography. When you shock or violate expectations so severely, you may never regain attention, and your credibility—especially in the area of good sense—suffers as a result.

■ Whenever machines are involved, have a Plan B in case the technology fails. Imagine what will happen if the slide projector jams, the light on the overhead projector burns out, or the videotape machine eats your tape. An alternate plan, usually in the form of a handout, saves your speech. Demonstrating your composure in case of equipment failure is another way to enhance your credibility (anonymous, 1994).

Summary

As a speaker in a visually oriented culture, it is to your advantage to use visual support effectively. Visuals illustrate your ideas, keep your audience focused on your speech, and make abstract ideas more concrete. Although visuals are not new, the amount and kind of support available now is unprecedented.

To display your visuals, choose a means that suits your topic and the room in which you will speak. Overhead projectors, chalk or white boards, handouts, poster boards, flip charts, slides, and computer projectors are additional ways to present your visual aids. All have advantages and disadvantages, and you should take care to have a Plan B in case your equipment fails. These are all ways to display your visuals, but they are not the visuals themselves.

Choose from several types of visuals. Objects, persons, or models comprise three-dimensional visuals. In addition, you can sometimes incorporate touch, smell, and taste into your presentation. Choose text-based lists, or image-based charts, graphs, photographs, drawings, and maps. Finally, select audio or video clips when they would best clarify your ideas.

Emerging technologies, led by advances in computer engineering, are guiding us into a century in which you will have access to even more sophisticated presentational equipment. High-tech boards that can be connected globally are but one example. Even now, you can use word-processing programs, graphics packages, and presentation programs to create professional-appearing visuals.

Throughout, remember that visual support should enhance rather than replace your speech. For this reason, follow principles of design including readability, size and spacing, and color to your advantage. Furthermore, display visuals only when you are discussing them, and talk to the audience, not to the visuals. Carefully edit your tapes and videos, and make sure they are visible and audible for everyone.

In conclusion, don't overlook the importance of competent use of visual materials as a way to enhance your credibility. Keep in mind that professional-looking resources create more positive impressions than those that appear to be scribbled out just minutes before your presentation. Further, the disastrous case of equipment failure may actually increase your credibility, if your listeners see you handle the stressful situation with composure. Finally, demonstrate your good sense by selecting and presenting only visual support that does not violate your listeners' expectations.

JAFFE CONNECTION

Key Terms

multimedia presentations (224)
flip charts (227)
model (232)
text-based visuals (233)
flowcharts (233)
organizational charts (233)
image-based visuals (234)
line graphs (234)
bar graphs (234)
pie graphs (234)
picture graphs or pictographs (235)
diagram (236)

political maps (237)
geographic maps (237)
graphics programs (239)
presentation programs (239)
scanner (239)
transition (240)
build (240)
font (240)
serif font (241)
sans serif font (241)
points (242)

Access

WebTUTOR

for Audio Flashcards of Key Terms

Application and Critical Thinking Questions

1. Observe public speakers—for instance, professors in other courses—who regularly use visuals. What kind(s) of visual displays are most common? Which do you see used least? Evaluate the speakers' use of the visuals; that is, do they use them well, or should they read this chapter? Explain.

2. Which technology for displaying visuals will you probably use for your classroom speeches? Which would you not consider? In your future employment, what equipment do you think you'll use the most? The least? Why?

3. Think about speeches you've heard during the last week. What kinds of visuals, if any, did the speakers use? Are there instances where the use of visuals would have made it easier for you to listen to and understand the material?

4. Discuss with a small group of your classmates how you would best display a drawing in (1) a large auditorium, (2) a classroom, (3) a speech given outdoors, and (4) a presentation in someone's living room. (Several means may be appropriate.)

5. What kind of visual might work most appropriately for a speech on:
   - the circulatory system
   - the physical effects of smoking on the lungs
   - the fabled "silk" trading route
   - ozone depletion
   - changes in mortgage interest rates over two decades

6. Make a visual using a word-processing program on your computer. Experiment with fonts. If your software has a print preview function, look at the overall balance of the visual and adjust line spacing and font size as necessary.

7. Following the principles of design in this chapter, make a series of slides using a presentation program.

Internet Activities

1. Log on to the Internet and go to your *InfoTrac College Edition*. Do a PowerTrac search using the text words "using visual aids" or the key words "visual aids." Look for an article about visual aids in international or intercultural situations. Read it and summarize the information it presents about adapting visuals to foreign or heterogeneous audiences. Or read an article that gives advice on using visual aids successfully.

2. Do a search on www.alltheweb.com for all the words "visual aids font size." Read through a few sites and summarize the material on font size and spacing.

3. Browse the Internet using your favorite search engine, and find and read material on several sites about visual aids. Analyze the credibility of each site. (That is, does the URL contain an .edu or a .com? Why might that make a difference? Who wrote the materials? When? What links can you find? With this information, assess the overall usefulness of each site.) Take notes as you work and bring them to class so that you can discuss your findings with a small group of your classmates.

Hot Links at the Public Speaking Resource Center

Public Speaking Resource Center

The following links are maintained and can be accessed easily via Jaffe Connection at the Public Speaking Resource Center on the Wadsworth Communication Café web site at http://communication.wadsworth.com/publicspeaking/study.html

■ http://hammock.ifas.ufl.edu/txt/fairs/39421
Go here for a good summary of the material in this chapter, plus a strong section on the importance of visual aids. Jimmy Cheek and Carl Beeman authored the material, which is hosted by the Department of Agricultural and Extension Teaching, Florida Cooperative Extension Service, Institute of Food and Agricultural Sciences, University of Florida.

■ http://www.ifas.ufl.edu/~aee3030/visualaids.html
This site has good information on why and when to use visual aids.

■ http://www.sasked.gov.sk.ca/docs/comm20/mod10.html
This site offers an extensive description of how and when to use visual aids in a speech. Additionally, it gives exercises you could use to develop more effective visuals. Sponsored by Saskatchewan Education (1998).

Speech Interactive

Watch and listen to the following speech via Jaffe Speech Interactive on the Jaffe Connection CD-ROM. Observe the effective use of visual aids. You will have an opportunity to critique delivery of the speech and offer suggestions for improvement. Then, compare your Speech Evaluation Checklist and Speech Improvement Plan with the author's.

Jaffe Speech
Interactive

STUDENT SPEECH WITH VISUAL AIDS

Terrestrial Pulmonate Gastropods *by Shaura Neil*

In a flash, I am surrounded by a huge terrestrial pulmonate gastropod. The creature lunges at me; in a mad scramble for survival, I try to fight off the beast. All of a sudden . . . salt begins to fall from the sky. The ionic compound saves my life as the beast begins to wither up and die in front of me. I awaken from my dream and stare at the poster on my wall. I have just had a nightmare involving one of my favorite animals—the slug. In my nightmare salt saves me from a giant slug, but, in reality, it is salt that is the slug's worst nightmare.

If you live in Oregon, you've seen them, these snails-with-no-shells; and, like other Oregonians, you may have been tempted to send the little creatures to slug heaven by salting their slimy backs.

Because I have encountered slews of slugs, I decided to do some research on them—including ways to get rid of them.

Display first slide.

Today, I'll share some interesting facts about slugs and explain their contribution to the environment. Then, I'll describe their major predators and discuss inhumane and humane ways to rid your yard of these creatures.

In this speech, Shaura uses both PowerPoint-generated slides and a three-dimensional object; in one place she uses her hands to illustrate one of the slug's moves. Her computer is hooked up to an LCD display. Before she begins, the machine is on standby, but she reactivates it so that she can bring up a slide by clicking with the mouse.

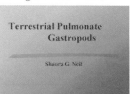

Terrestrial Pulmonate
Gastropods

Shaura G. Neil

Slugs are intriguing creatures. They have an average life span of one to six years and grow to be approximately one and a half to ten inches long. Slugs have amazing eating patterns; they spend most of their active hours devouring food and can masticate several times their own body weight in one day. What do they eat? Well . . .

Slugs will consume a wide variety of food, including lichens, green plants, worms, centipedes, certain insects, animal feces, AND . . . even other slugs.

Display next blank slide

To feed, a slug first extends its mouth over its desired substance, and then the slug uses its jaw to latch onto the food with its tongue. A slug's tongue contains over 27,000 sharp, backward-pointing teeth. Because a slug has teeth upon its tongue, it is nearly impossible for it to bite its own tongue.

Display next slide; format it so that it builds line by line as she discusses the material on it.

For locomotion, the slug crawls on its belly, or, to use a more scientific term,

Click to add the line "One foot."

its "foot." A slug's foot enables it to move because of a series of rippling muscles along the bottom of the foot that propel the slug along. The muscles move in a wavelike motion. Having only one foot can present a variety of problems for the slug.

Click to add the line "Speed: .025 mph."

Slugs can attain a maximum speed of .025 miles per hour. That's only 2 1/2 hundredths of a mile . . . which figures out to 44 yards an hour—less than 1/2 a football field in distance. And that's just the speediest slugs! Also, it can create quite an embarrassment when one slug trips another slug.

Click to add the line "Slug Slime."

A second crucial aspect of a slug's locomotion involves its "slug slime." This slime is vital because it simultaneously increases traction and "greases the skids" of the slug's path. The slime is used not only for movement, but for moisture control, mating, and self defense. How is it protective? When a slug feels threatened it secretes large amounts of the slime, generating a thick, protective coat. A slug's slime also absorbs water. This amazing feature explains why it is impossible to rinse slug slime from your skin after you have finished handling the beast.

Insert the blank slide.

The slugs mating ritual is quite unique. A slug's courtship can last for hours and involves ritualized bouts of lunging, nipping, and side swiping. Slugs are hermaphroditic, meaning that they contain both male and female reproductive organs. Perhaps unfortunately for the slug, slugs require another slug to mate with in order to receive a proper blend of genetic coding. However, the blend cannot be too drastic; a slug can only mate with other slugs of the same species. For example, a ba-

Shaura has inserted a plain slide like this after each slide in the slide show. She puts it on the screen until she comes to the place in her speech that requires the next visual.

Shaura presses her mouse to bring up this slide:

She extends her hands and, with them, makes the latching on motion of a masticating slug.

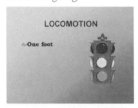

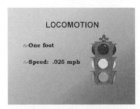

nana slug will only mate with another banana slug. This prevents the unghastly occurrence of slug mutts.

Slugs are not only fascinating creatures, they also contribute to the environment.

Display this slide.

Slugs disperse seeds and spores through their waste elimination, break down decaying plant matter, and help to reduce the population of dozens of other small pests, such as spiders and beetles. The absence of slugs would no doubt hurt the ecosystem.

Despite their contributions to the environment, slugs have many predators.

Small mammals, snakes, amphibians, some species of birds, carnivorous beetles, and other slugs all seek to devour the slug. Slugs have very few defense mechanisms against predators of species other their own. Slugs are colored to blend in with their surroundings and they can secrete their slime, as mentioned above. However, against other slugs, slugs have an amazing strategy. It is common for two slugs to engage in a life or death struggle. In this struggle the two slugs lock tongues. At the commencement of the battle the victor flips his opponent on its back, leaving it to fry in the sun. Do not become caught in the midst of a battle between two slugs.

Her transition summarizes her previous point and introduces her next one. She displays the next slide. Using a build feature allows her to bring up each point as she discusses it.

There remains one predator of slugs that has not been mentioned—the human. I am now going to bring out a visual aid. Those of you with weak stomachs please, look away.

(Bring forth from a paper bag a container of salt.)

Every year, hundreds of innocent slugs are brutally slaughtered through the use of salt by humans. The simple use of NaCl induces an unnecessary and excruciatingly painful death for the slug. Salt creates an ionic imbalance in the slug, impelling it to crawl out of its own slime and rapidly dehydrate. Because slugs have numerous nerve endings all over their body, salt causes undue pain as they die.

Insert blank slide.

There are alternatives to salt. Slug poison is less painful to the slug and can be found at a local hardware store. However, poison creates problems of its own. Poison can be fatal to children and to small pets if consumed. Consequently, parents, pet owners, and city dwellers are wisely cautioned not to use slug poison.

Used coffee grinds placed at the base of plants in a garden is very effective in deterring slugs. The aroma and texture of the grinds is unpleasant to slugs and they will avoid that territory. The only downfall of this method is that grinds must be replaced every day because, once they lose their aroma, they are useless.

Alcohol can also be an effective slug repellent. Slugs are attracted to beer, so if you set a bowl of beer set near a garden, the slugs will gravitate to it and drink alcohol in the beer, which is fatal. Once again, the drawback to this method is that the beer must be replaced daily. There is also the consideration of having to look at dead slugs . . . and dispose of them. Furthermore, family members may no longer want to eat out of a bowl that once held dead slugs. Still, beer is a more humane option than salt.

After learning all of these marvelous facts about slugs, it is my hope to prevent the further use of salt in eliminating them. I plead with you all to end this atrocity. As a slug-lover and an ambassador of peace for slugs everywhere I urge everyone to please, skip the salt.

VIDA 生命 LIFE

©1997 GRETCHEN ROSENBLATT

13

Choosing Effective Language

This chapter will help you:

- Explain how words are linked to culture and meaning

- Distinguish between the denotative and connotative meanings of words

- Define dialects and jargon, and explain when they are appropriate in public speaking

- Tell how the ability to name or label groups and issues is linked to power

- Give examples of epithets, euphemisms, and ageist and sexist language

- List six guidelines for effective language in public speaking

- Understand how alliteration, rhyme, repetition, personification, hyperbole, metaphor, and simile can make a speech more interesting

- Give guidelines for listening and speaking in linguistically diverse contexts

"Life" ©1997 By Gretchen Rosenblatt

The language you choose provides your listeners with more than just information. It also gives them clues about your region of origin, age, educational level, income level, gender, ethnicity, and occupation. For example, the following quotations came from a range of individuals: a professor, a person from the Middle Ages, a nonnative speaker of English, and a New Yorker. Read them and then match the individuals to their quotations.

I got a brothuh who's goin' into thoid grade. The kid's got no hang-ups whatsoeveuh.

Theatetus and the Eleatic stranger discover in the Sophist that defining accurately the "type" sophist is not easy. The difficulty of their task stems from the fact that the differences between the sophist and the philosopher are so minute that it is easy to mistake the one for the other.

When passenger of foot heave in sight, tootle the horn. Trumpet him melodiously at first, but if he still obstacles your passage then tootle him with vigor.

Whan that my fourthe housbond was on bere [funeral bier], I weep algate, and made sory chere, as wyves moten, for it is usage, and with my coverchief covered my visage.

You probably had little difficulty distinguishing (in this order) the New Yorker, the professor, the nonnative speaker of English, and the woman from the Middle Ages. The fact that you could successfully match the pairs shows that words and grammatical choices provide evidence of a speaker's social and personal identity. The quotation from medieval English additionally shows that language changes over time.

Throughout the years, you've developed a distinctive **voice**—a way of phrasing your ideas that expresses your unique view of the world and distinguishes your speaking style from that of your friends. Similarly, in public speaking you're developing a personalized way of communicating within the norms of the culture. As a result, your public voice differs from that of other speakers within your classroom.

In the study of rhetoric, language falls within the canon of style, which is the focus of this chapter. First, the chapter looks at some aspects of language itself and examines how our vocabularies both reveal and express cultural assumptions. Next, it provides tips for effective language choices in U.S. classrooms. Finally, it discusses ways of speaking in linguistically diverse settings.

Language Reflects Culture

Languages are verbal codes made up of a system of symbols that a community of language speakers uses to share their ideas. **Symbols** are signs that represent or stand for objects and concepts the community shares. However, in order for these signs to be meaningful, the persons who use them must understand them similarly. To illustrate, we sometimes use symbols in the form of simple drawings to convey ideas such as those depicted in Figure 13.1.

If you're familiar with these symbols, you know them as: (a) recycle, (b) no smoking, (c) a curve in the road, and (d) New Mexico. Some, such as the highway sign, are well known—all drivers learn its meaning in order to pass their licensing exam. Less familiar is the "zia," or sun symbol, which represents my home state of New Mexico. Obviously, if you're unfamiliar with a sign, you won't be able to decipher its meaning.

Voice
An individual's distinct way of using words and phrasing ideas to express a unique view of the world.

Languages
Verbal codes consisting of symbols a speech community uses to communicate with one another.

Symbols
Signs that represent or stand for objects and concepts.

FIGURE 13.1 Four signs or symbols: (a) recycle, (b) no smoking, (c) a curve in the road, and (d) New Mexico.

Although humans can represent some ideas by pictograms or drawings, they can't draw pictures to communicate every concept. So, each society has developed a language system made up of **words**—verbal symbols that stand for or represent cultural ideas. Each member of the culture learns the language in order to communicate and interact within the group.

> **Words**
>
> Verbal symbols that stand for or represent ideas.

Words and Meaning

In *New Words and a Changing American Culture,* Raymond Gozzi (1990) explains that words are the names we give to our "cultural memories." They serve as "markers of cultural attention" or shared experiences that we consider significant enough to name. Put another way, one or more people in a culture notice a phenomenon, formulate an idea about it, and label it—they encode their idea into a word. The process looks something like this:

Long ago humans:

1. Noticed a phenomenon—some creatures can fly.

2. Formed a concept—all these creatures have two legs, two wings, a beak, and feathers.

3. Created a label—for this category of flying animals, the label *bird* (English), *oiseau* (French), *pájaro* or *ave* (Spanish).

According to this theory, our vocabulary indicates what our society identifies as significant, and the labels we create carve out our interpretations of our world, forming the social realities in which we live, think, and act. An example might help. Think of the words you know for different kinds of snow. There's *snow,* of course, maybe *blizzard, downy flakes,* and *sleet,* but can you think of more words to represent snow? This task would be easier if you were an Eskimo, for Eskimos have named many different kinds of snow. Does that mean they perceive varieties of snow that you do not? Maybe. It almost certainly means that knowing subtle differences between kinds of snow is more significant in that culture than it is in others.

It's easy to see how humans create words for objects such as birds, snow, buildings, or chairs. However, words also label less tangible experiences, actions, feelings, and ideas. To understand this better, think of the meanings (if any) you attach to the word *Woodstock.* Before 1969, people familiar with the word associated it with a small town in upstate New York. However, after the 1969 rock concert held on a farm outside the town—plus recordings, films, books, interviews, and articles that surrounded those events—the word *Woodstock* came to symbolize a way of living, thinking, and acting characteristic of the "Woodstock generation." (To cartoon fans, Woodstock is the bird in the Peanuts cartoon strip.)

Our languages change to reflect cultural transformations. Did you know that more than 10,000 words have been added to English since 1961? They include *gridlock, yup-*

DIVERSITY IN PRACTICE

Dialects

A **dialect** is a variant form of a language. There are many English dialects: One is British English (BritSpeak); others include American English, Black English (ebonics), international English, and a variety of other regional and ethnic group variations (Dialects Doing Well, 1998). The dialect most common in institutions such as education, business, and broadcasting is **Standard English.** It is the language of print—and the version of English widely used by public speakers in the United States.

You may speak a dialect other than Standard English. Although your dialect functions well in many settings, you may choose to be bidialectical, meaning that you use one version of English around family and friends and another in public contexts. This is called **code switching.** Pauline Jefferson, for instance, uses Standard English when she transacts business with customers in her bank and when she makes public presentations for her co-workers. However, when she speaks before a small female audience in her local church, she switches codes, alternating between Standard English and ebonics.

For more information about this topic, log on to the Internet and use a search engine such as www.alltheweb.com to search for the exact term *code switching* or go to www.slanguages.com for a look at English slang terms that vary by city. Also, the site, http://www.americandialect.org, sponsored by the American Dialect Association, offers scholarly and less-academic links to information on dialects such as ebonics, the Ocracoke Brogue, and American Sign Language.

---

pie, microchip, junk food, and the *mall.* When your grandparents were growing up, there were no malls or junk food, no gridlock or microchips. They either didn't exist or they weren't important enough to name (Gozzi, 1990). In addition to creating new terms, English adopts words from other languages, including *coffee* from the Arabians, *ambiance* from the French, and *kamikazi* from the Japanese. And, meanings change over time. If you read a Shakespearean play, you'll be struck by the differences between the English of Shakespeare's time and the English of today.

Denotative Meaning

Words *denote* or "point" to an object or abstract idea; thus, the **denotative meaning** is what the word names or identifies. The following list might clarify this further. You'll find several categories followed by examples of words that denote or stand for objects or ideas within each:

- **Real objects:** rocks, buildings, clouds, daisies
- **Imaginary things:** unicorns, Martians, elves, Superman
- **Qualities of objects:** softness, generosity, tall, narrow
- **Feelings:** anger, envy, peace, love
- **States of being:** happiness, depression, contentment, gratitude
- **Abstractions:** justice, quarks, conscience, success
- **Actions:** exercising, singing, eating, studying

Dialect

A variant form of a language.

Standard English

The English dialect most commonly used in public speaking and in institutions in the United States.

Code Switching

Changing from one language code to another in order to adapt to different audiences.

Denotative Meaning

What a word names or identifies.

When you look up words in the dictionary, you find their denotative meanings. For example, the label *report card* denotes "a report on a student that is periodically submitted by a school to the student's parents or guardian" (*Webster's,* 1967).

However, some words stand for more than one idea; their meaning is **ambiguous** in that their context determines how we interpret them. For instance, the word *pot* has at least five meanings:

- A rounded container used chiefly for domestic purposes

- A sum of money, as in the total amount of bets at stake at one time (the jackpot)

- Ruin or deterioration, as in "her business went to pot"

- Slang for marijuana

- A shot in which a billiard ball is pocketed *(Webster's)*

You know that when you cook in a pot, you're thinking of the first meaning. But when you discuss legalization of pot, you're not talking about laws regulating cooking containers or billiard shots! The context determines the meaning.

As you plan language for your speech, make sure to use the correct word in the correct context to denote your intended meaning. Use a dictionary or thesaurus if you need to. Increasing your vocabulary and discriminating among shades of meaning between words is a good idea, for the greater your vocabulary, the more power you will have to communicate your thoughts precisely.

Connotative Meaning

Although words denote objects and concepts, they also carry emotional overtones or **connotative meanings.** That is, words not only stand for ideas, but they also represent feelings and associations related to the concepts. To illustrate, *report card* has different connotations for different individuals depending on their experiences. How do you feel about yours? Positive, because your parents rewarded you for good grades? Negative, because your parents nagged you to study more? Your reaction is the connotative meaning of *report card* for you. Language can be emotionally charged—either positively or negatively—and we commonly substitute a more neutral word for one with negative connotations. To discuss this further, we now turn to epithets and euphemisms.

Epithets

Epithets are words or phrases used to describe some quality of a person or group; they often have negative connotations. For example, one political party refers to the other as *extremist* because carefully conducted opinion polls show that voters respond negatively to the term. Within hours, the party under attack counters with the term *big government spenders,* another term that offends.

Some epithets are so powerful and so negative that it's difficult even to write them. Words such as *nerd, pig* (for police officers), *anti-choice, queer,* and *nigger* are negative epithets that function to frame perceptions about the group. For example, calling anti-abortion advocates "anti-choice" creates a negative image, whereas the group's self-chosen title, "pro-life," has positive connotations.

Members of labeled groups often try to lessen the negative power of the epithet by accepting and using the term themselves. For instance, police officers take the letters of the word *pig* and reinterpret them to form the slogan *Pride, Integrity, Guts.* Similarly, some homosexuals take the epithet *queer* and transform it for use in slogans such as "We're queer and we're here" or in labels such as Queer Nation. One who did so explained, "We have to take the power out of these words" (Ray & Badle, 1993).

Ambiguous

Word that stands for more than one object or idea; its meaning depends on the context.

Connotative Meaning

Emotional overtones, related feelings, and associations that cluster around a term.

Epithets

Words or phrases with powerful negative connotations, used to describe some quality of a person or group.

Use of jargon—a set of technical words associated with a topic—is appropriate in contexts where everyone knows the terms. However, undefined jargon in a speech to a lay audience is generally more confusing than enlightening. (Anita Cirulis)

Euphemisms

Euphemisms

Words or phrases that substitute inoffensive terms to discuss potentially offensive, embarrassing, or unpleasant things.

Euphemisms, in contrast, are words or phrases that substitute an agreeable or inoffensive term for a more direct one that might offend, embarrass, or suggest something unpleasant. We regularly use euphemisms for things we hesitate to speak of, such as bodily functions (going to the powder room), religion (the Man Upstairs), and death (passed away). Euphemisms also mask unpleasant situations, such as corporate layoffs. It sounds better for a company to "downsize" than to "fire" or "lay off" workers.

Public speakers often use euphemisms for controversial actions, ideas, and policies. For example, government officials call new taxes *revenue enhancement* or *investments in America* to soften the reality of planned tax increases. Similarly, military officers use the term *collateral damage* rather than *bombing of civilians* to describe the unpleasant results of a military action. Learn more about this subject by logging onto the Internet and using a search engine such as <u>www.dogpile.com</u> to search for the word *euphemisms*.

Watch for connotative language in your research. For example, a U.S. military leader calls an opponent a *warlord* rather than an *influential leader*. Politicians label their opponents *obstructionists* who *attack* and *destroy* legislation, whereas they, of course, *stand up for the rights of ordinary people*. By carefully choosing their words, these speakers hope to create perceptions that produce the spin or interpretation they want.

Jargon

Jargon

A specialized, technical vocabulary that serves the interests and activities of a particular group.

Jargon is a specialized, technical vocabulary and style that serves special groups (doctors, lawyers), interests (feminism, knitting), and activities (football, gardening). For example, football jargon has specialized meanings for *drive* and *down* and *safety*. When everyone in your audience knows the meaning of the specialized vocabulary, it's appropriate to use jargon. However, if you're communicating with nonspecialists, you'll need to define and clarify technical terms to avoid excluding listeners. By translating jargon, you demonstrate that you are rhetorically sensitive to your audience.

In summary, languages are systems of symbols—words that denote or stand for ideas and evoke feelings or connotative meanings that differ from person to person. Carefully choose your words, making sure that you use the correct word in context. Pay attention to connotative meanings—either positive or negative—that listeners might attach to your words. You can demonstrate that you are rhetorically sensitive by adapting your dialect and your jargon to your audience and the occasion. As you do this, you are taking into account the cultural implications of your terminology.

STOP AND CHECK

Think Critically about Denotative and Connotative Words

Test your understanding of meanings with these exercises:

1. Whenever they launch a new product, marketers carefully select terminology that will have positive connotations for consumers. Look up two or three advertisements in your favorite magazine, then list some of the words you find in each ad. What is the denotative meaning of each word on your list? Now jot down some of your personal connotations for each term. Evaluate the overall marketability of the term itself.

2. Work with your classmates to make a list of the car models represented within the class (Mustang, Accord, Sport, etc.). Within a small group identify the denotative meaning of each word. Then discuss the connotative associations you think the manufacturers hope will sell the car.

   For additional information, log on to the Internet and go to http://www.wuacc.edu/services/zzcwwctr/connotation.txt, a website from Washburn University that gives exercises to test how connotations differ among various individuals. For an additional exercise about denotative and connotative words, go to Chapter 13: Activities for Jaffe Connection at the Public Speaking Resource Center, http//communication.wadsworth.com/publicspeaking/study.html.

Public Speaking Resource Center

Ethical Language Choices

Language choices have ethical implications, because words and phrases can include or exclude, affirm or dismiss the value of individuals or whole groups (Johannesen, 1996). Furthermore, your word choices affect your own credibility. For example, Seiter, Larsen, and Skinner (1998) found that speakers who put down persons with disabilities or focused on the disability rather than on the individual lost credibility, likability, and persuasiveness. In this section, we'll look at ways your vocabulary choices both reveal your biases and influence your audience's ideas in two areas—age and gender.

Eliminate Ageist Language

The U.S. culture places a great deal of value on youth, and older people are not given the same respect they are in other societies. This can be seen in the **ageist language** used to portray older people (Freimuth & Jamieson, 1979). Here are a few common examples.

Ageist Language

Portrays older people in demeaning or unflattering ways.

1. Stereotypes. Common misconceptions are that older people are close minded, less capable mentally, unhealthy, physically unattractive, lonely, and poor. Language choices can perpetuate these stereotypes. Examples include *set in her ways, losing his marbles, ready for a nursing home,* and *well-preserved* (to describe an attractive elderly person).

2. Labels. Often you hear negative labels applied to elderly people. A few examples are *old duffer, little old lady* (in tennis shoes), *granny, gramps or pop, old biddy, old hag,* and *dirty old man.* What kind of mental images do you form as you read through this list?

In cultures where elderly citizens are highly respected, ageist language is not the issue that it is in the United States, where youth is valued. Here, ageist language can demean older people by subtly influencing listeners to perceive them negatively. (Joel Simon)

3. Dismissive language. Language can be applied to elderly people in ways that discount the importance of their ideas, as these examples show: *too old, senile, no longer in the thick of things, over the hill.*

4. Language that values youth. Such phrases as *feel younger* or *look ten years younger* subtly reinforce the notion that it's better to be younger.

Eliminate Sexist Language

Sexist Language
Negatively influences the way listeners see men and women.

In a similar way, **sexist language** can subtly influence the way we view women and men. In the last few decades, there has been an emphasis on removing sexist terms from English (Mura & Waggenspack, 1983; Hacker, 1998). In fact, your instructor will probably insist that you use gender-neutral terminology. Here are two examples of sexist language common in the past.

■ Generic "he" or "man." People who are now your grandparents' age were taught in high school English to use the pronoun *he* to designate a person of either sex, as this illustration from a 1938 speech text shows.

> When one has settled upon a subject and has some notion of what he wishes to do with it, his immediate concern is with the materials, the stuff out of which his speech is to be woven. He must have ideas and data with which to hold attention and to make and impress his point (Winans, 1938).

Such language arguably excludes females by making them invisible. The use of the suffix *man* creates similar problems. Replace words like *chairman, mailman, spokesman, caveman,* and *policeman* with gender-inclusive labels such as *chairperson, mail carrier, spokesperson, cave dweller,* and *police officer.*

■ Nonparallel language. Nonparallel language means that the two sexes are not treated equally in language. There are several types of **nonparallel language.** One occurs when a suffix is added to a male term in order to designate a female, as in actor-actress, and steward-stewardess. Another comes from marking job titles, as in a *male nurse* or a *female judge.* (Would you ever say a *female nurse* or a *male judge?*) Nonparallel language also occurs in differing terms of address; a woman may be known as *Mrs. Alberto Sanchez,* but men aren't called *Mr. Jane Andrews.* Similarly, couples may be perceived as *man and wife* but never as *woman and husband.*

Nonparallel Language

Does not treat the two sexes equally.

In short, terminology is not neutral. The words you select have the power to influence your listeners' perceptions, not only regarding issues but also regarding individuals and groups. The fact that some language choices demean or put down groups or individuals raises ethical questions and colors your listeners' views about you. Making sure that your word choices are inclusive is one way to show respect for diversity, and doing so will likely enhance your personal credibility.

STOP AND CHECK

Avoiding Language That Demeans

With a small group of your classmates, select a group that has been put down or demeaned by language use. This may include women, specific ethnic groups, religious groups, or groups with alternative lifestyles.

1. Make a list of some terms that outsiders have used to label members of the group.

2. Then list some labels the group places on itself.

3. Assess the connotative meanings associated with the words on each list.

With a few classmates, talk about ways you can select language sensitively with respect to the specific group you've chosen.

To investigate this topic further, log on to the Internet and use a search engine such as www.dogpile.com or www.alltheweb.com to search for an exact term such as *sexist language, ageism,* or *racism.* If you are using Jaffe's Web Tutor, you can participate in an online discussion about strategies for avoiding language that demeans.

Use Effective Language in Public Speaking

Several principles in the canon of style will help you use language more effectively in your public speeches. As you select the wording for your speeches, choose language that is accurate, appropriate, concise, clear, concrete, and interesting.

Be Accurate

Be accurate in your word choices. One form of inaccuracy is to use similar sounding, but incorrect, words called **malaprops**—named after the fictional Mrs. Malaprop in Richard Sheridan's comedy, *The Rivals.* This character consistently used the wrong word, to the great amusement of her audience. Children are noted for their use of malaprops or cute sayings. For example, a little boy who was discussing eating habits with his mother asked, "If you're a *vegetarian,* why don't you fix our cat?" He obviously confused the word with *veterinarian.*

Malaprops

Using one word in place of another that sounds like it but has a different meaning; often humorous.

Malapropism is cute for children, but embarrassing for adults. One government cabinet officer, speaking before a group of physicians, stated alcohol could lead to *pso-*

riasis [sir EYE uh sis] of the liver. Soon, she realized that her listeners were chuckling. When she recognized her mistake, she laughed, too, and quickly acknowledged that, of course, she meant *cirrhosis* [sir OH sis] of the liver. She knew the difference between psoriasis (a skin disease) and cirrhosis; her mistake was simply a slip of the tongue. (For additional examples of malaprops, log on to your *InfoTrac College Edition* and do a Power-Trac search for the text term *bloopers* or *malaprops*.)

In addition, it is a wise policy not to use a dictionary word without knowing the context in which it's commonly used. For example, a Japanese student told about a car wreck that, in her words, "*distorted* the car door." Her Japanese–English dictionary came up with distort to convey the idea that the car was "bent," "caved in," or "dented." Although the word does mean "crooked," "deformed," or "contorted," no native speaker of English would use *distorted* in the context of a dented fender.

Finally, strive to use standard grammatical choices in contexts that call for Standard English. Nonstandard forms such as *me and him* (instead of *he and I*) or *they was* (instead of *they were*) can create negative impressions in a job interview or other public presentation. The key is to adapt your grammar to fit the occasion. To check a grammatical form, go to http://www.bartleby.com/index.html, a site sponsored by Columbia University to assist you in composing a message in Standard English.

Be Appropriate

Match your language to the topic, the audience, the situation, and yourself as an individual. Generally, language in public settings is more formal and contains less slang than you would use in conversations; however, your audience and the situation should have the final influence over your linguistic choices. For example, the wording and level of formality you would use to express your ideas would differ when you address homeless people gathered in a park or members of an alumni association at a formal banquet, even when the topic is the same. And language used in a lecture differs from language used in a tribute delivered at a funeral.

Also, the use of a dialect is appropriate for some individuals, but not others. For example, an African-American might use the dialect known as ebonics when it's expected and appropriate; however, a Euro-American or an Asian-American is usually wise to avoid ebonic forms, even in the same setting.

Be Concise

Verbiage
Nonessential words.

Directness is valued in the U.S. culture. We commonly eliminate words considered unnecessary. In fact, padding your speech with nonessential words is called **verbiage.** Here's an example from a caller on a radio talk show: "What they did is they took the issue and distorted it, and how they did it is they did it by . . ." He would have been more concise had he said, "They distorted the issue by . . ."

Students often clutter their speeches with too many words. This example from a student speech on the value of learning a second language shows both how he actually gave the speech and how he could have given it:

As he gave it:

I became interested in this topic *upon the constant hounding of my father urging me* to take a foreign language, preferably Japanese, *the reason being is because* my major is business, and the Japanese are dominating the international business scene.

As he might have given it:

I became interested in this topic because my father constantly hounded me to take a foreign language—preferably Japanese. He reasoned that my major is business, and the Japanese are dominant players on the international business scene.

If you've ever tried to make sense of complicated instructions, you know the importance of using words accurately, regardless of whether you're translating from one language into another or using words from your own language that you don't really understand. (Anne Dowie)

Although brevity or conciseness is valued in the U.S. culture, many other cultures value flowery words and language; what we may consider verbiage, other groups may regard as good verbal skills as Diversity in Practice: Understanding Aristide explains.

Be Clear

The purpose of public speaking is to clarify ideas, rather than to make them more difficult to understand. One of the best ways to make ideas clear is to avoid jargon, which we've already discussed. However, as you research your topic, you will probably find a number of technical words in your sources. Avoid using technical terms that you don't understand, or define any jargon you must use. Jesse failed to do this in his discussion of how AIDS is transmitted.

DIVERSITY IN PRACTICE

Understanding Aristide

When Jean-Bertrand Aristide, the President of Haiti, speaks, American congressional leaders and administration officials are often confused. According to *U.S. News & World Report,* he "speaks a cultural tongue Americans don't understand" (Zimmermann & Goode, 1994, p. 32). He is a master of competitive oratory, a type of speechmaking that features indirect language, laced with proverbs and metaphors, and he commonly uses a stylistic device called "throwing pwent" in which he is intentionally indirect and ambiguous. Contrast this with the public speaking tradition explained in this chapter that emphasizes clarity, concrete wording, and elimination of vague terminology, and you can see the potential for misunderstandings on both sides.

For more information about this topic, log on to your *InfoTrac College Edition* and look up the key words *ambiguous language.* Read one of the articles you find there.

> We've all been taught that AIDS is perinatal and that it is transmitted through sexual contact.

Following the speech, someone asked what *perinatal* meant. Jesse didn't know; the word came from an article he'd read, and he had not looked it up. (*Perinatal* actually means "associated with the birth process, the period immediately before, during, or just after the time of birth.") If he'd taken the time to find out what the word denoted, Jesse could have said instead,

> We've been taught that AIDS is transmitted from mother to child perinatally—that is, during the birth process—and that it is transmitted through sexual activity.

This version would have been more effective, for the brief definition clarifies, rather than obscures, the word's meaning.

Be Concrete

Concrete Words
Specific, rather than general or abstract, terms.

Another important aspect of style, one that can help your listeners form precise understandings, is to choose **concrete words**—those that are specific rather than abstract, particular rather than general. Think of words as ranging along a scale of abstraction such as this:

abstract/general	entertainer
	musician
	instrumentalist
	woodwind player
concrete/particular	saxophonist

If you say, "She plays a saxophone," your ideas are much more concrete than if you say, "She's an instrumentalist." But "She's an instrumentalist" is more concrete than "She's an entertainer." The more distinct and specific the words you choose, the more vivid your images and the more precise your meanings.

This excerpt from Bob's speech on electronic drums is exceptional for its use of concrete language:

> Picture your stereotypical rock drummer: shaggy, smells, looks, and sometimes acts like a lower primate, body type—lean and wiry, definitely the fast-twitch kind of muscles, and they aren't in the head. And it always seems that they're the first in the band to OD. On the Muppets TV show, the drummer's name was "Animal," and they kept him chained to his set of drums.

As you can see, concrete images help you picture the sights, movements—even the smells—of drummers. This is an example of language that appeals to listeners' senses.

Vague Words
Imprecise terms that have indefinite boundaries.

Vague words are those with indefinite boundaries. Put simply, they are words that do not precisely define a concept. For example, what is a hill? When does it become a mountain? Who is old? A child thinks a nineteen-year-old is old, but a nineteen-year-old thinks old is being forty-five. What is large? Small? Compared to what? A giant pizza is not on the same scale as a giant building. You can lessen your use of vague words by choosing specific details to define or illustrate what you mean. Let's say you're speaking of a "small" inheritance. Give a dollar figure that shows what you consider "small." One listener may think $2,000, whereas another has $20,000 in mind.

Be Interesting

A major reason you speak is to help your listeners see, feel, and remember the information you are presenting. Colorful, vivid language helps keep listener attention and inter-

Create vivid images by using concrete words. Saying that Natalya is a violinist is more specific than calling her a *musician;* but musician is more specific than the term *entertainer.* (Anita Cirulis)

est. There are a number of ways to make the language of your speech more memorable: alliteration, rhyming, repetition, personification, hyperbole, metaphors, and similes.

STOP AND CHECK

Choosing More Accurate Wording

The purpose of this exercise is to raise your awareness of vague words that we typically use in place of more precise ones. For example, *get* is a common verb that can often be replaced with a more concrete term. In the blank that follows the sentences below, replace the *get* or its past tense *got* with more precise wording. You can complete this activity online under Chapter 13: Activities for Jaffe Connection at the Public Speaking Resouce Center, http://communication.wadsworth.com/publicspeaking/study.html

Can you *get* the telephone, please?   _____
What did you *get* for your birthday?   _____
Why did you *get* angry about that?   _____
I'm *getting* ready to outline my speech.   _____
He *got* a thousand dollars just for giving one speech! _____
It *got* cold last night.   _____
He *gets* nervous just before he speaks.   _____
After I studied the calculus problem for over an hour, I finally *got* it!   _____
You can *get* information 24 hours a day on the Internet. _____
After he *gets* here, we can leave.   _____

Alliteration

Alliteration
Words with recurring initial sounds.

Alliteration is the use of words that have the same recurring initial sounds. For instance, the keynote speaker at a conference used the alliterative phrase "*Choose change or chase* it" to organize her presentation. Another speaker referred to the writer, Harriet Beecher Stowe, as "very *proper*, *primly* dressed, and *precisely* spoken" (Carnahan, 1999). In another example, Natalie used alliteration in a speech about seat belts: "Don't let *fate* *forecast* your *future*. Buckle up."

One way to help listeners remember the main ideas in a topical message is to alliterate the main points. A speech coach used this alliterative pattern:

Good team members have:

Commitment.

Communication.

Competitiveness.

Rhyming

Rhymes
Words that end in the same sound.

As you know, **rhymes** are words that end in the same sounds. You can rhyme single words, phrases, or lines. For an example of a speech that is rhymed throughout, listen to a recording made by a rap artist. Although it is possible to rhyme an entire speech, you will probably use rhymes in more limited ways. This excerpt from the drum speech shows how Bob rhymed three words within one sentence:

So I want to examine this new world of the push-button beat and pose the question to you: "What or who would you rather have in your band, a *mean* and *clean* drum *machine* or a stereotypical rock drummer?"

You can also use rhymes effectively for wording the main points of your speeches. Here are two examples:

We are faced with two choices:

Retreat.

Compete.

Workplaces typically have three generations of employees (Peters, 1999):

Boomers

Bloomers

Zoomers

As you might imagine, this stylistic device often enables listeners to remember major points more easily.

Repetition

Repetition
Saying the same word or phrase at the beginning or at the end of clauses or sentences.

Technically, there are two ways to use **repetition.** One is to repeat the same word or phrase at the beginning of clauses or sentences. For example, Ronald Reagan's (1986) tribute to the Challenger crew of seven astronauts who lost their lives when their spacecraft exploded included these repetitive clauses: "We will cherish each of their stories, *stories of* triumph and bravery, *stories of* true American heroes." Another type of repetition restates the same phrase at the end of a phrase or a sentence. Lincoln's famous phrase, "government of *the people,* by *the people,* for *the people*" is an example. This speech excerpt, which shows two repeated phrases, comes from a talk by a Native American speaker (Archambault, 1992):

> This idea is not original with me. It was taught to us by a great leader of the Lakota people—my people—Chief Sitting Bull. *He taught us* that Indian children could succeed in modern society and yet retain the values of their culture, *values such as* respect for the earth, for wildlife, for rivers and streams, for plants and trees; and *values such as* caring for each other and for family and community. *He taught us* that we must leave behind more hope than we found.

Personification

Personification means giving human characteristics to nonhuman entities. These entities include animals, countries, natural objects and processes, and social processes. Native American Chief Seattle (1853, 1971) used personification in an 1853 speech before the Governor of the Washington Territory:

> Yonder sky that has wept tears of compassion upon my people for centuries untold, and which to us appears changeless and eternal, may change.

Personification
Giving human characteristics to nonhuman entities.

Hyperbole

Hyperbole (hype) is the use of exaggeration for effect. For example, politicians say things such as, "If we don't do something about health care, there will be *no more* jobs." Or "If we don't do something about AIDS, there will be *no more* people." They use these exaggerations to indicate that the problems are serious and deserve government attention.

Although hyperbole can be effective, excessive hype can lessen the speaker's credibility. Some exaggerations border on the ridiculous, and people feel the speaker is overreacting or lying. Moreover, instead of focusing on the policy the discussion often changes focus to the hyperbole itself. *No* jobs? Really? *No* more people? At all? In the classroom, Zack's use of hyperbole similarly created a negative impression:

> Imagine a world where you have no trees, total pollution, and a landfill in every neighborhood. This is where we are heading because of our abuse of the land and lack of concern for ways to replenish the earth and her resources. There is a way where each person . . . could help, maybe even solve the problem. It's called recycling.

Hyperbole
Using exaggeration for effect.

His point that recycling will contribute to the preservation of natural resources is a good one. However, the use of *no* trees, *total* pollution, and *every* neighborhood overstates the case; furthermore, although recycling may help, it will not *solve the problem* of environmental pollution in and of itself. Thus, Zack's exaggerations led some listeners to think he was not exercising good reasoning. Because this was his introduction, they discounted his ideas from the very beginning.

Metaphor

The use of metaphor is discussed extensively in other places throughout this text (see Chapters 8 and 18). To review, **metaphors** are implied comparisons in which one thing is spoken of as being something else; the words *like* and *as* are not used. To Professor Michael Osborn (1997), speech students are builders who frame and craft their speeches, or they are weavers who intertwine verbal and nonverbal elements into a successful performance, or they're climbers who scramble over barriers or obstacles such as speech anxiety on their way to a successful speech. In a speech given at Kansas State University on the anniversary of women's suffrage, newscaster Bernard Shaw (1993) used a metaphor comparing democracy to food preparation.

Metaphors
Implied comparison in which one thing is spoken of as being something else.

Democracy is not a smooth sauce. . . . Democracy is the lone dish in constant need of seasoning, stirring, tasting. Democracy is never . . . never done.

One danger in using metaphors is the possibility of beginning with one comparison and ending with another. This is called a **mixed metaphor.** By way of illustration, a panelist on a television news broadcast said the following about deploying U.S. troops to another country:

> We must solve the root problem, or the line will be drawn in the sand, and we'll be back in the soup again.

As you can see he combined three images: "root" compares the problem to a plant; the "line drawn in the sand," an uncrossable boundary; and "soup," a food. By going in three directions with his comparison, this speaker left his listeners with no clear image.

Simile

Similes are similar to metaphors in that they compare two items that are unlike in most ways but alike in one essential detail. However, they differ from metaphors in that they explicitly state the connection, and they contain the word *like* or *as*. Jesus often used similes in his teachings, as this example demonstrates:

> The kingdom of heaven is like a grain of mustard seed, which a man took, and sowed in his field. Which indeed is the least of all seeds: but when it is grown, it is the greatest among herbs, and becomes a tree, so that the birds of the air come and lodge in the branches thereof (Matthew 13:31–32).

Similarly, Chief Seattle (1853, 1971) used vivid similes, as this excerpt from his speech indicates:

> [The white] people are many. They are like the grass that covers vast prairies. My people are few. They resemble the scattering trees of a storm-swept plain. . . . There was a time when our people covered the land as the waves of a wind-ruffled sea cover its shell paved floor, but that time long since passed away with the greatness of tribes that are now but a mournful memory.

When you read through speeches, you will see some metaphors and similes emerge and reemerge. Some arise from our experiences of being human. For instance, all human groups experience day and night, sickness and health, seasonal changes, and family relationships. Osborn (1967, 1977) calls these **archetypal symbols,** because all humankind understand them. Other comparisons relate to cultural modes of transportation (the ship of state) and sports (the game of life), and as the culture changes, new metaphors linked to electronic technology are emerging (experiencing static, feeling wired).

Language and Pluralistic Audiences

In classrooms across the country, students with the following linguistic diversity commonly sit side by side:

- Some are monolingual (speak one language only).
- Others are bidialectical (speak two English dialects).
- A few are multidialectical (speak three or more English dialects).
- Some are bilingual (speak two languages).

Mixed Metaphor
Combining metaphors from two or more sources, beginning with one comparison and ending with another.

Similes
Short comparisons that use the word *like* or *as* to compare two items that are alike in one essential detail.

Archetypal Symbols
Recurring metaphors and similes that arise from shared human and natural experiences.

■ A few are multilingual (speak three or more languages).

Communicating in a linguistically diverse setting can be complicated and frustrating. However, you can plan ways to adapt to multilingual situations that will be beneficial to everyone involved.

Adapt to Multilingual Situations

When you speak to a linguistically diverse audience, don't assume you'll be instantly understood. Take a hypothetical student, Ryan, whose only language is Standard English. His classmates include people who speak Spanish and English, Japanese and English, ebonics and Standard English, and Mandarin Chinese and English. Because he wants to speak effectively, he adapts his speech by using a few simple strategies:

■ Before preparing his outline, he tries to "hear" the terminology and jargon related to his topic in the way a nonnative speaker of English might hear it.

■ When possible, he chooses simple words that most people would understand; however, he does not talk "down" to his audience.

■ He identifies words that might be confusing and uses them on visual aids, which he displays as he talks.

■ He defines difficult words and jargon terms as he goes along.

■ He builds in redundancy or repetition by saying the same idea in a number of different ways.

Put simply, being mindful of linguistic diversity allows Ryan to strategically select language that communicates effectively with listeners from various linguistic backgrounds.

When you're an audience member who's listening to a nonfluent speaker, you must put forth more effort than normal in order to make the experience satisfying, both to the speaker and to yourself. Remember that the major goal of any speech is communication of ideas, not perfection of language skills. So as you listen, try to understand the message by concentrating on the ideas rather than on each specific word. This may require a special kind of patience as well as the ability to take the perspective of the communicator. **Perspective taking** means that you put yourself in the other person's shoes. That is, you try to imagine what it would be like to give a speech in a foreign language to a group of native speakers of that language. Also, keep in mind that nonfluency is linked to inexperience in your language, not to lack of intelligence or lack of education (Lustig & Koester, 1993; Simons, Vazquez, & Harris, 1993; Thiederman, 1991a, 1991b). These additional tips can help you listen more effectively:

Perspective Taking
Putting yourself in the other person's shoes.

■ Approach the speech with a positive attitude, expecting to understand.

■ Listen all the way through. Make special efforts to keep your mind from wandering in the middle of the speech. It may help to take notes.

■ Practice *respons*-ibility in co-creating meaning. Plan to give appropriate nonverbal feedback to demonstrate your interest, patience, and support for the speaker.

■ Control your negative emotional responses. Let's face it, it is difficult to deal with linguistic barriers, and people often get frustrated or bored when there are language differences.

■ Don't laugh, even if the speakers do, at their language skills. Often they laugh nervously to relieve tension.

Speaking through an interpreter requires certain adaptations in language and delivery. (Bob Daemmrich/The Image Works)

Adapt to an Interpreter

Although using an interpreter may seem remote now, you may eventually have to communicate through someone who translates your words into another language, including sign language. If you have occasion to use an interpreter, here are a few things to remember.

- Keep your language simple. Do not use overly technical words or uncommon vocabulary.

- In advance of the speech, provide your interpreter with an outline of your speech so that he or she may check the meaning of any unfamiliar words. The interpreter may also use it during your speech as a guide to what you will say next.

- When your interpreter translates into another language, speak in short units. Don't try entire paragraphs; rather, speak one or two sentences, then allow the interpreter to speak.

- Consider looking at the interpreter as he or she speaks. This will indicate that you are ready for the translation; it also signals the audience to look at the interpreter rather than at you.

- Because it takes two to three times longer to speak through an interpreter who translates into another language, shorten your speech accordingly.

Jaffe Speech Interactive

Remember that using interpreters is not easy, but without them, you would not be able to communicate your ideas effectively. Consequently, work on maintaining a positive attitude throughout the speaking event. (Appendix C provides an example of a classroom speech, delivered in Spanish and interpreted into English by a fellow student.)

Summary

Language is a tool that humans use to communicate with one another and build complex societies. We use words to name our cultural memories—meaning that we label those things we notice and need to know in order to survive; in short, we name the events, people, and things we find important. Languages are dynamic, with words being added, borrowed, and discontinued in response to social changes.

Words denote or stand for objects, actions, and ideas; jargon, a technical vocabulary common to members of an occupation, can confuse outsiders who don't know their meaning. More importantly, words have connotative meanings that consist of the feelings and associations that the word implies. Epithets generally carry negative connotations, whereas euphemisms put negative things more positively. In recent years, people have become concerned about the power of words—especially those used in ways that hurt others—and have worked to eliminate sexist, ageist, racist, and other demeaning speech from acceptable vocabulary.

Your speaking effectiveness will depend largely on how well you can put your ideas into words. Thus, there are several guidelines for using language effectively in public speaking. First, be accurate in both your vocabulary and grammar. Further, use language that is appropriate to the audience, the occasion, and yourself. Eliminate extra words and phrases that make your speech less concise. Define jargon in an effort to be clear, and select concrete words that will allow your listeners to form more precise meanings. Finally, choose words that are interesting, and consider using alliteration, rhyme, repetition, personification, hyperbole, metaphors, and similes that draw from shared cultural references.

Finally, it is probable that you will be in a public speaking situation where you either speak in a second language—necessitating the use of an interpreter—or listen to a speaker who has the accent of another language. In these situations, it is most important to communicate ideas rather than have linguistic precision. If you listen to a speaker from another linguistic background, take the responsibility of listening with an open mind in a supportive manner.

JAFFE CONNECTION

Key Terms

voice (252)
languages (252)
symbols (252)
words (253)
dialect (254)
Standard English (254)
code switching (254)
denotative meaning (254)
ambiguous (255)
connotative meanings (255)

epithets (255)
euphemisms (256)
jargon (256)
ageist language (257)
sexist language (258)
nonparallel language (259)
malaprops (259)
verbiage (260)
concrete words (262)
vague words (262)

alliteration (264)
rhymes (264)
repetition (264)
personification (265)
hyperbole (265)
metaphors (265)
mixed metaphor (266)
similes (266)
archetypal symbols (266)
perspective taking (267)

Access

**for Audio Flashcards
of Key Terms**

Application and Critical Thinking Questions

1. Interview a member of a specific occupation, and make a list of jargon terms associated with the job (e. g., carpenters, waiters, foresters, pharmacists, truckers, bankers). Discuss your list with a classmate. How many terms do you know? Which terms are unfamiliar? If you were listening to a speaker from that occupation, how might she or he translate the jargon so that you would better understand?

2. Find a speech by a Native American or a speaker from another culture. W. C. Vanderwerth's book, *Indian Oratory* (University of Oklahoma Press, 1971), is a good source for historical Native American oratory. Locate the metaphors and similes in it. Note the differences, if any, between the metaphors of that culture and your own.

3. Study Bob Pettit's speech, "Who/What Would You Want in Your Band? Or, Why Did I Spend 25 Years Playing Drums?" at the end of this chapter. Note the vivid use of language in the speech. How effective is his use of jargon?

4. When (if ever) might you use an interpreter in the future? When might you listen to a speech delivered with the assistance of an interpreter? (Consider speeches you might watch on television.) When (if ever) might you give a speech in a second language? When might you listen to a speaker who is presenting a speech in a second language?

5. If you know a second language, prepare a short speech in your own language, then work with an interpreter who presents your speech in English as you give it in your language. For example, Maria prepared her speech in Italian and had an Italian-speaking classmate interpret when she gave it to the class—some of whom spoke Italian, some of whom didn't. Paula prepared her speech in Romanian and brought her cousin to class to translate, because all her classmates were monolingual.

Internet Activities

1. Log on to your *InfoTrac College Edition* and do a PowerTrac search for the journal *Vital Speeches*. Locate and read a speech by a Native American speaker, paying special attention to the speaker's language choices.

2. Do a PowerTrac search for the subject *jargon* and read one of the articles you find there. What do you learn about the use and misuse of jargon? Share your findings with your classmates.

3. Use a web search engine such as www.alltheweb.com or www.dogpile.com and look up the word *ebonics*. Download and print off at least two articles and bring them to class with you. In a small group discuss one of the following questions; afterwards, share your group's conclusions with the entire class:

    ■ Identify some ways that ebonics differs from Standard English.

    ■ What controversies swirl around ebonics? Why do you think the dialect is controversial?

    ■ What do linguists say about the dialect?

    ■ What are the pro arguments for instruction in ebonics?

    ■ What are the arguments against instruction in ebonics?

4. Go to the site http://www.nec.com/company/foundation/necfound/htm/ whatsnew/commndis.htm. Here you'll find a helpful fact sheet about ways to communicate with and about people with disabilities. Read it and summarize your findings in a class discussion.

5. One of the most respected scholars of American dialects is William Labov of the University of Pennsylvania. Use your Internet searching skills to find his home page and other sites that show the extent of his scholarly research on dialects.

Hot Links at the Public Speaking Resource Center

The following links are maintained and can be accessed easily via Jaffe Connection at the Public Speaking Resource Center on the Wadsworth Communication Café website at http://communication.wadsworth.com/publicspeaking/study.html

Public Speaking Resource Center

■ http://www.aber.ac.uk/~dgc/sem06.html This website, created by Daniel Chandler, Lecturer in the Education Department at the University of Wales, defines denotation and connotation and elaborates extensively on both. Moreover, it offers links to other language concepts such as encoding/decoding, similes/metaphors, and so on.

■ http://www-rcf.usc.edu~cmmr/News.html The Center for Multilingual, Multicultural Research provides links to the full text of news articles on topics related to education, society, and language, such as the debate over bilingual education.

STUDENT SPEECH WITH COMMENTARY

Who/What Would You Want in Your Band? Or Why Did I Spend 25 Years Playing Drums? *by Bob Pettit*

Bob, a rock drummer who returned to college to get an engineering degree, first gave this speech in an introductory level public speaking class. His vivid and colorful use of language make it interesting throughout.

According to a record producer in the cartoon strip Doonesbury, "Drummers are extinct." Now, by drummers here, I'm not talking some type of weird dinosaur or puff-chested bird, but rather drummers as we've all come to know and love them, ala Ringo and Bongo, the dudes that beat the skins and drive the tunes with the bad beat. And what's making them go extinct is computers. Nowadays, the drum machine is the heppist of session cats. Computerized drums are getting all the good gigs. And if you've got ears, you've heard the new sound. It is everywhere—on radio, TV, blasting from big portables. You can't escape it, even if you'd like to. The beat is intense and relentless, inhuman. A lover like it would drive you insane. And it makes a drummer like me wonder why I've bothered to spend the last twenty some years playing drums. Fact is, twenty years ago 100% of the drums heard on record were real drums played by real drummers. Nowadays, as an article in *Rolling Stone Magazine* points out, "On any recent record, there's a good chance that . . . the drums aren't real." So, I want to examine this

At the outset, Bob gains attention by playing off the word extinct. He skillfully and vividly moves from one part of the introduction to the next—establishing at the outset the jargon style he will employ throughout the speech.

new world of the push button beat and pose the question to you: "What or who would you rather have in your band, a mean and clean drum machine, or a stereotypical rock drummer?"

In the old days a musician "paid his dues" in the school of hard knocks. Being hungry was where it was at. You got lean and mean, and you had to want it bad. "Wood shedding," "working on your chops," and "playing your axe" were the only ways out of the rut, or should I say "groove?" For me the groove got so deep it started to look more like a rectangular hole six feet in the ground.

Now, I had my successes, but the good times were countered by the bad times, and I finally reached the point where I realized both me and my dog were getting skinny. They say starvation is a sure sign you're in the wrong business, but not in music. There, it's just some kind of musical purgatory one must pay to get a soulful sound. But, wait a minute, computers don't eat, and computers don't starve. Then, how come they sound so good?

Well, some people don't think they do. An editorial in *High Fidelity Magazine* calls on the industry to, "Throw away those machines." And *Rolling Stone* claims computers will never take the place of the quote, "crazed inspiration" and the "spontaneous performance" of a "bare chested drummer pounding out a beat." It seems drummers are still in demand in spite of themselves.

Picture your stereotypical rock drummer: shaggy, smells, looks, and sometimes acts like a lower primate, body type—lean and wiry, definitely the fast-twitch kind of muscles, and they aren't in the head. And it always seems that they're the first in the band to O. D. On the *Muppets* TV show, the drummer's name was "Animal," and they kept him chained to his set of drums. I suppose they threw him bones and scraps from the butcher shop every few days or so. (I worked with a female vocalist who thought that was exactly what should have been done with me, but that is another story, and beside the point.)

The point is, that in spite of a reputation for difficulty, real drummers are still in demand. As the columnist for *High Fidelity* put it, he, " . . . longs for the hollow crack of a snare drum."

On the other hand, the computer does have a lot of things going for it. For one thing, it always shows up, it never acts like a prima donna, and it doesn't get drunk on stage. *And* it has Perfect Time. That means it *never* slows down or speeds up. *Rolling Stone* reports that one programmer "added an imperfection to humanize" a drum part. The record producer noticed immediately and made him take it out. He said, "If I'd wanted a timing error, I'd hire a drummer!" Ouch!!

So, there is no doubt computers "do got the beat," and though they may not always get respect, they are being taken seriously. *Rolling Stone* admits they have "taken over Top Forty" and *High Fidelity* describes them as having "come of age." And *Down Beat Magazine,* that old standard of the jazz world, calls them "electronically sophisticated . . . musically adaptable" and having "great digitally stored drum sounds."

There is one thing both sides agree on. The electronic drums save time and money. In the recording studio, the machine gets it right the first time, everytime, and you don't have to send it a check afterwards.

An example of the impact of drum machines can be seen in what happened to the band Nu Shooze. They got their start playing nightclubs in Portland, Oregon. In those days, they used regular drums. But when it came time to make a record album, they used computerized drums and fired their drummer, who then got a job washing dishes on the grave-yard shift at Ho Fung's Bar & Grill. Just kidding. . . . Actually, their drummer incorporated the computer's sound into his own beat, and that, according to *Down Beat,* is the trend of the future; real drummers playing real drums, and using real computers. It's a combination that's making people get up

---

Bob does not state his first main point immediately. He approaches it indirectly by describing a drummer's life. Notice how his use of jargon enhances his credibility.

Here he uses nonstandard English—which arguably enhances, rather than detracts from, his credibility. Notice the purgatory metaphor.

Bob uses a number of humorous images here.

Notice the signposts—words and phrases that connect the ideas to one another and to the speech as a whole.

Again, he intentionally uses a nonstandard grammatical form that helps create his persona. Bob briefly explains Down Beat Magazine, *the less familiar of the three he's citing.*

Notice his use of repetition here.

and dance—all around the world. The fans know what makes them shake their booties round. And they're buying the records by the millions.

So, to wrap it up, progress has finally caught up with the ancient and primal art of drumming. Ready or not, the electronic drum has arrived. And while the traditionalists may grumble, the new technology is being embraced by progressive performers and fans alike. So, we are back to the question of what would *you* prefer in your band, a lean and clean drum machine, or your stereotypical drummer?

Well, what do you think? I think the future holds promise for everything authentic, whether it's the sound of skin-on-skin jungle drums, or those crazy bongo machines.

(Reprinted by permission of the author.)

His use of rhetorical questions as he concludes, invites the audience to participate mentally throughout the entire speech.

14

Delivering Your Speech

This chapter will help you:

■ Describe how personal appearance, clothing, and accessories can affect public speaking

■ List three functions of gestures, and explain how each can be used in public speaking

■ Understand how eye contact makes a difference in your delivery

■ Describe elements of your voice that influence your message

■ List four methods of delivery

■ Discuss ways to use technology effectively in speech delivery

"Carnaval" ©1995 by Joshua Sarantitis, Emmanuel Montoya, and Precita Eyes Mural Arts Center

Compare politicians you've seen—Bill Bradley, Bill Clinton, Hillary Clinton, George W. Bush, Jesse Ventura, J. C. Watts. Each, arguably, has a similar message ("I have a vision that will lead America forward; vote for me"). Similar words, yes, but each politician creates a different impression based on personal appearance, manner, vocal quality—in short, delivery.

Delivery—the way you perform your speech—includes not only your words but also the way you present them nonverbally. To deliver your speech competently, you must understand effective nonverbal communication and develop skills for using your appearance, your gestures, and your voice to create a positive impression. In the last three decades researchers have learned a great deal about nonverbal communication, gaining insights you can apply to your own delivery. The chapter discusses personal appearance, movements or mannerisms, and vocal variations that can enhance or detract from your verbal message. It then elaborates on the four major types of delivery introduced in Chapter 2 and concludes with ways to adapt your delivery when you use technology.

Maximize Your Personal Appearance

Erving Goffman (1959) develops the concept of **impression management** in his influential book, *The Presentation of Self in Everyday Life*. In it, Goffman compares our self-presentation to a dramatic stage performance in which we attempt to create and maintain impressions of ourselves as if we were on a stage, using a combination of props and personal mannerisms to accomplish this. Your listeners form initial impressions based on the way you look: your physical appearance, your clothing, and your accessories.

Make the Best of Your Physical Appearance

You have several relatively permanent physical features that disclose information about you. For example, by just looking at you, others can infer your sex, general age range, racial background, height, weight, and body type. Unfortunately, some audiences respond to personal appearance in a stereotypical manner. As Chapter 6 pointed out, an audience may disregard younger speakers or pay less attention to women or minorities.

Physical features or conditions can also make you reluctant to speak publicly—less-than-perfect skin, crooked teeth, visible birthmarks, above-average or below-average weight or height, poor eyesight, a cane or wheelchair (Bippus & Daly, 1999). Because this culture saturates us with images of physically perfect bodies, any perceived difference often causes anxiety, as if you're in the limelight being scrutinized. Remember, however, that people do see your features, but they generally don't focus on them throughout your entire speech. If you worry about your appearance, one of your best strategies is to have an interesting topic and a good opening statement that draws people's attention to your subject rather than to your looks.

Regardless of features, you can pay special attention to grooming, which is vital in this culture (Arthur, 1997). In fact, the proverb "Cleanliness is next to godliness" shows that neatness can be almost as significant as natural beauty. And you can enhance your presentation by smiling and gesturing appropriately. Moreover, your listeners don't only see your physical characteristics; your clothing and accessories are an important part of the total impression you create.

Choose Appropriate Clothing and Accessories

Dirk always wore black—typically a black tee shirt with the name of a rock band and a picture on the front showing a creature with fangs that dripped blood. However, on

Governor Jesse Ventura's outrageous accessories delighted his supporters, ignited his critics, and left a lot of people wondering about his ability to govern the state of Minnesota. You can hear one opinion by listening to the Persuasive Speech by Jenny Chung on Jaffe Speech Interactive on the Jaffe Connection CD-ROM. (Titan Sports/Sygma)

Jaffe Speech
Interactive

speech days he wisely chose a more conservative black polo shirt. Some authors—notably John Molloy (1976) of *Dress for Success* fame—have made a fortune telling people that their clothing choices influence the way others perceive them. This principle applies to your classroom, where a good general rule is to select typical clothing that is slightly more formal than normal. For example, instead of a sweatshirt with writing on it, substitute a plain pullover sweater on speech day. Resist the temptation to wear your favorite baseball cap turned backward. Clothing that is too tight or too revealing is less appropriate than more conservative wear.

Before you speak anywhere, it's a good idea to check out clothing expectations. Let's say your job requires you to give a presentation at an unfamiliar organization. You wisely find out in advance if members generally wear tailored or less-formal clothing. One student who was asked to speak at a staff retreat at her university was embarrassed when she failed to do this:

> I was overdressed! I didn't realize it was a retreat setting, and everyone was dressed very casually.
>
> Seana

Accessories—the objects you carry or add to your clothing—include jewelry, glasses, briefcases, notebooks, or folders. Not long ago, one of my classes reminded me that accessories do matter. Out of laziness, I'd been carting around my materials in a cardboard box. My students advised me that a leather briefcase would be a more impressive carrier! In your classroom and elsewhere, the basic rules for accessories are that they are simple, appropriate, and of the best quality you can afford.

There are ethical implications in impression management. That is, we may try to create an impression that truly reflects who we are, or we may try to deceive our audiences to one degree or another. Speakers who present verbal and nonverbal messages that they themselves believe are termed **sincere.** In contrast, speakers who make strategic choices to control nonverbal messages in order to create false or misleading impressions are termed **cynical.** They don't believe their own messages!

Accessories
Objects you carry or add to your clothing.

Sincere
Speakers presenting verbal and nonverbal messages they themselves believe.

Cynical
Speakers presenting verbal or nonverbal messages they don't believe, attempting to create a false image.

STOP AND CHECK

Managing Impressions

You can probably think of public personalities who try to appear genuinely interested in people when they only want their time, money, or votes. Consider the ethics of politicians who wear flannel shirts to "connect" with common people. What about lawyers who hire consultants to advise and coach their clients to select clothing, mannerisms, and nonverbal techniques aimed to create an impression of innocence in jury members' minds. Using the following questions, discuss with a small group of your classmates whether or not these actions—and others like them—are ethically appropriate.

1. Is it wrong to imply that the politician, really a Harvard Law School graduate, is just like the blue-collar workers he's speaking to?

2. Are lawyers and consultants acting ethically if they believe their client is guilty?

3. What if they believe their client is innocent?

4. In what ways do sincere politicians and lawyers contribute to the political or judicial process?

5. How do cynical politicians and lawyers contribute positively to the political or judicial process? Negatively?

You can participate in an online discussion about impression management by clicking on the Public Speaking Now icon at the Public Speaking Resource Center, http://communication.wadsworth.com/publicspeaking. Follow directions for accessing our threaded discussion and chat.

Develop Effective Mannerisms

Your manner—or the way you speak, move, and look at the audience—is an area of nonverbal communication over which you have a great deal of control. Mannerisms discussed in this section include gestures and eye contact.

Control Your Gestures

Body movements range from large motions, such as posture, walking, and gesturing, to very small movements, such as raising one eyebrow. More than thirty years ago, Ekman and Friesen (1969) classified the functions of **gestures** into several categories, which nonverbal scholars still use: emblems, illustrators, and adaptors.

Emblems

Emblems are gestures that stand for words or ideas. You'll occasionally use them in public speaking, as when you hold up a hand to ask for quiet. Your forefinger to your lips in a "sh-h-h-h" gesture functions in the same way. Not surprisingly, emblems vary across cultures. For instance, Ethiopians put one forefinger to their lips when silencing a child, but they use four fingers when they are communicating with adults. The sign that stands for "A-OK" in the United States refers to money in Japan (Richmond & McCroskey, 2000). It's an obscene gesture in some Latin American countries, as Richard Nixon discovered when he exited a plane in Latin America and responded to a reporter's question, "How was the trip?" by signaling "A-OK!"

Gestures
Body movements or motions, whether large or barely noticeable.

Emblems
Three are especially important in speech delivery: gestures that stand for words or ideas; a head nod means yes.

Illustrators

Illustrators are gestures that illustrate or add emphasis to your words, and you will likely use them in your speaking. Illustrators function in a variety of ways:

- To accent words and phrases. For example, "We should *all* vote" [extend your hands and arms outward].

- To show spatial relationships. For example, "It's about *this* [extend your hands to show the distance] wide."

- To point to objects. For instance, "Look at this [point to the area on the map] part of the ocean."

Illustrators
Gestures that add emphasis to or illustrate verbal messages.

Adaptors

If you use too many **adaptors,** a third kind of gesture, you may alert your audience to your nervousness, because adaptors can betray stress or fear. There are three kinds of adaptors:

- **Self-adaptors** are those in which you touch yourself. Fidgeting with your hair, licking your lips, scratching your face, and rubbing your hands together during your speech are a few examples.

- **Object adaptors** involve touching things. Here you play with your keys or jingle change in your pocket, pull at necklaces or earrings, twist a ring, or tap your pencils or note cards.

- **Alter-adaptors** are gestures you use in relationship to the audience. For instance, if you fold your arms across your chest during intense questioning, you may be subconsciously protecting yourself against the perceived psychological threat of the questioner.

Because adaptors indicate anxiety or other stresses, especially when they appear to be nervous mannerisms, strive to eliminate them.

Adaptors
Gestures that betray stress or fear.

Self-adaptors
Touching yourself when you're stressed; scratching, for example.

Object Adaptors
Nervously touching or playing with items such as pens or jewelry.

Alter-adaptors
Gestures, such as folding your arms protectively, that betray nervousness about the audience.

Make Eye Contact

> I find it hard to listen to speakers who look down, not giving full attention to the audience.
>
> Larisa

It's important to look at the audience in U.S. culture in order to communicate honesty and trustworthiness. The phrase "Look me in the eye and say that" is partly premised on the cultural notion that people won't lie if they're looking directly at you. **Eye contact** also communicates friendliness. In interpersonal relationships, for instance, one person who avoids the other's gaze signals a lack of interest in developing a relationship.

You may need to practice making direct eye contact. Tempting as it is to look at your notes, the desktops in the front row, the back wall, or out the window, all these gazes communicate that you're uncomfortable. Avoid this impression by looking around the room in at least three general directions: at the listeners directly in front of you, those to the left, and those to the right. Because of your peripheral vision, you can generally keep most listeners within your vision as you change the direction of your gaze.

Finally, look at various people within the room—not just at one or two. And resist the urge to make more eye contact with audience members you perceive as powerful. For example, you may want to look more at your instructor than at your classmates, at

Eye Contact
Looking audiences in the eye; a way to communicate friendliness in U.S. culture.

Although cultures differ in the amount of eye contact considered appropriate, in the United States it's important to engage your audience directly. How would you respond if this speaker gave his entire speech looking in the direction shown in each picture? (Karen Preuss)

men more than at women, but try to avoid these behaviors. As part of a job application process, one would-be professor who addressed the faculty members made noticeably more eye contact with male faculty members than with female professors—largely ignoring the female department chair. Needless to say, he wasn't hired!

What is typical in the United States is not universal. For instance, Japanese communicators use less direct eye contact. It's not unusual to see downcast or closed eyes at a meeting or a conference; within Japanese culture this demonstrates attentiveness and agreement rather than rejection, disinterest, or disagreement. Additionally, Nigerians as well as Puerto Ricans consider it disrespectful to make prolonged eye contact with superiors (Richmond & McCroskey, 2000). For additional information on gestures and eye contact, log on to your *InfoTrac College Edition* and search for the key words *eye contact, nonverbal gestures,* or *body language.*

Vary Your Vocal Behaviors

When friends call on the phone, you recognize their voices instantly because of distinctive vocal features. And even without seeing someone—as when you listen to the radio—you can identify speakers as young or old, male or female, southerners or New Yorkers, native or nonnative speakers of English. Moreover, you can often detect moods such as boredom, hostility, or enthusiasm. Understanding two important aspects of vocal behaviors will help you be a better public speaker: pronunciation and vocal variation.

Pronounce Your Words

Pronunciation, the way you actually say words, has several components including articulation and stress or accenting. Your pronunciation can reveal your regional origin, ethnicity, or social status.

Articulation
The way you enunciate or say specific sounds.

Stress
Accenting syllables or words.

Articulation and Stress

Articulation is the way you say individual sounds such as *this* or *dis, bird* or *beerd.* Some speakers reverse sounds—saying *aks* instead of *ask.* **Stress** is the way you accent syllables or whole words—"poe-LEESE" (police) or "POE-leese," for example. Some people alter both articulation and stress, for instance, comparable (COM-purr-uh-bul) becomes "come-PARE-uh-bul"; potpourri (poe-per-EE) becomes "pot-PORE-ee." When you're in doubt about a pronunciation, consult a dictionary. You'll find that some words such as status have two acceptable pronunciations—"STAY-tus" and "STATT-us." When the dictionary provides two variations, the first is considered preferable (PREFF-er-uh-bul)!

Regional Origin

You've probably noticed regional variations in pronunciation and articulation. The following list illustrates just a few:

- There are differences in the *extent* to which sounds are held. Southern speakers typically draw out their sounds, resulting in the "southern drawl."

- Many Bostonians add an *r* at the end of a word such as *tuba*. Listen to a speaker from Massachusetts, and you'll hear *tuber.*

- Speakers from different regions often articulate sounds differently. Go to Brooklyn and you'll hear *oi* instead of *er* (*thoity* means *thirty*).

Ethnicity

Ethnicity is another factor that may affect pronunciation. Dialects such as ebonics have distinctive articulation and stress patterns. And nonnative speakers of English have accents that reflect articulation and stress patterns from their first language. In a multilingual world and in pluralistic classrooms, there are bound to be accents, and as travel and immigration continue to shrink the world, you'll hear even more in the future. Unfortunately, we tend to judge one another on the basis of regional and ethnic dialects and accents; see the letter in Diversity in Practice: Immigrants, Don't Be in Such a Hurry to Shed Your Accents on the next page, which argues for acceptance of a variety of accents.

Social Status

Differences in pronunciation often indicate social status. This is the premise for the classic movie *My Fair Lady*. Eliza Doolittle *says* the same words as Professor Higgins, but her pronunciation marks her as an uneducated member of the lower class. The professor takes her on as a project. By changing her pronunciation—and some other nonverbal variables, such as dress and grooming—she eventually passes as a Hungarian princess.

Use Vocal Variation

Around 330 B.C., Aristotle understood the importance of vocal characteristics in creating an impression on listeners. We continue to discuss these three important components of voice identified in his text *Rhetoric:* volume, pitch, rate—and the variations in each.

> It is not enough to know what we ought to say; we must also say it as we ought. . . . It is, essentially, a matter of the right management of the voice to express the various emotions—of speaking loudly, softly, or between the two; of high, low, or intermediate pitch; of the various rhythms that suit various subjects. These are the three things—volume of sound, modulation of pitch, and rhythm—that a speaker bears in mind (Aristotle, trans Roberts, 1984).

What kinds of impressions do **vocal variations** create? For one thing, listeners like speakers with pleasing vocal variations. One student summarized delivery skills that leave positive impressions on him:

Vocal Variations
Changes in volume, rate, and pitch that combine to create impressions of the speaker.

DIVERSITY IN PRACTICE

Immigrants, Don't Be in Such a Hurry to Shed Your Accents

This letter to the editor appeared in the *New York Times*, March 21, 1993.

To the Editor:

You report that immigrants in New York City are turning to speech classes to reduce the sting of discrimination against them based on accent. . . . I'd like to tell all my fellow immigrants taking accent-reduction classes: As long as you speak fluent and comprehensible English, don't waste your money on artificially removing your accent.

I am fortunate enough to be one of the linguistically gifted. I even acquired an American accent before I left China for the United States five years ago. From the day I set foot on this continent till now, the praise of my English has never ceased. What most people single out is that I have no, or very little accent. However, I know I do have an accent. . . . I intend to keep it because it belongs to me. I want to speak and write grammatically flawless English, but I have no desire to equip myself with a perfect American accent. . . .

America is probably the largest place for accents in English because the entire nation is composed of immigrants from different areas of the world. This country is built on accents. Accent is one of the most conspicuous symbols of what makes America the free and prosperous land its own people are proud of and other people long to live in.

I work in an urban institution where accents are an integral part of my job: students, faculty and staff come from ethnically diverse backgrounds. Hearing accents confirms for me every day that the college is fulfilling its goal to offer education to a multicultural population.

I wonder what accent my fellow immigrants should obtain after getting rid of their own: a New York accent? a Boston accent? Brooklyn? Texas? California? Or go after President Clinton's accent?

Fellow immigrants, don't worry about the way you speak until Peter Jennings eliminates his Canadian accent.

YanHong Krompacky

An audience stays in tune when the speaker's voice changes, adding life to the message. An animated speaker is also more interesting than a "block" of ice. The speaker must be interested in what he/she is saying in order to be convincing.

David

In addition, several studies (Burgoon et al., 1989; Ray, 1986) conclude that audiences typically associate vocal characteristics with personality traits. For instance, here are just a few common associations:

loud and fast speakers: self-sufficient, resourceful, dynamic

loud and slow: aggressive, competitive, confident

soft and fast: enthusiastic, adventuresome, confident, composed

soft and slow: competitive, enthusiastic, benevolent

Is there a relationship between your voice and your credibility? Various studies indicate that audiences make a number of associations about your trustworthiness based on your voice. Speak faster, and you may be considered more intelligent, objective, and knowledgeable. If you're a male, you may be seen as dominant, dynamic, and sociable. Speak with a moderate rate, and you may give the impression of composure, honesty, people orientation, and compassion (Burgoon et al., 1989).

Make vocal variations work for you. For example, use a slower rate when you're giving key points and speed up for background material (Davidson & Kline, 1999). Change your vocal inflections if your audience appears to be losing interest; that is, add pitch variation and slightly increased volume and rate to communicate enthusiasm (Hypes, Turner, Norris, & Wolfferts, 1999).

Meanings can vary depending on your tone of voice, rising or falling inflection, or stressed words. For instance, a movie character is accused of shooting a clerk in a convenience store. When the sheriff asks, "Why did you shoot the clerk?" the suspect responds, "I *shot* the clerk?" (pause) "*I* shot the clerk?" At the trial, the sheriff testifies that the accused confessed twice, clearly saying, "I shot the clerk." The sheriff's vocal cues indicate a statement of fact, whereas the suspect's rising voice inflection and stressed words indicate that he's asking a question—drastically changing the meaning of the literal words. For additional tips on vocal variation, log on to the Internet and search for the exact phrase *vary your voice* on www.alltheweb.com.

Pause for Effect

Finally, consider your use of pauses. Pauses can be effective, or they can be embarrassing—to both you and your listeners. Effective pauses are intentional; that is, you purposely pause between major ideas, or you give your audience a few seconds to contemplate a difficult concept. Judith Humphries (1998) urges speakers to slow down and use lots of pauses as this quotation illustrates,

> [C]onsider this: when does the audience think? Not while you're speaking, because they can't think about an idea until it's delivered. They think during the pauses. But if there are no pauses, they won't think. They won't be moved. They won't act upon what you say. The degree to which you want to involve the audience is reflected in the length of your pauses (accessed on *InfoTrac College Edition*).

In addition, use pauses as punctuation marks. For example, at the end of the body of the speech, you might pause slightly, move one step backward, then say, "In conclusion . . ." Your pause functions as a comma that signals a separation in your thoughts.

In contrast, ineffective pauses or hesitations disrupt your fluency and sometimes signal that you've lost your train of thought. **Unfilled pauses** are silent; **filled** or **vocalized pauses** are your "uh" or "um," "like" and "you know" sounds. Beginning public speakers, as well as many professionals, use vocalized pauses. However, too many "ums" can be distracting, so work to keep them to a minimum (Rose, 1998). (For additional information, look up the exact phrase "unfilled pauses" on the Internet search engine www.alltheweb.com.)

Unfilled Pauses
Silent pauses.

Filled (Vocalized) Pauses
Saying "um" or "uh" or other sounds during a pause.

Put It All Together

Chapter 1 defined communicative competence as the ability to communicate in a personally effective and socially appropriate manner (Spitzberg, 1994). The key is to find what delivery works best for you in a given situation. For instance, consider these two presentation styles: confident and conversational. A **confident style** incorporates vocal

Confident Style
A way of speaking characterized by effective vocal variety, fluency, gestures, and eye contact.

STOP AND CHECK

Think Critically about Delivery

Political candidates often illustrate the link between delivery and effective speaking (Brookhiser, 1999; Shipman, 2000). For example, Ronald Reagan was called the "Great Communicator," and Bill Clinton's speaking skills are legendary. In contrast, Republican candidate 2000, Steve Forbes, and Democratic front-runners, Vice President Al Gore and Senator Bill Bradley, were all termed "charismatically challenged." Bradley's delivery was described as, "somewhere between that of a dentist's drill and the hum of a refrigerator . . . " (Simon, 1999, p. 16). Gore's delivery was widely referred to as wooden, earnest, solemn, uptight, in fact, he tended to discount delivery and focus instead on speech content. Enter the consultants. Bradley's handlers spun his style as "authentic" and "genuine," an implied repudiation of the previous administration's style. In contrast, Gore's consultants sat beside him, watching and rewatching videotaped speeches, analyzing his volume, his rate, his gestures, his facial expressions. They coached him to loosen up . . . leave the podium, spread his arms, smile, wear cowboy boots, trade in his blue suit for warmer brown more casual clothing. Gore admitted what good public speakers know—no matter how wonderful his ideas, his message would go largely unheard if the audience slept through his delivery.

Within small groups in your classroom discuss the following questions:

1. What do you think of Bradley's decision to capitalize on his unremarkable delivery? Of Gore's makeover? What qualities are important in a president? How does presidential image matter?

2. On MTV's campaign coverage, young people were once asked their impression of one candidate. A person responded, "Uh, uh, old." What difference is it if a President looks old?

3. President William Taft (1909–1914) weighed around 300 pounds. Could he be elected today? Why or why not? Is this good or bad?

4. Why have no women yet been elected to the Presidency? When will the United States elect its first female President?

5. Could Abraham Lincoln—with his looks and awkward mannerisms—be elected in this television-dominated society? Why or why not?

6. How do you judge your classmates' abilities based on the way they present themselves?

You can also discuss these questions online. Click on Public Speaking Now at the Public Speaking Resource Center for directions on accessing threaded discussion and chat.

Public Speaking Resource Center

Conversational Style

Speaking that's comparatively calmer, slower, and less intense, but maintains good eye contact and gestures.

variety, fluency, good use of gestures, and eye contact to create an impression of dynamism as well as credibility. If you're naturally outgoing, this style may best fit your personality. However, in some situations—funerals, for example—you'd choose a more **conversational style,** one that's calmer, slower, softer, and less intense, but still maintains good eye contact and gestures (Branham & Pearce, 1996). Listeners associate this style with trustworthiness, honesty, sociability, likableness, and professionalism, and it may actually fit you better if your personality is more laid-back. But someone who generally speaks more conversationally can adapt for occasions—a rally, for instance—where excitement runs high and people expect a more enthusiastic delivery. Both styles are persuasive.

Whoopi Goldberg uses her distinctive vocal features along with variation in rate, volume, and pauses to create a style that's uniquely her own. (AP/Worldwide Photos)

Don't worry if you are not yet a dynamic, confident speaker. Instead, work on creating your personal delivery style—using your appearance, mannerisms, and vocal variations to your advantage. Then, choose a mode of delivery that fits the specific context.

Select the Appropriate Type of Delivery

Tim forgot that his classroom speech was due until his name was called, so he just stood up and "winged" a talk. Quianna memorized her speech (located at the end of Chapter 7) because, as a member of the University of Alaska speech team, she presented it more than twenty-five times in competition. The attorney general read her commencement address at the Ivy League school, and excerpts of it were reprinted in the *New York Times*. Juan Gonzalez prepared his closing arguments carefully, but when he actually faced the jury, he delivered his final appeal using only his legal pad with a few scrawled notes. These speakers illustrate the four major types of delivery, introduced briefly in Chapter 2: impromptu, memorized, manuscript, and extemporaneous.

Impromptu Delivery

Use impromptu delivery when you must think on your feet. This mode requires the least amount of preparation and rehearsal, because impromptu speeches are given spur of the moment, meaning that you don't prepare them in advance. However, in a sense, your entire life—your knowledge and experience—prepares you for these speeches. Let's say you attend a wedding reception, and you're asked to tell a funny story spontaneously about the bride and groom. You won't have time to spend weeks in preparation. Instead, you'll think quickly and draw from your experience with the couple to find material for your speech.

Most people shudder at the thought of speaking without preparation and rehearsal, especially if their performance will be rewarded or punished in some way—such as by a grade or a job evaluation. However, a few students give an impromptu speech when the professor has assigned one that's to be carefully prepared. Bad strategy!

Memorized Delivery

Memorized delivery used to be common. Roman orators, for example, planned their speeches carefully, then memorized exact words and phrases. As a result, they could give the same oration over and over. In many oral cultures, tribal orators memorize the stories and legends of the tribe. This ensures that the exact stories continue throughout succeeding generations.

College students who successfully memorize speeches are those, such as Quianna and her teammates, who repeat each speech dozens of times in intercollegiate speech tournaments. However, you'll rarely hear memorized speeches in the classrooms or in offices, boardrooms, churches, and clubs of contemporary cultures. Consequently, it's not advisable to memorize your speeches. Regardless of this advice, some students think that memorizing will help them overcome their fears. One international student confided:

> I think if I memorize the entire speech including the pauses, gestures, posture, etc., I will feel more comfortable delivering the speech and I will be less nervous.
>
> Lambros

However, the opposite often happens. Standing in front of their audiences, beginning speakers often forget what they've memorized. Some pause (ineffectively), look toward the ceiling, repeat the last phrase in a whisper, repeat it aloud, then look hopelessly at the instructor. When this happens, they end up embarrassed.

Jaffe Speech
Interactive

Another drawback is that memorized speeches are generally not delivered conversationally. Put simply, these speeches sound memorized, not natural. Rather than focusing on a dialogue with the audience, the speaker appears to be focusing on recalling the words of the speech. For a model of memorized delivery, access the Informative Speech on the 25th Amendment to the United States Constitution by Loren Rozokas. This speech is located on Speech Interactive on the Jaffe Connection CD-ROM. The text of this speech is located in Appendix C.

Manuscript Delivery

When you write your speech out and read it, you're using manuscript delivery. In general, reading your speech is not recommended. In fact, Hypes et al. (1999) call this "the most inactive method of presenting," one that enables a speaker to impart a lot of information—most of which the audience soon forgets. Active speaker-listener interactions, in contrast, keep the participants' attention longer, involve them mentally, and make the speech more enjoyable.

Despite the disadvantages, on some occasions—especially formal ones such as commencement addresses—manuscript delivery is acceptable, even necessary. Further, you may use a manuscript if you speak on radio or television when exact timing is essential.

For competent manuscript delivery, type your entire script in capital letters, using triple spacing. Then, go over your speech, using a highlighter or underlining the words you wish to accent. Make slashes where you plan to pause. Finally, practice the speech until you can read it in a natural manner, with as much eye contact as possible. Conversational delivery is essential, because most people don't like to be read to, especially if you never pause or look up!

Although manuscript delivery is sometimes appropriate, you generally won't speak in such formal settings nor will you appear on radio or television. And manuscript delivery is inappropriate for most classroom speeches. The final type of delivery—extemporaneous—is generally the preferred mode, and this is the method you'll most commonly use.

Extemporaneous Delivery

In contrast to impromptu speeches, you prepare extemporaneous speeches carefully in advance. However, you don't plan every single word. Instead, you outline your major ideas, and you use note cards with cue words during your delivery. To illustrate how a professional speaker prepares for extemporaneous delivery, consider the case of Ted Robinson, a Honolulu clergyman (Krauss, 1993):

> Robinson works all year long on his forty talks. Every summer he takes a one-month study leave, during which he spends about two weeks collecting ideas and setting up forty separate file folders for forty different topics. Throughout the year, he adds ideas to his files. On a weekly basis, he prepares in the following way:

- On Wednesday he pulls up the folder with the topic of the week, looks at the ideas he has collected, then spends his time narrowing his purpose.

- On Thursday he organizes a tentative outline, admitting, "Often, the hardest part is to start. Sometimes it takes another day to jell."

- On Friday he enters his empty church, goes to the pulpit and preaches the sermon—twice. As he does, he rewrites, crosses out, changes, and omits ideas on his tentative outline.

- On Saturday he follows the same procedure—two more times in an empty building. Finally, at 9:00 that evening, he sits down with a 5 x 8 file card and jots down a key word outline, which he then memorizes.

- On Sunday he reviews his outline and heads off to deliver his talk.

Let Robinson act as a model. Begin the process of researching and organizing your speech well in advance. Give yourself plenty of time to let your ideas jell. Write out your outline, and put the main ideas onto note cards (see Chapter 11). Then, practice, practice, practice—aloud, to your friends, as you drive. On the day of the speech, review your outline and your notes and go to class with the confidence that comes from thorough preparation.

Of the four types of delivery, three—impromptu, manuscript, and extemporaneous—are used with some regularity in the United States. Each has its strengths and weaknesses. In general, extemporaneous delivery is most commonly used in public presentations, and it is the one you will use in most of your classroom speeches.

Adapt Your Delivery with Technology

Technology provides many delivery aids that can amplify your voice and record your words in audio or video form. Because microphones are so common and because instructors as well as employers often videotape speeches, knowing basic principles for delivering your speech, using technological aids, is important. Increasing numbers of nonprofessionals—politicians, doctors, educators, social activists, and the like—are mastering these valuable skills. And to prepare you for speaking in an electronic culture, this chapter closes with tips for using technology.

Using Microphones

Microphones allow people with ordinary voices to project their words over greater distances. Because you'll probably use microphones (mikes) at some point, let's review several types of mikes as well as guidelines for using them effectively.

The types of mikes available fall into two basic categories: fixed and portable. Each type has advantages and disadvantages. **Fixed microphones** are attached to a podium or a stand. Although they project your voice adequately and allow you to use both hands, they limit your movements, forcing you to stay within the pickup range of the mike. Generally, these mikes have a short, flexible "neck" that you can adjust upward or downward

Fixed Microphones
Attached to a podium or stand.

Portable Microphones
Handheld or clip mikes that can be carried around.

Lavaliere Mikes
A type of portable mike worn like a necklace.

Pickup Range
The greatest distance at which a mike can be held so that it picks up sound and transmits it effectively.

or from side to side a few inches. **Portable microphones** include handheld versions (corded or cordless) and small clip mikes that attach to your clothing. **Lavaliere mikes** are portable mikes that fasten around your neck by a thin cord. These all give you considerably more freedom to move around the room. However, handheld mikes limit you slightly because you have only one hand free to gesture or handle notes.

No matter which microphone you use, there are several guidelines to follow. Test it before you speak, and ask the sound technician to make necessary adjustments at that time. Remember that each mike has its own **pickup range**—the distance you can hold it from your mouth, pick up the sound, and transmit it effectively. This is especially important to consider with a fixed mike. If you find the microphone is not projecting your voice well, move it toward you; don't bend toward it, assuming an unnatural posture. Speak in a conversational voice. Too much volume may distort your words, so step away from the mike if you intend to raise your voice. Finally, be careful not to touch or jar the microphone or mike stand, which can create intrusive and grating sounds.

Adapting for Videotaped Speeches

The simplest kind of video recording requires only one camera operator, using a portable handheld or fixed camera with a single camera angle. More sophisticated presentations require a variety of professionals including producers, stage managers, lighting directors, makeup artists, directors, and editors who work together to create a polished product. Regardless of the level of sophistication, cameras call for slight adjustments in appearance and movement. For example, the choices you make about your personal appearance can add to or subtract from an overall positive impression:

- Makeup is commonly used to minimize shine and to conceal or camouflage blemishes for both men and women. However, strive to look natural rather than made up.

- Wardrobe consultants suggest that some clothing choices are better than others for filmed speeches (Ross, 1989). For instance, blue or gray tones photograph better than solid black or white, and busy patterns and very small plaids or stripes may be distorted on film. Further, off-white or pastel shirts or blouses appear better than stark white, and shiny, highly reflective fabrics may cause glare.

- Some accessories are more appropriate than others. "Less is more" with jewelry—in both amount and flashiness. Also, choose simple ties in conservative colors.

As you can see, the choices you make in makeup, clothing, and accessories can strengthen your overall presentation or become the focus of your listeners' attention. Furthermore, because the camera is a close-up medium, you need to adapt your gestures and eye contact, at least slightly, when your speech is videotaped. Here are a few guidelines:

- Because the camera can zero in on your face by using extreme close-up (ECU) shots, every blink, every small eyebrow movement will show. With this in mind, be aware of your facial expressions, and control those that do not contribute to your verbal message.

- Control your body movements. In general, sweeping gestures, walking, scratching, touching your hair, nervous mannerisms, and other nonessential motions detract.

- Work to be graceful and fluid in the movements you do use. Relax so that you appear comfortable.

- If you're working with several cameras, look at the one with the red light on.

A good strategy is to study videotaped speeches—of both effective and ineffective speakers. Mute the sound, then closely inspect the speaker's gestures and eye contact to find elements that contribute to an overall positive or negative impression.

Using a TelePrompTer

If you have ever spoken on television, you may have used a **TelePrompTer,** a handy machine that eliminates your worries about forgetting your speech. TelePrompTer screens, located just beneath the camera lens, project your script line by line, allowing you to read it while looking directly at the camera (somewhat like reading the credit lines that unroll on your television screen at the end of a program). During a rehearsal session, work with a technician who controls the speed of the lines so that the text unrolls at your speaking rate. The technician can circle key words or underline phrases that you want to emphasize. Because this is a special form of manuscript delivery, practice reading so that your delivery sounds conversational, as if you were simply talking to your audience.

TelePrompTer
Screen, located beneath the camera lens, on which the words of the speech scroll up during a filmed speech.

Summary

The intention of this chapter was to increase your knowledge of the nonverbal elements of communication so that you can make choices that will create positive impressions as you deliver your speech. The notion that good speakers manage nonverbal aspects of delivery, affecting listeners' impressions, is at least as old as Aristotle—and he surely didn't invent the idea. Modern scholars continue to explore specific aspects of appearance, mannerisms, and vocal variations that create positive or negative impressions in audiences.

You can make strategic choices in the way you dress, in your grooming, and in the accessories you use to communicate messages of competence. Your mannerisms—gestures, eye contact, and vocal variation—are also important in creating impressions of dynamism, honesty, and other characteristics of credibility. As you make wise choices and learn to use nonverbal communication effectively, your competence in public speaking increases correspondingly.

Of the four major types of delivery, extemporaneous is most common in the classroom. Memorization, common in oral cultures and in competitive speech tournaments, is less frequently used elsewhere. You may speak spontaneously in the impromptu style, or you may read from a manuscript. More commonly, you'll join the ranks of extemporaneous speakers—preparing in advance but choosing your exact wording as you actually speak.

You may use technology as you present your speech. The most common aid to delivery is the microphone; consequently, it is important to know the types of mikes and how to use them effectively. Speeches recorded on videotapes call for careful choices in clothing, accessories, and makeup. They also require control of body movements. Finally, TelePrompTers help you read a script as you're being filmed.

As with all attempts to influence others, the attempt to manage impressions has ethical implications. Speakers who believe in both the verbal and nonverbal messages they are sending are said to be sincere, but those who are trying to create false or misleading impressions are termed cynical.

JAFFE ● CONNECTION

Key Terms

delivery (276)

impression management (276)

accessories (277)

sincere (277)

cynical (277)

gestures (278)

emblems (278)

illustrators (279)

adaptors (279)

self-adaptors (279)

object adaptors (279)

alter-adaptors (279)

eye contact (279)

articulation (280)

stress (280)

vocal variations (281)

unfilled pauses (283)

filled (vocalized) pauses (283)

confident style (283)

conversational style (284)

fixed microphones (287)

portable microphones (288)

lavaliere mikes (288)

pickup range (288)

TelePrompTer (289)

Application and Critical Thinking Questions

1. The combination of environment, appearance, and mannerisms forms a "front." Whether intentional or unwitting, the front influences the way observers define and interpret the situation. With this in mind, why do some people appear to be something they're not? For instance, why did the Iraqis appear to be stronger than they were before the 1991 Gulf War? Why do some speakers appear to be competent or trustworthy, and you later discover they do not have these characteristics? What are the ethical implications of fronts? Have you ever tried to put on a front (anonymous, 1993)?

2. Create the text for an ad selling one of the products listed below. Bring it to class and exchange it with a classmate. Demonstrate the type of vocal variation you would use if you were delivering an ad for:

   ■ a used car dealership

   ■ a perfume

   ■ a vacation to South America

   ■ a brand of cola

3. If possible, videotape one of your speeches, then watch yourself on video. Specifically pay attention to the gestures you use, noting when you use emblems, illustrators, or adaptors. Plan specific strategies to improve your gestures, eliminating those that create negative impressions and strengthening those that produce favorable impressions.

   Watch the tape again. This time, evaluate your eye contact. Throughout your speech, notice the way you use your voice. Check for appropriate rate and volume. Also, be alert for pauses, and count the number of "ums," if any. Discuss with a partner from class how you can improve these nonverbal aspects of delivery.

   If you can't videotape a speech, create a worksheet that identifies the elements of delivery mentioned in the chapter. Give it to a classmate just before your speech and have him or her specifically note your gestures, eye contact, and use of your voice during your speech; afterwards, discuss with that person strategies you can use to improve in problem areas.

4. With a small group of your classmates, make a set of guidelines for delivery that's appropriate to your classroom's unique culture. For example, would you change the advice about clothing or accessories presented in this chapter? What might you add that's not covered here? Prepare for this discussion by doing InfoTrac and Internet Activities 1 and 2 that follow.

5. Some colleges and universities are offering public speaking courses online. With a group of your classmates, discuss the pros and cons of this practice. How might it work? What would be the drawbacks? Would you take such a course? Why or why not? Prepare for this discussion by doing InfoTrac and Internet Activity 4, which follows.

Internet Activities

1. Use your *InfoTrac College Edition* to do a PowerTrac search for the subject *public speaking*. Read a couple of the articles that discuss speech delivery and list the tips you find in it. Then use the information you find to help your group do Exercise 4 in the Application and Critical Thinking Questions.

2. Try a key word search for *gestures* using PowerTrac and read an article that discusses gestures in public speaking or presenting. Take notes that you can use for Exercise 4 of Application and Critical Thinking Questions.

3. Using the www.alltheweb.com text search tool, look for the exact term *canon of delivery* and study one of the web pages you find on it.

4. Using www.alltheweb.com, search for all the words *public speaking course online*. Use the information you find there to aid your discussion of the questions in Exercise 5, Application and Critical Thinking Questions.

Hot Links at the Public Speaking Resource Center

Public
Speaking
Resource
Center

The following links are maintained and can be accessed easily via Jaffe Connection at the Public Speaking Resource Center on the Wadsworth Communication Café website at http://communication.wadsworth.com/publicspeaking/study.html

http://maine.maine.edu/~zubrick/tren5.html This page is a good reference for nonverbal communication topics. It appears on Joe Zubrick's faculty website at the University of Maine at Presque Isle.

http://www.collegegrad.com/ezine/16interv.shtml This page from JobHunter E-Zine argues the importance of nonverbal communication in job interviews. Its often humorous principles also apply to public speaking.

15

Telling Narratives

This chapter will help you:

- Explain how narratives function to explain, to persuade, and to entertain

- Apply three tests for narrative reasoning

- List elements of narratives

- Give guidelines for using language effectively in narratives

- Identify the five parts of an exemplum

Detail from "Balance of Power" ©1996 by Susan Kelk Cervantes, Juana Alicia and Raul Martinez

Place yourself in Jonesborough, Tennessee, on a warm fall day. You're in a tent with hundreds of people listening to a man dressed in overalls narrate the story of his boyhood in Mississippi with a thick southern accent. From the "Tall Tales Tent" down the street and the "Family Tales Tent" next to yours, you occasionally hear bursts of laughter and applause. You are just one of some 8,000 visitors who annually trek to the storytelling festival in this, Tennessee's oldest town. If you can't visit Jonesborough, check your local listings for a closer festival hosted by one of 225-plus storytelling organizations nationally (Watson, 1997). Or turn on public radio and listen to Garrison Keillor's stories of Lake Wobegon on his weekly program, *Prairie Home Companion.*

Storytelling is universal; it has existed in every culture during every era. As a result, we live in a "story-shaped world" (Wicker, 1975). We tell stories about real people and real events, and we make up narratives of imaginary worlds peopled with imaginary characters. Lawyers frame their prosecution or defense arguments as narratives, and politicians present their political visions in story form. Coaches, teachers, members of the clergy, and comedians . . . all routinely tell stories. The scholar Roland Barthes states the importance of narrative in this way (quoted in Polkinghorne, 1988, p. 14):

> The narratives of the world are numberless. . . . Narrative is present in every age, in every place, in every society; it begins with the very history of [humankind] and there nowhere is nor has been a people without narrative. All classes, all human groups, have their narratives, enjoyment of which is very often shared by [others] with different, even opposing, cultural background. . . . Narrative is international, transhistorical, transcultural: it is simply there, like life itself.

Ordinary citizens as well as international leaders use narrative reasoning; it is especially common among women and speakers from ethnic groups such as African-Americans and Native Americans (Cortese, 1990). In fact, stories are so much a part of every culture, that Walter Fisher (1984a, 1999) calls us **homo narrans,** the storytelling animal. This chapter begins with a discussion of narrative functions, followed by tests for narrative reasoning or merit. The last half of the chapter discusses important components of narrative and concludes with a useful organizational pattern, the exemplum.

Homo Narrans
A Latin phrase that identifies humans as storytelling animals.

Narrative Functions

Storytelling
An oral art form we use to preserve and transmit commonly held ideas, images, motives and emotions.

Storytelling is "an oral art form for preserving and transmitting ideas, images, motives and emotions with which everyone can identify" (Cassady, 1994, p. 12). Stories tell about the past, highlight human emotions and drives, and illuminate cultural ideals. Tales from a variety of groups illustrate facets of the cultures, identify common themes, and show cultural differences, leading audiences to self-awareness and cross-cultural understandings at the same time (Anokye, 1994). Here we look at three functions of stories: to inform, to persuade, and to entertain.

Informative Narratives

What's it like to go to that college? What happens to the money I donate to a charity? What took place during the *Titanic*'s last hours? Answers to questions such as these often come in the form of narratives. Before you entered college, did you talk to students who explained campus life by telling stories about classes, professors, registration, and social events? From hearing both positive and negative tales, you began to anticipate the good as well as the bad of college life. Hearing about a single mother whose child got medicine because of your charitable donation leaves you satisfied that your gift was used wisely. And the fate of the *Titanic*—whether presented in oral, written, or filmed versions—still fascinates millions of people globally. The scholar Didier Coste (1989) says that our narratives present our culture's understandings of natural, social, and ultimate things.

Explaining Nature

We use stories to explain natural phenomena. Why are cats and dogs enemies? The Kaluli tribe from Papua New Guinea explains this in a myth. Where do babies come from? Parents dust off the "birds and the bees" story for a new generation. How did the world come into being? Scientists across international borders weave together facts and ideas into narrative accounts such as the big bang theory. When combined with evolutionary narratives, these accounts can profoundly affect our perceptions of the world (Spangler & Thompson, 1992). Of course, many cultural groups modify or reject outright these scientific stories; instead, they offer explanations (often irreconcilable) of their own. Did O. J. Simpson kill his wife? Prosecutors and defense lawyers offered competing explanations that listeners weighed and compared, finally accepting the murder story that made the most sense to them.

Explaining Society and Institutions

Stories also explain how our institutions or cultural structures came into being. Think of your history texts: They're peopled with characters who faced dramatic choices, overcame hardships, invented useful as well as harmful machines, and made mistakes. These stories explain the founding of our country, its wars, blameworthy scenes of slavery as well as praiseworthy scenes of the Constitutional Convention. (Naturally, history books from other countries have different explanations of some of the same events.) Frequently, historical facts are obscured by myths, and a variety of scholars offer alternative explanations. For example, "Afrocentric" historians and feminist "her-storians" tell different narratives from those told by "malestream" scholars.

Organizations and groups as well as cultures have unique stories that explain their history and traditions. Your college has a story, as does your family. Couples relate the saga of their relationship in story form (Sternberg, 1998). An *InfoTrac College Edition* search for the keyword *storytelling* yielded hits that described narratives in courtrooms, social work settings, business boardrooms, churches, health care facilities, and ceramics studios. One hit led to a speech by a communication professional whose job involves "corporate storytelling"; put simply, he helps men and women tell their organizations' stories in clear and compelling ways (Gresh, 1998).

Explaining Ultimate Things

Another genre of philosophical and religious stories attempts to explain ultimate realities—to answer such questions as: Who are we? What is our purpose on earth? What happens after death? How should I live a moral life? These stories explain the rituals that give meaning to religious adherents, rituals that are usually based in historical events. Jewish people, for instance, narrate the story of the Maccabees as they light Hanukkah candles. Muslims tell of the Prophet's flight to Medira during the fast of Ramadan. Christians remember the death and resurrection of Jesus as they celebrate Easter. In short, religious beliefs and practices are grounded in stories that followers have preserved over generations, stories that give ultimate meaning to the lives of adherents. (Diversity in Practice on the next page explores narrative traditions in Native American cultures.)

In short, listening to stories is one way we learn about processes and concepts, a way we answer our own questions and tell others about nature, society, and ultimate things.

Native American groups have a variety of narrative traditions, but stories are important to all of them. Here a Cherokee storyteller shares cultural lore with young members of the tribe. (Larry Migdale/Stock, Boston)

Myths
Powerful ancient stories told to communicate a culture's answer to ultimate questions about life's purpose and meaning.

DIVERSITY IN PRACTICE

Native American Narrative Traditions

Several native groups of North America differentiate among stories in the following ways (Bierhorst, 1985):

> **Eskimos** distinguish between *old* stories and *young* stories.

> **Winnebago** natives tell both *waikan* (sacred) or *worak* (narrated) tales.

> **Pawnees** differentiate between *false* stories, which are fiction, nonfiction, or a mixture of both, and *true* stories, which are the old, sacred tales.

> **Tlingit** natives tell *tlagu* stories (of the long ago) and *ch'kalnik* tales (it really happened).

You can see from these labels that cultural groups distinguish between different kinds of stories. Some ancient stories, called **myths,** communicate the group's answers to the ultimate questions of life; they differ from stories that aim to entertain or serve less significant functions. For this reason, R. C. Rowland (1990) calls them the most powerful narratives—they are the stories people use to define the good society and to solve problems that are not subject to rational solutions.

For examples of Native American stories, log on to the Internet and search for the exact phrase *Native American tales.*

Persuasive Narratives

Do you think I should take this vitamin?

My cousin did, and she . . .

How should children treat other people's belongings?

Once upon a time, a little girl named Goldilocks went to the home of three bears . . .

Do angels exist?

Well, one day the most interesting thing happened to me! It was like this . . .

Persuasive stories motivate listeners to choose some behaviors and avoid others, to act and to keep on acting—to volunteer their time on a regular basis, for instance. Stories (about UFOs, for example) also convince people that something is or is not true. Finally, narratives present hopeful visions of the future that audiences will want to aspire to and bleak scenarios they'll want to avoid.

Motivational Narratives

You have undoubtedly heard stories that provide models or examples of successful people (who behave in certain ways or adhere to social norms and values) or people who fail (who suffer the consequences of socially unacceptable actions). Either way, these **exemplary narratives** persuade people within a culture to choose some actions and avoid others. These examples illustrate the exemplary function.

> **Exemplary Narratives**
> Provide examples or models of culturally appropriate or inappropriate ways to live.

- Clara "Mother" Hale opened Hale House in Harlem to care for drug babies and babies with AIDS. Her story models what ordinary people can do when they decide to fight injustice.

- Dave Roever is badly scarred as a result of his Vietnam injuries. His personal testimonial about facing adversity provides a positive model for others in difficult circumstances.

- The fictional character Pinocchio serves to caution children not to lie.

- A personal story about a spending spree and your resulting credit problems motivates your listeners to use their credit cards wisely.

Exemplary narratives told publicly are powerful partly because they flesh out culturally admired traits that can be quite abstract. For instance, what is courage? Go hear Dave Dravecky tell his life story. In the prime of his baseball career, this athlete lost his pitching arm and shoulder to cancer. Or listen to Christopher Reeve, who played Superman in the movies before he suffered a broken neck. The lessons these men learned through their ordeals are models for others who face life challenges of their own.

Stories model actions such as hard work by people like Yolanda Tavera, who grew up as a migrant child following the crops, but now coordinates migrant education for an entire school district. Motivational speakers describe entrepreneurs like Bill Gates, who dropped out of Harvard and founded the Microsoft Corporation. Although the characters change, the plot is similar in every case: the people begin with little except vision and perseverance and end up successful in their fields. Others would be wise to follow their example.

Not all stories model how we should live; some provide a cautionary message, showing us how NOT to behave. These narratives are also powerful because of their emotional content. A police officer tells horror stories about teenagers whose careless driving killed carloads of innocent people. Her hope is that the emotional impact of the stories will influence beginning drivers to take care behind the wheel. Health professionals tell frightening tales of people who practiced unsafe sex, with dire consequences. The purpose of each story is to influence people to avoid specific behaviors.

Christopher Reeve, who played Superman in the movies before suffering a broken neck, tells his personal story for a variety of purposes. Depending on the occasion and the audience, his listeners may be inspired to persevere under adversity or to support funding for spinal cord injuries. (Lisa Quinones/ Black Star)

Speakers also use stories to influence listeners' beliefs, actions, or attitudes. In fact, narrative reasoning is so effective that Aristotle classified it as a type of **deliberative speaking,** the kind of speaking that gives people information and motivates them to make wise decisions regarding future courses of action. Persuasive stories function in two ways. They provide a rationale *for* a particular course of action, a proof of its *necessity*. At other times, they provide good arguments *against* a particular course of action.

Some stories are unpleasant to hear, for their telling exposes a societal wrong that needs to be righted. Speakers often use emotionally involving narratives to motivate others to intervene, to make a difference, to improve the lives of the needy. What follows is a persuasive narrative told by Ganga Stone (n.d.), founder of a volunteer network that cooks and delivers more than 1,200 meals daily to needy people.

> I hugged the heavy bag of donated groceries and began to climb the five long flights of stairs to Richard's studio apartment. I remember feeling a strong sense of satisfaction knowing that I was bringing help to a dying man who was all alone. That satisfied glow disappeared the instant I saw him.
>
> Richard lay propped up in a bed, his swollen features all distorted by AIDS-related disease. He hadn't eaten in two days, so when I approached his bedside he eagerly grabbed the grocery bag. I watched him reach again and again in the bag to find something, anything, that he could eat . . . now. Bread mix, oatmeal,

Deliberative Speaking

A form of speaking that gives people the information and motivation they need to make wise decisions regarding future courses of action.

canned beans, a box of macaroni and cheese—there was nothing ready to eat and no way he could get out of bed to cook. He finally gave up.

Then he looked up at me still clutching the empty bag, the useless assortment of ingredients strewn across the bed and floor. For a moment we just stared at one another. Then I made a promise I wasn't sure how I would keep. But I promised to bring him meals for as long as he needed, and I vowed that no one else in the same situation would ever have to face the unthinkable combination of AIDS and starvation. That was nearly seven years and 300,000 meals ago.

Ms. Stone tells this personal narrative with persuasive intentions. If she can effectively persuade listeners to identify with both Richard and herself, a woman determined to change a negative situation, they will feel her compassion and look for personal ways to relieve the suffering of people like Richard. If they become concerned enough, they may tell the story to others, inviting more and more people to attack such problems.

Not only do persuasive stories change individuals, they also contribute to changes in policies on wider levels. On the campus level, for example, speakers who publicly narrate stories about a series of muggings have convinced administrators to establish policies that correct the problem. On the national level, widely circulated tales about oil spills led to tighter regulations for oil tankers. International tales of human rights abuses led the United States to send military personnel to Kuwait, Somalia, and Bosnia.

Visionary Narratives

Narratives do more than recount the past or the present. Science fiction, for instance, paints bleak scenarios of out-of-control technology or, conversely, depicts a bright future if machines are harnessed and controlled. Stories about the future can give hope, as shown when a physician comforts parents with an "after surgery, this child will walk again" narrative. On a more mundane level, investors pour millions of dollars into stocks such as amazon.com based, not on past earnings, but on visions of future wealth.

Inspiring narratives also suggest ideals that go beyond your listeners' current beliefs and experiences, confronting them with possibilities and visions, expanding their understandings of themselves and their lives (Kirkwood, 1992). Through the **rhetoric of possibility,** you show what might be, and you move others to envision a future that they then make real. A famous example is Dr. Martin Luther King, Jr.'s 1963 call to be a nation in which all are judged, "not by the color of their skin, but by the content of their character." His vision inspires us to this day, but it's still not a reality, and we must continue to work together to make that vision come true. To see how the vision still lives, log on to the Internet and search for the exact phrase *I Have a Dream.* Follow links to a couple of sites from the more than 20,000 hits you will get.

Rhetoric of Possibility
Points out what can be, not what is.

In short, persuasive stories can influence a few people or millions. They act as examples of both wise and unwise behaviors; they provide a rationale *for* or *against* a policy, and they present a vision of what might be.

Entertaining Narratives

Let's face it: not all stories are full of profound meanings. Sometimes we tell tales just to relax and have a good time. For example, storyteller Jackie Torrence (1998) calls some stories "Jump Tales," for they end with a "BOO!" and we tell them because we love the shivers they give. Children's stories, urban legends, and television sitcoms are examples of narratives that feature unusual or quirky characters in unusual or quirky situations. Humorous stories also come in the form of extended jokes or in exaggerated situations carried to the extreme (Cassady, 1994).

Entertaining stories are told in gatherings, large and small. Friends tell friends the funny things they saw or did during the day. Parents and grandparents tell silly stories;

campers entertain one another as the campfire dies down. You've probably told your share of entertaining stories to at least a few people. Log on to the Internet and search for *silly stories* or *jokes,* for *scary stories, urban legends,* or *campfire tales.* The number of hits you get in each category should give you some idea of the popularity of entertaining stories. (www.alltheweb.com turned up more than one million hits for *jokes!*)

In short, the great rhetoric scholar, Kenneth Burke (1983), summarizes the variety of narratives we use as "the imaginative, the visionary, the sublime, the ridiculous, the eschatological (as with . . . Purgatory . . . [or] the Transmigration of Souls), the satirical, every detail of every single science or speculation, even every bit of gossip . . ." (p. 859). We are indeed storytelling animals.

STOP AND CHECK

Your Narrative Purposes

Of all the stories you've recounted within the last 24-hour period, estimate the percentage you told for the following purposes:

___ to inform
___ to persuade
___ to entertain

Do you think these percentages will change when you're out of college and working full time in your chosen career? If so, what kind(s) of stories will you probably tell more? What kind(s) will you tell less frequently? Discuss with a small group of your classmates how you will probably use narratives to do the following in your career area:

- Explain natural things
- Explain organizational or social realities
- Explain ultimate things
- Motivate people to believe or act in specific ways
- Present a vision of the future
- Entertain an audience

Evaluating Narrative Reasoning

Stories aren't equally valuable, and we need to test them to see if they are sensible and worthy of being told. Some are true and honest; others are false, mistaken, or downright lies (Burke, 1983). But how do we judge them? And if we're faced with competing narratives, how do we weigh and decide which is best? To answer these questions, narrative theorists offer three major tests of narrative logic (Fisher, 1999).

1. Is the story coherent or understandable? That is, does it hang together in a logical way? Do the events within the story itself follow one another in a predictable sequence? Do the characters act and interact in ways that are probable, given their personalities and cultural backgrounds? Or do some things seem out of character or out of order?

2. Is the story a true or faithful representative of what you know about the world and the way it works? In other words, does it make sense within the larger cultural framework? If it is a myth, folktale, or hypothetical story, does it contain important truths that demonstrate appropriate ways to live?

3. Does the story deserve to be told? Is the message important or worthwhile? Does it draw conclusions or motivate people to behave in positive ways that result in ethical outcomes for individuals and for society as a whole? Put simply, it's important to evaluate the desirability of passing on the narrative.

We have to weigh priorities when we choose whether or not to repeat a story; one that creates problems for the individuals involved and their families can provide a good example for other people. For instance, members of the press debated whether or not to print excerpts from videotapes made by the two killers at Columbine High School just before their bloody rampage. Reporters weighed the positive effects of informing society about the mind-set of dangerous teens against the negative effects of publicizing atrocious behaviors. *Time* magazine led with the story, but *Newsweek* and *U.S. News & World Report* passed on it. Gossip about a political candidate's marriage or the suicide attempts of a British princess also pose questions of narrative merit. If details of a person's private life are merely entertaining, many people refuse to relate them; however, if the story reveals a person's character or tendency to behave negatively, it might be appropriate to tell.

Good stories aren't necessarily true—fiction has its place—but stories that are blatantly false and result in harm to others are wrong to tell. History provides many examples of leaders who spread lies, with disastrous consequences. Here's one: In the Middle Ages, people circulated narratives about Jews poisoning the water supply of villages, stories that resulted in the murders of many Jewish people and produced irreversible negative consequences on individuals and on society as a whole.

Guidelines for Narratives

Because you have been hearing and telling stories all your life, the elements of the narrative schema are probably quite familiar. This section covers five important elements of a good story: the purpose, characters, sequence, plot, and language.

Identify Your Purpose

If you give a narrative speech, or if you only tell a narrative as part of a larger speech, still consider your purpose carefully. What function do you want the narrative to fulfill? Is its major purpose to inform, persuade, or entertain? Will it present a vision of possibilities that your audience has not yet considered? Remember that even when a story is mainly told for entertainment purposes, it generally conveys a lesson or point.

Develop Your Characters

It almost goes without saying that stories contain characters. Many narratives involve fictional characters such as animals or natural objects that are personified or given human traits—for instance, talking trees. Moreover, obviously imaginary characters such as dragons, talking train engines, genies in bottles, and other fanciful characters are widely used to convey important cultural values. Aesop's fables, for instance, have communicated western cultural wisdom for more than 2,000 years. Coyote stories, similarly, communicate the wisdom of various Native American groups.

Depending on your purpose, stories that are about actual people who act, meaning they move, speak, form relationships, and interact with others, are more effective. These characters are motivated by their distinctive personality traits, their ethnic and religious backgrounds, their educational experiences, and their social backgrounds, and these factors influence their choices.

Develop the Plot

Plot
The story's action

Characters in a good story face some sort of challenge that tests their assumptions, values, or actions. The way they respond to the challenges and the resulting changes in their lives form the **plot** or action of the narrative. During this period of change, natural processes, such as growing up, occur. The characters also meet physical, psychological, and economic challenges; they have accidents; they begin and end relationships; they lose their possessions in a tragic fire. How they deal with these challenges provides the point of the story.

Select Vivid Language

Narrative speaking requires careful attention to language. Vivid word choices and details bring the story to life and enable your listeners to feel as if they are there. Detailed descriptions in stories do more than simply convey information. They help create the scene and provide a sense of authenticity by providing specific names, places, and times that meet your listeners' psychological preference to set events in space and time (Tannen, 1989). Consider these features of style as you plan the language of your narratives: use of details, constructed dialogue, and listing.

Provide Detailed Descriptions

Details are important in several places. At the beginning, when you orient the audience to the plot of the story, include enough descriptive material so your audience will have a sense of the context. When you come to the key action, provide important details your audience can use to clearly understand the changes taking place within the characters. Finally, use a cluster of details in the climax of the story to drive home your main point.

The opening details function to set the story in a time and a place. For this reason, mythical stories often begin with the formulaic phrase, "Once upon a time in a faraway land." Listeners who have heard fairy tales, immediately pull up their mental "fairy tale schema" and listen to the story through that filter. Setting a true-life narrative in a specific place and time functions to draw listeners into the world of the story. A college student who started her narrative, "When I was a junior in high school, I was enrolled in a very small private school in the mountain country of Montana," immediately activated her listeners' "personal experiences" schema. Regardless of the actuality of the tale, details about the setting help listeners place themselves psychologically in the story's space.

A word of caution: take care to include just the right amount of details. Certain details are vital, but others are irrelevant for a variety of reasons. First, there may be *too many details*. For instance, just ask a child to tell you about a movie he saw, and you will probably get bogged down in details, maybe even missing the point of the story entirely, because young storytellers don't always separate *relevant* details from *interesting* ones. In addition, details can be inappropriate if they reveal more than listeners want to know. For instance, narrators can disclose intimate or horrifying information that causes listeners to focus on the details and miss the point. For these reasons, evaluate details carefully in light of your specific audience, then edit out irrelevant or inappropriate material.

Construct Dialogue

Constructed Dialogue
Created conversation between characters that adds realism to a story.

Created or **constructed dialogue** between major characters adds realism to a narration. By adding vocal variety that conveys the personalities and the emotions of the characters during your delivery, you further increase, not only your involvement, but your listener's involvement as well. For example, compare these two ways to report actions:

> He told me to move my car, but I didn't, because I was only going to park for a moment. The next thing I knew, he threatened me.

Kitbidin Atamkulov goes from village to village recounting the epic tale of Manas, the Kirghiz hero. His use of vivid language and concrete details makes the story memorable to both old and new generations of listeners. (Franz Lanting/ Minden Pictures)

Contrast the different effect it would have on your audience if you create a dialogue, then use different "voices," volume, and rate for each character, like this:

> He rolled down his car window and yelled, "Hey, kid, move your pile of junk!"
>
> I turned down my radio and explained through my open window, "I'll just be here a minute. I'm waiting for my mother."
>
> He jerked open his car door, stomped over to my car, leaned into my window and said slowly through clenched teeth, "I said, (pause) 'Move . . . your . . . pile . . . of . . . junk, *kid*!'"

As you can see, creating a scene with vivid, memorable dialogue is far more likely to involve your listeners in your dilemma, causing them to place themselves in the scene with you. By increasing listeners' emotional involvement in the story, you keep their attention and have greater potential for communicating the point of your speech.

Create Lists

Lists increase rapport with an audience because they introduce specific areas of commonality with the speaker. For instance, saying, "I packed my bags and checked twice to see if I had forgotten anything," gets across the message, but specific details that are familiar to fellow travelers enliven it, as this example illustrates:

> As I packed for Europe, I was afraid I would forget something vital. I looked through my bag for the seventh time. Toothpaste? Check. Toothbrush? Check. Toilet paper? (I'd been told to bring my own.) Check. Deodorant? Yep. Yet something seemed to be missing—as I was to discover in an isolated village in Germany.

Again, the details involve listeners actively as they create mental images for each item in the list. As you can see, the language of narrative does make a difference. Because narrative is one way of appealing to emotions, it is vital that your audience is involved in the story, and word choices that increase audience involvement make your story more powerful and memorable.

STOP AND CHECK

Analyzing a Folktale

Using the Hot Links at the end of this chapter, log on to the Internet and download a folktale from another culture. Compare the way it's constructed with the guidelines presented here. What is the purpose of the story? Are the characters real or imaginary? What details provide clues to their personality and motivations? What is the plot of the story? How does the storyteller incorporate vivid language, use of details, dialogue, and lists? How is the story similar to one that's typical of narratives from your culture? Is it different? If so, how?

Bring your analysis to class and prepare to discuss your conclusions with a small group of your classmates.

The Exemplum Pattern

Exemplum

An organizational pattern in which a narrative is used to illustrate a quotation.

A common narrative pattern, used by speech teachers for hundreds of years, is the **exemplum** (McNally, 1969). It has five elements. When you use this schema, include all five elements; without them, the narrative is just another narrative. The five parts of the exemplum follow one another in this pattern:

1. State a quotation or proverb.

2. Identify and explain the author or source of the proverb or the quotation.

3. Rephrase the proverb in your own words.

4. Tell a story that illustrates the quotation or proverb.

5. Apply the quotation or proverb to the audience.

Select your narrative from personal experiences, from historical events, or from episodes in the life of someone else. Choose one that represents, illustrates, or explains something important to you, perhaps a turning point in your life. Identify a lesson or point to your story, then find a quotation that supports this point. You can use a commonly quoted saying, such as "silence is golden," or you can go to sources of quotations (listed topically and by author) that are found in the reference section of the library or online. As Chapter 8 pointed out, a subject index such as www.yahoo.com links you to many such sources including *Bartlett's Familiar Quotations*, Classic Quotations, and Words of Women.

Jessica Howard's (2000) classroom exemplum built on her personal experiences as big sister to a Down Syndrome child. Here are her main points.

1. **Quotation.** "When one door of happiness closes, another opens; but often we look so long at the closed door that we do not see the one which has opened for us."

2. **Source.** Helen Keller was born in 1880; 19 months later, she contracted a fever that left her blind and deaf. When she was seven, her tutor, Anne Sullivan, taught Helen to communicate through sign language, Braille, and other alternative methods of sharing ideas. Helen learned to speak and to read lips using her hands. She eventually graduated from several colleges with high honors. Throughout her life, she overcame obstacles in an extraordinary way, never letting her disabilities thwart her ambitions.

3. **Paraphrase.** Ms. Keller's life shows that when circumstances close one pleasant option, it's easy to focus on the loss and fail to see possibilities that open up in another area.

4. **Narrative.** Before I turned thirteen, my mom told us she was pregnant with her fourth child. We three girls teased her because she was thirty-eight years old, but deep down we were all excited. Unfortunately, complications arose and tests re-

vealed that the baby was a boy who had Down Syndrome. I could tell you in my own words how I felt, but I came across a metaphor by Emily Kingsley, mother of a child with a disability, that captured my emotions.

Kingsley says a pregnancy is like planning a trip to Italy. An excited traveler buys guidebooks and makes plans to see art and buildings and remnants from ancient Rome. She even learns handy Italian phrases. After months of eager planning the day arrives, and she packs her bags and gets on the plane. Several hours later the plane lands, not in Italy, but in Holland where she discovers she must stay! Holland is not a terrible place, but this traveler wanted to go to Italy, and it takes her awhile to adjust. Pretty soon, though, she gets guidebooks and begins to explore the slower-paced, less flashy country she's in. She notices the windmills, the tulips, the Rembrandts. Her friends are busy, coming and going from Italy—bragging about their wonderful time there, and she listens longingly as they share experiences she will never have. Her pain at the loss of her dream never leaves, but she learns to enjoy the special, very lovely things Holland offers.

That is exactly what it was like when my brother was born. Our family knew what it was like to have "normal" children, so having one with Down Syndrome was different. It wasn't terrible, just different. We love him with all our hearts; he's adorable and loving and has a happiness and contentment that I envy. These past six years with my brother have taught me so much about not taking good health for granted, about what's really important in life, and about how much our perspective can change our attitudes.

5. **Lesson.** Our lives confront us with many happenings we don't want; often plans change because of some outside force we cannot control. Learning to roll with the punches you're thrown in life is a great quality. In the long run, God has everything under control, so if your plans don't work out, don't spend your life mourning your loss. "When one door of happiness closes, another opens; but often we look so long at the closed door that we do not see the one which has opened for us."

In summary, an exemplum builds around a quotation that you develop by telling a narrative. This pattern is useful when your speech goal is to reinforce cultural values.

Summary

In every society narrative is present as a form of reasoning or sense making. Narratives both reflect and shape cultural beliefs and values, and hearing narratives from other cultures highlights both commonalities and differences between groups. Narratives in all cultures function in three ways: to inform, to persuade, and to entertain. Explanatory narratives provide answers for why and how things are the way they are. Exemplary narratives are stories with a moral or point that listeners should—or should not—imitate. Other persuasive narratives provide a reason to do something, or a reason NOT to pursue the action. In addition, narratives help us envision possibilities that we had not imagined before. Finally, some narratives are just plain fun and we listen to them to be entertained. Some stories are better than others, but every good story should be coherent, it should represent some aspect of the real world, and it should be worthy of being told. To evaluate a story's merit, consider its effect on society, its effect on individuals, and its overall truthfulness about life.

Five elements should be developed in a narrative—purpose, characters, sequence, plot, and language. Vivid language is especially important because it brings characters to life and makes the action more compelling, causing listeners to identify with more elements of the story. The exemplum is an excellent way to organize a narrative speech that is constructed around a quotation. It begins with the quotation, provides information about the source, and paraphrases the saying. An illustrative story forms most of the speech that concludes with a stated lesson or moral to the story.

JAFFE CONNECTION

Key Terms

homo narrans (294)
storytelling (294)
myths (296)
exemplary narratives (297)
deliberative speaking (298)

rhetoric of possibility (299)
plot (302)
constructed dialogue (302)
exemplum (304)

Application and Critical Thinking Questions

1. What narratives do you use to explain the world of nature? The social world? Your family? Other groups to which you belong? The ultimate meanings in life?

2. Do your stories ever clash with the narratives of others? If so, what do you do about these differences?

3. Share with a group of classmates a few examples of exemplary narratives you heard while you were growing up. In what ways were they intended to influence your behaviors? How successful were they?

4. In what settings have you heard inspiring life stories? Have you ever shared your personal saga of overcoming some challenge? If so, describe the occasion. Where might you give one in the future?

5. Think of stories that you have only heard orally. Who are the "legends" in your family, your sports team, your religious group, living group, or university? What lessons do their stories provide? What values or actions do they help you remember and perpetuate?

6. Many speeches are given in the form of a narrative, or an extended narrative takes up a significant part of the speech. Chief Joseph's speech in Appendix C is one example. Read through it to see how he uses a story to drive home his point.

7. The exemplum pattern is useful in a variety of settings. With a small group of your classmates, sketch out themes and suggest the types of supporting narratives that would be appropriate on each of the following occasions:

   ■ A sports award banquet

   ■ A luncheon meeting of a club such as Rotary or Kiwanis

   ■ A religious youth group meeting

   ■ A scholarship presentation ceremony

   ■ A Fourth of July celebration

   ■ A keynote address to a conference focusing on issues relevant to female physicians

Internet Activities

1. Do a PowerTrac search on your *InfoTrac College Edition* for the journal *Asian Folklore Studies,* and read an article in it. Briefly summarize the article to share with your classmates.

2. On your *InfoTrac College Edition*, do a PowerTrac search for the key word *storytelling*. Read a couple of articles and look for tips that can help you tell stories more effectively.

3. Do a PowerTrac search for the journal *Vital Speeches,* and look for the narrative speech entitled "Storytelling: The Soul of an Enterprise" by Sean Gresh (December 1, 1998, issue). Read the speech (the story of his life and career choices), then decide how effective you think it was with the specific audience in the particular situation.

4. Use the search engine www.alltheweb.com to search for the exact phrase *African American tales,* then read some of the stories you find there.

5. Use the search engine www.dogpile.com and ask it to fetch *folklore*. Link to hits that interest you.

Hot Links at the Public Speaking Resource Center

Public Speaking Resource Center

The following links are maintained and can be accessed easily via Jaffe Connection at the Public Speaking Resource Center on the Wadsworth Communication Café web site at http://communication.wadsworth.com/publicspeaking/study.html

■ http://www.storyconnection.net/diannes_story.htm
Dianne de Las Casas is a professional storyteller whose site lets you see the many opportunities available to storytellers today. Read her story and follow her links to professional associations for storytellers. She is actively involved with integrating the ancient art of storytelling with today's technological innovations via the Internet and the World Wide Web.

■ http://haldjas.folklore.ee/folklore
Folklore is an electronic journal of folklore published by the Estonian Language Institute. Articles in this journal will help you better understand how hearing tales from other cultures illuminates both likenesses and differences among cultural groups.

■ http://virtual.park.uga.edu/~clandrum/folklore.html
Cindy Landrum of the University of Georgia sponsors this site with links to oral lore, social and folk custom, and material culture. Click onto a definition of folklore, or see examples of folktales and explore the ethnic or social groups from which a particular item, belief, or story originates.

Speech Interactive

Watch and listen to the following speech via Jaffe Speech Interactive on the Jaffe Connection CD-ROM. You will have an opportunity to critique Gail's delivery of the speech and offer suggestions for improvement. Then, compare your Speech Evaluation Checklist and Speech Improvement Plan with the author's.

Jaffe Speech Interactive

Spanking? There's Gotta Be a Better Way *by Gail Grobey*

Gail gave this narrative speech in an argumentation class. Besides being a narrative speech, it's an example of invitational rhetoric (see Chapter 18); she invited her classmates, many of whom disagreed with her claim that spanking is wrong, to understand her perspective by telling this story.

My daughter Celeste [displaying the photograph] has always been a rather precocious child. She's picked up all kinds of concepts and language from listening to her future-English-teacher mom talk and has learned how to apply them. When given the opportunity, she'll wax lyrical in her piping four-year-old voice at some length about the Joker's role as antagonist in Batman and how Robin functions as a foil or why the conflict between the villain and the hero is necessary. She's constantly telling me when I'm stressed about school or work or the mess in the kitchen, "Mom, just breathe. Just find your center and relax in it."

Yes, she's a precocious child, but this time let me place the emphasis on child. Her temper is fierce and daunting, like her mother's! She can get very physical in her anger, striking out destructively at anything she can get her hands on. She can also be manipulative (which is really more like her father)!

At times, my patience is driven to the very end, and so I can understand why some parents turn to spanking. There are times when there seems to be no other alternative, when I can't think of any other way to get through to this completely irrational being. And there are a lot of things about me that would make me the ideal spanking parent: my temper, my impatience, my obsessive need to control. And after all, I was a spanked child. But when she was born, and I saw that tiny body and the light in her eyes, I made a conscious commitment never to strike my child.

As she's grown, that commitment has been challenged. About a year ago, she pranced into my room chanting in the universal language of preschoolers, "Look what I found! You can't have it." I looked down and in her hand was a large, inviting, bright red pill with irresistible yellow writing on it. I recognized it at once as one of my mother's blood pressure pills, and quite naturally, my first impulse was to snatch it.

I also recognized, however, that she was looking for just such a reaction from me. She had lately begun establishing clear patterns of button-pushing. I would say, "Give it to me." To which she would naturally reply, "No!"

And so it would begin. She was prepared to throw and fully enjoy the temper tantrum that would inevitably follow and tax me to the end of my patience. I repressed my impulse to aggressively take command and instead, bent down on one knee and asked her with casual awe, "Wow. Where'd you'd find it?"

She eyed me suspiciously, backing up. She said, "On the kitchen floor. It's mine. I'm keeping it."

All I could think of was how easy it would be to tip her over the edge into a major fight. (The big ones always begin over something small and silly — me attempting to exercise control over something and her asserting that this is not acceptable. We both get lost in our rage.) It would have been so easy to just grab the pill and move into fight mode. But I held firm to creativity over violence.

"Oh, Celeste," I said, "thank you so much. You are a real hero. You found that dangerous pill and picked it up before the dogs could eat it and make themselves sick. You saved them! What a hero!"

The change on her face was instant. She voluntarily and proudly relinquished the pill and dashed off to tell her grandma what a noble deed she'd just done. I remember saying out loud, "Whew. That was close!

Gail begins by setting a picture of Celeste on the table she's standing behind, and she introduces the major characters, her daughter Celeste and herself, using vivid details. Her listeners have plenty of mental images of the child and her relationship to her mother early in the speech.

Because she knows her audience pretty much disagrees with her position, she shows that she understands their frustration and their desire to deal with children who are angry and obnoxious.

Here is the point of climax, and Gail again clusters vivid details that enliven the scene. Her use of constructed dialogue, delivered with the vocal variations that would actually occur in the scene, kept the audience's attention.

Celeste "frames" the issue in terms of ownership and control, and Gail tries to see things from her child's perspective.

Here is an excellent example of re-sourcement (see Chapter 18) in which Gail reframes the discovery of the pill as a safety issue.

It seems like such a small thing, but I see it as representative of the greater whole. It's one of my proudest moments as a parent: Celeste and I both walked away with the feeling that we had accomplished something important. She experienced a boost in self-esteem, and I ended up holding firm to my commitment and reinforcing to myself my belief that there is always an alternative way to deal with children, no matter how small the situation or problem. One never needs to resort to violence.

Gail's narrative provides an excellent example that others can use as a model for nonviolent childrearing. Choosing to tell a narrative, rather than building a case with examples, statistics, and other evidence, was probably more effective with her specific audience.

16

Informative Speaking

This chapter will help you:

■ Describe the global importance of information

■ Analyze an audience's knowledge of your subject

■ Create several types of informative speeches including demonstrations and instructions, descriptions, reports, and explanations

■ Use guidelines to make your informative speeches more effective

"Nuclear Family" ©1976 by Michael Rios

Walk into a thriving corporation and you will see employees giving reports, providing instructions, demonstrating techniques and products, and updating their coworkers on the latest information related to their organization. Go into a school and you'll see students and teachers making announcements, discussing facts, defining terms, and explaining complex concepts. Now, take a moment and picture yourself fifteen years down the road. Where are you working? What instructions or directions are vital to your success? What information will you pass along to your coworkers or the public? What new information do you need to be healthier, more productive, or happier? This list suggests a few ways that ordinary people speak to inform:

- A member of the student government reports a committee's findings about the possibility of bringing a well-known entertainer to campus.

- A nurse demonstrates to first-time fathers how to wash a newborn.

- A teen explains to younger students some strategies for saying no to sex.

- Accountants present the annual audit to a client company's board of directors.

This chapter first examines the global importance of information. It then turns to audience analysis and distinguishes four levels of audience knowledge that should affect your informative strategies. Next, it describes demonstrations and instructions, descriptions, reports and explanations and includes skeletal outlines of speeches in these categories. General guidelines for informative speeches conclude the chapter.

Information Is Important Globally

Information Age

Thanks to technological innovations more information is available today than in any other era.

Electronic Superhighways

Television, telephones, and computers linked up through networks.

Information Explosion

A metaphor comparing rapid information output to a bomb that scatters fragments of disconnected pieces in all directions.

Information Overload

A human response of being overwhelmed by the sheer amount of available data.

Our age has been called the **Information Age.** This means, among other things, that a greater number of people in our country and around our globe know more about issues, people, places, theories, objects, and processes than any other humans throughout history have known. It also means that enormous industries exist to distribute information through print and electronic channels with data bank storage and cable linkages that connect televisions, telephones, and computers into **electronic superhighways** (Elmer-Dewitt, 1993). You may experience the resulting **information explosion** as a bombardment of fragments of disconnected, irrelevant facts.

An example might clarify this concept. In one five-minute newscast, you can learn about a train derailment in France, a fire in Tennessee, and a coup in a central Asian country—but do any of these facts affect you personally? Surf the Internet and you'll have access to more information than you can read in a lifetime. But what's really important and what's trivial? What do you need to know in order to live better, and what's simply interesting? Sorting through the bits of data may leave you feeling overwhelmed with **information overload,** for the sheer amount of material is staggering!

Similarly, your audience can feel overwhelmed unless you, as a speaker, connect disparate facts and ideas and help listeners integrate new information with old. When you do this successfully, you not only help them make sense of their world, but you also provide your listeners with basic information they can use to make wise decisions (Fancher, 1993). Let's say you gather and present data that clearly describe and explain various types of mutual funds, including their benefits and pitfalls. You've empowered audience members by giving them information they can use to invest wisely.

Having access to information is so important that world leaders consider the ability to both give and receive information to be a global human right that deserves to be protected by international law. Indeed, Article 19 of the Universal Declaration of Human Rights (1948) states:

"Knowledge is power" could be the motto of these educators who provide health and child care information to mothers in Kenya. (Sean Sprague/PANOS Pictures)

Everyone has the right to freedom of opinion and expression; this right includes freedom to hold opinions without interference and to seek and impart information and ideas through any media and regardless of frontiers (Quoted in Harms & Richstad, 1978).

Article 19 recognizes the potential dangers of an **information imbalance** in which some people or groups know a great deal and others know very little. People who are kept in ignorance, with vital facts concealed from them, may lack fundamental understandings of their world. Here are a few examples: Radio Free Europe broadcast messages to people in Communist-controlled countries during the Cold War, providing listeners behind the Iron Curtain with information that their governments withheld. Throughout the world, public health educators give people information that may save their lives. One example is women in central Africa and Southeast Asia who empower one another with facts they can use to protect themselves against sexually transmitted diseases. In addition, groups in the United States are refurbishing used computers to send to children in Third World countries.

In short, some people think of information as a resource or commodity that's scarce and valuable. This culture has it in abundance; other nations have less. Some groups and social classes within the United States have access to the information they need to be successful and healthy; others have limited access to the same knowledge. Finally, some individuals know how to take advantage of the information that is widely available; others do not (Maxwell & McCain, 1997).

Information Imbalance
Some people or groups have very little access to information in contrast to others that have it in abundance.

Analyze Your Audience's Current Knowledge

When Dwight took public speaking, he saw an article in the *World Press Review* entitled "Longing for the Days of Harem." His curiosity was piqued; he knew little about harems, and he was pretty sure his classmates were similarly unfamiliar with them. So he decided to give an informative speech on the topic, but in order to his classmates' understandings, he first had to find out what they already knew and believed about harems. Then he adjusted his speech accordingly (Edwards & McDonald, 1993). Audiences can

FIGURE 16.1 Early in your planning, assess your audience's current levels »of knowledge about your topic and identify misconceptions or outdated information they may have. Doing so will help you devise strategies that will make your information more useful to your listeners.

have no information, a minimum of information, forgotten or outdated information, or misinformation (see Figure 16.1), and each level of understanding calls for different strategies.

Presenting New Information

Some audiences are unfamiliar with your subject; they've never even heard of it, so the information you present will be novel. Your task, then, is to provide a basic overview of your topic. For instance, what do you know about detoxihol? DEET? Harems? Emmaline Pankhurst? Starlight plastic? I've heard speeches on each of these topics, and each speaker succeeded only because he or she followed the following guidelines:

1. Provide basic, introductory facts—the who, what, when, where, and how type of information.

2. Define unfamiliar terminology and jargon clearly.

3. Give detailed, vivid explanations and descriptions.

4. Make as many links as you can to the audience's knowledge by using literal and figurative analogies—comparing and contrasting the concept with something that's already familiar to them.

Presenting Supplemental Information

The great inventor Thomas Edison once said, "We don't know a millionth of one percent about anything." This means that audiences often have vague or superficial knowledge about your subject but lack detailed, in-depth understandings. This type of listener doesn't want you to rehash basic information; they want supplemental information. To illustrate, an audience somewhat familiar with Nelson Mandela's life will be more impressed if you provide little-known information that gives additional insight into his character. Another example: most people learned in elementary school to select foods from several food groups, so a speech describing the major groups is redundant. However, the same audience may lack information about specific elements of nutrition such as antioxidants—information that would help them choose foods more wisely. Specific strategies to use with audiences whose information is limited include:

1. Dig deeper into your research sources to discover additional, less well known details and facts.

2. Go beyond the obvious and add in-depth descriptions and explanations to what is already familiar.

3. Narrow a broad topic and provide interesting and novel information about just one aspect of it. For example, explore only Mandela's childhood or focus on his educational background alone.

Presenting Review or Updated Information

This category of listeners once studied your subject, but they've forgotten some or most of what they learned, or they lack current, updated information. Your speech can function as a review that refreshes the audience's memories, reinforces their knowledge, and keeps their information current. This type of informative speech is typical in school or job settings. For instance, students may have studied the five canons of rhetoric, but they need to review them if they want to ace the test; workers may have read or heard about sexual harassment laws in companywide seminars held two years ago, but a workshop on new regulations keeps them updated. With audiences in this category, you'll be more effective if you use these strategies:

1. When you review material, approach the subject from different angles—help listeners conceptualize it from different perspectives.

2. Be creative; use vivid supporting materials that capture and hold attention.

3. When appropriate, use humor, and strive to make the review interesting.

4. For both reviews and updates, present the most recent available information. Mills (1999) reports that our current proliferation of information results in 100 percent new knowledge every five years (at least in high-tech areas); consequently, what's learned earlier quickly becomes outdated. Overstated? Perhaps. But it's true that people who want to stay current must become lifelong learners.

Countering Misinformation

A final type of audience has misconceptions and misunderstandings about a subject that you can elucidate by clarifying definitions and facts and by countering misunderstandings. For instance, the saying, "A dog is a human's best friend," is well known and widely accepted in the United States. However, a 1999 cover story in *Atlantic* magazine informs readers of scientific evidence that suggests dogs don't really like their owners; instead, they fake devotion in order to manipulate their humans. If this is true, many or most people in your audience misunderstand dog behaviors! In other examples, Arab students sometimes speak to counter their classmates' misconceptions about Arab culture, and politicians clarify specific policy positions their opponents have distorted. When countering misunderstandings, you are presenting material that is inconsistent or contradictory to what they "know," and you will be wise to consider the following:

1. Prepare for emotional responses—often negative reactions. (Think about it. Who wants to hear that her beloved Fido is really a con artist?) Consequently, present the most credible facts you can find and tone down the emotional aspect.

2. Look for information derived from scientific studies, especially quantification, when that type of support would be most convincing.

3. Define terminology carefully; consider explaining the origin of specific words or ideas.

4. Counter the negative prejudices against and stereotypes related to a specific topic (such as Arab culture) by highlighting positive elements of the subject.

In summary, the amount of information your audience brings to your speech should make a difference in the strategies you select to present meaningful information. By assessing their knowledge about your subject in advance, you can more effectively craft a speech that meets their need to know.

Public
Speaking
Resource
Center

STOP AND CHECK

Analyze Your Audience's Knowledge

To determine your audience's prior knowledge—or lack thereof—regarding your topic, answer the following questions about your topic. (Refer back to Chapter 6 if you need to construct a questionnaire to determine your audience's knowledge about your topic.) You can answer these questions online under Chapter 16: Forms and Checklists for Jaffe Connection at the Public Speaking Resource Center, http://communication.wadsworth.com/publicspeaking/study.html

I. Put an "X" in the blank that is most like your classroom audience; put a "O" in the blank that's next most like them.

_____ no information   _____ limited information

_____ forgotten information   _____ outdated information

_____ misinformation:

specify _____

II. On the scale below, estimate the percentage of audience members who have direct experience with the topic.

|-------|-------|-------|-------|-------|-------|

10% or less 25%   33%   50%   66%   75%   90%+

III. Does most of the audience have an attitude that would make it difficult for them to listen?   _____ yes   _____ no
If yes, specify _____

IV. Will the audience probably be interested in the topic?
_____ yes   _____ no

If no, what can you do to spark interest? _____

V. What potential benefit will audience members gain by knowing this information? _____

_____

Types of Informative Speeches

Informative speeches fall into several categories. Demonstrations and instructions, descriptions, reports, and explanations are some of the broad categories of informative speaking you may be called upon to give—both in college and in your eventual career. This section gives specific guidelines for these types of speeches.

Doing Demonstrations and Providing Instructions

Instructions provide answers to the question: "How do you do that?" On the day her company went public, the entrepreneurial Martha Stewart became a billionaire. What's her line of work? She gives demonstration speeches on television and creates instructional books and magazines. She's like thousands of teachers, coaches, and salespeople who both *show* and *tell* others how to do a procedure, how to use a specific object, or how to complete a task. Ms. Stewart, like other successful instructors, understands and implements a number of guidelines for giving demonstrations and instructions—guidelines that can help you succeed when you must give a "how-to" speech. (Unfortunately, no one can guarantee that you'll earn millions!)

When you give **demonstrations,** you both show and explain how to do a process or how to use an item. The following tips will help you.

Demonstrations
"How-to" speeches that both show and tell.

1. Your first step in preparation is to think through all the required stages or steps. As you proceed, ask yourself the following questions: What comes first? What's absolutely essential? Which step is easiest? Which is hardest? What does the audience already know how to do? Where will the audience most likely be confused? Which step takes the most time? Which take practically no time at all (Mannie, 1998; Demonstrative Speech, n.d.)?

2. Next, work on the content of your speech. Organize the essential steps sequentially, and concentrate on clarifying and simplifying the ones that will probably cause difficulty or confusion. During this time, carefully preplan the environment to facilitate learning—this may mean your audience will have to move their chairs or stand up and spread out around the room. Or you may have to furnish supplies if you want them to do the project with you.

3. Plan your visual support. Ask yourself if actual objects are practical (see Chapter 12); if not, plan videotapes or other supplementary visuals. Then practice working with your props so that you can use them and still maintain rapport with your audience (Flynn, n.d.). The following outline shows the necessity of visual aids during demonstrations. If this speaker had simply tried to describe how to create a cartoon face, he'd have surely failed! However, he drew cartoon features onto a transparency as shown in Figure 16.2, then he uncovered feature by feature as he progressed through his speech.

Specific Purpose: To inform my audience about specific cartoon features they can easily draw to create a cartoon character almost instantly.

Central Idea: By drawing in simple cartoon shapes for eyes, noses, mouths, hair, and facial outlines, almost anyone can easily draw a cartoon.

   I. First, select the eyes.

  II. Then, draw a nose.

 III. Choose a mouth.

 IV. Add hair.

  V. Outline your character's face.

FIGURE 16.2 For his speech on drawing cartoon faces, one speaker put a number of facial features on a transparency. He uncovered each row as he discussed the separate elements, and his listeners created personal cartoons, feature by feature, as he went along.

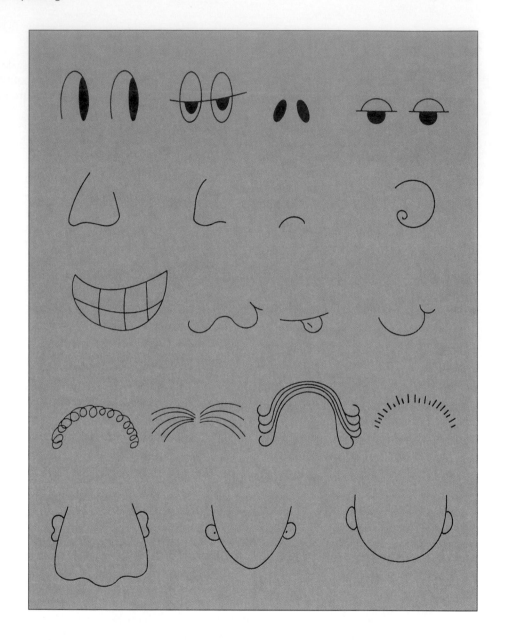

Before he started, he had each classmate take out a pencil or pen and a blank sheet of paper. (He'd brought along several blank sheets of paper and several writing instruments, just in case.) Then, as he spoke, each student created her or his own cartoon.

4. Make sure you time the entire process. If a task takes too long to accomplish in the time allotted for your speech, a better strategy is to demonstrate the process yourself and provide handouts with step-by-step instructions for listeners to use at home. One student failed to do this. She chose to have each listener complete a complicated origami project—folding a crane—in a seven-minute speech; twenty-two minutes later, her audience still had half-folded cranes when the class period ran out! Demonstrating the crane and providing each student with an instructional handout and a piece of origami paper would have been more successful.

Another strategy for a lengthy process is to prepare several versions of the item, stopping each at a different point of completion. Cooking and art demonstrations illustrate this well; a cooking instructor, for example, begins to crystallize onions. But rather than take the twenty minutes necessary to complete the process, he sets the pan aside, reaches for onions he's finished earlier, then proceeds with the next step. Similarly, a sculptor does an essential step in creating a pot; then she leaves it to dry and takes up a pot she prepared in advance that's ready for the next step.

Not all "how-to" speeches require a demonstration. You can give people tips on how to resolve conflict or how to listen more effectively, on how to select a caterer for a major celebration or how to manage time effectively. In these cases, your focus is on providing instructions or pointers that will help audience members accomplish a specific goal. Diversity in Practice: Japanese Seminars on Fathering on the next page illustrates the widespread nature of providing instructions.

Giving Descriptions

Descriptions answer the question: "What's it like?" Before you can describe an object, place, or event to someone else, you must first observe it carefully yourself. As you do, look for details, then select vivid imagery and sensory words that help people understand what your subject looks, smells, feels, or tastes like. A guide in an art museum, for example, walks her group from painting to painting, pointing out details of color, form, and texture within each painting that her audience would probably not see at first glance. Descriptions of places, objects, and events, range from personal to global (see Figure 16.3). Because your listeners will probably be more interested in topics that are close to their daily lives in location, time, and relevance, be explicit about how any topic relates to their perceived interests and needs.

Describing Places

People seek out useful information about places. A student visiting a campus, for example, needs to know how the place is laid out, and a college guide describes various parts of the campus as he shows the visitor around. Descriptions of different countries or sites such as national parks or tourist attractions similarly attract audiences, and travel agents or park rangers are just two types of professionals who describe places.

When you describe a place, provide vivid details that help your listeners form precise images of the site. Take advantage of visual aids including maps, drawings, slides, brochures, or enlarged photographs, and consider a spatial or topical organizational pattern. By way of illustration, here are the main points of a speech about Thailand given by a Thai student:

Specific Purpose: To inform my audience about the beauty of Thailand and the many tourist attractions in it.

Central Idea: Thailand is a beautiful country with many scenic attractions that complement the human-made wonders to be found there.

I. Geographic features
    A. Inland areas
    B. Famous beaches

II. Tourist attractions
    A. Cities
    B. Temples and shrines

DIVERSITY IN PRACTICE

Japanese Seminars on Fathering

Some "how-to" speeches occur in a series of lectures, seminars, or workshop presentations that take place over a period of time. In Takasuki, Japan, for example, the Sunstar Corporation hired Mieko Hosomi, a newspaper editor, to present a series of "how-to" lectures for a group of about forty company executives—not on the art of making better shampoos and other toiletries, but on the art of being better fathers. When a recession in Japan led to a five-day, rather than a six-day work week, many companies began to hire speakers like Mrs. Hosomi to help men, who know how to be workaholics, learn how to focus their energies on fathering as well (Sanger, 1993).

One Japanese corporation sponsored a series of lectures informing men about effective parenting skills. (Pite/Liaison International)

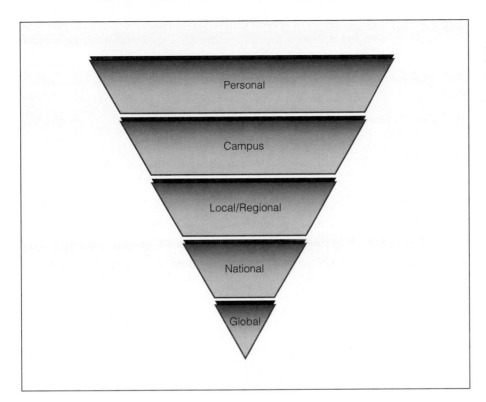

FIGURE 16.3 People need useful information on a variety of levels. However, they will most likely be interested in personal topics or in topics that you connect to their daily concerns.

If you're searching for an international topic, places are good choices. Students have described Italian villas, African deserts, and the Taj Mahal, as well as local museums, Disney World, Carnegie Hall, the Mississippi River delta, and the Holocaust Museum in Washington, D.C.

Describing Objects

Descriptions of objects, including natural objects (stars, glaciers), human constructions (the Vietnam War Memorial), huge things (the planet Jupiter), or microscopic matter (microbes), are common. Students have described inanimate (computers) or animate (panda bears) objects by providing information about the origin of the object, how it's made, identifying characteristics, how it works, how it's used, and so on.

Topic choices can range from personal to international. On the personal level, students have described body features such as skin or fingernails. They've talked about campus objects such as a historical tree or a memorial plaque and explained cultural artifacts such as the Golden Gate Bridge, CD players, and guitars. International topics have included the Great Pyramids and the Great Wall of China.

Describing Events

Events or occurrences can be personal (birthday customs), community (local festivals or celebrations), national (elections), and international (the Russian launch of Sputnik or the bombing of Hiroshima). Chronological, narrative, and topical organizational patterns are typically used. The first two patterns work well for step-by-step events such as the launch of Sputnik or planning a wedding. The topical pattern is also useful for describing happenings that consist of several different components (birthday customs, for instance). Here is an example of a topical outline for a speech describing a sporting event.

Specific Purpose: To inform my audience of the different events that occur in a rodeo.

Central Idea: Rodeos are athletic contests with people and animals competing in a variety of events.

   I. Bull riding

  II. Barrel racing

 III. Bronco busting

 IV. Calf roping

When you describe events or happenings in concrete details and vivid language, your listeners can place themselves at the event. In other words, you speak so that they participate vicariously.

Presenting Reports

Think of a report as a way to answer the question: "What have we learned about this subject?" Giving reports is a global business that employs millions of people; around the clock, reporters collect and organize news and information about people and issues of public interest. For example, investigative reporters search for the answers to questions such as, "What are scientists learning about the causes of breast cancer?" And campus reporters pass along the information that university task forces have come up with. In classrooms and boardrooms, here and abroad, people give reports. This section discusses two common topic areas: people and issues.

Reporting about People

What individuals have shaped our world? What did they accomplish? How did they live? You can answer such questions by providing sketches of influential historical or contemporary characters. Biographical reports can be about philosophers (Kierkegaard), military men and women (Genghis Khan, the Amazons), artists (the Impressionists), writers (Toni Morrison), and so on. Don't overlook villains (Machiavelli) as well as heroes (Mother Teresa) for biographical subjects.

Generally, chronological, topical, or narrative organizational patterns best fit a biographical report. Fei Fei's outline is organized topically with two points: (1) Confucius's life and (2) his influence. She then uses chronological subpoints to develop her first point—Confucius's life.

Specific Purpose: To inform my audience of the life and ideas of the Chinese philosopher whose teachings influence more than a billion people globally.

Central Idea: Confucius, who lived in China about 2,500 years ago, developed a life-affirming philosophy that has influenced many Asian cultures.

   I. Confucius's life

     A. Birth and youth

     B. Early career

     C. Period as a wandering scholar

     D. Later years

II. Confucius's influence
   A. His teaching method
   B. Concepts of *li* and *ren*
   C. Five relationships

In addition to individual subjects, don't overlook groups of people such as skinheads, the Mafia, aborigines, and Motown musicians as potential subjects. Here is an outline of a student speech on the Amish that is organized topically:

Specific Purpose: To inform my audience about Amish people by describing their beliefs and explaining challenges facing their group.

Central Idea: The Amish are a religious group with written and unwritten rules for living that are being challenged by education and tourism.

 I. The Amish people
   A. Number and location
   B. Historical information

 II. Amish beliefs
   A. Written ordinances—Dortrecht Confession of Faith (1632)
   B. Unwritten rules of local congregations—Ordnung

III. Challenges to Amish culture
   A. Education and teacher certification
   B. Tourism attention

As you develop your major points, keep in mind your audience's questions: "Why should I listen to a speech about this person or group?" "What impact has this subject had on society?" "How does knowing about this individual or group tie into my concerns?" When you answer these questions, your listeners will better understand the relevancy of the person or group. For links to biographical information on thousands of individuals, both contemporary and historical, visit the Internet site http://www.libraryspot.com/biographicalinfo.htm

Reporting about Issues

Newspapers and magazines are good sources for a list of current issues that we discuss within our communities and our society as a whole. We debate welfare reform, immigration policies, legalization of marijuana, humanitarian aid to war-torn nations, plus local and campus problems—all complex and controversial. Generally, addressing issues allows us to create policies aimed at solving the problems and answering the question "What should we do about this problem?" Here are a few examples of controversial issues:

- What have we learned about the effects of marijuana on the body?

- What do we know about the effectiveness of various programs for rehabilitating juvenile offenders?

- What are the issues each side emphasizes in their support of or opposition to taxing the Internet?

Think of this speech as an investigative report, where you research the facts surrounding an issue and then present your findings. Your major purpose is to enlighten your listeners so that they have a factual foundation to use in formulating their own conclusions. Thus, reports are not intended to persuade or advocate one position or another. (However, you may follow up your report by giving a persuasive speech on the same topic.)

Often informative speakers report on both sides of controversial issues such as the use of Native American mascots for sports teams. (Regis Lefebure/The Stock Market)

Informative speeches about issues are common assignments in public speaking classrooms. As you prepare, look for the answers to such questions as: What exactly is the problem or issue? What are the current beliefs or theories commonly held about the issue? What is the extent of the problem (how many people does it affect)? How did this situation develop? What solutions are proposed? What are the arguments on both sides of the issue? Generally, pro-con, cause-effect, problem-solution(s), narrative, and topical patterns work well for investigative reports. Here is one student's pro–con outline for a speech that explores the controversy surrounding the use of Native American symbols in sports.

Specific Purpose: To inform my audience about the supporters' and opponents' views regarding Native American symbols used in sports.

Central Idea: There are several arguments both for and against using Native American symbols for sports nicknames and mascots.

I. There are many arguments against the use of Native American symbols as nicknames and mascots.
  A. Use of the symbols is offensive toward the native people.
  B. Using Native American symbols perpetuates racist stereotypes.
  C. Non-Indians do not have the right to use sacred Indian symbols.

II. A large group of people supports the continuance of such symbols.
  A. Schools choose Indian mascots because they represent school values.
  B. Many people simply do not want to change.
  C. Using these symbols gives schools an opportunity to educate students on the Indian heritage they represent.

Issues for speech topics can be personal (eating disorders), campus (tuition hikes), local (potholes), national (teens and guns), and global (trade with nations that violate human rights). Many global decisions, such as what to do with nuclear waste, have long-lasting effects. Others, although less significant, are related to larger controversies. For example, the discussion of plastic surgery for Miss America contestants is associated with issues of women's rights and stereotypes of female beauty.

Explaining Concepts

Katherine Rowan (1995) of Purdue University focuses her research on explanatory or **expository speaking**—known more simply as the "speech to teach." Every day expository speakers set forth, disclose, unmask, or explain an idea in detail in order to increase listener's understandings. Science and history teachers define terms and explain concepts daily, parents answer the endless "whys" of four-year-olds with explanations. Effective expository speakers identify the hurdles listeners are likely to encounter in their attempt to comprehend the concept. They then plan ways to overcome the barriers and make meanings clear.

Expository Speaking
The "speech to teach" that sets forth, discloses, unmasks, or explains an idea in detail so that listeners understand it.

Defining Terms

Definitions answer the questions: "What is it?" or "What does it mean?" Providing definitions is common in educational and workplace settings—for example, a philosophy professor defines *justice,* a speech professor elucidates the concept of *confirmation* as it's used in the academic discipline, and an employer defines *sexual harassment* for new employees. In addition, inspirational speakers commonly define words. Examples: a priest defines *peacemaking;* a commencement speaker defines *integrity;* a coach defines *commitment.* In short, although we see people act in ways we classify as just or as sexual harassment, we can neither see nor touch justice or harassment, and defining these terms helps us as a society discriminate between appropriate and inappropriate behaviors.

One effective organizational pattern for a speech of definition presents first the denotative then the connotative meaning of a word. (Chapter 13 discusses denotation and connotation in detail.)

I. **Denotative Meaning:** Focus on the *denotation* of the term as found in various reference books such as a thesaurus or etymological dictionary. The *Oxford English Dictionary* or another unabridged dictionary provides the most thorough definitions available. In addition, check through books in a specific academic discipline to see how scholars in that field define the term; the definition of *confirmation* you find in a dictionary will not be identical to the definition you'd find in a book on interpersonal communication. You can develop the denotative point of your speech by presenting the following:

   ■ Provide synonyms and antonyms that are familiar to your audience.

   ■ Explain the use or function of something you're defining.

   ■ Give the etymology of the word. What's its source historically? How has the concept developed over time?

   ■ Compare an unknown concept or item to one that your audience already knows. For example, "an Allen wrench" might be unfamiliar to some listeners, but "a wrench that looks like a hockey stick" or "an L-shaped wrench" helps them select the specific tool, given a line up of wrenches (Boerger & Henley, 1999).

II. **Connotative Meaning:** Focus on the *connotation* of the term, using realistic life experiences as creatively as you can. Here, draw from anything you can think of that will elucidate or clarify the idea.

   1. Relate a personal experience that demonstrates the idea.

   2. Quote other people as to what the term means to them.

   3. Tell a narrative or give a series of short examples that illustrate the concept.

   4. Refer to an exemplar—a person or thing that exemplifies the term.

   5. Connect the term to a familiar political, social, or moral issue (von Till, 1998).

For example, in the denotative section of her student speech on *destiny*, Terez Czapp provided the dictionary definition then explained the etymology of the word like this:

> The Roman saying, *"Destinatum est mihi,"* meant, "I have made up my mind." In Rome, destiny meant a decision was fixed or determined. Later the word reappeared in both Old and Middle French in the feminine form *destiné*. Finally, from the Middle English word *destinee*, we get the modern form of the word.

Next she provided a transition to the connotative section—an extended example of a near-fatal car wreck that devastated her family—by saying, "However, it isn't the word's etymological history that is meaningful to me. You see, destiny is a depressing reminder of a car accident. . . ." Terez closed with a quotation by William Jennings Bryan, "Destiny is not a matter of chance, it is a matter of choice. It is not a thing to be waited for, it is a thing to be achieved." Including both denotative and connotative meanings provided a fuller picture of the concept of *destiny*.

Giving Explanations

Think of explanations as translation speeches in which you take a complex or information-dense concept and put it into common words and images that elucidate or clarify it. Explanations commonly answer questions about processes—"How does it work?"—or about concepts—"What's the theory behind that?" or "Why?"

How does a telephone work? How do Koreans greet one another? How is a levee constructed? To answer questions like these, you'll describe stages, ordered sequences, or procedures involved in processes—both natural and cultural. You can explain how something's done (bungee jumping, resolving conflict), how things work (elevators, cuckoo clocks, microwave ovens), or how they're made (mountain bikes, a pair of shoes). Not surprisingly, chronological patterns are common, as this outline demonstrates. Marietta was born in the Philippines and adopted by an American family when she was sixteen years old.

> **Specific Purpose:** To inform my audience about the process of adopting a child from another country.
>
> **Central Idea:** The four parts of the adoption process are application, selection, child arrival, and postplacement.
>
> I. Application—the family and a social worker evaluate the adoptive home.
>
> II. Selection—the agency provides pictures and histories of available children.
>
> III. Child arrival—the child arrives with an "Orphan Visa."
>
> IV. Postplacement—for up to a year, the family and a social worker evaluate the placement, after which time the adoption is finalized.

You can also explain concepts. What do we know about intelligence? What's in the mind of a serial killer? What is Johari's Window? These questions relate to concepts or abstractions—the principles, theories, and ideas we form mentally to explain both natural and social realities. For example, although we cannot know for certain what causes some people to kill repeatedly, we formulate theories or explanations for the unusual behaviors of serial killers.

Because concepts are sometimes difficult to define and explain, your major challenge is to make the complex ideas and theories understandable and relevant to the lives of your listeners. Here are some guidelines to follow for speeches about concepts.

■ Simplify complex ideas by breaking them down into their component parts. For example, subdivide intelligence into categories that include social intelligence, spatial intelligence, and musical intelligence (Gardner, 1993).

■ Carefully define your terminology, avoiding technical jargon. Exactly what falls into the category of spatial intelligence? Use examples that clarify this component of intelligence, or show the items from the tests that measure spatial intelligence.

■ Clarify confusing details by using analogies, both figurative and literal, to compare the concept to something that listeners already understand. In this case, you might compare spatial intelligence to running a maze.

■ Use detailed examples of concrete situations that illustrate the actions of people who test high in various kinds of intelligence.

The following example demonstrates a typical topical organizational pattern for an explanatory speech.

Specific Purpose: To inform my audience of core values of many groups in sub-Saharan Africa.

Central Idea: Four major value clusters are characteristic of many cultural groups in sub-Saharan Africa.

  I. Spiritual force

  II. Ancestralism and cyclism

  III. Communalism

  IV. Rationality

Here are a few concepts that students have defined or explained in their "speech to teach": black holes, time, Afrocentrism, success, and False Memory Syndrome (thinking you remember something that happened—often as a result of psychotherapy—when the event did not occur).

We sometimes clash over theories, concepts, and ideas. For instance, exactly what does compassionate conservatism mean? People's ideas differ. What caused the dinosaurs to become extinct? Theories vary. What constitutes a date rape? Few people give the same answer. The purpose of explanatory speaking is not to argue for one definition or another, but to clarify the concept, sometimes by comparing and contrasting differing definitions and theories regarding it.

Guidelines for Informative Speaking

A common complaint about informational speaking is that it's not interesting (Goodall & Waaigen, 1986). To keep your audience's attention and to be both understandable and relevant, remember these guidelines for producing listenable messages (Rubin, 1993).

1. **Do an obstacle analysis of the audience.** Identify the parts of the message that are difficult to understand, then work specifically on ways to make those sections clear. Next, identify internal barriers that might prevent your audience from learning your material. Choosing a scientific topic for an audience who thinks science is difficult and boring, or challenging an audience's current misconceptions about a subject they hold dear are examples of topics that meet with psychological resistance. Plan strategies to deal with each obstacle (Rowan, 1995).

2. **Organize the material carefully.** Be kind to your listeners by stating your major points clearly and building in transition statements and signposts such as **next** and **in addition** that enable them to identify the flow of ideas. Use structures such as lists, comparisons-contrasts, or cause-effect patterns. Provide internal previews and summaries along with connectives that show how your material is linked—words and

Discourse Consistency

Using a repetitive style such as alliteration of main points throughout the speech.

phrases such as *because* and *for example, therefore* and *as a result.* (See Chapter 10). **Discourse consistency** also helps. This means you use a repetitive style such as beginning every section with a question or alliterating your main points throughout the entire speech (Rubin, 1993).

3. **Personalize your material for your audience.** Help listeners see the connection between your topic and their experiences, goals, beliefs, and actions. When they see the relevance of information to their personal lives, they're more likely to listen and learn effectively.

4. **Compare the known to the unknown.** Be audience centered and start where your listeners are, with what's familiar. Put simply, begin with their existing knowledge, then build on this foundation and show similarities and differences between what they already know and your topic.

5. **Choose your vocabulary carefully.** You may have heard lectures or reports that were full of technical information given in incomprehensible jargon; if so, you probably failed to understand the topic clearly. To clarify your ideas, define your terms and explain them in everyday, concrete images. Avoid trigger words—those with negative connotations—that might set off negative reactions in your audience.

Repetition

Saying the same thing more than once.

Redundancy

Repeating the same idea more than once, but developing it differently each time.

6. **Build in repetition and redundancy. Repetition** means that you say the same thing more than once. **Redundancy** means that you repeat the same *idea* several times, but you develop it somewhat differently each time. Phrases such as *in other words,* or *put simply* are ways to build in redundancy. Repeat and redefine the critical parts of the message in order to reinforce these crucial points in your listeners' minds (Thompson & Grandgenett, 1999).

7. **Strive to be interesting.** In your preparation, occasionally try to distance yourself from the speech and hear it as if it were delivered by someone else. Do you find yourself drifting off? If so, where? Think of ways to enliven your factual material. Providing detailed descriptions, for example, engages your audience dialogically, because you give your listeners descriptions they can use to form mental images as you talk.

If you follow these guidelines, you will increase your listeners' motivation and interest in the topic. And your careful attention to details will help them understand the material more clearly.

Review Loren Rozokas' informative speech on Speech Interactive on the Jaffe Connection CD-ROM. How well did Loren follow these guidelines? You can submit your answers online under Chapter 16: Activities for Jaffe Connection at the Public Speaking Resource Center, http://communication.wadsworth.com/publicspeaking/study.html

Public Speaking Resource Center

STOP AND CHECK

Obstacle Analysis and Strategic Plan

As you prepare your speech, ask yourself the following questions:

■ What concepts or steps may be obstacles for this audience?

■ What psychological barriers are likely?

■ What's the best way to overcome these obstacles?

■ Are the steps in order? Or are my main ideas clear?

- Where might I use alliteration, rhyming, or another form of discourse consistency?

- Where are my signposts and transitions? Should I use more?

- How, specifically, have I connected this material to the lives of my classmates?

- What do they already know that I'm building upon?

- Is my language clear?

- Where should I repeat an idea verbatim?

- Which ideas have I presented in a number of different ways?

- Would I be interested in listening to my speech if someone else were giving it? If not, how could I make it more interesting?

Summary

We live in an Information Age where having the ability to give and receive information is empowering; those who lack information do not have the basic knowledge they need to perform competently in complex societies. Because of this, a variety of people in a variety of settings give informative speeches. Their goals are to present new information, to supplement what's already known, to review or update material, or to correct misinformation.

There are several categories for informative speaking that answer listeners' questions such as "How do you do that?" or "What's that mean?" These include demonstrations and instructions, descriptions, reports, and explanations. Throughout your topic selection, consider the importance of providing information on personal, campus, local, national, and international topics.

Finally, remember the keys to informative speaking. Do an obstacle analysis that identifies elements within the topic or within the listeners that might prove to be barriers, then work to overcome those obstacles. Organize the speech and provide links that connect the material. Relate your topic to your listeners, and make vocabulary choices that clarify your ideas. Think of creative ways of presenting your information, and throughout your talk, tie abstract concepts to concrete experiences that are familiar to your listeners. Finally, include repetition and redundancy to reinforce the critical points of the message.

JAFFE CONNECTION

Key Terms

Information Age (312)
electronic superhighways (312)
information explosion (312)
information overload (312)
information imbalance (313)

demonstrations (317)
expository speaking (325)
discourse consistency (328)
repetition (328)
redundancy (328)

Access

**for Audio Flashcards
of Key Terms**

Application and Critical Thinking Questions

1. For your classroom speech consider a topic from the field of communication. For example, in interpersonal communication, topics such as how to work through conflict, how to become independent from parents, or how to successfully navigate the early stages of a romantic relationship are useful. From nonverbal communication come makeover speeches or speeches about time or touch. From mass communication, you could explain how camera angles communicate meaning or how emotions are expressed in e-mail messages. Your information could help your classmates communicate better.

2. Descriptions can be speeches in themselves, or good descriptions can be elements of larger speeches. To improve your descriptive skills, identify a place, an object, or an event, then make a list of vivid words that provide information about the look, the feel, the smell, the taste, or the sound of the item or place. Then give your description to a small group of your classmates.

3. Using Figure 16.3 on page 321, identify information in each category that would be profitable to your classmates. That is, what will they be better off knowing on the personal, campus, local or regional, national, or global levels? How is such information valuable?

4. Within a small group in your classroom, discuss implications of the unequal distribution of information. Examples: What if only some societies know how to make sophisticated weaponry? What if some have information that benefits them economically and others do not? What if only some individuals or groups know their cultural history? What if only women were to have access to health information and men were excluded? What if only people under 35 years of age, with incomes over $80,000 a year, knew how to use computers to advantage?

5. In a small group, think of creative ways to present an informative speech that reviews audience knowledge about one of these familiar topics:

    - Good nutrition
    - What to do in case of fire
    - How to read a textbook

6. Working with a small group, generate a list of speech topics in each of the four categories listed below. For example, your audience

    - Is totally unfamiliar with these topics (medieval manuscripts, an unfamiliar composer)
    - Has some knowledge of the topics, but not a lot (Singapore, the history of MTV)
    - Has studied this topic, but needs a review (the five canons of rhetoric)
    - Has outdated information (a new computer program)
    - Has major misconceptions regarding the topics (tarantulas, Islam)

    Select a subject in two different categories and discuss how you would modify your speech strategies to accomplish your general purpose with each topic.

Internet Activities

1. Log onto your *InfoTrac College Edition* and do a PowerTrac search for the journal *Vital Speeches*. Skim the list of speeches and identify ten titles that appear more informative than persuasive. For example, "[Alzheimer's is] a Frustrating Disease" and "Marketing to Women 50+ on the Internet" seem comparatively more informative than "Dying Should Not Be an Event: Eliminating the Federal Estate and Inheritance Taxes" or "Violence among Our Children: What Can Be Done?" which appear to take a specific position. Read one of the speeches you've identified as informative and evaluate how well the speaker follows the guidelines for informative speaking found in this chapter.

2. Use www.alltheweb.com and search for the exact term *informative speaking*. Find a site from either a speech team (also called forensics team) or from a university professor that provides additional information about speaking to inform.

3. Use the same search engine and search for the exact term *tour guides*. What can you learn about career opportunities for people who describe places, people, or events?

4. To better understand the way Martha Stewart has used her skills in giving instructions to earn millions, log on to and browse her website at http://www.marthastewart.com Categories include cooking, gardening, weddings, and so on.

Hot Links at the Public Speaking Resource Center

The following links are maintained and can be accessed easily via Jaffe Connection at the Public Speaking Resource Center on the Wadsworth Communication Café web site at http://communication.wadsworth.com/publicspeaking/study.html

Public
Speaking
Resource
Center

■ http://mauicc.hawaii.edu/staff/stjohn/publicspeakers/explanatory.html
Ron St. John's site provides links to many additional web pages that provide excellent information about explanatory speaking.

■ www.forensicsonline.com/speech/
This is a site sponsored by an organization for competitive speaking in high school. It provides helpful guidelines for expository speeches that are ten minutes in length.

■ www.howstuffworks.com
This is a great site that explains step-by-step procedures and shows diagrams of hundreds of things you can use for speeches of demonstration. Examples include inside a smoke detector, how medical school works, diagrams of cell phones, birdhouses, and jakebrakes.

■ http://www.brown.edu.tn~che/che498/presen/html
These notes on effective presentations, prepared for engineering students, provide good suggestions for ways to clarify highly technical subjects.

Japanese Writing *by Ariko Iso*

This speech was given by Ariko Iso, a student from Japan for whom English was a second language. In it she explained an interesting aspect of her culture. Ariko distributed the handout illustrated in Figure 16.4 before she spoke, asking her listeners to leave it face down until she told them to turn it over.

How many of you have tee shirts that have writing in a foreign language? Can you understand the meaning of the words or symbols? Many of you raised your hands, because recently, foreign words have become part of fashionable clothing. Have you seen a *Pepsi* can recently? You may have noticed that the word Pepsi is written in several languages. Although English is spoken throughout the world, it is good to know other languages and writing systems. By knowing about other languages, we can know about the different cultures more directly.

After I came to America, some of my friends asked me to write their names in Japanese. I can write down their names very easily, but if they ask me about my language in detail, I am confused myself, because Japanese writing has three kinds of characters. Each of them has its own characteristics and its own usage.

Today, I will explain the three kinds of Japanese characters. I will especially focus on those that came from Chinese characters and show you how they are made.

First, let's look at Japanese writing in general. Japanese writing has three kinds of characters—*kanji,* or Chinese characters, *hiragana,* or Japanese characters, and *katakana,* or Japanese characters used to distinguish words that came from foreign countries. Chinese characters are the basic ones. We imported Chinese characters to Japan in 600 A.D. However, the Japanese people made them more simple and symbolic. Each symbol stands for a word or idea.

The other two types of Japanese characters, *hiragana* and *katakana,* are similar to the English alphabet, so I will call them the Japanese alphabet. The symbols themselves do not have meaning; instead, they only stand for combinations of sounds, much like the letters *m* and *a* stand for the sound "ma." When we put the characters together, they form a word. They are like a puzzle; there are only single pieces before we put them together.

Secondly, I will explain the difference between *hiragana* and *katakana.* Both of these alphabets stand for the same sounds, but the usages are different. *Hiragana* is used for real Japanese words that are not represented by Chinese characters. Katakana is used for the words from foreign countries. For example, when we imported Buddhism from China, all of the books and Buddhist scriptures were translated using *katakana.* Today, we use it for a lot of foreign words that we have brought directly into our language—words like *basketball, school, coffee, TV,* names of people, places, and brands. We pronounce them with al-most the same sounds that you use in English. Thus, they are English, but also Japanese.

Finally, Chinese characters, or *kanji,* are the most interesting. We use over 2,000 Chinese characters in our writing. However, there are two or more ways to pronounce each character, and each of these pronunciations results in a different word with a different meaning. Their number is almost the same as the number of stars.

Each *kanji* character looks very interesting. They are both artistic and functional. Originally, Chinese characters pictured objects. Please turn over your handout and look at the top row of figures (Figure 16.4). You can see that many *kanji* characters are symbols of objects. Look at how the eye changed to form the kanji character meaning *eye.* Trace over the dotted lines to make your own character for *eye.* Please move to

One of Ariko's primary challenges is to help her audience understand how this topic relates to them, so she begins by linking her subject to familiar objects.

She previews her major ideas.

She begins by naming the three types of characters and providing brief historical information.

Her first major point follows the guideline presented in the text of comparing the unfamiliar (Japanese writing) to the familiar (the English alphabet).

Here she moves to the less familiar by showing how the two types of Japanese symbols contrast to the English alphabet. However, she continues to connect the topic to the here-and-now world of her audience.

She now comes to the most unfamiliar aspect of her topic, which she develops by using familiar items—eyes, rivers, trees.

Ariko uses her handout to get her audience members actively involved in her subject.

FIGURE 16.4 Ariko uses her handout to get audience members actively involved.

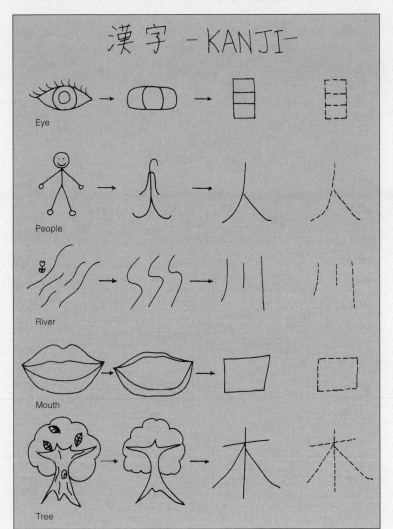

the next line. A picture of a person was drawn in a simplified way to form the character on the right that means person. In much the same way, the sketch of a river becomes the character that means river. The character representing the word for *mouth* is similar. Finally, you can see in the last row how the character that depicts a tree evolved from a line drawing of a tree. Let's practice by tracing the rest of the symbols.

It is a great help to memorize all of the Chinese characters. The five characters I've presented are very simple, but complicated Chinese characters are created by combining simple symbols.

I hope you enjoyed the process of making *kanji* characters and gained some knowledge of Japanese and Chinese characters that are used in my language. Briefly, there are three kinds of characters that we use in writing Japanese: *Kanji*, the Chinese characters, are the basic ones; *hiragana* is used for real Japanese words; and *katakana* for words taken from foreign languages.

See if you can find Japanese characters in things around you in your daily life—you may even recognize one that you learned today!

Her conclusion contains a brief review.

Ariko's ending relates to her introductory strategy in which she linked her subject to everyday items.

17

Persuasive Speaking

This chapter will help you:

- Find a subject for a persuasive speech

- Decide on a claim of fact, value, or policy

- Narrow the focus of your speech in light of your listeners' beliefs, attitudes, and actions

- Identify organizational patterns for your speeches including problem-solution, direct method, comparative advantages, criteria satisfaction, negative method, and Monroe's Motivated Sequence

Detail from "Desaparecidos Pero no Olvidados" ©1999 by Carlos Madriz, Josh Short, and Mabel Negrette

If you watch C-SPAN on cable TV, you see persuasive speakers in action on a daily basis. Televised coverage of the House of Representatives, for instance, shows the "gentlewoman from Hawaii" and the "gentleman from New York" arguing against a proposed amendment that the "gentleman from Indiana" supports. Or tune into *Court TV* and you'll see defense and prosecution lawyers present conflicting narratives that each side hopes will persuade the jury. Flip to a talk show and hear representatives of various viewpoints argue for their beliefs and lifestyles. All these examples underscore the importance of persuasion in our society.

Persuasion is vital in a democracy that values citizen participation and freedom of speech. Indeed, Aristotle designated three arenas in which rhetoric, or the art of persuasion, functioned in a healthy democratic society: law courts, governing assemblies, and ceremonial and ritual occasions where the culture's core beliefs and values are reinforced. However, the role of persuasion varies across cultures, as the Diversity in Practice on the next page illustrates.

This chapter focuses specifically on the purposes and types of persuasive speaking. In it, you will find information on selecting a topic, using what your listeners know and how they behave to narrow your speaking purpose, and selecting strategies and organizational patterns that will be effective in conveying your ideas and arguing for your positions.

Select Your Persuasive Topic

Choosing a persuasive topic for your classroom speech can be daunting! Even if you have some ideas for subjects, you may not know how to focus clearly on one specific purpose and one central idea. In this section, we will look at strategies you can use to find a subject. Then, we'll look at ways to select your claim and tentatively formulate your central idea.

Finding Your Subject

It is important to find a need that you can address by speaking out. Select a topic that matters to you—especially in the area of persuasion, it's pretty hard to persuade others if you yourself are neutral about the subject. So begin by considering your strong beliefs and feelings; then ask yourself what would improve society in general or people's lives in particular. These guidelines lead to a series of questions you can ask yourself as you search for an appropriate topic (Mullins, 1993).

- **My strong beliefs:** What ideas and issues would I argue for? What ideas and issues would I argue against?

- **My strong feelings:** What makes me angry? What are my pet peeves? What arouses my pity? What makes me sad? What do I fear?

- **My social ideals:** What changes would I like to see in society? What current problems or conditions could improve if we believed that there is a problem, that there are solutions, and that we can be part of those solutions?

- **My personal ideals:** What can make life more meaningful for others and myself? What activities will expand our horizons? What improves our health? What leads to more fulfilling personal relationships?

Here are some examples of classroom topics: censorship, high insurance rates, white supremacists, affordable housing, international child sponsorship programs, the joys of hot air ballooning learning another language. You can see that they reflect strong beliefs and feelings and that the topics relate to social or personal needs.

DIVERSITY IN PRACTICE

Persuasion in Other Cultures

Not every culture places the same value on persuasion as a means of publicly discussing issues and formulating reasoned conclusions. These examples, from historical and contemporary societies, illustrate this.

Rome

During Rome's long history as a republic, representatives of the people publicly debated issues that affected the entire community. However, by the first century A.D., emperors such as Nero and Caligula were dictators who made binding decisions and pronouncements, whether or not the senators approved; dissenters often met with torture or death. Although the Senate formally existed, Caligula mocked its power when he declared his horse to be a senator!

The Soviet Union

When the Communists ruled the former Soviet Union, party leaders made decisions and spoke for the people. They strongly discouraged ordinary citizens from dissenting from the "party line," often through use of coercive force that could result in months or years in Siberian work camps.

Athabaskan Speakers

Speakers in this oral-based society of native Alaskans think it rude to explicitly state the conclusions they want listeners to draw. It is enough for them to simply present a set of facts and let audience members draw their own conclusions. This emphasis on information rather than persuasive strategies distinguishes their norms from those found in this text (Rubin, 1993).

International Negotiation

Many cultures are realizing the benefits of persuasive speaking—at least in their dealings with representatives of the West. Because of trade negotiations, the existence of the United Nations, peace talks, and other international exchanges, many nations with different persuasive traditions are adopting strategies of Western rhetoric. Their leaders are often educated at American universities, and they adapt their rhetorical strategies to communicate their nation's views to international audiences. For example, Takakazu Kuriyama, the Japanese Ambassador to the United States (1992–1995), studied at Amherst College (Massachusetts) and Lawrence University (Wisconsin). He intentionally adopted some U. S. rhetorical strategies when he dealt with members of Congress and representatives of the U.S. media (Ota, 1993).

 To read one of Mr. Kuriyama's persuasive appeals, log on to the Internet and go to http://www.japantimes.co.jp/100/frame100.html. He wrote article 59.

Examine your strong beliefs and feelings, your social and personal ideals for topics. Gary believes that hot air ballooning enriches his life, and he uses his enthusiasm to convince his classmates that the sport is worth consideration. (Russ Schleipman/OffShoot Stock)

STOP AND CHECK

Select Your Topic

Fold a piece of paper into fourths and label each quarter, using one of the following categories.

- My strong beliefs
- My strong feelings
- My social ideals
- My personal ideals

Next, make a list of possible topics within each section.

Afterwards, consider your classroom audience. Circle a topic in each section that would be most appropriate, given this particular group.

Analyze the topics you've circled, and put an *X* by those you could discuss within the allotted time.

Finally, select the best topic, given your audience and the time constraints.

Making Persuasive Claims

Selecting your subject is only the first step. After you know your topic area, ask yourself what claim you want to defend. A **claim** is an assertion that is disputable or open to challenge—a conclusion or generalization that some people won't accept, a statement that requires some sort of evidence or backing to be believed. We commonly make three types of claims: fact, value, and policy.

Claim
An assertion that's disputable or open to challenge.

Factual Claims

Here you argue what exists or does not exist, what's led to a current situation, or what will or will not happen; you assess their validity using terms such as *true* or *false*, *correct* or *incorrect*, *yes* or *no*. The following three types of **factual claims** are common:

Factual Claims
Arguments about existence, causation, or predictions.

1. **Debatable points** (there is life on other planets; Lee Harvey Oswald acted alone in killing President Kennedy)

2. **Causal relationships** (secondhand smoke leads to lung disease; television violence influences children to commit violent acts)

3. **Predictions** (this mutual fund will gain value; Y2K will shut down global economies and cause widespread anarchy)

All these claims generate differences of opinion. Is there life on other planets? Science fiction writers seem to think so, but no one really knows if this is, in fact, true. What, if anything, links smoking to disease? Television violence to violent children? Studies often find correlations between two things, but correlation is not the same as causation. Finally, claims about future happenings are open to debate. Remember how, before January 1, 2000, some people predicted that computer glitches would cause mild or catastrophic damage, so they prepared by stocking up on peanut butter and taking cash out of their bank accounts, or by buying guns in order to defend themselves after President Clinton declared martial law and took over the country? A few weeks later, the same people found themselves making peanut butter cookies or admitting that the president did not make a grab for power. Catastrophic problems simply did not materialize.

Value Claims

When you judge or evaluate something using terms such as *right* or *wrong* (it's immoral to burn the flag), *good* or *bad* (those hamburgers are awful), *beautiful* or *ugly* (Judy Chicago's art is wonderful), you're making a **value claim.** Value conflicts are hard to resolve when the people arguing disagree on **criteria,** or standards for deciding whether or not something is right or wrong, fair or unfair, humane or inhumane.

Value Claims
Arguments about right or wrong, moral or immoral, beautiful or ugly.

Criteria
The standards you use for making evaluations or judgments.

Take a current movie that you loved and your friend hated. You each evaluated the movie and came to very different conclusions. Why? Because you each had different criteria for deciding what makes a "good" or a "bad" movie. Let's say your criteria include romance, beginning-to-end action, and stunning visual effects—which this movie had. However, your friend likes movies only if the characters are realistic and the plot is unpredictable. Your movie fails to meet her criteria. You can argue for hours about the merits of the movie, but unless one or the other adjusts the criteria, you'll never agree.

Policy claims

These claims consider whether individuals or groups should act or not, and how they should proceed if they decide to do so. In short, **policy claims** often deal with problems and solutions, assessed by terms such as *should* and *would*. You'll commonly hear two major types of policy arguments:

Policy Claims
Arguments about the need or the plan for taking action.

1. **Arguments against the *status quo*** (a Latin phrase that means *the existing state of affairs*) are arguments for change, whether in policies or individual behaviors. (Congress should adopt a flat tax system; you should write your senator and urge a vote on the flat tax.)

2. **Arguments supporting the *status quo*** are arguments for the way things are—arguments against change. (The administration should not raise tuition.)

For instance, many people believe that taxation within the United States could be improved, and they argue against the status quo by, first, identifying the problematic area of taxation, then proposing a solution that both makes improvements and is workable. Some Campaign 2000 candidates argued for lowered taxes or changed inheritance tax laws; others urged the adoption of a flat tax or replacement of income taxes with a value-added (sales) tax. Each candidate then had to show the feasibility of her or his plan—why it would work, why it would be most efficient.

In short, within a single topic area, you can argue facts, defend a value question, or formulate a policy to solve a problem related to the topic. Whatever you decide on as your major claim will be the tentative formulation of your central idea.

Let's say you decide to speak about ocean pollution—specifically, dumping garbage in the ocean. You have the option of focusing on facts, values, or policies surrounding the issue as the following illustrates.

Claim		Tentative Central Idea
Fact	Argue a debatable point.	Dumping garbage in our oceans is not excessive.
	Attempt to prove a cause-effect relationship.	Dumping waste products in the ocean poses health risks to seaboard residents.
	Make a prediction.	If we do not take seriously the issue of dumping garbage in the ocean, our beaches will become too contaminated to use.
Value	Argue something is right or wrong, good or bad, beautiful or ugly.	It is wrong to dump garbage in the ocean.
Policy	Propose a policy change.	We should stop dumping garbage in ocean waters.
	Propose a behavioral change.	Write your representative and voice your concerns about dumping garbage in the oceans.
	Argue against a policy change.	There is no good reason to stop disposing of garbage in oceans.

In summary, select the subject of your speech from topics and issues that concern you—from the personal level to the international level. Then, tentatively formulate your central idea by deciding if you want to argue a factual claim, a value claim, or a policy claim.

STOP AND CHECK

Make Fact, Value, and Policy Claims

To better understand that discussions surrounding a controversial topic contain a mixture of factual, value, and policy claims, work alone or with a small group of classmates and choose a controversial topic such as euthanasia, gays in the military, affirmative action, environmental protection, or sex education. Then write out a factual claim, a value claim, and a policy claim relating to your topic. Afterward, share your claims with the class as a whole.

- Write a factual claim dealing with a debatable fact, causation, or a prediction.

- Assess questions of good or bad, developing criteria for a decision.

- Decide whether or not the status quo needs to be changed, and frame your policy claim accordingly.

To understand how the same topic can be developed in different ways, compare the speech outline on sleep deprivation with the text of the speech on the same topic that appears at the end of the chapter.

Narrow Your Persuasive Purpose

Although the general purpose of your speech is to persuade, narrow your focus and specific purpose in light of what your listeners already know and do, how they feel, and what they consider important. Because all these factors are interrelated, keep in mind that one speech may, in reality, have multiple purposes that exist on a number of levels. For instance, while you are trying to convince your listeners about hazards of dumping garbage in the ocean—focusing on their beliefs—you may also be reinforcing their health-related values and the negative attitudes they currently hold toward pollution.

This section will present specific strategies to use when you target your audience's beliefs and actions, their values, or their attitudes. (Chapter 18 will provide detailed information on creating persuasive appeals.)

Focusing on Beliefs and Actions

What we think is true affects how we act. Our beliefs and actions, in turn, are influenced by our values and our attitudes. To illustrate, people who take vitamins regularly believe that the vitamins actually have beneficial effects on their health; in addition, they feel it is good, even moral, to take care of their health. They also have positive attitudes toward good nutrition. This combination of beliefs, values, and attitudes leads them to act by both purchasing and consuming vitamins. Figure 17.1 shows some possible combinations of belief and action that you should consider as you narrow the focus of your speaking intention.

Unconvinced

Unconvinced audience members neither believe nor act. Take acupuncture as an example. Some listeners know nothing about this Chinese medical treatment; others know, but they don't believe it will help them. Still others have misconceptions about the practice. With all these listeners, you must produce enough evidence **to convince,** to persuade them to believe your factual claims before you call for action. The following general strategies are useful when your listeners are unconvinced:

To Convince
A persuasive purpose that targets audience beliefs.

- Begin with logical appeals. Build your factual case carefully, using only evidence that passes the test for credible supporting material.

- Prove your competence by being knowledgeable about the facts. Further, show that you have respect for your listeners' intelligence and for their divergent beliefs.

- Use comparatively fewer emotional appeals.

Unmotivated or Unfocused

Sometimes your audiences are already convinced, often because they know a lot about your subject. However, they don't act on their beliefs due to **apathy** or indifference (unmotivated listeners) or lack of specific know-how (unfocused listeners). Topics such as

Apathy
Indifference due to lack of motivation.

FIGURE 17.1 Your audience members approach your topic with various combinations of beliefs and actions.

	Don't Believe	Believe
Don't Act	unconvinced	unmotivated, unfocused
Act	inconsistent	consistent

donating blood are in this category. Your purpose, then, is to actuate, or move them to behave in ways that are consistent with their beliefs, using two different persuasive strategies.

- When your audience is unmotivated, give them good reasons to act. Use emotional appeals to show that behaving as you propose will fulfill their needs and satisfy them emotionally.

- When they lack focus, provide a detailed plan that spells out specific steps they can take to implement your proposals.

In both instances, show listeners that you have their best interests in mind as you appeal for action.

Inconsistent

When people act in ways that differ from their beliefs, they experience what various theorists call inconsistency, or **dissonance.** One influential theory of persuasion, called **dissonance theory** (Craig, 1998; Festinger, 1957), argues that humans, like other living organisms, seek balance or equilibrium. When challenged with inconsistency, they feel psychological discomfort, and they try to return to a place of psychological balance. Inconsistency between belief and action is one of the best motivators for change. (For additional information about this subject, log on to your *InfoTrac College Edition* and do a keyword search for *cognitive dissonance,* or use www.alltheweb.com to search for the exact phrase *cognitive dissonance*; use the Advanced Search feature to limit your hits to those with .edu in the URL. Then read one of the articles you find there.)

Sometimes people question or change their beliefs, but continue to behave as if they were still convinced. For example, consumers lose faith in products that they continue to purchase; students continue to major in subjects that they know are not right for them; people persist in binge drinking, even though they think it's dangerous. With inconsistent audiences, either strengthen or reinforce wavering beliefs or persuade listeners to modify their actions to match their changed beliefs.

This list summarizes a few specific strategies that you can use when your listeners' actions are inconsistent with their beliefs.

- Support faltering beliefs by concentrating on logical appeals, using as much persuasive evidence as you can muster. Include emotional appeals as well, giving reasons for listeners to want to strengthen their wavering beliefs.

- When you want behaviors to change, appeal to emotions such as honesty and sincerity. Use narratives or testimonials that exemplify how you or someone else succeeded in a similar situation.

Consistent

When people act in ways that are consistent with their beliefs, they may need encouragement to "keep on keeping on." This type of audience is common in places like service clubs, religious organizations, and political rallies. Here, your narrowed purpose is to reinforce both their beliefs and actions by following this set of guidelines.

Dissonance
Inconsistency or clash.

Dissonance Theory
Theory that humans seek stability or equilibrium; when faced with inconsistency they seek psychological balance that may motivate them to change in order to be consistent.

Inconsistency between belief and action is one of the best motivators for change. For example, this woman may know that smoking is harmful, but she still smokes. Highlighting her dissonance is a good way to persuade her to make at least an effort to quit. (Barbra Alper/Stock, Boston)

■ Help listeners maintain a positive attitude about their accomplishments. Use examples and testimony that illustrate how their efforts are making a difference in the world.

■ Relate yourself personally to their fundamental beliefs and values.

Throughout this section, we have explored ways that audience beliefs and actions influence both your persuasive purposes and the methods you use to present your ideas. Although you continue to employ a variety of appeals in every speech, each type of audience requires somewhat different emphases and strategies.

Focusing on Values

As noted earlier, value claims argue that something should be judged or evaluated as moral or immoral, beautiful or ugly, right or wrong, and so on. This is a value claim: *Keeping the minimum wage at its present level is wrong.* In order to make an evaluation, you first establish the criteria or standards on which to judge an economic policy by answering questions such as these:

■ How do we make and apply moral judgments in the economic realm?

■ What criteria do we use?

■ Where do these criteria come from?

■ Why should we accept these sources?

Within a single audience, listeners often vary widely in their views on issues such as gambling. Some perceive legalized gambling as harmless entertainment; others strongly believe it poses social dangers. (Okonlewski/The Image Works)

If your listeners agree with your criteria, it's easier for them to accept your evaluation. However, you can see that value questions are often conflict laden, for the standards used to make many value judgments are not universally accepted.

Because each individual's beliefs and experiences affect his or her value judgments, within a single audience they may vary so widely that some listeners view a topic as unethical whereas others view it as ethical. Furthermore, because values are assumptions about what is good, questions of value often generate strong emotional responses that are difficult to change. Remember the Ethical Quality Scale presented in Chapter 6? It is nearly impossible in one speech to move listeners from viewing a topic as highly unethical to the point where they evaluate it as highly ethical. Here are some tips for arguing a claim of value:

■ Establish the criteria you have used to make your evaluation.

■ Appeal to your audience's emotions. Use examples to help listeners identify with the issue. Appeal also to related values such as fairness, generosity, kindness, or freedom.

■ As Chapter 8 pointed out, appeals to authority can be persuasive if the audience accepts the source as authoritative. Some audiences are moved by appeals to cultural traditions, words of philosophers, poets, scientists, or scriptures.

Focusing on Attitudes

As Chapter 6 pointed out, we can have positive, negative, or neutral attitudes about subjects, which we typically measure along a scale such as this:

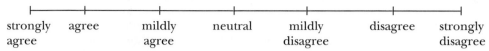

Spanking, used moderately, can be an effective method of disciplining children.

| strongly agree | agree | mildly agree | neutral | mildly disagree | disagree | strongly disagree |

Let's take a hypothetical student, Xavier, who is strongly against spanking. When he addresses an audience that shares his negative attitude, he simply bolsters the listeners' attitudes by emphasizing unpleasant or harmful aspects of spanking.

However, when Xavier faces a neutral audiences that's neither positive nor negative, he must adjust his strategies. He first asks himself why they are neutral. Do they lack information? Or are they apathetic? Do they need to understand how the subject touches their lives directly? His purpose with neutral listeners is to create or produce a stronger attitude, in this case a negative attitude, in his listeners.

When his listeners hold an opposite attitude—they all think spanking children is a good way to discipline children, his strategies again change. If they're mildly or moderately positive toward spanking, his overall strategy will be to lessen the positive and enable the audience to see negative aspects of the subject. If they're strongly for spanking, he faces a hostile audience. Knowing this, Xavier sets modest goals and aims for small attitude changes.

Perhaps the most distressing speaking situation arises when you face an audience that's hostile toward you personally. In these cases, it's important to emphasize common ground between yourself and your listeners. The following guidelines will help you plan effective speeches targeted toward attitudes:

- When listeners are positive, strengthen their emotional ties to the topic by using examples, connotative words, and appeals to needs and values that evoke emotional responses. Establish common ground throughout your speech (see Chapter 18).

- With uninformed audiences, present factual information early in the speech so they have a basis to form an evaluation. Then use emotional appeals to create either a positive or negative attitude toward the topic.

- With apathetic audiences, use emotional appeals. Link the topic to listeners in as many ways as you can. Appeal to values such as fairness and justice.

- When your audience is mildly negative, approach listeners directly. Make a clear case with objective data; present the positive facets of your subject, and link it to personal and community values your audience accepts. This way, even if they disagree with you, they will at least understand the rationale for your position.

- With negative audiences in general, approach your subject indirectly by establishing common ground on which you can all agree. For instance, begin with a statement with which everyone agrees and explain why there is agreement. Then make a statement that most would accept and explain why this is so. Move gradually to the point on which they think they disagree. By this time, they have already seen that they agree with you on many points, and as a result, they may be less negative toward your proposal (anonymous, 1993).

Generally, attitudes change incrementally. This means that listeners don't move rapidly from one extreme to another; rather, they change gradually over time. Each new encounter with the subject is only one small step that produces a slight attitude shift. Eventually, the small shifts add up to a measurable attitude change. Many people in the United States, for instance, once had a neutral attitude toward congressional term limits. However, over a period of months and years, after many speeches and much media coverage, many citizens began to view limitation of congressional terms positively.

Although we have discussed beliefs and actions, attitudes, and values as separate entities, the truth is that they're intertwined. Keep in mind the interrelated aspect of these cultural factors as you analyze your audience, select the specific purpose for your speech, and choose supporting material that will be persuasive.

Adapt to the Audience's Attitude

Analyze the following public speaking situation: An anthropology major is going to present a speech on government funding for archaeological digs. Her claim is that the study of archaeology is important enough to receive government funding because knowing about other human cultures helps us to better understand our own.

Divide into three groups within the classroom. Each group will discuss how the speaker should prepare for one of the following audiences:

1. A group of anthropology majors who agree with her and are highly positive toward her topic.

2. An audience that knows nothing about anthropology, but know that they are concerned about how their tax money is spent.

3. Listeners who feel that archaeology is a waste of time.

Questions

1. How will the speaker analyze the particular audience?

2. What purpose should she select for that group?

3. What specific strategies will she use to make her points?

4. What kinds of reasoning and evidence should she use?

5. What should she emphasize and why?

If your instructor requests, you can complete this activity online and submit your individual response via email. Go to Chapter 17: Activities for Jaffe Connection at the Public Speaking Resource Center, http://communication. wadsworth.com/publicspeaking/study.html

Public Speaking Resource Center

Choose a Persuasive Pattern

After you have analyzed your audience by considering their positions regarding your issue, you then begin to look at the organizational pattern that will best communicate your ideas. In this section, we discuss common patterns used in persuasive public speaking.

Problem-Solution Pattern

You've already seen the problem-solution pattern in Chapter 9. It's commonly used in both informative and persuasive speaking. The goal of informative speaking is to increase your audience's understanding of the issue and the proposed solution or solutions. In persuasive speeches, however, your purpose is generally to convince or to advocate the implementation of a specific policy. When the intent is to convince listeners that there is indeed a problem, the outline looks like this:

Specific Purpose: To persuade my audience that there are too many air disasters, but that the problem can be solved by concentrating efforts in three areas.

Central Idea: Global air traffic has too many disasters and near disasters that could be minimized by working to eliminate the sources of the problems.

  I. There are too many air disasters and near disasters around the globe.

    A. The problem involves near misses and crashes.

      1. The problem is extensive (statistics).

      2. This has negative implications for travelers.

B. There are several causes of this problem.
   1. There are communication problems between crews and air traffic controllers.
   2. Weather is a consideration.
   3. Mechanical and maintenance failures cause disasters.

II. The problem can be minimized.
   A. Airplanes should be more carefully inspected and maintained.
   B. Both crew members and air traffic controllers should continue to receive on-the-job training both in communication and in understanding the effects of weather.
   C. Engineers and researchers should continue to develop state-of-the-art equipment to prevent some of these disasters.

When you aim less at convincing your audience or a problem, and instead argue for a particular solution, a good strategy is to present several possible solutions, then advocate or argue that one is best. This adds a third point to the outline.

I. Problem and need

II. Possible solutions

III. The one best solution

This is how a more complete outline looks:

Specific Purpose: To persuade my audience that incineration is the best solution to the problem of medical waste.

Central Idea: Of the three methods of medical waste disposal—steam sterilization, ocean dumping, and incineration—incineration is the best.

I. More and more medical waste is being generated, creating a need for a safe method of disposal.
   A. There are several waste products from medical procedures.
   B. The problem is extensive (statistics).
   C. Some of the waste products pose risks.

II. There are three ways to dispose of medical waste.
   A. One is the steam sterilization process.
   B. The second is ocean dumping.
   C. The third is incineration.

III. Incineration is the best solution.
   A. It completely destroys the product.
   B. Fire purifies.

Direct Method Pattern

In the **direct method,** sometimes called the **statement of reasons pattern,** you make a claim, then directly state your reasons to support it. Each point, thus, provides an additional rationale to agree with your views. It's a good pattern to use when listeners are apathetic or neutral, either mildly favoring or mildly opposing your claim. Consider it when your goal is to convince, although you can also use it to organize a speech **to actuate** (or motivate the audience to do something).

This outline is from a speech to actuate. You can see that each main point gives listeners an additional reason to act. The speaker, additionally, moves to a climax by beginning with the least important reason and ending with the most important.

Specific Purpose: To persuade my listeners to drive 55 miles per hour.

Central Idea: If everyone drove 55 miles per hour, we would save fuel, money, and lives.

Everyone should drive 55 miles per hour.

Direct Method or Statement of Reasons Pattern

A method that makes a claim, then states reasons that provide a rationale for the ideas.

To Actuate

Motivate the audience to do something.

You could use the direct methods pattern to organize a speech supporting the adoption of school uniforms. What other organizational patterns would work for this topic? (Mugshots/ The Stock Market)

   I. It will save fuel.

  II. It will save money.

 III. It will save lives.

The intention of the following speech was to convince listeners that a particular policy should be enacted. The major points are factual claims of prediction that provide reasons to agree with the major claim.

Specific Purpose: To persuade my listeners to believe that all primary and secondary students should wear uniforms to school.

Central Idea: All students should wear school uniforms to eliminate social distinctions, save money, and prevent crime.

All precollege students, even those in public schools, should wear uniforms.

   I. This will eliminate social distinctions between rich and poor

  II. It will save money.

 III. It will prevent clothing-related crime.

As you can see, this pattern is a variant of the topical pattern. It's easy to use, both in speeches intended to convince and in those intended to actuate.

Comparative Advantages Pattern

A method that shows the superiority of a proposal by comparing its advantages to those of the competition.

Comparative Advantages Pattern

Use a **comparative advantages pattern** for policy speeches arguing that one proposal is superior to competing proposals by comparing its advantages to those of the competition. Study the following outline from a speech to convince an audience of the superiority of osteopathic doctors:

Specific Purpose: To persuade my audience that a Doctor of Osteopathic Medicine (D.O.) is superior to a chiropractor for many reasons.

Central Idea: D.O.s are better than chiropractors because of their training and their ability to do surgery.

Doctors of Osteopathic Medicine (D.O.s) are superior to chiropractors.

I. They can do everything chiropractors do, and more.

II. Their training is superior because it includes courses comparable to those in medical schools.

III. Many D.O.s perform surgeries in hospitals with which they are affiliated.

You can also use the comparative advantages method when you want your listeners to act. For instance, in hopes of recruiting students, a representative of a small private college compares the advantages of her institution over larger state schools. Look for this pattern in advertisements, sales speeches, and campaign speeches, as these outlines demonstrate:

Specific Purpose: To persuade my audience to purchase a [certain kind of car].

Central Idea: Buy [this car] because of its repair record, resale value, and fuel economy is better than those of its competitors.

Buy [a certain make of automobile].

I. It has a better repair record than its competitors.

II. It has a higher resale value than comparable cars.

III. It is more economical than its major competitors.

It's easy to see that this pattern is related to reasoning by comparison and contrast, for you continually compare and contrast your proposal or product to other proposals and products the audience already knows.

Criteria Satisfaction Pattern

As defined earlier, criteria are standards that form a basis for judgments; the **criteria satisfaction pattern** first sets forth the standards to judge a proposal, then shows how the solution, candidate, or product meets or exceeds these standards. Because it describes the standards for evaluation at the outset, it is useful in speeches that argue value claims.

Take, for example, the problem of hiring a new professor. The criteria section of an argument for a specific candidate answers the question, "What qualities does a good professor have?" The search committee might believe that a professor should have good teaching skills, good interpersonal skills, and good research and writing skills. The second part of the speech—the satisfaction section—shows how the proposed candidate satisfies all the criteria. In this case, the candidate has a record of good teaching evaluations, she works well with people, and she has written two books and published several articles in academic journals.

The following outline demonstrates the criteria satisfaction pattern for the argument that using community service is a workable punishment for criminals:

Specific Purpose: To persuade my audience that community service meets all the criteria for a good punishment for nonviolent criminals.

Central Idea: Community service is a punishment that fits the crime, reduces recidivism, and is cost effective.

Criteria Satisfaction Pattern

Good for value speeches; sets forth the standards for judgment, then shows how the proposed solution meets or exceeds these standards.

What does a good punishment for nonviolent felons look like?

I. The punishment fits the crime.

II. It reduces recidivism.

III. It is cost effective.

Community service is the best punishment for nonviolent crimes.

I. The punishment can be tailored to fit the crime.

II. It keeps felons out of prison where they can be influenced by career criminals.

III. It is far less costly to administer than incarceration.

You may find the criteria satisfaction pattern especially useful for controversial issues; this is so because at the outset you establish common ground with your listeners by setting up criteria on which you all agree. As in the direct methods pattern, consider building to a climax by developing the most persuasive criteria last.

Negative Method Pattern

Negative Method Pattern

Point out shortcomings of other proposals, then demonstrate why your proposal is the one logical solution remaining.

When you use the **negative method pattern,** you concentrate on the shortcomings of every other proposal; then you show why your proposal is the one logical solution remaining. In other words, point out the negative aspects in competing proposals; then, after you've dismantled or undermined everyone else's plan, you propose your own. This pattern is often used to argue a policy claim that's one among many.

Specific Purpose: To persuade my audience that global legalization of drugs is the only way to control the supply and demand of illicit drugs.

Central Idea: Because of the failures of drug enforcement agencies and education, we need to regulate drugs through legalization.

We need a solution to the problem of drugs around the world.

I. More drug enforcement agencies are not the answer.

II. Better education is not the answer.

III. Global legalization of drugs is the only way we will regulate supply and demand.

As you can see, you have many persuasive patterns from which to choose. As you plan your speech, use the pattern that is most appropriate to both your material and your audience. These patterns, obviously, are not exhaustive, but they are among the most common you'll find in public speeches, advertisements, and other persuasive messages. Finally, we turn to perhaps the most widely used pattern: Monroe's Motivated Sequence.

Monroe's Motivated Sequence

Monroe's Motivated Sequence

A call to action in five steps: attention, need, satisfaction, visualization, and action.

Alan Monroe, a professor at Purdue University for many years, developed and refined a pattern that is commonly used in persuasive speaking, especially in speeches with the purpose of actuating behavior. As you will see, **Monroe's Motivated Sequence** is a modified form of a problem-solution speech.

Before people act, they must be motivated to do what they know they should. Because of this, it's important to provide emotional reasons as well as logical ones. Monroe's pattern includes the word *motivated*, because it has several built-in steps to increase motivational appeals. (Note that this pattern is not a formula in the sense that you have to include each element that Monroe describes. Rather Monroe suggests various ways that you can develop each point in the speech.) Here are the five easily remembered steps in the sequence, as explained by Monroe himself (1962).

1. **Attention Step:** At the outset of the speech, as in any speech, you must gain the audience's attention and draw it to your speech topic.

2. **Need Step:** This step is similar to the problem part of a problem-solution speech. Monroe suggests four elements in establishing the need: (a) statement—tell the nature of the problem; (b) illustration—give a relevant detailed example or examples; (c) ramifications—provide additional support such as statistics or testimony that show the extent of the problem; and (d) pointing—show the direct relationship between the audience and the problem. What are the personal implications for each listener?

3. **Satisfaction Step:** After you've demonstrated the problem, how extensive it is, and how it will affect the audience, propose a solution that will satisfy the need you have created. This step can have as many as five parts: (a) statement—briefly state the attitude, belief, or action you want the audience to adopt; (b) explanation—make your proposal understandable (visual aids may help at this point); (c) theoretical demonstration—show the logical connection between the need and your solution; (d) practicality—use facts, figures, and testimony to show that the proposal has worked effectively or that the belief has been proved correct; and (e) meeting objections—show that your proposal can overcome any potential objections your listeners have.

4. **Visualization Step:** This step is unique from other patterns. In it, you ask the audience to imagine what will happen if they enact the proposal or if they fail to do so. (a) Positive—describe the future if your plan is put into action. Create a realistic positive scenario showing what your solution provides. Use appeals to pathos—safety needs, pride, pleasure, and other emotions. (b) Negative—have the listeners imagine themselves in an unpleasant situation because they did not put your solution into effect. (c) Contrast—compare the negative results of not enacting your plan with the positive results your plan will produce.

5. **Action:** In the final step, call for your listeners to act in a specific way: (a) call for a specific, overt action, attitude, or belief; (b) state your personal intention to act; and (c) end with impact.

As you might imagine, this pattern is good for a sales speech. It is also effective in policy speeches and other claims that include a "should" or an "ought."

STOP AND CHECK

Use Monroe's Motivated Sequence

Working alone or with a small group, plan a short outline for a speech intended to motivate your audience to action. Choose one of these general topic categories:

- **Sales:** Convince your classmates to buy a specific product.
- **Public service:** Ask your listeners to donate time or money to a worthy cause.

Summary

The best subjects for persuasive speeches come from the things that matter most to you personally. For this reason, ask yourself questions such as, What do I believe strongly? What arouses strong feelings within me? What would I like to see changed? What enriches my life? Your answers will generally provide you with topics that you're willing to defend. Choosing your subject is only the first part of topic selection. You then decide whether you will argue a claim of fact, value, or policy.

We consistently argue for our ideas in an attempt to influence one another's beliefs, actions, values, and attitudes, and we strategically organize our speeches and adapt our ideas to different types of audiences. However, assumptions and actions are always interwoven. The result is that while you are motivating listeners to act, you are also trying to reinforce their positive attitudes and beliefs. Throughout the entire time, you rely on underlying values to support your calls to action.

Choose from a number of common patterns to organize your major points. Consider the problem-solution pattern and its variant in the Monroe's Motivated Sequence—both of which define a problem and identify a solution. The direct method, also called the statement of reasons pattern, directly lists arguments that support your claim. The criteria satisfaction pattern is good for value speeches because you first set up criteria or standards for judgment, then show how your proposal meets these standards. The comparative advantages method shows the advantage of your proposal over similar proposals; the negative method, in contrast, shows the disadvantages of every proposal but your own.

JAFFE CONNECTION

Access

for Audio Flashcards of Key Terms

Key Terms

claim (339)
factual claims (339)
value claims (339)
criteria (339)
policy claims (339)
status quo (340)
to convince (341)
apathy (341)
dissonance (342)

dissonance theory (342)
direct method or statement of reasons pattern (347)
to actuate (347)
comparative advantages pattern (348)
criteria satisfaction pattern (349)
negative method pattern (350)
Monroe's Motivated Sequence (350)

Application and Critical Thinking Questions

1. Consider the relationships between beliefs and actions, and identify topics that might fall into each category. For instance, for the "unfocused" category, people often believe that they should learn to study more effectively, but they don't know how to proceed. For the "unconvinced" category, people don't know enough about oat bran, so they don't eat it regularly.

2. Listen to at least one persuasive speech on television, taking notes on the speaker's arguments. (C-SPAN is a good source for such speeches.) What kinds of claims does the speaker make? How does she or he support the claims? Who are the intended audiences? How effectively does the speaker adapt to the audience's beliefs, actions, attitudes, and values?

3. Read the excerpts from President Clinton's speech at the Vietnam War Memorial in 1993, found in Appendix C. Evaluate Clinton's effectiveness in dealing with an audience consisting of many hostile listeners.

4. With a small group in your classroom, identify areas in which national attitudes have changed—or areas in which your personal attitudes have changed. How did persuasive public speaking contribute to those changes?

Internet Activities

Internet Activities

1. Use your *InfoTrac College Edition* to do a PowerTrac search for the journal *Argumentation and Advocacy*. Browse the hits and read an article that interests you. (For example, the winter 1998 issue featured an article on Chicano murals and another on talk radio.)

2. Do a PowerTrac search for the journal *Vital Speeches* on your *InfoTrac College Edition*. Outline a persuasive policy speech you find there.

3. To explore hostile speaking in greater depth, log on to the Internet and search for the exact phrase *speaking to a hostile audience* on www.alltheweb.com.

Hot Links at the Public Speaking Resource Center

The following links are maintained and can be accessed easily via Jaffe Connection at the Public Speaking Resource Center on the Wadsworth Communication Café web site at http://communication.wadsworth.com/publicspeaking/study.html

Public Speaking Resource Center

■ www.ridgeweb1.mnscu.edu
Log on to Ridgewater College's site and click on Keith Green's faculty page. Follow links to Speech 121 then to Public Speaking Handout: Monroe's Motivated Sequence. Professor Green of Ridgewater College provides excellent information on Monroe's Motivated Sequence including ideal audience responses to each stages and pitfalls to avoid.

■ http://www.sasked.gov.sk.ca/docs/comm20/mod6.html
Saskatchewan Education created this page, which briefly overviews persuasive speaking, including topics, purposes, formats, and critical listening to persuasive communication. Activities are included.

■ http://www.ifas.ufl.edu~all030/persuasionout.html
This site provides an excellent description of the difference between informative and persuasive speeches.

The following speeches, both on the same subject, show how differently two people approach a topic depending on their purpose, their audience, and the context in which they speak.

STUDENT OUTLINE WITH COMMENTARY

Sleep Deprivation *by Angela Croff**

Topic: Sleep Deprivation

General Purpose: To Persuade

*Reprinted with permission.

Angela submitted this content outline on the topic of sleep deprivation for a classroom speech. Her purpose is to convince her college audience, which vaguely believes sleep is important, but routinely gets less sleep than needed. So she piles up facts and statistics that will help listeners understand the serious consequences of going without sleep.

The introduction gains attention, relates to the audience, establishes Angela's credibility, and previews her three main points. She uses the direct method pattern.

Angela's entire speech focuses on the problem, specifically the effects of sleep loss. She presents three main effects—financial, relational, and workplace. Is this the order you'd choose for the points? Why or why not?

In her first point, she piled up one number after another. Here she chooses words with negative connotations, terms such as "childish" and "paranoid" and "explosive," characteristics we want to avoid.

Sleep deprivation relates to safety. Her examples reinforce the idea of interconnectedness. One person's lack of vigilance can be deadly to others. To points B and C, she could search for research connecting sleep deprivation and workplace violence.

Specific Purpose: To persuade (convince) my audience that sleep deprivation has three negative consequences.

Central Idea: When sleep is deprived, individuals suffer financially and relationally, and society as a whole suffers.

■ Introduction

   A. We need food, water, shelter . . . and sleep to survive.

   B. We are similar to rats in our need for sleep; without food, rats last 16 days; without sleep they last only 17 days.

   C. As I began to study the effects of sleep deprivation on society, I found many interesting facts.

   D. Sleep deprivation affects society in three specific ways: our financial lives, our personal relationships, and our work environments all suffer.

■ Body

   A. First of all, sleep deprivation affects us financially.

      1. Americans waste $70 billion a year in lost productivity, accidents, and medical bills.

      2. Americans fill over 14 million prescriptions a year to help them sleep; they also spend millions on OTC drugs, 33 million in grocery stores.

      3. In 1977 there were three sleep disorder clinics, now there are 377; we waste billions of dollars and hundreds of hours of labor building clinics because we aren't sleeping right.

   B. Second, sleep deprivation affects our individual relationships.

      1. Because society is made up of interrelated individuals, when one person struggles, we all do.

      2. When sleep deprived, individuals have trouble controlling their emotions and behaviors.

         a. Small disagreements can become potentially explosive.

         b. Sleep deprivation leaves us feeling sluggish, tired, irritable, and depressed.

         c. Volunteers in an experiment, after going sleepless for some time, exhibited childish, masochistic, and paranoid behaviors; they also injured themselves.

         d. Sleep deprived individuals have increasingly aggressive behaviors.

   C. And finally, sleep deprivation affects safety in our working environments.

      1. Volunteers, who were asked to refrain from sleeping for a certain amount of time, became listless, serious, and grim; they did poorly on tasks of vigilance, reaction time, and simple arithmetic.

         a. Imagine yourself as a truck driver, a fireman, or a schoolteacher.

         b. All of these jobs require vigilance, reaction time and simple arithmetic skills.

      2. Examples of lives lost due to sleep deprivation are those of the Challenger space shuttle and Exxon Valdez oil spill.

■ Conclusion

A. In conclusion, I ask you to consider the facts and statistics I have presented.

B. Sleep deprivation really is a factor that affects our work, our personal relationships, and our lives.

C. Let those poor research rats be a warning to you, and go get some sleep!

STUDENT SPEECH WITH COMMENTARY

Sleep Deprivation *by Sonja Ralston**

Introduction

Since Congress has finally achieved a budget surplus, they've been able to devote their time to more important things, like declaring this week National Sleep Awareness Week. The March 22, 1999, *USA Today* in part of a 19-article series on sleep deprivation warned that we are faced with a new national debt measured, not in dollars, but in lost hours of sleep.

William Dement, a sleep researcher at Stanford University, explains that a sleep debt accumulates night after night: if you skip one hour a night for eight nights, you'll owe your body as if you had stayed up all night long. And if you think only college students carry a sleep balance (akin to their credit card balance) somewhere deep in the red, keep in mind that James B. Mass, a sleep researcher at Cornell University, noted in the May 27, 1998, *Houston Chronicle*, "It's a national crisis." And it's affecting more than just our moods; every year the national sleep debt costs us $166 billion and 13,000 lives.

Before we can drift off for a good night's sleep we must first wake up to some of the alarming effects of sleep debts, then we can open our eyes to better understand their causes, and finally cozy up to some solutions at both the personal and the societal levels.

Body

Unlike your loan shark, Big Tony, when you default on a debt to your body it can't exactly smash your kneecaps with a baseball bat. Instead it retaliates with the effects of sleep debts, which range from general fatigue to something as fatal as sleeping behind the wheel, and everything in between.

According to the December 12, 1998, edition of the *Tokyo Daily,* those most severely affected are "shift workers, parents of young children, and young adults, most notably students." However, it can affect anyone, especially those with high levels of stress in their lives, and according to a survey released last week by the National Sleep Foundation, 65 percent of adults are suffering from sleep deprivation, more than twice the number reported in 1991.

According to the *Orange County Register* of September 12, 1998, "an estimated 23 million Americans are afflicted with migraine headaches," the most common cause of which is a basic lack of sleep. And while these painful headaches can affect our moods and our productivity, they can also seriously affect our memories. Not getting enough sleep in and of itself can impair your memory, but that, in conjunction with frequent migraines, is enough to permanently damage your short-term memory retention. In the September 1998 edition of *American Health for Women*, Dr. Robin West, a psychologist at the University of Florida, Gainesville notes that being stressed

*Reprinted with permission.

Her conclusion appeals mainly to beliefs, but the final reference to the introduction does call for action.

Sonja's speech was given in competition, so she prepared and revised it over a period of time. She updates her information to include timely current events. Throughout, she'll use the metaphor of a debt. Her purpose, like Angela's, targets beliefs, but, unlike Angela, she describes societal and personal solutions.

She links herself to authoritative sources, and relates her topic to the audience before she mentions social consequences.

To add more vivid images, she selects sleep-related words.

The loan shark metaphor injects humor. Her problem section first presents effects rather than causes.

Internet news sources allow her to sit in her Texas dorm room and access national and global news and opinion from places such as Japan, California, Louisiana, and Canada.

By introducing national statistics first, Sonja hints at the range of the problem. Then she hones in on short term memory, which is especially relevant to this group. Audiences tend to act if they understand what they will gain or lose by acting.

The "effects" section of the speech contains some of the same material Angela used.

strains the memory, but "add lack of sleep to the mix, and it's no wonder we're literally losing our minds." Being tired makes it hard to focus, which makes it difficult to get information into our short-term storage banks.

Also, our cumulative sleep debts have a serious impact on the monetary debt of American companies, who, according to the aforementioned *Houston Chronicle* article, lost $150 billion every year through the decreased productivity of their sleepy employees. People also spend money on sleep aids and caffeine pills.

Not surprisingly, people who carry high sleep debts are also more susceptible to disease and micro-sleep. Dr. Max Hirshkowitz, Director of Baylor, a sleep lab, explains in the May 27, 1998, *Sacramento Bee* that "micro-sleep" is the instantaneous dozing off which lasts less than a minute, but at 60 mph, five seconds is long enough. Micro-sleep is the attributed cause of such disasters as the Chernobyl explosion, the Exxon-Valdez crash, and the 25 to 50 people killed every day in this country by those sleeping behind the wheel. That article goes on to exclaim, "that's like a 747 crashing every other week, with no survivors." Sadly, the National Highway Safety Administration reports that there will be a twenty-percent increase in that number Sunday, the day we "spring ahead" into daylight savings time. So from headaches and memory loss to monetary costs and micro-sleep, sleep debts affect us all in some way.

Translating the numbers into concrete images makes her material more interesting. The inclusion of daylight savings time, which began a few days later, updates her speech.

After summarizing the effects of sleep deprivation, she turns to the causes. If you were crafting this speech, would you start with causes or effects? Why? Notice the structure of the speech; she previews three points, signposts each one, then summarizes at the end.

Now that we understand why we need to be alarmed by letting our sleep balance plunge below zero, we can open our eyes to better examine the three causes of sleep debts. First, as Dr. Stanley Coren, a neuropsychologist at the University of British Columbia, explains in the August 2, 1998, edition of the *Boston Globe,* the "chronic lack of sleep experienced by the American population is a direct result of the industrial revolution." In the nineteenth century, the hours of the day were extended due to the widespread use of electric lights and the elimination of the midday nap. Experts at the National Sleep Foundation say we need between eight and nine hours of sleep a night to function at our peaks, and most of us are only getting seven or less.

Having too much to do is another cause of sleep deprivation. Daily chores, TV, the Internet, caffeine, and simple insomnia, which affects over 35 million Americans, are all demands on our sleep time, and with 24-hour Wal-Marts, 120 channels on cable, and the world at the tips of our keyboards, there's always something to do, so sleep loses out.

And with all this, Dr. Judith Leech, head of the Ottawa Hospital sleep lab, presents the third cause in the April 19, 1998, edition of the *Ottawa Citizen.* She says that in addition to how much we sleep, "how well we sleep" is important. A fitful night of tossing and turning, although it may last ten hours, does us about as much good as six hours of deep, sound, relaxing sleep. So, the industrial revolution, too much to do, and poor sleep quality all influence our insufficient sleeping habits.

Here's the transition to the solution section; Sonja's first suggestion is exaggerated and unrealistic and acts as a humorous counterpoint to Dr. Costriotta's depressing conclusion.

Now that we understand both the causes and the effects of sleep debts, we can cozy up to some solutions on both the societal and personal levels. Dr. Richard Costriotta, director of the University of Texas-Houston sleep lab, exclaims: "Welcome to the 90's" where more than half of us are sleep deprived and there's nothing we can do about it. Well, that's not quite true.

To completely eliminate this plague in our society, I propose that we undo the industrial revolution, destroy all the light bulbs, and revert to an agrarian society. Okay, so that's not really plausible, but there are steps we can take to eliminate our sleep deprivation without diminishing the last two centuries of progress.

First, we need to recognize the limitations of societal solutions. While some may say that big businesses will never be sensitive to the needs of their employees, an article in the March 28, 1999, *Times-Picayune* tells about several companies in the New Orleans area that have implemented nap time as part of the daily work routine. This drastically diminishes the sleep debts of their employees and increases productivity and benefits to the company.

If you're not lucky enough to work for one of these companies, don't worry, because most of the solutions lie on the personal level. In his 1999 book, *Power Sleep,* Dr. James Maas lists several tips for putting your sleep balance back in the black.

- First and foremost, make an appointment with sleep and don't be late.

- Secondly, turn the bedroom into a conducive sleeping environment; eliminate distractions such as the TV, computers, and work out equipment; make it quiet and dark, and lower the temperature so it's a few degrees cooler than the rest of the house.

- Next, establish a routine before bed; take a warm shower, eat a light snack with warm milk, unwind, and allow yourself 20 minutes to fall asleep.

- Finally, he advises to avoid evening exercise and caffeine and nicotine, if not altogether, at least within 4 hours of bedtime, because these activities lead to increased heart rate, which makes it difficult to relax.

By following these simple steps, we can eliminate our sleep debts and be happier, healthier, more productive individuals.

Conclusion

Today we've taken a look at our National Debt. Our national sleep debt, that is: first we woke up to some of its alarming effects, then we opened our eyes to better understand its causes, and finally we cozied up to some simple steps that both businesses and all of us can take.

Unlike so many other plagues that haunt our society today, we know both what causes and what cures sleep deprivation, so the real tragedy here is that two-thirds of us are still suffering unnecessarily.

So, before National Sleep Awareness Week and this tournament are over, take the time to pay off your sleep debt before your body declares biological bankruptcy. Sleep tight and don't let your sleep debt bite.

You've seen how often she cites credible sources; this is important when her major aim is to convince listeners that the problem is more serious than they think.

People often fail to act, even if they're convinced they should, because they don't know how to start, so providing easy and practical tips, such as these, is a good strategy.

Her conclusion is brief but very effective. She quickly reviews her arguments and calls for action by playing off the debt metaphor.

18

Persuasive Reasoning

Methods

This chapter will help you:

- Describe the elements of Toulmin's model of reasoning

- Define *logos,* or rational proofs

- Explain these types of reasoning and identify tests for each: analogy (metaphor and parallel case), inductive, deductive, and causal

- Recognize fallacious reasoning

- Define *pathos,* or emotional proofs

- Understand how appeals to emotions and needs are aspects of *pathos*

- Define *ethos,* or speaker credibility

- Identify ways that *ethos* functions as a reason to believe

- Explain how reasoning strategies vary across cultural groups

- Identify elements of invitational rhetoric

"For the Roses/Para las Rosas" ©1985 by Juana Alicia

A few years ago, a sixteen-year-old Japanese exchange student dressed up as a character in a movie and left his host home to attend a Halloween party. Unfortunately, Yoshihiro Hattori approached the wrong house. Bonnie Peairs (pronounced PEERS), finding the strangely dressed teen at her doorstep, called her husband, who reached for his gun and yelled "Freeze." Yoshihiro, whose English was limited, continued to advance, holding what turned out to be a camera. Seconds later, he lay dead of a gunshot wound.

The following year, Hattori's parents listened in disbelief as a jury acquitted Rodney Peairs, concluding he acted in "a reasonable manner." Mr. Hattori called the verdict "incredible, unbelievable." In Japan, the press found the decision beyond belief. Professor Masako Notoji expressed shock that twelve people could think it reasonable to shoot someone before talking to him. She explained, "We are more civilized. We rely on words." The key word here is *reasonable*. The evidence that seemed rational to jurors was nonsensical to Japanese onlookers (Gun crazy, 1993; Sanger, 1993).

Throughout your lifetime, you've reasoned your way through everyday matters, making sense of your world and making decisions that affect your life. Based on observations made in the course of everyday living, you've formed a number of conclusions that seem sensible to you. You may not think much about how you reason; you just "know" when something makes sense and when it does not. However, you may find that your conclusions aren't universally shared, and you may have felt compelled to explain them. Consequently, you'll benefit if you understand and apply the three types of reasoning common in the Western tradition, as Aristotle explained in *Rhetoric* (trans. Roberts, 1984).

> Of the modes of persuasion furnished by the spoken word there are three kinds. The first kind depends on the personal character of the speaker [*ethos*]; the second on putting the audience into a certain frame of mind [*pathos*]; the third on the proof, or apparent proof, provided by the words of the speech itself [*logos*].

Ethos, pathos, and *logos* overlap to form a totality of "good reasons." In other words, emotion can be reasonable; reason can have emotional underpinnings; and it is both reasonable and emotionally satisfying to believe a credible speaker. Moreover, in specific times, places, and situations, you will emphasize one reasoning type over the others. For instance, if you're explaining an economic recession, you'll use different kinds of reasoning or proofs than if you're explaining the accidental death of a young child to her kindergarten peers.

Using *logos, pathos,* and *ethos* effectively will empower you both as a speaker and as a critical listener within this culture. However, winning an argument is not always possible or desirable, and this chapter concludes with principles and forms of invitational rhetoric.

Use Toulmin's Reasoning Model

Watch a show such as *Law and Order,* and you'll see prosecutors charge a defendant with a crime based on evidence that warrants their prosecution. Every week, defense lawyers stand and rebut these charges by attacking the claim, the evidence, the link to their client, and so on. Professor Stephen Toulmin (1958; Toulmin, Rieke, & Janik, 1984) diagrammed elements of an argument based on interchanges typically found in courtrooms. His linear model, shown in Figure 18.1, illustrates important aspects of reasoning and clarifies the relationships among claims, evidence or data, warrants, qualifiers, and conditions for rebuttal that characterize traditional reasoning in U.S. culture. Learning to qualify your claim, justifying it with evidence, and planning ways to deal with counterarguments will make your speeches more persuasive.

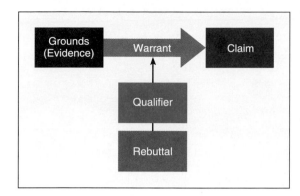

FIGURE 18.1 Toulmin's model of argument. (Adapted from Macmillan Publishing Company, Inc., from *An Introduction to Reasoning,* Second Edition, by Stephen Toulmin, Richard Rieke, and Allan Janik. Copyright © by Macmillan Publishing Company.)

Claims

As Chapter 17 pointed out, claims are disputable assertions that require evidence or backing in order to be accepted (Mullins, 1993). To review, factual claims argue about what exists, what causes something else, or what the future will bring. Value claims deal with the rightness, the goodness, or the worth of a thing. Finally, policy claims argue over actions or proposals for change.

Grounds, Data, or Evidence

To support your claims, select facts, examples and narratives, quotations, statistics, and literal and figurative comparisons, as described in Chapter 8. Evidence is also called **data** or **grounds,** and providing your listeners with evidence allows them to weigh your data and decide whether or not your conclusions make sense. Without sufficient and credible data, your claims will simply be unsupported **assertions.**

Data or Grounds
Evidence offered to support a claim.

Assertions
Claims put forth without any supporting evidence.

Warrants

The justification or reasoning that both you and your listeners use to connect your evidence with your claim is called a **warrant.** Switch your TV on to a police drama and watch the reasoning the officers use to justify an arrest. Officers must produce a warrant, which they can only get if they have sufficient data or grounds to make the arrest. Consider this scenario: The fingerprints on the gun (evidence) match the suspect's prints (additional evidence); the logical conclusion is that the suspect held the gun (claim of fact), because each person has unique fingerprints (the warrant that connects or links the evidence to the claim).

Warrant
Justification or reasoning that connects the claim and the evidence.

Qualifiers

Avoid words such as *always* or *never* when you make claims. Instead, use **qualifiers,** the words and phrases that limit or narrow the scope of your claim. Some common qualifiers are "in most cases," "in males between the ages of seven and nine," "among voters with a college degree," and "usually." For example, instead of asserting "one in eight women will get breast cancer," add a qualifier such as "women *who live to the age of 110* have a one in eight chance of getting breast cancer" in order to have a more defensible claim.

Qualifiers
Words and phrases that limit or narrow the scope of a claim.

The relationship between Chinese women's strength and possible steroid use has been a question at several summer Olympic competitions. (Wide World Photos)

Rebuttal

Not all listeners will agree with your claims. As a "listening speaker," try to hear the arguments your audience members will raise, then prepare to counter their arguments directly. This preparation is the **rebuttal** aspect of the model. It might help you to think of rebuttals as arguments your audience raises that begin with the phrase, "*But* what about . . . ?" Demonstrating that you've considered these counterarguments and that you still have good reasons for your claim enhances your persuasiveness.

In summary, if you learn to recognize the type of claim you are making, qualify it, provide evidence to warrant it, then deal with rebuttals, you will be more effective in presenting your ideas to others and having them recognize your views as reasonable.

Rebuttal

Arguments that counter or disagree with a claim.

Public
Speaking
Resource
Center

STOP AND CHECK

Evaluating Claims—A Case Study

During summer Olympic competition, the question often surfaces: Are Chinese female athletes on steroids? Read the following elements of the argument, and then answer the questions below. You can answer these questions online and, if requested by your instructor, submit them via email. Go to Chapter 18: Activities for Jaffe Connection at the Public Speaking Resource Center, http://communication.wadsworth.com/publicspeaking/study.html

- Chinese female athletes have voices in the low range, compared to other women.

- They are comparatively large.

- They are heavily muscled.

- Their country has been advised by coaches from the former East Germany, which was found to provide steroids to its female swimmers for many years.

- George Steinbrenner of the Yankees baseball team said that it was impossible to build such a strong team in just two years without some explanation.

- Scientists admit that steroids can be administered in training so that they will leave no traces during the competition.

- The Chinese female swimmers used steroids in their training programs.

Questions
1. What is the claim?

2. Is the claim one of fact, value, or policy?

3. What is the warrant?

4. What possible rebuttal might an objector make? [Hint: *But what about* the population of China?]

5. Is there enough evidence, in your opinion, to warrant the claim?

6. What else might cause the swimmers' characteristics?

Use Logos or Rational Proofs

Logos includes the verbal arguments you make relating to your subject. Also known as rational proofs, these arguments include analogy, inductive, deductive, and causal reasoning. As you might expect, these are not the only methods of sense making, as Diversity in Practice on the next page explains.

Logos
Verbal arguments, arguments from the words of the speech itself.

Reasoning by Analogy: Figurative and Literal

Chapter 8 described an **analogy** as a comparison between one item that is less familiar or unknown and something concrete that the audience already knows. In public speeches you can use both figurative (metaphor) and literal (parallel case) comparisons to draw conclusions. For example, we ask: How should we think about the role of the U.S. in the world? If we use a figurative analogy or metaphor, we might compare our role to that of a policeman, kindly big sister, or a bystander or onlooker. The comparison that those in power choose affects our global policies. We also consider questions such as, What kind of health care system should we adopt? If we use a literal analogy, we'll look around for a parallel case (a real country or state with a workable system) and decide whether or not that country or state is enough like ours to make their system work similarly well for us.

Analogy
Comparison of one item that's less familiar or unknown to something concrete and familiar.

Figurative Analogies (Metaphors)

When **reasoning by metaphor,** you figuratively compare two things that are generally different but share a recognizable similarity (Whaley, 1997). Metaphors are fundamentally dialogical, for they require that your listeners participate actively and make sensible connections between the two things you compare. For example, what images do these metaphors evoke in you?

Reasoning by Metaphor
Comparing two things that are generally different but share a recognizable similarity.

- Jesse Jackson's supporters form a "Rainbow Coalition" within a "patchwork quilt" society.

- The separation between Church and State is a "wall" or a "dance" or a "two-way street" (Voth, 1998).

- A teacher sees herself as a "police officer" or a "gardener" or an "ship's captain" in the classroom.

Metaphors can guide actions. For example, what if a teacher who keeps her classroom "shipshape" begins to think of herself as "sowing and nurturing seeds of learning" (Jaffe, 1998)? Metaphors can also arouse strong emotions, especially when they elicit positive images. For instance, Jesse Jackson's patchwork quilt evokes images of home, warmth, love, and security.

Use of analogy is a fundamental, universal form of reasoning. The scholar Brian Wicker (1975), for instance, sees metaphor as an older, more poetic way of seeing the world, related to the modes of thinking of poets and storytellers—a continuation of

The Influence of Culture on Reasoning

Culture influences our reasoning strategies in a number of ways that can easily lead to misunderstandings between cultural groups (Hilliard, 1986).

- **Topics considered appropriate for discussion varies across cultures.** Some groups, for instance, would not debate such issues as gay rights, day care, or euthanasia. Openly speaking about sex is unthinkable to some cultural groups.

- **Cultural groups conceptualize issues differently.** Although people in mainstream U.S. culture think of issues as problems and solutions to be defined, proposed, tested, and eliminated or enacted, others see problems as the result of fate, evidence of a bad relationship with the deity or deities, or proof that people are out of harmony with one another.

- **The norms for structuring and framing a discussion vary.** Rather than looking at causes and effects or pro and con arguments, then making claims and counterclaims, some cultural groups ground their discussions in the historical perspectives of the various participants. Still others rely on narrative structures to frame their speeches. In the United States, it's typical to frame debates as having a winner and a loser. But other cultures approach issues as an opportunity for a community of equals to cooperate in reaching consensus.

- **Levels of explicitness differ across cultures.** In U.S. institutions, we tend to spell out conclusions explicitly and concretely. In contrast, some cultures tolerate much more ambiguity in their conclusions; and their speakers influence others through subtle metaphors and indirect suggestions.

- **Forms of proof are often dissimilar.** What's considered rational or irrational, what counts as evidence, and what constitutes a good reason varies from culture to culture. In contrast to reliance on facts, statistics, and studies by experts, some cultural groups find good reasons in narratives, analogies, traditional sayings, authoritative texts, and the words of wise, experienced elders.

- **The communication style varies.** The bias in mainstream U.S. culture is toward linear, analytical models of reasoning as depicted in the Toulmin model. Other cultural groups reason more holistically through drama, intuition, and emotional expressiveness.

To better understand the influence of diversity on reasoning, log on to www. yahoo.com on the Internet. Under the general category Society and Culture, »follow links to Cultures and Groups. There you'll find co-cultural groups including vegetarians, Goths, 20-somethings, and people of color. Compare some topics the different groups discuss or look at reasoning strategies a particular group uses to justify its positions.

our oral heritage. Aristotle associates metaphor with mental brilliance as seen in this quotation from *Poetics* (trans. Bywater, 1984):

> . . . the greatest thing by far is to be a master of metaphor. It is the one thing that cannot be learnt from others, and it is also a sign of genius, since a good metaphor implies an intuitive perception of the similarity in dissimilars (1459.5)

In the following quotation, Asa Hilliard (1986) claims that metaphorical reasoning is typical of African and African-American speakers.

> Early use was made of proverbs, song, and stories. Direct or symbolic lessons were taught through these. . . . Parenthetically, it is interesting that racist psychologists claim that Black people are not capable of "Level II Thinking," the kind of abstract thinking which is reflected in proverbs and analogies. To the contrary, this is our strong suit. . . . Psychologists . . . miss the extensive use of proverbs and analogies among us (p. 287).

Literal Analogies (Parallel Cases)

Whereas metaphor shows likenesses between two *different* things, reasoning by **parallel case** or **literal analogy** finds likenesses between two *similar* things. We often use this type of reasoning to formulate policies by asking what another person or group decided to do when faced with a problem similar to our own. Here are some examples.

Parallel Case or Literal Analogy
Compares likenesses between two similar things; argues that what happened in a known case will likely happen in a similar case.

- How should your school solve parking problems on campus? Look at case studies of schools that solved similar parking problems, then infer that the other schools' experiences will be a good predictor of what might or might not work for yours.

- How should a local hospital keep health care costs under control? Look at cost-saving measures instituted by a hospital in a similar location.

- How should the state of South Carolina deal with welfare reform? Well, which states are most like South Carolina? What did they do? What positive or negative outcomes resulted from policies enacted in those states?

In summary, we commonly use actual cases based on real experiences to formulate policies and make predictions about the future. Then we predict that what happened in a known case will happen in a similar case that we project.

Testing Analogies

Reasoning by metaphor is not generally considered a "hard" proof, so you must make sure that your listeners can sensibly connect your concept and the thing you use for comparison. Check to see that the comparison does, in fact, illuminate, clarify, and illustrate your idea. Parallel case reasoning is different, you can test it more directly by considering the following two questions.

1. Are the cases really alike? Or are you "comparing apples to oranges"?

2. Are they alike in essential details?

Reasoning Inductively

The **inductive reasoning** process begins with when you use specific instances or examples then formulate a reasonable generalization or conclusion from them. Put another way, induction is reasoning from the particular to the general. Inductive reasoning is characteristic of many ethnic speakers who ground their knowing and reasoning in personal experiences that arise out of their relationship with others. Patricia Sullivan (1993), for instance, explains that African-American leaders tie knowledge to human experiences, human actions, and the human life world.

Inductive Reasoning
Starts with specific instances or examples, then formulates a reasonable conclusion.

> Knowledge does not exist for its own sake, or in the abstract, but exists as grounded in human experience. What is relevant is relevant because it makes a difference in people's lives.

Here is an example of induction from a 1999 *Newsweek* feature about young Latinos (Hayden, 1999):

- Thirty-year-old physicist, Juan Malcadena, of Argentinean descent, won a MacArthur Foundation "genius" grant.
- Astronaut John Olivas, age 33, is a fourth-generation Mexican-American.
- Basketball star Rebecca Lobo is of Cuban descent; she's twenty-five years old.
- Ted Cruz, the first Latino to clerk for the chief justice of the United States, is the twenty-nine-year-old son of a Cuban immigrant.
- Twenty-two-year-old singer Shakira, a native of Colombia, is making an album to show that Latinos "can do good rock."
- Puerivan-born Luigi Crespo, age 27, is the executive director of the Republican National Hispanic Assembly.

> **Generalization:** Members of the Latin Gen X, also called Generation Ñ, is "cruising the American mainstream, rediscovering their roots, and inventing a new, bicultural identity" (Leland & Chambers, 1999, p. 53).

Because you can only be sure of a conclusion when you're able to observe 100 percent of a population, it is ideal to look at every example before you form a conclusion. However, you can rarely observe every member of a specific group. (Imagine trying to survey every member of Generation Ñ!) Instead, you select a representative sample, survey the characteristics of that sample, formulate conclusions, then generalize your findings to the larger population it represents. Take care here. If you only study middle-class Latinos, don't assume that your conclusions apply to all members of Generation Ñ.

The three major tests for inductive reasoning are all linked to the tests you used to evaluate examples (see Chapter 8).

1. Are enough cases represented to justify the conclusion? Or are you forming a conclusion based on only a few cases?

2. Are the cases typical? That is, do they represent the average members of the population to which the generalizations are applied? Or are they extreme cases that may show what could happen, but not what usually happens?

3. Are the examples from the time under discussion, or are they out of date?

Reasoning Deductively

Deductive Reasoning
Starts with a principle (the premise) and applies it to a specific case.

Inductive reasoning moves from specific examples or particulars to conclusions or generalizations, but **deductive reasoning** does the opposite. It begins with a generalization or principle, called the premise and moves logically to an application in a specific case. (See Figure 18.2 for an example of the relationship between inductive and deductive reasoning.) In formal logic the deductive reasoning process is often shown in a syllogism such as this:

Major premise:	All Catholic bishops are unmarried.
Minor premise:	He is a Catholic bishop.
Conclusion:	Therefore, he is not married.

When you're sure of the major premise, you can state your conclusion with confidence. Because it is a principle that members of the Catholic clergy cannot marry and remain in the priesthood, you can be sure that a particular individual who has risen to the level of bishop is unmarried.

FIGURE 18.2   You observe a number of spaniels and inductively reason that they make good pets. Using that premise you deduce that Curly—the dog you want to buy—will be a good pet.

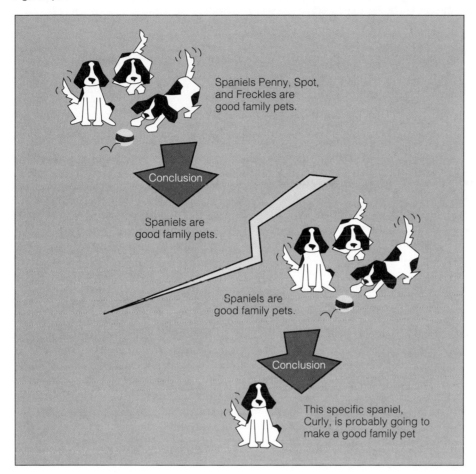

In contrast, many premises are less certain. Although some, such as "all men are mortal," are 100 percent true, others, such as "Generation Ñ is cruising the mainstream culture," are not valid in all cases. For this reason, it's wise to qualify both your premises and your conclusions:

> Many young Latinos are entering the mainstream while recovering their roots. Yvonne Serres is a twenty-five-year-old woman of Mexican descent.

> She has a good chance of forging a bicultural identity.

When you reason deductively, you rarely provide the entire syllogism in your argument, leaving your listeners to fill in the unstated premises. Aristotle called this an **enthymeme.** For example, you might say, "Married? He's a Catholic bishop!" and let your audience make the necessary connections. Or (sitting around the table discussing seventeen-year-old Ryan's recent marriage), "Tiffany and Ryan may find themselves divorced in a few years." Your listeners use their common generalizations about teen marriages to make sense of what you've just said. The complete syllogism in this case is

> Teen marriages have a higher divorce rate.
> Tiffany and Ryan are marrying at age seventeen.

> Therefore, they have a higher chance of getting divorced.

Enthymeme

Omitting part of the syllogism in an argument and letting listeners supply what's missing; inherently dialogical.

Using enthymemes is inherently dialogical, for your listeners must form conclusions based on their knowledge of what you don't say. However, if they know nothing about your subject—the rules regarding the Catholic clergy, for example—they'll miss your meaning.

There are two major tests for deductive reasoning:

1. In order for the conclusion to be valid, the premises must be true or highly probable.

2. In order to be reasonable, the conclusion must follow from the premise.

Reasoning Causally

Causal Reasoning

Links two factors in such as way that the first factor occurs before the second and leads to the second as a matter of rule.

One speaker made this assertion: "There were nine million immigrants last year, and there were nine million Americans out of work." Both of these facts can be verified by counting. However, if the speaker links the two, stating or implying that one results in or leads to the other, the speaker is then using **causal reasoning,** and the statement sounds like this: "There were nine million Americans out of work because there were nine million immigrants." In the first statement, the two conditions exist together in time—perhaps by chance; in the second statement, the second condition *results from* the first and would cease to exist without it.

Because the belief in causation is a core Euro-American belief, this type of reasoning is common here. However, in order to be a cause, one factor must precede another and be linked in such a way *that the second factor follows as a matter of rule.* Thus, it is evident that the lack of oxygen to the brain (first factor) causes death (second factor)—this link is observed time after time. But other causal links are not as well proved, sometimes because many other factors may be linked to the effects. The causes of unemployment are much more complex than the flood of immigrants. The key to causal reasoning is to produce enough reasons to warrant the link or connection between the two factors.

Test causation by asking a series of questions to assess if the reasoning is valid.

1. Is there a real connection? Does one follow as a result of the first, or do the two events simply exist together in time?

2. Is this the only cause? The most important cause? Or are there other factors?

3. Is the cause strong enough for the effect?

In summary, you use a variety of reasons to warrant your claims including figurative and literal analogies, inductive and deductive reasoning, and causal links. All of these types of reasoning fall under the category of *logos,* or rational proofs. (See Diversity in Practice on the next page for information on gender patterns in reasoning.)

Recognizing Logical Fallacies

Fallacy

Failure in logical reasoning that leads to unsound or misleading arguments.

A **fallacy** is a failure in logical reasoning that leads to unsound or misleading arguments. As a speaker and as a critical listener, examine the arguments you hear to avoid being taken in by common fallacies such as the following.

Unsupported Assertion

Unsupported Assertion

A claim presented without evidence.

In the **unsupported assertion** fallacy, the claim is offered without supporting evidence. Have you ever argued for a grade? ("I deserve an A, so why did I get a B?") If you really want to achieve a grade change, you'll have to produce some pretty convincing data to show that you deserve the A. Otherwise, your record will remain the same.

DIVERSITY IN PRACTICE

Gender and Reasoning

Although both men and women reason inductively, a number of feminist philosophers believe inductive reasoning is a *major* way that women draw conclusions. Women typically describe specific experiences of real people—the rape victim, the family without medical insurance, the student athlete whose sport was eliminated—then generalize from these examples. In short, women's reasoning is grounded in personal experiences that arise out of their interpersonal relationships (Griffiths, 1988; Jaggar, 1989; McMillan, 1982).

A common stereotype of women is that they reason with their hearts rather than their heads—an overgeneralization that may have some basis in fact. Studies of women's patterns of thinking show the importance of emotion in their reasoning process. Alison Jaggar (1989), for example, believes that emotions are essential to knowing. Although they are obviously different from "dispassionate investigation," emotions complement logic, and they are intertwined with rational proofs. Feelings, in this view, are not inferior to reason; furthermore, they are not something that women must overcome in order to think clearly. Instead, emotions can be a source of knowledge in themselves, and "truth" or "knowledge" without them is distorted (Griffiths, 1988).

Not all scholars believe that fundamental differences exist between men and women, Frank (1997) argues that evidence, linear thinking, and deductive logic are not inherently masculine; both men and women use them. Moreover, intuitive and emotional arguments are not inherently feminine; men often reason through experiences, emotions, and empathy.

The Laboratory for Complex Thinking and Scientific Reasoning, directed by Kevin Dunbar of McGill University, analyzed videotapes and audiotapes of women and men's online thinking and reasoning during laboratory meetings by following a number of women scientists over extensive time periods. They found no major differences in inductive, deductive, or causal reasoning processes. However, they did find that, when given an unexpected finding, men scientists tend to assume they know the cause, whereas women track it down (Women, science & cognition, n. d.).

Whatever differences there may be, Asen (1999) argues that "difference must be viewed as a *resource for*—not an *impediment to*—meaningful dialogue." To learn more about gender and reasoning, log on to the Internet and go to http://www.psych.mcgill.ca/perpg/fac/dunbar/women.html. Or read David Frank's 1997 article or related articles in the journal, *Argumentation and Advocacy,* available on your *InfoTrac College Edition*.

Ad Populum or Bandwagon

This appeal to popular reason is another failure of evidence; rather than providing sound rational arguments, the speaker justifies a belief or action by phrases such as "Everyone's doing it" or "We all think this way." Think of how often the majority is wrong.

Ad Hominem (Personal Attack)

Rather than evaluate the claim, the evidence, and the warrant or reasoning behind it, an ***ad hominem*** attack discounts or demeans the messenger. For instance, in the movie

Ad Populum or Bandwagon

An appeal to popular opinion.

Ad Hominem

An attack on the messenger rather than the message.

Field of Dreams, townspeople gather to discuss library books. One woman wants to ban a book; another argues that it should be kept. The first woman, instead of giving reasons against the book, attacks the messenger: "At least my husband doesn't plow under his crop and build a baseball diamond!" To which the second woman responds, "Well, at least I'm not a Nazi book burner like you." Both women ignore the issues relating to literary merit and censorship.

False Analogy

False Analogy

Comparing two things too dissimilar to warrant the conclusion.

The two things compared are not similar enough to warrant the conclusion in the fallacy of **false analogy.** Look again at the *Field of Dreams* example. The second woman compares the first to a Nazi, but wanting to remove the writings of one author from a local library is nowhere near the actions of the Nazis during World War II.

Post Hoc

Post Hoc

A fallacy of causation; a false cause.

The entire phrase describing this fallacy is **Post Hoc,** *Ergo Propter Hoc* (literally: after this, therefore because of this). This fallacy of causation argues that because one event follows the other, the first must be the cause of the second. For instance, Maria's speech on lottery winners (at the end of Chapter 8) told of Daisy who was sued for half of her $2.8 million winnings by her son's teenaged friend. Before she bought her ticket, Daisy asked him to pray that she'd win; afterward, the teen felt that his prayer had caused her fortune. (The judge, however, ruled that there is no way to prove this.)

Overgeneralization

Overgeneralization

A fallacy of induction; generalizing too broadly, given the evidence.

This fallacy of inductive reasoning extends the conclusion further than the evidence warrants. For example, let's say you have a bad experience with a specific brand of computer, so you judge the whole line of computers (or worse, the entire company) as bad based on your one negative experience. People overgeneralize about blind dates, about partisanship of politicians, about student cheating, about members of religious groups, and so on. Jumping to a conclusion based on minimal evidence is **overgeneralization.**

Red Herring Argument

Red Herring

Introducing a side issue with the intent of drawing attention from the real issue.

The speaker dodges the real argument and intentionally digresses from the issue by introducing an unrelated side issue in an attempt to divert attention. The term derives from the days of fox hunting when a dead fish was dragged across the trail of a fox in order to set the dogs off in a different direction (Gass, 1999). Any time you think, "That's beside the point," or "That's irrelevant," you're probably hearing a **red herring** argument.

False Dichotomy

False Dichotomy

An either-or fallacy that ignores other reasonable options.

The **false dichotomy** fallacy presents an either-or choice that overlooks other reasonable possibilities. As examples, you might hear: Either graduate from college or work in a low-paying job, or either athletes should be role models or we should ignore their private lives entirely. Such false choices overlook the range of possibilities between the two extremes.

In summary, an argument can be fallacious because it fails to produce evidence for the claim or the support it presents as faulty. Fallacies also attack the messenger instead of the message. Furthermore, fallacies of analogy, of causation, and of induction are common. Learning to recognize them will help you think more critically about the arguments you make and those you hear every day.

STOP AND CHECK

Identifying Fallacies

Working alone or with a group of classmates, copy the list of common fallacies presented here, then give an example of each. Use material from television shows (re-runs of *Seinfeld, Mad About You,* or *Home Improvement,* for example), personal experiences, talk radio callers, and the like. Share your examples with other class members. You can complete this activity online and submit it to a classmate via email. Go to Chapter 18: Activities for Jaffe Connection at the Public Speaking Resource Center, http://communication.wadsworth.com/publicspeaking/study.html

    If you need more information or additional examples of fallacies, go to the Internet site http://commfaculty.fullerton.edu/rgass/fallacy31.htm, sponsored by Dr. Robert Gass, University of California, Fullerton. Professor Gass provides definitions and examples of these and other common fallacies as well as an assignment and links to other sites that explain fallacious reasoning.

Include Pathos or Emotional Proofs

Contrast the following situations:

■ You're listening to a speaker who has all her facts and figures straight, and she provides evidence that passes all the tests: Her examples are representative; her statistics come from reputable sources, and she cites knowledgeable experts, but you still feel that there's no good reason for you to act. In other words, you're unmotivated—you are neither interested nor concerned.

■ You're listening to a second speaker who similarly provides excellent evidence and sound reasoning. However, she links her topic to your core beliefs, values, personal goals, and emotions. You find yourself beginning to care about her subject, and you want to believe and act as she proposes.

The second speaker realizes what good speakers have always known—**motivation** is an internal, individualistic or subjective factor that results when listeners understand how topics affect their lives in a personal way. In short, we look for emotional and psychological reasons to believe and act. And in the end, our subjective reasons may be as powerful an influence as our logical ones; this demonstrates the power of emotions—which Aristotle called **pathos**—in reasoning.

    Although you often respond subconsciously to emotional appeals, your responses can be conscious, and your thoughts may run something like this:

    "She's right, that's *exactly how it feels* to go to bed hungry—and we shouldn't let it happen!"

    "Writing my resume carefully *will help me* get a better job."

    "I have to protest over *such a fundamental issue* as freedom of speech."

    "I've experienced *frustration* just like that! I can relate!"

Pathos relies on two major, but intertwined, types of appeals: appeals to emotions and appeals to needs.

Appealing to Emotions

According to Aristotle, **emotions** are all the feelings that change people in ways that affect their judgments. Two general categories of emotions apply to speechmaking: Positive emotions are those we want to be part of our lives, and negative emotions are those

Motivation
Internal, individualized factor that results when we understand how topics affect our lives in a personal way.

Pathos
Appeals or reasons directed toward audience emotions.

Emotions
Feelings that change people and affect their judgments; we tend to seek positive emotions and avoid negative ones.

we want to avoid or prevent. Political campaign ads provide an illustration of both kinds of emotions. Politicians try to engender hope if they're elected and fear of the consequences if they're not.

Positive Emotions

Psychologists say that we "approach" rather than "avoid" pleasurable emotions. Most people agree that love, peace, pride, approval, hope, generosity, courage, and loyalty are desirable. Additionally, we feel good about our core beliefs and values such as freedom and individualism. By appealing to positive feelings, you can often motivate your listeners to accept and act on your claims.

One of the best ways to appeal to emotions is to use narratives and examples, as this excerpt from a student speech demonstrates. Marieta, originally from the Philippines, was adopted into an American home when she was a teenager (Cribbins, 1990).

> You might be thinking that adopting an international child is a lot of work. Well, it is, but I believe it is worth it. My parents say that bringing me into their family is one of the most gratifying things they have ever done. And their generosity has obviously benefited me. If it were not for my parents, I would not be able to continue my college education. I wouldn't have any parents or sisters to call my own. As far as I know, I would probably still be in an orphanage because I wouldn't have a place to go.

This personal story emphasizes generosity and hope as well as the underlying values of self-sacrifice for the good of others, education, family, and belonging. It provides a powerful argument for international adoption.

Negative Emotions

Some emotions are unpleasant, and we avoid these negative feelings, such as guilt or shame, hatred, fear, insecurity, anger, and anxiety. Appeals to negative emotions can be forceful—and sometimes disastrous. Consider the rhetoric of hate groups who appeal to their audiences' weaknesses, angers, fears, and insecurities.

Don't reject the use of negative emotions entirely, however. Fear, anger, and guilt, for instance, can motivate us to avoid real dangers—a fact that the campaign against drunk driving uses effectively. Think of a story you've heard or a television ad you've seen that shows adorable children killed by drivers who "just this once" drove drunk. Don't they make you want to do something about the problem?

One way to arouse listener emotion is to use analogies. In this case Mike Suzuki uses anger to explore the use of Native American symbols as sports mascots. He wanted his fellow students (at a Catholic university that was undergoing a mascot change) to identify with the Native Americans' perspective, so he employed the following analogy:

> Opponents feel that non-Indian people do not have the right to use sacred Indian symbols. Phil St. John, a Sioux Indian and founder of the Concerned American Indian Parents group, said the behaviors of Indian mascots at sporting events were comparable to a Native American tearing apart a rosary in front of a Catholic church. Can you imagine someone dressing up as the Pope and swinging a cross wildly in the air at one of our football games? This is how some Native Americans feel when their sacred symbols are used in sports.

As you might imagine, it's easy to overdo negative appeals. For instance, excessive appeals to guilt or fear may turn the audience away from a speaker's beliefs. Here is how one listener reacted to a speech by a famous environmental activist (Roczak, 1992).

> [The activist's] presentation is meant to instill unease. In my case, she is succeeding, though not in the way she intends. She is making me worry . . . for the fate of this movement on which so much depends. As much as I want to

endorse what I hear, [her] effort to shock and shame just isn't taking. . . . I find myself going numb.

He advises environmentalist speakers to evaluate the psychological impact of their appeals to fear and guilt, then, consider presenting a "politics of vision" that connects environmental goals to positive emotions—to what is "generous, joyous, freely given, and noble" in people.

Appealing to Needs

One of the most widely cited systems of classifying needs follows the work of Abraham Maslow (1987). Maslow ranked needs into levels, each building on the others (see Figure 18.3). Everyone must satisfy basic needs to survive. Although succeeding levels are important, they become less and less vital for survival. Briefly, Maslow's five levels and how they relate to public speaking are as follows:

1. **Basic needs:** It's been said that we can live forty days without food, four days without water, and four minutes without air. Thus, food, water, and air are basic survival needs. Shelter, sex, rest, and stress release are others.

    To appeal to this level in your speeches, show how your topic will help your listeners satisfy their basic survival needs.

2. **Security needs:** Once we have the basics, we need to feel secure and safe with them. The second level includes the need for self-preservation as well as secure employment as a means of obtaining the other needs. In addition, we need to feel we are able to take control of our circumstances.

    In your speeches, you can explain how to gain peace of mind, job security, safety and comfort, and better health.

3. **Needs to love and belong:** Included here are our needs for love and affection that can be met through meaningful, stable relationships with others, including friends, families, and social groups on whom we can depend.

    You can address these needs in your speeches by showing how your topic helps your listeners be better friends, creates a stronger community, or builds ties between people.

4. **Esteem needs:** We need approval and recognition from others. We need to see ourselves as competent, respected individuals who can be proud of what we do. This category includes self-respect and reputation.

    Demonstrate that you respect your listeners, and mention their accomplishments when appropriate. Find ways to make listeners feel competent to carry out your proposals. Let them know that their ideas, opinions, and concerns are significant.

5. **Self-actualization needs:** At the final level, we seek to reach our highest potential through personal growth, doing good deeds, creating unique works, and overcoming obstacles.

    Challenge your listeners to look beyond themselves and reach out to others. Encourage them to dream big dreams and accomplish unique things. The Army's slogan "Be all that you can be" is an example of an appeal to self-actualization.

Return to the excerpt from Marieta's speech on international adoption found on the previous page. Identify the different levels of Maslow's hierarchy of needs you find in her appeal. (To learn more about Maslow's work, log on to the Internet and go to www.alltheweb.com. Do a search for the exact term *Abraham Maslow* and look for additional levels that have been added to his hierarchy.

FIGURE 18.3   Maslow's hierarchy of needs. (Adapted from *Motivation and Personality,* 3rd ed., by Abraham H. Maslow. Revised by Roger Frager, James Fadiman, Cynthia McReynolds, and Ruth Cox. Copyright 1954, © 1987 by Addison-Wesley, Longman, Co. Copyright © 1970 by Abraham Maslow. Reprinted by permission of Prentice-Hall, Inc., Upper Saddle River, NJ.)

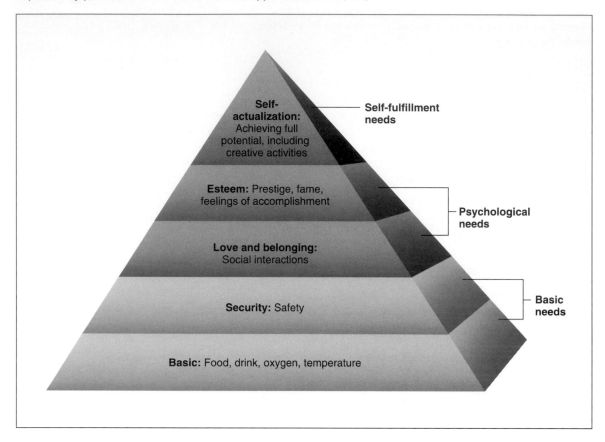

Understanding Complex Motivations

As we've seen, using pathos is complex, because needs, wants, values, and emotions overlap. As you create emotional appeals, keep in mind four important factors that result in motivational variation from individual to individual (Griffiths, 1988).

1. Sometimes you must choose between two desirable goals or feelings—job security or the ability to reach your potential, for example. In contrast, you may have to choose between two undesirable things—"the lesser of two evils."

2. Motives vary according to the circumstances of our lives. Someone who's just broken up a significant relationship may worry more about belonging and self-esteem than a couple in a long-term relationship. You probably find that what motivates you is different from what motivates your parents, and your parents, in turn, respond to different appeals than do your grandparents.

3. We sometimes respond out of mixed motives. The alumna who donates out of loyalty to your school may also like the pride she feels when a building is named in her honor. Someone participating in an angry protest march may be acting out of underlying anxiety, fear, or frustration.

4. Motivations are often group centered, meaning that what we want for ourselves, we want for others—including our family, friends, members of our clubs, religious

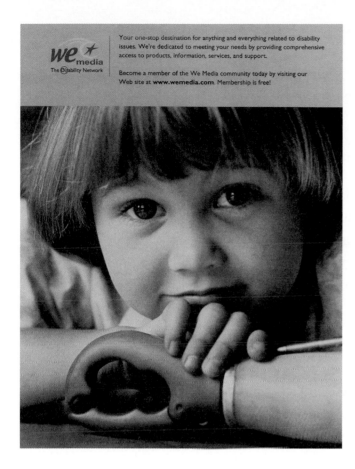

Examine this ad. What rational appeals are here? What emotional appeals? Are the appeals balanced? Why or why not? (Courtesy of We Media)

groups, schools, towns, states, society, and world. For this reason, speeches about child abuse in other countries motivate listeners who want security for themselves and their own families, as well as for strangers.

Testing Emotional Appeals

Emotions, although essential, are not always trustworthy, and it's appropriate to examine them to see if they make sense. Let's say you are using fear to motivate your audience. Ask yourself if the fear is justified or if you're making your listeners unduly fearful. Are you creating or playing on irrational fears? Although emotion is important in argument, excessive appeal to emotion can cloud logical reasoning.

As a listener, ask questions such as these: Why do I feel guilty? Is my guilt reasonable? Is this speaker using my feelings to manipulate me into action? Although the speaker is causing me to feel angry, is anger my primary emotion? Could it be that I am really fearful instead? That is, are her ideas challenging my cherished beliefs and creating anxiety that I am masking with anger toward her (anonymous, 1993)?

Further, is emotion being used ethically? Generally, it is considered unethical to appeal to emotions in an attempt to bypass logical reasoning. For example, does an appeal to national pride create an argument for going to war in a way that clouds a more rational argument against military involvement? Does a speaker use fear to motivate listeners to act for his own profit rather than for the audience's good?

STOP AND CHECK

Evaluating Pathos in Campaign Ads

A memorable political campaign ad was aired only once during the 1964 race between Democrat Lyndon Johnson and Republican Barry Goldwater. The Vietnam War was heating up, the Cold War was in full swing, and millions of Americans feared a final countdown that would unleash a nuclear attack. The Democrats took advantage of Goldwater's reputation as a military "hawk" in their ad, which showed a young girl pulling the petals off a daisy, while an off-screen narrator counts down—"10, 9, 8, 7, 6 . . ."

■ What does the ad imply Goldwater would do as president?

■ What emotion is stirred?

■ If you were a college student dreading the draft, how might you respond?

■ Is there enough information here for you to make a reasoned voting decision?

Other historical campaigns featured emotional appeals. President Ronald Reagan was famous for the ad "It's Morning in America," which showed scenes of happy families and beautiful homes. President Clinton's campaign featured his birthplace in Hope, Arkansas, and Clinton presented himself as "The Man from Hope."

■ What emotions are aroused here?

■ What values are represented?

■ What do the ads imply that Reagan and Clinton will do as president?

■ Is there enough information here for you to make a reasoned voting decision?

Develop Ethos or Speaker Credibility

Proof

A reason to believe.

Ethos

Personal credibility or character traits that make a speaker believable and worthy of the audience's confidence.

A third type of **proof**—or reason to believe—comes from your personal qualities, as Chapter 6 pointed out. In fact, Aristotle (trans. Roberts, 1984) believed that your character—a proof he called **ethos**—is the most effective means of persuasion you possess. Here is his explanation of speaker credibility.

> Persuasion is achieved by the speaker's personal character [ethos] when the speech is so spoken as to make us think him [or her] credible. We believe good [people] more fully and more readily than others: this is true generally whatever the question is, and absolutely true where exact certainty is impossible and opinions are divided (1356, 4ff).

This simply means that people will place their confidence in you if they see you as personally believable, trustworthy, and of good character. Their inner dialogue—or reasoning—might look something like this:

> She really knows what she's talking about—she has obviously done her homework! In addition, she seems to have good intentions towards me; I trust her. Thus, I believe it when she tells me that . . .

In contrast, audiences frequently use a speaker's ethos as a reason not to believe what he or she is asserting to be true. Their reasoning may run something like this:

> He has no clue as to what he is talking about. I feel he isn't being entirely up front. He seems so arrogant—like he really doesn't care about us—he just wants us to sign up for his pet project. I don't trust him. Therefore, I don't really believe his information about . . .

We evaluate speakers in four areas: good sense, good character, goodwill, and dynamism. You can increase your ethos by demonstrating these characteristics.

Demonstrating Good Sense

Good sense is a cluster of characteristics made up of several components.

- **Intelligence:** Show that you understand your subject and have up-to-date information about it. Discuss related historical developments, and link your topic to contemporary national and international issues. Listeners will recognize that you're not "bluffing your way" through your speech.

- **Sound Reasoning:** Support your claims with trustworthy evidence and logical connections between ideas. Avoid fallacies and excessive appeals to emotions.

- **Composure:** Demonstrate composure by remaining calm rather than losing your poise in a stressful situation. For example, if you're agitated during a classroom presentation, your audience may wonder why you can't control yourself. However, if you are composed and controlled, they'll perceive you more favorably. However, note the differences in cultural expectations about composure described in Diversity in Practice on the next page.

Exhibiting Good Character

Character counts. Your listeners will believe you more readily if they trust you, so demonstrate honesty, integrity, and trustworthiness by documenting your sources and giving facts that square with what they know to be true. Choose topics that matter to you, and stick by your convictions, even when they are unpopular. Politicians get into trouble with constituents when they appear to be poll-driven and pander to the beliefs of a particular audience, waffling from one position to another according to what's popular instead of sticking by their core beliefs.

Expressing Goodwill

Your listeners want to know you're concerned about them, that you can speak to them in their "own language." Kenneth Burke (1950), one of the twentieth-century's most respected rhetoricians, stressed the importance of "identification" with an audience. According to Burke, a variety of "divisions" separate us, but **identification,** sometimes called **co-orientation,** has the power to bring people with diverse beliefs and behaviors together.

But how do you identify with your audience? One way is to find areas of **common ground**—to emphasize ways you are similar to audience members. When your listeners share your beliefs, values, attitudes, and behaviors, it's easy to find areas of commonality to draw on. However, diversity issues make identification more difficult. When your listeners differ from you and from one another, consider closely the areas you do share, and then apply this principle: Find areas of common ground and build on them. For instance, you share with every audience the needs for safety and self-esteem.

In this example, Susan Au Allen (1993), president of the U.S. Pan Asian American Chamber of Commerce, emphasizes common ground with her largely African-American audience.

> So I salute you, a cherished ally. . . . We are Japanese, Filipinos, Chinese, Asian Indians, Koreans, Vietnamese, Laos, Thais, Cambodians, Hmongs, Pakistanis, and Indonesians. Each has a distinct beautiful ethnic cultural heritage, but our goals are the same as yours. We want to remove racial barriers, we want equal opportunity for our members, and we want to create greater horizons for those who follow.

Identification or Co-orientation

Concerns shared among speakers and listeners that help overcome divisions and bring diverse people together.

Common Ground

Specific areas or concerns that both speakers and audiences consider important.

Composure in Other Cultures

Concepts of ethos depend on the cultural context. For example, credible speakers in the African-American tradition are forceful and emotional, rather than calm and composed (Kochman, 1990). Good speakers are genuinely intense in their expressions, and sometimes their emotions threaten to override the order and procedure common in the Euro-American style of public speaking. For this reason, listeners brought up in the Euro-American culture may consider these speakers loud.

Similarly, Janice Walker Anderson (1991) found that Arabs traditionally expect effective speakers to show their emotion and to heighten the audience's emotions through the rhythm and sounds of words. Overstating a case indicates the speaker's sincerity, not distortion; in contrast, a soft tone indicates the speaker is weak or dishonest.

Although you'll usually rely on commonalities, in some cases your differences make you more credible, depending on the topic. For example, Gary suffered a stroke when he was seventeen years old; consequently, when he spoke about strokes and stroke victims, his words were much more persuasive because of his disability. When Ariko (whose speech is found at the end of Chapter 16) spoke on Japanese writing, her Japanese origin made her more credible.

Showing Dynamism

Dynamism or forcefulness is a fourth trait that influences credibility. Chapter 14 pointed out that dynamism is linked to traits of extroversion, energy, and enthusiasm. This doesn't mean that you are not credible if you're not dynamic; however, your visible enjoyment of your topic, your enthusiasm, and your liveliness contribute to your ethos. Think of it this way: Wouldn't you be more likely to believe someone who states ideas forcefully, rather than apologetically?

In conclusion, simply because other cultures do not name these proofs in the way that Aristotle described them does not mean that they do not exist in some form within the culture. Across the globe, public speakers appeal to their listeners' rationality, their emotional responses, and their assessment of speakers as trustworthy.

STOP AND CHECK

Evaluating Ethos

Log on to your *InfoTrac College Edition* and do a PowerTrac search for the journal *Vital Speeches*. Read two speeches and identify ways the speaker demonstrates good sense, good character, and goodwill.

Invitational Rhetoric
Inviting audiences to enter and understand the rhetor's world, then share their own perspectives; focuses on mutual understanding and mutual influence, not winning or change per se.

Incorporate Principles and Forms of Invitational Rhetoric

In highly controversial cases, marshaling your best arguments will probably not resolve disagreements. Take an issue such as euthanasia. Others may disagree heartily with your point of view, so you may find it more satisfying to practice **invitational rhetoric,** a form

Due to her courage and persistence in spite of house arrest, Nobel Peace Prize winner Aung San Suu Kyi of Myanmar (Burma) has great credibility in the movement to resist her country's dictators. (World Wide Photos).

of "sense making" identified by Sonia Foss and Cindy Griffin (1995). Rather than focusing on winning an argument, invitational rhetors invite their audiences to enter their world, understand it as they do, then present their own perspectives. Change may or may not result. Foss and Griffin identify three principles and two forms associated with invitational rhetoric.

Combining Three Principles

It's typical to think of traditional argument as verbal dueling in which one person wins the war of words; in contrast, invitational rhetoric focuses on mutual understanding and mutual influence that are based in the principles of equality, individual value, and self-determination.

1. **Equality:** Rather than trying to impose your "superior" views on others, as an invitational rhetor, you'll see your listeners as equals. You won't select strategies to overcome their resistance; however, you will identify possible barriers to understanding and try to minimize or neutralize them. In short, you'll be open to one another's viewpoints.

   For example, say it's an election year. Within your classroom are active supporters of three different candidates for president. You all have formulated what you think are good reasons for your choices. As an invitational rhetor, you share the path you've traveled in making your decision, and you invite your classmates to share theirs.

2. **Nonhierarchical Value of All**: By approaching your audience as equals, you respectfully look for the value in their conclusions as well as your own. You won't at-

tempt to demean their position and point out their deficiencies, and you'll try to maintain a positive relationship with those who differ from you.

Back to the election. By not seeing yourself as intellectually or morally superior by virtue of your viewpoints, you respectfully accept the value of your classmates' conclusions, and you try to see the point of their reasoning. There's no yelling, no put-downs, no character assassination of the various candidates.

3. **Self-Determination**: Invitational rhetoric may or may not result in change. If your listeners change their opinions or their behaviors, it won't be because you shamed or scared them into accepting your views. And you may modify your own positions as a result of their insights. In some instances, you and your listeners may agree to disagree while remaining respectful of one another.

You and your classmates may eventually split your votes, but regardless of who's elected, you will have insights into the reasoning involved in each position, and you may have learned more about working effectively in the political climate that will follow the election.

Including Two Forms

How does invitational rhetoric look in action? Two general forms are typical of this alternative way of approaching issues: (1) offering perspectives and (2) creating conditions that result in an atmosphere of respect and equality.

Offering Perspectives

Re-sourcement
Creatively framing a divisive issue or viewpoint in a different way that may be less threatening.

You explain what you currently understand or know, and you show a willingness to yield, examine, or revise your conclusions if someone offers a more satisfying perspective. When confronted with hostile or very divergent viewpoints, **re-sourcement** is one way to respond creatively by framing the issue in a different way.

If this sounds complicated, read Gail Grobey's speech found at the end of Chapter 15. By telling a narrative, Gail offers her perspective on not spanking children (to listeners who believed in spanking), and she reframes her daughter's discovery of a prescription pill. She calls it an act of heroism (saving the dog from danger) rather than accepting the ownership frame her daughter presents (it's mine, and you can't take it away).

Creating Conditions

Absolute Listening
Listening without interrupting or inserting oneself into the talk.

Reversibility of Perspectives
An attempt to think from the other's perspective as well as one's own.

When you practice invitational rhetoric, you use two basic means to create conditions in which your audiences can feel safe, valued, and free to offer their own perspectives. First, you use **absolute listening,** or listening without interrupting or inserting yourself into the talk; this allows others to discover their own perspectives. You hear people out without criticism or counterarguments. Second, you use **reversibility of perspectives.** As others present their ideas, you attempt to think from their perspectives rather than seeing only your own. The Native American saying "Don't judge people until you've walked a mile in their moccasins" demonstrates this perspective taking.

Invitational rhetoric, a form of reasoning that is often associated with women, is a model of cooperative, dialogical communication in which you and your audiences generate ideas. Because it is rooted in affirmation and respect, it's arguably an ethical way of coming to conclusions. Further, because you're not intent on controlling the ideas of others, you can disagree without going to war.

Summary

You draw upon a variety of reasoning strategies to make simple daily decisions or to argue about complex national policy questions. Although it is often impossible to prove a claim beyond any doubt, you have several methods of reasoning to support your ideas.

Toulmin's linear model of reasoning shows that claims of fact, value, and policy are based on various kinds of evidence, with a connecting link or warrant that justifies them. Listeners weigh the evidence, data, or grounds to see if it is sufficient and trustworthy enough to lead to the conclusion. To avoid overstating your claim, it is important to limit its scope by using qualifiers. Further, your arguments may be more persuasive if you rebut or counter the possible objections your listeners may have.

Aristotle presented three kinds of proofs thousands of years ago. The first, *logos,* or rational proof, comes from your words. Use analogies, both figurative and literal, to reason by comparison. Reason inductively by drawing generalizations or conclusions from a number of examples. Then, deductively apply these generalizations to particular cases. Finally, causal reasoning links things that exist in time in such a way that the second is a result of the first. All of these methods require the application of specific tests; otherwise, they may lead to fallacious or faulty conclusions.

Pathos, or emotional proofs, involves appeals to your listeners' positive and negative emotions as well as their needs. The chapter presented five basic needs: survival, security, belonging and love, esteem, and self-actualization. Emotions combine to form motivations that are both complex and mixed.

The third proof, *ethos,* comes from your personal credibility. To be believable, you should have good character, good sense, goodwill, and dynamism. Ethos varies across cultures.

Finally, an alternative way to make sense of complex issues is to practice invitational rhetoric based on equality, individual value, and self-determination rather than on control. You offer your perspectives and create conditions in which others are free to offer theirs. Use absolute listening and reversibility of perspectives as means of hearing and learning from the viewpoints of others. Change may or may not result.

Key Terms

data or grounds (361)

assertions (361)

warrant (361)

qualifiers (361)

rebuttal (362)

logos (363)

analogy (363)

reasoning by metaphor (363)

parallel case or literal analogy (365)

inductive reasoning (365)

deductive reasoning (366)

enthymeme (367)

causal reasoning (368)

fallacy (368)

unsupported assertion (368)

ad populum or bandwagon (369)

ad hominem (369)

false analogy (370)

post hoc (370)

overgeneralization (370)

red herring (370)

false dichotomy (370)

motivation (371)

pathos (371)

emotions (371)

proof (376)

ethos (376)

identification or co-orientation (377)

Access

WebTUTOR™

**for Audio Flashcards
of Key Terms**

common ground (377)

invitational rhetoric (378)

re-sourcement (380)

absolute listening (380)

reversibility of perspectives (380)

Application and Critical Thinking Questions

1. Find a letter to the editor in your local newspaper written by a citizen about a controversial topic. Identify the types of reasoning the author uses, then evaluate his or her arguments. Do they pass the tests for reasoning given in the text? Assess the effectiveness of the argument overall.

2. Find and discuss examples of reasoning that use emotional appeals—effectively and ineffectively. Look at letters to the editor (refer to Yan Hong Krompacky's letter in Chapter 14) or use ads from current magazines. What appeals do you find to positive and negative emotions? To needs?

3. Watch a law and order movie or show on television and see if you can diagram the argument or case against the suspect using Toulmin's model. Who is arrested? For what (the claim)? On what evidence (the data or grounds)? What's the warrant (the link: think causal reasoning, inductive reasoning, deductive reasoning, parallel case reasoning, testimony by a credible source, emotional arguments)? Is the claim or charge limited or qualified? What are rebuttal arguments (the defense)?

4. Read the speech that comes at the end of this chapter. Stop and answer the questions posed throughout.

5. With a small group within your classroom, make a list of possible speech topics that relate to each of the levels of need in Maslow's hierarchy.

6. With your classmates watch the classic movie *Twelve Angry Men* or *The Castle* (a 1999 movie from Australia) and focus on the persuasiveness of the arguments stemming from logical and emotional appeals and from the credibility of each speaker.

7. Visit the hot link site from the University of Richmond (see Hot Links) that connects you with sites related to computers in the classroom. Select either a pro or con position, and using the Toulmin model as your framework, work with a partner to create a complete argument. Then refute another set of partners in a classroom discussion.

Internet Activities

1. Log onto your *InfoTrac College Edition* and do a PowerTrac search for the journal *Argumentation and Advocacy*. Read an article related to *logos*, or rational proofs, that interests you there.

2. Use your *InfoTrac College Edition* PowerTrac feature to search for the key term *fallacy*. Read a "facts and fallacies"-type article about a subject that interests you, and identify the types of fallacies presented in it.

3. Stephen Toulmin is a major figure in argumentation. Go to a search engine such as www.alltheweb.com or www.dogpile.com and search for the exact term *Stephen Toulmin*. Find out more about this important thinker whose work is studied by beginning speakers across the nation and the globe.

4. Go to http://www.reagan.com/plate.main/ronald/speeches/rrspeech00.html. President Reagan was scheduled to present the State of the Union Address on January 28, 1986. However, the Space Shuttle Challenger exploded before the

stunned eyes of a watching nation (including many schoolchildren who were watching the first teacher launched into space), and Reagan delivered this speech instead. Read it, especially noticing how he adapts his argument for different groups within his national audience.

Hot Links at the Public Speaking Resource Center

The following links are maintained and can be accessed easily via Jaffe Connection at the Public Speaking Resource Center on the Wadsworth Communication Café web site at http://communication.wadsworth.com/publicspeaking/study.html

Public Speaking Resource Center

- http://www.homepages.dsu.edu/nelsonj/advcomp/analyzin.htm
  This page on analysis of audience needs was prepared by an composition professor who describes Maslow's hierarchy in greater depth.

- http://www.richmond.edu~educate/stohr/syllabi/readings.html
  This page, created by the University of Richmond Department of Education links to many sources, both pro and con, about using computers in the classroom.

STUDENT SPEECH

Sample Student Speech: The Benefits of Hunting, *Anonymous*

This speech contains both sound and faulty reasoning. To guide your analysis, stop throughout your reading and answer the questions inserted between points in the text.

Animals, I'm sure, have a place in everyone's heart. No one would like to see animals live pitiful lives and die by the hundreds from overpopulation and starvation. Well, this has happened before, and it could very well happen again if hunting is once again abolished by people who are uneducated about its true benefits.

If the welfare of animals means anything to you, it is essential that you listen closely to the biological facts that support hunting as being beneficial to wildlife, for, in order to conserve wildlife, we must preserve hunting.

In the next few minutes, I will tell you about the damages resulting when people's right to hunt in certain areas is taken away. I will inform you of the uneducated ideas of animal activists and, finally, explain the differences between hunters and poachers.

> ***a.*** *What about the use of the phrases "I'm sure," "everyone," and "no one"? What effect does the use of the term "uneducated" have?*
>
> ***b.*** *What claim is the speaker making?*

So many people are unaware of the damage that occurs to the wildlife when hunting is taken away from a particular area. The best example of this happened in the state of Massachusetts. There, an animal rights group rallied and petitioned against deer hunting. Their efforts led to the banning of hunting in Massachusetts. During the period in which deer hunting was allowed, the deer population was around 100,000. Within the first year after the law was enacted, the population soared to 150,000.

Sounds good? Well, it wasn't! The overabundance of deer created a famine. Deer began to eat forest trees, gardens, and roots. They ate down to the foliage, leaving the plants unable to grow back the next year. Three years after the law went into effect, the deer population went from 150,000 to only 9,000. It took the state 10 years to return the deer population to normal. Eventually, the hunting ban was reversed, and the deer population has remained at its carrying capacity. I think it is hunting that plays a major role in keeping species from overpopulation.

    c. *What kind of reasoning is the speaker using? Does it pass the tests? Do you think her conclusion is obvious? Why or why not?*

    d. *She says in her introduction that she will present biological facts about hunting. Does she do so to your satisfaction?*

People often argue that animals were fine before man invented guns. However, before the white men came over here with guns, there weren't sprawling cities like Los Angeles and Portland to take up most of the animals' habitat. In those days, there was far more land for the animals to live on. Today, modernization has pushed the animals into a smaller wildlife area, leaving them less food and less room for breeding. Therefore, it is easier for the animals to overpopulate. Hunting has played a major role in keeping the animal population at a normal number. If hunting is taken away, the animals are sure to overpopulate.

It has been proven that humankind, even in its earliest form, has always hunted animals. Here in North America, before white people and guns came over, Indians hunted animals on a consistent basis. They killed hundreds of buffalo by herding them over cliffs every year. They caught school after school of salmon that migrated up the rivers. These hunts have always played a major role in population management, whether or not you choose to label it as a law of nature.

    e. *What argument does the speaker attempt to rebut? Does she do so to your satisfaction?*

However, people argue that Indians needed to hunt animals to live; whereas, today's North Americans don't need to kill animals to survive. So what if we can survive on fruit and vegetables? Humans are born omnivorous, meaning it is natural for us to eat both meat and plants. What is inhumane about eating an animal for food? Weren't we designed to do so?

    f. *Here is the second argument she attempts to counter or rebut. How well does she do it? Explain your answer.*

People also argue that the laws of nature will take care of animals. Hunting has always been a major part of the laws of nature. Without mountain lions there to kill rabbits, the rabbit population would be a long-gone species because of overpopulation. Humans as well as mountain lions are animals. Our predation is as important to other animals, such as deer, as the mountain lion's predation is to rabbits.

    g. *What is the third argument the speaker attempts to refute? What kind of reasoning does she use?*

    h. *Which of the three arguments do you think she did the best job of refuting? Which argument did she refute the least adequately?*

Animal activists harass hunters all the time. These people have false perceptions of what hunting really is, and who hunters really are. At a rally against deer hunting a woman speaker argued that "Hunters are barbarians who are in it for the kill. Hunters would use machine guns if they could. Plus, the deer are so cute." I think that argument is pathetic and holds absolutely no validity.

Another instance of hunter harassment occurred at Yellowstone National Park. An animal activist was not satisfied with only verbal harassment, so he struck the hunter on the head twice. Are animal activists really the peaceful and humane people they claim to be? And they still believe that hunters are bloodthirsty, crazy, and inhumane!

    i. *Do these two examples pass the tests for their use? Are they typical? How does the speaker generalize from them? How might she make her point instead?*

Many of these misperceptions about hunters come from the association of hunters with poachers. Hunters are not poachers!

Poachers are people who kill animals when they want, regardless of laws and regulations that were set to protect the animals. These are the kind of people who hunt elephants for their ivory tusks or kill crocodiles for their skins. Poachers kill deer in areas that are off-limits, during off-limited hunting seasons. These people are criminals who are extremely harmful to wildlife.

Hunters would turn in a poacher in an instant if they caught one. Poachers give hunting a bad image in the eyes of the public. It's too bad that the animal activists don't go after the poachers who are extremely harmful to animals, and stop pointing a finger at hunters who follow the laws and regulations.

> *j.*   *Why does the speaker contrast hunters to poachers? In what ways, if any, is this an effective argument?*

If hunting is banned, just imagine a drive through the mountains on a road covered with emaciated skeletons of cadaverous deer who died of starvation. No longer can you take a picture of Bambi, your favorite deer that you saw every year at Yellowstone National Park. For Bambi and his family were overpopulated, and they slowly wilted away until their final day. Too bad there weren't a few healthy bucks taken by hunting that year to keep Bambi and family at a cozy carrying capacity where there was plenty of delicious food for all of them.

> *k.*   *Here, the speaker uses a great deal of pathos. Identify emotional language and images. Is this effective? Why or why not?*

The argument that animal activists use against hunting is fabricated mainly from emotions. If they are personally against killing an animal, I can respect that. But they have no place trying to ban hunting. It is proven by biological facts that hunting is necessary for wildlife management. It provides millions of dollars that fund the construction of programs that help wildlife. It keeps species from overpopulating and starving to death. In order for wildlife to flourish at an optimum population number, hunting must continue to be a major part of wildlife management.

> *l.*   *What does she put in her summary that does not appear anywhere else in her speech? If she had included it in the body of her speech and provided some evidence for that point, would her speech be stronger?*

Questions

Now answer the following questions about the speech as a whole:

1. Overall, how would you grade the reasoning in this speech? Defend your grade.

2. How would you assess this speaker's credibility? How knowledgeable does she seem to be, and why? Does she show good sense throughout? Where (if at all) does she demonstrate goodwill toward listeners? Is there any way to assess her good character? Where (if at all) does she identify with her listeners?

3. How might you respond if you were an animal activist in her audience?

4. Where did you feel you would like to see sources cited?

You can answer these questions online and if requested by your instructor, submit them via email. Go to Chapter 18: Activities for Jaffe Connection at the Public Speaking Resource Center, http://communication.wadsworth.com/ publicspeaking/study.html

Public Speaking Resource Center

SOURCE: This speech was given at Oregon State University, Corvallis, on March 6, 1992.

The ability to work well in small groups is essential because classrooms, businesses, and other organizations, here and abroad, regularly use cooperative work teams and groups to accomplish their work. In fact, in a recent survey conducted by Pennsylvania State University, 71.4 percent of corporate executives polled listed the ability to work in teams as a desirable quality in recent graduates (Galvin & Cooper, 2000). Task-oriented teams can produce excellent results, but they can also be dysfunctional and frustrating for participants, especially those who are unaware of the dynamics inherent in group work. This appendix first presents some advantages and disadvantages of group work. Next, it gives specific tips for working in two types of groups: investigative groups and problem-solving groups. A description of formats commonly used to present group findings publicly concludes this appendix.

Advantages and Disadvantages of Group Work

You've probably heard the saying "Two heads are better than one." In fact, some people who work on difficult problems believe "The more heads the better." However, if you're trying to accomplish a task with a group plagued by scheduling conflicts, dominating members, or nonparticipants, you may be tempted to work alone! Truth be told, the many advantages of group work must be balanced against the disadvantages.

Advantages of Groups

Groups and teams have several advantages (Beebe & Masterson, 1990; Cooper, 1995; Scott & Brydon, 1997):

- *Groups have access to more information and knowledge than do single individuals.* It stands to reason that the more people there are, the more experiences they've had and the more knowledge they have as a whole. For example, one person is an expert in one area, and another provides different expertise. Together, they pool their resources and generate more information than either one could produce individually.

- *The various viewpoints people bring to the group offer possibilities for more creative ideas to emerge.* By combining personalities and thinking and learning styles, the group as a whole can respond more creatively to an issue than if it relied on the ideas of one person. Diversity within a well-functioning group can also increase the members' understandings of multicultural perspectives.

- *Group work provides a deeper level of involvement and learning.* When all participants do research, discuss their findings with others, and listen to the information discovered by their teammates, they can do three to four times as much research in approximately the same time frame. In addition, during discussions they can ask and answer questions that clarify confusing ideas and sharpen their critical thinking skills. Consequently, many people learn better in small groups.

- *Many people enjoy working in small groups.* They are more motivated and have more positive attitudes when they don't have to deal with a subject or problem alone. In short, social interactions with others in the group make teamwork satisfying; not only do participants learn about an issue, they learn about one another.

- *Working in small groups results in the co-creation of meaning.* Because of the nature of information sharing and decision making, small groups are inherently dialogical. Ideally, all members participate in discussing, refining, and evaluating ideas and solutions.

Disadvantages of Groups

Despite their many advantages, group work carries with it a number of disadvantages you should recognize and avoid whenever possible.

- *Working in groups takes more time.* Scheduling meetings and working around the schedules of other busy people takes time that often frustrates task-oriented group members.

- *Some members of the group do more work than others.* It's true that some group members rely on others and do less work than they would if they were responsible for the entire project. The result is that hard workers often resent the slackers.

- *Some members of the group may monopolize the discussion and impose their ideas on others.* Dominators can take over a group for a number of reasons: One is linked to personality; some people are more extroverted and opinionated. Another is linked to gender; women often defer to men in mixed gender groups (Tannen, 1990).

- *There is a tendency toward groupthink* (Janik, 1971). Groupthink happens when the members pressure one another to conform to a decision (which may be unwise) in order to avoid conflict. A classic case occurred when President Kennedy and his advisors proceeded with the disastrous Bay of Pigs invasion of Cuba. Although an objective outsider might have predicted the unfortunate outcome, no one on the advisory team was willing to challenge the group's decision.

In summary, although group work offers many advantages, it also has disadvantages. However, these can be minimized by having group members be accountable to one another, by giving all members a chance to voice their opinion, and by avoiding agreement simply for the sake of peace.

Teaming up to Investigate a Subject

Educators commonly ask students to team up to study a subject and present what they've learned to the entire class. For example, Eisen (1998) reported that biology students learned to do "science thinking" in small groups, and their presentations of their findings honed organizational and speaking skills they'll use throughout their careers as scientists.

Investigative reporters (students and professionals alike) also team up to probe complex social issues. Because a seven-to-ten-minute report (described in Chapter 16) can only overview a controversy, many instructors ask students interested in a specific topic such as social security or the abolishment of recess to study the issue in teams. The group then presents their findings in an extended period of time. In addition, reporters for a newsmagazine such as *Newsweek* or *Time* commonly work together on a major feature. One or two write the actual story, but you can find names of additional contributors at the end of the article. You'll also find sidebars and smaller, supplementary stories alongside the featured one, each written by a different member of the investigative team.

The advantages of teamwork, explained earlier in this chapter, converge in investigative teams. Obviously, a team can cover a national issue in a national magazine much better than a single reporter can. Similarly, students typically learn more and become more involved in a subject when they investigate it with others. Besides, the group shares the research burden, allowing a particular student to focus mainly on one area. Not only do team members learn more, others in the class benefit from the variety of perspectives they hear and the in-depth coverage they get when the group shares its findings publicly.

To research and report a topic effectively, the team should have several meetings that progress from the initial getting acquainted with one another and the subject, moving through the research stage, and concluding with the final presentation.

DIVERSITY IN PRACTICE

Gender Tendencies in Group Interactions

In her book, *You Just Don't Understand: Women and Men in Conversation,* Deborah Tannen (1990, 2000) identifies several differences in the conversational styles associated with men and women. John Cowan (2000) traces these differences to boys' and girls' playground experiences that he humorously suggests were "at least a light-year apart" (p. 307). However, gender-associated characteristics are tendencies, not absolutes, and researchers who take a "gender similarities" approach suggest that men and women, especially college students, may be more alike than different (Grob, Meyers, & Schuh, 1997). Nevertheless, Tannen's conclusions are widely discussed, and tendencies, like these that follow, have implications for male-female communication in small-group contexts.

■ Men engage in "Report Talk." Their speaking is informative, and they rely more on facts, figures, and definitions, and less on personalized information. In contrast, women tend to engage in "Rapport Talk" that stresses relationships. They personalize their information with examples and stories.

■ Men's interactional goals are to gain power, status, and respect— whether or not they offend other group members. Women's goals, in contrast, are to help others and build relationships between people. They are less concerned about persuading others in the group.

■ Men speak in a "dominant way," meaning that they interrupt and display their knowledge and expertise. They also control the topic and set the agenda. On the other hand, women express more agreement, making connections and smoothing relationships. Cowan (2000) says that men offer "assertion followed by counterassertion," whereas women offer "inquiry followed by counterinquiry" (p. 307). Although women suggest more topics than men, men choose which topic to discuss.

■ Men explain more than women, and their explanations are lengthy. Women can and do explain, but they have fewer opportunities to do so in mixed gender groups.

■ Men speak more. Conversational time is one-sided in their favor. Women listen more and speak less in mixed gender groups.

To learn more about Professor Tannen's work, go online and visit her web page at http://www.georgetown.edu/tannen/, or go to www.alltheweb.com and search for the exact phrase *Deborah Tannen.* There you'll find interviews, excerpts from her books, and other interesting information about gender differences in communication that affect men's and women's talk in small groups.

First Meeting: Getting Acquainted

When you first gather, get to know one another and find out each person's interest in the topic. (This is a good time to exchange phone numbers or e-mail addresses.) Then have each person share his or her knowledge about the subject. Leadership can develop informally, or you can designate someone to guide the meeting and keep people on task. One important role is that of a **gatekeeper;** this person makes sure that quiet people participate and that no one dominates the discussion. Another important role is that of a **recorder,** a person who takes notes (minutes) on what transpires during the meeting.

During this meeting, divide your subject into subtopics and have each member select specific aspects to research in depth. For instance, you might include a definition, the history, numbers and types of people affected, regions or areas affected, proposed solutions, or arguments for and against each solution. If the group is to be successful, it must hold members accountable. Consequently, before your meeting breaks up, ask all present to identify the areas and specify the methods (interviews, library research) they will use to investigate their subtopics. Then set a date, place, and time (beginning and ending times) for the next meeting.

Additional Meetings: Discussing the Subject

Begin each new meeting by approving the minutes of the previous meeting. Organize your group's work; using an explicit **agenda** that lists in order the items you'll discuss is helpful. Proceed by holding team members accountable for summarizing their work and answering questions the others ask. After everyone has contributed, discuss the following: What questions do we still have as a group? Are there gaps in our research? If so, where? What patterns or recurring themes are we finding? Are we beginning to detect a way to organize our final presentation?

Continue to use the gatekeeper role and have important discussion items recorded in minutes. In every meeting, focus on your final goal, which is to present your material publicly. To achieve this objective, work together to organize and outline your material into a coherent form. Review organizational patterns in Chapter 9, and think of creative ways to introduce and conclude your presentation (Chapter 10). Identify possible visual aids (assigning a person to create each one), and put someone in charge of requesting the equipment you will need for your presentation.

Before the group separates, have everyone state specifically what he or she will do during the period before the next meeting to forward the goals of the group. Always conclude by agreeing on a date, place, and time for your next meeting.

Final Meeting: Polishing the Presentation

In previous meetings you have researched various aspects of a complex topic. You've also used skills from the canon of arrangement or organization to shape your final product. Now, get together in one last meeting to make sure all the details are finalized. Give each group member a written outline or other record of what you've done. Rehearse the final presentation to make sure everyone knows her or his role and to iron out any glitches that arise. Check that visuals are made and equipment is ordered, then congratulate one another on a job well done.

Teaming up to Solve a Problem

What is a problem? Professor Jack Henson (n.d.) defines a **problem** as *the difference between what is* (the present condition) and *what should be* (the goal). Put another way, a problem is the gap that exists between what we want and what we now have. Several years ago, Antioch College in Ohio confronted the issue of sexual offenses on campus by holding a two-year-long series of campuswide small-group discussions. Leaders announced the resulting policy on sexual behaviors with a flurry of media attention. Both parties on a date must give verbal and willing consent at each increasing level of physical intimacy—they should ask first, even for a kiss. By following these rules, people aren't forced to participate in sexual activity against their will.

Although their solution is atypical, Antioch College's problem represents the type of issue we discuss in organizations, on local, national, and global levels. Our challenges include child care on campus, wheelchair accessibility, global trade imbalances, elder abuse, safe water, and so on. When problems arise, we often form discussion groups, task forces, and committees in which we typically use a problem-solving method identified a hundred years ago by the educator John Dewey and modified several times since it was first explained.

The analytical, linear process of appraising problems and generating solutions presented here is typical of Euro-American culture. In many public contexts, following a structured, rather than a random, approach results in more effective group work. However, don't think of this process as strictly linear, proceeding from point to point in one direction only; your group may circle back to previous steps, and you may revise as you go along. What follows is a modification of John Dewey's original five steps.

Step One: Define the Problem

It's important at the outset to state the problem clearly. If you fail to do this, your work will be more difficult later, for it's hard to find a solution for something that is vague. Some problems are simple to define; for instance, "Whom shall we hire as the new basketball coach?" is easy to pinpoint when group members have in hand the previous coach's letter of resignation. However, many, even most, problems require narrowing the topic in ways similar to what you have done for your speeches throughout the term, following these three general suggestions:

- State the issue as a policy question, using the word *should*. For example, "Which athlete should we honor as outstanding gymnast? What should we do to prevent sexual offenses?

- Leave the question broad enough to allow for a variety of answers; put simply, use an open rather than a closed question. Thus, "Should the student council repair acts of vandalism in the student union building?" (yes or no) is less effective for group discussion than the more open question "How should the student council ensure that campus buildings remain free from vandalism?"

- State the question as objectively as possible, avoiding emotionally charged language. "How can we get rid of this unfair grading system?" is less effective than "What changes, if any, should be made in the current methods of assigning grades?"

Step Two: Analyze the Problem

After you know the problem, begin collecting pertinent information using the guidelines described in Chapters 7 and 8. Look for the facts—including causes and effects—values, and policies that relate to your topic. Divide the relevant issues among group members and have them consult oral, print, media, and Internet sources for information by asking questions such as these:

- What are the factual issues involved? What's the history of the problem?
- What causes the problem? Which are primary causes? Which are secondary factors that contribute to it?
- What effects result from the problem?
- What values apply? Is it wrong or right? In what respects?
- Are any relevant policies involved? Any historical precedents?

So far, your group has defined the problem and analyzed related issues. You have also explored facts, possible causes, and resulting effects of the problem; finally, you have analyzed underlying values and related historical policies. Now you're ready as a group to explore possible solutions.

Step Three: Set Criteria for Deciding on a Solution

Because solutions must be realistic in terms of time, money, and ease of enactment, set up standards for determining an acceptable solution before you even begin to suggest possible solutions. As part of your consideration, Charles Kepner and Benjamin Tregoe suggest two vital factors: (1) What must we do? That is, what is *required?* (2) What do we want to do? In other words, what is *desired?* By way of illustration, we must solve the problem with less than $10,000; we want to solve it with less than $5,000. We must have the policy in effect by the beginning of the next school year; we want to have it implemented by the end of the spring term. As you might imagine, when you work within budget and time constraints, you'll automatically rule out some solutions as too costly or too time consuming!

Step Four: List Possible Solutions

During this period, your group's task is to generate as many ideas as possible. Because you're seeking possibilities, don't worry if all these suggestions aren't practical. Hold your judgment until later. One common way to generate ideas is through the process of **brainstorming,** in which group members offer a number of ideas for consideration. Don't overlook a mind map as described in Chapters 5 and 7 as a valuable way to record these ideas. Here are some tips for a successful brainstorming session:

- Have a recorder write down all the ideas presented; a chalkboard, overhead transparency, or flip chart is helpful for this.
- Record all the ideas without judging any of them.
- Make sure that each person in the group has an opportunity to contribute at least once.
- Piggyback off one another's ideas—that is, encourage group members to use one proposal as a jumping-off point for another.

After a successful brainstorming session, in which you all generate a number of ideas, begin to evaluate each idea against the criteria you set up earlier. Often your brainstorming session will lead you to rethink your criteria. Don't hesitate to circle back and make revisions at this time.

Step Five: Select the Best Solution

So far, your group has a good idea of the problem—its causes, effects, and history. You've decided on what is necessary for a good solution, and you've generated a number of ideas. It's now time to select the best solution, so you begin to evaluate the suggested solutions against the criteria you've set. You'll probably eliminate some ideas easily, because they're too expensive, they are too time consuming, or they don't fit your criteria for other obvious reasons. After you have pared down your options, analyze and weigh the merits of those that remain in order to find the one that members of your group can agree on.

Presenting Your Group's Findings

Prepare to report on your findings—both in writing and orally. First, summarize the work you completed in each step. Then present the solution you've chosen, justifying your choice. Provide information on why you predict it will work, why it will be cost effective, and why it will be easy to implement. The next step is to present your findings to an audience who will probably be involved in its implementation. In general, there are three basic ways to present your conclusions.

A Final Report

When you choose this format, one member speaks for the entire group. A group giving an investigative report on a topic such as abolishing recess would all gather data and work together to write up their findings, but only one member of the group would actually speak publicly.

A problem-solving team would designate a presenter to define the problem and briefly explain background information related to it. Then, the presenter summarizes the decision-making process, identifies the criteria decided on for the solution, describes alternative solutions that were considered, and explains and justifies the group's final choice.

To illustrate, let's look at ways Antioch College might announce the new dating policy. To communicate with the college leadership as well as the public, the task committee writes a final report that details the procedures used and gives the underlying rationale for the decision. The committee chairperson then presents these to the board of trustees and to the student council for approval. A press release generated from the final report goes to newspapers in the area. Television stations pick up the story and send reporters to interview the committee spokesperson to gain additional information about the policy.

A Panel Discussion

In this format, all your group's members sit on a panel and discuss the issue in dialogical interactions. During your discussion, a leader or moderator asks a series of questions, and you take turns providing your insights on each one. In short, all members contribute from their store of information and opinions. Afterward, the moderator may open the discussion to the audience and encourage listeners to participate in a dialogue with panelists during a question-and-answer period. In this way, both your group and your audience cooperate in co-creating meaning.

A classroom group that had studied a current issue such as whether or not to abolish recess each does research on the topic. They all locate pro and con arguments, find examples of schools that had abolished recess and those that decided to keep it, get quotations from experts on both sides of the issue, interview schoolchildren and teachers, and discuss among themselves their personal experiences with recess periods. In a group planning meeting, they share their findings and identify a series of questions to discuss, then on the day of their presentation, each member contributes to each question during their group's allotted half hour. Afterwards, they invite audience questions.

The entire problem-solving group at Antioch College might appear in a town hall session at the college. There, in a free-flowing manner, each committee participant would discuss the policy and the process the group went through to reach it; the committee chair acts as emcee. After the proposal is presented, audience members ask questions regarding implementation, consequences for breaking the rules, and so on.

A Symposium

In this format, each member of the group selects only one aspect of the problem and prepares and delivers a speech about it. After all the speakers have finished, the moderator usually opens up the floor for a question-and-answer period from the audience.

If a group investigating the topic of abolishing recess chooses a symposium format, their presentation would divide the topic into smaller topics, and each person would discuss only one. The first speaker could lead off by telling the history of recess; the second might overview the controversy surrounding recess. The third presenter might give a case study of a school that decided to abolish recess, and a fourth could relate a case study of a school that kept recess—after almost canceling it. The final speaker summarizes the issue. After they've all finished, a moderator opens up the floor for a question-and-answer period from the audience.

To inform parents of Antioch College's new policy, the committee might present a symposium during Parents' Weekend. Interested family members come to hear four task group members discuss the policy. The first discusses the history of the problem. The next speaker describes the campuswide discussions that took place over a two-year period. Another committee member details the specifics of the new dating code, and the final speaker tells why the committee believes this solution is workable. Parents are then encouraged to ask questions.

Appendix B: Speaking on Special Occasions

Special occasion speaking occurs at celebrations, more solemn occasions, and occasions that reaffirm group values. These speeches share the general purposes common to all public speaking: to inform, to persuade, to entertain. But an important additional function, called the *integrative function* (Goodall & Phillips, 1984), helps bind members of the organization to one another and connects them firmly to their shared goals. This type of persuasive speaking reinforces and maintains the common belief-attitude-value cluster that influences the specific actions of group members.

This appendix provides guidelines for speeches of introduction, farewell, announcement, award presentation and acceptance, nomination, and commemoration or goodwill. Diversity in Practice on the next page describes some features of organizational culture that can affect your speech.

Introductions

Whenever people meet for the first time, they seek information about one another, and speeches of introduction enable strangers to have the knowledge they need in order to interact effectively. Introductions, thus, answer the audience's question, "Who is this person?" You may introduce a classmate, a newcomer to your workplace, or a speaker at a special event. Regardless of the type of introduction, keep your remarks brief. Chapter 2 provided guidelines for introducing a classmate. Here are some tips for introducing an unfamiliar person into your school or work environment.

- Provide the newcomer's name and job title.

- Give a few relevant details about the educational and occupational background as well as the personal characteristics the new person brings to the group or organization.

- Close by welcoming the newcomer to the group.

Here is a sample introduction of a student life employee, new to the campus. Notice that it briefly presents her qualifications and provides the students, to whom she's a stranger, information about her background and some of her interests that will help them relate to her.

We are pleased to welcome a new Director of Student Life for the university: Janeen Bronstein. Janeen received both her bachelor's and master's degrees from Brandeis University. As an undergraduate, she decided upon a career in student life, so she worked as a resident advisor in her university's dormitories, and during two summers she administrated camping programs in upstate New York. She sought out activities that would give her a broad national and international perspective; for example, she spent a summer in Washington, D.C., where she was an intern in the Justice Department. That makes sense. One of her roles at the university will be to help us work out our problems and disputes. Prior to coming here, she served as Director of Student Life at our sister campus in Japan. Fortunately for us, she decided to trade in Toyko's subway crush for the complex freeway system of our metro area. Janeen comes with the highest recommendations from both the administrators and the students with whom she's worked.

Janeen, welcome. We know you will continue your tradition of interpersonal and administrative excellence and will be a wonderful addition to our student life staff.

To introduce a guest speaker, include some information about the occasion that precipitated the invitation as well as about the actual speaker. Here are some elements to include in such speeches:

- Greetings and/or a welcome to the group

- A statement about the occasion

- Announcement of the speaker's name and subject

- A brief account of the speaker's background, education, training, achievements, personality, or any other salient information that relates to the topic or the audience

DIVERSITY IN PRACTICE

Organizational Culture

When you apply the concept of culture to organizations, you conceive of the organization as a small society within the dominant culture. And you understand that the organizational culture is comprised of the group's history, politics, and economic system as well as art, music, dress, language, and rituals that members of the culture know and newcomers must learn. Consequently, an organization's cultural environment includes (Pacanowsky & O'Donnell-Trujillo, 1983):

- **History**—the founders, the founding date, the founding mission

- **Political system**—the way power is distributed, who leads and who follows, and when

- **Distribution of wealth**—pay equity, merit pay, bonuses, stock options, and dues or collections

- **Art and music and dress**—group logos, songs, or uniforms

- **Language**—jargon or special in-group terminology

- **Rituals**—banquets, picnics, award ceremonies, installations, commencements

- **Folklore**—the narratives and myths, the heroes and villains, described in the stories passed from person to person within the organization (Bormann, 1985).

These last two aspects of culture are particularly relevant to public speaking. W. B. Ouchi (1998), author of *Theory Z: How American Business Can Meet the Japanese Challenge,* underlines the fact that an organization's symbols, ceremonies, and myths communicate the beliefs and values of the group. The organizational narratives—told and retold from generation to generation—explain what is valued, believed, and remembered. Knowing these symbols and stories is an important part of understanding the organization; using them in public speaking can act as a powerful form of proof to members of the organization. You can read a special occasion speech given by William Ouchi online at http://208.215.167.139/sij-98-12/keynote03.htm

Afterwards, be prepared to make a few brief remarks that provide closure. Briefly thank the speaker, and make a simple, short remark relating to the central idea of the speech. For further information about introductions, the website located at http://ecglink.com/newsletter/introspk.html presents a good checklist.

Farewells

Saying good-bye is never easy; departures result in a disruption that affects those left behind, to a greater or lesser degree. This is true whether or not the person was well liked. For example, consider the varied emotions that arise when a popular professor leaves for a position in another university, a beloved rabbi retires, an unpopular manager is fired, the seniors on the football team graduate. All these departures signal changes in the social patterns of an organization. Because of this, farewell speeches function to ease the inevitable changes facing both the departing individual and the group.

People who leave give farewell speeches, and a remaining member of the organization says good-bye for the group. Both speakers should express emotions, especially appreciation, sadness, hope for the future, and affection for the other members of the group. Balance the sadness inherent in the occasion by remembrances of happy times; recounting humorous stories is one way to do this.

When you bid a group farewell because you are leaving, include some or all of these elements:

- Remind group members of what they've meant to you personally.
- List some lessons you learned from being with them.
- Tell humorous stories that you'll carry with you as happy memories.
- Express both your sadness at leaving and your hopes for the future.
- Invite people to write or visit you in your new location.

When you bid farewell to a departing member or members of an organization, you speak not only for yourself but also for the group. Remember these elements in your speech:

- Recognize the person's accomplishments that benefited the group.
- Recognize positive personal characteristics that you will remember.
- Use humorous anecdotes.
- Express your personal sadness and the group's sense of loss.
- Wish the person well in his or her new location.
- When appropriate, present a gift as a remembrance.

Announcements

Announcements are brief speeches that keep individuals and groups knowledgeable about the goings-on of organizations and groups to which they belong by providing facts about upcoming events or developments of interest to a specific audience. In clubs and organizations, churches and faculty meetings, announcements are an agenda staple because they answer the questions, "What's happening?" or "What's new?"

Essential to these short speeches are details regarding the who, where, when, and how much it costs, as the following outline of essential points shows:

- First, draw your listeners' attention to the event.
- Provide such details as who, what, when, and where the event takes place.

■ Give both the cost and the benefits of attending.

■ End with a brief summary of important information.

Here's a sample announcement:

> Remember when you were a little kid, and figures from the Peanuts cartoon strip were everywhere? I had a Snoopy tee shirt and couldn't wait for the annual "Great Pumpkin" show on TV. Well, you can return briefly to these beloved characters from childhood if you attend the campus production of "You're a Good Man, Charlie Brown."
>
> This play will be performed April 8 through 12 at Woodmar Theater here on campus. Evening performances begin at 8:00 P.M. In addition, there will be 3:00 matinee performances on Saturday and Sunday afternoons. Tickets are $10.00—$5.00 with your student body card. You can purchase them in advance at the ticket window in Bauman Auditorium, or you can purchase them at the door at the time of the performance. This is a small price to pay for an evening with such memorable characters as Linus and Lucy.
>
> Remember, "You're a Good Man, Charlie Brown," April 8 to 12, with both evening and weekend matinee performances. You can get your tickets at the ticket office or at the door. It's worth it all just to see Snoopy dance!

Award Presentations

Award rituals express the common values of a group. Ordinarily, we recognize individuals for meritorious work or for character traits that embody our ideals. It's common to present recipients with a permanent memento of some sort. When you present an award, emphasize the shared beliefs, values, and commitments of the group. In general, award presentations include similar elements:

■ Name the award and describe its significance. What personal traits or accomplishments does it honor? In whose name is it made? Why is it given? How often is it awarded? How are the recipients selected?

■ Summarize the reasons the recipient was selected to receive the award.

■ Relate the appropriateness of the award to the traits of the recipient.

■ Express good wishes to the recipient.

In some cultures, groups rarely single out one individual to praise over others. (New Zealanders, for instance, have the saying "The tall poppy gets mown down.") Consequently, the members of these groups tend to feel uncomfortable having their personal characteristics publicly acknowledged; knowing this, present the award or honor to the entire group rather than to an individual.

Acceptance Speeches

Accept an award with a brief speech in which you express gratitude to those who selected you, thank other people who helped you become eligible for such an honor, and reinforce the cultural values that the award demonstrates, as these guidelines and sample acceptance speech show.

■ Thank those who honored you.

■ Acknowledge others who helped you get it.

■ Personalize what it means to you.

■ Express appreciation for the honor.

Thank you Professor Geffner for those kind words, and thank you, committee, for selecting me as the Outstanding Speech and Hearing Student this year. As you know, there are many other students who are deserving of honor for their scholarship and their service to the clients in our speech clinic, and I know that each one deserves to receive recognition.

Of course, no student can accomplish anything were it not for the support of a dedicated faculty—and the faculty we have here at St. John's University has been outstanding. I have been impressed, not only with their academic credentials, but also with the personal interest each one takes in the lives of each student who majors in speech pathology and audiology. Thanks also to my parents, who supported me both financially and emotionally through these past four years. I appreciate you all.

Next year I will be attending graduate school at Northwestern University. I'm sure that when I'm homesick for New York, I will remember this honor and be inspired by your confidence in me.

Thank you once again.

Nominations

Whenever you may have the opportunity to nominate a candidate for an elected office, think of the nomination as a short persuasive speech that does two things: It introduces your candidate to the group, and it presents brief arguments explaining why she or he should be elected. Be sure to:

■ Name the office, and tell its importance to the organization as a whole.

■ List the reasons why the candidate is right for the office.

Because a nomination is a persuasive speech, two organizational patterns discussed in Chapter 17 work especially well: a direct method or statement of reasons pattern and a criteria satisfaction pattern, as these two brief outlines demonstrate:

Vote for Trung Vo-Vu for the office of treasurer.

  I. He has been the treasurer of three organizations.

 II. He is a business major.

III. He has worked part-time in a bank, and he understands money management.

A president must have three important traits.

  I. She must have demonstrated leadership ability.

 II. She must be able to represent the organization to outside groups.

III. She must have the ability to lead people to consensus when opinions differ.

Gisella Cassalino excels in all three areas.

  I. She has been vice-president of this organization and currently serves as president of the county's Partners with Disabilities organization.

 II. She is a communication major who gives public presentations with ease.

III. She has served on a committee that mediates student grievances.

Commemorative Speeches

Commemorative speeches emphasize the common ideals, history, and memories the participants hold. Although the basic purpose of commemorative speeches is to inspire listeners by reinforcing their beliefs and values, they are often entertaining as well.

Frequently, guest speakers give commemorative speeches. In addition to reinforcing the ideals of the group to which they speak, they also aim to create or increase goodwill toward the organization they represent. A single large corporation may provide speakers for more than 1,000 events annually. You can hear goodwill speeches at breakfast, luncheon, and dinner meetings or at conventions and commencement ceremonies.

Although each speech is different, they all share some characteristics; speakers typically follow these guidelines:

■ **Build the speech around a theme.** Find out in advance if one has been selected for the meeting; if so, prepare your remarks around it. If not, select your own inspiring theme. Farah Walters (1992), President and Chief Executive Officer, University Hospitals of Cleveland, explains her theme in this excerpt from a keynote address she gave before an organization called WomenSpace.

Before preparing these remarks, I asked the leadership of WomenSpace if there was anything special that I should address. I was told that there might be some interest in learning a little more about who I am and how I got to be the head of one of America's largest academic medical centers; and I was asked if I would give my assessment of where women are today in the professional world, and where I think women will be in the years ahead. I will touch upon those topics, but in a particular context. And that context is in the title of my talk—"In Celebration of Options."

■ **Inspire listeners.** Inspiration is often linked to positive emotions and values such as hope, courage, respect, perseverance, and generosity. See how many positive emotions and values you can identify in this excerpt from Barbara Bush's (1990) commencement address at Wellesley College.

Wellesley, you see, is not just a place, but an idea, an experiment in excellence in which diversity is not just tolerated, but is embraced. . . . Diversity, like anything worth having, requires effort. Effort to learn about and respect difference, to be compassionate with one another, to cherish our own identity, and to accept unconditionally the same in others. You should all be very proud that this is the Wellesley spirit.

■ **Pay special attention to language.** In order to make your speech both inspiring and memorable, select words and phrases that are vivid, moving, and interesting. Begin by describing scenes in detail in order for your hearers to form images in their minds; select words that are rich in connotative meanings. This excerpt from President John Kennedy's (1988) inaugural address shows the power of inspiring language.

And so, my fellow Americans; ask not what your country can do for you—ask what you can do for your country.

My fellow citizens of the world; ask not what America will do for you, but what together we can do for the freedom of man.

Finally, whether you are citizens of America or citizens of the world, ask of us here the same high standards of strength and sacrifice which we ask of you. With a good conscience our only sure reward, with history the final judge of our deeds, let us go forth to lead the land we love, asking His blessing and His help, but knowing that here on earth God's work must truly be our own.

■ **When it is appropriate, use humor.** For certain speeches, such as after-dinner speeches whose major purpose is to entertain, humor is almost essential. This example comes from the beginning of Donald Keough's (1993) commencement address at Emory University.

President Laney and faculty and new graduates and nongraduates and those who would be graduates except you still have overdue library books and outstanding library fines; those who parked their cars three years ago and are still searching for them; family, friends, high school teachers who said you'd never amount to a thing—and you wish they were here so they could see you now in these black robes that make you look like Supreme Court justices; relatives who wish you well, parents and spouses who sold the family silver and took out second mortgages to get some of you here, I am honored and proud and delighted to be a part of Emory University's 148th commencement.

■ **Be relatively brief.** These speaking occasions are generally not times to develop an extensive policy speech or to provide detailed information. Rather, they are times to reinforce important values and to state major themes.

In summary, special occasion speeches function to integrate the members of the group to one another and with the community in which they exist. You'll hear these talks in a variety of organizations—from clubs and volunteer associations to business, educational, and religious institutions. You may have numerous opportunities to introduce newcomers, present awards, give announcements, and make other short speeches on special occasions.

The Solitude of Self: An example of the wave pattern (Chapter 9)

Elizabeth Cady Stanton *(From an analysis by Cheryl Jorgensen-Earp)*

A fine example of a repetitive pattern is found in this speech, delivered before the Senate Committee on Woman's Suffrage in 1892. Stanton's introduction previews the four general subtopics she will cover. Each subtopic is followed by a number of major points, and each major point is developed by examples. The following is a sample of three of her major points (the "crests" of the wave in the wave pattern) and the examples she uses to tie them together. There is an intense use of repetitive style even in her examples.

Major point: Seeing then, that life must ever be a march and a battle, that each soldier must be equipped for his own protection, it is the height of cruelty to rob the individual of a single natural right.

To throw obstacles in the way of a complete education is like putting out the eyes;
To deny the rights of property, like cutting off the hands.
To deny political equality is to rob the ostracized of all self-respect;
    of credit in the market place;
    of recompense in the world of work;
    of a voice in those who make and administer the law;
    a choice in the jury before whom they are tried,
    and in the judge who decides their punishment.
Shakespeare's play Titus Andronicus contains a terrible satire on woman's position in the 19th century. Rude men (the play tells us) seized the king's daughter, cut out her tongue, cut off her hands, and then bade her go call for water and wash her hands.

Major point: What a picture of woman's position! Robbed of her natural rights, handicapped by law and custom at every turn, yet compelled to fight her own battles, and in the emergencies of life to fall back on herself for protection.

The girl of sixteen, thrown on the world to support herself;
    to make her own place in society,
    to resist the temptations that surround her
    and maintain a spotless integrity.
She does not acquire this power by being trained to trust others and distrust herself. If she wearies of the struggle, finding it hard work to swim up-stream, and allows herself to drift with the current, she will find plenty of company, but not one to share her misery in the hour of her deepest humiliation. If she tries to retrieve her position,
    to conceal the past,
    her life is hedged about with fears
    lest willing hands should tear the veil from what she fain would hide.
Young and friendless, she knows the bitter solitude of self.

Major point: How the little courtesies of life on the surface of society, deemed so important from man towards woman, fade into utter insignificance in view of the deeper tragedies in which she must play her part alone, where no human aid is possible.

Stanton's speech contains a number of major wave crests, rather than a single recurring theme. This demonstrates how variable the wave pattern can be. It may have many major points supported by small waves, a few major points supported by large waves, or a mixture of the two.

Source: Jorgensen-Earp, C. R. (n. d.). Making other arrangements: Alternative patterns of disposition (pp. 2–3). Student handout, Lynchburg College, Lynchburg, VA.

El Equipo Perfecto (The Perfect Team): A speech given in Spanish and interpreted in the classroom (Chapter 13)

Uriel Plascencia; *interpreter, Heather Hunt*

Uriel's first language is Spanish, and he prepared a narrative speech (Chapter 15) in Spanish then, in advance of the speech, he worked with a fellow student, going over his speech with her. On the day he spoke, she translated his words as he paused between ideas. One key to speaking through an interpreter is for Uriel to look directly at the audience at all times and to speak in his natural rate. Immediately, as Heather finishes one phrase, he should go right into the next. He might want to use fairly long phrases in some places and short phrases in others, depending on the point he wants to make. An interpreted speech sounds like this:

Cuando estaba en mi último año de Preparatoria, yo tuve buenos amigos. Nuestra amistad era muy fuerte que estabamos juntos much tiempo. (When I was a senior in high school, I had some very good friends. Our friendship was so strong that we spent a lot of time together.) Nosotros éramos como un equipo en todos los aspectos porque estábamos en las mismas clases, hacíamos juntos nuestra tarea, practicábamos deportes y platicabamos mucho. Nosotros nunca tuvimos problemas serios. (We were like a team in all aspects because we spent time in classes doing our homework, playing sports, and talking. We never seemed to have any serious problems.)

En el principio del segundo semestre, se abrió un campeonao de voleibol. (In the beginning of the second semester, there were openings for intramural volleyball.) Yo no pensaba estar en estos juegos porque yo estaba muy ocupado con mis estudios. (I didn't think about being in those games because I was very busy with my studies.) Dos de mis amigos hicieron un equipo y me invitaron a formar parte del equipo, yo acepté estar en el equipo. (Two of my friends made a team and they invited me to be a part of the team; I decided to play with them.) Ellos me dijeron la hora y el día de huestros partidos. (They told me the time and the days that we were supposed to play.) Un día, ellos me llamaron por telefono para saber si yo iba a venir al partido y yo les dije que sí. (One day, they called me to find out if I was coming to the game, and I said yes.) Antes del partido, ellos me dijeron que yo iba a jugar el segundo juego. (Before the game, they told me that I was going to play the second set.) Cuando ellos terminaron de jugar el primer juego, yo fui a la cancha para hacer cambios y ellos no quisieron cambiarme. (When they finished playing the first set, I came to the court to switch players, and they didn't want to switch the team.) Ellos no quisieron que yo jugara con ellos. (They didn't want me to play with them.) Yo me sentí in poco mal y trate de entenderlos porque nosotros teniamos planes para el futuro. (I felt a little bad, and I tried to understand because we had plans for the future.) Ellos ganaron el juego y nos fuimos juntos de ahí. Ellos no se disculparon y no me dijeron nada acerca de esto. (They won the game and we left from there together. They didn't apologize or even talk to me about it.)

Ellos me volvieron a llamar por teléfono para saber si yo iba a venir a los juegos finales y yo dije que sí. Yo fui muy emocionado a los juegos finales porque yo quería que fueramos los campeones. (They called me again to find out if I was coming to the finals and I said yes again. I came to the game very excited because I wanted to win the finals.) Antes del juego, ellos me dijeron qua yo iba a jugar el segundo juego. Ellos me volvieron hacer la misma cosa que la ultima vez. (Before the game, they told me that I was going to play the second set. They made me the same promise as the last time.) Yo fui a la cancha para hacer cambios y ellos no quisieron cambiarme. (I came to the court to switch with another player, but then they didn't want to switch.) Ellos me rechazaron enfrente de muchas personas porque habia mucha gente durante los juegos finales. (They rejected me in front of many people because there were a lot of people during the finals.) Ellos insinuaron que no me necesitaban. (They meant they didn't need me.) Yo estaba muy decepcionado y me sentí muy estúpido enfrente de ellos. Yo me fui de la cancha y no pude entender por que ellos me hicieron esto. (I was very disappointed and I felt so stupid in front of them. I left from the court, and I couldn't understand why they made this promise to me.) Nosotros no habíamos tenido problemas y no supe cuál era el problema. (We hadn't had any problems, and I didn't know what was wrong.) Yo me esperé para ver si ellos banaban (I waited there to see if they would win,) pero no ganaron y me fui imediatamente de ahí. (but they didn't and I left immediately.)

Yo estaba pensando todo el día acerca de cual fue el problema porque yo pensaba que nuestra amistad era más fuerte que un estupido juego. (I thought the whole day about what was wrong because I believed our friendship was stronger than a stupid game.) Ellos no podían decir que yo era un mal jugador porque yo era mejor que ellos. (They couldn't say that I was a bad player, because I was actually a better player.) Yo me sentí muy triste porque ellos no me habían hecho algo como esto antes. (I felt very bad because they had made a promise like this before.) Yo trate de entender la situacion pero no pude. (I was trying to understand the situation but I couldn't.)

Al siguiente día, (the next day) uno de mis amigos me estaba buscando para disculparse. El sabía lo que hizo y trato de explicarme y disculparse. (one of these friends was looking for me to apologize. He knew what he had done and he tried to explain to me and apologize.) Yo lo perdoné. (I forgave him.) Cuando me amigo trato de disculparse, yo no lo estaba escuchando. Yo estaba escuchando mi corazon y a Dios. (When my friend was trying to apologize, I didn't listen to him. I was listening to my heart and God.) Yo aprendí de Dios a perdonar y esta es la razon por que yo lo perdone. (I learned from God to forgive, and this is the reason why I forgave him.) Nosotros somos amigos otra vez. (We are friends again.) El aprendió una lección y estoy seguro que él no lo volverá a hacer a nadie. (He learned a lesson, and I am sure that he won't do this again to anybody.)

The Twenty-Fifth Amendment: An informative speech that was memorized and videotaped (Chapter 14)

Jaffe Speech
Interactive

Loren Rozokas; *American Legion Oratorical Contest Award Winner.*

You can watch speech on Jaffe Speech Interactive on the Jaffe Connection CD-ROM.

Riding only two cars behind President John F. Kennedy through the streets of Dallas, Texas, on November 22, 1963, Vice President Lyndon B. Johnson could hear the shots that killed his chief. Before the day was over, Johnson was sworn in as President of the United States and assumed command in the nation's capital.

The road to ratification of the 25th Amendment proved a long journey. The amendment, which addresses presidential chain of command, in case of death or resignation by a President, was noted in the original constitution, but the wording was vague and led to confusion in its interpretation.

Perhaps the problem stemmed from the fact that the office of vice president was only important in the event of the death of the president.

From the very beginning, the founding fathers provided that executive power would rest in the hands of the president. They created the office of vice president, almost as an afterthought, in order to provide for a successor should the president die or resign. While they provided the vice president with an auspicious title, the power they provided was limited.

Some delegates at the convention, such as Massachusetts' Elbridge Gerry, felt the whole idea of a vice president was unnecessary. His opposition was so intense that he refused to sign the constitution. Interestingly enough, he later served as vice president under James Madison.

Even the election of the vice president was dubious. In the beginning, the top two contenders ran against each other; one became president, while the runner up settled for a job with no power.

Because so many of the top office seekers did not get along, this caused great friction. Many vice presidents were virtually ignored by the chief executive in power.

As second in command, in 1880, Chester A. Arthur noted, "Being vice president isn't the most comfortable position to hold, you are a man waiting to fill another man's shoes." Within months of this statement, Chester Arthur got a chance to try those shoes on when his chief commander, James Garfield, died in September 1881.

Article 2, Section 6, of the Constitution was so obscure in its definition that when William Henry Harrison died in 1841, only a month after his inauguration, a problem immediately arose. John Tyler assumed the presidency. Congress believed Tyler was acting as the president, but, in fact, was not a true president. Tyler contended that, if he had the presidency, then he was indeed the president.

Research by constitutional historians, poring over the minutes and notes of the original drafters, determined that Tyler was wrong in his assumption. The early constitution made no provision whatsoever that a vice president would become the top officer in the land upon the death, resignation, or removal of the president.

In short, Presidents Tyler, Fillmore, Johnson, Arthur, Roosevelt, Coolidge, Truman, and Johnson were not constitutionally certified presidents when they assumed the presidency as vice presidents. In fact, they were only acting presidents. Of all the presidents to succeed the office because of a vacancy, only Gerald Ford was bona fide president because of the ratification of the 25th Amendment.

This item of presidential succession took 127 years to clear up.

An Indian's View of Indian Affairs: An example of narrative reasoning (Chapter 15)

Chief Joseph

Chief Joseph of the Nez Percé Indian tribe told this story on January 14, 1879, before a large gathering of cabinet officers, congressional representatives, diplomats, and other officials. His speech shows that Congress has good reasons to act in behalf of his people.

My name is In-mut-too-yah-lat-lat (Thunder Traveling over the Mountains). I am chief of the Wal-lam-wat-kin band of Chute-pa-lu, or Nez Percé (nose-pierced Indians). I was born in eastern Oregon, thirty-eight winters ago. My father was chief before me. . . .

Our fathers gave us many laws, which they had learned from their fathers. These laws were good. They told us to treat all men as they treated us; that we should never be the first to break a bargain; that it was a disgrace to tell a lie; that we should speak only the truth; that it was a shame for one man to take from another his wife, or his property without paying for it. We were taught to believe that the Great Spirit sees and hears everything, and that he never forgets . . . .

We did not know there were other people besides the Indian until about one hundred winters ago, when some men with white faces came to our country. They brought many things with them to trade for furs and skins. They brought tobacco, which was new to us. They brought guns with flint stones on them, which frightened our women and children. Our people could not talk with these white-faced men, but they used signs which all people understand. These men were Frenchmen, and they called our people "Nez Percé," because they wore rings in their noses for ornaments. Although very few of our people wear them now, we are still called by that name. . . . Our people were divided in opinion about these men. Some thought they taught more bad than good. An Indian respects a brave man, but he despises a coward. He loves a straight tongue, but he hates a forked tongue. The French trappers told us some truths and some lies.

The first white men of your people who came to our country were named Lewis and Clark. They also brought many things that our people had never seen. They talked straight, and our people gave them a great feast, as a proof that their hearts were friendly. These men were very kind. They made presents to our chiefs, and our people made presents to them. We had a great many horses, of which we gave them what they needed, and they gave us guns and tobacco in return. All the Nez Percé made friends with Lewis and Clark, and agreed to let them pass through their country, and never to make war on white men. This promise the Nez Percés have never broken. No white man can accuse them of bad faith, and speak with a straight tongue. It has always been the pride of the Nez Percé that they were the friends of the white men. When my father was a young man there came to our country a white man [Reverend Mr. Spaulding] who talked spirit law. He won the affections of our people because he spoke good things to them. At first he did not say anything about white men wanting to settle on our lands. Nothing was said about that until about twenty winters ago, when a number of white people came into our country and built houses and made farms. At first our people made no complaint. They thought there was room enough for all to live in peace, and they were learning many things from the white men that seemed to be good. But we soon found that the white men were growing rich very fast, and were greedy to possess everything the Indian had. My father . . . had suspicion of men who seemed anxious to make money. I was a boy then, but I remember well my father's caution.

Next there came a white officer [Governor Stevens], who invited all the Nez Percés to a treaty. . . . He said there were a great many white people in our country, and many more would come; that he wanted the land marked out so that the Indians and white men could be separated. If they were to live in peace it was necessary, he said, that the Indians should have a country set apart for them, and in that country they must stay. My father, who represented his band, refused to have anything to do with the council, because he wished to be a free man. He claimed that no man owned any part of the earth, and a man could not sell what he did not own.

Mr. Spaulding took hold of my father's arm and said, "Come and sign the treaty." My father pushed him away, and said, "Why do you ask me to sign away my country? It is your business to talk to us about spirit matters and not to talk to us about parting with our land." Governor Stevens urged my father to sign his treaty, but he refused. "I will not sign your paper," he said. "You go where you please, so do I; you are not a child, I am no child; I can think for myself. No man can think for me. I have no other home than this. I will not give it up to any man. My people would have no home. Take away your paper. I will not touch it with my hand . . . ."

Chief Joseph continues the speech, detailing years of treaty negotiations between the Nez Percé and the whites. His conclusion recognizes that the inevitable has happened; his people are powerless against the white settlers. But his final plea is for equal justice under law for the Indian as well as for whites.

Source: From Indian oratory: Famous speeches by noted Indian chieftains, by W. C. Vanderwerth. Copyright © 1971 by the University of Oklahoma Press, pp. 259–284.

Microwave Ovens: Another example of a content outline (Chapter 11)

Mike Moody

Mike, an engineering major, gave this speech in his introductory speaking class. He arranged with his physics professors to use an animated computerized model of a microwave oven, which he displayed on a terminal that was large enough for his classmates to see (Chapter 12). His challenge with a technical topic was to translate the jargon into clear terminology (Chapter 13) and to present his information in an interesting and understandable way (Chapter 16). Remember that a content outline does not record everything Mike says. He elaborated on each point and used gestures such as rubbing together his hands to review the concept of friction.

General Purpose: To inform

Specific Purpose: To inform my audience about how microwave ovens work and about corresponding effects associated with them.

Central Idea: Microwave ovens cook from the inside out rather than the outside in as with conventional ovens.

I. Introduction
   A. The microwave oven is a very popular household appliance today.
      1. As the August 1996 issue of *Consumer Reports* magazine says, 20 years ago, fewer than 8% of America's households had a microwave oven; today, about 90% do.
      2. The September 1996 issue of *Food Processing* magazine reports that more than 80% of the 7 million ovens sold annually in the U.S. are purchased as replacements.

   B. You've all probably seen and used microwave ovens and you know what would happen to this bag if I left the oven on long enough.
      Visual aid [bag that has been in an oven too long].
      1. Do you know why?
      2. Like many devices we use, the microwave oven is a mystery that consumers simply take for granted.
   C. I learned the theory behind microwave ovens in a college level physics course, in a thermodynamics course, through interviews, and by reading additional books and articles.
   D. Today I will explain the conceptual difference between conventional and microwave cooking, the basic theory behind microwave ovens, and some effects related to microwaves.

II. Body
   A. Conventional ovens utilize a central concept of thermodynamics called conduction.
      1. Louis Bloomfield, Professor of Physics at the University of Virginia and author of Q&A page, "How Things Work: Microwave Ovens" states that "A normal oven heats food by exposing it to hot air. It cooks the food from the outside in."
      2. In his book, Physics for Scientists and Engineers, Paul A. Tipler explains this type of heating as conduction; or "thermal energy (heat) is transferred by interactions among atoms or molecules . . . this energy is transported along the [food]."

   B. In contrast, microwaves are a type of electromagnetic wave.
      1. Their heat is generated by friction caused by the rubbing of all the dipole molecules of water.
      2. Charge/pole-visuals (computer generated, animated to show the action).
         a. Professor Bloomfield also states, "A microwave oven heats the food by heating the water in that food. It cooks foods from the inside out."
         b. In the Science and Technology section of *The Buckwellian* web page, Chip Audette explains that "the rubbing of the agitated molecules causes friction . . . which heats the food."
      3. In summary, microwave ovens emit electromagnetic waves in the form of microwaves and activate the dipole movement of the water molecules.

      a. Most ovens operate at a frequency of 2.45 GHz.

      b. Chip Audette states that the "frequency was chosen because it is especially effective at agitating water molecules."

   4. There are 4 main components to microwave ovens:

      a. [diagram of microwave oven] power controls, magnetron, wave guide and heating chamber.

   5. Microwaves have many different effects.

      a. The size of the heating chamber dictates how many "hot spots" it has. [animated computer visual showing the "hot spots"]

      b. Microwaves affect metal: you've heard the warnings!

         1. Professor Bloomfield says that "microwaves cause electric currents to flow through any metal object so thin or narrow that it can't tolerate the current, or if the object has sharp ends so that the charges leap off as sparks."

      c. Microwaves cause cellular and molecular damage, but no more than conventional ovens and far less than frying food; also, the chemical composition is not affected because the only thing happening is vibrating water molecules.

III. Conclusion

   A. To conclude this brief and simplified investigation of how microwave ovens work, let's consider what I have discussed.

      1. What is the basic difference between conventional and microwave cooking?

      2. How does food heat up in the microwave oven?

      3. What are some of the effects related to microwaves?

   B. Instead of having the confused "I don't have any clue why my food heats up in a microwave oven" look, you can now impress everyone the next time you're sitting at dinner in Marriot or hanging out in your room by showing them how to find the "hot spots" in a microwave oven (after explaining how the electromagnetic waves affect the dipole movement of the water molecules, of course): cook a phone book.

Memorial Day Address, 1993: An example of a speech delivered to a hostile audience (Chapter 17)

William J. Clinton, *President of the United States*

When President Clinton went to the Vietnam War Memorial in May of 1993, he faced a sizable number of Vietnam veterans who greeted him with placards along with boos and shouts—which they continued as he spoke. Just one year earlier, he had been criticized for his draft history and his public protest against the Vietnam War. As you read the speech, identify all the ways that the president tries to emphasize the common beliefs and values he and his listeners share.

Thank you, thank you very much. General Powell, General McCaffrey and my good friend Lou Puller, whom I did not know was coming here today, I thank you so much.

To all of you who are shouting, I have heard you. I ask you now to hear me. I have heard you.

Some have suggested that it is wrong for me to be here with you today because I did not agree a quarter of a century ago with the decision made to send the young men and women to battle in Vietnam. Well, so much the better. Here we are celebrating America today. Just as war is freedom's cost, disagreement is freedom's privilege. And we honor it here today.

But I ask all of you to remember the words that have been said here today, and I ask you, at this monument, Can any American be out of place? And can any Commander in Chief be in any other place but here on this day? I think not.

Many volumes have been written about this war and those complicated times, but the message of this memorial is quite simple: These men and women fought for freedom, brought honor to their communities, loved their country and died for it.

They were known to all of us. There's not a person in this crowd today who did not know someone on this wall. Four of my high school classmates are there, four who shared with me the joys and trials of childhood and did not live to see the three score and ten years the Scripture says we are entitled to.

Let us continue to disagree if we must about the war, but let us not let it divide us as a people any longer.

No one has come here today to disagree about the heroism of those whom we honor. But the only way we can really honor their memory is to resolve to live and serve today and tomorrow as best we can and to make America the best that she can be. Surely that is what we owe to all those whose names are etched in this beautiful memorial.

As we all resolve to keep the finest military in the world, let us remember some of the lessons that all agree on. If the day should come when our service men and women must again go into combat, let us all resolve they will go with the training, the equipment, and the support necessary to win, and, most important of all, with a clear mission to win.

Let us do what is necessary to regain control over our destiny as a people here at home, to strengthen our economy and to develop the capacities of all of our people, to rebuild our communities and our families where children are raised and character is developed. Let us keep the American dream alive.

Today let us also renew a pledge to the families whose names are not on this wall because their sons and daughters did not come home. We will do all we can to give you not only the attention you have asked for but the answers you deserve.

Today I have ordered that by Veterans Day we will have declassified all United States Government records related to POW's and MIA's from the Vietnam War—all those records except for a tiny fraction which could still affect our national security or invade the privacy of their families.

As we allow the American public to have access to what our government knows, we will press harder to find out what other governments know. We are pressing the Vietnamese to provide this accounting not only because it is the central outstanding issue in our relationship with Vietnam, but because it is a central commitment made by the American government to our people. And I intend to keep it.

You heard General Powell quoting President Lincoln: "With malice toward none and charity for all, let us bind up the nation's wounds."

Lincoln speaks to us today across the years. Let us resolve to take from this haunting and beautiful memorial a renewed sense of our national unity and purpose, a deepened gratitude for the sacrifice of those whose names we touched and whose memories we revere and a finer dedication to making America a better place for their children and for our children, too.

Thank you all for coming here today. God bless you, and God bless America.

Source: Speech at the Vietnam War Memorial in Washington, DC, May 1993.

Bibliography

Abt, J. (1991, December 4). Sharks. Student speech. Jamaica, NY: St. John's University.

Allen, M., Berkowitz, S., Hunt, S., & Louden, A. (1999, January). A meta-analysis of the impact of forensics and communication education on critical thinking. *Communication Education, 48,* 18–30.

Allen, S. A. (1993, February 15). To be successful you have to deal with reality: An opportunity for minority business. *Vital Speeches, 59,* 271–273.

American Library Association. Retrieved July 22, 1999, from the World Wide Web: http://www.ala.org/org/html.

Anderson, J. W. (1991). A comparison of Arab and American conceptions of "effective persuasion." In L. A. Samovar & R. E. Porter (Eds.). *Intercultural communication: A reader* (5th ed, pp. 96–106). Belmont, CA: Wadsworth.

Anokye, A. D. (1994, Fall). Oral connections to literacy: The narrative. *Journal of Basic Writing, 13,* 46–60.

Anonymous. (1993). Text review, 1/e.

Anonymous. (1994). Manuscript review, 1/e.

Archambault, D. (1992, May 1). Columbus plus 500 years: Whither the American Indian? *Vital Speeches of the Day, 58,* 491–493.

Aristotle. (1954, 1984). *Poetics.* (I. Bywater, Trans.). New York: The Modern Library.

Arthur, A. (1997, July). Keeping up public appearances: Master the fine art of public-speaking and give a great presentation every time. *Black Enterprise, 27*(12), 54(1). Accessed online: *InfoTrac College Edition.*

Asen, R. (1999, Winter). Toward a normative conception of difference in public deliberation. *Argumentation and Advocacy, 35*(3), 115(1). Accessed on *InfoTrac College Edition.*

Augustine. (1958). *On Christian doctrine: Book IV* (D. W. Robertson, Jr., Trans.). New York: Liberal Arts Press. (Original work written 416.)

Ayres, J., & Hopf, T. S. (1989). Visualization: Is it more than extra-attention? Communication Education, 38, 1–5.

Ayres, J., Hopf, T., & Ayres, D. M. (1994). An examination of whether imaging ability enhances the effectiveness of an intervention designed to reduce speech anxiety. *Communication Education, 43,* 256.

Barrett, H. (1991). *Rhetoric and civility: Human development, narcissism, and the good audience.* Albany: SUNY Press.

Bartanen, M. & Frank, D. (1999, Summer). Reclaiming a heritage: A proposal for rhetorically grounded academic debate. *Parliamentary Debate: The Journal of the National Parliamentary Debate Association, 6(1),* pp. 31–54.

Beatty, M., McCroskey, J. C., and Heisel, A. D. (1998, September). Communication Apprehension as temperamental expression: A communibiological paradigm. *Communication Monographs, 65,* 197–219.

Becker, C. B. (1988). Reasons for the lack of argumentation and debate in the Far East. In L. A. Samovar & R. E. Porter (Eds.). *Intercultural communication: A reader* (5th ed., pp. 243–252). Belmont, CA: Wadsworth.

Becker, R. A., & Keller-McNulty, S. (1996). Presentation myths. *The American Statistician, 50*(2), 112(4). Accessed online through *InfoTrac College Edition.*

Beebe, S. A., & Masterson, J. T. (1990). *Communicating in small groups: Principles and practices* (3rd ed.). New York: Harper-Collins.

Behnke, R. R. & Sawyer, C. R. (1999). Milestones of anticipatory Public Speaking Anxiety. *Communication Education, 48,* 165–172.

Bentley, S. C. (1998, February). Listening better: a guide to improving what may be the ultimate staff skill. *Nursing Homes, 47(2),* 56(3). Available on *InfoTrac College Edition.*

Berger, P. (1969). *A rumor of angels: Modern society and the rediscovery of the supernatural.* Garden City, NY: Doubleday.

Bierhorst, J. (1985). *The mythology of North America.* New York: William Morrow.

Bippus, A. M. & Daly, J. A. (1999). What do people think causes stage fright:? Naïve attributions about the reasons for Public Speaking Anxiety. *Communication Education, 48,* 63–72.

Bitzer, L. F. (1999). The rhetorical situation. In J. L. Lucaites, C. M. Condit, and S. Caudill (eds.). *Contemporary rhetorical theory: A reader* (pp. 217–225). New York: The Guilford Press.

Blakeslee, S. (1992, March 15). Faulty math heightens fears of breast cancer. *The New York Times,* sec. 4, pp. 1, 2.

Bloch, M. (1975). *Political language and oratory in traditional society.* London: Academic Press.

Boerger, M. A., & Henley, T. B. (1990, Spring). The use of analogy in giving instructions. *Psychological Record, 49*(2), 193(1). Accessed on *InfoTrac College Edition,* January 13, 2000.

Bolton, R. (1990). Active listening. In J. Stewart (Ed.), *Bridges not walls: A book about interpersonal communication* (5th ed., pp. 175–190). New York: McGraw Hill.

Bormann, E. G. (1985). Symbolic convergence theory: A communication formulation. *Journal of Communication, 35,* 128–138.

Branham, R. J., & Pearce, W. B. (1996). The conversational frame in public address. *Communication Quarterly, 44*(4), 423(17). Accessed online: *InfoTrac College Edition.*

Brookhiser, R. (1999, November 22). Weird Al: A troubled and alarming vice president. *National Review, 60*(22), 32(3).

Brownell, W. W., & Katula, R. A. (1984). The Communication Anxiety Graph: A classroom tool for managing speech anxiety. *Communication Quarterly, 32,* 243–249.

Burgoon, J. K., Buller, D. B., & Woodall, W. G. (1989). *Nonverbal communication: The unspoken dialogue.* New York: Harper & Row.

Burke, M. B. (1992). Polar bears. Student speech. Jamaica, NY: St. John's University.

Burke, K. (1950). *A rhetoric of motives.* Upper Saddle River, NJ: Prentice Hall.

Burke, K. (1983, August 12). Dramatism and logology. *The Literary Supplement,* 859.

Bush, B. (1990, June 1). Choice and change. Address delivered at Wellesley College commencement, Wellesley, MA.

Campbell, G. (1776, 1963). *The philosophy of rhetoric* (L. Bitzer, Ed.). Carbondale: Southern Illinois University Press.

Cantor, P. A. (1999, October 4). Pro wrestling and the end of history. *The Weekly Standard, 5(3),* 17–22.

Carnahan, J. (1999, June 15). Born to make barrels: Women who put their stamp on history. Address given at the Trailblazer's Awards Ceremony, University of Missouri, St. Louis. *Vital Speeches of the Day, 65*(17), 529–531.

Carrell, L. J. (1997). Diversity in the communication curriculum: Impact on student empathy. *Communication Education, 46,* 234–244.

Cassady, M. (1994). *The art of storytelling: Creative ideas for preparation and performance.* Colorado Springs, CO: Meriweather Publishing.

Christensen, M. D. (1998, March). An idea is only the bait. *The Writer, 111(3),* 20–21.

Cicero, M. T. (1981). (H. Caplan, Trans.). *Ad c. herennium: De ratione dicendi (Rhetorica ad herennium)*. The Loeb Classical Library. Cambridge, MA: Harvard University Press.

Cloud, J. (1999, November 1). An end to the hatred. *Time Magazine*, 154(18), 62.

Columbia Encyclopedia. (1993). Culture. Edition 5, 9710. Available online at: *InfoTrac College Edition*, Article A 17557559.

Condon, J. C., Jr. (1978). Intercultural communication from a speech communication perspective. In F. C. Casmir (Ed.). *Intercultural and international communication* (pp. 383–406). Washington, DC: University Press of America.

Cooper, P. J. (1995). *Communication for the classroom teacher* (5th ed.). Scottsdale, AZ: Gorsuch Scarisbrick Publishers.

Cortese, A. (1990). *Ethnic ethics: The restructuring of moral theory*. Albany, NY: SUNY Press.

Coste, D. (1989). *Narrative as communication*. Minneapolis: University of Minnesota Press.

Cowan, J. (2000). Lessons from the playground. In K. M. Galvin & P. J. Cooper (Eds.), *Making connections: Readings in relational communication* (2nd ed.). Los Angeles: Roxbury.

Craig, B. (1998, April 15, last updated). Cognitive dissonance theory: Leon Festinger. COMM 3210 Online Syllabus. Available online at http://spot.colorado.edu/~craigr/3210syll.htm#top.

Cribbins, M. (1990). International adoption. Student speech, Oregon State University, Corvallis.

Cuomo, M. (1999). New York Governor Mario Cuomo challenges President Reagan's portrayal of America as a "Shining City on a Hill." In R Torricelli & A. Carroll (Eds.). *In our own words: Extraordinary speeches of the American century* (pp. 354–359). New York: Kodansha International.

Curtis, D. B., Winsor, J. L., and Stephens, R. D. (1989). National preferences in business and communication education. *Communication Education, 38*, 6–14.

Daniel, J. L., & Smitherman, G. (1990). How I got over: Communication dynamics in the black community. In D. Carbaugh (Ed.), *Cultural communication and intercultural contacts*. Hillsdale, NJ: Lawrence Erlbaum.

Davidson, J. (1993, March 6). Overworked Americans or overwhelmed Americans? You cannot handle everything. *Vital Speeches of the Day, 59*, 470–473.

Davidson, W., & Kline, S. (1999, March). Ace your presentations. *Journal of Accountancy, 187*(3), 61(1). Accessed January 3, 2000: *InfoTrac College Edition*.

Delroy, K.-K. (1992). Ritual studies as a medium for communication. Paper presented at the Ethnography of Communication Conference, Portland, OR, August 13–15, p. 4.

Demonstrative speech (how-to). (n.d., accessed 2000, January). Available online at http://www.brazosport.cc.tx.us/~comm/demon.html.

DePaulo, B. M., Blank, A. L., Swain, G. W., and Hairfield, J. G. (1992). Expressiveness and expressive control. *Personality and Social Psychology Bulletin, 18*, 276–285.

Detz, J. (1998, April–May). Delivery plus content equals successful presentations. *Communication World, 15*(5), 34(3). Available: *InfoTrac College Edition*.

Dialects doing well. (1998, February 18). InSCIght on Apnet. Available online at http://www.apnet.com/inscight/02181009/graphb.htm.

Dickens, C. (1932). *A tale of two cities*. In T. H. Briggs, et al. (Eds.), *Romance* (p. 249). Boston: Houghton Mifflin.

DiMaggio, M. (1994). You have my deepest sympathy: you just won the lottery. Student Speech. Jamaica, NY: St. John's University.

Dwyer, K. K. (1998, April). Communication Apprehension and learning style preference: Correlation and implications for teaching. *Communication Education, 47*, 137–150.

Echo in introductions and conclusions. (n. d. accessed December 15, 1999) Instructional web page available online at: http://www.stlcc.cc.mo.us/fv/webcourses/eng020/testlocation/mensepage/Echo.html.

Eckenhoff, E. A. (1998, December 15). As you enter the new millennium: Character and the need to build it. [Transcript.] *Vital Speeches of the Day, 65* (5), 158(3). Available online at *InfoTrac College Edition*.

Edwards, R. & McDonald, J. L. (1993). Schema theory and listening. In A. D. Wolvin & C. G. Coakley (Eds.). *Perspectives on listening* (60–77). Norwood, NJ: Ablex.

Eisen, A. (1998). Small group presentations in teaching "science thinking" and context in a large biology class. *Bioscience, 48*(1), 53(5).

Ekman, P., & Friesen, W. V. (1969). The repertoire of nonverbal behavior: Categories, origins, usage, and coding. *Semiotica, I*, 49–98.

Elmer-Dewitt, P. (1993, April 12). Electronic superhighways. *Time*, 50–55.

Engnell, R. (1999). What is a central idea? Communication 100 course handout. Newberg, OR: George Fox University.

Faludi, S. (1992, January 26). Speak for yourself. *The New York Times Magazine*, pp. 10ff.

Fancher, M. R. (1993, August 8). Will journalism travel on the information highway? *Seattle Times*, p. A2.

Farmer, G. (1999, June 1). Cyberbabble and other facts: Life for the new millennium. [Transcript]. *Vital Speeches of the Day, 65* (16), 509(3). Available online at *InfoTrac College Edition*.

Festinger, L. (1957). *A theory of cognitive dissonance*. New York: Row, Peterson.

Fisher, W. R. (1984a). Narration as a human communication paradigm: The case of public moral argument. *Communication Monographs, 51*, 1–22.

Fisher, W. R. (1984b). The narrative paradigm: An elaboration. *Communication Monographs, 52*, 347–367.

Fisher, W. R. (1999). Narrative as human communication paradigm. In J. L. Lucaites, C. M. Condit, & S. Caudill (Eds.), *Contemporary rhetorical theory: A reader* (pp. 265–287). New York: The Guilford Press.

Flynn, L. R. (n.d., accessed 2000, January). Demonstration or "how-to" speech topics. Accessed online at www.colin.cc.ms.us/flynn/Speech/Demo Speech.htm.

Font. (n.d., accessed 2000, January 3). Publications: Glossary of terms. Available on-line: http://www.asme.org/pubs/glossary.html.

Foss, S. & Griffin, C. (1995). Beyond persuasion: A proposal for an invitational rhetoric. *Communication Monographs, 62*, 2–18.

Foster, G. D. (1999, June 15). Ethics in government: The challenges ahead. [Transcript]. *Vital Speeches of the Day, 65* (10), 583(4). Available online at *InfoTrac College Edition*.

Frank, D. A. (1997). Diversity in the public space: A response to Stepp. *Argumentation and Advocacy, 33*, 195(3).

Friemuth, V. S., & Jamieson, K. (1979). Communicating with the elderly: Shattering stereotypes. Urbana, IL: ERIC Clearinghouse on Reading and Communication Skills.

Galvin, K. M. & Cooper, P. J. (2000). Perceptual filters: Culture, family, and gender. In K. M. Galvin & P. J. Cooper (Eds.). *Making connections: Readings in relational communication* (2nd ed., pp. 32–33). Los Angeles: Roxbury.

Gardner, H. (1993). *Multiple intelligences: The theory in practice*. New York: Basic Books.

Gass, R. (1999). Fallacy list: SpCom 335: Advanced argumentation, California State University, Fullerton. Available online at http://commfaculty.fullerton.edu/rgass/fallacy31.htm.

Gates, H. L. (1992). *Loose canons: Notes on the culture wars*. New York: Oxford University Press.

Giller, E. (n.d., accessed 1999, December 28). Left brain/right brain religion. http://www.sabbath.com/acfl.htm.

Gingerich, J. (1999, February 24). Peter Ilich Tchaikovsky. Student speech, Goshen College, Goshen, IN.

Goffman, E. (1959). *The presentation of self in everyday life*. Garden City, NY: Doubleday Anchor Books.

Goodall, H. L., & Phillips, G. M. (1984). *Making it in any organization*. Upper Saddle River, NJ: Prentice Hall.

Goodall, H. L., & Waaigen, C. L. (1986). *The persuasive presentation: A practical guide to professional communication in organizations.* New York: Harper & Row.

Goodman, G., & Esterly, G. (1990). Questions—The most popular piece of language. In J. Stewart (Ed.), *Bridges not walls: A book about interpersonal communication* (4th ed., pp. 69–79). New York: McGraw Hill.

Goody J. & Watts, I. The consequences of literacy. In D. Crowley & P. Heyer (Eds.) (1991). *Communication in history: Technology, culture, society* (pp. 48–56). New York: Longman.

Gozzi, R. (1990). *New words and a changing American culture.* Columbia, SC: University of South Carolina Press.

Gray, G. W. (1946). The precepts of Kagemni and Ptah-hotep. *Quarterly Journal of Speech 31,* 446–454.

Greenhouse, S. (1999, April 17). A crusade of children: Canadian teen-ager enlists his peers in a fight against child labor. *New York Times,* National Edition, A 13.

Gresh, S. (1998, December 1). Storytelling: The soul of an enterprise. Address given to the Rotary Club, Andover, MA, September 25, 1998. *Vital Speeches of the Day, 65*(4), 122(4). Accessed online through *InfoTrac College Edition.*

Griffin, C. W. (1998). Improving students' writing strategies; knowing versus doing. *College Teaching, 46(2),* 18(5). Available. *InfoTrac College Edition,* Wadsworth.

Griffiths, M. (1988). Feminism, feelings, and philosophy. In M. Griffiths & M. Whitford (Eds.), *Feminist perspectives in philosophy* (pp. 131–151). Bloomington, IN: Indiana University Press.

Grob, L. M., Meyers, R. A., & Schuh, R. (1997). Powerful/powerless language use in group interactions: Sex differences or similarites? *Communication Quarterly, 45*(3), 282(22). Available online through *InfoTrac College Edition.*

Gun crazy. (1993, May 25). Editorial. *New York Times,* p. A22.

Hacker, D. (1998). *A writer's reference* (4th ed.). New York: Bedford/St. Martin's.

Hacker, D. (1998). *Research and documentation in the electronic age.* Boston: Bedford Books.

Harms, L. W., & Richstad, R. J. (1978). The right to communicate: Status of the concept. In F. L. Casmir (Ed.), *Intercultural and international communication.* Washington, DC: University Press of America.

Harnack, A. & Kleppinger, E. (1998). *Online!: A reference guide to using Internet sources, 1998 edition.* New York: St. Martin's Press. Website located at http://www.smpcollege.com/online-4styles^help.

Hart, R. P., & Burks, D. O. (1972). Rhetorical sensitivity and social interaction. *Speech Monographs, 39,* 90.

Harthorn, J. (1998, February 9). Multiple sclerosis. Student speech. Newberg, OR: George Fox University.

Hawkes, L, (1999). *A guide to the World Wide Web.* Upper Saddle River, NJ: Prentice-Hall.

Hayden, T. (1999, July 12). Critical Más: 20 for 2000. *Newsweek, 84*(2), 56(2).

Henson, J. (n.d.). Problem solving using group challenges. Available online at: http://www.bvte.ecu.edu/ACBMEC/p1998/henson.htm. Accessed February 1, 2000.

Hilliard, A. (1986). Pedagogy in ancient Kemet. In M. Karenga & J. Carruthers (Eds.). *Kemet and the African world view* (p. 257). London: University of Sankore Press.

Howell, W. (1990). Coping with Internal-Monologue. In J. Stewart (Ed.) *Bridges not walls: A book about interpersonal communication* (5th edition, pp. 128–138). New York: McGraw Hill.

Humphrey, J. (1998, May 15). Executive eloquence: A seven-fold path to inspirational leadership. *Vital Speeches, 64*(15), 468(4).

Hybels, S., & Weaver, R. L. (1992). *Communicating effectively* (3rd ed., p. 118). New York: McGraw-Hill.

Hypes, M. G., Turner, E. T., Norris, C. M., & Wolfferts, L. C. (1999, January). How to be a successful presenter. *The Journal of Physical Education, Recreation & Dance, 70*(1), 50(4).

Internet Source Validation Project. (1999). Available: http://www.stemnet.nf.ca/~dfurey/validate/termsi.html. Accessed July 1999.

Irvine, J. J. & York, D. E. (1995). Learning styles and culturally diverse students: A literature review. ED382722 UDO3046 Eric Documents Abstract. Available online at: http://ericae.net/faqs.

Jaasma, M. A. (1997, summer). Classroom Communication Apprehension: Does being male or female make a difference? *Communication Reports, 10,* 218–228.

Jaffe, C. I. (1998, November). Metaphors about the classroom. A paper presented to the National Communication Association. New York

Jaggar, A. M. (1989). Love and knowledge: Emotion in feminist epistemology. In A. Garry & M. Pearsall (Eds.), *Women, knowledge, and reality: Explorations in feminist philosophy* (pp. 129–155). London: Unwin.

Jamieson, K. H. (1988). *Eloquence in an electronic age.* New York: Oxford University Press.

Janik, I. (1971, November). Groupthink. *Psychology Today,* 43–46.

Jenefsky, C. (1996, October). Public speaking as empowerment at Visionary University. *Communication Education, 45,* 343–355.

Jensen, J. V. (1997). *Ethical issues in the communication process.* Mahwah, NJ: Lawrence Erlbaum Associates.

Jensen, K. K. & Harris, V. (1999). The public speaking portfolio. *Communication Education, 48,* 211–227.

Johannesen, R. L. (1996). *Ethics in human communication,* 4th ed. Prospect Heights, IL: Waveland Press.

Jordan, B. (1992, July 14). Excerpts from addresses by keynote speakers at the Democratic convention. *The New York Times,* p. A12.

Jorgensen-Earp, C. (1993, September 28). Telephone interview.

Jorgensen-Earp, C. (n.d.), "Making other arrangements:" Alternative patterns of disposition. Unpublished course handout. Lynchburg, VA: Lynchburg College.

Kao, E. M., Nagita, D. K., & Peterson, C. (1997). Explanatory style, family expressiveness, and self-esteem among Asian American and EuroAmerican college students. *Journal of Social Psychology, 137,* 435–444.

Kendall, K. E. (1988). Does the public speak publicly? A survey. *World Communication, 17,* 279–290.

Kennedy, J. F. (1988). Inaugural address. In J. Podell & S. Angovin (Eds.), *Speeches of the American presidents* (pp. 603–605). New York: H. W. Wilson.

Keough, D. R. (1993, May 10). The courage to dream: Seize the day. *Vital Speeches of the Day,* 599–601.

Kepner, C. H., & Tregoe, B. B. (1965). *The rational manager: A systematic approach to problem solving and decision making.* New York: McGraw-Hill.

Kiewitz, C., Weaver III, J. B., Brosius, H-B., & Weimann, G. (1997). Cultural differences in listening style preferences: A comparison of young adults in Germany, Israel, and the United States. *International Journal of Public Opinion Research, 9 (3),* 233–248. Available: *InfoTrac College Edition,* Article A21283282.

King, M. L. (1963, August 28). I have a dream. Address given at the March on Washington. Available online at http://www.mecca.org/~crights/dream.htm.

King, M. L. (1999). Dr. Martin Luther King, Jr. electrifies a nation with his call for an end to segregation and racial discrimination. (Speech given at the March on Washington, August 28, 1963, Washington, D.C.). In R. Torricelli & A. Carroll (Eds.). *In our own words: Extraordinary speeches of the American Century* (pp. 234–237). New York: Kodansha International.

Kirkwood, W. G. (1992). Narrative and the rehtoric of possibility. *Communication Monographs, 59,* 30–47.

Kirshenberg, S. (1998, November). Info on the Internet: User beware! *Training & Development, 52(11),* 83(2). Available: *Infotrac College Edition,* Article A53392425. Accessed November, 1999.

Kleiner, C. (1999, May 17). Wrestling's cult following. *U.S. News & World Report*, 56–57.

Kochman, T. (1990). Cultural pluralism: Black and white styles. In D. Carbaugh (Ed.). Cultural communication and intercultural contacts (pp. 219–224). Hillsdale, NJ: Lawrence Erlbaum.

Krauss, B. (1993, March 28). Some secrets to a soulful, shining Sunday sermon. *The Honolulu Advertiser*, p. A3.

Learning styles, culture and hemispheric dominance. (n.d., accessed 1999, December 28). Available: http://geocities.com/~mathskills/brain.htm.

Lee, M. (1995, June 20). Paralegal career. Student Speech. Jamaica, NY: St. John's University.

Leland, J., & Chambers, V. (1999, July 12). Generation Ñ. *Newsweek, 84*(2), 52(7).

Li, V. (1992, April 27). The glass ceiling. Student speech. Jamaica, NY: St. John's University.

Lieggi, L. K. (1999, July 20). Personal interview. Dundee, OR.

Lundeen, S. W. (1993). Metacognitive listening. In A. D. Wolvin & C. G. Coakley (Eds.). *Perspectives on listening* (106–123). Norwood, NJ: Ablex.

Lustig, M. W., & Koester, J. (1993). *Intercultural competence: Interpersonal communication across cultures.* New York: HarperCollins.

McClearey, K. (1997). Text review. University of Southern Illinois, Edwardsville.

McGuire, M., & Slembek, E. (1987). An emerging critical rhetoric: Hellmut Geissner's Sprechwissenschaft. *Quarterly Journal of Speech 73*, 349–400.

McKeon, R. (1998). Creativity and the commonplace. In T. B. Farrell (Ed.). *Landmark essays on contemporary rhetoric* (pp. 33–41). Mahwah, NJ: Hermagoras Press.

McMillan, C. (1982). *Women, reason, and nature: Some philosophical problems with feminism.* Princeton, NJ: Princeton University Press.

McNally, J. R. (1969). Opening assignments: A symposium. *The Speech Teacher, 18*, 18–20.

Mabry, M. (1999, July 12). No money, no meds. *Newsweek, 84(2)*, pp. 32–35.

Machrone, B. (1993, Fall). Ziff-Davis/Personal computing. Advertising supplement to *The New York Times.*

MacIntyre, A. (1981). *After virtue: A study in moral reasoning* (2nd ed.). South Bend, IN: University of Notre Dame Press.

MacIntyre, P. J., & MacDonald, J. R. (1998). Public speaking anxiety: Perceived competence and audience congeniality. *Communication Education, 47*, 359–365.

Maes, J. D., Weldy, T. B. & Icenogle, M. L. (1997, January). *Journal of Business Communication, 34*(1), 6–14. Available online as InfoTrac document: A19218840.

Mannie, K. (1998, December). Coaching through demonstration: Focus only on the key points of the skill. *Coach and Athletic Director, 68*(5), 74(2). Accessed on *InfoTrac College Edition*, January 2000.

Marsella, A. J. (1993). Counseling and psychotherapy with Japanese Americans: Cross-cultural considerations. *American Journal of Orthopsychiatry, 63*, 200–208.

Martel, M. (1984.) *Before you say a word: The executive guide to effective communication.* Upper Saddle River, NJ: Prentice Hall.

Maslow, A. H. (1987). *Motivation and personality* (3rd ed.). San Francisco: Harper & Row.

Maxwell, L., & McCain, T. A. (1997, July). Gateway or gatekeeper: The implication of copyright and digitalization on education. *Communication Education, 46*, 141–157.

Messenger, J. (1960). Anang proverb riddles. Journal of American Folklore, 73, 235.

Mills, D. W. (1999). Applying what we know: Student learning styles. Available online at http://crsnet.org/crsnet/articles/student-learning-styles.html.

Molloy, J. T. (1976). *Dress for success.* New York: Warner Books.

Monroe, A. H. (1962). *Principles and types of speech* (5th ed.). Chicago: Scott, Foresman.

Mullins, D. (1993). Guest lecture. St. John's University, Jamaica, NY.

Mura, S., & Waggenspack, B. (1983). Linguistic sexism: A rehtorical perspective. In J. L. Golden, G. F. Berquist, & W. F. Coleman (Eds.), *The rhetoric of western thought* (3rd ed., pp. 251–260). Dubuque, IA: Kendall/Hunt.

Murray, D. M. (1998, May). Write what you don't know. *The Writer, 111*(5), 7–9.

O'Mahoney, B. (1999). The copyright website (1995–1999). Available: http://www.benedict.com/index.html, Accessed November 1999.

Ong, W. J. (1982). *Orality and literacy: The technologizing of the word.* New York: Methuen.

Osborn, M. (1967). Archetypal metaphor in rhetoric: The light-dark family. *Quarterly Journal of Speech, 53*, 115–126.

Osborn, M. (1977). The evolution of the archetypal sea in rhetoric and poetic. *Quarterly Journal of Speech, 63*, 347–363.

Osborn, M. (1997). The play of metaphors. *Education, 118*(1), 84(4). Available online at *InfoTrac College Edition.*

Ota, A. K. (1993, July 11). Japan's ambassador to U. S. sets welcome new tone. *Seattle Times*, p. A12.

Ouchi, W. B. (1998, Fall). The concept of organizational culture in a diverse society. SIETAR International. Available at: http://208.215.167.139/sij-98-12/keynote03.htm.

Pacanowsky, M. E., & O'Donnell-Trujillo, N. (1983). Organizational communication as cultural performance. *Communication Monographs, 50*, 126–147.

Pearce, W. B. (1989). *Communication and the human condition.* Carbondale: Southern Illinois University Press.

Pease, B. (1998, March 9). What's all this international business travel stuff, anyhow? (Preparations before going to business trips abroad, part 2). *Electronic Design, 46*(6), 146(4). Accessed online through *InfoTrac College Edition.*

Pennebaker, J. W., Rime, B., & Blankenship, V. E. (1996). Stereotypes of emotional expressiveness of northerners and southerners: A cross-cultural test of Montesquieu's Hypothesis. *Journal of Personality and Social Psychology, 70*, 372–380.

Peters, D. A. (1999, April 1). Boomers, bloomers, and zoomers. *Vital Speeches, 65* (12), 379(6).

Peterson, M. S. (1997). Personnel interviewers' perceptions of the importance and adequacy of applicant's communication skills. *Communication Education, 46*, 287–291.

Podell, J., & Angovin, S. (Eds.). (1988). *Speeches of the American Presidents.* New York: H. W. Wilson.

Porter, R. E., & Samovar, L. A. (1994). An introduction to intercultural communication. In L. A. Samovar & R. E. Porter (Eds.). *Intercultural communication: A reader* (7th ed., pp. 4–25).

Preparing the delivery outline. (1999, December 14). Speech assignments web page link: Riverdale School Speech Class, Upper Grades. http://www.teleport.com/~beanman/english/delivout.html.

Quintilian. (1920–1922). (H. E. Butler, Trans.). The instituto oratoria of Quintilian (4 vols.). The Loeb Classical Library. Cambridge, MA: Harvard University Press.

Radel, J. (1999, July, last update). Effective presentations. Kansas University Medical Center on-line tutorial series. Available online: http://KUMC.edu/SAH/OTEd/jradel/effective.html.

Ray, G. B. (1986). Vocally cued personality prototypes: An implicit personality theory approach. *Communication Monographs, 53*, 266–276.

Ray, J., & Badle, C. (1993, February 3). Hosts of "Queer Talk" speaking on a talk radio call-in show. WABC, New York.

Readability. (n. d., accessed 2000, January 3). Planning, design, and production. Available online: http://ibis.nott.ac.uk/guidelines/ch2/chap2-G-4.html.

Reagan, R. (1986, January 31). Memorial service for the crew of the space shuttle *Challenger.* Houston.

Reynolds, J. (1995–1996). The Dangers of DEET. Forensics Competition. Spokane, WA: Whitworth College.

Reynolds, S. (1996, December). Selling to another language. *Communication World, 14*(1), 11(1). Accessed online through *InfoTrac College Edition.*

Richmond, V. P., & McCroskey, J. C. (1995). Communication: Apprehension, avoidance, and effectiveness (4th ed.). Scottsdale, AZ: Gorsuch Scarisbrick. Used with permission.

Richmond, V. P., & McCroskey, J. C. (2000). *Nonverbal behavior in interpersonal relations* (4th ed.). Boston: Allyn & Bacon.

Riding, R. & Cheema, I. (1991). Cognitive styles—an overview and integration. *Educational Psychology, 11,* 193–215. Available on *InfoTrac College Edition.*

Roach, C. A. & Wyatt, N. J. (1995). Listening and the rhetorical process. In J. Stewart (Ed.). *Bridges not walls: A book about interpersonal communication* (5th ed., pp. 171–176). New York: McGraw-Hill.

Robinson, T. E. (1997, July). Communication Apprehension and the basic public speaking course: A national survey of in-class treatment techniques. *Communication Education, 46,* 188–197.

Roczak, T. (1992, June 9). Green guilt and ecological overload. *New York Times,* p. A23.

Rodrigues, D. & Rodrigues, R. J. (2000). *The research paper and the world wide web,* 2nd ed. Upper Saddle River, NJ: Prentice Hall.

Roper Starch. (1999). How Americans communicate. Poll commissioned by the National Communication Association. Available: http://www.natcom.org/research/Roper/how americans-communicate.htm.

Rose, R. R. (1998, October 24). A definition. Filled Pause Research Center. Available: http://www.alltheweb.com, the exact phrase "filled pause."

Rosellini, L. (1999, May 17). Lords of the ring. *U.S. News & World Report,* 52–58.

Rosellini, L. (1999, November 1). An unlikely friendship, a historic meeting. *U.S. News & World Report, 127*(17), 68.

Ross, R. S. (1989). *Speech communication: The speechmaking system* (8th ed.). Upper Saddle River, NJ: Prentice Hall.

Rowan, K. E. (1995, July). A new pedagogy for explanatory public speaking: Why arrangement should not substitute for invention. *Communication Education, 44,* 235–250.

Rowland, R. C. (1990). On mythic criticism. *Communication Studies, 41*(2), 101–116.

Rubin, D. L. (1993). Listenability – oral-based discourse + considerateness. In A. D. Wolvin & C. G. Coakley (Eds.), *Perspectives on listening* (pp. 261–268). Norwood, NJ: Ablex.

Sanger, D. E. (1993, May 25). After gunman's acquittal, Japan struggles to understand America. *New York Times,* P. A1, 17.

Sanger, D. E. (1993, November 12). In Japan's astounding future: Life with father. *New York Times,* p. A4.

Sawyer, C. R. & Behnke, R. R. (1999, Winter). State anxiety patterns for Public Speaking Anxiety and the behavior inhibition system. *Communication Reports, 12,* 33–41.

Schrof, J. M. & Schultz, S. (1999, June 21). Social anxiety. *U.S. News & World Report, 126*(24), 53.

Schwandt, B., & Soraya, S. (1992, August 13–15). Ethnography of communication and "Sprechwissenschaft"—merging concepts. Paper presented at the Ethnography of Communication Conference, Portland, OR.

Schweid, B. (1999, November 23). State Dept. rebukes Arafat claim. *Washington Post* online. Available: www. washingtonpost.com/wp-srv/aponline/19991123.

Scofield, S. (1999, August). An end to writer's block. *The Writer, 111*(8), 7–9.

Scott, M. D., & Brydon, S. R. (1997). *Dimensions of communication: An introduction.* Mountain View, CA: Mayfield.

Scott, S. (1996, November). Instant access in forensics: Issues created by the Internet and electronic information systems in forensic competition. Paper presented at the meeting of the Speech Communication Association, San Diego.

Seattle. (1853, 1971). The Indian's night promises to be dark. From *Indian oratory: Famous speeches by noted Indian chieftains,* by W. C. Vanderwerth. Copyright 1971 by the University of Oklahoma Press, pp. 118–122.

Seiter, J. S., Larsen, J., & Skinner, J. (1998). "Handicapped" or "handi-capable?" The effects of language about persons with disabilities on perceptions of source credibility and persuasiveness. *Communication Reports, 11*(1), 21–31.

Seymour, J. (1996, March 12). PC presentations: The schlepp factor. (Equipment for on-the-road presentations). *PC Magazine, 15*(5), 91(2). Accessed online through *InfoTrac College Edition.*

Shaw, B. (1993, February 1). An attitude about women: Democracy is not a smooth sauce. *Vital Speeches of the Day, 59,* 245–247.

Shipman, C. (2000, December/January). Searching for Al. *George Magazine,* 102(9).

Simon, R. (1999, November 29). The levels of his game. *U. S. News & World Report, 127*(21), 16(3).

Simons, G. F., Vazquez, C., & Harris, P. R. (1993). *Transcultural leadership: Empowering the diverse workforce.* Houston: Gulf Publishing Co.

Sitkaram, K. S., & Cogdell, R. T. (1976.) *Foundations of intercultural communication.* Columbus, OH: Charles E. Merrill.

Smith, A. L. (Molefi Asanti). (1970). Socio-historical perspectives of black oratory. *Quarterly Journal of Speech, 61,* 264–269.

Smith, D. (1996, February 7). Discussion leader: Globalization of the general education cirriculum. George Fox University. Newberg, OR.

Spangler, D., & Thompson, W. I. (1992). *Reimagination of the world: A critique of the new age, science, and popular culture.* New York: Bear & Company.

Brian Spitzberg, B. H. (1994). A model of intercultural communication competence. In L. A. Samovar & R. E. Porter (Eds.). *Intercultural communication: A reader, 7th ed.* (347–359). Belmont, CA: Wadsworth.

Staley, C. C. & Staley, R. S. (2000). Communicating in organizations. In K. M. Galvin & P. J. Cooper (Eds.). *Making connections: Readings in relational communication* (2nd ed., pp. 287–294).

Sternberg, R. (1998). *Love is a story: A new theory of relationships.* New York: Oxford University Press.

Stewart, E. C., & Bennett, M. J. (1991). *American cultural patterns: A cross-cultural perspective* (rev. ed.). Yarmouth, ME: Intercultural Press, Inc.

Stone, G. (n.d.). Promotional Letter. New York: God's Love, We Deliver.

Stowers, R. H. and White, G. T. (1999, June). Connecting accounting and communication: A survey of public accounting firms. Communication Quarterly, 62, 23–31. Available: http://www. infotrac-college.com/wadsworth.

Streicher, J. (1996, 1999, updated). The five stages of culture shock. Student speech, George Fox University, Newberg, OR.

Sullivan, P. A. (1993). Signification and African-American rhetoric: A case study of Jesse Jackson's "Common Ground and Common Sense" speech. *Communication Quarterly, 41,* 1–14.

Tannen, D. (1989). *Talking voices: Repetition, dialogue, and imagery in conversational discourse.* Cambridge: Cambridge University Press.

Tannen, D. (1990). *You just don't understand: Women and men in conversation.* New York: William Morrow.

Tannen, D. (1995). *Talking from 9 to 5: Men and women in the workplace: Language, sex, and power.* New York: Avon.

Tannen, D. (2000, January 24). Guest appearance. *Hardball with Chris Matthews.* MSNBC. 5:00 p.m. PST.

Tembo, M. S. (1999, April). Your mother is still your mother. *World and I, 14(4).* Available on *Infotrac College Edition.*

Thiederman, S. (1991a). *Bridging cultural barriers for corporate success: How to manage the multicultural workforce.* New York: Lexington.

Thiederman, S. (1991b). *Profiting in American multicultural marketplaces: How to do business across cultural lines.* New York: Lexington.

Thinking and learning skills. (1999, December 24). University of Toronto. Available online at http://snow.utoronto.ca/learn2/introll.html.

Thompson, F. T., & Grandgenett, D. J. (1999, Fall). Helping disadvantaged learners build effective learning skills. *Education, 120*(1), 130–135.

Torrence, J. (1998). *Jackie tales: The magic of creating stories and the art of telling them.* New York: Avon Books.

Toulmin, S. (1958). *The uses of argument.* Cambridge, MA: Cambridge University Press.

Toulmin, S., Rieke, R., & Janik, A. (1984.) *An introduction to reasoning,* (2nd ed.). New York: Macmillan.

Tournier, P. (1990). The world of things and the world of persons. In J. Stewart (Ed.), *Bridges not walls: A book about interpersonal communication* (5th ed., pp. 163–167). New York: McGraw-Hill.

Transcript. (1992, March 29). Heckler stirs Clinton anger: Excerpts from the exchange. *The New York Times,* p. A9.

Truth, S. Ain't I a woman? in *Norton's anthology of women's literature,* p. 253.

Ugwu-Oju, D. (1993, November 14). Pursuit of happiness. *The New York Times Magazine.*

Vatz, R. E. (1999). The myth of the rhetorical situation. In J. L. Lucaites, C. M. Condit, and S. Caudill (Eds.). *Contemporary rhetorical theory: A reader* (pp. 226–231). New York: The Guilford Press.

Von Till, B. (1998). Definition speech. In C. Jaffe (Ed.), *Student resource workbook for public speaking: Concepts and skills for a diverse society* (2nd ed., p. 89). Belmont, CA: Wadsworth.

Voth, B. (1998, Winter). A case study in metaphor as argument: A longitudinal analysis of the wall separating Church and State. *Argumentation and Advocacy, 34*(3), 127(13). Accessed on *InfoTrac College Edition.*

Wallace, K. R. (1955). An ethical basis of communication. *The Speech Teacher, 4,* 1–9.

Walters, F. (1992, November 15). In celebration of options: Respect each other's differences. *Vital Speeches of the Day,* 265–269.

Watson, B. (1997). "The storyteller is the soybean...the audience is the sun." *Smithsonian, 27*(12), 60(8).

Webster's seventh new collegiate dictionary. (1967). Springfield, MA: G & C Merriam Co.

Weider, D. L., & Pratt, S. (1990). On being a recognizable Indian. In D. Carbaugh (Ed.), *Intercultural communication and intercultural contacts* (pp. 45–64). Hillsdale, NJ: Lawrence Erlbaum.

Whaley, B. P. (1997, Spring). Perceptions of rebuttal analogy: Politeness and implications for persuasion. *Argumentation and Advocacy, 33*(4), 16(19).

Whitworth, R. H. & Cochran, C. (1996). Evaluation of integrated versus unitary treatment for reducing Public Speaking Anxiety. *Communication Education, 45,* 306–314.

Wicker, B. (1975). *The story-shaped world: Fiction and metaphysics, some variations on a theme.* Notre Dame, IN: University of Notre Dame Press.

Wierbicka, A. (1991). *Cross-cultural pragmatics: The semantics of human interaction.* Berlin: Mouton de Gruyter.

Wills, J. W. (1970). Speaking arenas in ancient Mesopotamia, *Quarterly Journal of Speech, 56,* pp. 398–405.

Winans, J. A. (1938). *Speechmaking.* New York: D. Appleton-Century Co.

Wirth, D. (1999, October 29) Arachnophobia: Overcoming your fear. Student Speech. Goshen, IN: Goshen College.

Women, science, & cognition. (n.d., accessed January 18, 2000). Available online at: http://www.psych.mcgill.ca/perpg/fac/dunbar/women.html.

Yankelovich, D. (1999). *The magic of dialogue: Transforming conflict into cooperation.* New York: Simon and Schuster.

Zediker, K. (1993, February). Rediscovering the tradition: Women's history with a relational approach to the basic public speaking course. Panel presentation at the Western States Communication Association, Albuquerque, NM, February.

Zimmerman, T., and Goode, E. (1994, October 3). The mind of Aristide. *U.S. News & World Report,* 32.

Zuckerman, L. (1999, April 17). Words go right to the brain, but can they stir the heart? Some say popular software debases public speaking. *The New York Times,* National Edition. A17, 19.

Index